The Mystery to a Solution

The Mystery to a Solution

Poe, Borges, and the Analytic Detective Story

John T. Irwin

The Johns Hopkins University Press
Baltimore and London

The Johns Hopkins University Press
2715 North Charles Street
Baltimore, Maryland 21218-4319
The Johns Hopkins Press Ltd., London

Library of Congress Catalog-in-Publication Data

Irwin, John T.
The mystery to a solution : Poe, Borges, and the analytic detective story / John T. Irwin.
    p.   cm.
  Includes bibliographical references and index.
  ISBN 0-8018-4650-1 (hc : acid-free paper)
  1. Poe, Edgar Allan, 1809–1849—Fictional works. 2. Borges, Jorge Luis,
1899–   —Fictional works. 3. Detective and mystery stories—History and criticism—
Theory, etc. 4. Literature, Comparative—American and Argentine. 5. Literature,
Comparative—Argentine and American. I. Title.
PS2642.F43178   1994
813′.3—dc20   93-15474

A catalog record for this book is available from the British Library.

For my father and mother,

William Henry Irwin, Sr., and Marguerite Hunsaker Irwin,

for my aunt,

Eleanora Hunsaker,

for

William Ralph McKee and Frances Manning McKee,

for

Mary Farrell Camerer,

and for my goddaughter,

Donna Elizabeth Robinson

I see at last that I am face to face
with my South American destiny.
I was carried to this ruinous hour
by the intricate labyrinth of steps
woven by my days from a day that goes
back to my birth. At last I've discovered
the mysterious key to all my years, . . .
the missing letter, the perfect pattern
that was known to God from the beginning.
In this night's mirror I can comprehend
my unsuspected true face. The circle's
about to close. I wait to let it come.

           Borges, "Conjectural Poem"

Besides, rereading, not reading, is what counts.

           Borges, "Utopia of a Tired Man"

Contents

Contents

Preface

THIS BOOK IS IN PART a product of the form of design called chance. After finishing *American Hieroglyphics* in 1980, I began work on a study of my favorite American fiction writer. The book was tentatively titled *An Almost Theatrical Distance: Figuration and Desire in the Fiction of F. Scott Fitzgerald*. Several months into the project, an old friend, Joe Riddel, asked me to be part of a program he was organizing on American modernist poetry at the English Institute. I had written my dissertation on Hart Crane's *The Bridge* and had always wanted to do a book-length study of his poetry, and Joe's call seemed like a perfect opportunity both to oblige a friend and to initiate a project long contemplated and long delayed. I put aside the Fitzgerald manuscript (temporarily, so I thought) and began work on Crane, a project that continued for almost a year after the paper's presentation in Cambridge in August 1980. By the summer of 1981, I was well on my way to finishing a book called *"Apollinaire Lived in Paris. I Live in Cleveland, Ohio": Approaches to the Poetry of Hart Crane* when another request to speak led me in a different direction. Kent Ljungquist and Ben Fisher of the Poe Studies Association asked me to give a talk on a Poe panel at the MLA convention in December 1981. Poe had been the main subject of *American Hieroglyphics;* there were still aspects of his work I wanted to deal with; and writing the talk would, I thought, be a respite from the almost continuous work on Crane and eventually return me to that project after the Christmas holidays, refreshed by the change and ready for another year's work. . . .

That was twelve years ago. Appropriately enough, given the kind of manipulation of sequences discussed in the present book, the projects on Fitzgerald, on Crane, and on Poe and Borges that were begun in one order are being finished in the reverse order.[1] But the genesis of these three projects, one giving way to another over an eighteen-month period, is, as I said, only partly a matter of chance, for what led me to write about these four authors, to be attracted or distracted from one to the next, was an interest in a single structure they all shared, a structure governing their relationship to their art and thematized in their work. One might best describe this structure as growing out of each writer's engagement with Platonic idealism, specifically, their more or less conscious understanding of the allegory of the cave as a womb fantasy that translated the notion of origin (and thus of the self) from a physical to a mental plane and their further understanding that this fantasized return to origin could be assimilated to another structure governing their relationship to their art: that sense of the male artist's ability (personified in the muse) to conceive and give birth to the work, the artist's identification with the muse as mother. What animates the art of these four writers in varying ways is a structure whose underpinning is the desire for a total return to the matrix (the space of origin and of original power), but a return *wholly on the son's own terms.*

The full elaboration of this structure, whose initial outline is sketched in the present book, must await the completion of the Crane and Fitzgerald projects, but for the present it is sufficient to note that the central topic of this book grows out of the allegory of the cave's valorizing of mind at the expense of body, that is, out of Poe's sense of his detective Dupin as a kind of Platonic embodiment, a sedentary mastermind whose very lack of physical exertion emphasizes the mastery of mind over the material world. Indeed, one might argue that Platonism's valorizing of mind represents the return, in a philosophically respectable form, of what Freud calls the child's belief in and desire for "the omnipotence of thoughts." And one might further argue that Poe's invention of the detective story represents the artist's residual belief in, and desire for, just such omnipotence in his art, for a magical direct control of his will over the real world, embodied in a modern, scientifically acceptable guise as the figure of the master analyst. As an image of the limitless potential of mind, Dupin is in effect an adult mask for one of the most powerful of childhood wishes, the desire of a physically helpless being for mental dominance, the wish for the world to conform absolutely to our dreams, for thinking to make it so. And this childish wish receives its most powerful philosophical statement in the notion of a separate world of ideas or ideal forms more real than the physical world of fate and death, a realm compared to which our world is a shadowy illusion. To the extent that such an *idea*-lized realm represents the mind's revenge against the physical world, a dream of mental dominance achieved by dematerializing that world while maintaining its visible outlines, the Platonic or Berkeleyean element in these four writers is a philosophical defense mechanism against the frustrations and constraints of the physical world, on the one hand, and against the dangerous and humiliating demands of the body, on the other.

In creating the detective story, Poe produced the dominant modern genre, and I mean this not merely in the sense, so often cited, that it is the genre with the most titles listed or the most copies printed in any given year, but that it is preeminently the genre of an age dominated by science and technology, an age characterized by mental-work-as-analysis. In the detective scenario and the figure of the mastermind Dupin, Poe gave us at once the most appealing format and the most glamorous mask for mental work and the mental worker. From psychoanalyst to literary critic, from particle physicist to diagnostician, the most (self-)satisfying description of what one does (and thus what one is) seems to fall naturally into the scenario of a knotty problem and its solution—the patient amassing of clues, the false leads, the painstaking analysis, and the ultimate triumph— culminating with the observation (hopefully made by someone other than oneself), "Why, you're really more interesting than you look. In fact, you're like a detective." But we should note that in creating the detective story Poe also gave us a cautionary tale about the mastery of mind and our modern scientific world. For Victor Frankenstein and C. Auguste Dupin are products of the same period and the same impulse, except that Dupin is his own monster. Which is to say, he is the first great characterless character, the name for a mental position in an entirely plot-driven scenario, the image of a man of whom one could remark that what he does is the sum total of what he is, a man who foreshadows our present world in which the manipulation of electronic gadgets takes the place of thought and in which machines are all too often more interesting than people. And Poe turns the detective story into such a cautionary tale by setting as the task for the mind's exhibition of its mastery the analysis of its own structure. In baiting this task with a narcissistic hook, Poe makes it seem as if the Delphic injunction "Know thyself" had been inscribed on the obverse side of a coin whose reverse bore the inscription "Those whom the gods would destroy, first they make blind."

Poe's underlying project in the Dupin stories, as he makes clear at the start, is the analysis of self-consciousness within the larger project of differentiating the human. But since Poe understands self-consciousness as an infinitely reflexive structure, no image of the self can achieve absolute closure, and Poe is interested in the way that figurations of self-consciousness exhibit within themselves an awareness of their own conditionality. Like my earlier book, *American Hieroglyphics,* this one addresses a problem of ontotheology (the metaphysical quest for the Absolute), tracking the way that Poe and Borges transform this into a quest not for God but for the structure of the self, transform it from a metaphysical quest into the epistemological question of *figuring* the absolute, that impossible task of imaging something that, because it is infinite, cannot be bounded by a line. The present study locates itself within a branch of the history of ideas best designated as the history of the critique of figuration. And it is on this deeper level of significance of the detective genre that Borges's project situates itself. For exactly one hundred years after Poe had originated the form, Borges set out to double that origin, apparently feeling that the genre's deepest meaning had never really been addressed by the tradition that grew out of Poe's work.

In examining Poe's and Borges's detective story projects, this book combines history, literary history, biography, psychoanalysis, and practical and speculative criticism as it traces the issues underlying the detective genre into other works by Poe and Borges and into areas of inquiry as distant and various as the history of mathematics, classical mythology, handedness, the three/four oscillation, the double-mirror structure of self-consciousness, the mythography of Evans and Frazer, the structure of chess, automata, the mind-body problem, the etymology of "labyrinth," and scores of other topics. And throughout, the book strives to honor the aesthetic effect of the genre that is its subject by incorporating into its method the dynamics of a detective story—the uncovering of a mystery, the accumulation of evidence, the tracing of clues, and the final solution that ties the threads together.

It was precisely because writing this book led me into areas of interest outside my own field of expertise that it took so long to complete. And certainly these forays into other disciplines would have been impossible without the advice and encouragement of colleagues and friends in those fields. Evans Harrell, a former colleague in the Johns Hopkins mathematics department, helped me understand the web of mathematical and social issues surrounding the development of algebraic analysis, and he generously read and commented on the sections of the manuscript dealing with these issues. Two former colleagues in the Hopkins classics department, Diskin Clay and Lowell Edmunds, helped me find my way through the classical material, and Lowell Edmunds also read the sections dealing with Oedipus and Theseus, the double axe, the allegory of the cave, and Pythagorean mathematics, and made many useful suggestions.

In trying to acknowledge all the debts incurred in writing a lengthy manuscript, one inevitably runs the risk of forgetting someone, but in looking back over the last decade, there are several other people whose contributions stand out in my memory and whom I wish to thank: first of all, my colleagues in the Spanish department at Hopkins—particularly Harry Sieber and Eduardo Gonzalez—for advising me on the Borges material; Jean McGarry in the Writing Seminars who read the manuscript in its early stages and made perceptive comments; Ron Paulson in the English department for his suggestions about the Hogarth material; Richard Macksey in the Humanities Center for being a constant intellectual resource during the course of the project; several members of the Poe Studies Association, especially Ben Fisher, Kent Ljungquist, Richard Kopley, and G. R. Thompson, for advice and encouragement at crucial moments; and a recent visitor to Hopkins, Edgar Krebs, who, though his field is anthropology, is a skillful critic of Borges's work and was able to provide valuable insights about the Buenos Aires literary scene and the local influences on Borges's writing. Over the years the writing of this book has been materially assisted by several leaves from the Johns Hopkins University and, more recently, by a fellowship from the Guggenheim Foundation, both of which institutions I wish to thank.

In order to sustain one's interest in and energy for a project that lasts twelve years, a writer needs the reaction of readers to the work in progress, and I was able to get this by publishing sections of the book in magazines. I want to thank Richard Macksey at *MLN*, Edgar Dryden at the *Arizona Quarterly*, Richard Poirier at the *Raritan Review*, Staige Blackford at the *Virginia Quarterly Review*, Gordon Hutner at *American Literary History*, Ralph Cohen at *NLH*, Robert Lima at *Critica Hispanica*, Richard Burgin at *Boulevard*, Vicente Massot at *La Nueva Provincia* (Bahía Blanca), and Claudio Escribano, general editor, and Jorge Cruz, editor of the literary supplement, at *La Nación* (Buenos Aires), for taking parts of the book and for granting me permission to reprint them here. In addition, I want to thank Gustavo Pérez-Firmat for inviting me to read part of the book at a session on the continuity of North and South American literature at the American Studies Association convention in 1989 and for including that talk in the collection he edited entitled *Do the Americas Have a Common Literature?* (Duke University Press, 1990), and Richard Kopley for inviting me to speak at the Pym Conference in 1988 and for including a section of the book in his collection *Poe's Pym: Critical Explorations* (Duke University Press, 1992). My next-door neighbor Val Purvis, whose specialty is computer technology, helped me get the manuscript safely through my word processor and assisted in producing many of the book's illustrations, for which I am especially grateful. Finally, let me thank several of my past and present graduate students who served as research assistants and helped prepare the manuscript for publication, in particular, Jennifer Toner, Meredith McGill, Ned Washburn, and Tim Dean.

During the composition of this book, I had the rare privilege of spending some time with one of its subjects. Poe, of course, resides in Baltimore, but Borges paid a visit here in April 1983 to give the Pouder lecture at Johns Hopkins. With the passage of time, the memories of that visit have resolved themselves into a series of seemingly random mental tableaux. On the day of Borges's arrival, we gave a dinner party for him, and as often happens when you finally meet someone whose work you have admired for a long time, what stays in your memory from that meeting is a purely accidental detail. Although I'm sure there must have been interesting stretches of conversation that evening, the only thing I remember is that during the first course the meat in the oven suddenly began to smoke, setting off a smoke detector. While people rushed from the table trying to find where the alarm was coming from and what was wrong (I believe it was Jack Barth who found it at the head of the stairs and turned it off), Borges sat through it all smiling and (my main memory of that evening) swinging his head rhythmically from side to side like Stevie Wonder, trying to locate the source of the sound. When you have known someone only through their writings and those writings are as artful and intelligent as Borges's, you get a sense of the author as almost superhuman. But that evening sitting across from the man who had written all those stories, poems, and essays, a man grown old now and blind, gentle and slightly fragile, the achievement of that writing seemed all the more magnificent for his humanness.

The next day Borges attended a special session of my Poe-Borges seminar and answered questions about his work. And the day after, he and his companion (and later, wife) María Kodama, my colleague Bob Arellano, and I visited the Poe house on Amity Street and Poe's grave in the Westminster churchyard in downtown Baltimore. At the Poe house, the curator gave us a guided tour that, under normal circumstances, includes the tiny third-floor garret bedroom where Poe is thought to have written "Berenicë." But the staircase from the second to the third floor was so cramped and winding that we wondered whether Borges could make it up and down the stairs. Borges, who was game for anything, would have none of our objections, and up we went. In the single third-floor room directly under the eaves, a person of normal height could barely stand upright, so we put Borges in a chair next to the dormer window. There was a stuffed raven on a perch standing on the window sill, and someone guided Borges's hand to the bird's head. He patted it and began to recite "The Raven" from memory. Borges would have gone through the whole poem if there had been time; but we still had to visit the gravesite and there was his lecture that evening on Whitman, so we started down. María Kodama went first to guide Borges. Since the ceiling of the stairwell was extremely low, Borges had to sit down on the top step and then, with María placing his feet securely two steps below, slide himself down to the next step while I steadied him by gripping the collar of his overcoat. As Borges bumped his way step by step down the coffinlike staircase, I imagined Poe coming up this claustrophobic passageway to his room every day, and I suddenly knew where he experienced the sensations described in "The Premature Burial." So Poesque was the setting that for a moment I even imagined, in that telegraphic shorthand of nineteenth-century newspaper headlines dear to the author of *Pym,* what might have happened if Borges's coat collar had slipped from my grasp. FAMOUS WRITER STUCK IN STAIRWELL. CROWD TRAPPED IN ROOM ABOVE TURNS DESPERATE. CANNIBALISM ENSUES. As it happened, Borges made it to the bottom of the stairs in high spirits, clearly enjoying the adventure.

At Poe's grave a small crowd of reporters, photographers, and television newspeople had already gathered. Although the day had started out sunny, by the time we arrived it was cold and gray with a raw wind blowing. The usual protocol in visiting Poe's grave is to bring at least two bouquets of flowers, one for the marble monument in the front of the churchyard beneath which Poe is buried along with his wife and mother-in-law, and a second bouquet for the original gravesite in back of the church where there is still a tombstone bearing Poe's name. The apparent reason for this two-bouquet procedure is that, in disinterring Poe's body, there is a chance the gravediggers might not have gotten the right corpse, and consequently if one leaves a bouquet at both sites, the flowers are sure to find him in one place or the other. Whenever I visit the grave, I am reminded of the final image of Dick Diver in *Tender Is the Night* fading into the landscape: "In any case he is almost certainly in that section of the country, in one town or another."

After putting flowers at both sites, I photographed Borges sitting at the base of the monument running his hand across the bas-relief of Poe's face. By this point we had been in the churchyard about twenty-five minutes, and Borges was clearly feeling the cold. We started back to the car with a reporter following for one last question. With Borges in the passenger seat, the reporter, who was holding the door open on that side and leaning in, asked, "Señor Borges, could you feel the spirit of Poe here today?" Visibly trembling from the cold, Borges replied in his best English manner, "Well, sir, I certainly felt something," and then closed the car door, unaware that he'd almost slammed it on the reporter's head. Borges turned to the other occupants of the car with the air of a small boy who had done his duty and deserved a treat and said, "Now let's go back and get some hot chocolate."

The next day Borges and María Kodama were scheduled to fly out of Baltimore. I had taken several photographs of Borges over the course of the visit, but I wanted one last picture with him. I had been a chess player all my life, and I knew that Borges had been as well. I took along a chess set so we could be photographed playing a game, and Borges was delighted with the idea. I asked him what color he wanted to play, and he chose black, saying that he didn't like making decisions and that having to move first would overwhelm him with possibilities. I set up the opening moves of the Ruy Lopez in honor of item (g) in Pierre Menard's bibliography, and we had the picture taken. Since there was still an hour or so before we had to leave for the airport, we had time for a final conversation about his work. I knew that his visit to Baltimore was simply one stop on a long tour, and I asked him if he was tired and homesick for Buenos Aires. He said that whenever he got tired, he thought about the Argentine writer Lugones who, when he was growing old in the 1930s, felt that nobody read his work anymore, that he was ignored and forgotten, and who in consequence grew so lonely that he finally took his own life. Borges said that no matter how tired he got on these trips, the sense that people cared about him and his work was invigorating. The conversation turned to Poe and his influence, and for a moment Borges grew silent and then in lowered voice, as if confiding a secret, said, "I have always had this fear that some day I would be found out, that people would see that everything in my work is borrowed from someone else, from Poe or Kafka, from Chesterton, Stevenson, or Wells." I said that every writer borrowed from other writers and that the greater the writer, the more he borrowed. Besides, I added, no one cares if a writer borrows his material as long as he makes it his own. I reminded him of Kipling's poem "When 'Omer Smote 'Is Bloomin' Lyre" and its image of Homer borrowing preexisting folksongs for the *Iliad* and *Odyssey*. Soon we were ready to leave for the airport, and on the way there the conversation somehow turned to the noises cowboys make to herd cattle and whether those sounds differ from country to country. My final memory of the visit is driving down the highway with Borges, taking turns imitating either a Texas or a gaucho cattle call.

What these memories of Borges's visit ultimately make me realize is that the final and perhaps greatest debt I owe in writing this book is to Borges himself. For if Borges found his visit to Hopkins tiring but invigorating, I found, time and again, that the memories of that visit invigorated me during the years I worked on this project. I first read Borges's work in 1964. He seemed to me then, and still seems, the most original fiction writer of the second half of the twentieth century, the writer whose work bears the same relationship to the last half of the century that Joyce's does to the first, which is to say, the author without whose work it would be impossible to explain how the writings of his contemporaries got to look that way. What stays in my memory from his visit is the courtliness of his manners (clearly a nineteenth-century courtliness), his wit, his sense of fun, and his modesty. Alastair Reid had once remarked that Borges "wielded his modesty like a club," and yet that last conversation I had with him left me with the impression of someone who seemed not at all sure of what his ultimate place in literature would be and who thought that modesty was the best policy and certainly the one closest to his own temperament.

As I mentioned at the start, this book is in part a product of the form of design called chance. Almost thirty years ago in June 1965, when I was an ensign in the Navy stationed in Hawaii and working in cryptography, I played in a weekend chess tournament, the Oahu Championship. In the fourth round I was paired against a player named Fred Borges. I had bought a copy of *Labyrinths,* the New Directions anthology of Borges's work, the year before, and I mentioned to my opponent, as we filled out our score sheets before the game, that he had the same last name as the South American writer. This drew a blank, so I added, rather pointlessly, that I thought the name was Portuguese in origin. He said it was and pushed down the button that started my clock. The game that followed (a Morra Gambit in the Sicilian Defense) was the best chess game I have ever played in my life, involving at one point an eight-move combination to secure the positional advantage of a rook on the seventh rank.[2] I had thought so long before making the first move of the combination that I had left myself only fifteen minutes to make the last thirty-five moves needed to reach the time control. I won the game and went on to tie for second and third place in the tournament with a USCF senior master behind a grandmaster. As Casey Stengel used to say, you could look it up. Clearly, I had been playing way over my head because I was never to have that much success with tournament chess again, but that game in the fourth round made such a lasting impression that it indelibly linked the name Borges to the game of chess in my mind. Some fifteen years later when I began rereading Borges with the idea of teaching his fiction, that associative link resurfaced, attracting my attention to the line in Borges's first detective story, "In a guessing game to which the answer is chess, which word is the only one prohibited?" It was the following up of that thread that led me to this book, indeed, led me through a maze to a different chess game with another Borges. The book that follows, in homage to the genre Poe invented, mirrors to some degree the structure of a detective story, but it also mirrors, as an homage to Borges's doubling of Poe, the structure of a labyrinth. What this book demands of the reader is patience and trust—patience as the paths of inquiry begin to fork, as digressions shear off from the main line, and then digressions from di-gressions; and trust that these paths will eventually rejoin the main line and ultimately lead to the goal. What it offers in return, I hope, is a mounting sense of excitement as each new piece of information is added to the puzzle and the overall design begins to emerge. Prepare, then, to enter the maze, and at the first fork in the path, bear to the left.

The Mystery to a Solution

1   *Detective Fiction as High Art; Conserving a Sense of the Mysterious; Lacan, Derrida, and Johnson on "The Purloined Letter"; Russell's Paradox*

LET ME START WITH A simple-minded question: How does one write analytic detective fiction as high art when the genre's central narrative mechanism seems to discourage the unlimited rereading associated with serious writing? That is, if the point of an analytic detective story is the deductive solution of a mystery, how does the writer keep that solution from exhausting the reader's interest in the story? How does he write a work that can be reread by people other than those with poor memories? I use the term *analytic detective fiction* here to distinguish the genre invented by Poe in the Dupin tales of the 1840s from stories whose main character is a detective but whose main concern is not analysis but adventure, stories whose true genre is less detective fiction than the quest romance, as one of the masters of the adventure mode, Raymond Chandler, implicitly acknowledged when he gave the name Mallory to an early prototype of his detective Philip Marlowe. For Chandler, the private investigator represents a plausible form of modern knight-errant. In "The Simple Art of Murder" he says that the detective story is the detective's "adventure in search of a hidden truth, and it would be no adventure if it did not happen to a man fit for adventure."[1] The emphasis in Chandler's remarks, as in his fiction, is on the detective's character and his adventures, with the revelation of a hidden truth simply serving as a device to illuminate the former and motivate the latter. But in the analytic detective story the situation is different. As a character, Dupin is as thin as the paper he's printed on, and his adventures amount to little more than reading newspaper accounts of the crime and talking with the prefect of police and the narrator in the privacy of his apartment.

What gives the analytic detective genre its special appeal is that quality the Goncourt brothers noted on first reading Poe. In an 1856 journal entry they described Poe's stories as "a new literary world" bearing "signs of the literature of the twentieth century—love giving place to deductions . . . the interest of the story moved from the heart to the head . . . from the drama to the solution."[2] Precisely because it is a genre that grows out of an interest in deductions and solutions rather than in love and drama, the analytic detective story shows little interest in character, managing at best

1

to produce caricatures—monsters of idiosyncrasy from Holmes to Poirot. In its purest form it puts all its eggs in the basket of plot, and a specialized kind of plot at that. The problem is that this basket seems to be one that can be tipped out in a single reading.

Related to this difficulty is another. If the writer does his work properly, if he succeeds in building up a sense of the mysterious, of some dark secret or intricately knotted problem, then he has to face the fact that there exists no hidden truth or guilty knowledge whose revelation will not seem anticlimactic compared to an antecedent sense of mystery and the infinite speculative possibilities it permits. Borges, a contemporary master of the analytic detective genre, explicitly acknowledges this difficulty in his story "Ibn Hakkan al-Bokhari, Dead in His Labyrinth." He notes that one of his characters, "steeped in detective stories, thought that the solution of a mystery is always less impressive than the mystery itself. Mystery has something of the supernatural about it, and even of the divine; its solution, however, is always tainted by sleight of hand."[3] In a similar vein, Borges praises Chesterton's detective stories because "Chesterton always performs the tour de force of proposing a supernatural explanation and then replacing it, losing nothing, with another one from this world," a procedure that provides, in Borges's terms, a rational solution at the same time that it conserves a suprarational aura of mystery.[4] But, as Borges notes, the case is different with Poe who, though writing "stories of pure, fantastic horror" as well as detective stories, "never combined the two genres" (*BR*, 89). Poe "never invoked the help of the sedentary French gentleman Auguste Dupin . . . to determine the precise crime of 'The Man of the Crowd'" (*BR*, 89).

But if in the analytic detective story the solution is always in some sense an anticlimax that in dissipating the mystery exhausts the story's interest for us, an interest in speculative reasoning that the mystery empowers, how does one write this kind of story as a serious (i.e., rereadable) literary form? How does one both present the analytic solution of a mystery and at the same time conserve the sense of the mysterious on which analysis thrives?

Obviously, if I didn't consider Poe's Dupin stories to be, on the one hand, archetypes of analytic detective fiction, and on the other, serious literary works that demand and repay rereading, there would be no sense in my evoking at this length the apparent incompatibility of these modes and thus the writer's problem in reconciling them. All of which brings me to the task of uncrumpling that much-crumpled thing, "The Purloined Letter," in order to consider the way that this problem of a mystery with a repeatable solution, a solution that conserves (because it endlessly re-figures) the sense of the mysterious, lies at the very origin of the genre.

My approach to "The Purloined Letter" will be along what has become in recent years a well-worn path. I want to look briefly at three readings of the story that form a cumulative series of interpretations, each successive reading commenting both on the story and on the previous reading(s) in the series. They are Jacques Lacan's "Seminar on 'The Purloined Letter'" (1957), Jacques Derrida's "The Purveyor of Truth" (1975), and Barbara Johnson's "The Frame of Reference: Poe, Lacan, Derrida" (1978). Each of these essays presents a lengthy, complex argument in which "The Purloined Letter" is treated as a pretext, read as a parable of the act of analysis. However, I am not so much interested here in following the convolutions of their individual arguments as in isolating a thread that runs through all three, a clue to conduct us through labyrinthine passages. And that thread is the position that each essay takes on what we might call the numerical/geometrical structure of the story.

Let us begin with Lacan. He says that the story consists of "two scenes, the first of which we shall straightway designate the primal scene, and by no means inadvertently, since the second may be considered its repetition."[5] The first, or primal, scene takes place in "the royal *boudoir*" (41), the second scene in "the Minister's office" (42). And according to Lacan, each of these scenes has a triangular structure, composed of "three logical moments" (43) "structuring three glances, borne by three subjects, incarnated each time by different characters":

> The first is a glance that sees nothing: the King and the police.
>
> The second, a glance which sees that the first sees nothing and deludes itself as to the secrecy of what it hides: the Queen, then the Minister.
>
> The third sees that the first two glances leave what should be hidden exposed to whomever would seize it: the Minister, and finally Dupin. (44)

Thus in the royal boudoir the king doesn't see the incriminating letter which the queen in her haste has hidden in the open, leaving it with its address uppermost in plain sight on a table; and the queen, seeing that the king doesn't see the letter, mistakes his blindness for the letter's concealment, thus leaving herself vulnerable to the minister who sees both the king's glance and the queen's and realizes that the letter can be seized before the queen's very eyes precisely because she dare not do anything to attract the king's attention to it.

Similarly, in the second scene at the minister's residence, the letter, having been turned inside out and readdressed in a female hand, is once again hidden in plain sight in a card rack on the mantelpiece. And this time the police, who have searched the minister's quarters repeatedly without noticing the letter, represent that first glance that sees nothing; while the minister, who mistakes the blindness of the police for the con-

cealment of the letter, represents the second glance, and Dupin represents the third glance that sees what the first two miss, that the letter
hidden in the open is his for the taking. The figure who participates in
both these triangular scenes is the minister, and his shifting from the
position of the third glance in the initial scene to that of the second glance
in its repetition exhibits the special vulnerability to self-delusion, to a
blind spot, which the possession of the letter conveys.

In considering Derrida's critique of this reading in his essay "The
Purveyor of Truth," bear in mind that Derrida is motivated less by an
interest in Poe or "The Purloined Letter" than by a desire to score points
off Lacan. As Johnson points out, Derrida, in a lengthy footnote in his
book *Positions,* sketches out the argument that will become "The Purveyor
of Truth" and in this note he explicitly refers to Lacan's multiple "*acts of
aggression*" against him since the publication of *De la grammatologie* in
Critique in 1965.[6] Thus Derrida takes the case of "The Purloined Letter"
for one of the same reasons Dupin did—the minister once did Dupin "an
evil turn" (3:993) at Vienna, and Dupin sees the affair of the letter as an
opportunity to get even. The wit of Derrida's essay lies in the way that it
uses Lacan's reading of "The Purloined Letter" against itself, for if Lacan
believes that with his interpretation of the story he has gained possession
of Poe's "Purloined Letter," has made its meaning his own, then Derrida
will show him that the possession of the letter, as Lacan himself pointed
out, brings with it a blind spot. In his essay Derrida sets out to repeat the
encounter between Dupin and the minister with himself in the role of
Dupin and Lacan in the role of the minister.

Derrida attacks Lacan's reading of the story on a variety of points, but
the one that concerns us is Lacan's notion of the triangular structure of
each of the tale's two scenes. Derrida agrees that the story consists of two
scenes, but not the two on which Lacan focuses. He points out that the
scene in the royal boudoir and the subsequent one at the minister's residence are two narrated scenes within the framing artifice of the story, but
that the story itself consists of two scenes of narration—the first being the
prefect's initial visit to Dupin during which the prefect recounts the
events in the royal boudoir, and the second the prefect's subsequent visit
during which Dupin recounts the events at the minister's residence. While
the narrators of the *two narrated scenes* in the royal boudoir and at the
minister's residence are respectively the prefect and Dupin, the narrator
of the *two scenes of narration* at Dupin's lodgings is Dupin's unnamed companion. Thus, according to Derrida, Lacan reduces the four-sided structure of the scene of narration—what Derrida calls "the scene of
writing"—to the three-sided structure of the narrated scene "by over-
looking the narrator's position, the narrator's involvement in the content

of what he seems to be recounting."[7] In ignoring the presence of the narrator of "The Purloined Letter," Lacan cuts "a fourth side" out of the narrated figure "to leave merely triangles" (54). And he does this, says Derrida, precisely because as a psychoanalyst Lacan projects upon Poe's story the structure of the Oedipal triangle in his desire to read "The Purloined Letter" as an allegory of psychoanalysis or an *"allegory of the signifier"* (Johnson, 115).

Since in his critique of Lacan's interpretation of "The Purloined Letter" Derrida aims to get even with him by being "one up," and since Lacan in his reading of the numerical structure of the tale has already played the numbers one, two, and three (the tale is composed of two scenes, the second of which, by repeating the triangular structure of the first, creates a sameness or oneness between the two), then being one up means playing the next open number (four), hence Derrida's contention that the structure of the scenes is not triangular but quadrangular. However, whether Derrida arrives at this quadrangular structure by adding one to three or by doubling two is a problematic point, a point on which Johnson focuses in her critique of Lacan's and Derrida's readings of the tale.

As Johnson notes, Derrida objects to the triangular configuration that Lacan sees in the repeated scenes because this structure, derived from the Oedipal triangle, represents in Derrida's opinion a characteristic psychoanalytic attempt to dismiss or absorb the uncanny effects of doubling, a doubling Derrida maintains is everywhere present in the tale. Doubling tends, of course, to be a standard element of the analytic detective story, in that the usual method of apprehending the criminal involves the detective's doubling the criminal's thought processes so as to anticipate his next move and end up one jump ahead of him. And the number associated with doubling is usually four rather than two, for what we refer to as doubling is almost always splitting and doubling. Which is to say, the figure of the double externally duplicates an internal division in the protagonist's self (but with the master/slave polarity of that division characteristically reversed), so that doubling tends to be a structure of four halves problematically balanced across the inner/outer limit of the self rather than a structure of two separate, opposing wholes. Thus in the first Dupin story, "The Murders in the Rue Morgue," the narrator says that while observing Dupin in the exercise of his "peculiar analytic ability" (2:533), he entertained "the fancy of a double Dupin—the creative and the resolvent" in accordance with "the old philosophy of the Bi-Part Soul" (2:533). And in "The Purloined Letter" the minister, as both poet and mathematician, is represented as having this same dual intellectual power. In matching wits with the minister, Dupin first doubles his opponent's thought processes—a mental operation that Dupin illustrates by telling the story

of the schoolboy who always won at the game of even and odd—and he
then replays, in effect temporally doubles, the scene in which the minister
originally seized the letter, but with himself now in the minister's role, thus
shifting the minister into the role played by the queen in the original event
and evoking the destabilizing reversal-into-the-opposite inherent in doubling.

As Johnson notes, Derrida thinks that

> the problem with psychoanalytical triangularity . . . is not that it contains the
> wrong number of terms, but that it presupposes the possibility of a successful
> dialectical mediation and harmonious normalization, or *Aufhebung*, of desire.
> The three terms in the Oedipal triad enter into an opposition whose resolution
> resembles the synthetic moment of a Hegelian dialectic. (122)

But that synthetic moment, that successful dialectical mediation of desire
is precisely what the destabilizing effect of doubling constantly subverts,
for in the Oedipal triangle each of the three positions functions as one
pole of a mutually constitutive opposition with one of the other positions
and thus each position is subject to being reversed into its opposite. There
exists in the Oedipal triangle, then, no privileged position that is above or
outside the uncanny effects of doubling, no exempt, objective position
from which to mediate or regularize the subjective interaction of the
other two.

As with Derrida's reading of Lacan, the wit of Johnson's reading of
Derrida lies in the way that she doubles Derrida's own insights back upon
themselves to make them problematic. Thus in dealing with Derrida's
attempt to be one up on Lacan by playing the number four to Lacan's
three, Johnson assimilates their opposed readings of the tale's numerical
structure to the game of even and odd. Derrida opts for a quadrangular
structure (he plays the even number four) in order to evoke the uncanni-
ness, the oddness of doubling, while Lacan opts for a triangular structure
by playing the odd number three, in order to enforce the regularizing or
normalizing effect of the dialectical triad. In this game of even and odd,
Derrida and Lacan end up as reciprocal opposites, as specular doubles of
one another: Derrida asserts the oddness of evenness, while Lacan affirms
the evenness of oddness. Given the destabilizing reversal-into-the-
opposite inherent in doubling, Johnson sees the opposition between Derrida's and Lacan's interpretations as an "oscillation" between the former's
"unequivocal statements of undecidability" and the latter's "ambiguous
assertions of decidability" (146).

As to Johnson's own position on "The Purloined Letter," her reading
of Lacan and Derrida is meant to free her from having to take a position
on the tale's numerical structure, or more exactly, to free her from having

to take a *numerical* position on that structure. Johnson's strategy is to call into question the whole concern with numbers. At one point she asks, "But can what is at stake here really be reduced to a mere numbers game?" (121), and a bit later she answers, "Clearly, in these questions, the very notion of a number becomes problematic, and the argument on the basis of numbers can no longer be read literally" (121). As Johnson sees it, taking a position on the numerical structure of the tale means, for Lacan and Derrida, taking a numerical position, choosing a number, but that means playing the game of even and odd, the game of trying to be one up on a specular, antithetical double. And playing that game means endlessly repeating the structure of "The Purloined Letter" in which being one up inevitably leads to being one down. For if the structure created by the repeated scenes in the tale involves doubling the thought processes of one's opponent in order to use his own methods against him—as Dupin does with the minister, as Derrida does with Lacan, and as Johnson does with Derrida—then the very method by which one outwits one's opponent is the same method that will be used against oneself by the next player in the game, the next interpreter in the series, in order to leave the preceding interpreter one down.

Is it possible, then, to interpret "The Purloined Letter" without duplicating in the interpretive act that reversal-into-the-opposite inherent in the mechanism of seizing the letter as it is described in the tale? Is it possible to generate an insight without a blind spot, without a flaw that allows the insight subsequently to be turned against itself? Clearly, the desire for such an invulnerable insight is at work in Johnson's essay and accounts for the disconcerting level of self-consciousness she maintains regarding her own methodological stance, her own critical assumptions. For Johnson the refusal to take a numerical position on the structure of the tale, to play the next open number (five), for example, is an effort to avoid the game of trying to be one up by adding one to the opponent's numerical position, as Derrida does in playing the number four to Lacan's three; for that game will simply turn into an oscillation between even and odd running to infinity. But is it possible for Johnson to avoid becoming involved in this numbers game simply by refusing to choose a specific number with which to characterize the geometrical/numerical structure of the tale? Doesn't the very form of her essay—as a critique of Derrida's critique of Lacan's reading of "The Purloined Letter"—involve her in the numbers game? In situating her essay as the third of three critical readings following those of Lacan and Derrida, Johnson places herself in that third position which, in the structure governing the wandering of the purloined letter, is the position of maximum insight, but also the position in which the observer is subject to mistaking his insight concerning the subjective interaction of the other two glances for an objective viewpoint above such interaction. Indeed, how are we to describe the relationship between Johnson's interpretation and those of Lacan and Derrida? Are they linked in a triangular structure in which Lacan and Derrida face off as antithetical doubles, while Johnson, by refusing to become involved in the game of even and odd, occupies a position of "successful dialectical mediation" above them, a Hegelian synthesis of their positions? Or are they involved in a quadrangular structure in which Lacan and Derrida are reciprocal halves of one pole of a mutually constitutive opposition (i.e., the pole of trying to be one up on a specular double), while Johnson occupies the other pole of this opposition by doubling back Lacan's and Derrida's methods against them in order to avoid this game of one up? Johnson's final comment on her own methodology invokes the image of Derrida's quadrangular frame: "My own theoretical 'frame of reference' is precisely, to a very large extent, the writings of Lacan and Derrida. The frame is thus framed again by part of its content; the sender again receives his own message backward from the receiver" (146).

Johnson's essay is at odds with itself, as she would be the first to admit. Indeed, it is precisely her strategy to present the opposing aspects of her essay—its explicit refusal to take a numerical position on the structure of the tale coupled with its implicit assumption of a numerical position in representing its relationship to the two earlier essays—as an aporia, a trope of undecidability not unlike the one Paul de Man describes in the passage Johnson uses as the epigraph to her book *The Critical Difference*, whose final chapter is her essay on Derrida and Lacan. In that epigraph de Man evokes the aporia between grammar and rhetoric by citing as an example the case in which Edith Bunker asks her husband Archie if he wants his bowling shoes laced over or under—to which the irascible Archie replies, "What's the difference?" In terms of grammar Archie's reply asks for the difference between two alternatives, but in terms of rhetoric his reply means "Whatever the difference is, it's not important enough to make a difference to me." De Man remarks, "The same grammatical pattern engenders two meanings that are mutually exclusive: the literal meaning asks for the concept (difference) whose existence is denied by the figurative meaning" (Johnson, v). It is in this same vein that Johnson at the end of her essay, after having described the opposition between Derrida's and Lacan's positions as "the oscillation between unequivocal statements of undecidability and ambiguous assertions of decidability," concludes,

"Undecidability" can no more be used as a last word than "destination." . . . The "undeterminable" is not opposed to the determinable; "dissemination" is not opposed to repetition. If we could be sure of the difference between the determinable and the undeterminable, the undeterminable would be comprehended within the determinable. What is undecidable is whether a thing is decidable or not. (146)

What are we to make of these words? By which I mean not just what do these words say grammatically but what do they convey rhetorically, for what purpose are they being said in this context? I think the key lies in Johnson's statement that "'Undecidability' can no more be used as a last word than 'destination.'" At the point she says this, Johnson is nearing her own destination, the end of her essay, and is faced with the formal requirement of saying a last word and thus with the question of whether a last word can be said in the oft-renewed critical discussion of "The Purloined Letter." Having to say a last word, she says in effect, "The last word is that there is no last word." This type of statement, which says one thing grammatically and means its opposite rhetorically, occurs again and again in her essay. As we noted, it is the strategy at work when Johnson refuses to take a numerical position on the structure of the tale at the same time that she implicitly assumes a numerical position in relation to the two earlier readings, which her own essay retrospectively groups into a series along with itself. It is at work again when she turns Derrida's insights on doubling back upon themselves to tell Derrida that it is impossible to be one up on his specular double Lacan, for though what she says on a grammatical level is that it is impossible to be one up in such an encounter, the rhetorical effect of her statement is to leave her one up on her specular double Derrida. And this strategy is at work once again when she decisively concludes, "What is undecidable is whether a thing is decidable or not."

These instances of an aporia between grammar and rhetoric occur in statements that are in one way or another self-reflexive, statements that are themselves included in the class of things to which they refer. A simple example of a self-including statement is the sentence "All statements containing seven words are false." Because the sentence is itself a statement made up of seven words, we are faced with a paradox: if this statement is true, it is false, and if it is false, it is true. Similarly, in an aporia between grammar and rhetoric we are faced, as de Man notes, with a single grammatical pattern that engenders two mutually exclusive meanings. By very reason of the fact that they include themselves in the class of things to which they refer, such statements double back upon themselves and exhibit the uncanny reversal-into-the-opposite inherent in doubling.

One thinks in this connection of Russell's paradox. Distinguishing between two kinds of classes (those that do not include themselves as members and those that do), Russell calls the first class "normal" and the second "non-normal," and he then doubles back upon itself this distinction between nonself-including and self-including classes by asking whether *the class of all normal classes* is a normal or a non-normal class. By definition *the class of all normal classes* includes within itself all normal classes. Consequently, if it is itself a normal class, it must be included in itself. But self-inclusion is the distinguishing characteristic of a non-normal class. *The class of all "normal" classes* is, then, a concept whose form and content are at odds: the concept involves, on the one hand, a formal notion of *class* as absolutely inclusive, which is to say, as ultimately self-inclusive (*the class of all*), that is contradicted, on the other hand, by the content, by the specific definition of the "*classes*" which the former is to include completely within itself. As a result, the class of all normal classes is normal only if it is non-normal, and non-normal only if it is normal. Part of the endless fascination of paradoxes of self-inclusion is, of course, that they seem to reflect in the facing mirrors of language and logic the mysterious nature of self-consciousness as that which seeks to include wholly within itself an exact representation of that which, by its very essence, cannot wholly include itself.

At the very start of her essay Johnson sets the tone for all the self-including statements that are to follow when she remarks that in Poe's tale, Lacan's reading, and Derrida's critique,

> It is the *act of analysis* which seems to occupy the center of the discursive stage, and the *act of analysis of the act of analysis* which in some way disrupts that centrality. In the resulting asymmetrical, abyssal structure, no analysis—including this one—can intervene without transforming and repeating other elements in the sequence, which is thus not a stable sequence, but which nevertheless produces certain regular effects. (110)

The key phrase, of course, is "no analysis—including this one." It has about it the brisk American quality of Mark Twain's "No general statement is worth a damn—including this one"—a general statement that is worth a damn only if general statements aren't worth a damn. The very fact that Johnson makes an analytic statement that includes itself, which is to say, an analysis of her own analysis, in the sentence immediately following her statement that it is the act of analysis of the act of analysis that skews analysis in Poe's tale, Lacan's reading, and Derrida's critique, is her way of announcing her strategy at the start. It is not that Johnson will do anything different in her essay from what Lacan and Derrida have done in theirs. Indeed, it is not clear that she thinks anything different can be done at this point inasmuch as Lacan and Derrida have already replayed the tale's structure in a critical register by acting out the game of even and odd in their opposing positions. What will be different in her version is that these positions will be repeated with a complete awareness of their implications, a total critical self-consciousness that aims to create an insight without a blind spot. For what is at issue here is not so much whether one's critical argument is logically true or false, or one's reading of the tale perceptive or dull, but whether one's interpretive stance is methodologically self-aware or methodologically naive. In its translation from fiction to criticism, the project of analyzing the act of analysis becomes in effect the program of being infinitely self-conscious about self-consciousness. Or put another way, if the structure that we find in "The Purloined Letter" involves doubling an opponent's thought processes in order to turn his own methods against him, then the only defense against having the same strategy repeated against oneself by the next player is to produce an insight or take a position that is already self-consciously doubled back upon itself, as is the case with the type of self-including statement that says one thing grammatically but conveys its opposite rhetorically. For a position that includes itself and its opposite seems to leave no ground on which it can be undermined.

The commitment to an increasingly self-conscious analytic posture that animates this cumulative series of interpretations produces at last a kind of intellectual vertigo, a not uncharacteristic side effect of thought about thought—the rational animal turning in circles trying to catch itself by a tale it doesn't have. And certainly no one enjoyed producing this vertiginous effect more than did Poe, an effect that he imaged as a dizziness experienced at the edge of a vortex or on the brink of a precipice. That the dizzying, self-dissolving effect of thought about thought—what Johnson calls the "asymmetrical, abyssal structure" of analyzing the act of analysis—forms the continuing theme of the Dupin stories is announced in the opening sentence of the first tale, "The Murders in the Rue Morgue." The story begins with the narrator's lengthy prefatory remarks on the nature of the analytical power, remarks that conclude by presenting the narrative as a "commentary upon the propositions just advanced" (2:531). But those prefatory remarks start with this curious proposition: "The mental features discoursed of as the analytical are, in themselves, but little susceptible of analysis" (2:527). Inasmuch as this statement initiates the narrator's own brief analysis of the analytical power, it is self-reflexive: as an analytic statement about the nonsusceptibility of analysis to being analyzed, it is included in the class of things to which it refers, but what it says in effect is that analytic statements cannot wholly include themselves. In analyzing the act of analysis, self-conscious thought turns back upon itself to find that it cannot absolutely coincide with itself. This insight about the nature of thought is at least as old in our tradition as the philosophies of Zeno and Parmenides and as new as Gödel's proof and

Borges's (and Carroll's) map of natural size. It is the paradoxical insight that if one considers the act of thinking and the content of thought as two distinguishable things—as it seems one must in dealing with self-consciousness, with thought that is able to represent itself to itself, able to take itself as its own object—then the attempt to analyze the act of analysis, to include wholly the act of thinking within the content of thought, will be a progression of the order $n + 1$ to infinity. Which is to say that there will always be one more step needed in order to make the act of thinking and the content of thought coincide.

2 Borges and the Paradox of Self-Inclusion; Infinite Progression/Regression; Indivisibility and Totality; Microcosm/Macrocosm; Möbius Strip

THE PARADOX OF ANALYTIC SELF-INCLUSION, of absolute self-consciousness, that lies at the heart of Poe's detective stories is one of Borges's recurring themes. In his essay "Time and J. W. Dunne" (1940), Borges gives a brief list of some of the paradox's philosophical incarnations, beginning with Indian philosophy's "radical negation of introspection" about eight centuries ago:

> Schopenhauer rediscovers it around 1843. "The knower himself," he repeats, "cannot be known precisely as such, otherwise he would be the known of another knower" (*Welt als Wille und Vorstellung*, 2:19). Herbart also played with that kind of ontological multiplication. Before he was twenty he had reasoned that the self must be infinite, since the fact of one's knowing oneself postulates another self which also knows itself, and that self in turn postulates another self.[1]

In his essay "Avatars of the Tortoise" (1939), Borges traces this trope of an infinite progression/regression inherent in self-consciousness back to the "*regressus in infinitum*" (*OI*, 112) of Zeno's paradoxes. He notes that although Aristotle refutes these with "a perhaps disdainful brevity," he nevertheless makes use of them in "his famous *argument of the third man* against the Platonic doctrine, which seeks to demonstrate that two individuals who have common attributes (for example, two men) are mere temporal appearances of an eternal archetype":

> Aristotle asks if the many men and the Man—the temporal individuals and the Archetype—have common attributes. It is obvious that they do: they have the general attributes of humanity. In that case, states Aristotle, it will be necessary to postulate *another* archetype that includes them all, and then a fourth. . . . Zeno of Elea uses infinite regression to deny movement and number; his refuter uses infinite regression to deny universal forms. (*OI*, 110–11)

In a footnote to the preceding passage, Borges adds,

> In the *Parmenides*—which is undeniably Zenonian in tone—Plato invents a very similar argument to show that the one is really many. If the one exists, it partakes of being; therefore, there are two parts in it, one and being; but each

of these parts also has in turn both one and being, so that it is made up of two parts, and every part has these two parts, for the same principle goes on forever. Russell (*Introduction to Mathematical Philosophy* [1919], p. 138) substitutes an arithmetical progression for Plato's geometrical progression. If the one exists, the one partakes of being; but as one and being are different, two exist; but as being and two are different, three exist, etc. (*OI*, 111)

The "geometrical progression" of Plato's argument resembles the mechanism of splitting and doubling, with its simultaneous infinite regression/progression around an ambiguous limit or boundary. In demonstrating that "the one is really many," Plato begins by dividing the one into two parts, one and being, and then proceeds to make the same split in each of the parts *ad infinitum*. As a result, the dividing line by which the one is originally split (and by which all the parts are similarly split) can be interpreted either as an internal limit between parts of a whole (the One) or as an external limit between separate wholes (one and being). (It seems clear that if each part partakes of one and being, all the "parts" possess the characteristics of unitary existence and are thus separately existing wholes.)

The way in which "the one is really many" and the many, one, ultimately comes down, of course, to the way in which those two distinct "things"—thinking and being—are one. In comparing Russell's arithmetical and Plato's geometrical progression, Borges evokes two common reciprocal images of the oneness of thought and being, of the relationship of the individual mind to the universe of things—subtraction/addition and division/multiplication. In Russell's arithmetical progression a part, the one, is subtracted (i.e., differentiated) from the concept of being and then added again, as an independent unit, to the concept of being in order to form a total. And this notion of totality (considered as an independent conceptual unit differentiated from the total) is then named "two." But as that unitary concept of totality named "two" attempts to include itself within (in effect, to add itself to) the total, it generates a further concept of totality named "three." And this process, by the continual addition of a unitary constant to the total, progresses to infinity. Arithmetical progression images the relationship of the individual mind to the universe as the addition of one more separate thing to the totality of separate things. Which is to say that this progression by means of a constant quantity expresses the sense of *equality* among the things constituting the totality, the sense that each of these is, simply in terms of unitary wholeness, equal to any other individual one.

Geometrical progression, on the other hand, images the relationship of the individual mind to the universe as the multiplication, the mental doubling and redoubling, of the totality of things by the individual consciousness, and this progression by means of a ratio expresses the sense of each mind's (theoretical) equality with the sum total of all things. As an image of the relationship of mind to the universe, arithmetical progression tends to evoke a greater sense of the difference, the uniqueness, of each mind within the totality; while geometrical progression—in which each mind, in being equal to the totality, tends to become identical with every other mind—raises the specter that all difference (both between minds and between mind and the universe) is an illusion.

Borges dramatizes the latter state in his tale "Tlön, Uqbar, Orbis Tertius" (1940). The inhabitants of the imaginary planet of Tlön, being "congenitally idealist,"[2] come to believe "that there is only one Individual, and that this indivisible Individual is every one of the separate beings in the universe, and that those beings are the instruments and masks of divinity itself" (F, 27). At one time the thinkers of Tlön had maintained "that equality is one thing and identity another" (F, 27), but since theirs is a "monism, or extreme idealism" that does "not conceive of the spatial as everlasting in time" (F, 24), that denies in effect the being or spatial persistence of material things, there exists, in the absence of matter, no principle of differentiation between mental equality and mental identity, which is to say, no principle of differentiation between ideal archetypes (the mind) and real objects (the universe) or between one mind and another (since there are no bodies to differentiate them). Consequently, "if equality entails identity" (F, 27), every being in the universe is the "one . . . indivisible Individual." And in this "pantheistic idealism" (F, 28), each mind totally represents the whole. (Of course, in such a world the apparent differences between things implied by such phrases as "every being" and "each mind" would have to be consigned to the category of illusion.)

But what is involved in this notion of a totality that contains within it a complete representation of itself, a whole made up of parts each of which is equal to the whole? Wouldn't each of these parts, in order to be a complete representation, have to contain within itself a representation of all the other parts that are contained within and equal to the whole, and wouldn't this process go on to infinity? Borges evokes this microcosmic/macrocosmic regression in tales like "The Aleph" (1945) and "The Zahir" (1947). The Aleph, for example, is "a small iridescent sphere of almost unbearable brilliance . . . probably little more than an inch" in diameter but containing "all space . . . actual and undiminished" (A, 26). Gazing at it, the narrator experiences the endless alternation of container and contained that occurs when the part equals the whole:

> I saw the Aleph from every point and angle, and in the Aleph I saw the earth
> and in the earth the Aleph and in the Aleph the earth; . . . and I felt dizzy and
> wept, for my eyes had seen that secret and conjectured object whose name is
> common to all men but which no man has looked upon—the unimaginable
> universe. (*A*, 28)

The narrator adds that this "strange sphere" is named for "the first letter
of the Hebrew alphabet" perhaps because in "the Kabbala, that letter
stands for the *En Soph,* the pure and boundless godhead," a letter whose
shape is that "of a man pointing to both heaven and earth, in order to show
that the lower world is the map and mirror of the higher," or perhaps
called the Aleph because in "Cantor's *Mengenlehre,* it is the symbol of
transfinite numbers, of which any part is as great as the whole" (*A*, 29).

Clearly, this microcosmic sphere is a physical image of the individual
mind's theoretical absoluteness, its idealized state as a total representation
of the universe. How else are we to understand the otherwise meaningless
remark that this sphere little more than an inch in diameter contains "all
space . . . actual and undiminished" except as an evocation of the metaphysical (i.e., metaphorical) space of thought? The fact that Borges's microcosmic objects are also described as mirrors is a further indication of
their status as physical images of mind. At the end of "The Aleph," for
example, Borges compares the sphere to the Oriental mirror within
whose crystal "the whole world was reflected" and to "Merlin's universal
mirror, which was 'round and hollow . . . and seem'd a world of glas' (*The
Faerie Queene*, 3:2, 19)" (*A*, 30).

From being images of the mind as microcosm, Borges's mirrorlike
devices become images of the microcosmic potential of every object in the
universe. In "The Zahir" the narrator observes,

> Tennyson once said that if we could understand a single flower, we should
> know what we are and what the world is. Perhaps he meant that there is no fact,
> however insignificant, that does not involve . . . the infinite concatenation of
> cause and effect, . . . that the visible world is implicit in every phenome-
> non. . . . The Cabalists pretend that man is a microcosm, a symbolic mirror of
> the universe; according to Tennyson, everything would be.[3]

Indeed, this universal microcosmic status would seem to follow inevitably
from the existence of even one microcosmic subject, one absolute mind,
since a microcosm such as the Aleph (which images the theoretical absoluteness of thought as an absoluteness of visual representation that abol-
ishes the limitations of perspectival consciousness) presents each object
from an infinite number of spatial and temporal perspectives at once, an

infinity of perspectives that reflects the object's relationship to every other object in the universe. It is as if each object were surrounded by a timeless, 360-degree globe of consciousness, so that it becomes a kind of spherical mirror. The narrator of "The Aleph" says that within the small iridescent sphere "each thing (a mirror's face, let us say) was infinite things, since I distinctly saw it from every angle of the universe" (*A*, 26–27). And the narrator of "The Zahir" notes that where once he had to visualize separately the obverse and reverse of the microcosmic coin, "Now I see them simultaneously. . . . It is as though my eyesight were spherical, with the Zahir in the center" (*L*, 163).

But if everything in the universe is a potential microcosm, then the universe becomes an abyss of geometric progression in which microcosmic subjects and objects endlessly and emptily multiply one another. In his essay "Partial Enchantments of the *Quixote*" (1949), Borges considers the way the ideal of microcosmic self-inclusion threatens to produce, in literary works that reflect on their own representational status, this abyss of repetition. Discussing the self-reflexive character of the *Quixote*—the way, for example, that in Part Two of the book "the protagonists of the *Quixote* who are, also, readers of the *Quixote*, have read Part One"—Borges cites a series of literary precursors who anticipate this aspect of Cervantes' novel: "We inevitably remember the case of Shakespeare, who includes on the stage of *Hamlet* another stage, where a tragedy almost like that of *Hamlet* is being presented" (*OI*, 44–45). Also night 602 from *A Thousand and One Nights:* "That is when the Sultan hears his own story from the Sultana's mouth. He hears the beginning of the story, which embraces all the other stories as well as—monstrously—itself" (*OI*, 45). What is common to both these examples is that they exhibit the failure of self-inclusion, the failure to produce an absolutely exact self-representation. In the case of *Hamlet* "the imperfect correspondence of the principal work and the secondary one lessens the effectiveness of that inclusion" (*OI*, 45), while in the case of *A Thousand and One Nights* the narrative line, which threatens to double back to its beginning and thus render the work "infinite and circular," makes this self-including gesture at night 602, so that the work thus rendered infinitely circular would be simply a "truncated story" (*OI*, 45).

One could object, of course, that the failure of self-inclusion in both these instances is not the fault of the method but of the author, that, for example, Shakespeare could have created a perfect correspondence between "the principal work and the secondary one." As if in response to this objection, Borges concludes the essay with an example of self-inclusion that presupposes an exact correspondence between the object and its self-contained representation. The example, taken from Josiah Royce's *The World and the Individual* (1899), supposes that on "a portion of the surface of England" one builds a "precise map of England":

> The map, in order to be complete, according to the rule given, will have to contain, as a part of itself, a representation of its own contour and contents. In order that this representation should be constructed, the representation itself will have to contain once more, as a part of itself, a representation of its own contour and contents; . . . and so on without limit. (*OI*, 46)

That the failure of self-inclusion results not from human error but from a flaw in the project itself is made clear by Royce's specification that the resemblance between the country and the map be "absolutely exact" (*OI*, 46), in effect, ruling out any error in representation at the start—a specification whose absoluteness creates the infinite regression of map within map and thus prevents the task of achieving absolute exactness from ever being completed. Moreover, the *regressus in infinitum* turns into a literal *reductio ad absurdum* as the continuing diminution in the size of these representations (nested one within another) brings us to a vanishing point where representation becomes meaningless. In citing this example, Borges gives us an instance of spatial self-inclusion so easily visualizable that it renders perspicuous the logical criteria of self-inclusion, criteria he means for us to apply to the more complex problem of temporal self-inclusion presented by *Hamlet* and *A Thousand and One Nights*.

Gazing, then, at this map of England built upon "a portion of the surface of England," what do we see? First, self-inclusion involves in this case the *spatial containment* of the representation within the boundaries of the thing represented. Which is to say, the boundaries of the map and those of the country do not coincide. But in what does this difference between a thing and its self-included representation consist? It must be either a difference in detail or a difference in size or both, for if there were a difference in neither, the map and the country—given that one is constructed upon the surface of the other—would be indistinguishable. Borges's favorite image of this state of no-difference is the map of natural size described by the German professor in Lewis Carroll's *Sylvie and Bruno Concluded* (1893). The professor says that in his native country the cartographers, seeking absolute exactness, finally made a map whose scale was one mile to the mile: "'It has never been spread out, yet,' said Mein Herr: 'the farmers objected: they said it would cover the whole country, and shut out the sunlight! So we now use the country itself, as its own map, and I assure you it does nearly as well.'"[4]

While Royce specifies, on the one hand, a difference of size between country and map, he stipulates, on the other, that the map "represent, down to the minutest detail, every contour and marking, natural or artificial, that occurs upon the surface of England" (*OI*, 46). Which is to say, the map will reproduce not only the details of the country, but also the proportional relationship between them. Thus in Royce's example the infinite regression of representation within representation combines both an arithmetical component (the series proceeds by the continual addition of a constant unit, i.e., one more map) and a geometrical component (the series maintains a constant ratio or proportion between the successive representations and the thing represented).

In imaging self-inclusion as the physical containment of the representation within the space of the thing represented, Royce's example renders the distinction between form and content endlessly reversible by undermining one of the principal oppositions on which our understanding of the form/content distinction is based—the outer/inner relationship between container and contained. Since the country of England includes as part of its contents "a representation of its own contour and contents" (its own form/content structure), we are faced with a situation in which the country's content (the area contained within its bounding outline) physically encompasses its own form (its "contour"), so that the form is now an inner to the content's outer, a reversal endlessly repeated as the maps nest one within another.

This continual reversal of the inner/outer relationship between content and form becomes even more complex in the case of temporal self-inclusion precisely because the notion of containment as applied to a temporal form is more problematic. If, for example, in writing the play within a play in *Hamlet*, Shakespeare had created an exact correspondence between the principal work and the secondary one, then the performance of this *Hamlet* could never be completed. It would become trapped in a kind of perpetual stutter at the point in act III, scene II where the play within a play begins, always starting over there, never able wholly to include itself. To phrase the problem in this way is, of course, to figure the temporal progress of the drama as if it were a line in space and thus to imagine the kind of containment involved in temporal self-inclusion as if it were the enclosing of an area by the circumference of a circle or the bounding outline of a map. But is there some other way of imagining containment, the inclusion of one thing within another, than in spatial terms? To understand what is at issue here, imagine a literary work that makes its self-including gesture at the end of the narrative line rather than at its midpoint as in *Hamlet* and *A Thousand and One Nights*. In Borges's first detective story, "The Garden of Forking Paths" (1941), one of the characters speculates about just such a work: "I kept asking myself how a book could be infinite. I could not imagine any other than a cyclic volume, circular. A volume whose last page would be the same as the first and so have the possibility of continuing indefinitely" (*F*, 97). At the time he wrote, Borges had a striking example of such a circular work fresh at hand in Joyce's *Finnegans Wake*. The book had appeared in 1939, and Borges had discussed its linguistic innovations in a brief essay published in *Sur* in November of that same year (*BR*, 347). (Interestingly enough, Borges included a character named Finnegan in his second detective story, "Death and the Compass," published three years later.) In *Finnegans Wake* the unfinished last sentence ("A way a lone a last a loved a long the"[5]) is meant to lead us back to, and be completed by, the opening words of the book ("riverrun, past Eve and Adam's, from swerve of shore to bend of bay, brings us by a commodious vicus of recirculation back to Howth Castle and Environs" [3]), a circularizing of the temporal line of the narrative that enacts the "recirculation" of the temporal river back through its origin (Eve and Adam) evoked in the book's closing and opening passages.

But here two further questions arise. First, how does a work *temporally include* an exact representation of itself within itself? And second, what differentiates the work from its temporally included self-representation? To visualize the problem, imagine that the words of *Finnegans Wake* were written in one long line on a Möbius strip, so that the unfinished last sentence ultimately led back into the book's opening words. Our first reading of the book would inevitably bring us to the point where the narrative line, in circling back to its beginning, launched us automatically into a second reading. And that second reading would, then, constitute in relation to the first an exact self-representation which the work temporally includes by making its form initiate its own repetition, its end lead back into its beginning. And, of course, that second reading, in order to be an exact representation, would lead inevitably to a third, and so on. In temporal self-inclusion, then, the work formally embodies, which is to say, it implicitly enacts, its own continual rereading as a representation of the work's temporal (repetitive) mode of representationality. The difference between the work and its temporally included self-representation is not a difference of physical size or detail, as in the case of spatial self-inclusion, since obviously there are just as many words in the second reading of the text as in the first. Rather it is a difference of two (or more) separate times of reading that cannot be made to coincide no matter how exactly the text is repeated.

If we try to describe the second reading of the work in spatial terms, we find it has a dual status. In relation to the first reading it is a content, a temporal contained, to that reading's temporal container, an inner to its outer; while in relation to the third reading the second is a temporal container to the third's contained, an outer to its inner. In using spatial imagery to represent the process of temporal inclusion, I want to call attention to one of our most basic spatial assumptions about the act of rereading: If we imagine the form/content structure of a literary work as a container/contained relationship, then we inevitably think of our entrance into the work as a passage from outer to inner, from surface to depth, as in the classical trope of chaff and fruit that figures linguistic interpretation as the husking of an outer shell of words to reach an inner kernel of meaning. Within this image complex, the temporal movement from reading to rereading bears an implicit spatial vector pointing from surface to depth, and since rereading is imagined as the process of going deeper into a work, the temporal opposition earlier/later as applied to successive readings is coded as the spatial opposition outer/inner, that is, an earlier reading is experienced as an outer to a later reading's inner. But in works that circle back to enact the temporally repetitive nature of narrative representation, the problematic character of this spatial imaging of temporal inclusion is structurally evoked as the continual oscillation, in the act of rereading, of the inner/outer relationship between form and content.

One reason, then, for suggesting the Möbius strip as an image of temporal self-inclusion was to provide a more accurate spatial representation of the reversible form/content status of rereading. For the Möbius strip is not simply a circle, but a circle with a loop in it that turns the two sides of the strip into one continuous surface along its length, its lengthwise circulation continually reversing the distinction between inner and outer exhibited at its width. Since the strip's special character is precisely a function of the opposition between its two-sided width and its one-sided length, the Möbius strip is constitutively at right angles to itself. And as such, it evokes the way that a self-including structure is essentially at odds with itself, a condition frequently imaged as a contradiction in dimensionality. As we shall see, Poe created his own version of the loop in the Möbius strip, some twenty years before Möbius, with the everting of the purloined letter, the turning of the letter inside out like a glove.

3 Container/Contained; The Everting of the Letter; The Game of Even and Odd; Simple and Odd; Revenge on a Double; One Bad Turn

THE EXAMPLES OF SELF-INCLUSION discussed so far and the questions they raise provide a background against which to examine the type of self-inclusive gestures made in and by Poe's "Purloined Letter." The tale is one of the earliest and most sophisticated of a group of American symbolist works in which textual self-inclusion is a function of the coincidence of the text's title and the name of the central symbolic object the tale presents. In such works—*The Scarlet Letter* and *Moby-Dick* are other examples—the qualities the text attributes to the symbolic object are for the most part the attributes of the text itself. The object called the purloined letter, described by and thus contained in the story called "The Purloined Letter," is a self-included linguistic representation of the text's own representational status, in effect a symbol of the conditions of linguistic representationality. This aspect of the letter is made clear by its most distinctive feature: the document is always hidden in the open. On the original occasion, in the royal boudoir, the queen conceals the letter in plain sight on the surface of a table, having first turned the letter so that its "address" is "uppermost" and its "contents thus unexposed" (3:977). And on the second occasion, at the minister's residence, the minister hides the letter in a card rack dangling from the mantelpiece, "full in the view of every visiter" (3:991), although he has first taken the precaution of refolding the letter "in a reversed direction," turning it like "a glove, inside out," before readdressing and resealing it (3:992).

What this aspect of the letter symbolically evokes is the principal mystery of writing—that letters (written characters) on the surface of a sheet of paper somehow physically "contain" or "conceal" something metaphysical (thought)—a mysterious concealment/containment symbolized even more explicitly by Poe in another form of writing he was obsessed with, the encrypted message. But if the notion of containment implies that the contained (thought) is physically located inside the container (writing), a container that stores it (that holds it in place yet conceals that thought from direct view), then where on a sheet of paper is that physical difference between an inside and an outside located? Where is the depth on that surface?

In symbolizing the representational status of letters (writing) through the physical attributes of a single letter (missive), Poe presents us with what seems to be an obvious example of the alignment of the container/contained distinction with the physical difference between outer and inner. The letter is a single sheet of paper folded so that its message is on the inside and its address on the outside. And this equation of the letter's inner meaning with its physical inner surface is emphasized when the queen, in hiding the letter, turns the unfolded sheet so that the side with the address is uppermost and the side with the "contents" is "unexposed." The address written on the outside surface of the sheet represents the openness, the physical visibility, of writing as opposed to the unseen thought the writing conceals.

But this missive's concealment of its message, as a figure of writing's physical containment of its metaphysical content, is evoked only to be undercut. For on the two occasions when the letter is hidden in the open, we are confronted with a form of concealment that does not involve placing the missive out of sight inside a container. This conscious undermining of the equation of an "inner" meaning with a physical inside is itself emphasized when the minister hides the letter by everting it, by turning it inside out like a glove. In reversing the outside/inside relationship between container and contained, Poe indicates that the way writing physically "contains" thought is by hiding it *on* and not *inside* the written surface. For it clearly makes no difference to this form of concealment whether the letter's outside is exposed to view (as in the royal boudoir) or its inside (as in the minister's residence). Moreover, since the scenario of seizing the letter hidden in plain sight symbolizes the act of reading (in which one seizes the meaning concealed on the surface of writing), the turning of the letter inside out (the reversal of container and contained), considered as a figure of the *repetition* of this symbolic scenario of reading, evokes the form/content oscillation that occurs in *rereading* a work such as "The Purloined Letter" (a work that, because it includes a representation of its own formal status as writing as part of its content, already involves another form/content oscillation like that noted earlier in both spatial and temporal self-inclusion).

In reading this type of self-including work, one confronts a mirror image of the self, a figure of an individual consciousness that is constituted precisely by its mutually reflective relationship to a self-included (mental) representation of its own representational (symbolic/linguistic) status. And consequently the purloined letter's arraying of the question of how writing physically contains the metaphysical becomes in this context a figure of the body/mind relationship within the self, the problematic way the body physically contains or grounds intellection.

Since the self-including gesture of analyzing the act of analysis involves a doubling back in which self-consciousness, attempting to be absolutely even with itself, finds that it is originally and essentially at odds with itself, it is not surprising that in "The Purloined Letter" Dupin, in illustrating the way one doubles the thought processes of an opponent, gives as an example "the game of 'even and odd'" (3:984). In this game "one player holds in his hand a number" of marbles "and demands of another whether that number is even or odd. If the guess is right, the guesser wins one; if wrong, he loses one" (3:984). Dupin then tells the story of an eight-year-old boy who was so good at this guessing game that he won all the marbles at his school. The boy's "mode of reasoning" involved "an identification of the reasoner's intellect with that of his opponent" (3:984), and this doubling of the opponent's thought processes was achieved by a physical doubling of his appearance. The boy explained to Dupin: "I fashion the expression of my face, as accurately as possible, in accordance with the expression" of the opponent "and then wait to see what thoughts or sentiments arise in my mind or heart, as if to match or correspond with the expression" (3:984–85). The narrator comments that "the identification . . . of the reasoner's intellect with that of his opponent, depends . . . upon the accuracy with which the opponent's intellect is admeasured" (3:985), and Dupin, agreeing with this observation, adds,

> The Prefect and his cohort fail so frequently, first, by default of this identification, and, secondly, by ill-admeasurement, or rather through non-admeasurement, of the intellect with which they are engaged. They consider only their *own* ideas of ingenuity; and, in searching for anything hidden, advert only to the modes in which *they* would have hidden it . . . but when the cunning of the individual felon is diverse in character from their own, the felon foils them, of course. This always happens when it is above their own, and very usually when it is below. They have no variation of principle in their investigations. (3:985)

Now what are we to make of this? If, as Dupin says, the reason that the prefect and his men so frequently fail in admeasuring the opponent's intellect is that "they consider only their *own* ideas of ingenuity," that they are unable to imagine or conceive of the workings of a mind "diverse in character from their own" (always the case when the level of the mind is above their own and usually the case when it is below), then is there anything that occurs in the rest of Poe's tale that would lead us to believe this observation of Dupin's about the reason for the prefect's failure? Which is to say, if the prefect and his men can only catch felons whose minds are similar to their own and if what they need in this case is the ability to imagine the workings of a mind radically different from theirs, then does Dupin's method of outwitting the minister provide any evidence that this ability to imagine a radically different mind really exists? In fact, isn't all of the tale's emphasis on the resemblance between Dupin and the minister, on their possessing the same dual creative/resolvent power, part of a plot line in which Dupin outwits the minister only because their minds are so much alike? Isn't it precisely because the minister has hidden the letter at his residence in the same way that the queen hid it in the royal boudoir—by turning it and leaving it out in the open—that Dupin already knows where to look for the letter when he visits the minister? And doesn't Dupin recover the letter by replaying the same scenario by which the minister originally stole it?

Isn't all this simply a device to make us realize that it is impossible to imagine or conceive of a mind whose workings are radically different from one's own? We don't have any direct access to another's thought. Our ideas of the workings of another person's mind may be derived from what he says or does or tells us he is thinking, but our ideas of another's mind are still *our* ideas, a projection that we make of that mind's otherness to our own based on the only immediate experience that one has of psychic otherness, the self's original otherness to itself, that difference that constitutes personal identity.

In "Morella" (1835) Poe quotes Locke's definition of personal identity as "the sameness of a rational being" (2:226). But one immediately thinks, "Sameness as opposed to what?" For in differential terms, it makes no sense to speak of a rational being's continuing sameness with itself unless there is also a sense in which a rational being is continually different from itself. In "Morella" Poe says, "Since by person we understand an intelligent essence having reason, and since there is a consciousness which always accompanies thinking, it is this consciousness which makes every one to be that which he calls 'himself'—thereby distinguishing him from other beings that think, and giving him his personal identity" (2:226). It is this difference of thought from itself—which Poe evokes here as the difference between thinking and "a consciousness which always accompanies thinking"—that enables a rational being to recognize its sameness with itself and thus recognize its difference from others. It is precisely because the self's thought of another mind's otherness to itself reflects the otherness of thought to itself that the effort to imagine an opponent's thought processes produces a specular, antithetical double. And consequently, for all that "The Purloined Letter" purports to be about the way in which one effects "an identification of the reasoner's intellect with that of his opponent," it is in fact about that psychic difference which permits thought to be identified with itself, that difference which constitutes self-identity precisely *because* it prevents thought from being absolutely even with itself. And it is this difference that Poe evokes at the very start of the

Dupin stories when he says that the "mental features discoursed of as the analytical are, in themselves, but little susceptible of analysis."

As is often the case in his fiction, Poe, using the picture language of radicals, emblemizes this latent meaning on the level of etymology, a level to which he directs our attention in "The Purloined Letter" when he has Dupin, in arguing against those who equate analysis with algebra, remark, "If a term is of any importance—if words derive any value from applicability—then 'analysis' conveys 'algebra' about as much as, in Latin, *'ambitus'* implies 'ambition,' *'religio'* 'religion,' or *'homines honesti,'* a set of *honorable* men" (3:987). Since in each of these examples an English word has a meaning different from that of its Latin root, the inference seems clear: In "The Purloined Letter" "if a term is of any importance," we should submit it to philological analysis to see if the root from which it derives has different or additional meanings compared to its English form, meanings that might alter, reverse, or deepen the significance of the passages in which this term appears.

Let us apply this principle suggested by Dupin's remark to two interlocking pairs of words in the tale. On his first visit, the prefect introduces the affair of the letter like this: "The fact is, the business is *very* simple indeed, and I make no doubt that we can manage it sufficiently well ourselves; but then I thought Dupin would like to hear the details of it, because it is so excessively *odd*." To which Dupin replies, "Simple and odd" (3:975). Dupin's emphatic repetition of the words is meant to fix them in our minds so that later when he describes the game of even and odd, we hear the echo and link the pairs. And to make sure that we do not miss the connection, Dupin, immediately after mentioning the game of even and odd, says, "This game is simple" (3:984).

Simple, even, odd—what are their roots? The word *simple* comes from the Latin *simplex,* meaning "single," "unmixed," "not compounded."[1] The word *even* derives from the Anglo-Saxon *efne,* meaning "flat," "level," and ultimately from the Indo-European base **im-nos-,* meaning "what is the same," and containing the adverbial base **im-,* meaning "just like" (W, 503). The word *odd* derives from the Old Norse *oddi,* meaning a "point of land, triangle, hence (from the third angle) odd number" (W, 1017). Three words and at the root of each a number—simple, single, *one;* even, things just alike, *two;* odd, a triangular point of land, *three.* And these three words, grouped into two pairs (simple/odd, even/odd), contain, as it were, four syntactic places between them which the three words fill by one of the words being repeated. The doubling of the word *odd* links the two pairs. It gives them their element of sameness, evoking that condition of being at odds with itself, that difference from itself, that constitutes the sameness of a rational being. The three words—both through their meanings and through the way that they are paired and linked—are an emblem of the numerical structures that govern the tale, which is to say, of the numerical steps or geometrical patterns that self-consciousness goes through in trying to analyze itself.

Dupin says that the game of even and odd is simple, and throughout the Dupin stories Poe associates simplicity with the highest, purest form of ratiocination. In his prefatory remarks to "The Murders in the Rue Morgue" the narrator, contrasting the games of chess and draughts, argues that in chess with its variety of pieces and moves "what is only complex is mistaken . . . for what is profound" (2:528). But in the simple game of draughts "the analyst throws himself into the spirit of his opponent, identifies himself therewith, and not unfrequently sees thus, at a glance, the sole methods (sometimes indeed absurdly simple ones) by which he may seduce into error or hurry into miscalculation" (2:529). In this same vein, Dupin suggests to the prefect on his first visit that "the very simplicity" of the affair of the letter constitutes its oddness: "Perhaps the mystery is a little *too* plain. . . . A little *too* self-evident" (3:975). And later Dupin says that the minister, in hiding the letter, "would be driven, as a matter of course, to *simplicity,* if not deliberately induced to it as a matter of choice" (3:989). As in that "game of puzzles . . . played upon a map" (3:989), the minister, says Dupin, would choose a hiding place that would "escape observation by dint of being excessively obvious," relying on the fact that "the intellect suffers to pass unnoticed those considerations which are too obtrusively and too palpably self-evident" (3:990). But what is that simple thing whose very simplicity makes it so odd, so mysterious because so obvious, hiding out in the open "immediately beneath the nose of the whole world" (3:990)? What but self-consciousness, that condition of being at odds with itself that constitutes the sameness, the simplicity of a rational being?

By definition a number is odd if, when the number is divided by two, there is a remainder of one. And by that definition the first odd number is three. In that simple game of even and odd in which self-consciousness analyzes itself, the question inevitably arises as to whether, when the mind's desire to be absolutely even with itself is divided into the mind's essential condition of being at odds with itself, the one that is always left over is the same as the number one that precedes two, the same as that mythic, original, undivided unity prior to all paring/pairing. Or put another way, when the mind tries to make the act of thinking coincide absolutely with the content of thought only to find that there is always one more step needed to achieve this coincidence, is the infinite progression that results simply the antithetical mirror image of a Zenonian infinite regression which, by dividing a quantity in half, then dividing the half in half, then dividing the quarter in half and so on to infinity, seeks a lower limit, a part that cannot be halved again, a thing so small that, being indivisible, it represents an undivided unity, an original one?

Poe is too good both as philosopher and philologist not to know that the simple thing that is self-consciousness could never be as simple as that. Indeed, if the mind were ever able to make the act of thinking and the content of thought coincide so that there was no difference between them, then self-consciousness, that identity constituted by thought's difference from itself, would simply go out like a light. Such an undifferentiated one would be indistinguishable from zero. Though the root of the word *simple*, the Latin *simplex*, means "single," "unmixed," "not compounded," the roots of the word *simplex*—the Latin words *semel*, meaning "once," "a single time," and *plico*, meaning "to fold, fold together"[2]—make it clear that to be unmixed or uncompounded does not mean to be undifferentiated. For in the picture language of these radicals we can see that a thing that is single-fold is something—like a sheet of paper, a letter—that in being folded a single time is doubled back upon itself. That the image of self-consciousness as a *simple* fold doubling an inscribed surface back on itself was in Poe's mind when he plotted the folding/refolding of the purloined letter can be inferred from an 1845 poem on folding money called "Epigram for Wall Street" attributed to him:

> I'll tell you a plan for gaining wealth,
> > Better than banking, trade or leases—
> Take a bank note and fold it up,
> > And then you will find your money in *creases!*
> This wonderful plan, without danger or loss,
> > Keeps your cash in your hands, where nothing can trouble it;
> And every time that you fold it across,
> > 'Tis as plain as the light of the day that you *double* it!   (1:378)

The infinite progression implicit in the analysis of the act of analysis is evoked at the end of "The Purloined Letter" with the revelation of Dupin's revenge on the minister. This attempt by a mastermind to get even with his specular double clearly serves as a figure of the analytic mind's attempt at mastery, its attempt to be absolutely even with itself. Knowing that the minister "would feel some curiosity in regard to the identity of the person who had outwitted him" (3:993), Dupin leaves him a clue by substituting for the purloined letter one containing a quotation from Crébillon's "Atrée" copied out in his own handwriting, a hand with which the minister "is well acquainted" (3:993). In signing his deed, Dupin marks it as revenge, which is to say, he insures that the minister will interpret his actions not simply as the paid intervention of a gifted amateur sleuth or an intellectual duel to decide the cleverest man in Paris, but rather as repayment for the evil turn the minister did Dupin at Vienna. For I take it that the satisfaction of revenge requires—except in those cases where it is carried out on a substitute—a moment of revelation in which the object of revenge learns by whom, and for what, he is being paid back, a point that Poe underlines by having Dupin choose his quotation-signature from just such a revelatory moment in an eighteenth-century revenger's tragedy.

And yet from what we know of the minister it is inconceivable that once he learned of Dupin's revenge he would let the matter rest there—and equally inconceivable that his double would not know this. For though it might seem that with Dupin's revenge the score between them is even at one apiece (one bad turn at Vienna repaid by one bad turn at Paris), if the minister allows Dupin's trick to go unanswered, then Dupin will have had the last turn; and as proverbial wisdom assures us, the last word or last laugh is not just one word or one laugh like any other. The power to bring a series of reciprocal actions to an end, like the power to originate, involves the notion of a one that is simultaneously more than one. Consequently, we are left with the paradoxical situation in which Dupin's outwitting of the minister will constitute an evening of the score between them at one apiece only if the minister *does not* allow Dupin's trick to end the series, does not allow it to be that one last turn that in its finality is always more than one. It is not so much that one bad turn deserves another as that one bad turn demands another if it is to be experienced as simply one turn. All of which emphasizes the mutually constitutive contradictoriness of trying to *get even* with a specular double by being *one up on him*.

4 Borges's "Death and the Compass"; The Color Red; Via Negativa/Via Positiva; *Indivisibility versus Totality;* The Three/Four Oscillation

SO FAR WE HAVE LOOKED at three analytic readings of "The Purloined Letter" by Lacan, Derrida, and Johnson, as well as at Poe's own self-conscious thematizing within the story of the numerical/geometrical structure enacted in its interpretation. We must now add another element to this discussion by looking at a literary reading of Poe's tale that antedates the earliest of the three analyses by at least fifteen years: the reading that Borges gives of "The Purloined Letter" when he rewrites its numerical/geometrical structure in his own detective story "Death and the Compass" (1942). In the opening paragraph Borges explicitly links the tale to the Dupin stories, remarking that the detective Erik Lönnrot "thought of himself as a pure logician, a kind of Auguste Dupin" (*A*, 65). The plot of "Death and the Compass" revolves around a series of murders. All the obvious clues suggest that the number in the series is three, but all the less than obvious clues—the kind that police inspector Treviranus would miss, but Erik Lönnrot would not—point to the number four. We learn at the end of the story that the series of crimes has been planned by Lönnrot's archenemy, the criminal Red Scharlach, who, seeking to lure Lönnrot unawares to his own destruction, has counted on the fact that the detective would solve the arcane clues Treviranus missed and that Lönnrot's intellectual pride would blind him, would make him think that because he was one jump ahead of the police, he was one jump ahead of the criminal as well.

Lönnrot and Scharlach are, of course, doubles of one another, as their names indicate. In a note to the tale Borges says, "The end syllable of Lönnrot means red in German, and Red Scharlach is also translatable, in German, as Red Scarlet" (*A*, 269). Elsewhere Borges tells us that *Lönnrot* is Swedish, but neglects to add that in Swedish the word *lönn* is a prefix meaning "secret," "hidden," or "illicit."[1] Thus Lönnrot, the secret or hidden red, pursues and is pursued by his double Red Scharlach (Red Scarlet), the doubly red.

Scharlach's motive is revenge. In their final confrontation, he reminds Lönnrot that three years earlier the detective had arrested Scharlach's brother in a gambling dive and that in the ensuing shootout Scharlach had escaped, as he says, with "a cop's bullet in my guts" (*A*, 75). In hiding, delirious with fever for nine days and nights, Scharlach swore to "weave a maze around the man" who sent his brother to prison (*A*, 76). This elaborate revenge on "a kind of Auguste Dupin" for the arrest of a brother is probably an allusion to the fact that in "The Purloined Letter" the Minister D—— has a brother with whom he is sometimes confused because they "both have attained reputation in letters" (3:986). Since Dupin gets even with the minister, are we to see Scharlach's revenge on Lönnrot as an attempt to even the score for that earlier revenge on a brother criminal?

The maze Scharlach weaves around the detective begins with the murder of Rabbi Marcel Yarmolinsky on the third of December at a hotel in the north of the city. Yarmolinsky is a Talmudic scholar, and among his effects the police find "a treatise . . . on the Tetragrammaton" (*A*, 67) and in his typewriter a sheet of paper bearing the words "*The first letter of the Name has been uttered*" (*A*, 67). The second murder occurs on the night of January 3 in the west of the city. The victim, Daniel Simon Azevedo, is found lying on the doorstep of a paint store beneath "the shop's conventional red and yellow diamond shapes" (*A*, 68–69). Chalked across the diamond shapes are the words "*The second letter of the Name has been uttered*" (*A*, 69). The third murder occurs on the night of February 3 in the east of the city. The victim, whose name is either Gryphius or Ginzberg, telephones Treviranus offering to give him information about the murders of Yarmolinsky and Azevedo, but the call is interrupted by the arrival of two men who forcibly remove Gryphius-Ginzberg from the sailor's tavern where he has been staying. It is Carnival time and the two men are wearing harlequin "costumes of red, green, and yellow lozenges" (*A*, 70). Tracing the interrupted phone call, Treviranus arrives at the tavern to find scrawled on a market slate out front "*The last letter of the Name has been uttered*" and in Gryphius-Ginzberg's room "a star-shaped spatter of blood" and "a 1739 edition of Leusden's *Philologus Hebraeo-Graecus*" with the following passage underlined: "The Jewish day begins at sundown and ends the following sundown" (*A*, 71). On the night of March 1 Treviranus receives a sealed envelope containing "a letter signed by one 'Baruch Spinoza'" (*A*, 72) and a map of the city. The letter writer predicts that on the third of March there will not be a fourth murder because the locations of the three previous crimes in the north, west, and east form "the perfect sides of an equilateral and mystical triangle" (*A*, 72), as demonstrated by a triangle drawn in red ink on the map.

Appropriately, the letter predicting that only three men will be killed is sent to Treviranus, the first two syllables of whose name recall the Latin words for "three" and "man"—*tres, vir*. The inspector's name probably alludes as well to the *tresviri capitales*, a group of three magistrates who "exercised general control over the city police" in republican Rome. According to the eleventh edition of the *Encyclopaedia Britannica*, "Caesar increased their number to four, but Augustus reverted to three. In imperial times most of their functions passed into the hands of the *praefectus vigilum*"[2]—an etymological-historical link between Borges's Treviranus and Poe's prefect. Not to mention the fact (which Borges must have noticed) that the emperor who restored the number of the *tresviri capitales* from four to three also gave his name to the detective C. (César) Auguste Dupin. In "An Autobiographical Essay" (1970), Borges reports that he used part of the proceeds from a literary prize he received in 1929 to acquire "a secondhand set of the Eleventh Edition of the *Encyclopædia Britannica*" (*A*, 233), by no means an insignificant detail in the life of a writer obsessed with encyclopedias, a writer who says that some of his earliest memories are of "the steel engravings in *Chambers's Encyclopædia* and in the *Britannica*" in his father's library (*A*, 209). It is worth noting that in the eleventh edition of the *Britannica* the entry for *tresviri* occurs on the page facing the entry for Gottfried Reinhold Treviranus (1776–1837), a German naturalist. Not unpredictably, Inspector Treviranus's first words in the story point to the numerical image that lies at the Latin root of his name:

> "We needn't lose any time here looking for three-legged cats," Treviranus said, brandishing an imperious cigar. "Everyone knows the Tetrarch of Galilee owns the world's finest sapphires. Somebody out to steal them probably found his way in here by mistake. Yarmolinsky woke up and the thief was forced to kill him." (*A*, 66)

The only historical Tetrarch of Galilee, as the entry for *tetrarch* in the *Britannica* informs us, was Herod Antipas—the Herod of the gospels— whose reign (4 B.C.–A.D. 39) began under the emperorship of Augustus Caesar and bracketed the life of Christ. At the death of Herod the Great in 4 B.C., his realm was divided among his three sons: half went to Archelaus, with the title "ethnarch"; a quarter to Philip, with the title "tetrarch"; and a quarter to Herod Antipas, with the same title. As with Treviranus's initial image of a four-legged animal with only three legs, his reference to the Tetrarch of Galilee—with its historical resonance of a quadripartite realm divided among three people by doubling the portion of one of them—evokes the numerical structure that governs the tale. That Borges intends the historical allusion (and means for us not to miss it) seems clear from an exchange between Lönnrot and the editor of a Yiddish newspaper at the scene of Yarmolinsky's murder: "'Maybe this crime belongs to the history of Jewish superstitions,' Lönnrot grumbled. 'Like Christianity,' the editor from the *Jüdische Zeitung* made bold to add" (*A*, 67). Need I add that the entry for *tetrarch* in the eleventh edition of the *Britannica* occurs on the page facing the entry for *Tetragrammaton*?

Treviranus sends the map with the red triangle and the letter suggesting that the number of murders will be three to Lönnrot who has now, he believes, the final clue needed to capture the murderer. Since the letters in the Tetragrammaton are four rather than three, and since the Jewish day begins at sundown so that the three murders were committed not on the third but the fourth day of each month, and since in both the second and third murders a diamond shape is prominently displayed, Lönnrot concludes that the series of murders is not threefold but fourfold and that the shape which the locations of the crimes describe on the map is not a triangle but a diamond. Using a pair of dividers and a compass, Lönnrot pinpoints the location of the planned fourth murder in the south of the city, "the deserted villa Triste-le-Roy" (A, 73), and he arrives there well in advance of the murderer, so he thinks, in order to catch him in the act. But, of course, at the villa Triste-le-Roy—a building of intricate doublings, a kind of House of Usher designed by Zeno the Eleatic—Scharlach is already lying in wait and captures Lönnrot easily. Completing his triumph, Scharlach explains the maze to his prisoner. "The first term of the series came to me by pure chance," says Scharlach (A, 76). He and some of his associates—among them Daniel Azevedo, the second victim—had planned to commit a jewel robbery at the hotel where Rabbi Yarmolinsky was staying. Double-crossing his friends, Azevedo tried to commit the robbery a day early, got into Yarmolinsky's room by mistake, and killed the rabbi when he tried to ring for help. From the newspaper accounts of the crime, Scharlach learned that Lönnrot was seeking the key to Yarmolinsky's death in the rabbi's writings, and so he planned the series of murders to encourage Lönnrot's belief that Yarmolinsky had been sacrificed by a group of Hasidic Jews in search of the secret and unutterable Name of God, a trick to keep Lönnrot looking in the wrong direction while being led to his destruction. Appropriately, the second victim was the double-crosser Azevedo, while the third murder was simply a ruse with Scharlach himself playing the role of the victim Gryphius-Ginzberg.

Realizing that he has been outwitted and is about to be killed, Lönnrot tries to have the last word by finding a flaw in Scharlach's maze. Using a ploy favored by mathematicians and logicians—that Scharlach's plan, though successful, violates the principle of economy of means—Lönnrot says,

> In your maze there are three lines too many. . . . I know of a Greek maze that is a single straight line. Along this line so many thinkers have lost their way that a mere detective may very well lose his way. Scharlach, when in another incarna-

tion you hunt me down, stage (or commit) a murder at A, then a second murder at B, eight miles from A, then a third murder at C, four miles from A and B, halfway between the two. Lay in wait for me then at D, two miles from A and C, again halfway between them. Kill me at D, the way you are going to kill me here at Triste-le-Roy. (*A*, 78)

In his note to the tale, Borges identifies "the straight-line labyrinth at the story's close" as a figure taken from "Zeno the Eleatic" (*A*, 269).

This concluding image of infinite regression as the endless subdivision of a line inverts, of course, the figure of infinite progression evoked in the tale by the movement from a triangular to a quadrangular maze, which is to say, the figure of infinite progression as the endless addition of sides to a polygon—the figure that symbolizes the attempt to integrate the process of thinking into the content of thought as the attempt to incorporate an "objective" point of view outside a structure (e.g., the fourth point from which one views a triangle) into a more inclusive, more self-conscious formulation by making that viewpoint another angle of the structure. As we noted earlier, in the mind's quest to comprehend itself totally, to be absolutely even or at one with itself, infinite progression and infinite regression represent reciprocal paths to the idealized ground of the self, to its original, essential unity—infinite progression pursuing an absolute unity figured as totality, infinite regression pursuing an absolute simplicity figured as indivisibility. Part of the numerical mystery of individual self-consciousness is that although it is only one thing in a world of many things, for its individual possessor it is the one thing that is everything. And this absoluteness of self-consciousness for its possessor not only underlies the absolute means employed in quest of the self's origin (i.e., infinite progression/regression) but also projects itself naturally into the quest for a universal origin figured as a personified Absolute Consciousness, that Infinite Being whose consciousness is the one thing that is everything for every thing. This problem of the one and the many, of sameness and difference, obsessed Poe, and in his most thorough treatment of it in *Eureka* he was led, on the one hand, to deny that either the absolutely limited or the absolutely limitless was humanly conceivable and, on the other, to affirm his belief in an ultimate return of all things to an original unity, an ultimate blending "of individual Intelligences . . . into One" where man "shall recognize his existence as that of Jehovah."[3]

Translated into a religious context, infinite regression and infinite progression, as reciprocal modes of reaching an ultimate origin conceived as either a lower or an upper limit of consciousness, suggest the *via negativa* and the *via positiva* of mystical theology. In the *via negativa* one seeks an unmediated encounter with the divine origin by subtracting attributes from, by denying affirmative predicates to, the idea of God until one finally achieves a personal experience of the transcategorial nature of Being. Of this method Borges remarks, "To be one thing is inexorably not to be all the other things. The confused intuition of that truth has induced men to imagine that not being is more than being something and that, somehow, not to be is to be everything" (*OI*, 148). In the *via positiva* one takes the opposite path, constantly adding affirmative predicates to the concept of God until that concept becomes an absolute totality, although what one experiences in this path seems once again to be the trans-categorial nature of Being. In his essay "From Someone to Nobody" (1950), in which he sketches the historical oscillations in the concept of the Judeo-Christian God, Borges describes the reciprocal character of these two methods as "magnification to nothingness" (*OI*, 147).

Given Borges's interest in the way the classical pursuit of a microcosmic and a macrocosmic limit becomes the religious quest for the origin and end of all things, it is not surprising that as Lönnrot gets caught up in the quest for the sacred and unutterable Name of God, the meeting at the fourth point of the compass (a proleptic figure of infinite progression) comes to seem like a face-to-face encounter with the deity. And inasmuch as Lönnrot will die at the fourth point, it does turn out to be the place where he will meet his maker (his mental double). Agreeing to Lönnrot's request that he trap him in a straight-line labyrinth in their next incarna-tion, Scharlach takes a step back and shoots Lönnrot with his own gun—shoots him in the head, one would guess, the only spot to drop a pure logician. In his note to the tale, Borges says, "The killer and the slain, whose minds work in the same way, may be the same man. Lönnrot is not an unbelievable fool walking into his own death trap but, in a symbolic way, a man committing suicide" (*A*, 269). Given the presence of the color red in the names of slayer and slain and their talk of repeating their duel in another incarnation, one is reminded of Emerson's poem "Brahma," from which Borges quotes in his 1947 essay on Whitman:

> If the red slayer think he slays,
>   Or if the slain think he is slain,
> They know not well the subtle ways
>   I keep, and pass, and turn again.
>
> Far or forgot to me is near;
>   Shadow and sunlight are the same;
> The vanished gods to me appear;
>   And one to me are shame and fame.[4]

A question, however, still remains. Does Borges, in rewriting the numerical/geometrical structure of "The Purloined Letter" in "Death and the Compass," see that structure as threefold and triangular (as does Lacan) or fourfold and quadrangular (as does Derrida)? Certainly Scharlach's labyrinth seems to be fourfold and diamond-shaped. But inasmuch as the murder of Gryphius-Ginzberg was a ruse in which the criminal doubled as the victim, there were really only three crimes, and these three—the murders of Yarmolinsky in the north, Azevedo in the west, and Lönnrot in the south—form a triangle on the map. And if the labyrinth is really threefold and triangular, then all the obvious, simple clues indicating that there would only be three murders are the correct ones. But if the correct number is three, then what becomes of the name that is being uttered letter by letter? If it is not the four-letter name of God that Borges means to evoke, then is it the three-letter name of Poe, the creator of the detective genre?

Before deciding the structure is threefold and triangular, however, we should recall that there finally turn out to be three crimes only because one of the doubles correctly interprets all the arcane clues and presents himself at the fourth point at the expected moment. Is the numerical structure Borges rewrites from "The Purloined Letter," then, that of the two interlocking pairs of words (simple/odd, even/odd), a structure in which three things are made to fill four spaces by doubling one of them— and all as part of the mind's quest for an original undivided one, for a mythic absolute simplicity? Inasmuch as Lönnrot's search for God's "Secret Name" (*A*, 75) at the fourth point of the quadrangle symbolizes this quest, it is significant that the Tetragrammaton, "God's unspeakable name" (*A*, 68), has the same structure in all its various spellings (JHVH, IHVH, IHWH, YHVH, YHWH) as that of the two interlocking pairs of words in "The Purloined Letter," which is to say that three different letters are made to fill the name's four spaces by doubling one of them (H). In the case of both the sacred name and the interlocking pairs of words, the repeated letter or word occupies the second and fourth spaces—the numbers usually associated with doubling. One might also note, given the quadrangular aspect of Scharlach's maze, that two is the only number for which doubling and squaring are the same operation.

5   Doubling the Dupin Stories; Poet and Mathematician; Master/Slave Reversal

BORGES'S REWRITING OF THE numerical/geometrical structure of "The Purloined Letter" in "Death and the Compass" assumes an even greater significance when we realize that it was part of a larger project in which he set out to double Poe's three Dupin stories with three detective stories of his own—but with this difference: where Poe's detective solves the mystery and outwits the culprit, Borges's detectives, at least in the first two stories, are outwitted by the people they pursue, trapped in a labyrinth fashioned from the pursuer's ability to follow a trail until he arrives at the chosen spot at the expected moment. We should note, however, that Borges consistently undercuts the notion that the culprit's triumph, his being one up on his opponent, ultimately makes any real difference. "And one to me are shame and fame" might almost be the motto of these encounters.

The first Dupin story, "The Murders in the Rue Morgue," was published in 1841; Borges's first detective story, "The Garden of Forking Paths," was published exactly one hundred years later. As historian of the detective genre Howard Haycraft notes, there were "several events which marked the Centennial of the Detective Story in 1941." One was the first issue of *Ellery Queen's Mystery Magazine;* another was the publication of Haycraft's own magisterial *Murder for Pleasure: The Life and Times of the Detective Story.*[1] And yet another, it seems certain, was the original publication in Argentina of Borges's first detective story, whose English translation, he recalls, "won a second prize in *Ellery Queen's Mystery Magazine*" (A, 273). (The English translation of "The Garden of Forking Paths" by Anthony Boucher appeared in the August 1948 issue and was awarded the prize as the best foreign story published in the magazine that year.[2]) The second Dupin story, "The Mystery of Marie Rogêt," first appeared in 1842–43 in serial form, while Borges's second detective story, "Death and the Compass," was first published in 1942. The English translation of this story was also submitted to *Ellery Queen's Mystery Magazine* but, as Borges ruefully notes, "was flatly rejected" (A, 273). The third Dupin story, "The Purloined Letter," was published in 1844, but Borges's third story, "Ibn Hakkan al-Bokhari, Dead in His Labyrinth," was not published until

1951. In a note to the story's English translation Borges accounts for this break in the pattern, commenting that after his "first two exercises of 1941 and 1942" his third effort "became a cross between a permissible detective story and a caricature of one. The more I worked on it, the more hopeless the plot seemed and the stronger my need to parody" (*A*, 274). It is as if in reaching the third term of this series, Borges felt that his attempt to double Poe's three detective stories—perhaps with the idea of going one up on the inventor of the genre—had become enmeshed in that triangular/quadrangular labyrinth Poe created in "The Purloined Letter."

Certain it is that in Borges's final detective story the allusions to "The Purloined Letter" are numerous, culminating in an explicit reference. In the tale two friends, Dunraven and Unwin, try to decipher the mystery of Ibn Hakkan al-Bokhari's death in his own labyrinth. At one point Unwin says, "Don't go on multiplying the mysteries. . . . They should be kept simple. Bear in mind Poe's purloined letter, bear in mind Zangwill's locked room." To which Dunraven replies, "Or made complex. . . . Bear in mind the universe" (*A*, 116). That the name Dunraven alludes to the author of "The Raven" was confirmed by Borges during his visit to Hopkins in 1983; while the name Unwin probably alludes to the unwinable game of trying to be one up on a specular double. At any rate, both are appropriate, since we are told in the story that Dunraven is a poet and Unwin a mathematician.

These two occupations recall the discussion of the dual character of the Minister D—— in "The Purloined Letter." Thinking they have confused the minister with his brother who has also "attained reputation in letters," the narrator identifies D—— as "a mathematician, and no poet." To which Dupin replies, "You are mistaken; I know him well; he is both" (3:986). As we noted earlier, the minister's dual character as poet and mathematician mirrors that "double Dupin" whose reciprocal powers ("the creative and the resolvent") remind the narrator in "The Murders in the Rue Morgue" of "the old philosophy of the Bi-Part Soul" (2:533). Borges echoes this reciprocal relationship when he has the poet Dunraven suggest a mathematical solution to the mystery of the labyrinth and the mathematician Unwin counter with a poetic one. Dunraven asks whether, in trying to solve the mystery, Unwin has considered "the theory of series" or "a fourth dimension of space," and Unwin replies, "No . . . I thought about the labyrinth of Crete. The labyrinth whose center was a man with the head of a bull." To which Dunraven, not to be outdone in his own field, adds, "On coins and in sculpture the Minotaur has a bull's head. Dante imagined it as having the body of a bull and a man's head" (*A*, 123).

Since the minimum number needed to constitute a series is three (even if there are only two items in a series, the idea of their serial relationship is already a third thing), Dunraven's question about whether the solution might involve "the theory of series" or "a fourth dimension of space" suggests in effect that the key to the mystery turns upon choosing between the numbers three and four—a mathematical approach Unwin seems to reject in proposing the poetic myth of the Minotaur as the key. But as the two decipherers discuss the myth, the poetic solution turns into a mathematical one, indicating that this solution is an affair of "numbers" in both the poetic and mathematical senses. (One recalls that in "The Philosophy of Composition" [1846] the author of "The Raven" [1845] depicts the writing of the poem as a matter of almost mathematical calculation.) Unwin's reference to the Minotaur evokes the creature as a solitary figure at the center of the labyrinth, a figure whose solitariness Borges had emphasized some years earlier in his tale "The House of Asterion" (1947) by making the Minotaur in effect an image of solipsism. But in "Ibn Hakkan al-Bokhari" the creature's solitary condition is immediately represented as double. Not only does the Minotaur (a man with a bull's head) have a divided nature, but this division is doubled and its polarity reversed in Dante's reciprocal version where he has "the body of a bull and a man's head." In this example of splitting and doubling, we move almost imperceptibly from the solitary uniqueness of the Minotaur, through his divided nature, to a double version of that split considered as two reciprocal combinations of four parts (animal head / human body, human head / animal body).

But in this progression from one to two to four, what becomes of the number three? Unwin says that the story of the Minotaur gave him the key to the mystery when he realized that "a fugitive does not hide himself in a maze" (A, 122). Which is to say that the man claiming to be the fugitive Ibn Hakkan—this "red-haired king" (A, 274) who arrived in Cornwall with his slave "the color of night" and his lion "the color of the sun" (A, 117) and built an enormous crimson labyrinth in which to hide from the ghost of his cousin Zaid whom he had robbed and murdered—was lying. One builds a labyrinth not to hide from but to lie in wait for a pursuer. Unwin concludes that the man pretending to be Ibn Hakkan was really the king's vizier Zaid, who had stolen the king's treasure and then, knowing that Ibn Hakkan would pursue him, had built the labyrinth in order to trap him. And the piece of information that leads him to this conclusion is that when the bodies of the lion, slave, and king were found in the labyrinth, each of their faces had been crushed with a rock. Unwin says that Zaid "had to do it that way; one dead man with his face bashed in would have suggested a problem of identity, but the beast, the black man, and the king formed a series, and, given the first two terms, the last one would seem natural" (A,

124). Since Zaid in his role as Ibn Hakkan was known by sight to the Cornwall villagers, he had to obliterate the face of the real Ibn Hakkan in order to exchange places with him and then, in order to hide the singularity of that mutilation, he had to crush the faces of the slave and lion.

As "the theory of series" (associated here with the number three) suggests to Unwin the real identities of the murderer and the victim, so the real motive for the crime is presented in another triad. Responding to Dunraven's suggestion that Zaid had acted not out of greed but out of "hate and fear" for his master, Unwin says, "He really wanted to see Ibn Hakkan dead. He pretended to be Ibn Hakkan, he killed Ibn Hakkan, and in the end he *became* Ibn Hakkan" (*A*, 125). Thus the passive servant Zaid (the word *vizier* means "a porter" or "bearer of burdens" in Arabic) overcomes his opposite, the active master, by identifying himself with the object of his hatred and fear, duplicating Hakkan's methods in order to use them against him. But with the death of the master through this doubling of mastery back upon itself, the servant becomes the thing he hated—or as Unwin puts it, in a kind of dialectic triad, Zaid pretended to be Hakkan, he killed Hakkan, and at last became Hakkan.

The fact that the doubling of Ibn Hakkan by his vizier represents a master/slave reversal and that Unwin locates the triad of king, slave, and lion within the context of "a problem of identity" recalls Hegel's notion of the origin of personal identity as a master/slave conflict within a split and doubled consciousness. In the section on "Independence and Dependence of Self-Consciousness" in *The Phenomenology of Mind* (1807), Hegel describes the way the slave, through his relationship to the master, becomes conscious of "having and being 'a mind of his own'":

> In the master, the bondsman feels self-existence to be something external, an objective fact; in fear self-existence is present within himself; in fashioning the thing [i.e., in labor, service], self-existence comes to be felt explicitly as his own proper being. . . . For this reflexion of self into self the two moments, fear and service in general, as also that of formative activity, are necessary.[3]

Later, in his discussion of the freedom of self-consciousness, Hegel describes the concentration of the roles of master and slave within a single self:

> In Stoicism, self-consciousness is the bare and simple freedom of itself. In Scepticism, it realizes itself, negates the other side of determinate existence, but, in so doing, really doubles itself, and is itself now a duality. In this way the duplication, which previously was divided between two individuals, the lord and the bondsman, is concentrated into one. Thus we have here that dualizing of self-consciousness within itself, which lies essentially in the notion of mind;

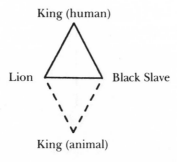

Figure 5.1

but the unity of the two elements is not yet present. Hence the *Unhappy Consciousness*, the Alienated Soul which is the consciousness of self as a divided nature, a doubled and merely contradictory being. (250–51)

Just as the attempt to be one up on a specular double inevitably leaves the winner one down, so for Hegel the internalized struggle between master and slave is "a struggle against an enemy, victory over whom really means being worsted, where to have attained one result is really to lose it in the opposite" (252).

Given the Hegelian resonance of Borges's tale, the triad of king, black man, and lion takes on an added significance. As the king of the beasts, the lion is the master in relation to other animals but a slave in relation to his human master, the black man; while the black, a man treated like an animal, is a slave in relation to the king. But the "king" whom the black man serves is himself a servant, pretending to be a king by exercising mastery over the black man and the lion. In terms of a Hegelian triad, the role of the king represents the dialectical elevation of the human over both the animal world (lion) and the animal in man (slave). But since the impostor Zaid finally becomes Ibn Hakkan by exercising the ultimate form of animal mastery over him (murder), the servant's accession to the king's role involves in effect a reversal into the role of the lion, the king of the beasts. Borges thus evokes the triangular structure of Hegelian dialectic in order to undercut it through the addition of a fourth figure, a double, who turns the dialectical triangle on its head to produce an inverted mirror image (see fig. 5.1).

For all the tale's emphasis on the trio of bodies found in the labyrinth, the story's numerical structure is not based on the number three but on three plus one as suggested by Dunraven's remark that the solution to the mystery might involve a choice between three and four—"the theory of series" or "a fourth dimension of space." In his final detective story, then, Borges in effect repeats the oscillating three/four structure of his second

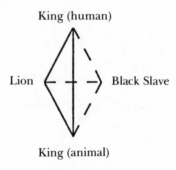

King (human)

Lion   Black Slave

King (animal)

Figure 5.2

story, "Death and the Compass," the structure he had rewritten from Poe's "The Purloined Letter."

In "Death and the Compass," a quadrangular labyrinth constructed within the compass's circle contains three bodies (Yarmolinsky, Azevedo, Lönnrot) arranged in a triangle, as well as a fourth figure (Scharlach), who has created the labyrinth and doubled as a victim. Similarly, in "Ibn Hakkan al-Bokhari" a circular labyrinth contains three bodies (lion, slave, king), whose interlocking master/slave relationships evoke the triangular structure of Hegelian dialectic, plus a fourth figure (Zaid), who built the labyrinth, posed as the victim, and, in killing the king, inverted the dialectical triad, transforming it into a quadrangular structure composed of two triangles sharing the same base but facing in opposite directions. Or, put another way, if we represent the dialectical struggle between the king as a figure of human mastery and as a figure of animal mastery in man by a line drawn between these two positions in the preceding diagram, then the triangle formed on the left with the lion as its apex represents the triumph of the animal mode of kingship (see fig. 5.2).

Yet in this scheme the lion is not a symbol of simple animal mastery, for it remains part of an opposition with its master, the black slave. The lion symbolizes, then, the triumph not of pure animal instinct but of animal instinct contaminated by, because lodged in a differential, master/slave relationship with, the dark repressed shadow-self; so that this symbolic lion is a slave-king that kills not out of brute necessity but for a human reason—revenge.

6 *Jung; The Three/Four Oscillation in Alchemy and the Cabala; The Duel/Marriage of Opposites; Red King and White Queen*

IF THE TRIADIC STRUCTURE DISCUSSED in the preceding section begins to sound more Jungian than Hegelian, we should remember that though Borges's thinking owes much to Hegel (as indicated by references to him in both the fiction and criticism), Borges's interest in triads was also influenced by his extensive reading of Jung, in whose work, particularly of the 1930s and '40s, the triad is part of a larger structure Jung calls the "vacillation between three and four." In a 1969 interview, Borges, noting that he has "always been a great reader of Jung," adds, "I read Jung in the same way as, let's say, I might read Pliny or Frazer's *Golden Bough*, I read it as a kind of mythology, or as a kind of museum or encyclopedia of curious lores."[1] In his essay "Kafka and His Precursors" (1951), Borges cites Jung's *Psychology and Alchemy* (published in 1944 but composed for the most part of material that had appeared in the 1930s), in which the psychoanalyst gives a brief summary of alchemy's relationship to the dilemma between three and four.

Explaining that alchemy "is pre-eminently concerned with the seed of unity which lies hidden in the chaos" of matter and "forms the counterpart to divine unity," Jung observes that this "seed of unity has a trinitarian character in Christian alchemy and a triadic character in pagan alchemy," but "according to other authorities it corresponds to the unity of the four elements and is therefore a quaternity."[2] Jung maintains that "the overwhelming majority of modern psychological findings speaks in favour of the latter view. The few cases I have observed which produced the number three were marked . . . by an unconsciousness of the 'inferior function.'" While Jung contends that "the number three is not a natural expression of wholeness," he notes that

> side by side with the distinct leanings of alchemy (and of the unconscious) towards quaternity there is always a vacillation between three and four. . . . In alchemy there are three as well as four *regimina* or procedures, three as well as four colours. There are always four elements, but often three of them are grouped together, with the fourth in a special position—sometimes earth, sometimes fire. . . . This uncertainty has a duplex character—in other words,

43

the central ideas are ternary as well as quaternary. . . . Four signifies the feminine, motherly, physical; three the masculine, fatherly, spiritual. Thus the
uncertainty as to three or four amounts to a wavering between the spiritual and
the physical—a striking example of how every human truth is a last truth but
one. (*PA*, 26–27)

Jung's alchemical version of the problem of the one and the many reads
like an occult exercise in counting from one to four: The seed of unity
(one) reveals itself as a "duplex" uncertainty (two) about whether the
unity's essential "character" is ternary (three) or quaternary (four). And
like Poe's simple game of even and odd (of specular oneupmanship in
which one more step is always needed to achieve an absolute analytic
coincidence of the self with itself), this duplex "vacillation between three
and four" figures, within Jung's reading of alchemy's numerical structure,
the task of analytic self-integration as a work always one step away from
closure—"a striking example of how every human truth is a last truth but
one." Jung interprets alchemy as a kind of ur-psychoanalysis whose goal is
the discovery of that hidden "seed of unity" that confers "human wholeness" (*PA*, 27) on its possessor, and he includes in this interpretation two
related bodies of arcane knowledge that were of particular interest to
Borges—gnosticism and the cabala.

A brief sampling of Jung's remarks on the dilemma between three and
four in these areas will give us a clearer sense of how Borges, in constructing his tales, used Jung's work as "a kind of mythology . . . or encyclopedia
of curious lores." In the first two sections of his book *Psychology and Religion* (originally published as essays in 1937 and 1942) Jung discusses the
Christian idea of God as a trinity of spiritual persons and argues that this
triune structure represents the repression of a fourth element in an ancient quaternity symbol, the element of the physical. Citing quaternity
structures such as the elements (earth, air, fire, water), the qualities (wet,
dry, warm, cold), the directions of the compass, the Pythagorean tetractys,
and the "Pythagorean idea that the soul is a square,"[3] Jung points out that
the quaternity is a "presumably prehistoric symbol, always associated with
the idea of a world-creating deity" (*PR*, 57), that is, one whose primary
manifestation is the physical world. He further contends that the Christian Trinity represents an intellectualization or sublimation of the concept of god in that the deity is conceived as wholly metaphysical (three
disembodied spiritual persons) and thus as wholly distinct, not to say
radically separated, from a physicality no longer viewed as part of god but
as a principle opposed to him, a principle of material evil at odds with the
uncontaminated goodness of pure spirit. Yet, as Jung notes, "the orthodox Christian formula is not quite complete, because the dogmatic aspect

Figure 6.1

of the evil principle is absent from the Trinity and leads a more or less awkward existence on its own as the devil," a being who possesses, in orthodox Christian formulations, "an autonomous personality, freedom, and eternality," possesses "metaphysical qualities so much in common with God that he can actually subsist in opposition to him" (*PR*, 59).

Jung interprets the metaphysical character of the prince of the physical world as an oblique expression of an "inner relationship," a "(negative) affinity of the devil with the Trinity" (*PR*, 59). He sees this as an unconscious acknowledgment that the Trinity and the devil, the three metaphysical persons plus the "recalcitrant fourth" (*PR*, 187) (a figure associated with the physical world yet possessing "metaphysical qualities . . . in common with God") represent the divided parts of an original quaternity in which the metaphysical and the physical formed a harmonious whole. The devil is, in effect, the dark shadow of God in the lower world of physical nature—the "ape of God" (*PR*, 172), as Jung says—and as such he is "the true, personal 'counterpart of Christ'" (*PR*, 59), the person of the Trinity who entered the physical world by means of his incarnation to combat his dark brother Satan. Jung represents the relationship between the Trinity and the devil in a geometric figure with which we are already familiar (*PR*, 175) (see fig. 6.1).

He points out that "two corresponding elements cross one another" in this "quaternity schema. On the one hand . . . the polaristic identity of Christ and his adversary, and on the other the unity of the Father unfolded in the multiplicity of the Holy Ghost" (*PR*, 178). But Jung also suggests that we can read the quadrangular figure as a shape composed of two opposing triangles, for since the devil is "the aping shadow of God" (*PR*, 177), he must in some sense be a dark mirror image of the Trinity: "Medieval representations of the triune God as having three heads are based on the three-headedness of Satan, as we find it, for instance, in Dante. This would point to an infernal Antitrinity, a true 'umbra trinitatis' analogous to the Antichrist" (*PR*, 172).

Jung's interest in religious notions of the relationship between the Trinity and the devil is, of course, psychoanalytically oriented, in that he reads this cosmic opposition between metaphysical and physical as a projection of the relationship between these two principles within the self—the opposition of mind and body, reason and instinct, conscious and unconscious. For Jung, the conflict between God and the devil appears, then, as a psychodrama in which the mind—"an *imago Dei* in man" (*PR*, 190), a "divine" seed of unity hidden in the chaos of matter—struggles against the prime evil of physicality (death) to establish the radical separateness of its metaphysical (mental) destiny from that of its mortal body. (In terms of establishing the "independence" of self-consciousness, Jung's psychoanalytic reading of the struggle between God and the devil and Hegel's dialectic struggle between master and slave bear a structural resemblance—which may be only to say that Jung was a reader of Hegel or Hegel a reader of cabalistic texts.) However, the desire of the self to be god, this illusion of separate destinies for mind and body, amounts, says Jung, to a violation of "human wholeness," a rejection or repression of the bodily and the unconscious that leaves man forever in conflict with himself and the natural world.

But Jung notes that the relationship between the Trinity and the devil (which depicts the metaphysical and physical as locked in unending opposition) is not the only form that the ancient quaternity symbol takes in Christian doctrine. There is also the relationship between the Trinity and the Virgin, a relationship which, in its substitution of the Virgin for the devil as the personification of physical nature, represents a reconciliation of mind and body, a restoration of wholeness by means of a *coniunctio* (to use the alchemical term), a union of God and the Virgin, of "the masculine, fatherly, spiritual" signified by three and "the feminine, motherly, physical" signified by four. Jung points out that in iconographic representations of the king and queen of heaven, "the king is usually represented as the triumphant Christ in conjunction with his bride, the Church. But the all-important point is that the king, being Christ, is at the same time the Trinity, and that the introduction of a fourth person, the Queen, makes it a quaternity" (*PR*, 71). Since the Virgin Mary was assumed bodily into heaven, she is "the only mortal being permitted to unite with the body before the resurrection of the dead. . . . Consequently the quaternity of the natural elements appears not only in close conjunction with the *corpus mysticum* of the bridal Church or Queen of Heaven . . . but in immediate relationship to the Trinity" (*PR*, 71). Mary "represents the earth, which is also the body and its darkness," and as the earth she is a figure "characterized by the four cardinal points, and hence as the globe with the four quarters, . . . or as the 'four-square' Heavenly City" (*PR*, 71).

The mystical marriage of the king and queen has, on "the physical plane," its alchemical equivalent in "the coniunctio of Sol and Luna,"[4] "the marriage of the red man and the white woman" (*MC*, 230), of *rex* and *regina*, sun and moon, to use a few of the alchemical terms for this male/female pair whose union symbolizes the coincidence of opposites. And just as the opposition between the Trinity and the devil (between three and four) is visually represented by the opposing figures of triangle and square, so the conjunction of Sol and Luna is also symbolically evoked in terms of these same two geometric shapes, but with a circle added as a symbol of perfect union. Jung quotes an alchemical formula for the *coniunctio* invoking these symbols: "Make a round circle of man and woman, extract therefrom a quadrangle and from it a triangle. Make the circle round, and you will have the Philosophers' Stone" (*PR*, 54). In this connection Jung interprets the medieval project of squaring the circle as "a symbol of the *opus alchymicum*," since "it breaks down the original chaotic unity into the four elements and then combines them again in a higher unity. Unity is represented by a circle and the four elements by a square. . . . The spirit . . . is the *ternarius* or number three which must first be separated from its body and, after purification of the latter, infused back into it. Evidently the body is the fourth" (*PA*, 124–25). In *Psychology and Alchemy* Jung reproduces illustrations from various seventeenth-century alchemical treatises depicting both the conjunction of Sol and Luna and the squaring of the circle as a composition of triangle, square, and circle (*PA*, 125–26, 372). One of the more interesting of these for our purposes (because it recalls Lönnrot's use of a pair of dividers to turn the mystic triangle into a quadrangle within the compass's circle) is from Michael Maier's *Scrutinium chymicum* (1687) and shows an alchemist squaring a circle "to make the two sexes one whole" (*PA*, 126) (see fig. 6.2). As we shall see presently, the linking of these three geometric figures to depict the marriage of opposites sheds light on their use in "Death and the Compass."

Borges would have been particularly interested in Jung's speculations on the Trinity, for the subject of the triune God's incomprehensible nature had intrigued him since at least as early as the 1931 essay "A Vindication of the Cabala" in which he discusses the mystery and concludes,

Hell is merely physical violence, but the three inextricable persons convey intellectual horror, a strangled, specious infinity like that of opposite mirrors. Dante tried to depict them as the reverberating of diaphanous circles of di-

Figure 6.2

verse colors; Donne, as entangled serpents, rich and inseparable. *Toto coruscat trinitas mysterio*, wrote Saint Paul; the Trinity shines in full mystery. (*BR*, 23)

And as late as 1975, in his tale "The Mirror and the Mask" from *The Book of Sand*, Borges is still playing with the image. The High King of Ireland tells his court poet:

"We are the figures of a fable, and it is good to remember that in fables the number three prevails."

"The wizard's three gifts, triads, and the unquestionable Trinity," the bard made bold to murmur.[5]

There is, of course, a direct link between Borges's essay "A Vindication of the Cabala" and "Death and the Compass," for one of the books by Rabbi Yarmolinsky that the police find at the scene of his murder is entitled *Vindication of the Kabbalah* (*A*, 67), and in their final confrontation Scharlach tells Lönnrot that the maze of events he constructed to trap him was suggested by the newspaper report that Lönnrot was "looking for the key to Yarmolinsky's death in his writings" (*A*, 77). As part of this plan, the letter and map sent to Treviranus represent the first three events as forming "the perfect sides of an equilateral and mystical triangle" (*A*, 72), and the signature on the letter—"Baruch Spinoza"—suggests that, like the work of the seventeenth-century Dutch philosopher Spinoza, this "Euclidean reasoning" (*A*, 72) is compounded of Jewish and Cartesian elements. One thinks in this regard of Spinoza's *Ethics*, a work which, as its

Latin title indicates (*Ethica Ordine Geometrico Demonstrata*), presents a philosophical argument in the form of a geometrical proof, complete with definitions, axioms, propositions, and corollaries. In adopting what he considered the simplest and least subjective form of presentation, Spinoza said that he intended to "write about human beings" as though he "were concerned with lines, and planes, and solids."[6] In the first two parts of the *Ethics*—entitled "Concerning God" and "Of the Nature and Origin of the Mind"—Spinoza discusses the essence "of the eternal and infinite being" (2:82) and then derives from the divine essence the nature of the human mind, the kind of analytic procedure of which Jung, defending his psychoanalytic reading of the Trinity, remarks, "The medieval mind finds it natural to derive the structure of the psyche from the Trinity, whereas the modern mind reverses the procedure" (*PR,* 147).

All of this serves to shed light on a detective story such as "Death and the Compass" in which the analytic impulse—carried to its natural limit in attempting a totally self-conscious knowledge of self-consciousness—inevitably turns into a quest for the Absolute Self. In analyzing the letter and map forwarded to him by Treviranus, Lönnrot treats the geometric figure with its Trinitarian associations not as a simple triangle but as a triangle inscribed in a circle, that is, he interprets the figure's vertices (the crime scenes located in the north, west, and east) as representing three of the compass's four cardinal points. And precisely because he sees the triangle circumscribed in this manner, he reads the figure as *incomplete,* as lacking that fourth point which he supplies with the aid of "a pair of dividers and a compass," pronouncing as he finishes the task "the word Tetragrammaton" (*A,* 72).

The link between the four letters of the Tetragrammaton and the four points of the compass suggested by Lönnrot's procedure exists in both alchemy and the cabala in the figure of Adam Kadmon. Commenting on the passage quoted above in which man and woman, triangle and quadrangle, are manipulated within the compass of a circle to produce the Philosophers' Stone, Jung explains, "This marvellous stone," which "was symbolized as a perfect living being of hermaphroditic nature corresponding to the Empedoclean *sphairos*" and the "all-round bisexual being in Plato," was, "as early as the beginning of the fourteenth century, . . . compared . . . to Christ, as an *allegoria Christi*," a comparison based in part on the Biblical image of Christ as the stone the builders rejected that has now become the head of the corner:

> From the Latin treatises it is also evident that the latent demiurge, dormant and concealed in matter, is identical with the so-called *homo philosophicus*, the second Adam. He is the spiritual man, Adam Kadmon, often identified with

Christ. Whereas the original Adam was mortal, because he was made of the corruptible four elements, the second Adam is immortal, because he consists of one pure and incorruptible essence. (*PR,* 55)

The chain of associations in this passage seems clear enough: The manipulation of triangle and quadrangle within a circle produces the Philosophers' Stone; the Stone is Christ and Christ is Adam Kadmon, the spiritual, second Adam in whom the four corruptible elements are transformed into the incorruptible fifth essence (i.e., the quintessence). But in alchemy the association of Adam with the four elements is also an association with the four compass points.

In a section of *Psychology and Alchemy* originally published in 1937, Jung quotes a passage from Zosimos on the significance of the letters in Adam's name:

> With reference to his body they named him symbolically after the four elements of the whole heavenly sphere. For his letter A stands for ascent [ἀνατολή: the East] or the air; D for descent [δύσις : the West] . . . because it [the earth] is heavy; A for arctic [ἄρκτος : the North]; and M for meridian [μεσημβρία : the South], the midmost of these bodies, the fire that burns in the midst of the fourth region. (*PA,* 363)

Since the letters of Adam's name are keyed to the cardinal points and since Christ, the second person of the Trinity, is the second Adam, there is, then, through the figure of Adam Kadmon a direct link between the letters of God's unutterable name and the four points of the compass, a link facilitated by the fact that the Tetragrammaton and the name Adam have similar structures, each consisting of three letters (YHV, ADM) made to fill four spaces by doubling one of them. The difference, of course, is that in the Tetragrammaton the repeated letter (H) occurs in the second and the fourth spaces, while in Adam's name the repeated letter (A) occurs in the first and third.

In his book *Mysterium Coniunctionis* (1955–56), Jung discusses the connection between Adam Kadmon and the Tetragrammaton in terms of the oscillation between three and four:

> In the Cabalistic view Adam Kadmon is not merely the universal soul or, psychologically, the "self," but is himself the process of transformation, its division into three or four parts (trimeria or tetrameria). The alchemical formula for this is the Axiom of Maria: "One becomes two, two becomes three, and out of the Third comes the One as the Fourth." The treatise of Rabbi Abraham Cohen Irira . . . says: "Adam Kadmon proceeded from the Simple and the One, and to that extent he is Unity; but he also descended and fell into his own nature, and to that extent he is Two. And again he will return to the

One, which he has in him, and to the Highest; and to that extent he is Three and Four." This speculation refers to the "essential Name," the Tetragrammaton, which is the four letters of God's name, "three different, and the fourth a repetition of the second." In the Hebrew word YHVH (written without vowels), *he* is feminine and is assigned as a wife to *yod* and to *vau*. As a result *yod* and *vau* are masculine, and the feminine *he*, though doubled, is identical and therefore a single unit. To that extent the essential Name is a triad. But since *he* is doubled, the Name is also a tetrad or quaternity. (*MC*, 429–30)

In the passage quoted from Rabbi Abraham Cohen Irira, the figure of Adam Kadmon (the primordial, prelapsarian man) is part of a myth of return, a myth in which complexity or multiplicity (the world of physical nature) is symbolized by numeration, and the direction of the numerative sequence is interpreted as a figurative return to the unity from which the sequence originated. This One to which the sequence returns is symbolized by the numbers three and four, whose association with the original unity is explained by the number of letters ("three different, and the fourth a repetition of the second") in the "essential Name" of God, the origin of all things. Yet, as Jung makes clear, this symbolic return to unity primarily involves a mystical conjunction or "double marriage" (*MC*, 430) in which the masculine *yod* and *vau* are joined to the feminine *he*. The *Kabbala denudata* notes that "the first *he* is the spouse of the *yod;* and the second, the spouse of the *vau*. The first emanated from *yod*, directly, and the second from *vau*, in a converse and reflex way" (*MC*, 429n). Thus the joining of the letters is not simply a double marriage but a marriage born of doubling, an incestuous union in which the masculine *yod* and *vau* are wedded to their own feminine (antithetical) emanations. This balancing of a direct and a reflex movement in the generation of emanations, of feminine mirror images, suggests the simultaneous progression/regression characteristic of a double-mirror structure, the kind of structure Borges had in mind when he described "the three inextricable persons" of the Trinity as "a strangled, specious infinity like that of opposite mirrors." That the double marriage of masculine and feminine letters in God's name (a marriage of doubles) is incestuous is only to be expected, given that incest is a structural correlative of doubling. Which is simply to say that incest is the form of (re)union necessarily implied by the notion of an originary (self-generative) being, a being that must double itself in order to reproduce—a fact apparent in the procession of persons within the Trinity, and in the incarnation of Christ (where the same being is father and son), and even in the figures of Adam and Eve (where the original man's mate is a being created from a part of his own body).

The figure of Adam Kadmon links the Tetragrammaton not only to

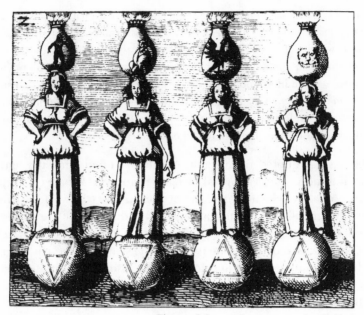

Figure 6.3

the four cardinal points but also to the geometric shape that connects these four directions in Borges's "Death and the Compass," the diamond figure formed by two equilateral triangles sharing the same base line but with apices pointing in opposite directions. As we noted earlier, in the cabala Adam's body is compounded of the four elements, with each letter keyed to one of them. Moreover, in alchemy each element has a symbol, based on the shape of a triangle: earth ▽, water ▽, air △, and fire △—a fourfold manipulation of a three-sided shape that represents yet another instance of a vacillation between, or a union of, three and four. In *Psychology and Alchemy* Jung reproduces an illustration from J. D. Mylius's *Philosophia reformata* (1622), correlating the four stages of the alchemical process—"*melanosis* (blackening), *leukosis* (whitening), *xanthosis* (yellowing), and *iosis* (reddening)" (*PA*, 229)—with the symbols of the four elements (see fig. 6.3). And he also includes an illustration from Abraham Eleazar's *Uraltes chymisches Werk* (1760) in which the alchemical process is represented by a union of the symbols for water and fire within a circle, a union that produces a geometrical figure resembling the Star of David (*PA*, 316) (see fig. 6.4). This figure for the *coniunctio* ⊗ bears an obvious relationship to the diamond figure created by the two triangles inscribed within the compass's circle ⊖ in "Death and the Compass," in that the Star of David figure is formed from the latter shape by simply sliding one of the two triangles with the same base line upward or downward onto the

Figure 6.4

other so that their bases no longer coincide. Indeed, one can also see that the geometric figure symbolizing the alchemical work is not only a union of the symbols for water ∇ and fire $\triangle$, but the basis for the symbols of the other two elements. The line added to the figure of a triangle to produce the symbols for earth $\overline{\nabla}$ and air $\overline{\triangle}$ is simply that portion of the opposing triangle's base which intersects it in the Star of David figure: earth $\overline{\nabla}$, air $\overline{\triangle}$.

In *Psychology and Alchemy* Jung reproduces from the *Hermaphroditisches Sonn- und Mondskind* (1752) another symbolic representation of the alchemical work in which the figure formed by the two triangles is more elongated (*PA,* 37) (see fig. 6.5). One can see in this version an additional link between the Star of David figure (which symbolizes the alchemical work as a mystical conjunction of opposites) and the geometric figure that Yeats used to visualize one of the principal occult symbols in his work, the gyres $\bowtie$ (a two-dimensional representation of twin cones rotating against one another), a symbol that Yeats claimed to have found in Hermetic philosophy and that represents the unity of opposites as a dynamic reversal or oscillation of opposites, circumference spiraling to center, center spiraling to circumference, upward and downward endlessly. Note as well that a further elongation of this figure (moving the bases of the triangles farther apart) would produce an hourglass shape formed by two triangles joined at their apices $\bowtie$, a shape that is the polar opposite of the diamond figure formed by two triangles sharing the same base $\diamondsuit$ in "Death and the Compass." We will have more to say later about the relationship of these two figures in "Death and the Compass," but for the present let us visually summarize the stages leading from one to the other (see fig. 6.6).

Now consider again for a moment the illustration from Mylius's *Philosophia reformata* showing the correlation of the four stages of the alchemical work with the four elements (see fig. 6.3). Notice that the fourth stage, known as the *iosis* or *rubedo* (reddening), is associated with the element fire and that the symbolic creature associated with this stage (contained in the

Figure 6.5

vas on the woman's head) is a lion, most probably a red lion. This fourth
stage represents the completion of the marriage of Sol and Luna, of Red
King and White Queen, the completion of a transformation process that
began with the *melanosis* or *nigredo* (blackening) symbolized by the figure
of a corpse, black man, or ape in the first *vas*. This first stage represents the
breakdown or separation of the elements, a *mortificatio* or *putrefactio* that
is the destiny of the earthy. The second stage—the *leukosis* or *albedo*
(whitening)—represents a washing (*ablutio, baptisma*), a purification by
water that effects a resurrection or rebirth (symbolized by the figure
emerging from an egg in the second *vas*). This second stage is "the silver or
moon condition, which still has to be raised to the sun condition. The
albedo is, so to speak, the daybreak, but not till the *rubedo* is it sunrise" (*PA,*
232). The transitional stage between the *albedo* and the *rubedo*—the *xanthosis* or *citrinitas* (yellowing)—is associated with the element air (as suggested by the figure of a bird in flight in the third *vas*) and perhaps
represents the raising of the temperature in the *vas* through the forced
injection of air with a bellows. About the fifteenth or sixteenth century the
citrinitas "gradually fell into disuse" and "the colours were reduced to
three" (*PA,* 229), the dilemma between three and four thus affecting the
stages of the alchemical work as well.

   With the omission of the third stage, "the *rubedo* then follows direct
from the *albedo* as the result of raising the heat of the fire to its highest
intensity. The red and the white are King and Queen, who may also
celebrate their 'chymical wedding' at this stage" (*PA,* 232). The marriage
of the Red King and White Queen is also referred to in some alchemical
texts as the marriage of "the red slave" and "the white woman" (*MC,* 147),
the substitution of "slave" for "king" being a reminder, at the end of the

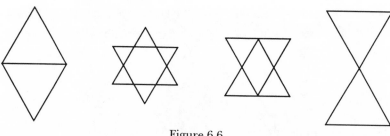

Figure 6.6

transformation process, of the process's origin—that first stage (symbolized by the black man, ape, or corpse) in which the solar king is enslaved in matter. For this reason the first stage, *nigredo*, is also known as the condition of the *sol niger*, the black sun. In a similar manner, the solar red lion whose image appears in the fourth *vas* of the illustration from Mylius is a figure that evokes the mutual presence in one another of beginning and end, of the first and last stages of the transformation process. Noting that the king of the beasts was "known even in Hellenistic times as a transformation stage of Helios," Jung explains that the red lion "represents the king in his theriomorphic form, that is, as he appears in his unconscious state. The animal form emphasizes that the king is overpowered or overlaid by his animal side and consequently expresses himself only in animal reactions. . . . According to the statements of the alchemists the king changes into his animal attribute, that is to say he returns to his animal nature, the psychic source of renewal. . . . The lion is the 'potency' of King Sol" (*MC*, 297–98).

From this brief summary of the "curious lores" available in Jung's work, it should be clear that Borges is manipulating alchemical and cabalistic images not only in his second detective story but in his third as well. For like the mystic equilateral triangle with its Trinitarian associations and the diamond-shaped figure linked both to the Tetragrammaton and to the cardinal points in "Death and the Compass," the "red-haired king," the "black slave" (*A*, 274), and the lion "the color of the sun" (*A*, 117) in "Ibn Hakkan al-Bokhari" are symbols borrowed from the alchemical "great work," the marriage of sun and moon, Red King and White Queen—the union that produces the ultimate goal of the alchemist's art, the Philosophers' Stone. Thus the description in the second story of the triangular/quadrangular figure as a labyrinth and the placing of the king, slave, and lion within a circular red labyrinth in the third story would correspond to the alchemical tradition of hiding the *lapis* or Philosophers' Stone at the center of a circular labyrinth, as shown in an illustration Jung reproduces from Van Vreeswyck's *De Groene Leeuw* (1672) (*PA*, 109) (see fig. 6.7). We should note in this regard that the Cornish villagers in "Ibn

Figure 6.7

Hakkan al-Bokhari" believe the crimson labyrinth contains a hoard of gold that Zaid had stolen from the king. Dunraven speculates that no gold was ever found because this treasure, unlike the inexhaustible "red gold of the Nibelungs" (*A*, 125), was used up to pay for the construction of the building. Red gold, as the color of the sun, is associated with the last stage of the alchemical process (the *rubedo*), an association emphasized by the fact that the product of this stage, the *lapis* or Philosophers' Stone, has the power to transmute base metals into gold. In terms of the alchemical work it is only appropriate, then, that along with the red-haired king, the black slave, and the lion the color of the sun, there should be, as a kind of vacillating fourth, a treasure of gold that is supposed to be hidden in the labyrinth but cannot be found.

Although in his second and third detective stories Borges is clearly using related groups of well-defined arcane symbols, in his note to "Death and the Compass" he says that the "repeated mention of the Kabbalah" in the story "provides the reader and the all-too-subtle detective with a false track" (*A*, 269). Of course, Borges does not mean that the cabalistic and alchemical symbols in "Death and the Compass" are not authentic, nor that an understanding of their significance is not important to an understanding of the story. Rather, he means that for all the tale's arcane symbolism, the tale's meaning is neither cabalistic nor alchemical, that it is not a story of the supernatural but of extremely clever rational analysis. The reader must know this symbolism's significance to understand that it forms part of a narrative structure whose meaning is the direct opposite of the alchemical procedure usually associated with these symbols (the marriage of the Red King and White Queen). For instead of being incorporated into a scenario that projects an ultimate union of opposites symbolized by the marriage of male and female principles, these symbols— the triangle and quadrangle manipulated within the compass's circle; the red king, black slave, and sun-colored lion lodged within a circular labyrinth—serve to enact the cyclically renewed battle of opposites, a struggle that runs to infinity. It is as if, to invoke an earlier example, the symbolism of the marriage of the king and queen of heaven (the union of the Trinity and the Virgin) were being used by Borges to represent the ongoing conflict between the Trinity and Satan, as if the imagery of a gender-heterogeneous union were used to figure a gender-homogeneous conflict.

The Cyclically Recurring Duel; The Two World Wars;

   Christian and Jew; Tetragrammaton and Swastika;

   Borges's Foreign Culprits; Differentiating the Human

THE CYCLICALLY RECURRING DUEL BETWEEN two opposing positions is, of course, an ongoing theme in Borges's work and one that leaves
its mark in one way or another on all three detective stories. As we noted
earlier, Lönnrot, in his final words to Scharlach, imagines the renewal of
their mental duel "in another incarnation," while trying in some small way
to reverse the outcome of their present encounter by arguing that Scharlach's plan, though successful, is not perfect. Similarly, the ending of "The
Garden of Forking Paths" involves a series of implicit reversals of its
significance as regards the tale's two antagonists. The capture and immi-
nent execution of the German spy Dr. Yu Tsun seems to give the victory to
his opponent Richard Madden, but, as Yu Tsun makes clear in his narrative, these events in fact mark the triumph of his plan for transmitting to
his chief in Berlin the name of the village the Germans are to bomb.
However, the apparent success of Yu Tsun's plan has been undercut at the
very start by the brief introduction Borges provides to the spy's narrative.
There he tells us that the secret Yu Tsun transmitted caused only a minor
delay in the British attack "against the German line at Serre-Montauban"
(*F*, 89), which is to say that Yu Tsun's plan, though successful, was part of a
losing cause. And, of course, a similar structure of reversal-into-the-
opposite governs the series of master/slave oscillations that link king,
vizier, slave, and lion in "Ibn Hakkan al-Bokhari." All of which suggests
that the cyclically recurring duel is a function of the reversal mechanism
inherent in mutually constitutive oppositions, that it is simply the continuing oscillation between active and passive differential poles as the inferi-
or side seeks to even the score.
    Given the presence of this temporal repetition-as-revenge structure in
the three detective stories, we should note that Borges specifically sets
each of his tales in relation to the First World War. "The Garden of
Forking Paths" occurs during the war (1916); "Death and the Compass"
occurs after the war (Rabbi Yarmolinsky had survived "three years of war
in the Carpathians" [*A*, 66]); and "Ibn Hakkan al-Bokhari" begins on "the
first summer evening of 1914" (*A*, 115), on the eve of the war. This linking
of the three tales to "the war to end all wars" is significant precisely be-

cause the first two stories were written and published during the Second
World War, when virtually the same opponents who had fought each
other in Europe a generation earlier had renewed the conflict as the
defeated side sought revenge for its loss and subsequent humiliation.
This sense of the Second World War as revenge, as an attempt to repeat
and reverse the outcome of the earlier war, was made clear during the
conflict by Hitler's demand that France surrender in 1940 at the same
place Germany had surrendered in 1918. And, of course, France's victory
in 1918 had been revenge for its defeat by Germany in 1870.

We should note in this regard that the two opponents in "Death and the
Compass" are specifically coded as Christian and Jew. In his note to the
English translation, Borges says that "the story is, as most of the names
imply, a Jewish one" (A, 269), and clearly one of Borges's aims in the tale is
to satirize the anti-Semitism of his Christian homeland in the context of
contemporary European events. At one point the narrator reports the
differing reactions of local newspapers to the series of murders:

> La Croix de l'Épée contrasted the present acts of violence with the admirable
> discipline and order observed by the last Congress of Hermits. Ernst Palast, in
> The Martyr, condemned "the unbearable pace of this unauthorized and stint-
> ing pogrom, which has required three months for the liquidation of three
> Jews." The Jüdische Zeitung rejected the ominous suggestion of an anti-Semitic
> plot, "despite the fact that many penetrating minds admit of no other solution
> to the threefold mystery." (A, 71–72)

In this connection one recalls the earlier exchange between the editor of
the Jüdische Zeitung and Lönnrot at the scene of Yarmolinsky's murder
when Treviranus, remarking, "I'm only a poor Christian. . . . I have no
time to waste on Jewish superstitions," elicits Lönnrot's response, "Maybe
this crime belongs to the history of Jewish superstitions," and the editor's
retort, "Like Christianity" (A, 67). Scharlach says that his plan for taking
revenge on Lönnrot by trapping him in a maze was suggested by the
words of an Irishman who, trying to convert Scharlach to "the faith of
Jesus" as the gangster lay delirious from a gunshot wound,

> kept repeating to me the saying of the goyim—All roads lead to Rome. At night,
> my fever fed on that metaphor. I felt the world was a maze from which escape
> was impossible since all roads, though they seemed to be leading north or
> south, were really leading to Rome, which at the same time was the square cell
> where my brother lay dying and also this villa, Triste-le-Roy. (A, 76)

Since the idea for the triangular/quadrangular maze that traps the Christian detective is explicitly associated with the Jewish gangster's resistance
to being converted to Christianity, one might read the oscillation between

triangle and quadrangle within the compass's circle as an expression of an ongoing struggle between the Christian God, symbolized by the Trinity, and the Hebrew God, symbolized by the Tetragrammaton. In which case the circle that contains the two figures would be an image not of harmonious union but of cyclically renewed strife.

That Borges means for us to interpret this image of a periodically recurring duel between Christian and Jew, evoked by the encounter of Lönnrot and Scharlach, in relation to the Nazi persecution going on at the time is supported by another of his tales, "The Secret Miracle" (1943). The story of Jaromir Hladik's execution by the Nazis in Prague begins with the image of an ongoing duel between two families played out through the medium of a game, one with special significance for Borges's detective tales, as we shall see. On the night before the Nazis entered Prague, Hladik

> had a dream of a long game of chess. The players were not two persons, but two illustrious families; the game had been going on for centuries. Nobody could remember what the stakes were, but it was rumored that they were enormous, perhaps infinite; the chessmen and the board were in a secret tower. Jaromir (in his dream) was the first-born of one of the contending families. The clock struck the hour for the game, which could not be postponed. The dreamer raced over the sands of a rainy desert, and was unable to recall either the pieces or the rules of chess. At that moment he awoke. (*L*, 88)

The sound of Nazi tanks filled the streets.

The connection between "Death and the Compass" and "The Secret Miracle" also turns upon a striking resemblance between the writings of Hladik and those of Rabbi Yarmolinsky. Yarmolinsky authored a *Vindication of the Kabbalah* and Hladik a *Vindication of Eternity;* Yarmolinsky did "a literal translation of the *Sefer Yeçirah*" (*A*, 67) and Hladik a "translation of the *Sepher Yezirah*" (*L*, 90); Yarmolinsky wrote a "*Study of the Philosophy of Robert Fludd*" (*A*, 67), while Hladik wrote "studies of the work of Böhme, of Ibn Ezra, and of Fludd" (*L*, 90). This resemblance in their work stems, obviously, from a basic similarity in their intellectual involvement with the cabala.

Given that the encounter between Lönnrot and Scharlach is meant to be read against the background of events in Nazi Germany, one wonders if the manipulation of alchemical and cabalistic symbols within the compass's circle in "Death and the Compass" is also meant to recall another, opposing manipulation of an ancient symbol within a circle, the Nazi swastika ⊗ . The swastika, or *svastika*, is a sign found among a wide variety of ancient cultures, though the word itself is Sanskrit in origin, deriving from *su* ("well") and *as* ("to be") and meaning "well-being" or "benediction." The *svastika*, as the eleventh edition of the *Encyclopaedia Britannica* notes, was "a symbol of good fortune" (*EB*, 3:844) in the ancient world and is often classified as a form of "pre-Christian cross" (*EB*, 7:506), a fact that explains why the principal description of the *svastika* in the *Britannica* occurs under the entry for "cross" and why a standard dictionary definition describes the swastika as having "the form of a Greek cross with each arm bent in a right-angle extension" (*W*, 1472). This sense of a pre-Christian or pagan cross suggests that the Nazis' adoption of the swastika as their symbol, apparently on the grounds of its association with the Aryan race, was also meant to be symbolic of the paganizing of a Christian country.

The *Britannica* points out that the *svastika* is often called the *Gammadion* because its form is "that of four Greek capital letters *gamma* Γ placed together" (*EB*, 7:506). The associative leap from a geometrical figure composed of "four Greek capital letters" and called *Gammadion* to a diamond-shaped geometrical figure whose four angles are linked to the Hebrew letters of the Tetragrammaton is not too difficult to make, particularly when this association suggests a scenario of repetition and reversal, a revenge structure in which the manipulation of an ancient symbol of good fortune to create the symbol of Nazi persecution is countered by Scharlach's manipulation of Christian and Jewish symbols to create a trap for the detective who imprisoned his brother. We should note that just as the Tetragrammaton is associated with the "vacillation between three and four" (three different letters made to fill four spaces by doubling one of them), so the *Gammadion* involves an oscillation between these same two numbers in that it is composed of a fourfold repetition of the third letter in the Greek alphabet, *gamma*.

The possible link between the *svastika* or *Gammadion* and the triangular/quadrangular labyrinth in "Death and the Compass" becomes even more meaningful when we recall that in the ancient world the *svastika* was frequently associated with labyrinths and mazes, so much so that it was sometimes taken as a labyrinth symbol. W. H. Matthews in *Mazes and Labyrinths: Their History and Development* (1922) cites the example of a Knossian coin that bears the image of "the Minotaur, or rather, a man with a bull's mask" on one side and a "'swastika' labyrinth" on the other.[1] And Janet Bord in *Mazes and Labyrinths of the World* (1976) reproduces a swastika labyrinth found on the reverse of a Knossian coin, as well as a swastika placed in the center of a labyrinth design on a Bronze Age cinerary urn (see fig. 7.1a and b).[2] In *Ilios* (1881) Heinrich Schliemann includes a drawing of a Sanskrit sign called *Nandyâvarta*, a kind of stylized *svastika* that makes clear the labyrinth associations of the basic symbol (see fig. 7.2).[3]

Figure 7.1a

Figure 7.1b

The *svastika*'s connection with the labyrinth is usually explained in terms of ancient rituals of sun worship. Schliemann cites the Orientalist Max Müller on the *svastika* as a sun symbol or sun wheel. Noting that "in ancient mythology the sun was frequently represented as a wheel," Müller points out that on some ancient coins "the place of the more definite figure of the sun is often taken by the *Svastika*" (Schliemann, 348). (Note that the *svastika* labyrinth on the Knossian coin reproduced in figure 7.1a contains a sun symbol at its center.) Schliemann interprets the *svastika* as "a wheel in motion, the direction of the motion being indicated by the crampons," and Müller theorizes that "the *Svastika*, with the hands pointing in the right direction, was originally a symbol of the sun, perhaps of the vernal sun" (Schliemann, 348).

The most common explanation of the link between *svastika* and labyrinth is that the labyrinth, with its winding underground passages, represents the underworld as the womb of earth into which the solar wheel or sun king descends at night to be reborn at dawn. Thus the *svastika* sign within a labyrinth, or the *svastika* as a labyrinth symbol, would represent the cycle or conjunction of opposites—sun and earth, day and night, life and death, or, transposed into a psychological register, spirit and matter, mind and body. Also, the four arms of the *svastika* make it an obvious symbol of such sun-related quaternities as the seasons and the directions. In *Psychology and Religion* Jung cites the paleolithic "'sun wheels' of Rhodesia" (*PR*, 57 n. 43) as evidence that the "quaternity" is a "prehistoric symbol, always associated with the idea of a world-creating deity."

The *svastika*'s connections with quaternity symbolism, the labyrinth, and the conjunction or cyclic recurrence of opposites (especially those of sun and underworld, day and night) suggest a basic resemblance between its symbolic function and that of the alchemical/cabalistic marriage of Sol and Luna (the conjunction of the lights of day and night) whose imagery

Figure 7.2

Borges evokes in constructing the triangular/quadrangular labyrinth in "Death and the Compass." And this in turn suggests a unity underlying the opposites represented, on the one hand, by the swastika symbol of Nazi persecution and, on the other, by the cabalistic symbols used to trap Scharlach's Christian nemesis, a unity constituted precisely *through* opposition and evoked by Borges in the note to "Death and the Compass" when he says that "the killer and the slain . . . may be the same man" and that Lönnrot is "in a symbolic way, a man committing suicide."

Borges develops this notion of a suicidal duel within a divided self in "Deutsches Requiem" (1946). The condemned Nazi war criminal Otto Dietrich zur Linde confesses that he tortured the Jewish poet David Jerusalem to the point of madness and suicide in the concentration camp at Tarnowitz. But a footnote to the text tells us that there is no record of a "David Jerusalem" ever having been at Tarnowitz and suggests that the poet is "perhaps a symbol of several individuals" (*L*, 145n). Jerusalem is certainly a symbol, but not so much of several individuals as of a part of one individual. Jerusalem represents the humane part of Linde's self, the part he has driven to madness and self-destruction in enacting his Nazi beliefs. Linde writes, "I do not know whether Jerusalem understood that, if I destroyed him, it was to destroy my compassion. In my eyes he was not a man, not even a Jew; he had been transformed into a detested zone of my soul. I agonized with him, I died with him and somehow I was lost with him; therefore, I was implacable" (*L*, 145). But if Jerusalem represents "a detested zone" of Linde's soul, it is because the Jewish poet represents a desired zone that has been repressed. (Linde says that he admires Jerusalem's poetry, much of which he knows by heart and considers superior to Whitman's work in its exact "praise of Happiness" [*L*, 144].) And, of course, the dark reciprocal of this is that for the symbolic David Jerusalem, Linde would also represent a detested/desired zone of the soul. Linde describes Jerusalem, with his "jaundiced complexion" and "almost black beard," as "the prototype of the Sephardic Jew, although, in fact, he belonged to the depraved and hated Ashkenazim" (*L*, 144–45). Certainly,

Borges expects the reader to notice that embedded within the word *Ash-kenazim* is the word *Nazi* and to register that the distinction between Ashkenazim and Sephardim, between Northern European and Mediterranean, fair-skinned and swarthy, Jews bespeaks a superior/inferior differentiation within Judaism that bears an uncomfortable resemblance to the Nazi distinction between Aryan and Jew.

In this connection, recall that as part of his ruse to trap the detective, Scharlach arranges events to confirm Lönnrot's belief that the murders are being committed by a group of Hasidic Jews who are sacrificing other Jews in order to discover the secret name of God. But it is, of course, Scharlach himself who is responsible, either directly or indirectly, for the deaths of the two Jews, Yarmolinsky (killed during an attempted burglary planned by Scharlach) and Azevedo (killed by Scharlach for double-crossing him). If, as Borges suggests in the note to "Death and the Compass," the killer and the slain are the same man and Lönnrot is thus "in a symbolic way, a man committing suicide," then Scharlach is also a man committing suicide. Or, to put it another way, it is not only Otto Dietrich zur Linde who has been reading Nietzsche but Borges as well, reading the Nietzsche who mercilessly ridiculed Christian anti-Semites on the grounds that Christianity is itself a Semitic religion and that Christian anti-Semitism is simply a projection of unconscious self-hatred, a desire to destroy something in the self that ultimately turns into the destruction of the self. Is this the point of the remark made by the editor of the *Jüdische Zeitung* (who is himself an atheist) that Christianity, like the cabala, is a Jewish superstition?

If one characterizes the struggle between Lönnrot and Scharlach as an instance of a recurring duel between Christian and Jew, then it is significant that the protagonists of Borges's other two detective stories are also coded as non-Christian—the Chinese Yu Tsun (Confucian) and the Arab Zaid (Muslim). These religious oppositions are explicitly alluded to in both of the other tales. In "The Garden of Forking Paths" Yu Tsun's victim, Stephen Albert, before becoming a Sinologist, had been a Christian "missionary in Tientsin" (*F*, 95), the site of a famous massacre of Christian missionaries by the Chinese in 1870 (*EB*, 26:963). And of course Albert's given name is that of the first Christian martyr, Stephen. In a similar vein, the impostor Zaid in "Ibn Hakkan al-Bokhari" victimizes the Christian minister Mr. Allaby by making him an unwitting part of his plan to kill Ibn Hakkan. When Zaid begins building the labyrinth, the villagers object, and Mr. Allaby preaches a sermon based on "an Eastern story of a king whom the Divinity had punished for having built a labyrinth" (*A*, 117). But the next day Zaid, in his role as Ibn Hakkan, visits Allaby and tells him he is building the labyrinth to hide himself from the avenging ghost of the man he murdered, his cousin Zaid. The result of Zaid's story is that "no further sermon alluded to the sin of pride, and the Moor was able to go on contracting masons" (A, 117). Later, when the disfigured bodies of Ibn Hakkan, the slave, and the lion are discovered in the labyrinth, Allaby repeats Zaid's story to the authorities, and to the extent that this story provides a false track concealing Zaid's escape, Allaby becomes an unsuspecting accomplice in Zaid's plan. Indeed, one wonders if Borges means for the minister's name to be pronounced "alibi," or if, given the ease with which the Mohammedan dupes the Christian, he means the name as an ironic allusion to the Islamic "Allah be praised!"

But of course the larger question here is why Borges chose to make the culprits in his three detective stories religiously or ethnically different from the communities in which they find themselves—a question with several possible answers. As we noted earlier, in Borges's second and third detective stories, it is as if he had used the symbolism of the marriage of the king and queen of heaven to represent the ongoing conflict between God and the devil. Since Christianity has traditionally treated the gods of other religions as personifications of the devil, one might account for the non-Christian culprits of the detective stories in terms of a God/devil polarity inherent in a genre concerned with the disclosure of guilt and the punishment of crime. But I would suggest that Borges's choice of protagonists has a more complex significance than that, a significance rooted in Borges's interpretation of the coding of the killer's role in Poe's first detective story, the evocation of the killer animal as a linguistic alien, a foreigner.

In "The Murders in the Rue Morgue," when the neighbors break into Mme. L'Espanaye's house in response to her screams, they hear "two voices in loud and angry contention—the one a gruff voice, the other much shriller" (2:540). The witnesses agree that the gruff voice spoke French and that the shrill voice, "a very strange voice" (2:540), spoke a foreign tongue. But each witness identifies it as a different foreign tongue and always one that the witness does not himself speak. This leads Dupin to suspect that the murderer is alien not to any specific human language but to human language as such, that this "foreigner" (2:540) is not a man but an animal who resembles a man. The killer is, of course, an orangutan, a creature whose name literally means "wild man of the forest" in Malay.

Poe's decision to make the killer in his first detective story an animal capable of being mistaken under certain conditions for a man (specifically, a "foreigner") suggests that the project that Poe evokes at the very start of "The Murders in the Rue Morgue" (the analysis of reflexive self-consciousness) is part of a larger task of differentiating the human, the task of distinguishing man from animal by defining the essentially "hu-

man" (i.e., mental, self-conscious) element in man as opposed to the animal (bodily) element. As I argued in an earlier work,[4] this larger project is
a recurring theme in Poe (especially in *The Narrative of A. Gordon Pym*) and
in other writers of the American renaissance, most notably Melville. However, the usual scenario through which it is enacted seldom entails, as in
"The Murders in the Rue Morgue," an animal being mistaken for a man
but rather a man being mistaken for, being treated as, an animal.

This latter version frequently involves a journey of exploration or
commerce to foreign parts where the voyager encounters natives who
differ from him in race, culture, or religion—beings whom the voyager
must either recognize or not recognize as human. Recognizing the human
in this context implies both identification and acknowledgment—the
task, first, of identifying the natives as beings of the same species as the
voyager no matter how much they may physically or culturally differ from
him, and second, of acknowledging that this common humanity necessarily entails their humane treatment. This scenario evokes as its allusive
background the history of Western exploration since Columbus with its
Christianizing, scientific, and commercial motives, that is, evokes a long
history of voyagers who did not recognize (either in the sense of identify
or acknowledge) the humanity of the inhabitants of the lands they visited,
inhabitants whom they classified as sub- or nonhuman in comparison with
themselves, as animals in effect, and whom they thus felt free to slaughter
or convert, enslave or economically exploit as the need arose.

Note in this regard that although the actual killer in Poe's first detective
story is the ape, he is not alone in occupying the criminal's role. His human
master, the French sailor, had recently returned, we are told, from a
voyage to the East Indies during which he had captured the orangutan in
the interior of Borneo, intending to bring this animal slave back to France
to sell. In this example of splitting and doubling, the internal master/slave
division between mind and body in the detective's self is externally doubled by the split between the human master and the animal slave who
share the role of criminal. But with the difference that the master/slave
relationship has temporarily been reversed in the latter case by the ape's
breaking loose from its master's control to commit a crime (murder on the
animal's part, but also, by implication, criminal negligence on the sailor's).

We should also note in this connection that the only words that the
witnesses who break into Mme. L'Espanaye's house are able to distinguish
in the speech of the gruff, French-speaking voice are "sacré," "diable,"
and "mon Dieu" (2:541). This invoking of God and the devil as the human
master discovers the slaughter caused by the rebellious animal slave suggests Poe's sense that the God/devil opposition is simply the absolutizing,
within the West, of the task of differentiating the human, that work which

the analytic detective story pursues through a series of interconnected master/slave oppositions between mind and body, man and animal, domestic and foreign, and, of course, divine and diabolic.

All of which is simply to say that while in Poe's first detective story the analysis of self-consciousness is clearly lodged within the larger scenario of differentiating the human, it is within a specific variant that represents this differentiation through the case of an animal mistaken for a man rather than the more common one of a man classified as alien and treated like an animal. Borges's strategy in the detective tales, then, of making his culprits alien to their surrounding cultures constitutes in effect his interpretation both of Poe's choice of a killer in the first Dupin tale and of the link between Poe's detective story project and the task of differentiating the human thematized in works such as *The Narrative of A. Gordon Pym*. That Borges's culprits are foreign to the cultures in which they find themselves and yet successful in their duels with these cultures' official representatives may simply be his way of suggesting how culturally circumscribed it is to make the faculty of rational analysis both the means of determining, and the essential criterion of, the human element in the self, in effect his way of suggesting how much this is a criterion peculiar to the post-Enlightenment West.

The theme of differentiating the human will assume greater importance in our discussion of the detective story later on, but for the moment we must turn our attention elsewhere (since this inquiry progresses only through digressions that bring new elements to the puzzle) and consider the question of color in Borges's detective stories.

8   *The Four Colors; The Missing Fourth; The Suicidal Liebestod; Gender-Coding in the Detective Triad; Poe's Arcana; The Hidden Red King*

THE NOTION THAT IN HIS detective stories Borges consciously uses imagery associated with a gender-heterogeneous union of opposites (the king and queen of heaven) to depict a gender-homogeneous conflict of opposites (God and the devil) is supported by the complex color symbolism of "Death and the Compass." As we noted earlier, one form that the quaternity symbol takes in alchemy is the four colors linked to the stages of the alchemical work—black, white, yellow, and red (*PA*, 229). But Jung points out that there is another quaternity of colors associated with the marriage of the king and queen of heaven—yellow, red, green, and blue. Yellow or "gold, the royal colour, is attributed to God the Father; red to God the Son, because he shed his blood; and to the Holy Ghost green," the color of renewal (*PA*, 212–13); while "blue is the colour of Mary's celestial cloak; she is the earth covered by the blue tent of the sky" (*PR*, 71).

In "Death and the Compass" a precise set of colors is associated with the diamond figure. At the scene of Azevedo's murder, the words "*The second letter of the Name has been uttered*" are chalked across a paint shop's conventional yellow and red diamond shapes. The men who kidnap Gryphius-Ginzberg are wearing harlequin costumes covered with yellow, red, and green lozenges. And in the mirador of the villa Triste-le-Roy, just before his capture by Scharlach, Lönnrot notices that the diamond-shaped window panes are yellow, red, and green, experiencing at that instant "an awesome, dizzying recollection" (*A*, 75). At the scene of the second murder, then, there are two colors linked to the diamond (yellow and red); at the scene of the pretended third murder, a third color is added (green); and at the scene of the real third murder, these three colors are repeated. Moreover, in the original Spanish text of the tale, the sequence of colors is always the same—yellow, red, and green—an order that corresponds to that of the divine persons associated with these colors—Father, Son, and Holy Ghost. Recall in this connection that in his 1931 essay on the cabala Borges remarks on Dante's depiction of the persons of the Trinity as "diaphanous circles of diverse colors" (*BR*, 23).

Given a context that includes the image of "an equilateral and mystical triangle" and a search for the secret name of God carried out in cabalistic terms, the colored diamonds or rhombs in "Death and the Compass" are more than likely an allusion to the quaternity of colors symbolizing the union of Trinity and Virgin, particularly since the tale's repeated association of three colors with a four-sided figure suggests that there is a missing fourth color. During Borges's visit to my Poe and Borges seminar in April 1983, I asked him why he had selected the colors yellow, red, and green for repeated mention in the story. He replied that in choosing these colors he had done "his best to avoid the blue" (not "blue" but "the blue," as if the color had been expected in this sequence), because he felt the color blue was "too decorative." Indeed, one wonders if by "too decorative" he meant "too feminine." Given Jung's bipartite division of the quaternity into the male Trinity representing the spirit (rationality) and the Virgin representing the body (instinct), Borges's suppression of the color associated with the quaternity's female member could be read as a function of the analytic detective genre's traditional valorizing of rationality as a male principle, read as part of a scenario in which the exercise of pure reason is figured as a battle of wits between males that climaxes in a narcissistic *Liebestod* of the analytic self with its specular double. This would account for Borges's use of imagery associated with a gender-heterogeneous union of opposites to depict a gender-homogeneous conflict between doubles, for Borges clearly means us to read the latter's outcome in relation to the former's, to see the suicidal duel between two men "whose minds work in the same way" and who "may be the same man" as a consummation in which the two male opponents, in love with their own cleverness, their own mental image of a mind that mirrors theirs, enact a sexually repressed, intellectualized version of the marriage of opposites.

It is worth noting in this regard that in both *Psychology and Alchemy* and *Psychology and Religion* Jung presents a brief psychoanalytic interpretation of a passage from a medieval poem, *Pèlerinage de l'âme*, in which the poet Guillaume de Digulleville, during a Dantesque dream-vision of Paradise, symbolically differentiates the persons of the Trinity through the colors gold, red, and green. Arguing that by tradition there "belongs to the series yellow, red, and green" a "missing fourth colour," blue (*PR*, 70), Jung relates the absence of this color to the fact that the Mother of God is not mentioned in Guillaume's vision. He reads Digulleville's poetic vision as an expression of the medieval mind's difficulty in developing a rational understanding of the relationship between God and the Mother of God, an expression of a basic uneasiness about "this problem of the Trinity and the exclusion, or the very qualified recognition, of the feminine element, of the earth, the body, and matter in general, which were yet, in the form of Mary's womb, the sacred abode of the Deity and the indispensable instrument for the divine work of redemption" (*PR*, 72).

If Jung's explicated color symbolism influenced Borges's choice of colors for the diamond figures in "Death and the Compass," then Borges's avoidance or suppression of the color blue (considered as a signifier of the feminine) would suggest on his part a conscious manipulation of the gender coding of roles in his detective stories, a manipulation whose significance, I would argue, can only be fully understood when read in relation to the coding of these same roles in the Dupin stories. Certainly, one of the more striking structural features of the Dupin stories is Poe's consistent gendering of the triad detective/criminal/victim as male/male/female, the two active roles coded as masculine and the passive role as feminine (Mme. L'Espanaye and her daughter; Marie Rogêt; the Queen of France). Since the only female role in this triad is the victim's, the feminine element in Poe's stories is automatically excluded at the start from the active exercise of reason (from the battle of wits between detective and criminal), excluded by the very deed (the commission of the crime) that, in initiating the action, relegates the woman to the status of inert matter (a corpse) or manipulated object (a blackmail victim).

Over the century and a half since its beginning, the detective genre has gradually become an equal opportunity employer. From being restricted to the role of the victim in the tales that originated the genre, women eventually worked their way into the role of the criminal in the 1920s and '30s, until they had clearly become, in a writer like Chandler, the gender of choice to play the killer. And now, of course, women routinely fill the role of the detective. The trajectory of this progress has been from the wholly passive role of victim, to the semiactive role of criminal (the criminal is active in relation to the victim but ultimately passive in relation to the detective), and on to the fully active role of detective—a trajectory that runs from body to intellect, from the inert passivity of a corpse to the hyperactivity of a mastermind, a trajectory worth keeping in mind for future reference.

This historical progress in the detective story, whereby women eventually gained access to all the roles in the triad, makes Borges's practice in the genre all the more striking. For in Borges's triad of detective/criminal/victim, not only are the first two roles coded as masculine, but the third as well. Borges's detectives and criminals are all men, and so are all his victims—Stephen Albert; Yarmolinsky, Azevedo, Lönnrot; Ibn Hakkan and the black slave. The suppression of feminine roles is so complete that there exists no female character in Borges's detective stories important enough to have a proper name. Borges's reversal of the gender coding of the victim's role is part of his general strategy of doubling Poe's detective stories by opposition, a strategy we shall see more of later. But this specific reversal may express as well Borges's sense that, if the feminizing of the victim's role in Poe's tales signifies the victimizing or abasement of the feminine-coded nonrational elements in the self (the bodily, the instinctual, the unconscious) in relation to a masculine-coded rational analysis, then this structure ultimately ends by victimizing the masculine-coded rationality as well. It ends by reducing rationality to a narcissistic, self-destructive game of no-difference. Indeed, one might apply to the male triad of detective, criminal, and victim Borges's remark about the three male persons of the Trinity—that they "convey intellectual horror, a strangled, specious infinity like that of opposite mirrors."

Before leaving the subject of alchemical color symbolism, we should note that just as Christ, in the quaternity of colors symbolizing the relationship of the Trinity and the Virgin, is associated with the color red because of the shedding of his blood, so in the quaternity of colors linked to the stages of the alchemical work he is also associated with red both because, as the *lapis* of the Philosophers' Stone, he is the product of the *rubedo* (reddening), the fiery final stage of the process, and because, as the earthly man refined by spiritual fire, he is Adam Kadmon, the second Adam whose name in Hebrew (*adamah*) means "red earth," as Jung points out (*PA,* 362; *MC,* 440). Significantly, in "The Circular Ruins" (1940), one of the tales from the volume that included his first detective story, Borges alludes to this derivation of Adam's name in describing how a magician, who worships a "manifold god" whose "earthly name" is "Fire," first attempts to dream a man into existence: "In the cosmogonies of the Gnostics, the demiurges mold a red Adam who is unable to stand on his feet; as clumsy and crude and elementary as that Adam of dust was the Adam of dreams wrought by the nights of the magician" (*A,* 59). These associations of the color, as we shall see, have a direct bearing on Borges's detective stories, for if Borges consciously suppresses the use of blue in "Death and the Compass," he just as consciously emphasizes the use of red, an emphasis meant to make the reader notice that it is the dominant color symbol in all three stories, and not merely because of the genre's inherent connection with bloodshed.

But before we follow up this red thread, we must address a necessary, and by this point obvious, question. If Borges's aim in his detective tales is to double Poe's three Dupin stories with three of his own, why did he go to the trouble of introducing alchemical and cabalistic symbolism into this project? As with most questions about Borges's work, there are several related answers. First, many of Borges's arcane allusions echo references in Poe's own work, for Poe, like Borges, had a continuing interest in curious lore. For example, Borges's allusion to the literal meaning of Adam's name in "The Circular Ruins" recalls Poe's reference to this same derivation in "Some Words with a Mummy" (1845). There, the revivified

Egyptian mummy Allamistakeo, in response to a question about the Creation, says that the notion of a universal origin is something he never
heard of, although he does remember

> hearing something remotely hinted, by a man of many speculations, concern-
> ing the origin *of the human race;* and by this individual the very word *Adam,* (or
> Red Earth) which you make use of, was employed. He employed it, however, in
> a generical sense, with reference to the spontaneous germination from rank
> soil . . . of five vast hordes of men. (3:1190)

Note that Borges's reference to the derivation of Adam's name occurs in a
remark about "the cosmogonies of the Gnostics," while Poe's reference to
"*Adam,* (or Red Earth)" occurs in a discussion of the fictive Egyptian
practice of periodically revivifying a mummified historian to rewrite from
personal knowledge "the traditions of the day concerning the epoch at
which he had originally lived," a practice of "re-scription and personal
rectification" of tradition that Poe calls "the Kabbala" (3:1189–90).

Similarly, Borges's use of symbolism associated with the alchemical
marriage of Sol and Luna and the production of the Philosophers' Stone
recalls Poe's tale "Von Kempelen and His Discovery" (1849), a satire on the
California gold fever in which Poe pretends that a shadowy figure named
Von Kempelen "has actually realized, in spirit and in effect, if not to the
letter, the old chimera of the philosopher's stone" (3:1363), the arcane
substance with the power to transmute base metal into gold. It is indicative
of Poe's knowledge of alchemical symbolism that he locates Von Kempelen's laboratory in a house concealed within a "labyrinth of narrow and
crooked passages" (3:1362). Von Kempelen bears the same name and,
indeed, may be a relative of the man who invented the "Automaton-chess-
player" (3:1361) (a linking of alchemy, automata, and chess whose point
will become clear later). Most significant of all, Poe tells us that when the
police arrested Von Kempelen in his laboratory they found "a paper
parcel, in his coat pocket, containing what was afterwards ascertained to
be a mixture of antimony and some *unknown substance,* in nearly, but not
quite, equal proportions" (3:1362). As Jung points out, antimony was one
of the chemical elements traditionally associated with the arcane substance. The alchemist Michael Maier refers to the arcane substance in its
hidden or unrefined state as the "antimony of the philosophers" (*MC,*
332). It is the *prima materia* from which the Philosophers' Stone is produced, "the black earth in which the gold or the *lapis* is sown like the grain
of wheat . . . the black, magically fecund earth that Adam took with him
from Paradise, also called antimony" (*PA,* 327).

Poe reports that the "*unknown substance*" found mixed with the antimony was tested by various scientists to determine its nature but "that up

to this period, *all* analysis has failed" (3:1364), a failure Poe emphasizes by repeated mention. This last detail suggests another probable reason for Borges's use of alchemical symbolism in doubling the Dupin stories, for if Poe considers the goal of the alchemical work (the Philosophers' Stone) to be an unanalyzable substance, then alchemy is a symbolic analogue of that detective work whose goal is the analysis of an analytic power that, as Poe claims, is "but little susceptible of analysis" (2:527). In employing alchemical symbolism in his detective stories, Borges is simply making explicit a connection implicit in Poe's own writing.

The link between the alchemical work and the analysis of the self is, of course, the whole point of Jung's reading of alchemy as a combination of an outer work (the analysis of matter) and an inner work (the analysis of mind) whose goal, the Philosophers' Stone, symbolizes the wholeness of the self. But Borges had not only read Jung, he had read Goethe and Spengler as well, and the effect of Borges's linking of alchemy and analytic detection is to evoke the detective as a descendant of that Goethean symbol of modern Western rationality, the alchemist Faust, whose quest for a godlike knowledge-as-the-will-to-power can have diabolic results. Significantly, Poe notes in his description of Von Kempelen that the gentleman has a "defect in one of his feet" (3:1361), a detail that Mabbott interprets as "a jocular hint of diablerie" (3:1367) alluding to the devil's cloven foot.

What we must keep in mind about all this, however, is that although Borges incorporates into his detective stories symbols from the alchemical work (specifically, from the marriage of the Red King and White Queen [Sol and Luna]) these symbols function within a detective scenario (a duel between antithetical doubles) whose significance is exactly the reverse of that harmonious union with which they are associated in alchemy. Which is to say that though Borges has borrowed the *symbols* from alchemy, he has taken the *scenario* from some other source, a source in which the "mating" associated with the Red King and the White Queen represents the deadly climax of a battle of wits between two opponents. To discover this source, we must follow that red thread mentioned earlier, a clue to which Borges himself directs our attention.

In the note to the English translation of "Death and the Compass" he points out that "a thread of red . . . runs through the story's pages. There is the sunset on the rose-colored wall and, in the same scene, the blood splashed on the dead man's face. Red is found in the detective's and in the gunman's names" (A, 269), not to mention the triangle in red ink inscribed with a threadlike line on the map sent to Treviranus. Moreover, in the note to the English translation of "Ibn Hakkan al-Bokhari," he disingenuously suggests that because the tale became in the process of writing "a cross between a permissible detective story and a caricature of one," it should "be read for its humor," since he "can't expect anyone to take seriously or to look for symbols in such pictorial whims as . . . a red-haired king, and a scarlet maze so large that on first sight its outer ramparts appear to be a straight blank wall" (A, 274). Borges thus extends the thread of red from the pages of "Death and the Compass" into those of "Ibn Hakkan al-Bokhari" as a clue to lead us from "a scarlet maze" containing "a red-haired king" back to the maze created by Red Scharlach (Scarlet) to trap Erik Lönnrot, whose last name means "hidden red" and whose first name derives from the Old Norse *Eirìkr* meaning "honorable ruler" (W, 492)—in effect, the hidden red king. We should also note that the place Scharlach traps Lönnrot is called Triste-le-Roy, a name that apparently means "sad the king" in French if we take "Roy" to be the Old French spelling of *roi*. (We might note in passing that the proper name Roy in English derives from an assimilation of the Gaelic word *rhu*, meaning "red," to the French *roi* [W, 1271].) The word *Triste* is also clearly meant to evoke echoically the word *tryst*, an appointed (often secret) meeting place, usually a meeting place for lovers, as befits the suicidal *Liebestod* that occurs there in "Death and the Compass."

But who is this hidden red king concealed in the victim Lönnrot's name, this "red-haired king" killed in "a scarlet maze"?

Lewis Carroll's Red King; A Riddle Whose Answer Is Chess;

The Works of Herbert Quain; Simplicity and Complexity;

Mirroring Mirrors

ONE OF BORGES'S RECURRING SYMBOLS for the mystery of reflective self-consciousness is a figure taken from one of his favorite books—the Red King from Lewis Carroll's *Through the Looking-Glass* (1871). Carroll based the narrative action of *Through the Looking-Glass* on the moves of a chess problem, an action that involves Alice's progress as a white pawn across the chessboard, her eventual promotion to a white queen, and her checkmating of the Red King. This entire action takes place, of course, in a dream Alice has when she falls asleep in front of the drawing-room mirror. Significantly, when Alice first encounters the Red King within this dream, he is himself asleep in the garden of Looking-glass House and, as her companions inform her, dreaming of Alice. The Aleph-like oscillation of container and contained as Alice dreams the Red King who is dreaming Alice, turn and turnabout *ad infinitum*, evokes Alice's eventual checkmate of the King as a kind of self-negating duel with a specular double. The word *checkmate* ultimately derives from the Persian "*shāh*, king + *māt*, he is dead" (*W*, 250), so that the word *chess*, which derives from *check*, has as its ultimate origin a word meaning "king." (We should note in passing the structural resemblance between the delivery of checkmate in a game and the analysis of the analytic power. For just as the latter is always one step short of its goal, so checkmate always ends the game one move short of the killing of the king, with the king in check and unable to move out of it but with another move still needed to capture and remove him from the board.)

If the killing of the concealed red king enacted in Borges's second and third detective stories was indeed influenced by Carroll's *Through the Looking-Glass*, then one of the more curious passages in Borges's first detective story, "The Garden of Forking Paths," suddenly assumes greater significance. There the fugitive spy Yu Tsun and the Sinologist Stephen Albert are discussing Yu Tsun's ancestor Ts'ui Pên—"a chess player, a famous poet and a calligrapher" (*F*, 96)—who retired from public life in order "to write a novel with more characters than there are in the *Hung Lou Mêng*, and to create a maze in which all men would lose themselves" (*F*, 93). Yet when Ts'ui Pên "was assassinated by a stranger" (*F*, 93) some years later, "his heirs found only a mess of manuscripts," a "shapeless mass of contradictory rough drafts" (*F*, 96). After years of study, Albert concluded that "the book and the labyrinth were one and the same," the book Ts'ui Pên called *The Garden of Forking Paths* (*F*, 96). One of the clues that led him to this solution was "the curious legend that Ts'ui Pên had proposed to create an infinite maze" (*F*, 97). Questioning himself about "how a book could be infinite" (*F*, 97), Albert realized that Ts'ui Pên had constructed a labyrinthine work in which the narrative paths fork in time rather than in space:

> In all fiction, when a man is faced with alternatives he chooses one at the expense of the others. In the almost unfathomable Ts'ui Pên, he chooses—simultaneously—all of them. He thus *creates* various futures, various times which start others that will in their turn branch out and bifurcate in other times. This is the cause of the contradictions in the novel. (*F*, 98)

But there was still one difficulty. Albert says that of all the problems that challenged Ts'ui Pên, none disturbed him

> "more than the profound one of time. Now then, this is the *only* problem that does not figure in the pages of *The Garden*. He does not even use the word which means *time*. How can these voluntary omissions be explained?"
>
> I proposed various solutions, all of them inadequate. We discussed them. Finally Stephen Albert said: "In a guessing game to which the answer is chess, which word is the only one prohibited?" I thought for a moment and then replied:
>
> "The word is *chess*."
>
> "Precisely," said Albert. "*The Garden of Forking Paths* is an enormous guessing game, or parable, in which the subject is time. The rules of the game forbid the use of the word itself. To eliminate a word completely, to refer to it by means of inept phrases and obvious paraphrases, is perhaps the best way of drawing attention to it." (*F*, 99–100)

In describing Ts'ui Pên's labyrinthine book, Borges is, of course, presenting us with an image of his own writing, but through an added sleight of hand he also gives us a clue to the specific maze he has created for the reader in his detective stories.

In order to illustrate the principle that the only prohibited word in a riddle is the word that answers it, Stephen Albert gives the example of a riddle whose "answer is chess." But of course this example, taken within the larger context of Borges's three detective tales, contradicts the principle it is supposed to illustrate, for in using the word *chess* in his first detective story Borges in effect gives us the answer to the riddle presented in his second and third stories—the repeated scenario of killing the red king concealed within a maze (a chessboard). Moreover, since Borges gives us the answer before presenting us with the riddle, we treat the information, on our initial reading of the three tales, not as an answer but a clue, a hint to be on the lookout for a riddle whose answer is chess. It is only on a second reading, as we move from the third story back to the first, that we realize the three detective stories taken as a group are themselves the riddle. For if the scenario of killing the red king in the second and third stories is an allusion to the checkmate of the Red King in Carroll's *Through the Looking-Glass* (an allusion we catch precisely because we are looking for a riddle whose answer is chess), then in rereading the first story, we realize that Ts'ui Pên's labyrinthine book called *The Garden of Forking Paths* is itself an allusion to a bookish garden that is both a labyrinth and a chessboard— the garden of Looking-glass House.

When Alice enters the garden of Looking-glass House, she finds that its paths, which seem to lead straight to a distant hill, twist and turn "like a corkscrew," causing her to wander "up and down . . . trying turn after turn, but always coming back to the house, do what she would."[1] Besides calling to mind the labyrinthine garden of Ts'ui Pên's novel, Alice's dream of corkscrew paths that twist and turn but always lead back to the same spot reminds us of Scharlach's delirious dream, as he lay wounded at the "symmetrical" villa of Triste-le-Roy, that "the world was a maze from which escape was impossible since all roads" led "to Rome, which at the same time was the square cell" where his "brother lay dying and also this villa, Triste-le-Roy" (*A*, 76), a building whose mirror-image construction makes it a nightmare version of Looking-glass House.

It is only when Alice meets the Red Queen (whom she must approach by walking away from her, due to the reverse nature of Looking-glass world) that she escapes from the labyrinth of corkscrew paths and reaches the hill from which she can survey the garden. There she sees

> a number of tiny little brooks running straight across it from side to side, and the ground between . . . divided up into squares by a number of little green hedges, that reached from brook to brook.
> "I declare it's marked out just like a large chess-board!" Alice said at last. "There ought to be some men moving about somewhere—and so there are!" she added in a tone of delight. . . . "It's a great huge game of chess that's being played—all over the world—if this *is* the world at all, you know." (*AA*, 207–8)

Alice is given another glimpse of the reverse nature of Looking-glass House when she meets the White Queen, who bandages her own finger, screams loudly, and then pricks her finger on the clasp of her brooch—an example of what the White Queen calls "living backwards," a mode of life whose "one great advantage" is "that one's memory works both ways" (*AA*,

247). In keeping with the reversal of cause and effect that characterizes Looking-glass House, Borges, in providing us with a clue to his use of Carroll's book in the three detective stories, quite properly gives us the answer to the riddle before presenting us with the riddle itself—a gesture whose appropriateness is increased by the fact that *Through the Looking-Glass* is a book filled with riddles, although none as complex as the self-including structure Borges creates in his first detective story.

In "The Garden of Forking Paths," two men—Yu Tsun and Stephen Albert, murderer and victim—discuss within a garden the meaning of a fictive labyrinthine book called *The Garden of Forking Paths*, a book written by Yu Tsun's ancestor, who was murdered by a stranger (just as Albert will be). The Chinese novel is a "riddle" whose operation Albert illustrates by citing the prohibition against using the word *chess* in a riddle whose answer is chess, a prohibition borne out by the fictive Chinese book (a riddle whose answer is time) but contradicted by the actual short story. This structure becomes even more complex when we consider that both the fictive novel and the actual short story—each named for the garden-labyrinth—are based upon, and allude to, a garden in another book that is at once a maze, the scene of a chess game, and, in keeping with its looking-glass status, a place of temporal reversals and spatial inversions. But Borges has at least two more tricks up his sleeve in this game of mirroring mirrors. The level of complexity takes another jump when we recall that Borges's first detective story gave the title to his first volume of pure fictions, *The Garden of Forking Paths* (1941). Thus, we have a real book of fiction containing a real short story containing a fictive Chinese novel, all with the same title alternating between italics and quotation marks, one nesting inside the other like the Aleph inside the universe inside the Aleph in an endless oscillation.

And to this array of mirrors, Borges adds one more reflective, not to say deflective, surface. For among the stories included in the volume *The Garden of Forking Paths* is "An Examination of the Work of Herbert Quain," a discussion of a fictive author whose first book was a detective novel called *The God of the Labyrinth*. The novel's plot is outlined by the short story's narrator, "Borges":

> An indecipherable assassination takes place in the initial pages; a leisurely discussion takes place toward the middle; a solution appears in the end. Once the enigma is cleared up, there is a long and retrospective paragraph which contains the following phrase:
>
> "Everyone thought that the encounter of the two chess players was accidental." This phrase allows one to understand that the solution is erroneous. The unquiet reader rereads the pertinent chapters and discovers *another* solution,

the true one. The reader of this singular book is thus forcibly more discerning than the detective. (*F*, 74)

In explaining how the remark about "the encounter of the two chess players" forces the reader to reread the novel and discover another solution, Borges gives us a clue to a clue. For since "An Examination of the Work of Herbert Quain" precedes "The Garden of Forking Paths" in the 1941 volume, this passage prospectively describes the way in which Stephen Albert's remark—"a guessing game to which the answer is chess"— serves to initiate a retrospective reading of Borges's detective stories, a rereading that reveals their relationship to the garden-maze-chessboard of Carroll's *Through the Looking-Glass* and the checkmate of the Red King.

A similar mirroring of Borges's detective fiction occurs in Quain's other works. There is an unfinished novel (only its third part has been completed) called *April March* (the fourth and third months) whose prologue evokes "the inverse world of Bradley in which death precedes birth, the scar the wound, and the wound the blow" (*F*, 75), which is to say, a world like the one where the White Queen bandages her finger, screams in pain, and then pricks her finger on a brooch, or where the critical explication of a story precedes the story. The narrator Borges remarks,

> The worlds proposed by *April March* are not regressive; only the manner of writing their history is so: regressive and ramified, as I have already said. The work is made up of thirteen chapters. The first reports the ambiguous dialogue of certain strangers on a railway platform. The second narrates the events on the eve of the first act. The third, also retrograde, describes the events of *another* possible eve to the first day; the fourth, still another. Each one of these three eves (each of which rigorously excludes the other) is divided into three other eves, each of a very different kind. The entire work, thus, constitutes nine novels; each novel contains three long chapters. (The first chapter, naturally, is common to all.) The temper of one of these novels is symbolic; that of another, psychological; of another, communist; of still another, anticommunist; and so on. (*F*, 75–76)

Borges then provides us with a diagram to illustrate the forking of these three parallel but mutually exclusive plot lines that all spring from the same initial incident.

Obviously, the structure of *April March* mirrors in a reverse direction the endlessly branching, parallel time lines of Ts'ui Pên's imaginary book *The Garden of Forking Paths,* but the initial (though chronologically latest) incident in Quain's book—"the ambiguous dialogue of certain strangers on a railway platform"—is drawn not from the fictive Chinese novel but from Borges's real detective story. On his journey to see Stephen Albert, Yu Tsun's train pulls into an unmarked station:

> "Ashgrove?" I asked some children on the platform. "Ashgrove," they replied. I got out.
>
>   A lamp lit the platform, but the children's faces remained in shadow. One of them asked me: "Are you going to Dr. Stephen Albert's house?" Without waiting for my answer, another said: "The house is a good distance away but you won't get lost if you take the road to the left and bear to the left at every crossroad." . . .
>
>   The advice about turning always to the left reminded me that such was the common formula for finding the central courtyard of certain labyrinths. (*F*, 93)

This ambiguous dialogue of certain strangers on a railway platform, prospectively mirrored in the Quain piece, is retrospectively mirrored in part in Borges's third detective story when Dunraven and Unwin enter the crimson labyrinth: "Dunraven said that inside the house were many branching ways but that, by turning always to the left, they would reach the very center of the network in little more than an hour" (*A*, 116).

The narrator Borges completes his survey of Quain's writings with summaries of two other works: a two-act play, *The Secret Mirror,* whose second act parallels the first act but inverts its significance, and a collection of eight stories (the same number as in Borges's volume *The Garden of Forking Paths*) called *Statements,* from the third of which, the narrator says, "I was ingenuous enough to extract . . . my story of 'The Circular Ruins'" (*F*, 78). Perhaps it is to commemorate his borrowing the plot of this story from the author of *The Secret Mirror* that Borges uses a quotation from Carroll's *Through the Looking-Glass* as the epigraph to "The Circular Ruins."

The symbolic self-inclusion involved in Borges's describing the imaginary Chinese novel *The Garden of Forking Paths* within the text of the real story "The Garden of Forking Paths," and then including that story in the real volume of tales bearing the same name, carries to its logical conclusion the reflexive structure of Poe's "Purloined Letter." For this symbolic mirroring of the representational status of the whole work by a part of itself (a mirroring that is then re-reflected by the third use of the same title) evokes the infinite progression/regression inherent in any self-reflexive structure. As Bertrand Russell (an author from whom Borges borrowed many of his "pet subjects" [Burgin, 107]) notes in his *Introduction to Mathematical Philosophy* (1919), the mathematician "Cantor used reflexiveness as the *definition* of the infinite. . . . All *known* infinite classes . . . are reflexive. . . . All *reflexive* classes . . . are infinite."[2] Borges had discussed Cantor's work on infinite classes in his essay "The Doctrine of Cycles" (1936).

Borges filters the self-including structure of the Dupin stories (particularly that of "The Purloined Letter") first through the reflexive imagery of Carroll's book and then through the literary critical specularity of the Quain piece in order to produce the multiple mirrorings involved in his first detective story's thrice-repeated title. In effect, he creates out of the original structure of "The Purloined Letter" a kind of fall of the house of mirrors. And, indeed, he may well be giving us a clue to "The Purloined Letter"'s presence in the reflexive structure of Yu Tsun's narrative when he tells us that among his narrator's personal effects at the start of his adventure was "a letter" which Yu Tsun "decided to destroy at once" but which he "did not destroy" (F, 91). And this same allusion seems to recur when Yu Tsun notes that the final clue Stephen Albert needed to decipher the labyrinthine Chinese book was "a fragment of a letter" in Ts'ui Pên's own handwriting bearing the words: "I leave to various future times, but not to all, my garden of forking paths" (F, 97). So complex is the structure Borges has created in these stories it is no wonder he decided to give us the answer to the riddle at the very start.

But we must not think that being given the answer to a riddle is the same as being given the solution to a mystery, for in Borges's handling of the detective story, clues usually lead not to solutions but to other clues, in much the same way that the murderer Zaid, in escaping from the crimson labyrinth, finds himself trapped in the labyrinth of the world. If the killing of the red king in Borges's second and third detective stories is, as I have suggested, an allusion to the checkmating of the Red King in Carroll's *Through the Looking-Glass*, then this riddling evocation of a narrative based on a chess game is meant to allude in turn to the association of chess with the analytic detective genre from the very beginning.

At the start of "The Murders in the Rue Morgue," the narrator discusses games of mental acuity traditionally considered to be good training for the analytic faculty. Contrasting chess and draughts (checkers), the narrator argues that "the higher powers of the reflective intellect" (2:528) are better served by the simple game of draughts than the complex game of chess. In chess, he says, "where the pieces have different and *bizarre* motions, with various and variable values, what is only complex is mistaken . . . for what is profound" (2:528). It is a game that mainly favors the power of "*attention,*" one where "the more concentrative rather than the more acute player" wins (2:528). But in the relatively simple game of draughts "where the moves are *unique* and have but little variation, . . . the mere attention being left comparatively unemployed," the advantage goes to the player of "superior *acumen,*" which is to say, to the analyst who "throws himself into the spirit of his opponent, identifies himself therewith, and not unfrequently sees thus, at a glance, the sole methods (sometimes indeed absurdly simple ones) by which he may seduce into error or hurry into miscalculation" (2:528–29).

As anyone who has played both chess and draughts knows, the narrator's comments on the two games are largely nonsense. His discourse is simply a ploy to associate the differential opposition between simplicity and complexity with the whole question of analyzing the analytic power, an opposition that will come into full play when Poe introduces in the third Dupin story the "simple" game of even and odd with its lengthy accompanying explanation of the way one identifies one's mind with an opponent's, the principle he briefly enunciates here in relation to the simple game of draughts. What is striking within the strict economy of a Poe short story is the length of the narrator's commentary on chess in "The Murders in the Rue Morgue," an emphasis that fixes in the reader's mind the image of the game as being present (and somehow linked) to the analytic detective genre from the start. And indeed for all the narrator's disparagement of the game in the first Dupin story, by the time of the third story (some three years later) this link between chess and analytic detection seems to have become well enough established in Poe's mind for him to present us with a scenario strongly reminiscent of a chess game. Thus in "The Purloined Letter" there are a king and a queen and a battle between two knights (Dupin is a Chevalier, and one assumes that his double the Minister D—— is at least of equal rank), a battle for possession of a letter that concerns the queen's honor and that has the power, in the minister's hands, of turning the queen into a pawn. Suffice it to say that even if we put aside detective stories in which the actual game of chess figures in some way, or detectives like Chandler's Philip Marlowe who are chess fanatics, we are still left with the fact that the image of a chess game has become, within the tradition of the genre, one of the most common tropes for the battle of wits between detective and criminal.

Just as the narrator of "The Murders in the Rue Morgue" considers chess a game of extreme complication, so Borges associates it with two of his favorite images of complexity—the labyrinth and the paradoxes of Zeno—associations that seem to be rooted in his biography. In a 1971 interview Borges recalled studying "an engraving of the labyrinth in a French book" when he was a child, an engraving that showed the labyrinth as "a circular building without doors but with many windows": "I thought that if I used a magnifying glass I would be able to see the Minotaur," but "my eyesight was never very good. Later I discovered a bit more about life's complexity, as if it were a game. I'm talking about chess now."[3] In another interview two years earlier, Borges described the way in which his father introduced him to Zeno's paradoxes when he was a child:

> He was very fond of chess, . . . he took me to the chessboard, and he explained to me the paradoxes of Zeno, Achilles and the Tortoise, you remember, the arrows, the fact that movement was impossible because there was always a point in between, and so on. And I remember him speaking of these things to me and I was very very puzzled by them. And he explained them with the help of a chessboard. (Burgin, 9)

Chess is, of course, a game of endlessly forking paths, of constantly branching combinations of moves that make up the possible lines of play. In Edward Kasner and James Newman's *Mathematics and the Imagination*— a book Borges reviewed in *Sur* in 1940, remarking that it would become one of the small number of books he reread most often and filled with annotations[4]—the authors, after noting that "the total possible number of moves in a game of chess is: $10^{10^{50}}$,"[5] tell the story of the Grand Vizier Sissa Ben who asked the Indian king Shirhâm to give him, as a reward for inventing the game of chess, all the wheat that would accumulate by placing one grain on the first square of the board, two on the second, four on the third, and so on until all sixty-four squares were covered (*MI*, 173). While this geometric progression does not lead to infinity, it does produce a number so large ($2^{64} - 1$) that in any normal human context it might as well be infinite. In coming across this example of a chessboard used to illustrate the way the progressive doubling of a quantity quickly produces an astronomical number, Borges may well have been reminded of his father's use of the board to illustrate the infinite regression involved in continually halving the distance between two points, as in Zeno's straight-line labyrinth. And this early memory may have resurfaced again in Borges's reading of *Through the Looking-Glass*, for as Alice negotiates the chessboard-maze of the garden, she encounters an infinite regress of her own in the person of the Red King.

In chapter 4 Alice meets Tweedledum and Tweedledee, the mirror-image twins whose antithetical nature requires that they take opposing sides on every issue, the latter's rejoinders always beginning with the exclamation "Contrariwise!" In the company of these two, Alice comes upon the Red King asleep in the garden:

> "He's dreaming now," said Tweedledee: "and what do you think he's dreaming about?"
>
> Alice said "Nobody can guess that."
>
> "Why, about *you!*" Tweedledee exclaimed, clapping his hands triumphantly.

"And if he left off dreaming about you, where do you suppose you'd be?"

"Where I am now, of course," said Alice.

"Not you!" Tweedledee retorted contemptuously. "You'd be nowhere. Why, you're only a sort of thing in his dream!"

"If that there King was to wake," added Tweedledum, "you'd go out—bang!—just like a candle!" (*AA*, 238)

But as we noted earlier, the entire world of Looking-glass House is part of Alice's dream in front of the drawing-room mirror, a fact that evokes Martin Gardner's comment in *The Annotated Alice* that this "odd sort of infinite regress" in which "Alice dreams of the King, who is dreaming of Alice" is "like two mirrors facing each other" (*AA*, 239 n. 7), as emblemized by the presence of Alice's twin companions. The importance of this moment in the story is emphasized in the final chapter when Alice, awakened from her dream, faces the "serious question" of "who it was that dreamed it all": "It *must* have been either me or the Red King. He was part of my dream, of course—but then I was part of his dream, too!" (*AA*, 343–44).

10 *Who Is Albert?;* Dream of the Red Chamber; *Alice and the Red King; Borges and Averroes; Thinking the Absence of Thought; A Dream within a Dream*

IF THE UNDERLYING STRUCTURE SHARED by Borges's second and third detective stories involves the killing of a concealed red king in a chesslike battle of wits, then a question naturally arises: Does this same structure, with its Carrollian resonance, also underlie the action of Borges's first detective story, "The Garden of Forking Paths"? Is there a king concealed in the tale, and if so, is he associated with the color red? I would argue that the answer to both questions is yes, and that the episode from *Through the Looking-Glass* in which Alice encounters the sleeping Red King is the key to discovering the link between king and color in Borges's narrative.

We noted earlier that the victim Stephen Albert's given name probably alludes to the first Christian martyr, while his family name is the same as that of a town in northern France some fifty miles from the Belgian border, a town whose name Yu Tsun seeks to transmit to his chief in Berlin by means of Albert's murder and the subsequent newspaper publicity. However, given the tale's First World War setting, the victim's surname also probably alludes to one of the most famous figures in that war, King Albert of Belgium, the heroic monarch who refused to let Germany violate his country's neutrality by permitting its army unobstructed passage to the French border. Albert personally led the Belgian army in the field for four years with such gallantry and skill that he was hailed throughout the world as "le roi-chevalier." As Barbara Tuchman notes in *The Guns of August,* King Albert's rejection of the German ultimatum in the face of overwhelming odds and his military valor in defending his country marked "one of the rare appearances of the hero in history."[1] In the international press "his face became known to the world as a symbol of heroism and tragedy" (Tuchman, 17). Borges, of course, spent the years of the First World War as a teenager in Geneva, where his vacationing family had been trapped by the outbreak of hostilities. He thus experienced the figures and events of the 1914–18 war from a European as well as a South American perspective, and this immediate, personal impact of the war on Borges and his family seems to have left a lasting impression. It is also possible that Borges, having been present in Europe during the war, may have known a piece of curious lore concerning the French town of Albert during the July–August 1916 Somme offensive, the military operation that Yu Tsun's spy mission is meant to disrupt. Albert was the center from which the Allied drive started, and the tower of the town church was hit by shell fire, causing the "figure of the Golden Virgin on top of the partly demolished tower" to lean from its pedestal at a 90-degree angle. A picture of the tower, with its precariously leaning figure, made the cover of *The New York Times* Mid-Week Pictorial for August 17, 1916, with the caption "A Sign to the Soldiers" and the explanation that "the soldiers believe that the fall of this figure, which can be seen for miles around, will signal the approaching end of the war."[2] The town of Albert may have thus been connected in Borges's mind not only with the image of a king but with the figure of the Virgin (see fig. 10.1).

That King Albert, the Belgian monarch during the First World War, was on Borges's mind in 1941 when he wrote "The Garden of Forking Paths" can probably be explained by the fact that a year earlier, in May 1940, when the German army once again invaded Belgium on its way to France, Albert's son King Leopold III deserted the French and British armies that had come to his country's aid and unconditionally surrendered the Belgian army to the Nazis after a mere eighteen days resistance. As William Shirer notes,

> In the end the Belgian people . . . passed judgment on their sovereign. He was not recalled to the throne from Switzerland, where he took refuge at the war's end, until five years after it was over. When the call came, . . . his return provoked such a violent reaction among the populace that civil war threatened to break out. He soon abdicated in favor of his son.[3]

It must have seemed to Borges, writing in 1941, that one of his favorite themes, that of the traitor and the hero, had been played out in generational terms with this repetition and reversal of the heroic conduct of a father by the treacherous conduct of a son.

What seems clear in all this is that just as Yu Tsun used the victim Stephen Albert's patronymic to transmit the name of a town on the Belgian border to his chief in Berlin, so Borges uses it to transmit the name of King Albert of Belgium, "le roi-chevalier," to the reader, thus coding the murder of Stephen Albert as the killing of a concealed king. We should note in this regard that in describing Stephen Albert, Yu Tsun is clearly impressed by the nobility, not to say saintliness, of his character. But that still leaves us with the question of where the color red is in the tale and how it is linked to Stephen Albert. Carroll's episode of the sleeping Red King whose dream encompasses the dreamer Alice provides us with the associative link needed to find the red clue hidden in the text.

VOL. III., NO. 24. AUGUST 17, 1916.
PRICE TEN CENTS
The New York Times
MID-WEEK PICTORIAL
Double-Page Graphic Drawing of the Theatre of
ITALIAN VICTORY
Americans Fighting for France
A Sign to the Soldiers.
The leaning figure of the Golden Virgin on top of the partly demolished tower of the church at Albert, the centre from which the present allied drive on the Somme River was started. The soldiers believe that the fall of this figure, which can be seen for miles around, will signal the approaching end of the war.
(Central News Photo Service.)

Figure 10.1

Yu Tsun tells us that his great grandfather Ts'ui Pên "gave up temporal power to write a novel with more characters than there are in the *Hung Lou Mêng,* and to create a maze in which all men would lose themselves" (*F,* 93). The literary work to which Yu Tsun compares his ancestor's book— the *Hung Lou Mêng*—is an eighteenth-century Chinese novel whose title is usually translated as *Dream of the Red Chamber.* In Chinese, *Hung Lou* means "Red Chamber or Red Two Story Building, and suggests wealth, honour, and all the world's blessings."[4] Thus the title *Dream of the Red Chamber* is meant to suggest the illusory, dreamlike status of the mortal world, that world which in Chinese is literally called "the red-dust" (*DR,* xviii) and which the novel's hero Pao-Yu ultimately renounces "for the higher reaches of Buddhist paradise" (*DR,* xviii).

It is only fitting that Yu Tsun cites *Dream of the Red Chamber* in connection with his literary ancestor, for Borges clearly borrowed the name of his Chinese protagonist from a character in the eighteenth-century novel (one Chia Yu-Tsun)—*Dream of the Red Chamber* being thus the inscribed origin, the literary ancestor as it were, of Borges's Yu Tsun. And given that this Yu Tsun had been a "teacher of English at the Tsingtao *Hochschule*" (*F,* 89) before becoming a German spy, he seems all the more like his fictional precursor, for the Yu-Tsun of the novel begins as a destitute scholar, "born in a family of learning and position," who makes "a precarious living by copying and by writing letters for the illiterate" (*DR,* 13) but eventually becomes "an official, shrewd and without too many scruples" (*DR,* xxv).

The author of *Dream of the Red Chamber,* Tsao Hsueh-Chin, was born in Kiangsu province around 1719 and died in 1764. He

> probably began his novel about ten years before his death, for a poem by one of
> his close friends, dated 1757, alludes to his "writing his book at the Village of
> the Yellow Leaf." As he left no other writing, *Dream of the Red Chamber* must
> have been the "book." He did not, unfortunately, live to finish his novel. He had
> written only eighty chapters when he died. (*DR,* xvi–xvii)

One cannot help but notice a certain resemblance here to Ts'ui Pên, who at his death left an apparently "shapeless mass of contradictory rough drafts" (*F,* 96) of his own novel. Albert conjectures that Ts'ui Pên had told his friends at one point that he was retiring to write a novel and at another that he was retiring to build a labyrinth, and that his friends assumed these were separate projects, neither of which had been finished.

In 1792 the first printed version of *Dream of the Red Chamber* appeared, with forty additional chapters which the "editor" of the volume, Kao Ngoh, claimed to have compiled from fragments left by Tsao Hsueh-Chin but in reality had written himself (in most versions of the "completed" novel the two share the title page). As a result, the question of how well Kao Ngoh succeeded "in divining and carrying out the original designs of Tsao Hsueh-Chin" (*DR*, xviii) has become part of the novel's critical tradition. Indeed, the relationship of the two Chinese writers sounds as if it were the model for that between Ts'ui Pên, who leaves an apparently unfinished novel at his death, and Stephen Albert, who completes the former's work by realizing that the seemingly "contradictory rough drafts" are not fragments of an unfinished book but the temporally branching plot lines of a narrative maze.

Perhaps the best known episode in *Dream of the Red Chamber*, and certainly the one that would have recommended the work to Borges as an allusive background for "The Garden of Forking Paths," is the hero Pao-Yu's dream of seeing himself dreaming. Falling asleep, the young protagonist finds himself in a garden extraordinarily like his garden at home. Meeting several waiting-maids who uncannily resemble those of his own household, he follows them into the dwelling where he discovers a young man who looks just like himself lying in bed. Awakened by one of the maids, the young man on the bed says,

> "I have been having such an odd dream. . . . I thought I was in a great flower-garden, where I met some girls who called me nasty names and would not play with me. But I followed them back to the house, and there what should I find but another Pao-Yu, lying senseless on his bed, for all the world like an empty bag. His thoughts and feelings seemed all to have flown somewhere far, far away." When the real Pao-Yu heard this dream, he could not contain himself and cried out to the boy on the bed: "I came to look for a Pao-Yu; and now it seems that you are the one!" The boy on the bed rose and coming quickly toward him, embraced him, saying: "So you are Pao-Yu, and it was not a dream!" "A dream!" cried Pao-Yu. "No, indeed. It was more true than truth itself." But hardly had he finished speaking when someone came to the door, crying: "Mr. Pao-Yu is to go to his father's room at once." . . . The dream Pao-Yu rushed away, and as he left the room the real Pao-Yu called after him: "Come back soon, Pao-Yu! Come back." His maid Hsi-Jen was by the bed, . . . and said, laughing: "Where is this Pao-Yu that you are calling to?" Though he was no longer asleep, his mind was dazed and confused. "There he is," he said, pointing sleepily at the door. "He has just gone out." "Why, you are still dreaming!" said Hsi-Jen, much amused. "Do you know what it is you are staring at. . . ? It is your own reflection in the mirror!" (*DR*, xiii)

That Borges associated this episode from *Dream of the Red Chamber* with Alice's discovery of her mirror image within a dream (the Red King who dreams her as she dreams him) is confirmed by the fact that Borges included "'Pao Yu's Infinite Dream' by Ts'ao Hsüen-ch'in" in the *Anthology of Fantastic Literature* he edited with Silvina Ocampo and Bioy-Casares in 1940, placing it in a group of *"stories with a dreamed character"* that also included "a fragment from Lewis Carroll's *Through the Looking-Glass*."[5]

Besides Pao-Yu's dream, there are at least two other episodes involving mirror images in *Dream of the Red Chamber* that would have had special interest for Borges as precursors of Carroll's Looking-glass House. In the first, the hero Chia Pao-Yu meets his double Chen Pao-Yu, a young man who resembles him so closely that "had they worn the same clothes they would have taken one for the other's reflection in a magic mirror" (*DR*, 363). Chia Pao-Yu thinks that he has finally found "someone like himself," someone who can "understand him." But he finds that though "Chen Pao-Yu's exterior" is "exactly the same as his own," Chen Pao-Yu's ideas and "the burden of his conversation" are "as unlike his own as water" is "unlike fire" (*DR*, 363). In the other episode, a character named Chia Jui receives from his Taoist a magic mirror "made by the Goddess of Disillusionment of the Ethereal and Spiritual Palace in the Sphere of the Primordial Void" (*DR*, 91). The mirror has curative powers, but the Taoist warns that the youth must "not look into the right side" but "only use the reverse" (*DR*, 91). In the reverse side he sees "a gruesome skeleton staring at him with hollow eyes," but on the right side he sees a beautiful woman who beckons to him. On several occasions Chia Jui enters the mirror world of the right side and satisfies his desire for the woman: "When he was about to leave the illusive world of the mirror on his last visit, he was seized by two men and put in chains. 'Just a moment, officers,' Chia Jui pleaded. 'Let me take my mirror with me.' These were his last words" (*DR*, 91). This parting gesture of taking the mirror (the container of the illusory world of reflection) with him *into* the illusory world it contains (with the consequent reversal of outer and inner) is essentially the same structure as that of Pao-Yu's infinite dream and of the dreamer Alice's discovery that she is a figure in the dream of the Red King. However, we have one question still to answer. How exactly does the allusion in Borges's first detective story to the Chinese novel *Dream of the Red Chamber* (with its several resemblances to *Through the Looking-Glass*) link the color red to Stephen Albert?

Yu Tsun, in noting that his ancestor had set out "to write a novel with more characters than there are in" *Dream of the Red Chamber,* equates in effect Ts'ui Pên's literary labyrinth, *The Garden of Forking Paths,* with the eighteenth-century Chinese novel and its various mirror-image episodes. But, of course, in Borges's story Yu Tsun himself enacts a mirror-image episode. Just as his ancestor the novelist had been murdered by a stranger in his labyrinthine garden (in order to write his book, Ts'ui Pên had retired to the "Pavilion of the Limpid Sun" which was "set in the middle of an intricate garden" [*F*, 96]), so the decipherer of his ancestor's novel,

Stephen Albert, is also murdered by a stranger (Yu Tsun) in the middle of an implied labyrinth (since the directions to Albert's house are the same as those for reaching the central courtyard of certain mazes). And indeed as Yu Tsun approaches Albert's house, he has an uncanny sense of reliving an event from the past. These two moments distant in time that mirror one another equate or identify the victims (each killed by a stranger in a maze) with each other, the writer and the reader of the labyrinthine book. And if Stephen Albert is identified with Yu Tsun's great-grandfather Ts'ui Pên (the man whose existence ultimately made Yu Tsun's existence possible), then Yu Tsun's murder of Albert is the equivalent of Alice's checkmating the Red King (the figure whose dream, so the mirror-image twins claim, holds Alice in existence). And of course Yu Tsun's murder of Albert necessarily results in his own death, since he must allow himself to be caught in order to have his name connected with Albert's when the event is written up in the newspapers. Yu Tsun is thus "in a symbolic way, a man committing suicide." Significantly, the clue that allowed Albert to decipher Ts'ui Pên's novel and thus to become identified with him was, as we recall, "a fragment of a letter" Albert had discovered bearing the sentence "I leave to various future times, but not to all, my garden of forking paths." In token of Albert's identification with Yu Tsun's great-grandfather (and with the dreaming Pao-Yu in *Dream of the Red Chamber*, and with the dreaming Red King in Alice's dream), the piece of paper on which the clue is written "had once been crimson" but had faded with time until it was now "rose colored, tenuous, quadrangular" (*F*, 97)—the same fading of colors used to describe the labyrinth in "Ibn Hakkan al-Bokhari" (Dunraven recalls that when he was a boy the labyrinth "was not its present rose color but was crimson" [*A*, 119]).

We should note in this connection that the image Tweedledum uses to describe Alice's fate should the Red King awaken—"you'd go out—bang!—just like a candle!"—is one that Borges employs in a slightly different form to depict the instantaneous vanishing of a mental object at the moment the mind turns its attention from it. In the story "Averroes' Search" (1947), for example, the Arab philosopher Averroes, at the end of a day in which he has puzzled over and then misunderstood the meanings of the words *tragedy* and *comedy* in Aristotle's *Poetics*, prepares for sleep:

> Having unwound his turban, he looked at himself in a metal mirror. I do not know what his eyes saw, because no historian has ever described the forms of his face. I do know that he disappeared suddenly, as if fulminated by an invisible fire, and with him disappeared the house and the unseen fountain and the books and the manuscript. (*L*, 155)

Commenting on the abrupt conclusion of the story, Borges explains in a final paragraph that Averroes' lightless incineration was part of an attempt "to narrate the process of a defeat." Averroes, "closed within the orb of Islam, could never know the meaning of the terms *tragedy* and *comedy*. I related his case," but

> I felt that the work was mocking me. I felt that Averroes, wanting to imagine what a drama is without ever having suspected what a theater is, was no more absurd than I, wanting to imagine Averroes with no other sources than a few fragments from Renan, Lane and Asín Palacios. I felt, on the last page, that my narration was a symbol of the man I was as I wrote it and that, in order to compose that narration, I had to be that man and, in order to be that man, I had to compose that narration, and so on to infinity. (The moment I cease to believe in him, "Averroes" disappears.) (*L,* 155)

Just as the written character Averroes looks in the mirror only to see himself suddenly vanish from sight, so the writer Borges sees in this character who contemplates himself in a mirror, a mirror image of himself in the act of writing "Averroes," that is, in the act of projecting the written image of a writer (Averroes/Borges) who tries to imagine or mirror the mind of another writer (Aristotle/Averroes) by meditating on his works, his written image. In contemplating this process, Borges experiences a kind of master/slave reversal: he feels that the narration is mocking him. And the nature of the narrative's daimonism is suggested by the specific form of Averroes' incomprehension, his supposed failure to understand the meaning of the words *tragedy* and *comedy*, to grasp the very notion of the dramatic, the idea of the projection of the self as a persona, a mirror image, a double. It is precisely Averroes' imputed inability to understand the self's mutually constitutive, representational nature (symbolized by the Janus-like, reciprocal masks of tragedy and comedy), to understand the self as something essentially constituted by relatedness to an image of itself, that mocks Borges's art. For how can Borges, in imagining the mind of Averroes, really represent the absence of that knowledge (the meaning of tragedy and comedy) which he (Borges) possesses? The very form of Borges's representation (the mirror-image relationship between writer and written character, between the self and its dramatic mask) is at odds with the supposed content of that representation (the specified inequality in the two men's knowledge). Since this is an impossible situation to maintain, the desired specular relationship between author and character dissolves; the image vanishes from the mirror; the story breaks off.

Finally, insofar as this attempt to imagine the absence of an idea in the mind of one's specular double is a synecdoche for the mind's effort to imagine absolute otherness to itself, to imagine the total absence of mind (as indicated by Averroes' sudden annihilation), we can see why Borges characteristically depicts self-consciousness as an endless labyrinth or inextricable maze. For any representation of the total absence of thought is necessarily an illusion, precisely because the representation is itself a mental image and as such implies the continued presence of an *observer* of that image, the presence of the very consciousness whose absence it seeks to represent. As if trapped in an endless labyrinth of mirrors, self-consciousness literally cannot *imagine* a way out of itself, cannot think the absence of thought. And this is, of course, part of what makes the analytic power so little susceptible of analysis, for when thought tries to define itself by imaging its own limit (its total absence), that image always turns out to be a trick with mirrors, in the sense that it projects a symmetrical relationship between thought and its absolute negation, between thought and a nothingness that is both void of relationship itself and incapable of being incorporated into a differential relationship with thought.

There is, then, a logical connection between the realization of the infinitely progressive/regressive, double-mirror structure of thought (Alice dreaming the King dreaming Alice; Borges mirroring Averroes mirroring Borges) and the mirror illusion that one can actually image the absence of mind (Alice going out like a candle; Averroes vanishing in front of a mirror). For what the mirror illusion obliquely expresses, in implying the continued existence of the observer of that illusion, is the desire for an absolute consciousness that transcends thought's double-mirror structure (with its rhetorical dependence, as regards the figuration of the self, on the reflected image of a mortal body), transcends a structure that in its endlessly progressive/regressive self-reflection (a mirroring infinitely mirrored) conveys a sense of the self's groundlessness, its insubstantiality.

In "Deutsches Requiem," Borges makes clear the divine character of this desired observer in a passage imagistically linked to the moment of conscious self-projection or self-dramatization that ends "Averroes' Search." The narrator of "Deutsches Requiem," Otto Dietrich zur Linde, remarks, "The theologians maintain that if God's attention were to wander for a single second from the right hand which traces these words, that hand would plunge into nothingness, as if fulminated by a lightless fire" (*L*, 143). If this power to hold things in physical existence simply by thinking of them is a sign of divinity, then the Red King, whose dream keeps Alice from going out like a candle, represents for Borges a Berkeleyean absolutizing of thought that, in equating thinking and being, *percipi* and *esse*, projects an omniscient knower as the ground of the universe's existence. And since the Red King (who symbolizes this absolute consciousness) is explicitly presented as part of Alice's dream, as a projected apotheosis of Alice's mind, we can appreciate how precisely and subtly Borges has used Carroll's work in constructing "Death and the Compass," how he has reflected the theme of Poe's detective stories (the analysis of the act of analysis, the quest for an absolute knowledge of the mind) through the scenario of checkmating the Red King (the identification with, and overcoming of, the notion of absolute mind) in order to produce a tale in which a detective, who thinks of himself as "a pure logician, a kind of Auguste Dupin" (*A*, 65), goes looking for the "Secret Name" (*A*, 75) of God only to find himself engaged in a battle of wits with a double who seeks his death, a death which the logician imagines not as annihilation but as a cyclically recurring defeat in an endless struggle. In his essay "Valéry as Symbol" (1945), Borges, pointing out that "the man defined by Valéry's compositions . . . extols the mental virtues," argues that the character of Edmond Teste is a "mere *Doppelgänger* of Valéry. . . . That is to say, Valéry is a derivation of Edgar Allan Poe's Chevalier Dupin and the inconceivable God of the theologians" (*OI*, 74).

Alice's "serious question" about who "dreamed it all"—"me or the Red King"—is, then, a question about the survival of individual self-consciousness, and as Poe observes in "A Tale of the Ragged Mountains" (1844), "Novalis errs not in saying that 'we are near waking when we dream that we dream'" (3:946).

11 *Mirrors and Mazes; Mutually Constitutive Oppositions; Right/Left Reversal; The Fourth Dimension; Fortunatus's Purse; The Turn to the Left*

THE SETTING IN WHICH ALICE confronts her dual status as dreamer and figure in a dream is, appropriately enough, a garden maze. As Borges's favorite encyclopedia notes, the word *maze* derives from the Swedish "*masa,* to lounge, move slowly and lazily, to dream, muse. Skeat (*Etym.* Dict.) takes the original sense to be probably 'to be lost in thought,' 'to dream,' and connects with the root *ma-man-,* to think, cf. 'mind,' 'man,' etc." (*EB,* 17:942). Moreover, gardens have been, since at least the Middle Ages, a traditional literary locus for the dream vision as well as the setting for the most common form of labyrinth to survive into modern times—the hedge maze. (In a 1969 interview, Borges described the hedge maze at Hampton Court as "a kind of toy labyrinth" [Burgin, 23].) In *Mazes and Labyrinths,* W. H. Matthews notes that "an ingenious development of the hedge maze principle is the construction of indoor mazes lined with mirrors, by means of which the perplexity of the visitor is very greatly increased. Such 'mirror mazes' often find a place in fairs and exhibitions" (*ML,* 202). Matthews describes a temporary maze built for an English "garden fête":

> At the entrance was displayed a conventional labyrinth design, slightly modified to convey the misleading suggestion that it was a key to the maze, and below this were the following lines: "Beware the dreadful Minotaur / That dwells within the Maze. . . . Take one short peep, prepare to leap / *And run to save your life!*" At the goal was placed a chair facing an embowered mirror. (*ML,* 203)

Since the word *maze* derives from a root meaning "to be lost in thought," "to dream," and since a mirror is one of the most common physical images of mind, a "mirror maze" or a maze with a mirror at its center is clearly an appropriate place to evoke the doubly reflective condition of being lost in thought about thought, hence Carroll's choice of the garden maze of a house named for a mirror as the setting for Alice to confront the split and doubled nature of self-consciousness, a confrontation reflected yet again in his choice of her companions, the mirror-image twins Tweedledum and Tweedledee.

When Borges, in his story "The Circular Ruins," rewrote what he calls that "ancient idea . . . of the idealists, of Berkeley and the Hindus, and also of the Red King in Lewis Carroll"[1]—that the dreamer is himself the dream of another, who is in turn the dream of another, and so on—he used as an epigraph Tweedledee's words to Alice ("And if he left off dreaming about you"), words that Borges says were the origin of the idea for his story (Burgin, 53). Some twenty years later, in his poem "Chess" (1960), Borges again made use of Carroll's association of the game with the infinite regress of dreamer and dreamed. He says that just as the chess pieces "do not realize the dominant / hand of the player rules their destiny," so

> The player, too, is captive of caprice
> (the sentence is Omar's) on another ground
> crisscrossed with black nights and white days.
>
> God moves the player, he, in turn, the piece.
> But what god beyond God begins the round
> of dust and time and dream and agonies?   (*BR*, 281)

Since chess, like the labyrinth and the paradoxes of Zeno, is for Borges a symbol of the world's complexity, and since Poe, in evoking the simplicity he associates with the analytic power (and, by implication, with the analytic detective story), uses chess as an example of "what is only complex," Borges's decision to mirror Poe's detective stories through a work based on a chess game (*Through the Looking-Glass*) constitutes in effect an antithetical doubling in which he opposes the "complexity" of his stories, a hundred years deep into the tradition, to the "simplicity" of Poe's origin. Indeed, Borges's strategy seems particularly appropriate to an antithetical doubling of "The Purloined Letter"—and not just because of the mirroring implicit in its reflexive structure, or because it is the "simplest" of the three Dupin stories (the only mystery is how the minister has hidden the letter) and thus an obvious choice as the polar opposite of the complex stories Borges projects. But because, as we noted earlier, though the narrator in the first Dupin story disparages the complexity of chess compared to the simplicity of the analytic power, the plot of Poe's third story (with its king and queen and its two knights battling for possession of a letter capable of turning the queen into a pawn) bears nevertheless a striking resemblance to a chess game, indeed, bears a proleptic resemblance, as Borges must have noticed, to the passage in *Through the Looking-Glass* where Alice, playing the role of a pawn, is taken prisoner by the Red Knight and then rescued by the White Knight who defeats the former in single combat. The difference, of course, between Poe's and Carroll's versions is that while the queen in Poe's tale tries to keep from becoming a pawn, Alice in the role of a pawn tries to become a queen, an eventual promotion that allows her to checkmate the Red King.

It is within the context of this antithetical doubling, in which a late-comer in a genre opposes the complexity of the "world" (i.e., the difficulty of originality late in a tradition) to the "simplicity" of the genre's origin, that we can appreciate the deeper significance of the exchange quoted earlier between the two decipherers of Ibn Hakkan's fate, in which Unwin's commending the simplicity of Poe's purloined letter and Zangwill's locked room is balanced by Dunraven's speaking up for the complexity of the universe. One thinks in this regard of Borges's preface to the first edition of *Doctor Brodie's Report* (1970) in which he says that although he has tried "to write straightforward stories," he does "not dare state that they are simple; there isn't anywhere on earth a single page or single word that is, since each thing implies the universe, whose most obvious trait is complexity."[2] And yet is it merely ironic that Dunraven, whose name evokes Poe, should be the member of the pair to oppose the complexity of the universe to the simplicity of "Poe's purloined letter"? Not within the logic of a mutually constitutive opposition. For there it is not a matter of irony but of essence that a differential pole evokes its opposing position or that a character whose name alludes to Poe proposes a position the opposite of Poe's. In an opposition such as right/left, the significance of a given differential pole is precisely (and only) its relationship to its opposite. This implicit presence, within a pole, of its defining opposite is characteristic of the mechanism of splitting and doubling in which the doubles are external mirror images of an internal split within each, mirror images in that the master/slave polarities of the internal halves are reversed in the doubles. Thus the opposition between right and left is in effect the opposition between master Right (as opposed to slave left) / master Left (as opposed to slave right), or written algebraically R_l/L_r. Doubled but reversed (like a body and its mirror image), the poles cannot be made to coincide, precisely because their asymmetry is what constitutes their differential existence. It is this notion of a mirror asymmetry, metaphorized as the self-constituting difference between polar opposites, that I mean to evoke by the term *antithetical doubling*. And in order to understand what is involved in figuratively describing Borges's three detective stories as a mirroring or antithetical doubling of the Dupin tales, we must consider for a moment the kind of reversal inherent in the relationship between a body and its reflected image—the reversal of handedness.

Borges's interest in the right/left reversal characterizing mirror-image asymmetry can be judged from his essay "The First Wells" (1946). There he singles out as one of his four favorite works by H. G. Wells "The Plattner Story" (1897), a tale about "a man who returns from the other life with his heart on the right side, because he has been completely inverted, as in a mirror" (*OI*, 86–87). In Wells's story Gottfried Plattner vanishes one day without a trace when a mysterious green powder he has been analyzing suddenly explodes during a chemical experiment. Some days later, Plattner reappears, with another explosion, in the middle of his employer's garden. In explaining what is involved in Plattner's returning from the other life physically "inverted, just as a reflection returns from a mirror,"[3] Wells discusses the question of symmetry in two- and three-dimensional objects:

> There is no way of taking a man and moving him about *in space,* as ordinary people understand space, that will result in our changing his sides. Whatever you do, his right is still his right, his left his left. You can do that with a perfectly thin and flat thing, of course. If you were to cut a figure out of paper, any figure with a right and left side, you could change its sides simply by lifting it up and turning it over. But with a solid it is different. Mathematical theorists tell us that the only way in which the right and left sides of a solid body can be changed is by taking that body clean out of space as we know it,— taking it out of ordinary existence, that is, and turning it somewhere outside space. . . . To put the thing in technical language, the curious inversion of Plattner's right and left sides is proof that he has moved out of our space into what is called the Fourth Dimension, and that he has returned again to our world. (*PS,* 5)

Wells's remark that the reversal of "the right and left sides of a solid body" can only be accomplished by "taking that body clean out of space" and "turning" it in "the Fourth Dimension" recalls Möbius's speculation in the *Barycentric Calculus* (1827) that "two equal and similar solid figures, which are however mirror images of each other, could be made to coincide, if one were 'able to let one system make a half revolution in a space of four dimensions.'" But, Möbius adds, "since such a space cannot be conceived, this coincidence is impossible in this case."[4]

Using just the authors we have mentioned in this section, we could draw up a brief genealogy of the practice of imaging the reversal of mutually constitutive opposites as the physical reversal of the inner and outer surfaces of "a perfectly thin and flat thing" (like a sheet of paper) within a three-dimensional space, or as the reversal of the right and left sides of a solid body in a four-dimensional space. Which is to say, we could outline the tradition of depicting the metaphysical as if it were a higher dimension of the physical, a dimension in which mirror-image opposites can be made to coincide and three-dimensional objects manipulated like two-dimensional objects within the normal world.

Using Möbius's statement (1827) as an epigraph, we would begin our genealogy in 1844 with Poe's turning of the purloined letter inside out like a glove, a reversal of the inner/outer polarity of the written surface that symbolizes the way the metaphysical dimension of writing (thought) is at once inside and outside, at once contains and is contained by, the physical written surface. From "The Purloined Letter" we would draw a line of descent that passes through the discovery of the Möbius strip in 1865, to Carroll's Looking-glass House (1871) in which the left/right reversal of the mirror-image twins Tweedledum and Tweedledee, considered as a symbol of the oppositional nature of self-reflection, is associated with the metaphysical, inner/outer reversal that occurs when Alice and the Red King simultaneously contain each other in their respective dreams.

From *Through the Looking-Glass* we could extend the genealogical line to another work of Carroll's, *Sylvie and Bruno Concluded* (1893). There, Lady Muriel's German friend, Mein Herr, uses the Möbius strip to explain the construction of a puzzling object called Fortunatus's Purse. The narrator and Mein Herr are sitting with Lady Muriel in her garden when Mein Herr offers to show Lady Muriel how to make this purse with the pocket handkerchiefs she is hemming:

> "You shall first," said Mein Herr, possessing himself of two of the handkerchiefs, spreading one upon the other, and holding them up by two corners, "you shall first join together these upper corners, the right to the right, the left to the left; and the opening between them shall be the *mouth* of the Purse."
>
> A very few stitches sufficed to carry out *this* direction. "Now, if I sew the other three edges together," she suggested, "the bag is complete?"
>
> "Not so, Miladi: the *lower* edges shall *first* be joined—ah, not so!" (as she was beginning to sew them together). "Turn one of them over, and join the *right* lower corner of the one to the *left* lower corner of the other, and sew the lower edges together in what you would call *the wrong way*."
>
> "*I* see!" said Lady Muriel, as she deftly executed the order. "And a very twisted, uncomfortable, uncanny-looking bag it makes! . . . And how are we to join up these mysterious—no, I mean *this* mysterious opening?" (twisting the thing round and round with a puzzled air.) "Yes, it *is* one opening. I thought it was *two*, at first."
>
> "You have seen the puzzle of the Paper Ring?" Mein Herr said. . . . "Where you take a slip of paper, and join its ends together, first twisting one, so as to join the *upper* corner of *one* end to the *lower* corner of the *other*?" . . .

"Yes, I know that Puzzle," said Lady Muriel. "The Ring has only *one* surface, and only *one* edge. It's very mysterious!"

"The *bag* is just like that, isn't it?" I suggested. "Is not the *outer* surface of one side of it continuous with the *inner* surface of the other side?" (*LC*, 577–78)

After Mein Herr shows Lady Muriel how to complete the bag by sewing the four edges of a third handkerchief to the four edges of the "opening" created in sewing the first two handkerchiefs together, he explains the advantage of this curious container: "Whatever is *inside* that Purse, is *outside* it; and whatever is *outside* it, is *inside* it. So you have all the wealth of the world in that leetle Purse!" (*LC*, 579).

In the preface to *Sylvie and Bruno Concluded*, Carroll says that this book, like its predecessor *Sylvie and Bruno* (1889), is "an attempt to show what might *possibly* happen, supposing that Fairies really existed; and that they were sometimes visible to us, and we to them; and that they were sometimes able to assume human form: and supposing, also, that human beings might sometimes become conscious of what goes on in the Fairy-world" (*LC*, 512). To that end, Carroll supposes

> a Human being to be capable of various psychical states, with varying degrees of consciousness, as follows:—
>
> (*a*) the ordinary state, with no consciousness of the presence of Fairies;
>
> (*b*) the "eerie" state, in which, while conscious of actual surroundings, he is *also* conscious of the presence of Fairies;
>
> (*c*) a form of trance, in which, while *un*conscious of actual surroundings, and apparently asleep, he (i.e. his immaterial essence) migrates to other scenes, in the actual world, or in Fairyland, and is conscious of the presence of Fairies. (*LC*, 512)

As these categories suggest, *Sylvie and Bruno Concluded* is a book about the relationship between our normal consciousness of the physical world and a different, presumably higher, dimension of consciousness in which we become aware of another world. Moreover, since one does not change physical location in order to perceive or enter this other world but simply alters the level of psychic awareness, this book is also about the odd (usually invisible) presence in (and to) one another of the normal and the Fairy worlds. In effect, Carroll uses Fortunatus's Purse—this puzzling object whose inner and outer surfaces are continuous so that whatever is inside it is outside, and whatever is outside it is inside—as a symbol not only of a higher dimension in which opposites are reversed but also of the interpenetrability of the two realms—the way that the normal and the Fairy worlds (the physical world of objects and the metaphysical world of thought) are simultaneously inside and outside each other, like the universe and the Aleph. The narrator of *Sylvie and Bruno Concluded* experiences this interpenetrability during Mein Herr's explanation of the curious geometry of the purse to Lady Muriel, as instructor and pupil temporarily assume an uncanny resemblance to inhabitants of the Fairy world:

> She looked so strangely like a child, puzzling over a difficult lesson, and Mein Herr had become, for the moment, so strangely like the old Professor, that I felt utterly bewildered: the "eerie" feeling was on me in its full force, and I felt almost *impelled* to say "Do you understand it, Sylvie?" However I checked myself by a great effort, and let the dream (if indeed it *was* a dream) go on to its end. (*LC*, 579)

It is a short step in our genealogical chart from Carroll's *Sylvie and Bruno Concluded* of 1893 to Wells's "The Plattner Story" of 1897, with more than a slight family resemblance between the two. For in Wells's tale the interpenetrability of the normal world and the four-dimensional "Other-World" once again generates the story's action. Recovering from the initial shock of the explosion that launched him into the Other-World, Plattner finds that he can still see the three-dimensional world, although it has grown quite dim and the people in it "faint and silent as ghosts" (*PS*, 14). Plattner, on the other hand, is not only invisible (as is the world he now inhabits) to the people in the three-dimensional world, he is intangible as well. To his amazement, the people in the three-dimensional world can walk "*clean through him!*" (*PS*, 14). The only awareness they have of his new existence is in dreams, where "Plattner was seen, sometimes singly, sometimes in company, wandering about through a coruscating iridescence. In all cases his face was pale and distressed, and in some he gesticulated towards the dreamer" (*PS*, 10). Plattner's final revelation about this Other-World, "which, unseen and unapproachable to us, is yet lying all about us" (*PS*, 28), comes when he witnesses from his vantage point in the fourth dimension the death of someone in the three-dimensional world. As he stands watching the scene, a "shadowy black arm" like "a beam of darkness" stretched "across his shoulder and clutched its prey. He did not dare turn his head to see the Shadow behind the arm" (*PS*, 27).

From "The Plattner Story" and its ghostly fourth dimension in which a solid body's right and left sides can be reversed, the line of descent runs to Borges's third detective story and Dunraven's suggestion that the solution to the mystery of Ibn Hakkan's murder may involve "the theory of series" or "a fourth dimension of space." Dunraven suggests these possibilities not just because they are lines of inquiry that would interest a mathematician like Unwin but because Unwin had claimed that while the facts of the story of Ibn Hakkan, which Dunraven had recounted, "were true, or could be thought of as true, . . . told the way you told them they were obviously lies" (*A*, 122), which is to say that the facts need to be reinterpreted. And one of these is the false Ibn Hakkan's statement that he built the labyrinth in order to hide from the ghost of a man he had murdered. In this context, Dunraven's suggestion that "a fourth dimension of space" may be involved in the solution to the mystery would seem to be a half-serious attempt to provide a "scientific" basis—like the ghostly fourth dimension of "The Plattner Story"—for the notion of a murder committed by a disembodied spirit. But since the two detectives almost immediately dismiss the theory of a ghostly murderer, it seems much more likely that Dunraven's reference to a fourth dimension is meant to associate the kind of imagery that characterizes the interplay between the three-dimensional world and an imaginary higher dimension with the recurring motif of an oscillation between three and four, a conjecture supported by the fact that Dunraven's remark pairs the fourth dimension with "the theory of series," which is explicitly linked in the story to the number three (the three faceless bodies in the labyrinth). Thus just as the movement from three dimensions to four is associated with the inversion of the binary oppositions of the three-dimensional world (e.g., the reversal of the right and left sides of a solid body), so the oscillating three/four structure in Borges's stories is associated with the inversion (in a three-dimensional space) of the two-dimensional figure of a triangle as the means of moving from a three- to a four-sided configuration. In "Death and the Compass" this inversion is explicit. Lönnrot arrives at the quadrangular shape by projecting from the base of the triangle on the map another triangle pointing downward. In "Ibn Hakkan al-Bokhari," the inversion is implicit in Zaid's turning the dialectical triad of lion, slave, and king on its head through his doubling of Ibn Hakkan, a doubling that produces a four-sided figure (lion, slave, and king, plus the impostor Zaid) composed of a dialectical triad and its inverted image.

The reversal of right and left involved in Borges's antithetical doubling of the Dupin stories is not, however, a reversal of the physical opposition between the two sides of a solid body as in "The Plattner Story," but rather the reversal of a metaphysical opposition traditionally correlated with the difference between hands—that between right and wrong. In the Dupin stories, the detective's analysis inevitably prevails. But in Borges's detective stories the privileging of the right hand is reversed, and mastery shifts to the sinister side, a shift to which Borges gives us a clue by noting that the way to reach the center of certain labyrinths is "by turning always to the left" (*A*, 116).

12   *The Chess-Playing Automaton; The Privilege*
     of the Right Hand; The Oppositional Structure of Chess;
     The Intersecting of Mirror Folds; Chess as
     Emblem of Analysis

THE REVERSAL OF THE MASTER/SLAVE relationship between right and left in Borges's stories is almost certainly an allusion to another of Poe's works in which, within the context of a chess game, the opposition between the right and left hands is specifically linked to the relationship of a master to a slave. In the essay "Maelzel's Chess-Player" (1836), Poe presents a lengthy analysis of the chess-playing automaton invented by Baron Wolfgang von Kempelen in 1769 and exhibited during the 1820s and '30s in the United States by Johann Maelzel, an inventor of musical automata and a one-time friend and business partner of Beethoven. Poe's analysis— which critics frequently point to as a prefiguration of the analytic method of the Dupin stories and a trial run for Dupin's "voice"—is designed to solve the mystery of the automaton by showing that it is a hoax, that its chess playing is the work not of a mechanical but of a human agency. The automaton consisted of a slightly larger than life-sized figure of a turbaned Turk seated behind a wooden cabinet. The cabinet's interior was filled with machinery that could be exhibited during a public performance by means of panels in the cabinet's front. The chessboard was located on top of the cabinet directly in front of the automaton who, to the accompaniment of mechanical noises from the interior of the cabinet, moved the pieces with his left hand.

Poe contends that the automaton is not really actuated by the machinery in the cabinet but by a man ingeniously concealed behind the machinery. He suggests that once the exhibition of the machinery is completed and the panels in the front of the cabinet closed, the

> man within . . . gets up into the body of the Turk just so high as to bring his eyes
> above the level of the chess-board. . . . In this position he sees the chess-board
> through the bosom of the Turk which is of gauze. Bringing his right arm across
> his breast he actuates the little machinery necessary to guide the left arm and
> the fingers of the figure. (*P*, 14:24)

To support his contention, Poe points out first of all that the automaton's manner of playing chess exhibits the characteristics of mental rather than mechanical activity. For example, "the moves of the Turk are not made at regular intervals of time, but accommodate themselves to the moves of the antagonist" (*P*, 14:25), the assumption being that temporal regularity is essential to the workings of a machine and that the temporal variability displayed by the automaton in adjusting the intervals between its moves not only to those between the opponent's moves but to the moves' complexity is something beyond the scope of pure mechanism and instead in the realm of mind.

Poe's line of argument—in its elaboration of the antithetical qualities characterizing the opposition between a human mind and "a pure machine" (qualities such as temporal variability versus temporal regularity)—involves an implicit analysis of the human analytic power, and as such, prefigures the way in which the analytic power in the Dupin stories will take itself as the most natural, not to say inevitable, object of its own analysis.

In all, Poe educes some seventeen reasons for believing that the automaton is manipulated by a man hidden within it, but it is only with the last of these that we are particularly concerned. Noting that the "Turk plays with his *left* arm," Poe says, "A circumstance so remarkable cannot be accidental." The automaton's left-handedness

> cannot have connexion with the operations of the machine considered merely as such. Any mechanical arrangement which would cause the figure to move, in any given manner, the left arm—could, if reversed, cause it to move, in the same manner, the right. But these principles cannot be extended to the human organization, wherein there is a marked and radical difference in the construction, and at all events, in the powers, of the right and left arms. Reflecting upon this latter fact, we naturally refer the incongruity noticeable in the Chess-Player to this peculiarity in the human organization. If so, we must imagine some *reversion*—for the Chess-Player plays precisely as a man *would not*. These ideas, once entertained, are sufficient of themselves to suggest the notion of a man in the interior. A few more imperceptible steps lead us, finally, to the result. The Automaton plays with his left arm, because under no other circumstances could the man within play with his right—a *desideratum*, of course. (*P*, 14:36–37)

Poe goes on to argue that in order for the automaton to move the chessmen with its right arm it would be necessary for the man within, who is facing in the same direction as the figure, "either to use his right arm in an exceedingly painful and awkward position . . . or else to use his left arm brought across his breast. In neither case could he act with the requisite ease or precision" (*P*, 14:37). Consequently, the automaton uses its left arm because this allows the man inside to move with ease and precision, that is, to use his right arm by bringing it across his breast to manipulate the automaton's left hand.

It is hard to say which is odder—the argument itself or the fact that Poe uses it to conclude the essay. It is not especially surprising that Poe accepts the privileging of the right hand over the left, a privileging implicit in his statement that the automaton's left-handedness is remarkable precisely because in using this hand the automaton "plays . . . as a man *would not.*" (There is, of course, overwhelming statistical support for Poe's observation. Most studies of the question of the dominant hand put the number of right-handed people at somewhere between 85 and 90 percent of the population,[1] so that there is a sense in which right-handedness can be said to characterize human behavior.) What *is* surprising, however, are the conclusions Poe draws from this observation. He contends that in "the human organization" there is "a marked and radical difference in the construction, and at all events, in the powers, of the right and left arms," which is to say that the privileging of the right hand over the left is not an arbitrary effect of custom but a necessary aspect of human nature, of the psychophysical structure of the body. By contrast, in a mechanical organization such as the automaton the distinction between the right and left arms, Poe claims, is an indifferent one, since "any mechanical arrangement which would cause the figure to move, in any given manner, the left arm—could, if reversed, cause it to move, in the same manner, the right," the sign of this indifference being the ease with which the opposing functions are reversed in the machine. What this asserts in effect is that "a marked and radical difference" between the right and left arms (a difference whose most obvious expression is the superiority of the right arm to the left) is a distinctive characteristic of a human (master) organization as opposed to a nonhuman (slave) organization. And since what is at issue in Poe's essay is precisely the question of whether the chess-playing automaton is a *thinking* machine, a device of such subtle "arrangement" that it can, within the limited context of a chess game, mechanically duplicate the functions of mental analysis so as to reverse the master/slave relationship between mind and machine and defeat a human opponent, the fact that the automaton uses its left arm indicates to Poe that the machine has *not* achieved that human (i.e., independent, self-sufficient) organization whose mark of superiority over the nonhuman is precisely the mark of its control over itself—right-handedness.

We should note in this connection that in Poe's "The Gold-Bug" (1843) the difference between master and slave, between William Legrand and his black servant Jupiter, is presented at one point as the difference between someone who knows his right hand from his left and someone who does not. In the search for Captain Kidd's treasure, Jupiter is told by Legrand to drop the gold bug through the left eye of a skull nailed to a tree limb. When Jupiter hesitates, Legrand asks, "Do you know your right hand from your left?" Jupiter says that his left hand is the one he uses to chop wood (a comment that emphasizes his slave status as hewer of wood and drawer of water), and Legrand replies, "To be sure! you are left-handed; and your left eye is on the same side as your left hand" (3:821). But as it turns out, Jupiter drops the bug through the right eye rather than the left, either because he becomes confused or because the hand that he thinks is his left is in fact his right. Whether Jupiter is actually left-handed, as his master suggests, is not clear from the story, but what *is* clear is that the difference between master and slave, between the mind that gives the orders and the physical mechanism (the body) that carries them out, is associated here with the difference between right and left, a knowledge that "Massa Will" (as Jupiter calls him) possesses and that his body servant does not.

In the Maelzel essay Poe interprets the automaton's left-handedness, its playing "precisely as a man *would not*," as the necessary accommodation of a purely mechanical system of motion to a superior (i.e., immaterial) motive force—human will or desire, the "*desideratum*," to use Poe's word, of allowing the human operator to move his body, his personal physical mechanism, with ease and precision. Because the "marked and radical difference" in the construction of a human being's right and left arms is, according to Poe, directly related to a difference in "powers" within the psychophysical organism, anything in the automaton's design that prevents the human operator from acting at his best, that is, from using the favored right arm, is experienced not only as an impairment of mechanical precision but as a form of psychophysical unease, a thwarting of the will—the implicit assumption being that the right hand's superiority to the left is the mark, on the physical organism, of the mind's direct and immediate control of the body. Consequently, the automaton's left-handedness means that the mind's control in this case is indirect, mediated by some additional physical mechanism. It suggests that between the automaton's mechanical body and the mental power that animates it there is interposed another body (that of the concealed operator), the "peculiarity" of whose "human organization" (right-handedness) dictates the "*reversion*," to use Poe's word, exhibited by the automaton (left-handedness). In Poe's analysis, the chess-playing automaton with its human operator manipulating it from within becomes in effect a vehicle for representing various aspects of the body-mind relationship, a kind of sideshow version of the Cartesian angel driving a machine.

We are not particularly concerned here with the flaws in Poe's argu-

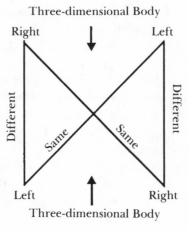

Figure 12.1

ment in the Maelzel essay. Indeed, his analytic method is often more a rhetorical device to create the appearance of logical rigor than an exercise in rigorous logic. While he was right both about the presence of a human operator inside the cabinet and about the way the operator concealed himself during the exhibition of the cabinet's interior, he was wrong about almost every other aspect of the automaton's operation, including the way the man inside observed the movements on the chessboard (this was accomplished by means of magnetic disks suspended on wires beneath the squares of the board, the disks rising and falling as the iron chess pieces were moved from square to square) and the way in which the Turk's arm was manipulated ("a mechanism on the pantograph principle . . . permitted the operator to guide the Turk's hand to any square of the board by moving a stylus to the corresponding square on the small board on which he followed the game himself "[2]). What *is* of special interest to us in Poe's analysis is the notion that the difference between mind and machine, between a human and nonhuman organization, is that a human organization possesses, or is capable of producing, "a marked and radical difference" *within* itself, a difference that creates the possibility of "parts" in the self, the possibility of physically representing the self's relatedness to itself. What Poe has done is to take the difference between the right and left sides of the body as the principal expression, within the physical organism, of that mental difference of the self from itself which constitutes self-consciousness, an internal difference whose projection onto the external world simultaneously constitutes the self's difference from others (as Poe argues in that passage from "Morella" where, citing Locke, he describes personal identity as the consciousness that "always accompanies thinking" and that allows us to recognize ourselves, "thereby distinguish-

Figure 12.2

ing" the individual self "from other beings that think" [2:226]).

In order to understand the implications of Poe's alignment of the physical difference between right and left with the mental difference that constitutes self-identity, we must keep in mind that he makes this correlation within the context of the game of chess, so that to pursue these implications we must consider for a moment the game's physical structure. In the usual situation where two opponents face each other across the board, the right hand of one player is directly opposed to his opponent's left hand and diagonally opposed to his opponent's right. If we diagram the players' face-to-face opposition in terms of the sameness and difference in the names of the hands that are, respectively, diagonally and directly opposed, we get figure 12.1.

Now consider the arrangement of the chessmen at the start of the game (see fig. 12.2). The player with the white pieces has the king side on his right hand and the queen side on his left, while the player with the black pieces has the king side on his left hand and the queen side on his right. Which is to say that the two kings face each other along one file and the two queens face each other along the adjacent file. If we diagram the position of the opposing kings and queens at the start of the game in terms of the sameness and difference of the pieces' names, we arrive at a configuration that is the reverse of the one depicting the opposition of the players' hands (see fig. 12.3). Here the pieces with different names are diagonally opposed, while those with the same name are directly opposed.

Let us look at one other opposition that sheds light on the relationship between the two diagrams—the face-to-face opposition of a human being and his mirror image. If we diagram this opposition in terms of the sameness and difference in the names of the hands that are directly and diagonally opposed, we get the configuration illustrated in figure 12.4. This figure is obviously similar to the one depicting the opposing posi-

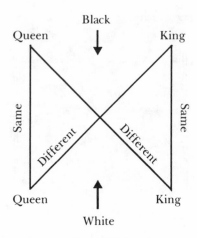

Figure 12.3

tions of the kings and queens at the start of a chess game, and the juxta-position of the two diagrams illustrates the way in which the initial align-ment of the opposing pieces exhibits what is known as mirror-image asymmetry—that is, the direct opposition of things with the same name and the diagonal opposition of things with different names. (Given this arrangement of the opposing chess pieces, it is not surprising, for exam-ple, that when Alice enters the world of mirror images in *Through the Looking-Glass,* she finds herself in the middle of a chess game.)

In this connection note that what the mirror image of a human body doubles is precisely the body's own bilateral asymmetry, the fact that the body's right and left halves are mirror images of each other. Just as there is no way, within three-dimensional space, of turning one's right hand to make it coincide with one's left, so there is no way of turning one's right hand to make it coincide with its reflected image. The only way to effect this coincidence within three dimensions would be if one could turn one's right hand inside out like a glove (the equivalent of turning the hand 180 degrees within a fourth dimension).

Since the mirror image of a right hand is configured like a left, the reflection in a mirror of the constitutive opposition between the right and left halves of the body necessarily involves a reversal into the opposite, that is, the reflected right as left, the reflected left as right. This self-reflection presents as an object of speculation the necessary presence of the opposing poles within one another. In such an opposition, the poles are joined by a mirror fold or mirror hinge, and the self-reflective mirror-ing of this opposition involves the intersection of a first mirror fold (be-tween the body's right and left halves) by a second mirror fold at right angles to it, the fold between the body and its mirror image (see fig. 12.5).

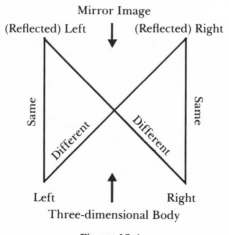

Figure 12.4

The designation of these mirror folds as "first" and "second" refers merely to their positions in a discursive sequence, for insofar as the poles are mutually constitutive, they must be simultaneously present in the differential moment. And since, in this configuration (12.5), each of the opposing poles is in turn differentiated into another bipolar opposition, we can make the further observation that it is *only* when a mirror fold is mirrored in (intersected by) another mirror fold that the two folds simultaneously come into existence—another way of saying that doubling is always splitting and doubling.

As the image of a body reflected in a mirror externally doubles the internal differentiation of the body into mirror-image halves, so the mirror asymmetry in the initial alignment of the opposing chessmen doubles in a facing configuration the internal asymmetry between the king- and queen-side alignment of each player's pieces. This "external" doubling of an "internal" halving in the arrangement of the chess pieces means that the square of the chessboard is in effect a figure composed of four quadrants created by two folds (along the horizontal and vertical axes), a figure that represents differentiation, the manifold, as a mirror-image folding/unfolding about the axes of dimensionality (see fig. 12.6.). (In comparing this diagram with the preceding one, we should keep in mind that since the mirror asymmetry in the initial arrangement of the white and black pieces is an attempt to represent, in the relationship of two opposing three-dimensional configurations, the relationship between a three-dimensional body and its two-dimensional reflected image, there will not be an exact correspondence between the two schemata.)

Now consider once again the situation at the start of the game with the two opponents facing one another across the board. They are about to do

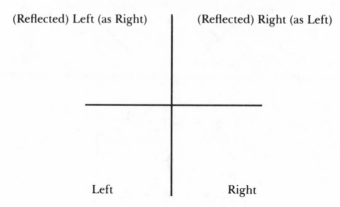

Three-dimensional Body

Figure 12.5

battle, each aiming to defeat the other by checkmating the opponent's king. But suppose for a moment that there were no chessboard between them and that this face-to-face encounter, instead of being a battle of wits, was a physical confrontation in which each opponent, trying to deliver a knockout blow, swung his privileged right fist at the other's chin. As one would expect in a facing encounter, these right-handed swings would be diagonally opposed. But now translate this confrontation back into a battle of wits on the chessboard, and suppose that each player, trying to deliver a knockout blow in the game, attacked his opponent's most important piece. The two king-side attacks would, of course, directly confront one another along the same side of the board. In contrast to the physical confrontation between two three-dimensional bodies (the face-to-face encounter of the players), the material structure of a chess game (the initial alignment of the pieces) physically represents the nonphysical battle of wits as the struggle of each player with his mirror image. The mirror asymmetry in the alignment of the opposing chess pieces at the start of the game is in effect an emblem of the analytic method employed by each player—the method of evaluating a move that one intends to make by considering in advance the opponent's strongest replies, and one's own response to each of these replies, and so on, alternating moves to the limit of one's concentration in a mental game played against an antithetical specular double, against a self-generated image of the other's mind created by treating one's own mind as other to itself.

In "The Murders in the Rue Morgue" Poe associates this mental division—this intentional opposing of the self to itself as a way of imagin-

Figure 12.6

ing another's mind—with the image of a battle of wits between a master-mind and an automaton. The marked change in Dupin's physical appearance as he exerts his analytic powers reminds the narrator of "the old philosophy of the Bi-Part Soul" and leads him to speculate on the existence of "a double Dupin" (2:533). Significantly, the narrator introduces his description of this change in appearance by reporting a boast of Dupin's that "most men, in respect to himself," wear "windows in their bosoms" (2:533). Mabbott suggests that this remark is based on a story Poe found in Horace Binney Wallace's *Stanley* (1838) about "Momus, god of laughter," reproaching "Vulcan for not making his human automata with windows in their bosoms" (2:570 n. 8); and Mabbott further notes that the classical source of this anecdote is Lucian's *Hermotimus*. But Dupin's remark also reminds us of Poe's contention that Maelzel's chess-playing automaton had an opening in its chest, veiled with gauze, through which the concealed human operator viewed the chessboard. Whether Dupin's comment refers to the story of Vulcan's automata or to Maelzel's chess player, the point is the same: Dupin's analytic power is of such superiority that, compared to him, other men are like automata, slavish mechanisms playing against, and ultimately manipulated by, a mastermind who has the power to see into their inmost beings. But what is most striking about all of this is that the narrator's description of Dupin's altered physical appearance as he exercises his analytic skill makes Dupin himself sound like an automaton: "His manner at these moments was frigid and abstract; his eyes were vacant in expression; while his voice, usually a rich tenor, rose into a treble which would have sounded petulantly but for the deliberateness and entire distinctness of the enunciation" (2:533). It is as if Dupin's body had suddenly become a physical medium for an alien spirit—which is simply Poe's way of presenting the relationship between

Dupin and other men, between the mastermind and the mechanical automata, as the external doubling of an internal split between mind and
body in Dupin, between a godlike pure spirit (a simple intellectual substance) and the complex bodily mechanism which that substance inhabits
and directs but to which it is essentially alien.

13
White and Black; The Temporal Privilege; Odd and Even;
The Alignment of Master Terms; Pythagorean Contraries;
Simplicity versus Complexity in the Automaton; Leibniz:
Imaging the Mind/Body Interface; The Other Side
of the Mirror

SO FAR WE HAVE CONSIDERED the physical structure of chess in terms of the intersection of four pairs of opposites—right/left, direct/diagonal, same/different, king/queen—but there are, of course, several other binary oppositions that structure the game, the most obvious being the white/black differentiation of the opposing sides. It is through this particular opposition that the privileging of one pole over the other within a binary system explicitly enters into chess, for the player of the white pieces starts the game with an advantage over the player of the black, not a material or spatial advantage but a temporal one. By convention white moves first; and all else being equal, white should thus be able to checkmate black one move before black can checkmate white. In terms of the game's structure, the advantage arises from the alternation of moves and thus from the necessity of one side having to move first. But the privileging comes from imposing on the question of the first move a preference associated with the color opposition that differentiates the two sides, that privilege of white over black, of light over dark that is at least as old in our tradition as the beginning of Genesis, where God creates the light, sees that it is good, and divides it from the darkness. Since white moves first and black second, the white/black opposition is aligned with the numerical opposition that governs alternation in a series, which is to say that all of white's moves are odd-numbered and all of black's even.

We should note in this regard that the game of even and odd which Dupin uses in "The Purloined Letter" to illustrate the method of effecting "an identification of the reasoner's intellect with that of his opponent" (3:984) bears a certain resemblance to the ritual for choosing colors that precedes most casual chess games. As we recall, in Poe's game of even and odd, "one player holds in his hand" a number of marbles "and demands of another whether that number is even or odd. If the guess is right, the guesser wins one; if wrong, he loses one" (3:984). In choosing colors at the start of a chess game, one player takes a white and a black pawn from the board, puts them behind his back, and then presents his opponent with his closed fists, each holding a pawn. The opponent chooses by tapping one of the fists with his hand, and he plays the color of the pawn held in that fist.

Poe describes the strategy employed in the game of even and odd by a certain schoolboy who excels in the "observation and admeasurement of the astuteness of his opponents":

> For example, an arrant simpleton is his opponent, and, holding up his closed hand, asks, "are they even or odd?" Our schoolboy replies, "odd," and loses; but upon the second trial he wins, for he then says to himself, "the simpleton had them even upon the first trial, and his amount of cunning is just sufficient to make him have them odd upon the second; I will therefore guess odd;"—he guesses odd, and wins. Now, with a simpleton a degree above the first, he would have reasoned thus: "This fellow finds that in the first instance I guessed odd, and, in the second, he will propose to himself, upon the first impulse, a simple variation from even to odd, as did the first simpleton; but then a second thought will suggest that this is too simple a variation, and finally he will decide upon putting it even as before. I will therefore guess even;"—he guesses even, and wins. (3:984)

The choosing of colors at the start of a chess game involves a similar strategy, a strategy that depends on the fact that it is virtually a reflex action for the player doing the choosing to tap the fist directly opposite the hand with which he chooses. Since white has the advantage of the first move, a player naturally wants to have the white pieces for himself and give the black pieces to his opponent. To accomplish this, an experienced chess player will, first, make an effort to be the one who holds the pawns. He will have already noted whether his opponent is right- or left-handed, and he will have made some estimate of his opponent's level of experience as a chess player. If he judges that his opponent is either inexperienced or the kind of unreflective person who thinks that the battle of wits begins with the first move rather than with the choice of colors, that is, the kind of person for whom the act of choosing colors will be a matter of reflex rather than reflection, then he will put the black pawn in the hand directly opposite the hand his opponent uses to make the choice. For example, if his opponent is right-handed, he will conceal the black pawn in his left fist. If, however, he judges that his opponent is an experienced player who is likely to be familiar with the strategy involved in the choice of colors and thus likely to recognize that the person holding the pawns is also an experienced player for whom this choice is not a matter of chance but of calculation, then he will reverse the previous strategy and conceal the black pawn in the fist diagonally opposite the hand his opponent uses to make the choice. Of course, if the person who does the choosing *is* an experienced player, then this opens up the possibility of a series of mirror-image reversals of strategy as each player estimates the other's subtlety on the basis of his own. But in practice this degree of complexity seldom applies, and as a rule of thumb the strategy of *direct* opposition with an inexperienced player and *diagonal* opposition with an experienced one markedly increases one's chances of getting the white pieces.

This method of selecting the colors in a chess game and the psychological maneuvering that accompanies it are certainly things that an experienced game player like Poe would have been at least as, if not more, familiar with than a children's guessing game played with marbles. (Indeed, Poe's game of even and odd sounds like something these children invented after reading Laplace on probability.) The ritual of guessing which hand holds the white pawn is significant in the present context in that it links the game of chess to Poe's game of even and odd, not simply because of the shared device of guessing the contents of a closed fist but because the difference between the white and black pawns is, in chess, the difference between making the odd-numbered and making the even-numbered moves. Moreover, this choice between white and black (odd and even) is physically presented as a choice between right and left in tapping the opponent's fist, so that Poe's game of even and odd is connected, through this ritual, to the physical structure of specularity, the direct/diagonal opposition of the hands of facing opponents.

While the advantage white is given at the start of the game consists in what might be called temporal odds (precedence in a series of alternating moves), the white side bears other marks of its privileged status, such as the fact that the player of the white pieces has his most important piece, the king, on his right-hand side, while the player of the black pieces has the king on his left. It is not unusual that the introduction of privileging into a system of intersecting bipolar oppositions tends to align the master terms in these oppositions on one side and the slave terms on the other, as, for example, with the alignment of white, odd, and right versus black, even, and left in chess.

Given the notion of chess as a kind of microcosmic world constituted by the intersection of a series of bipolar oppositions, one is reminded of Aristotle's summary in the *Metaphysics* of the Pythagorean belief that "the original constituents" of "Being" are a series of ten opposing pairs or contraries whose intersection creates the fabric of the universe. Noting that the Pythagoreans "consider number to be a first principle, both as the material of things and as constituting their properties and states," Aristotle remarks,

> The elements of number, according to them, are the Even and the Odd. Of these the former is limited and the latter unlimited; Unity consists of both

(since it is both odd and even); number is derived from Unity; and numbers, as we have said, compose the whole sensible universe.

Others of this same school hold that there are ten principles, which they enunciate in a series of corresponding pairs: (i.) Limit and the Unlimited; (ii.) Odd and Even; (iii.) Unity and Plurality; (iv.) Right and Left; (v.) Male and Female; (vi.) Rest and Motion; (vii.) Straight and Crooked; (viii.) Light and Darkness; (ix.) Good and Evil; (x.) Square and Oblong.[1]

The number of basic principles is ten because the "decad" was considered by the Pythagoreans "to be a complete thing and to comprise the whole essential nature of the numerical system" (Aristotle, 17:33–35), the number ten being the sum of the first four numbers as organized in the Pythagorean "tetractys" or equilateral triangle of fours ⸪ . In each of the ten pairs the master term (associated with order and harmony) comes first, and the slave term (associated with chaos) comes second. In this connection one is also reminded of the passage from Plutarch's *Isis and Osiris* describing the way in which, for the Pythagoreans, the master opposition of good and evil aligns the polarities of the other nine pairs:

> Under the good they set Unity, the Determinate, the Permanent, the Straight, the Odd, the Square, the Equal, the Right-handed, the Bright; under the bad they set Duality, the Indeterminate, the Moving, the Curved, the Even, the Oblong, the Unequal, the Left-handed, the Dark, on the supposition that these are the underlying principles of creation. For these, however, Anaxagoras postulates Mind and Infinitude, Aristotle Form and Privation, and Plato, in many passages, as though obscuring and veiling his opinion, names the one of the opposing principles "Identity" and other "Difference."[2]

Although Aristotle and Plutarch do not entirely agree in the names they assign to the Pythagoreans' ten basic contraries, it is enough for our purposes to note that several of the oppositions structuring the game of chess (odd/even, right/left, light/dark) appear in both lists and that several other chess-related oppositions can be assimilated to pairs that appear on one or the other of the two lists (e.g., king/queen to Aristotle's male/female, and direct/diagonal to Aristotle's straight/crooked and Plutarch's straight/curved). All of which is simply to point out that if the physical structure of chess is an embodiment of the game's characteristic analytic method, then to the extent that this method is a representation of self-identity as something constituted by the differential opposition between the self and its specular (mentally self-reflective) double, it is not surprising that the game's structure involves a network of intersecting bipolar oppositions: a mirrored proliferation, a multiplicative unfolding, of that basic mirror-fold structure which displays self-as-other, same-as-different. Nor is it surprising that this structure resembles and, indeed, shares several oppositions with a philosophical analysis of the "original constituents" of "Being" that images the basic relationship between mind and world as a series of paired contraries. For what is being evoked in both the structure of the game and the philosophical analysis is the sense that self-consciousness comes into existence not as a single, isolated mirror fold of the self upon itself but rather as a complex, simultaneously given network of intersecting oppositions in which the self finds itself located, or, more precisely, caught as in a net. We should note in this connection that Borges characteristically uses the image of a net to describe the intersecting paths of a labyrinth. In "Ibn Hakkan al-Bokhari," for example, he refers to the interior of the maze as a "network" (*A*, 116), and in his tale "The Maker" (1958), he describes the labyrinthine passages of a crypt as being "like nets of stone" (*A*, 157).

In the labyrinthine network of differences, the basic structural element is the simple mirror fold, but since this fold only comes into existence when it is intersected by another mirror fold, this constitutive mirroring of the self-reflexive by the self-reflective simultaneously (and limitlessly) multiplies the simplicity (L. *simplex*, "single fold") of the basic structural element as a complex (L. *complexus*, "a weaving or twining together") of differential oppositions. One could say, then, that the reciprocity of the simple and the complex is that of specularity (L. *speculum*, "mirror") and reticulation (L. *reticulum*, diminutive of *rete*, "a net"), a reciprocity clearly embodied in the physical structure of chess where the mirror-image asymmetry (both between the opposing sides and within each side) in the initial alignment of the white and black pieces plays itself out upon a mazelike network of white and black squares.

We might note in passing that the image of a network of bipolar oppositions figures prominently in the double-mirror scenario of Borges's poem "The Golem," a treatment of the automaton theme as a trope of master/slave reversal. The poem tells the story of a certain rabbi of Prague who, by the cabalistic manipulation of "letters in complicated variations" (*complejas variaciones*), finally "pronounced the Name which is the Key,"[3] thereby animating a "dummy" (*SP*, 111), a human "simulacrum" (*SP*, 113). But the animation of the golem, instead of conferring a measure of freedom on the creature, leaves it, "like ourselves"

> Locked in the sonorous meshes of the net [*red sonora*]
> Of After, Before, Tomorrow, Meanwhile, Yet,
> Right, Left, You, Me, and Different and Same.   (*SP*, 113)

The golem's role as a mirror image in this scenario is suggested by the creature's inability to speak, just as its slave status is evoked by its menial occupation of sweeping the synagogue. (One recalls that in the archetypal literary version of mirror doubling, the story of Narcissus in Ovid's *Meta-morphoses*, it is precisely the speechlessness of the reflected image that reveals its true character as a slave mimicking Narcissus's movements and not an independent being as Narcissus had at first thought.) In a final twist Borges shows that the specular, master/slave relationship between the rabbi and his mute "simulacrum" is itself a mirror image of the relation-ship between God and the rabbi, for the rabbi is simply a creature who, in "yearning to know that which the Deity / Knows" (*SP*, 111), has created a being in his own likeness.

In his analysis of the chess-playing automaton, Poe uses the opposition between simplicity and complexity as a means of differentiating mental and mechanical activity, just as he will later, in the Dupin stories, introduce this same opposition (which he uses to structure his analysis of the analytic power) into his discussion of chess as a game whose relative complexity, compared to checkers, makes it less useful as a mental exercise for devel-oping the "higher powers of the reflective intellect" (2:528), powers that Poe associates with a radical simplicity. In the Maelzel essay Poe reports that during the exhibition of the machinery inside the Turk's body prior to the chess game, the automaton was "rolled round" the room on casters (*P*, 14:27), with the result that "certain portions of the mechanism changed their shape and position in a degree too great to be accounted for by the simple laws of perspective":

> Subsequent examinations convince us that these undue alterations were attrib-utable to mirrors in the interior of the trunk. The introduction of mirrors among the machinery could not have been intended to influence, in any de-gree, the machinery itself. Their operation, whatever that operation should prove to be, must necessarily have reference to the eye of the spectator. We at once concluded that these mirrors were so placed to multiply to the vision some few pieces of machinery within the trunk so as to give it the appearance of being crowded with mechanism. Now the direct inference from this is that the machine is not a pure machine. For if it were, the inventor, so far from wishing its mechanism to appear complex, and using deception for the purpose of giving it this appearance, would have been especially desirous of convincing those who witnessed his exhibition, of the *simplicity* of the means by which results so wonderful were brought about. (*P*, 14:28)

The oddness of Poe's argument requires an explanation. He claims that the mirrors inside the automaton are placed so as "to multiply" to the spectators' vision the amount of machinery contained in the trunk, but he then proceeds to ignore the obvious implication of this—that in creating this appearance the inventor wants to convince the spectators that there exists literally no space for a human operator in an interior "crowded with mechanism"—an implication that could be easily interpreted as indicating, through the inventor's specific effort to convince us otherwise, that a human operator is in fact present. Instead, Poe reads the imputed mirroring of the automaton's machinery in terms of an opposition between simplicity and complexity. He says that the automaton cannot be "a pure machine," because if it were, its inventor would *not* have wanted "its mechanism to appear complex" but would have tried instead to convince the spectators "of the *simplicity* of the means by which results so wonderful were brought about."

Poe's interpretation of the inventor's wishes—far from indicating what would lead a spectator to infer that the automaton is not a pure machine—seems to run exactly counter to one's logical expectations. For if the interest excited by the automaton arises not from the likelihood that it is an exceptionally clever hoax but from the mere possibility that it is a machine actually capable of thought, then by as much as the inventor exaggerates the disproportion between the device's "wonderful" results and the simple means of producing those results, he increases the spectator's sense that the device is a fraud and thus decreases its attraction for the public. It would seem that from the standpoint of exhibiting the automaton to interested viewers the inventor's ends are best served by making the interior machinery appear as complex as possible in order to maintain, through a mysterious collocation of gears and levers, the illusion that somewhere within this labyrinth of parts the leap from mechanical to mental activity has actually been achieved, an illusion impossible to keep up if a simple arrangement of machinery allows the spectator to survey the workings at a glance and trace an unbroken chain of purely mechanical causes.

Does Poe's argument, then, make any sense at all? Only if we understand that Poe is more interested in a philosophical question—the analysis of the distinctive features of mental activity by means of a differential opposition between the mental and the mechanical—than he is in the actual configuration of the automaton. Which is merely to say that his principal interest in the automaton is as a vehicle for his epistemological theories. To judge from the thrust of his argument, Poe operates in a philosophical tradition that considers the mind or soul to be a simple substance—one without parts. (Since something without parts cannot be analyzed into its components, this sense of the mind may also account for Poe's remark in the first Dupin story that the analytic power, as a function of this simple substance, is "but little susceptible of analysis.") In suggesting, then, that if the automaton had been a genuine thinking machine, its inventor would not have tried to make the mechanism appear complex but emphasized instead the simplicity of its structure, Poe is merely taking the position that any mechanical device that has actually attained the power of thought must have also acquired, as a significant modification of its mechanical (i.e., complex) structure, the distinctive feature of the thinking substance—simplicity. Whatever has become like the mind must show in one way or another the essential quality of the mind's substantial ground.

In this connection we should remember that the person who introduces mirrors into the mechanism of the chess-playing automaton is Poe himself. He theorizes their presence within the device in order to account for certain changes in the "shape and position" of its machinery which he claims to have observed when the interior of the automaton was exhibited to the spectators, changes he cannot explain by "the simple laws of perspective." What Poe has done, of course, by this sleight of hand is to place at the center of the purported thinking machine the most common physical image of reflective mental activity (a mirror), thereby emphasizing the enormous gap between the complex mechanical action of part pushing against part (an action that, if it is to achieve its goal of thought, must produce reflection) and the relatively simple, though no less physical, action of mirroring that literally reflects the image of this complex mechanism back upon itself. This mechanical parody of self-reflection presents Poe's argument in emblematic form, for obviously a machine that cannot even attain the relative simplicity of physical mirroring could never achieve the radical simplicity of mental reflexiveness.

In many respects Poe's strategy is reminiscent of one used by Leibniz in *The Monadology* (1714) to exhibit the impossibility of deriving mental activity from mechanical motion: "It must be confessed," says Leibniz,

> that *perception* and that which depends on it *are inexplicable by mechanical causes*, that is, by figures and motions. And, supposing that there were a machine so constructed as to think, feel and have perception, we could conceive of it as enlarged and yet preserving the same proportions, so that we might enter it as into a mill. And this granted, we should only find on visiting it, pieces which push one against another, but never anything by which to explain a perception. This must be sought for, therefore, in the simple substance and not in the composite or in the machine. Furthermore, nothing but this (namely, perceptions and their changes) can be found in the simple substance. It is also in this alone that all the *internal activities* of simple substances can consist.[4]

The parallel between this approach and Poe's strategy of placing mirrors inside the automaton becomes even more striking when we recall that this "simple substance" Leibniz calls "the monad," a substance without parts, extension, figure, or divisibility, is described again and again in his work as "a perpetual living mirror of the universe" (*LS*, 544) precisely because each monad "expresses exactly all the others through the relations which it has to them" (*LS*, 545). Thus, Leibniz's method of contrasting mental and mechanical activity by inviting a human observer inside an imaginary automaton enlarged to the size of a mill amounts in effect to placing a mirror (the monad) inside a machine, a strategy that sheds light on Poe's larger project in the Maelzel essay of figuring the mind-body problem through the scenario of a human operator hidden inside a chess-playing automaton.

There is, of course, a further appropriateness in our invoking Leibniz in this context, for the monad, as a kind of universal mirror, is one of the philosophical ancestors of Borges's microcosmic Aleph, as Borges himself indicates in his essay "Pascal" (1947) (*OI*, 95). Borges mentions Leibniz frequently in both his stories and essays. No fewer than three of the nineteen items in Pierre Menard's fictive bibliography, for example, refer to the German philosopher in connection with such topics as the universal written character and the paradoxes of Zeno. Moreover, in his essay "The Analytical Language of John Wilkins" (1941), Borges explicitly associates Leibniz with the opposition between simplicity and complexity as it relates to different forms of philosophical analysis. Discussing Wilkins's "universal language" in which "each word defines itself," Borges points out that Descartes "had already noted in a letter dated November, 1629, that by using the decimal system of numeration we could learn in a single day to name all quantities to infinity, and to write them in a new language, the language of numbers" (*OI*, 102). In a footnote to this dream of a Dewey decimal system of the universe, Borges adds,

> Theoretically, the number of systems of numeration is unlimited. The most complex (for the use of divinities and angels) would record an infinite number of symbols, one for each whole number; the simplest requires only two. Zero is written 0, one 1, two 10, three 11, four 100, five 101, six 110, seven 111, eight 1000 . . . It is the invention of Leibnitz, who was apparently stimulated by the enigmatic hexagrams of the Yi tsing. (*OI*, 102n)

Leibniz's creation of a rudimentary binary computer language lends an added resonance to his interest in automata and thus to his possible influence on Poe's essay, particularly when we recall that the principal nineteenth-century automaton to which Poe compares Maelzel's chess player is Babbage's calculating machine.

The basic difficulty in dealing with the mind-body relationship lies, of course, in representing the interface between the two. In the passage from *The Monadology* quoted earlier, Leibniz maintains that perception is inexplicable by mechanical causes. Which is to say that although the mind is located in the body (and can even be linked to a specific area), Leibniz cannot satisfactorily image the way in which mind and body impinge on one another. He cannot convincingly describe the interface by which physical sensations are transformed into mental images, and mental impulses into physical motions. It was precisely this lack of an adequate image to explain the reciprocal cause-and-effect relationship between mind and body that led Leibniz to circumvent the problem by positing a preestablished harmony between the two.

However, in an earlier work, *New Essays on Human Understanding* (written in French in 1703–5 but not published until 1765), Leibniz did sketch out a rough theoretical model of the physical basis of thought, using the functions of reception, storage, recall, and combination as criteria for explaining mental activity. The model is of interest to us because the physical image that Leibniz proposes for the structure of the brain is that of a sheet or screen whose surface is meaningfully differentiated by folds, an image that provides an enlightening background to Poe's purloined letter and its folds. Commenting on a passage from Locke's *An Essay Concerning Human Understanding* in which Locke compares the mind to a dark room, Leibniz writes,

> In order to render the resemblance [between the understanding and a dark room] greater it would be necessary to suppose that there was in the dark room to receive the images a cloth [or screen], which was not smooth, but diversified by folds representing innate knowledge; that, furthermore, this cloth or canvas being stretched had a sort of elasticity or power of acting, and even an action or reaction accommodated as much to past folds as to newly arrived impressions of the images. And this action would consist in certain vibrations or oscillations, such as are seen in a stretched cord when it is touched, of such a kind that it gives forth a sort of musical sound. For not only do we receive images or traces in the brain but we also form them anew when we consider *complex ideas*. Thus the cloth, which represents our brain, must be active and elastic. This comparison would explain tolerably well what takes place in the brain; but as to the soul, which is a simple substance or *monad*, it represents without extension these same varieties of extended masses and has perception of them. (*LS*, 420)[5]

Clearly, the basic form of information storage that lies behind Leibniz's model is writing or drawing. For meaningful marks on a sheet of paper Leibniz substitutes meaningful folds in a sheet of cloth, a substitution that renders less apparent the difficulties involved in this model. For example, if the same surface must both receive impressions and store them, it is difficult to see why the activity of storing does not eventually exhaust the surface's ability to receive new images, difficult to represent the physical structure of an interface that can continually receive impressions without ever becoming filled with the stored material, as a sheet of paper becomes filled with marks. But this is only a minor difficulty compared to some of the others Leibniz must confront. At the very start he has to describe a surface that can receive images in a visual form and yet store them in a nonvisual form, a capacity implied, as I read it, in his description of the understanding as a dark room, a nonvisual storage space. Which is merely to say that if one were to dissect a brain, one would not find within the mass of gray matter a collection of tiny pictures constituting the memory. In order to explain how visual images received upon the surface are transformed into physical modifications of that surface ("impressions" or "folds"), Leibniz imagines the cloth or screen as being elastic—a quality that further serves to explain how images stored in the brain can be recalled, although the figure Leibniz uses to depict this process involves the reproduction of an aural rather than a visual sensation. He describes the surface's elasticity as being like that of a cord stretched to a specific tension so that it reproduces the same musical tone when touched.

What Leibniz provides in the final analysis is simply a disjointed series of illustrations tacked on to the basic trope of the brain as a receptive screen, a series of broad analogies each of which matches a physical property or motion to a mental activity. Yet when these analogies are considered as elements of a unified complex rather than as separate examples, then the very nature of the physical—the fact that a three-dimensional body excludes any other three-dimensional body from occupying the same space at the same time—defeats Leibniz's attempt to provide an image of the material ground of thought, for what this complex of analogies ultimately illustrates through its attribution of mutually exclusive mechanical motions to the same surface is the virtual impossibility of deriving mental activity from purely mechanical causes—a point Leibniz implicitly acknowledges when, in the second half of the passage's final sentence, he relinquishes the figure of a dimensional surface in favor of a dimensionless substance, the monad that "represents without extension these same varieties of extended masses and has perception of them." Since the principle of noncontradiction is physically grounded on the space-excluding character of extended bodies, the realm of the unextended, of the dimensionless, often functions rhetorically (as in this instance) as a trope of the transcendence of the principle of noncontradiction, a transcendence physically imaged as a pervasive interpenetrability, the metaphysical realm's immanence in the physical. In effect, then, it is the physical incompatibilities or contradictions in Leibniz's model of the material basis of thought that he renames, in the final sentence of the quoted passage, as the metaphysical, the "soul."

As an image of the border between physical and mental, Leibniz's "active and elastic" screen "diversified by folds" ultimately (though perhaps unintentionally) illustrates the same point as Poe's purloined letter folded so that its outer and inner surfaces are reversed: that the most accurate physical representation of the link between body and mind is the reversal or interchangeability of dimensional oppositions considered as the sign of the metaphysical's transcendence of the bodily. The turning of the purloined letter inside out symbolically depicts the relationship between the physicality of writing and the metaphysicality of thought as a continuous container/contained oscillation. And the reciprocity of writing and reading as, respectively, the bodily projection of an inner metaphysical content and the mental introjection of an outer physical form thus images the act of self-reflection—as Poe suggests in "The Purloined Letter" when he compares the turning of the letter to the turning of a glove (3:992). For the latter reverses not only inner and outer surfaces but also the mirror-image opposition between right and left hands. And since inner and outer are respectively coded as mind and body, Poe's equation of the inner/outer opposition with the mirror-image opposition of handedness associates the mind-body relationship with that between the body and its mirror image, thus evoking the double-mirror structure of self-consciousness in which external mirroring images internal reflection. In the external relationship of the body as master to its reflected image as slave, the mind finds a reverse representation of the relationship of the mind as master to the body as slave. In looking at the body's reflection in a glass, the mind sees a physical image of its own metaphysical condition, the condition of being simultaneously inner and outer to the physical. But, as one would expect with mirroring, it is an image in which the terms evoke their opposites. That is to say, the *physical reflecting surface,* which contains or encompasses the reflected image of the body within its border and is thus an *outer* to the image's *inner,* is an inverted figure of the *mental reflecting power* that is physically located in the body as an *inner* to the body's *outer;* while the individual's reflected image, contained within the reflecting surface's border, is in turn a figure of the self as container of the body, a figure of the mind's power to project itself, as a specular other, outside the body so as to include the body as part of that larger entity constituted by self-reflection (the self). What the self discovers in this double mirroring is its own divided status as *the mirror of self-reflection* and *the image in the mirror* (the part symbolically equal to the whole).

When Poe in "The Purloined Letter" equates the inner/outer (mind/body) opposition with the right/left opposition, he is in effect repeating an alignment made earlier in the Maelzel essay—the alignment of the master/slave opposition between the right and left hands with that between mental (human) and mechanical (nonhuman) activity, an alignment that he makes by first invoking "the radical difference" in the "powers" of the two hands and then remarking that the automaton, in moving the pieces with his left hand, plays "precisely as a man *would not*." In both cases the mirror-image opposition between right- and left-handedness is represented as the physical expression on the body of the mind's relationship to (its mastery of) the body, the visible sign of the mirror/image relationship between the reflecting (metaphysical) power and the reflected (physical) object. Moreover, one suspects that Poe's purpose in theorizing the presence of mirrors inside the automaton was not just to produce a mechanical parody of self-reflection but to provide the automaton with a form of internal mirroring that would correspond to the external mirror-image relationship between the mechanical chess player and its human opponent (a relationship evoked by the mirror-image structure of the game they play).

What seems clear, then, is that in the Maelzel essay Poe began to develop not only the specific network of bipolar oppositions he was to use later in analyzing the act of analysis in the Dupin stories, but also the alignment of their privileged terms. And what seems equally clear is that Borges, in doubling Poe's three detective stories with three of his own, adopted that same network of oppositions but reversed their privileging in order to make his triad of stories a mirror image of Poe's, perhaps in an attempt to reverse the master/slave relationship between the originator of the genre and his most self-conscious follower.

This reversal of Poe's privileged terms in Borges's detective stories accounts, then, not only for the triumph of the criminal over the detective (sinister over righteous) and for the related shift in the gender coding of the victim from female to male, but also for the triumph of complexity (the indeterminacy of the world) over simplicity (the analytic certainty of the mind), for Borges presents the outwitting of the detective by the criminal as less a victory of one mind over another than an entrapment of both minds in the fatal, labyrinthine net of the world. Indeed, given Poe's association of chess with complexity and draughts with simplicity, this reversal of privileged terms probably accounts as well for Borges's decision to reflect the structure of the Dupin stories through the complex chess game played out in the garden maze of Carroll's Looking-glass House, a strategy Borges seems to acknowledge in his poem "Edgar Allan Poe":

As if on the wrong side of the mirror,
He yielded, solitary, to his rich [*complejo / Destino*]
Fate of fabricating nightmares. Perhaps,

On the wrong side of death, solitary
And unyielding, he devises more
Magnificent and atrocious marvels still.   (*SP*, 173)

If Poe is on the other side of the mirror, it is because Borges has put him there by playing, with its complex inventor, the simple game of trying to be one up on a specular double.

14 *Diamond and Hourglass; Sir Thomas Browne; English, French, and Mere Spanish; "Tlön" and* Urn Burial; *Translation from Past to Present*

OF THE GEOMETRIC FIGURES INVOKED so far to image various aspects of self-reflection, two are clearly linked by being reciprocals of one another. The first is the diamond shape formed by two triangles sharing the same base but with their apices pointing in opposite directions ◊. We associated this figure (which Lönnrot inscribes on the map in "Death and the Compass") with the oscillation between three and four and with the infinite progression/regression characteristic of double-mirror structures, and we then linked it to Poe's game of even and odd (in which the analysis of mind is evoked as specular doubling) and to the two interlocking pairs of words in "The Purloined Letter" (simple/odd, even/odd) whose structure involves three different things being made to fill four spaces by doubling one of them. The second geometric figure is the hourglass shape formed by two triangles joined at their apices ⟊, a configuration that, when rotated 90 degrees ⋈, represents the direct and diagonal oppositions linking the mirror-image halves of two facing bodies or of a body and its reflected image. The diamond and hourglass shapes are reciprocals because they are formed by flipping the figure of a triangle 180 degrees upward or downward from its base ⟁. Our task now is to show, first, that these two figures associated with the schematic representation of specular self-consciousness are parts of a more complex geometrical pattern that images the intelligible continuity of the world; second, that both these figures are composed of a simpler geometric shape imaging the physical basis of the functioning of human intelligence; and, finally, to link all of these shapes to the Borgesian image of the labyrinth and to the symbolic action that takes place there.

To pursue this task, we must consider for a moment another author whose work not only influenced Borges's writing in general but also served as a specific link between the Dupin stories and Borges's three detective tales—Sir Thomas Browne. Borges recalls that his first published collection of prose contained "a quite bad essay on Sir Thomas Browne, which may have been the first ever attempted on him in the Spanish language" (*A*, 231), and he notes later that among their various "literary ventures" (*A*, 245) together, he and Adolfo Bioy-Casares "anno-

129

tated Sir Thomas Browne" (*A*, 246). Borges associates Browne's influence on his writing with the fact that at an early stage in his career he (Borges) played "the sedulous ape to two Spanish baroque seventeenth-century writers, Quevedo and Saavedra Fajardo, who stood in their own stiff, arid, Spanish way for the same kind of writing as Sir Thomas Browne in 'Urne-Buriall.' I was doing my best to write Latin in Spanish" (*A*, 231). The reference to Browne's *Urn Burial* is significant for several reasons. First, it recalls the ending of "Tlön, Uqbar, Orbis Tertius," the opening tale in the volume *The Garden of Forking Paths*. Appearing as characters in the tale, Borges and Bioy-Casares discover by chance a project, conducted by a secret society of intellectuals, to produce the encyclopedia of a fictive world named Tlön. The story, which chronicles the progress of their discovery and the subsequent "intrusion" of the "fantastic world" of Tlön "into the real one" (*F*, 32), ends:

> A scattered dynasty of solitaries has changed the face of the world. Its task continues. If our foresight is not mistaken, a hundred years from now someone will discover the hundred volumes of the *Second Encyclopaedia of Tlön*.
>
> Then, English, French, and mere Spanish will disappear from this planet. The world will be Tlön. I take no notice. I go on revising, in the quiet of the days in the hotel at Adrogué, a tentative translation into Spanish, in the style of Quevedo, which I do not intend to see published, of Sir Thomas Browne's *Urn Burial*. (*F*, 34–35)

One might explain Borges's decision to end the tale like this on the grounds that a major theme of *Urn Burial* is the difficulty of understanding the relics of the past and translating their meaning into the present, and that the reference thus evokes Borges's sense of the possible fate of his own writings a hundred years from now when the world has become Tlön and "English, French, and mere Spanish" have disappeared. But the decision to use the ending, the place of greatest formal importance in the story, for a reference to a work that is not mentioned anywhere else in the narrative (and whose appearance in the tale's last sentence is thus doubly striking because totally unexpected) suggests in a writer like Borges that there is more at work here. In fact, Borges's remark about "English, French, and mere Spanish" provides a clue to the significance of this final image of a modern writer (Borges) translating into the seventeenth-century Latinate Spanish of Quevedo a work originally written by Browne in seventeenth-century Latinate English. Browne and Quevedo had each tried, of course, to write his native language as if it were Latin (in his essay on Quevedo, Borges describes the Spaniard's style as a "return to the arduous Latin of Seneca, Tacitus, and Lucan—the tortured and crabbed

Latin of the *silver age*" [*OI*, 38]) because each felt the cultural or linguistic inferiority of his native tongue compared to a classical language, felt that to write great literature meant to write like the ancient Roman authors. In effect, Borges expresses the modern equivalent of this sense of cultural or linguistic inferiority in referring to his native language as "mere Spanish" in comparison to the great modern literary languages of English and French. The notion that Borges felt such an inferiority casts a different light on his remark about trying early in his career "to play the sedulous ape to . . . Quevedo and Saavedra Fajardo." For what Borges would have sought in these two writers was simply the linguistic means of playing the sedulous ape to Browne, whose work he greatly admired—the two seventeenth-century Spaniards being in effect stylistic equivalents for translating Browne's Latinate prose into Spanish.

During his visit to Hopkins in 1983, Borges confirmed this view in response to a question about his interest in Browne:

> When I was a young man, I played the sedulous ape to Sir Thomas Browne. I tried to do so in Spanish. Then Adolfo Bioy-Casares and I translated the last chapter of *Urn Burial* into seventeenth-century Spanish—Quevedo. And it went quite well in seventeenth-century Spanish. . . . We did our best to be seventeenth-century, we went in for Latinisms the way that Sir Thomas Browne did.[1]

That it was actually Browne rather than Quevedo to whom Borges "played the sedulous ape" seems only appropriate, since the phrase is a quotation from a passage in Robert Louis Stevenson's *Memories and Portraits* (1896) in which he describes how he taught himself to write by imitating various authors, especially Browne:

> I have thus played the sedulous ape to Hazlitt, to Lamb, to Wordsworth, to Sir Thomas Browne, to Defoe, to Hawthorne, to Montaigne, to Baudelaire and to Obermann. I remember one of these monkey tricks, which was called *The Vanity of Morals:* it was to have had a second part, *The Vanity of Knowledge;* and as I had neither morality nor scholarship, the names were apt; but the second part was never attempted, and the first part was written (which is my reason for recalling it, ghostlike, from its ashes) no less than three times: first in the manner of Hazlitt, second in the manner of Ruskin, who had cast on me a passing spell, and third, in a laborious pasticcio of Sir Thomas Browne.[2]

One wonders if Stevenson's plan for a two-part work was also an attempt to imitate Browne's juxtaposition of *Urn Burial* and *The Garden of Cyrus* published together in a single volume in 1658, which is to say, Browne's structuring of the two essays as reciprocal halves of one work, a conjecture supported by Stevenson's apparent allusion to the subject of *Urn Burial* in his remark about recalling the first part of his work "ghostlike, from its ashes."

Clearly, the concluding image in "Tlön, Uqbar, Orbis Tertius" of "Borges" revising "a tentative translation . . . in the style of Quevedo . . . of Sir Thomas Browne's *Urn Burial*" is based more or less on an actual passage in Borges's career—his youthful, admiring attempt to imitate Browne's style. Yet Borges describes the translation of *Urn Burial* as one that he does "not intend to see published," and in reality he and Bioy-Casares only translated one chapter of the work. Which leads one to suspect that this image of an unpublished translation of an admired English work is Borges's oblique way of pointing to another Borgesian "translation" from English into Spanish that he *does* intend to publish, indeed that he has already begun to publish with the last tale in the volume that "Tlön, Uqbar, Orbis Tertius" opens—a "translation" of the analytic detective story into his native tongue through an antithetical doubling of the Dupin tales. And Borges probably chose *Urn Burial* to evoke this other "translation" because of the work's connection with Poe's detective stories.

The epigraph to "The Murders in the Rue Morgue" is taken from the last chapter of *Urn Burial*, the same chapter that Borges and Bioy-Casares translated into Quevedian Spanish. It runs: "What song the Syrens sang, or what name Achilles assumed when he hid himself among women, although puzzling questions, are not beyond *all* conjecture. *Sir Thomas Browne*" (2:527). Poe uses this quotation to set the stage for a narrative in which "puzzling questions" that defeat ordinary intellects are found not to be beyond the "conjectures" of an extraordinary intellect. And Borges, in availing himself of this epigraphic link between the two writers in order to evoke his antithetical "translation" of Poe (through the opposing image of his submissive translation of Browne), takes further advantage of the fact that this epigraph is itself a translation, a free rewriting (as Browne points out) of a passage from the Latin text of Suetonius's life of Tiberius. Describing the emperor's devotion to "liberal studies" in Latin and Greek, Suetonius says that Tiberius

> made Greek verses in imitation of Euphorion, Rhianus, and Parthenius, poets of whom he was very fond, placing their busts in the public libraries among those of the eminent writers of old. . . . Yet his special aim was a knowledge of mythology, which he carried to a silly and laughable extreme; for he used to test even the grammarians, a class of men in whom, as I have said, he was especially interested, by questions something like this: "Who was Hecuba's mother?" "What was the name of Achilles among the maidens?" "What were the Sirens in the habit of singing?"[3]

One can imagine Borges finding the passage that follows this description particularly relevant to his own situation, for Suetonius goes on to tell us that although Tiberius "spoke Greek readily and fluently, yet he would not use it on all occasions, and especially eschewed it in the senate," apologizing to the senate on one occasion for "the necessity of employing" a Greek word, and on another suggesting that "a native word" be "substituted for the foreign one," and on still another forbidding a soldier, who "was asked in Greek to give testimony," from answering "except in Latin" (Suetonius, 1:393–95). One could argue that just as Borges—a writer of "mere Spanish" who as a young man played the sedulous ape to the Englishman Browne—feels about English, so the English writer Browne with his Latinate style felt about Latin, and Tiberius, who in private wrote imitative Greek verses but in public demanded that "a native word" be "substituted for the foreign one," felt about Greek—on the one hand, a feeling of admiration for the foreign language's lexical and literary richness, and on the other, a feeling of resentment that one's own language should be lexically or literarily inferior and that one should therefore have to imitate a foreign master.

It is in this context that we can understand the full significance of Borges's implicit linking of his unpublished Quevedian translation of Browne's *Urn Burial* and his published antithetical translation of Poe's Dupin stories, that is, his invoking the image of the former in the first story of a collection whose last story initiates the latter. For if Borges's fictive Quevedian translation of *Urn Burial*, his attempt to find an equivalent in Spanish for an English author's style, is associated with (and thus symbolically represents) that stage in his career when, as a young writer of "mere Spanish," he played the sedulous ape to a foreign master, then his parenthetical announcement that this translation is not to be published signals the end of that phase and points to the beginning of his effort to reverse the master/slave relationship between English and Spanish through the antithetical rewriting of Poe's Dupin stories. In evoking his passage from submissive imitation to active reinvention, from being Browne's sedulous ape to being Poe's antithetical double, Borges relies not only on the epigraphic link between *Urn Burial* and the Dupin stories, but also on the fact that the specific Dupin story bearing the epigraph is itself concerned with the struggle between a master and a sedulous ape. As Poe makes clear in "The Murders in the Rue Morgue," it was the orangutan's attempt to imitate its human master that originally triggered the animal's rampage:

> Returning home from some sailors' frolic on the night, or rather in the morning of the murder, he [the sailor] found the beast occupying his own bed-room,

into which it had broken from a closet adjoining, where it had been, as was
thought, securely confined. Razor in hand, and fully lathered, it was sitting
before a looking-glass, attempting the operation of shaving, in which it had no
doubt previously watched its master through the key-hole of the closet. Terrified at the sight of so dangerous a weapon in the possession of an animal so
ferocious, and so well able to use it, the man, for some moments, was at a loss
what to do. He had been accustomed, however, to quiet the creature, even in its
fiercest moods, by the use of a whip, and to this he now resorted. Upon sight of
it, the Ourang-Outang sprang at once through the door of the chamber, down
the stairs, and thence, through a window, unfortunately open, into the street.
(2:564–65)

Given that this tale, whose epigraph links Browne to Poe, has a special
relationship to Borges's project of thematizing his passage from being
Browne's ape to Poe's double, it seems only appropriate that at one point
in the story the difference between master and slave (sailor and ape) is
presented as the difference between someone who speaks French (one of
the two languages with which Borges contrasts "mere Spanish") and
someone who "speaks" an undetermined foreign tongue. We might also
note in passing that since the human activity the ape imitates is that of
looking at one's face in a mirror, the master/slave relationship between the
sailor and orangutan, like the mastermind/automaton relationship between Dupin and ordinary men, is simply another figuration, within the
tale, of that simultaneous conjunction/opposition of mind and body in
which, on the one hand, the "human" separates itself from the "animal"
through the differentiation of mind from body, while, on the other, the
mind's reflexive structure (its being at once the mirror and the image in
the mirror) is seen to derive from and depend upon the projec-
tion/introjection of the physical image of an (animal) body. It is because
the ape (whose mirror-gazing codes him as an animal parody of self-
reflection) effects a temporary master/slave reversal by escaping the sail-
or's control and performing acts in which he is mistaken for a human
(albeit a madman) that the mastermind must enter the affair to restore the
proper relationship between mind and body.

Once we see the connection between Borges's fictive Quevedian translation of *Urn Burial* and his real antithetical translation of the Dupin
stories, it becomes clear not only how the apparently incongruous, final
image in "Tlön, Uqbar, Orbis Tertius" grows out of what precedes it, but
also how much of that preceding material is itself an oblique allusion to
Borges's detective story project. As we noted earlier, at the end of the tale
Borges depicts the gradual displacement of the real world by the imaginary world of Tlön, in particular the displacement of language:

> Tlön may be a labyrinth, but it is a labyrinth plotted by men, a labyrinth
> destined to be deciphered by men.
>
> Contact with Tlön and the ways of Tlön have disintegrated this world.
> Captivated by its discipline, humanity forgets and goes on forgetting that it is
> the discipline of chess players, not of angels. Now, the conjectural "primitive
> language" of Tlön has found its way into the schools. Now, the teaching of its
> harmonious history, full of stirring episodes, has obliterated the history which
> dominated my childhood. Now, in all memories, a fictitious past occupies the
> place of any other. We know nothing about it with any certainty, not even that it
> is false. . . . If our foresight is not mistaken, a hundred years from now some-
> one will discover the hundred volumes of the *Second Encyclopaedia of Tlön*. (*F*,
> 34)

In essence the world of Tlön represents the future, a future that is
contained in and grows out of present imaginings but that will ultimately
turn out to be so different from the present that the question of communication between present and future seems problematic. In that future, as
Borges conceives it, English and French and Spanish will have become
dead languages, which is to say that they will be to the "primitive language" of Tlön what Latin was to English at the time Browne wrote *Urn
Burial*.

As we noted earlier, one of the themes of *Urn Burial* is the difficulty of
understanding the relics of the past and translating their meaning into
the present. The occasion of the essay, as Browne tells us in chapter 2, was
the discovery

> in a Field of old *Walsingham*, not many moneths past . . . [of] between fourty
> and fifty Urnes, deposited in a dry and sandy soile, not a yard deep, nor farre
> from one another: . . . Some containing two pounds of bones, distinguishable
> in skulls, ribs, jawes, thigh-bones, and teeth, with fresh impressions of their
> combustion. Besides the extraneous substances, like peeces of small boxes, or
> combes handsomely wrought, handles of small brasse instruments, brazen
> nippers, and in one some kinde of *Opale*.[4]

In carrying out his scholarly investigation of these remains—a mostly
conjectural inquiry into what can be known of the people whose ashes are
contained in these urns, their nationality, the time and circumstances of
their cremation and burial, the significance of their funerary rites and
interred objects—Browne produces not only a meditation on time and
mortality, on the persistence of physical objects versus the ephemerality of
their human significance, but also an oblique dissertation on the largely
imaginary nature of our knowledge of the past, an essay on the uncertainty of much of what we think we know about antiquity and on the certainty

that what we do know is so little compared to what has been lost that even if our knowledge were certain it would still present only a distorted or false perspective on the past. (One of the attractions of Tlön, of course, is that it provides "a fictitious past," a "harmonious history, full of stirring episodes" in place of a real past of which we know nothing with any certainty, not even that it is false.)

Although Browne admits that there is "nothing of more uncertainty" than "the time of these Urnes deposited, or precise Antiquity of these Reliques" (*SW*, 127), he nevertheless makes an educated guess (which we now believe to be wrong) that these are the remains of "*Romanes, or Brittains Romanized*" (*SW*, 131). Yet clearly this conjecture is nothing more than a reflection of the work's style into its content, for if Browne's purpose in writing Latinate English is to maintain a supposed continuity between English and classical literature, to establish the sense of an unbroken tradition in which English authors can see themselves as direct descendants of Latin writers, then Browne's suggestion that the remains belong to "*Romanes, or Brittains Romanized*" in effect presents these objects as a physical expression of the historical link between Rome and England. And the fact that Browne opts for a Roman or Romanized British origin for these remains, even though he acknowledges that there is just as much historical evidence for a Saxon or Danish origin, embodies his sense of the imaginary nature of history, his sense that historical knowledge is always a function of the kind of continuity the present is able to find, or needs to find, with the past—the need, for example, to show that English writing is related to the high literary tradition of the Romans rather than to the semibarbarous tradition of the Saxons or Danes.

If *Urn Burial* is about the difficulty the present has both in knowing the facts and understanding the meaning of the past, then Borges's "Tlön, Uqbar, Orbis Tertius" is in some sense the reciprocal of Browne's essay, in that it represents an attempt to imagine the present as having become just that kind of problematic past by imagining a future that has little or no linguistic, literary, or historical continuity with the present. And what seems clear is that the specific example of a literary-historical continuity that serves as the differential opposite for this vision of a possible future discontinuity (symbolized by Tlön) is the tradition of the analytic detective story, as Borges indicates when he describes Tlön as "a labyrinth plotted by men, . . . destined to be deciphered by men," its logical rigor "the discipline of chess players," that is, when he evokes this fictive world in a set of images he associates elsewhere with the detective genre. And this association of the chesslike, labyrinthine fiction named Tlön with the chesslike labyrinth of analytic detective fiction explains Borges's choice of another image in the concluding passage of "Tlön, Uqbar, Orbis

Tertius"—his prediction of the appearance of the *Second Encyclopaedia of Tlön* "a hundred years from now" when "English, French, and mere Spanish will disappear from this planet." For of course this prediction is made in a volume whose title story "The Garden of Forking Paths" (1941) appears in Spanish exactly a hundred years after the publication in English of the first analytic detective story "The Murders in the Rue Morgue" (1841), a tale about a French detective.

In fashioning his reciprocal version of Browne's attempt to exhume antiquity in *Urn Burial,* Borges thematizes a backward glance a hundred years into the past (the antithetical doubling of the Dupin stories) as a forward glance a hundred years into the future (the fictive world of Tlön), a procedure that raises not only the question of whether someone in the future will do for Borges what Borges has done for Poe (that is, retrospectively reanimate his work by doubling it a hundred years later) but also the question of whether, in a future as different from the present as Tlön is from the real world, any historical continuity between that future and our present would simply amount to a massive misinterpretation of the earlier time by the later. Which raises in turn the further question of whether Borges's reimagining of Poe's detective stories is a similar misinterpretation of an artifact from the past—a problem that, as we recall, Borges treats explicitly in "Averroes' Search," where Averroes' misunderstanding of Aristotle's terms *tragedy* and *comedy* becomes, in a characteristic form/content mirroring, a reflection of Borges's possible misunderstanding of Averroes.

15 The Garden of Cyrus; *The Quincuncial Network;*
Decussation and V Shape; The Fold of the Hand

IN INVOKING HIS UNPUBLISHED QUEVEDIAN translation of *Urn Burial* in "Tlön, Uqbar, Orbis Tertius," Borges not only thematizes his antithetical "translation" of the Dupin stories from English into Spanish and from the past into the present, he also suggests that the relationship between Poe's detective stories and his own is modeled on the antithetical pairing of Browne's two essays published in one volume in 1658, essays that, Janus-like, look in opposite directions—*Urn Burial* toward the past, *The Garden of Cyrus* toward the future. Commenting on the structural link between these works, Frank Huntley observes that they

> form a Platonic dichotomy: two parts opposed yet conjoined, with a rising from the lower or elemental *Urn Burial* (death) to the higher or celestial *Garden of Cyrus,* the "numerical character" of reality (life). . . . That Browne intended us to read the two essays together and in the order he gave them is seen most obviously in the deliberateness of their opposition in subject matter. One concerns death, the other, life; one the body, the other the soul; one passions, the other reason; one accident, the other design; one substance, the other form. . . . The first essay treats of time; the second, space. And together these two concepts delineate the character of God, in that time is an image of His Eternity, whereas number and geometrical figures in space are a key to His Wisdom.[1]

In the dedicatory preface to *The Garden of Cyrus,* Browne comments on this linking:

> That we conjoyn these parts of different Subjects, or that this should succeed the other; Your judgement will admit without impute of incongruity; Since the delightfull World comes after death, and Paradise succeeds the Grave. Since the verdant state of things is the Symbole of the Resurrection, and to flourish in the state of Glory, we must first be sown in corruption. Beside the ancient practise of Noble Persons, to conclude in Garden-Graves, and Urnes themselves of old, to be wrapt up in flowers and garlands. (*SW,* 160–61)

In modeling the relationship between Poe's detective stories and his own on the antithetical conjunction of Browne's two essays, Borges clearly

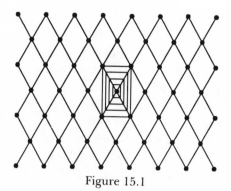

Figure 15.1

associates Poe's tales with the first essay and his own with the second. This association of the Dupin stories with *Urn Burial* is based not only on Poe's epigraphic linking of Browne's essay to the first Dupin tale but also on the fact that one of the themes of *Urn Burial*—the difficulty of translating the meaning of an artifact from the past into the present—points to the role of Poe's three tales as century-old artifacts in Borges's project of translating the original meaning of the detective genre from past to present. Similarly, Borges's three detective tales, considered as an attempt to resurrect the original spirit of the Dupin stories, are associated with *The Garden of Cyrus* and its imagery of the "verdant state" as "Symbole of the Resurrection." Indeed, Borges alludes to this latter association in naming his first story. In a kind of chiasmus of first and last, the epigraph to Poe's first detective story is taken from the last chapter of Browne's first essay *Urn Burial*, while the title of Borges's first detective story, "The Garden of Forking Paths," clearly derives from the full title of Browne's final essay, *The Garden of Cyrus or, The Quincunciall, Lozenge, or Net-Work Plantations of the Ancients, Artificially, Naturally, Mystically Considered.*

The initial subject of the essay is "Cyrus the Younger's method of planting trees by fives in the shape of the quincunx" (Huntley, 204), that is, in the shape of an X (a tree at each corner of a rectangle and one in the center) so as to produce a continuous plantation whose form is a network of lozenges or rhombs (see fig. 15.1). The garden that gives its name to Browne's essay was literally one laid out in a pattern of forking lines, and Browne's subsequent enumeration of the various objects exhibiting this "quincunciall, lozenge, or net-work" pattern reads like a list of the principal images not only from "The Garden of Forking Paths" but from Borges's other two detective stories as well.

In the opening chapter of the essay, Browne observes that while "in some ancient and modern practice the *area* or decussated plot" (L. *de-cussare*, "to cross in the form of an X") in the quincuncial plantation may be "a perfect square," the "Originall figure" is more likely to have been a "*Rhombus* or Lozenge" (*SW*, 165). This is significant for our purposes because later, in discussing the reticular pattern of "Chesse-boards," Browne maintains that while their present form is a network of squares, this was probably not their original design: "I wish we had their true and ancient description, farre different from ours, or the *Chet mat* of the *Persians*, which might continue some elegant remarkables, as being an invention as High as *Hermes* the Secretary of *Osyris*, figuring the whole world, the motion of the Planets, with Eclipses of Sunne and Moon" (*SW*, 172–73). Browne suggests not only that the original design of the chessboard was a quincuncial network of lozenges but that in this original form the chessboard was a Hermetic microcosm, "figuring the whole world." Later in the essay he again evokes the quincuncial network as a microcosmic symbol, noting that in the Egyptian hieroglyphics "*Orus*, the Hieroglyphick of the world, is described in a Net-work covering, from the shoulder to the foot" (*SW*, 188). Given the connection Browne makes between the quincunx plantation, the reticular design of the chessboard, and the net as a microcosmic image, one could predict, from Borges's association of gardens, chess, and networks with the figure of the maze, that Browne would find yet another example of the quincunx design in that "noble peece of Antiquity, . . . the Labyrinth of *Crete*," a structure "built upon a long quadrate, containing five large squares, communicating by right inflections, terminating in the centre of the middle square, and lodging of the *Minotaur*" (*SW*, 175). (We might note in passing that the association of the chessboard with the labyrinth was frequently embodied in medieval and renaissance game boards where the labyrinth design of the game of merels [the ancestor of tic-tac-toe] was often inscribed on one panel of a hinged board whose facing panel was inscribed for chess.[2])

We originally began our discussion of Browne's work and its relationship to Borges's detective stories in order to show that two geometrical shapes associated with the schematic representation of self-consciousness (the lozenge and the hourglass) were parts of a more complex geometrical pattern imaging the intelligible continuity of the world. By now it should be obvious that Browne's quincuncial network, considered as a microcosm "figuring the whole world," is that larger pattern. It is not hard to see how a net, with each of its strands linked to every other strand in a single unbroken fabric, is an appropriate figure of continuity, but what is perhaps less clear is its appropriateness as a figure of intelligibility. How does the image of a net present the world as an object whose shape is compatible—whose form meshes—with the shape of the mind? To ask this question is in effect to ask why or how the network's two component figures are appropriate schematic images of specular self-consciousness,

Figure 15.2

for it is simply the repetition of these components that produces the network pattern, the repetition of the diamond or lozenge shape (enclosed by the intersecting parallel lines) and the decussation (X) or hourglass figure (that represents the actual method of planting trees in the quincuncial arrangement) (see fig. 15.2). But these two figures, as we shall see, are in turn composed of a still more basic figure, one that visually represents the physical basis of the functioning of human intelligence—the V shape.

To understand how this simple figure evokes the physical ground of intelligence, we must examine the connection Browne makes in *The Garden of Cyrus* among numbers, letters, and geometrical shapes, specifically the number five (the number of trees in the quincuncial pattern), the letter V (the Roman symbol for five), and the geometrical decussation (the X shape in which the five trees are planted, one at each corner of a rectangle and one in the center). Browne views the quincuncial network of lozenges as an "Originall figure," that is, as the geometrical form of an orderly disposition of the physical world that is far older than simply the garden of Cyrus. Browne speculates that this pattern dates from "the Prototype and originall of Plantations," the Garden of Eden, for "since even in Paradise it self, the tree of knowledge was placed in the middle of the Garden, whatever was the ambient figure, there wanted not a centre and rule of decussation" (*SW*, 169). And the implication is that if the God-given design of man's original plantation was a quincuncial network, then this design must express the basic relationship between man and the world, knower and known, which is to say that this formal pattern imposed on physical nature schematizes the interface of mind and world in that it contains within itself the various modes of intelligible representation of the world (i.e., mathematics, language, geometry) joined together in the homogeneousness of their physical inscription as numbers, letters, and geometric shapes.

The notion that there is a necessary (because original) correspondence among numbers, letters, and geometric shapes is, of course, a belief shared by a variety of mystical philosophies, alchemy and the cabala among them. This belief grounds such practices as the numerical interpretation of the letters in a name (e.g., the Tetragrammaton) and the pictographic or geometric reading of the shapes of letters and numbers— practices based on a sense of the absolute noncontingency, and thus necessary meaningfulness, of every detail created by an absolute intelligence. At the beginning of his poem "The Golem," Borges associates this belief in correspondences with the Platonic doctrine of archetypes, although elsewhere he suggests its ultimately Pythagorean origin:

> If (as the Greek asserts in the *Cratylus*)
> the name is archetype to the thing,
> the rose is in the letters of "rose"
> and the length of the Nile in "Nile."

> Thus, compounded of consonants and vowels,
> there must be a terrible Name, which essence
> ciphers as God and Omnipotence
> preserves in consummate letters and syllables.

> Adam, and the stars, knew it
> in the Garden. The iron rust of sin
> (say the Cabalists) has effaced it
> and the generations have lost the word.   (*BR*, 274)

If Browne believes that the quincuncial network is a God-given design expressing the original relationship between mind and world, then its shape must in some way be the root at which the branches of intelligible representation are joined. It must be the spot at which numbers, letters, and geometric figures share a common medium or reduce to a single physical shape that allows them to be converted directly (and visibly) into one another. Browne indicates both the connecting point and the conversion mechanism in the network figure when he notes that the quincunx pattern owes its "name not only unto the Quintuple number of Trees, but the figure declaring that number," that is, the Roman letter V, "which being doubled at the angle, makes up the Letter X, that is the Emphaticall decussation, or fundamentall figure" (*SW*, 165). Thus the letter V, the written sign for the number five in Latin, by "being doubled at the angle" (by having a second, inverted V projected downward from the angle of the first) produces the geometrical figure for the quincunx plantation, the decussation or X shape whose five places (four end points and central intersection) embody the meaning of the number five. The Roman V is at

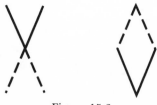

Figure 15.3

once, then, a *letter,* a *numeral* (the signifier of a number), and a *geometric shape* whose manipulation (to create the X figure) both embodies the meaning of that number (in its five places) and displays that arrangement of objects by fives which, through its repetition, unfolds the network pattern. And this sense of a necessary correspondence (as evidenced by the convertibility) of letter, number, and geometric shape is reinforced by the fact that the X produced by doubling the sign for the number five is itself the sign in Latin for the integer that is five doubled.

The ultimate root of the word *decussation* is, of course, the Latin word for ten, *decem.* As Huntley notes, Browne bases the numerical structure of his two essays on the figure of the quincuncial decussation considered as "the Roman X, the perfect number, made of two fives—Roman Vs— joined at their apices."[3] Thus, *Urn Burial* and *The Garden of Cyrus* are each composed of five chapters and "each essay is dated 'Norwich, May 1,' the fifth month" (*GC,* x). Moreover, if the trajectory of *Urn Burial* is downward, toward death and the grave, and that of *The Garden of Cyrus* upward, toward resurrection and the celestial sphere, then the decussation is an even more appropriate figure for their linking, since, according to Browne, in "Aegyptian Philosophy . . . the scale of influences was thus disposed, and the geniall spirits of both worlds . . . trace their way in ascending and descending Pyramids, mystically apprehended in the Letter X" (*SW,* 204). We should note in this regard that just as Browne has designed the conjunction/opposition of his two essays so that each is composed of five chapters but with the trajectory of one downward and the other upward in imitation of the two Vs (fives) joined at their apices, so Borges has designed the conjunction/opposition of Poe's detective stories and his own so that three stories are doubled by three but with the earlier group of tales oriented toward the right and the later toward the left.

It is not difficult to see in this V shape, which links together letter, number, and geometric figure, the basic form that composes the lozenge and hourglass figures. The hourglass is simply the Roman V "doubled at the angle," and the lozenge the Roman V doubled at the open end (see fig. 15.3). But now the question that was deferred from the network pattern to its components (the lozenge and the hourglass or X), and then deferred

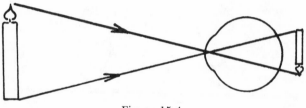

Figure 15.4

again to their component, the V shape, arises once more. What makes the V shape an appropriate image of intelligibility? Why or how does it visually represent the physical basis of the functioning of human intelligence? Browne starts us in the direction of the answer by noting the connection between the V shape and vision itself: "It is no wonder that this Quincunciall order was first and still affected as gratefull unto the Eye: For all things are seen Quincuncially" (*SW,* 202–3).

Browne associates two separate decussations with vision. The first is that of the light rays in the eye as the cornea and the lens—"the hole of the hornycoat" and "the Christalline humour" (*SW,* 203) in Browne's terminology—refract the rays to produce an inverted image on the retina, the V shape in effect governing the path of the light rays to the lens and then from the lens to the retina (see fig. 15.4). He then notes a second decussation associated with sight in that intersection of the optic nerves known as the optic chiasma (see fig. 15.5).

According to Browne, "ancient Anatomy" believed that the purpose of this neural decussation was to effect "a concurrence" (*SW,* 203), by which he apparently meant that its purpose was to reorient and integrate the separate images from each retina into a single image in the brain. (In fact, the optic chiasma is a kind of intermediate switching point in the process of effecting this concurrence rather than its immediate effecter, the retina of each eye being divided into a right and left half and the chiasma being the point at which the optic nerves from each eye divide, those from the right halves of the two retinas following a path to the right side of the occipital cortex and those from the left halves of the retinas following a path to the left side of the occipital cortex—a process of visual splitting and doubling.)

Just as Browne associates the decussation formed by the V shape doubled at its angle with the path of vision that runs from outer to inner, from object to brain, so he associates the reciprocal of this figure—the lozenge or rhomb formed by the V shape doubled at its open end—with the path that runs from inner to outer, the path by which an internal image is projected onto the external world in the painting of a picture, for example. Browne notes that "perspective picturers, in their Base, Horison, and

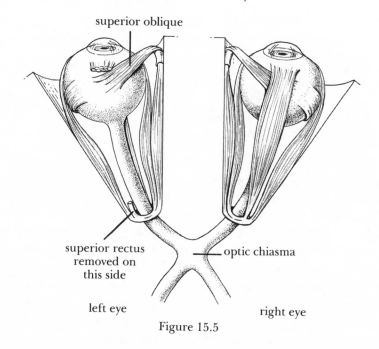

superior oblique

superior rectus
removed on
this side

optic chiasma

left eye

right eye

Figure 15.5

lines of distances, cannot escape these Rhomboidall decussations" (*SW*, 172), by which he means that in linear perspective the artist treats the picture plane as the base of two pyramids pointing in opposite directions, the apex of one being the eyepoint of the artist and the apex of the other being the central vanishing point toward which all the orthogonals perpendicular to the picture plane recede (see fig. 15.6).

The reciprocity of the decussation and the lozenge—a function of the reciprocal doubling of their component V shape at its angle and its open end in the unfolding of the network pattern—can be seen again in the geometric figures that Browne associates with the conjunction/opposition of body and soul. On the one hand, he finds the decussation present "in the whole body of man, which upon the extension of arms and legges, doth make out a square, whose intersection is at the genitals," not to mention "the phantastical Quincunx, in *Plato*, of the first Hermaphrodite or double man, united at the Loynes, which *Jupiter* after divided" (*SW*, 188–89); while on the other hand, he reminds us that "the Noble *Antoninus* in some sence doth call the soul it self a Rhombus" (*SW*, 209), although he notes elsewhere that in their operation the powers of the soul describe the reciprocal shape: "Things entring upon the intellect by a Pyramid from without, and thence into the memory by another from within, the common decussation being in the understanding as is delivered by *Bovillus*" (*SW*, 203).

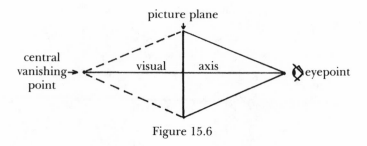

Figure 15.6

Browne's schematic figurations of intelligence and its associated structures—vision, imaginative projection, the interactions of understanding and memory, and of mind and body—are all ultimately based on a single figure, the V shape, doubled either at angle or at open end. And if we interpret this shape as the simplest possible geometric representation of a fold or hinge that doubles an entity back upon itself by folding it in half .̣Ṿ̣., then this doubling (at angle Ṿ , or open end ◌̇V̇) of a shape which is itself a representation of halving and doubling produces the same structure that we found embodied earlier in the game of chess, a structure that figures specular self-consciousness as the mirror doubling of the mirror-image halves of the bilaterally asymmetrical human body.

It is precisely in the context of the body's right hand / left hand mirror fold that the special appropriateness of the V shape as a figure of the physical basis of the functioning of human intelligence becomes clear, the clue being the shape's association with the number five. For in being both a sign for the number and a simple visual representation of a fold or hinge, the V shape points to its origin: the conjunction of these two signifieds in the hingelike structure of the five digits of the hand—that fold, formed by the four fingers and opposable thumb, which is the physical (i.e., necessary) embodiment of the essentially oppositional character of human knowledge. This fold of the hand is doubled in turn by the fold of its opposing hand, the opposition between right and left hands being at once a replication of the oppositional structure of the thumb and fingers of each hand and a function of the mirror fold between the right and left halves of the body. One might diagram this arrangement of opposable thumb and fingers, of opposing hands and arms, as the branching of a V-shaped fold into other V-shaped folds (see fig. 15.7). And if we move from the level of touch to sight, we find that the V shape, variously oriented, also describes the operation of binocular vision, in that the activities of scanning and focusing (the visual analogues of opening and closing the hand in order to grasp an object between thumb and fingers) can be geometrically figured respectively by a V whose open end represents the field of vision in the scanning mode and by an inverted V whose angle

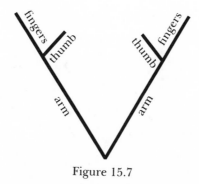

Figure 15.7

represents the intersection of the eyes' axes of vision in the focusing mode. The reciprocity of scanning and focusing would then be evoked either by the lozenge or the decussation, depending on the order in which the related activities are represented.

That Browne associated the V shape with the fold of the hand formed by fingers and thumb can be inferred from his description of the two principal battle formations of the Roman legions—"the *Cuneus* and *Forceps*, or the sheare and wedge battles, each made of half a *Rhombus,* and but differenced by position. The wedge invented to break or work into a body, the *forceps* to environ and defeat the power thereof, composed out of the selectest Souldiery and disposed into the form of an U, wherein receiving the wedge, it inclosed it on both sides" (*SW,* 174). The *forceps,* which operates by opening to receive the attacking force and then trapping it between its two sides, is clearly modeled on the opening and closing of the hand; and certainly Browne, as a physician, could not have missed the structural similarity that accounts for the same name's being applied to a medical instrument that either in its V-shaped form (tweezers) or its X-shaped, scissors form is simply a mechanical extension of the hand's grasping power.

What all of this ultimately suggests is that the V shape—considered as a geometric representation of the fold of the hand—is an appropriate figure of intelligibility precisely because the basic metaphor of human knowledge (basic because derived from the givenness of the body's structure, the physical basis of the functioning of intelligence) is one that figures thought as the mental grasping of an object. (The roots of the word *intelligible* are the two Latin words *inter,* meaning "between" or "among," and *legere,* "to gather, choose, pick," an origin that evokes the handling and selection of objects as the model of intellection.) In this context, then, to say that a thing is "intelligible" means that it exists as an object for the mind by being grasped between the poles of a differential opposition in a manner directly analogous to that in which a physical

Figure 15.8

object is grasped between the opposing poles of finger and thumb. And this sense of intelligibility as the grasping or enclosing of an object between opposing sides is carried through all the figures that the V shape composes—the forcepslike decussation, the enclosure of the rhomb, and the network pattern that images the world's continuous intelligibility as its containment or capture within a net whose structure is an endless repetition of the structure of the hand. Indeed, we can see, within the pattern of the quincuncial network, that geometrical figure employed earlier to show how the oppositional structure of thumb and fingers is replicated in the structure of the opposing hands and arms, its V shape branching into other V shapes (see fig. 15.8).

And if we take the image of a net literally as an openwork pattern of loosely knotted cords—that is, as a pattern whose basic linking element (the knot) is a self-interfering structure in which a line, looping back to grasp itself within itself, is thereby able to grasp some other thing within that loop—if we give it this literal interpretation, then the net is a particularly appropriate figure of self-consciousness, of that self-opposing structure which grasps itself by a process of simultaneous projection and introjection, by a loop that runs from the self into the world and then back to grasp the self and in so doing grasps the world within this loop as that physical other *from which* and *by means of which* the self is differentiated.

16 *Geometric Atomism; The Spherical Number Five; The History of a Metaphor; The Total Library*

IN ANALYZING THE NETWORK PATTERN into the basic V shape, Browne engages in a kind of geometric atomism. The V, functioning as an atomistic unit, produces a complex continuum (the quincuncial network) through the interplay of the sameness of its shape with the difference of its position or orientation in endlessly repeated combinations. That Borges would have been alert to the geometric atomism underlying Browne's analysis of the quincuncial network can be inferred from a passage in his 1939 essay "The Total Library" in which he cites Aristotle's discussion, in the first book of the *Metaphysics,* of Leucippus's cosmology. In commenting on Leucippus's notion that the world was formed "by the fortuitous conjunction of atoms," Aristotle, according to Borges,

> observes that the atoms required by this conjecture are homogeneous and that their differences derive from position, order, or form. To illustrate those distinctions he adds: "A is different from N in form; AN from NA in order; Z from N in position." In the treatise *De Generatione et Corruptione,* he attempts to bring the variety of visible things into accord with the simplicity of the atoms and he reasons that a tragedy is made up of the same elements as a comedy— that is, the twenty-six letters of the alphabet. (*BR,* 94–95)

Notice that since the geometric shapes used here to image atomistic units are letters, the intelligibility of physical nature is implicitly represented as the interpretability of a meaningful script, a divine writing. Further, the homogeneity of these atomistic shapes (as opposed to differences derived from position, order, or form) is largely a function of the fact that the three letters used as examples (A, N, Z) all have physical forms based on a wedge or V figure—A being an inverted V with a line across its middle, N being two Vs joined at one line end with their apices pointing in opposite directions 𝖭𝖫 , and Z being this same figure reoriented 90 degrees.

This linking of geometric atomism to writing is part of that philosophic tendency noted earlier to assume an original union or coincidence of the various modes of intelligible representation in a single figure that is at once a geometric shape, a letter, and the sign of a number. But in the present context where the letters chosen as illustrations are all variations or combinations of a basic wedge shape, this linking also suggests a specific form of writing, cuneiform script, whose signs are all based on a single geometric form. This style of writing, used extensively in the ancient world (especially by the Babylonians and Assyrians), derives its name from the Latin *cuneus*, "wedge," because "each character or sign is composed of a wedge (⊤ or ▬), or a combination of wedges . . . written from left to right," the shape being formed "by a single pressure of the stylus" in soft clay (*EB*, 7:629, 632). One might speculate that the linking of geometric atomism to the geometric character of letters suggests the derivation of the former from the latter: that an intelligible script, whose signs are either variations or combinations of a single geometric form, may have been the model for imagining the fundamental intelligibility of physical nature (its logical readability) as the "unfolding" of a simple shape into the differential complexity of the universe, a complexity produced by manipulating the "position, order, or form" of that basic shape in various combinations. And one might speculate further that if the V shape depicts intelligibility as the mind's grasp of an intellectual object between the poles of a differential opposition (modeled on the opposition of fingers and thumb), then the use of the V or wedge as the basic component in cuneiform writing suggests an associative transference in which the fold of the hand grasping the writing tool has been schematically translated into the wedge-shaped mark of the stylus, with the result that cuneiform script, a hatchwork of interlocking signs, becomes the physical expression of the mind's grasp of the world as a continuous network of differences (see fig. 16.1).

That Borges associates the V shape with writing seems clear from "Death and the Compass" where the diamond (formed by doubling the V at its open end) has each of its four angles (its four Vs) linked to a letter of the Tetragrammaton (one of which, of course, is the letter V). And certainly this associative link is encouraged not only by the fact that Browne uses the Latin name *cuneus* (the root of "cuneiform") for one of the dynamic forms of the V, but also by the fact that Browne, in analyzing the number five, gives a numerological interpretation of the Tetragrammaton's letters, an interpretation that, as he makes clear, is "Cabalisticall" in origin. In explaining the number five's "stability," he cites "the sphericity of its nature, which multiplied in it self, will return into its own denomination, and bring up the reare of the account" (*SW*, 207). Thus five is a spherical number because, when it is multiplied by itself, it always circles back to end in itself no matter how often the process is repeated (e.g., $5 \times 5 = 25$, $25 \times 5 = 125$, $125 \times 5 = 625$, etc.). Browne suggests the ultimate significance of this "sphericity" in noting that five is "one of the Numbers that makes up the mysticall Name of God, which consisting of

Figure 16.1

Letters denoting all the sphaericall Numbers, ten, five, and six; Emphatically sets forth the Notion of *Trismegistus,* and that intelligible Sphere which is the Nature of God" (*SW,* 207). Since the letters that compose the Tetragrammaton (Y, H, V) are respectively the tenth, fifth, and sixth letters of the Hebrew alphabet, and since ten, five, and six are all spherical numbers, these letters encode God's essence (His spherical intelligence) within His name, in the same way that, as Borges says in "The Golem," if "the name is archetype to the thing, / the rose is in the letters of 'rose' / and the length of the Nile in 'Nile'" (*BR,* 274).

Borges devotes one of his most famous essays, "Pascal's Sphere" (1951), to tracing the genealogy of the image of God as a perfect sphere, noting at one point that in "the *Asclepius,* . . . attributed to Trismegistus," Alain de Lille, "the twelfth-century French theologian . . . discovered this formula, which future generations would not forget: 'God is an intelligible sphere, whose center is everywhere and whose circumference is nowhere'" (*OI,* 7). In sketching the history of this metaphor, Borges shows that what began as a religious image—an image of God's immanence and transcendence, of the fact He "is in each one of his creatures, but is not limited by any one of them" (*OI,* 7)—was gradually secularized by being transferred from creator to creation. In 1584 Giordano Bruno wrote, "The center of the universe is everywhere and the circumference nowhere" (*OI,* 8). This secularization ultimately transformed it from a positive to a negative figuration, from an image of the omnipresence of the creator in his creation, of the closeness of God to man, to an image of the minuteness of man in the universe, of the distance of man from any absolute ground of meaning. By the seventeenth century "the absolute space that inspired the hexameters of Lucretius, the absolute space that had been a liberation for Bruno, was a labyrinth and an abyss for Pascal. He hated the universe, and yearned to adore God. But God was less real to him than the hated universe. . . . He compared our lives to those of shipwrecked men on a desert island," and he described the universe as "a frightful sphere, the center of which is everywhere, and the circumference nowhere," later changing the word "frightful" to "infinite" (*OI*, 8–9). "Perhaps," Borges concludes, "universal history is the history of the diverse intonation of a few metaphors" (*OI*, 9).

A similar shift in the intonation of a metaphor—from religious to secular, stable to vacillating, certain to uncertain—links Browne's numerological interpretation of the Tetragrammaton in *The Garden of Cyrus* to Borges's in "Death and the Compass." Browne introduces the subject of the Tetragrammaton into his essay precisely to explain "the stability" of the number five, a stability he associates with the number's spherical character of always returning to its origin at its endpoint, a character he derives from its ultimate source in the divine nature whose perfect sphericity is embodied in the letters of God's name, each linked to a spherical number. In contrast, Borges, in elaborating the numerical associations of the Tetragrammaton, is not interested in the numbers signified by each of its letters but rather in the number of letters that make up the Name— three different characters made to fill four spaces by doubling one of them—a structure that evokes not stability but vacillation, a shifting back and forth between three and four—the movement in one direction projecting an infinite progression, in the other an infinite regression. This dual movement involves, as we noted earlier, the secularization of another religious image, that of God as origin and end, omnipresent center and limitless circumference—a dual goal that can be reached either by the *via negativa* (which continually removes attributes from the divine nature in a kind of regression to indivisibility) or by the *via positiva* (which continually adds attributes to the divine nature in a kind of infinite progression to totality). But Borges's secular version of this figure concentrates on infinity as a physical reality rather than as a divine attribute, suggesting that for Borges, as for Pascal, God is "less real . . . than the hated universe." The detective's quest for the letters of God's secret name, a quest that becomes in Lönnrot's mind the search for a personal encounter with God, plays itself out through the alternative figures of a potentially infinite-sided polygon or an infinitely divisible line, figures in which the endlessness of the physical infinity to be traversed in search of the universe's creator codes the quest's metaphysical goal as unattainable and the quest as pointless and frightful.

This shift in the intonation of a metaphor is also the theme of Borges's essay "The Total Library." As we noted, the metaphor there imaged atomistic units as intelligible geometric shapes by likening them to the shapes of letters in a phonetic alphabet, whose various combinations produce a readable script that becomes in turn a figure of the continuous intelligibility of nature. As Borges shows, what began as an image figuring the necessary meaningfulness of every detail created by an absolute mind ultimately became, when allied to the notion of physical infinity, an image of random meaninglessness. For if the infinitely complex script of physical nature can be reduced to a finite number of components whose combinatory manipulation creates it, then is it not possible that that meaningful script might have been meaninglessly generated by the random permutations and combinations of these components over an infinite period of time? Borges regards this argument, which he says is "related to atomism and combinatory analysis, to typography and to chance," as "a typographical avatar of the doctrine of the eternal return which, adopted by the Stoics or by Blanqui, by the Pythagoreans or by Nietzsche, eternally returns" (BR, 94), and he cites three recent instances of it: Huxley's remark that "a half-dozen monkeys, supplied with typewriters, would produce in a few eternities all the books in the British Museum"; Lewis Carroll's observation in the second part of Sylvie and Bruno that "since the number of words in a language is limited, so is the number of their possible combinations, that is, of their books" (BR, 95); and Kurd Lasswitz's notion of reducing the basic set of written characters to

> twenty-five symbols (twenty-two letters, the space, the period, the comma), whose recombination and repetition would include everything it is possible to express: in all languages. The totality of such variations would take up a Total Library of astronomical size. Lasswitz urges mankind to construct that inhuman library, which chance would organize and which would itself eliminate intelligence. (BR, 96)

To evoke the sense of a library that contains everything "in its blind volumes," Borges, using a device borrowed from Whitman, produces a finite list of items whose heterogeneity conveys the sense of the randomness of an infinite collection (BR, 96). A forerunner of that masterpiece of listing Borges produces in "The Aleph" to suggest what it is like to gaze into the microcosmic crystal, this sampling of the library's items is the most interesting part of the essay; for just as the idea of a total library, analyzed in the 1939 essay, provides the subject for Borges's 1941 story "The Library of Babel," so many of the items in his library catalogue are associated with, or represent the seeds of, other Borges stories. The most important of these items for our present purposes are the three that conclude the list—"the song the sirens sang, the accurate catalog of the library, the proof that the catalog is fallacious" (BR, 96).

The phrase "the song the sirens sang," from the last chapter of Browne's Urn Burial, not only suggests Browne's connection with the subject of Borges's essay (i.e., the place of Browne's atomistic analysis of the quincunx within that tradition of typographical atomism Borges invokes to explain the notion of the total library), but also points to the use that Borges will make of Browne's speculations on the quincunx and its component V shape in his project of doubling Poe's Dupin stories. For of course "the song the sirens sang" is part of the Browne epigraph to "The Murders in the Rue Morgue," and the two items following this phrase on Borges's list ("the accurate catalog of the library, the proof that the catalog is fallacious") represent Borges's version of the analytic detective story's theme, which Poe states immediately following Browne's epigraph by having the narrator note, in beginning his analysis of the analytic power, that "the mental features discoursed of as the analytical are, in themselves, but little susceptible of analysis." The "accurate catalog" of the total library must itself be an equivalent totality, since its entries are in a one-to-one relationship to the library's items. It is a microcosm to the total library's macrocosm, a figuration of mind as mirror of the universe. And the item that immediately follows it—"the proof that the catalog is fallacious"—represents the inevitable critique of mind which demonstrates that thought cannot even represent itself absolutely to itself (cannot totally coincide with itself), let alone represent absolutely the totality of the universe (although as always the mind will attempt to demonstrate this non-absoluteness in a formally absolute manner).

Borges concludes that this "vast, contradictory library" whose books "affirm everything, deny everything, and confuse everything—like a raving god" is yet another example of the mind's habit of inventing "horrible fancies," fancies such as "the Platonic ideas, the chimera, the sphinx, the abnormal transfinite numbers (where the parts are no less abundant than the whole), masks, mirrors, operas, the monstrous Trinity: the Father, the Son, and the unresolvable Ghost, all articulated into one single organism" (*BR*, 96). This short list of horrible fancies recalls the longer sampling of items from the frightful library, and once again the list evokes themes and images that run through Borges's fiction. Indeed, in scanning this list one is struck, given the presence of the chimera and the sphinx, by the absence of that other classical monster associated with Borges's favorite symbol, the labyrinth. One would have expected the Minotaur in this company. The absence becomes even more striking when we consider that Borges ends the list of horrible fancies with "the monstrous Trinity," that imaginary Being composed of three persons with a single nature whom Borges treats as the metaphysical counterimage of an imaginary being like the Minotaur who combines two natures in a single person. Perhaps the presence of the chimera and the sphinx at a place where we would have expected to find the Minotaur will assume greater significance as we pick up "the thread of red" that Borges mentions in his note to "Death and the Compass" and follow it deeper into the labyrinth of his detective stories.

17 *The Quincuncial Labyrinth; Sidereal and Subterranean V Shapes; Taurus and Asterion; The House of the Double Axe; Bodily and Geographic Directionality; Reversing Privileged Directions*

AS WE HAVE SEEN, THE debt that Borges owes to Sir Thomas Browne's work is substantial. Not only is his antithetical doubling of the Dupin stories almost certainly modeled on the oppositional relationship between Browne's *Urn Burial* and *The Garden of Cyrus*, but several of the key structures in Borges's detective tales are clearly drawn from or influenced by Browne's speculations on the quincuncial network and its component V shape. It is only appropriate, then, that in examining the labyrinth symbol in Borges's detective stories we attend to two important associations Browne makes concerning the labyrinth and its inhabitant. One of these, mentioned earlier, is his suggestion that the shape of the Cretan labyrinth was based on the quincunx, an association underlying Borges's description of the diamond figure in "Death and the Compass" as a "labyrinth" and his image of the interior of the labyrinth in "Ibn Hakkan al-Bokhari" as a "network." The other, regarding the labyrinth's inhabitant, is a remark, almost in passing, that links the V shape to the figure of a bull among the stars and then links these images in turn to various labyrinth-related geometric shapes beneath the earth. Evoking the variety of V, X, and lozenge shapes in nature, Browne notes,

> But not to look so high as Heaven or the single Quincunx of the *Hyades* upon the head of *Taurus*, the Triangle and remarkable *Crusero* about the foot of the *Centaur;* observable rudiments there are hereof in subterraneous concretions, and bodies in the Earth; in the *Gypsum* or *Talcum Rhomboides,* in the Favaginites or honey-comb-stone, in the *Asteria* and *Astroites,* and in the crucigerous stone of S. *Iago* of *Gallicia.* (SW, 177)

In this "as-above-so-below" argument, Browne cites the correspondence between the geometric shapes of constellations in the heavens and of mineral "bodies in the Earth." He begins with "the single Quincunx of the *Hyades* upon the head of *Taurus,*" which is to say, with that constellation of five stars called the Hyades (where we count six stars nowadays, Hesiod only named five) disposed in the shape of a Roman V, a shape that the ancients interpreted as the outline of the bull's head in the constellation Taurus. In classical mythology Taurus was most often identified with the bull "that swam away with Europa,"[1] the bull in this case being the form Zeus took to carry off the maiden from Phoenicia to Crete where he fathered three sons by her—Minos, Sarpedon, and Rhadamanthys.[2] Minos eventually became king of Crete, and his wife Queen Pasiphae was the mother of the Minotaur. There were, however, several alternative myths connected with the constellation Taurus, and one of these, as R. H. Allen notes in his classic study *Star Names*, was a "myth of early spring" which "made Taurus *Amasius Pasiphaes*, the Lover of Pasiphaë," that is, the bull (sent by Poseidon) that fathered the Minotaur (*Minos + tauros*, the bull of Minos) (Allen, 379). Given the Borgesian context, we should also note that Taurus, as the first sign "in the early Hebrew zodiac," was "designated by A or Āleph, the first letter of that alphabet, coincidentally a crude figure of the Bull's face and horns" (Allen, 381). Moreover, the constellation that we call the Hyades, whose V shape of five stars outlines the head of the bull in Taurus, was known to the ancient Chinese astronomers as "*Pal*, a Hand-net" (Allen, 389).

That Browne associated Taurus with the myth of the Minotaur can be inferred from the group of constellations he cites next—"the Triangle and remarkable *Crusero* about the foot of the *Centaur*." The constellations we call the Southern Triangle and Southern Cross are both based on geometric shapes associated with the quincuncial network, the triangle being simply a closed V (half a lozenge as Borges shows in "Death and the Compass") and the cross a decussation. The two small constellations— Triangle and Cross—are located next to the front and hind feet respectively of the part-equine, part-human creature whose shape was seen in the outline of the constellation Centaur. The centaur, of course, is the figure in classical mythology whose form most closely resembles that of the Minotaur, their shapes being to some degree reciprocals of one another, the Minotaur having the head of a bull and the body of a man, the centaur the head and torso of a man and the body of a horse. The association of these biform creatures was underlined in classical mythology by the fact that the same hero defeated both. Theseus kills the Minotaur in the Cretan labyrinth, and he leads the Lapiths in defeating the centaurs at the wedding feast of Peirithous. Indeed, as Allen notes, the connection between the two was so close that "some ancient artists and mythologists" in their representations of the constellation changed the Centaur's "hind quarters to those of a bull, thus showing the Minotaur" (Allen, 150), in effect, changed them to that alternate version of the Minotaur composed of a man's head and torso and a bull's body. Consequently, in ancient Rome the constellation, although usually known as Centaurus, was also referred to on occasion as Minotaurus (Allen, 151).

In Browne's two groups of asterisms, there are three small constellations (Hyades, Triangle, Crusero) representing geometric shapes associated with the quincuncial network and two large constellations, one linked to the bull that fathered the Minotaur (Taurus) and the other to the Minotaur itself (Centaur). And these starry figurations of labyrinth and Minotaur are mirrored in turn by the "subterraneous concretions" Browne lists next, that is, by the names and crystalline shapes of various minerals in the earth—the *Talcum Rhomboides* evoking the rhomb or lozenge of the quincunx pattern, the honeycomb-stone suggesting the labyrinthine network, and the crucigerous stone of S. *Iago* balancing the celestial decussation of the *Crusero*. This reflection of labyrinth-related shapes from the astral into the subterranean realm is only appropriate, given that in most versions of the myth the Cretan labyrinth is underground and that the ancients considered the night sky to be a representation of the underworld. As Borges's favorite encyclopedia notes, "The rocks of Crete are full of winding caves, which gave the first idea of the legendary labyrinth. Later writers (for instance, Claudian, *De sexto Cons. Honorii*, 634) place it near Gortyna, and a set of winding passages and chambers close to that place is still pointed out as the labyrinth; these are, however, in reality ancient quarries" (*EB*, 16:32). The subterranean character of the labyrinth undoubtedly accounts for one of the suggested origins of the name, the Greek word λαῦρα meaning "the passage of a mine." However, the derivation most widely accepted nowadays "is from λάβρυς [*labrys*], a Lydian or Carian word meaning a 'double-edged axe' (*Journal of Hellenic Studies*, xxi. 109, 268), according to which the Cretan labyrinth or palace of Minos was the house of the double axe, the symbol of Zeus" (*EB*, 16:32). And this is the derivation Borges cites in *The Book of Imaginary Beings* (1969): "The worship of the bull and of the two-headed ax (whose name was *labrys* and may have been at the root of the word *labyrinth*) was typical of pre-Hellenic religions, which held sacred bull-fights."[3]

In his brief list of heavenly bodies and "bodies in the Earth," Browne emphasizes the link between the sidereal and subterranean realms through the names of two of the stones mentioned—*Asteria* and *Astroites*. Both are ancient names of gemstones, and although we are not sure which gems were intended, it seems likely that both names (which derive from the Greek root *aster*, "star") were applied to astriated stones whose crystalline structure reflects light into a starlike figure on the gem's surface, such as the star sapphire. Yet in this context of starry shapes associated with the Minotaur and crystalline shapes associated with the labyrinth, these two names—*Asteria* and *Astroites*—are clearly meant by Browne to recall the proper name of the labyrinth's inhabitant, the Minotaur Asterion. Derived from the same Greek root as the names of the gems, Asterion means "starry."

In "The House of Asterion"—a vision of the labyrinth from the Minotaur's point of view—Borges uses as an epigraph a sentence from Apollodorus's *Library:* "And the queen gave birth to a child who was called Asterion" (*L*, 138). In Borges's Spanish text the phrase translated as "gave birth" is *dió a luz*, an idiom that can mean "to give birth," "to bring out," "to publish," but that literally means "to bring to light" or "to give to the light." This imagistic linking of Asterion and the light is emphasized in the story itself when the Minotaur notes that although "everything is repeated many times" in the world, "two things in the world seem to be only once: above, the intricate sun; below, Asterion" (*L*, 139–40). We noted this same connection earlier between the Minotaur and the light on certain Knossian (Cretan) coins bearing the labyrinth design (see fig. 7.1a), a labyrinth whose center (the location of the Minotaur) was marked with the figure of a star or the sun suggesting the Minotaur's link either to a bull among the stars or to the solar bull.

There are, of course, a variety of theories about the meaning of the myth of the labyrinth, the Minotaur, and the Minotaur's slayer Theseus, some of which we will consider in trying to determine the myth's significance for Borges's detective stories. As a preliminary step let us recall just how pervasive the labyrinth image is in these tales. In "The Garden of Forking Paths," the Chinese novel composed by Yu Tsun's ancestor is described as "a symbolic labyrinth," an "invisible labyrinth of time" (*F*, 96). As we noted, the implication is that the structure of Borges's short story reflects the labyrinthine quality of the fictive novel whose name it bears, a notion hinted at both by Yu Tsun's remark that the directions to Stephen Albert's house resemble those "for finding the central courtyard of certain labyrinths" (*F*, 93), and by the temporal doubling of Ts'ui Pên's fate (murder by a stranger) in Stephen Albert's.

In "Death and the Compass" the triangular/quadrangular figure formed on the city map by the crimes' locations is described as a labyrinth, as is the figure of a line halved and halved again that Lönnrot proposes as a more economical version of Scharlach's maze. Moreover, the villa of Triste-le-Roy where the doubles meet is depicted as a labyrinth composed of endless repetitions and mirror images:

> Seen from up close, the house was a clutter of meaningless symmetries and almost insane repetitions: . . . one balcony appeared to reflect another; double outer staircases crossed at each landing. A two-faced Hermes cast a monstrous shadow. . . . Lönnrot explored the house. . . . He was multiplied to infinity in

facing mirrors. . . . On the third floor, the last floor, the house seemed endless and growing. (*A,* 74–75)

The same image of the house emerges from Scharlach's subsequent description of the period he spent "in this deserted villa, racked with fever," hiding from the police:

> The hateful two-faced Janus that looks on the sunsets and the dawns filled both my sleep and my wakefulness with its horror. I came to loathe my body, I came to feel that two eyes, two hands, two lungs, are as monstrous as two faces. . . . During those nights, I swore by the god who looks with two faces and by all the gods of fever and of mirrors that I would weave a maze around the man [Sp. *tejer un laberinto en torno del hombre*] who sent my brother to prison. (*A,* 75–76)

In this passage Borges links the basic structural element of a physical labyrinth (spatial doubling) to the bilateral asymmetry of the body—the external doubleness of the labyrinth, its "meaningless symmetries and almost insane repetitions" (personified by the images of "a two-faced Hermes" and "the hateful two-faced Janus") being in effect a function of the human body's arrangement of "two eyes, two hands, two lungs" horizontally opposed on either side of its vertical axis. And the implication is clear: the plight of a physical body trapped in a maze symbolizes the condition of a mind trapped in a body composed of bilateral mirror-image halves. Indeed, the correlation between the labyrinth's shape and that of its inhabitant is the first point Borges makes in his essay on the Minotaur: "The idea of a house built so that people could become lost in it is perhaps more unusual than that of a man with a bull's head, but both ideas go well together and the image of the labyrinth fits with the image of the Minotaur. It is equally fitting that in the center of a monstrous house there be a monstrous inhabitant" (*BIB,* 158).

Borges's manipulation of the labyrinth as a figure of the human dwelling place characteristically expands from the image of a house in which one becomes lost to that of a world where it is impossible to get one's bearings. And the usual transition between these two images is the figure of the labyrinth as a city. In Scharlach's description of his delirious stay at Triste-le-Roy, he invokes the image of Rome as the center of a labyrinth to which all the world's roads lead, and then superimposes this image on those of the quadrangular cell where his brother is imprisoned and the symmetrical villa where he hides from the police, in order to produce a composite figure of universal labyrinthine entrapment. The association of Rome with the labyrinth is appropriate not merely because the intersecting pattern of city streets suggests the network image used to describe a labyrinth's interior (note that a network is implied in Scharlach's figure of *weaving* a maze around the man who imprisoned his brother) but because Rome is a city built over a maze of subterranean passages (the catacombs), a labyrinth in which for centuries people have lost their way and fugitives have hidden from their pursuers. The appropriateness of this link between Rome and the labyrinth is increased by the fact that the catacombs were used as burial chambers and that the original labyrinth, the Egyptian one near Lake Moeris mentioned by Herodotus and Strabo, was intended in part as a necropolis (*EB,* 16:32).

A similar expansion of the labyrinth figure occurs in "Ibn Hakkan al-Bokhari." Questioning the notion that Ibn Hakkan had built the labyrinth as a hiding place, Unwin remarks, "A fugitive does not hide himself in a maze. . . . He has no need to erect a labyrinth when the whole world already is one. For anyone who really wants to hide away, London is a better labyrinth than a lookout tower to which all the corridors of a building lead" (*A,* 122). This progression of the labyrinth image from house to city to world is significant for our purposes because it arrays, in narrative terms, the analytic detective story's project of differentiating the human through the analysis of self-consciousness as the specific project of *physically locating the human.* In effect, it presents the problem of man's knowing his metaphysical "place" in the scheme of things as that of knowing his physical location in the natural world. Thus, Borges begins his essay on the Minotaur by noting that "the image of the labyrinth," a "house built so that people could become lost in it, . . . fits with the image of the Minotaur," for the confusion of differentiation personified by a creature half human and half animal is the symbolic equivalent of a confusion of orientation within the "house" of the world that prevents man from "finding" himself, from recognizing himself as human rather than animal.

In this scenario, where the problem of who and what we are is figured as the problem of where we are, the intersecting oppositions of the bodily labyrinth (front/rear, right/left) are projected onto the world labyrinth as the intersecting oppositions of the cardinal points (north/south, east/west). In Borges's second detective story, the "labyrinth" is formed by the four points of the compass, and the geographic directionality by which the antithetical doubles find one another at the fourth point is an external projection, a figuration, of that bodily directionality by which the self locates or discovers itself in the face-to-face encounter with its mirror image, that directionality constituted by the intersection of the body's bilateral mirror fold with the mirror fold between the body and its reflected image.

The intersecting oppositions of bodily directionality and geographic directionality are, of course, traditionally defined in terms of one another. The standard dictionary definition of *right,* for example, is "that side of one's body which is toward the east when one faces north, usually the side of the more used hand" (*W,* 1254); while the definition of *left* is "that side of one's body which is toward the west when one faces north, usually the side of the less-used hand" (*W,* 835). Similarly, the definition of *north* is "the direction to the right of a person facing the sunset" (*W,* 1001), of *south* the "direction to the left of a person facing the sunset" (*W,* 1394), of *east* the "direction to the right of a person facing north" (*W,* 456), and of *west* the "direction to the left of a person facing north" (*W,* 1660).

What occurs in a real labyrinth is that the correlation between bodily and geographic directionality is disrupted; one becomes disoriented, no longer knowing, as the word implies, where the east is in relation to oneself. Because a labyrinth is usually a subterranean structure, a person trapped within one is effectively cut off from the two great natural indicators of direction—the sun and the North Star. To be lost in a labyrinth, then, raises the specter of an ultimate loss of differentiation itself. It suggests that if an individual were permanently cut off from the geographic directionality that defines bodily directionality, he would eventually lose the ability to distinguish between right and left, to make those bodily differentiations by which the self locates itself.

Just as there is a privileged pole in each of the oppositions associated with bodily directionality (i.e., front over rear, right over left), so there is also a privileged pole in each of the oppositions associated with geographic directionality. Indeed, one reason for quoting at length the dictionary definitions of *right* and *left* and of the cardinal points was to display this privileging. In the definitions of *right* and *left* and of *east* and *west,* it is stipulated that one be "facing north"; while in the definitions of *north* and *south* the condition is that one be "facing the sunset" (west). This preference for north over south and west over east as the directions one faces in order to define the other cardinal points and the sides of the body can perhaps be explained in terms of practical navigation. The privileging of the north probably results in part from the fact that on a day-to-day basis the North Star is a more reliable approximate indicator of true north than the rising sun is of true east or the setting sun of true west, while the privileging of the west may well be a function of the fact that in the modern world the sun's setting is an event likely to be observed by more people on any given day than the sun's rising. Yet in the privileging of one pole of a differential opposition over another, there is always a cultural bias at work, and certainly the favored status of north and west in these definitions results in part from their being the directions most closely associated with both the geographic location and the historical designation of that culture represented by the dictionary, the modern, scientific culture of that industrialized portion of the northern hemisphere traditionally referred to as the West.

That the favored status of north and west in our present geographic symbolism is culturally determined can be inferred from the very etymology of the word *north*. Its classical roots are the "Oscan *nertrak,* on the left, Umbrian *nertru,* from the left," and Greek *"nerteros,* nether," the "basic idea of *north*" being "'left (with eastern orientation),' as Webster remarks."[4] Clearly, this etymology suggests an earlier, different geographic orientation of our culture in which the north, instead of being privileged, was identified with the unlucky or sinister left hand, an orientation in which, as one dictionary notes, the north was "so called from being to the left of worshipers praying to the East" (*W,* 1001). This orientation toward the sunrise, which puts the south on one's right and the north on one's left, can also be seen in various Middle Eastern languages. In Arabic, for example, "the word *šimâl* indicates the north and also designates the left side," north and left both being associated with ill fortune; while the name of the south, "thè Yemen, the flourishing land, the Arabia Felix of the classics" is "taken from the root *ymn* which implies ideas of success and happiness, and from it are derived the terms *yumn,* 'felicity' . . . and *yamîne,* 'right.' . . . The same mutual associations are also recorded in Hebrew, where the word for left is applied to the north and that for right indicates the south."[5]

The privileging of north and west in modern Western culture's geographic symbolism is significant in the present context because it links two seemingly unrelated strands in the labyrinthine network of Borges's detective stories. We noted earlier that in his doubling of the Dupin stories, Borges reverses the traditional privilege of right over left by having the criminal outwit the detective. And we also noted that the sinister figures in these stories are specifically coded as Easterners within the tales' Western settings. They are associated either with the Far East (as in the case of the Chinese Yu Tsun) or with the Middle East (as in the cases of the Jew Scharlach and the Moslem Zaid). This identification of the sinister with the oriental, of left with east, indicates the orientation of Borges's own geographic symbolism, which is to say, his reorientation, in these labyrinthine tales about labyrinths, of that traditional symbolism privileging north and west. For if left and east are identified (if the east is on one's left), then one must be facing south. Since in a network of bipolar oppositions the master terms tend to be aligned, reversing the privileging in one opposition usually means reversing it in several. Thus in "Death and the Compass," the triumph of Scharlach over Lönnrot (sinister over righteous, east over west) implicitly enacts the reversal of another master/slave

polarity, that geographic opposition evoked by the originating and culminating events of the narrative (the murder of Yarmolinsky and the
meeting of the doubles)—north and south. It is not without significance
that Borges has the Eastern criminal defeat the Western detective (who
thinks of himself as "a kind of Auguste Dupin") at the fourth point of the
compass in the south, for in effect Borges's encounter with Dupin's
creator—his antithetical doubling of the detective story's origin through
the repetition and reversal of the genre's traditional oppositions—is an
effort to reverse the master/slave polarity of north and south in the literature of the Americas. Borges aims to be an origin for South American
writing in the way that Poe was for North American. He seeks, through
this duel with a major writer, to establish for Latin American literature a
standard of excellence such that future Latin American writers will not
always have to look to the north to find major writing in the New World.
For Borges as a developing fiction writer in the late 1930s and early '40s,
this north/south encounter was the result of a more or less conscious
decision to avoid a traditional east/west cultural axis, to turn away from
the French influence that represented the artistic ideal for most of his
fellow Argentineans (an Argentine obsession he was to satirize in "Pierre
Menard, Author of *Don Quixote*") and turn toward the English language
and particularly North American fiction as the principal foreign literary
influence on his work. Yet given Borges's oft-stated admiration for North
American writers, what drew him specifically to Poe for his project of
antithetical doubling?

Poe and Borges as Southerners; A Military/Literary Heritage; Heroic Grandfathers; Pierre Menard; Faulkner as Mediating Influence; The Journey to the South

TO ASK WHAT DREW BORGES to Poe's work and why he was able to use Poe both as a point of access to North American literature and as a model of how one could achieve literary self-definition through a kind of antithetical regional identification are two questions that in some sense turn out to be the same question or at least to have the same answer. Clearly, one of the reasons that Borges as a South American was attracted to this particular North American writer was that Poe thought of himself as a Southerner. Although Poe had been born in Boston, he had been raised by his foster parents, the Allans, in Virginia, and he seems to have considered himself a Southern gentleman, even something of an aristocrat (albeit a fallen one), for the rest of his life—a regional (and social) designation that served in some degree to distinguish him in his own mind from the largely Northern literary establishment in which he moved and in terms of which he sought success.

The resemblance, not to say kinship, Borges felt with Poe as a Southerner seems to have involved a series of similarities that flowed out of this regional designation, the most important being the sense of a dual military/literary heritage. The American South is, of course, a region with a strong military tradition, and in the Civil War, the South thought of itself as the natural heir to the Royalist side in the English civil war—the aristocratic side whose wealth was based on land rather than commerce, whose cavaliers were equally adept at penning a witty sonnet or making a dashing cavalry charge that either carried all before it or ended in disaster. This image of the Southerner as cavalier, as the aristocrat who is both soldier and poet, sheds light on the career choice that confronted Poe at the age of seventeen when his foster father John Allan removed him from the University of Virginia and refused to finance him any longer. Although Poe was ultimately to support himself for most of his adult life as a writer and magazine editor, he initially tried to earn his living by following a career in the military. After leaving the university, Poe went to Boston and enlisted as a private in the army under the name Edgar A. Perry in May 1827. Poe spent the next two years in the service, ultimately rising to the rank of sergeant major, the highest noncommissioned rank. After securing a substitute, he was honorably discharged in April 1829. He then sought and received an appointment to West Point and reported for duty in June 1830.

According to his biographer Arthur Hobson Quinn, Poe felt that a military commission was the only way he could maintain the gentlemanly status to which he had been raised by Allan but which had been denied him by Allan's withdrawal of financial support. No doubt Poe, with his Virginia upbringing, felt as well a certain chivalric attraction to military life, and at this point he must have also thought that there would be enough free time in the army for him to continue his writing. In addition, Poe may have been led to this career by the fact that his paternal grandfather, David Poe, Sr., had been something of a local military hero. During the Revolutionary War, Poe's grandfather had served as "Assistant Deputy-Quartermaster General for the City of Baltimore with the rank of Major. . . . So well known were Major Poe's services that he became brevetted in the eyes of the public and was known for many years as 'General' Poe."[1] Quinn adds that in his seventies "General" Poe seems to have resumed his military career and "taken part in the defence of Baltimore in 1814 against the British attack" (Quinn, 18). The memory of his grandfather's services to the nation may well have influenced Poe's application to and acceptance by West Point, but whatever the reason for his decision, the discipline of West Point soon proved too much for the young man. Poe decided to leave and in January 1831 managed to get himself court-martialed for "Gross neglect of Duty" and "Disobedience of Orders" (Quinn, 173). He departed the academy in February and supported himself for the rest of his life as a writer, but he dedicated his *Poems by Edgar A. Poe, Second Edition* published in April 1831 to "The U.S. Corps of Cadets."

This passage in Poe's life must have had a special resonance for Borges, for like Poe he also had a paternal grandfather who was a local military hero and he seems to have felt an attraction for both the military and the literary life. In his 1970 autobiographical essay, Borges recalls that his grandfather, Colonel Francisco Borges, was "Commander-in-Chief of the northern and western frontiers of the Province of Buenos Aires" and that in 1874 at the age of forty-one he was killed in one of his country's civil wars when, riding on horseback toward the enemy lines, "he was struck by two Remington bullets" (A, 205–6). Ever the chronicler of historical firsts, Borges remarks, "This was the first time Remington rifles were used in the Argentine" (A, 206). And he adds with evident amusement, "It tickles my fancy to think that the firm that shaves me every morning bears the same name as the one that killed my grandfather" (A, 206).

The military heroes among Borges's ancestors were not, however, confined to his father's side of the family. In the same 1970 essay, he recalls that his maternal great-grandfather was

> Colonel Isidoro Suárez, who, in 1824, at the age of twenty-four, led a famous charge of Peruvian and Colombian cavalry, which turned the tide of the battle of Junín, in Peru. This was the next to last battle of the South American War of Independence. . . . Another member of my mother's family was Francisco de Laprida, who, in 1816, in Tucumán, where he presided over the Congress, declared the independence of the Argentine Confederation, and was killed in 1829 in a civil war. My mother's father, Isidoro Acevedo, though a civilian, took part in the fighting of yet other civil wars in the 1860's and 1880's. So, on both sides of my family, I have military forebears; this may account for my yearning after that epic destiny which my gods denied me, no doubt wisely. (*A*, 208)

He adds, "I was always very nearsighted and wore glasses, and I was rather frail. As most of my people had been soldiers—even my father's brother had been a naval officer—and I knew I would never be, I felt ashamed, quite early, to be a bookish kind of person and not a man of action" (*A*, 208). But his being a bookish kind of person was also a family inheritance. As Borges says in the same essay, "A tradition of literature ran through my father's family. His great-uncle Juan Crisóstomo Lafinur was one of the first Argentine poets. . . . One of my father's cousins, Álvaro Melián Lafinur . . . was a leading minor poet and later found his way into the Argentine Academy of Letters" (*A*, 210). And of course Borges's father had written a novel, as well as numerous sonnets and a translation of Omar Khayyam.

One can see Borges confronting his dual military and literary heritage (as well as the influence of Poe in this area) in that first story he wrote in a new manner in 1939 in the wake of his father's death and his own near death from blood poisoning, a new manner that the world would come to know as "Borgesian"—"Pierre Menard, Author of *Don Quixote*." The image of the French author Pierre Menard that emerges from what the narrator calls his "*visible* lifework" (*F*, 45), a bibliography of nineteen items made up for the most part of symbolist poems, arcane monographs, and translations, is that of a very minor writer indeed—effete, brittle, *précieux*, as the French say. The career evoked by this visible work seems to be very much Borges's sense of what his own literary career would have looked like to the world if he had died of septicemia in early 1939—a minor poet and essayist lionized in the Frenchified literary salons of Buenos Aires society. But this visible work was not the whole of Menard's literary creation; there was an invisible work as well, one of such sublimity in its conception that it could only be the creation of a major writer. (Indeed, part of the peculiarly poignant effect of placing "Pierre Menard" within the context of Borges's biography is the sense we get that Borges meant to evoke, in the difference between Menard's visible and invisible work, that feeling every young writer has had in contemplating the possibility of his own premature death—that sense of the difference between the way his career will look to the world on the basis of the few minor things he has published and the way that it would look if the world could see the great, but invisible because as yet unwritten, works he had planned.)

In his invisible work Menard had, of course, set out to reproduce Cervantes' *Don Quixote*, not "to compose another *Don Quixote*," not "to produce a mechanical transcription of the original," but "to produce pages which would coincide—word for word and line for line—with those of Miguel de Cervantes" (*F*, 48–49). And to make his task even more difficult, Menard decided that "to be, in the twentieth century, a popular novelist of the seventeenth . . . , to be, in some way, Cervantes and to arrive at *Don Quixote*" was "less arduous—and consequently less interesting— than to continue being Pierre Menard and to arrive at *Don Quixote* through the experiences of Pierre Menard" (*F*, 49).

What the narrator, who is in his own way as brittle as the Menard evoked by the visible work, seems to be most puzzled by is why someone like Menard, a minor symbolist, a connoisseur of arcana, would choose to reproduce *Don Quixote*, choose to emulate Cervantes. Not only is the work in a foreign language (and one which the narrator clearly feels is inferior to French), but it is crude, bawdy, filled with an earthy vitality that makes it seem doubly foreign to the world in which Menard lives. The narrator goes to some lengths to explain this choice, but we are perhaps in a better position to understand what Cervantes represented for Menard because of our sense of what Poe represented for Borges. For quite clearly the important fact about Cervantes in this context is that he was both a soldier and a writer (and of course compared to the Frenchman Menard, a south- erner), or more precisely a soldier who became a writer when his soldier- ing days came to an end, a writer who in the *Quixote* created a character who sets out to enact in real life the deeds of chivalrous valor he has read about in books, deeds that are simply literary inventions.

Borges makes sure the reader notices that the central fact about Cer- vantes is his being both a man of action and a man of intellect when he has the narrator remark that one of the three chapters of the *Quixote* which Menard set out to reproduce exactly was

Chapter XXXVIII of Part One "which treats of the curious discourse that Don Quixote delivered on the subject of arms and letters." As is known, Don Qui- xote (like Quevedo in a later, analogous passage of *La hora de todos*) passes judgment against letters and in favor of arms. Cervantes was an old soldier, which explains such a judgment. But that the *Don Quixote* of Pierre Menard—a contemporary of *La trahison des clercs* and Bertrand Russell—should relapse into these nebulous sophistries! (*F*, 52)

The narrator explains Menard's stance in this regard by invoking "his resigned or ironic habit of propounding ideas which were the strict reverse of those he preferred" (*F*, 52). No wonder then the narrator feels that though the "text of Cervantes and that of Menard are verbally identical, . . . the second is almost infinitely richer" (*F*, 52).

We might attribute something of this added richness to Borges's story of Menard as well if we were to substitute for the figure of the minor French poet and essayist Menard, who sets out to double the work of a major Spanish writer (Cervantes), the figure of a minor Argentine poet and essayist (Borges) who, at the start of his career as a fiction writer, sets out to double the work of a major North American fiction writer (Poe). After all, Poe, like Cervantes, had been at different times in his life both a soldier and a writer, and as such he probably felt, as Borges says of himself, a "yearning after" some "epic destiny" his gods had denied him. It is precisely the writer's yearning for some heroic action withheld by fate that Borges assimilates to Cervantes' debate between arms and letters, a debate Don Quixote decides in favor of arms, but that Borges, who was barred from a life of vigorous physical action by his nearsightedness and frailty and who must thus try to turn a fate into a power, sets out to decide in favor of letters. And what better model for that choice of letters over arms than someone who, like Poe, had rejected a military career for the life of a writer, and what better work of Poe's to double than one that thematized the dispute between action and intellection as the difference between a violent crime and its analytic solution, between the physicality of the former (the brutality of murder) and the mental subtlety of the latter? It is a difference Poe himself emphasized in "The Murders in the Rue Morgue." The killer is literally a hairy ape (his rampage being marked by both ferocious brutality and enormous physical dexterity), and the detective is a mastermind whose profound sedentariness is meant to highlight, by contrast with the physical activity of the killer, the detective's mental superiority to all mere brute force.

That Borges thought of his story "Pierre Menard, Author of *Don Quixote*" as an oblique gloss on his project of doubling Poe's detective stories can perhaps be judged from the fact that "Pierre Menard" was published in the same volume of fiction whose final story, "The Garden of Forking Paths," initiated this project. Need I add that the narrator of "Pierre Menard" remarks in passing that he had always considered Menard as a writer "essentially devoted to Poe" (*F*, 50). The narrator intends this remark as an explanation of why Cervantes was an oddly inappropriate writer for the refined symbolist Menard to emulate, but of course the Poe the narrator has in mind is the minor poet and essayist who, as he says, "engendered Baudelaire, who engendered Mallarmé, who engendered Valéry, who engendered Edmond Teste" (*F*, 50), the Poe whose writing could be thought of as having influenced Menard's "*visible* works" (*F*, 45). But the Poe Borges has in mind is the major fiction writer rather than the minor poet, the Poe whose writing influenced Menard's invisible work, that is, whose actual influence on Borges's work Menard's invisible project symbolizes. At one point in the tale Menard says that he chose the *Quixote* for his invisible project because he could rewrite it "without incurring a tautology" since it was "an accidental book," a book that was not "inevitable" (*F*, 50) in the way that, for example, the poetic "interjection of Edgar Allan Poe *Ah, bear in mind this garden was enchanted!*" was. Indeed, so inevitable does Poe's line seem that Menard says he "cannot imagine the universe" without it (*F*, 50). This last remark is, of course, meant in part to evoke the preciousness of the minor symbolist Menard. But clearly Menard's citation of the line from Poe's 1848 poem "To Helen [Whitman]," in its association of Poe with an enchanted garden, is also an allusion to Poe's link to the fantastic garden that gives its name to the volume in which "Pierre Menard" appears (*The Garden of Forking Paths*), to its title story, and thus to those other two gardens whose imagery Borges draws on in doubling the Dupin tales—Browne's *Garden of Cyrus* and Lewis Carroll's specular chessboard-garden in *Through the Looking-Glass*. If it was the non-inevitability of the *Quixote* that evoked Menard's invisible project, it seems to have been the inevitability of Poe's work that evoked Borges's.

We should note that Poe's influence on Borges—the exemplary influence of a Southern writer working within a Northern literary establishment that provided Borges with a model for his own engagement with North American literature, an engagement that in its imitative but antithetical dynamics gave Borges a sharpened sense of his own southernness—was probably mediated and reinforced by the work of another author from the American South who was Borges's contemporary, William Faulkner. Borges was a fan of Faulkner's work, and between 1937 and 1939 he reviewed three of his books—*The Unvanquished, Absalom, Absalom!,* and *The Wild Palms*—and in 1941 published a Spanish translation (done in collaboration with his mother) of the last of these. Of *The Unvanquished* Borges wrote, "Rivers of brown water, rundown mansions, black slaves, equestrian wars—lazy and cruel: the peculiar world of *The Unvanquished* is consanguineous with this America and its history, and it is also *criollo*. There are some books that touch us physically like the nearness of the sea or the morning. This—for me—is one of them" (*BR*, 93). One can sense Borges's already assimilating Faulkner's South, with its "equestrian wars," to his own south and to the image of his grandfather's death on horseback during one of the Argentine civil wars.

Faulkner's resemblance to Poe as regards a dual military/literary tradition would, of course, have accounted in part for Borges's interest in him. As Poe and Borges both had paternal grandfathers who were military heroes, so Faulkner's paternal great-grandfather had been a hero in the Confederate army during the Civil War. William C. Falkner, the "Old Colonel" as he was called, had led his regiment into battle at the First Manassas and come out a hero. After the war, he made his way in the world as a lawyer, planter, railroad builder, and politician. But perhaps the most interesting of his careers was as a writer. Among his literary efforts was a long poem called *The Siege of Monterey* about his experiences in the Mexican War, a successful play entitled *The Lost Diamond,* and a money-making novel, *The White Rose of Memphis.* Faulkner, of course, drew liberally on his own family history for his fiction, and the four generations of Faulkner men (from the Old Colonel down to the author) are models for both the Sartorises and the Compsons.

Faulkner's sense of the way in which one's ancestors could exercise a fateful influence on one's own life is the theme of *Light in August,* where the three main characters, Joe Christmas, Joanna Burden, and Gail Hightower, have all had their destinies determined by the lives of their grandfathers. Given how important a figure Colonel Borges was in the imagination of his literary grandson, we can imagine what Borges must have felt about Gail Hightower's lifelong obsession with his grandfather's tragic death during a cavalry raid in the Civil War. Indeed, Faulkner himself seems to have been a bit obsessed with the military heroics of his own great-grandfather, and when the chance came for Faulkner to serve in the military in World War I, his disappointment at being turned down by the Aviation Section of the U.S. Army because he was both too short and underweight, an almost literal figure of not measuring up to the stature of one's heroic ancestors, was to last his entire lifetime. Of course, Faulkner volunteered for and was accepted by the Royal Air Force, but the war ended while he was still in training in Canada. Like Borges, Faulkner seems to have yearned for an epic destiny which the gods denied him.

A literary taste Faulkner shared with both Poe and Borges was, of course, his predilection for the detective story. Faulkner is a major inheritor of Poe in this genre—*Absalom, Absalom!* representing in some sense the culmination of the gothic detective form begun by the Dupin tales. And as we know, Faulkner practiced the genre with a certain regularity: his efforts included the novel *Intruder in the Dust,* the short-story collection

Knight's Gambit, and the screenplay for Raymond Chandler's *The Big Sleep*, on which he collaborated with Jules Furthman and Leigh Brackett. One can perhaps see most clearly Faulkner's influence reinforcing that of Poe in Borges's "Ibn Hakkan al-Bokhari," where the situation of the two young men puzzling over the facts of a very old murder and constructing alternative stories to explain what really happened is strongly reminiscent of the situation of Quentin and Shreve in *Absalom, Absalom!* And in a sense Borges's self-definition as a writer depended upon his ultimately convincing himself of the very thing that Quentin, in the city of Poe's birth and his own death, never seemed able to convince himself—that he didn't hate the South.

Borges's most explicit examination of his own southernness as a writer, and consequently a particularly instructive instance of the influence of Poe on his work, is to be found in the short story with which he ends the 1956 collection *Ficciones*. In the preface to the collection Borges says that "The South" is "perhaps my best story" and that "it can be read as a direct narrative of novelistic events, and also in another way" (*F*, 105–6). One "other way" it can be read is as a figurative account of Borges's career as a writer. Like Borges at the time, the story's main character Juan Dahlmann works at a small municipal library in Buenos Aires and, like Borges's, Dahlmann's ancestors were military heroes: "His maternal grandfather had been that Francisco Flores, of the Second Line-Infantry Division, who had died on the frontier of Buenos Aires, run through with a lance by Indians from Catriel" (*F*, 167). Dahlmann's paternal grandfather had been a German emigrant, but Dahlmann had always "considered himself profoundly Argentinian" (*F*, 167), for though there was a "discord inherent between his two lines of descent," Dahlmann "(perhaps driven to it by his Germanic blood) chose the line represented by his romantic ancestor, his ancestor of the romantic death" (*F*, 167). Dahlmann had inherited a ranch in the south that belonged to the Flores family, and he had managed to save it "at the cost of numerous small privations" (*F*, 167) over the years. The ranch represents the south for Dahlmann, and the south represents the core of Dahlmann's nationalism by being associated with his heroic ancestor Francisco Flores who was killed by the Indians. As the narrator says, "An old sword, a leather frame containing the daguerreotype of a blank-faced man with a beard, the dash and grace of certain music, the familiar strophes of *Martín Fierro*, the passing years, boredom and solitude, all went to foster this voluntary, but never ostentatious nationalism" (*F*, 167). The opposition that Borges draws in the tale between the urban north and the rural south, between Buenos Aires (as a city of emigrants and the descendants of emigrants, a city of imitation Europeans) and the pampas (where all those traits that are distinctively Argentinean are to be found) amounts to a symbolic geography in which the journey to the south will be acted out.

Although Dahlmann had not seen the ranch in many years, "he contented himself with the abstract idea of possession and with the certitude that his ranch was waiting for him" (*F*, 167). And in February 1939, an accident and its aftermath lead him to make a trip there. The accident Borges gives Dahlmann is taken from his own biography, that brush with death from blood poisoning mentioned earlier. As Borges describes it in "An Autobiographical Essay,"

> It was on Christmas Eve of 1938—the same year my father died—that I had a severe accident. I was running up a stairway and suddenly felt something brush my scalp. I had grazed a freshly painted open casement window. In spite of first-aid treatment, the wound became poisoned, and for a period of a week or so I lay sleepless every night and had hallucinations and high fever. One evening, I lost the power of speech and had to be rushed to the hospital for an immediate operation. Septicemia had set in, and for a month I hovered, all unknowingly, between life and death. (Much later, I was to write about this in my story "The South.") When I began to recover, I feared for my mental integrity. . . . I wondered whether I could ever write again. I had previously written quite a few poems and dozens of short reviews. I thought that if I tried to write a review now and failed, I'd be all through intellectually but that if I tried something I had never really done before and failed at that it wouldn't be so bad and might even prepare me for the final revelation. I decided I would try to write a story. The result was "Pierre Menard, Author of *Don Quixote*." (*A*, 242–43)

Borges evokes the episode as a kind of symbolic death and rebirth. In the wake of the death of his father (whom he had always considered the fiction writer in the family) and his own near death, the old writing self (the minor poet and reviewer) is transcended and the new writing self (the fiction writer) comes into existence. Borges's biographer Rodríguez Monegal notes that this version of the accident differs, both by omission and alteration, from the account given by his mother, and that it also ignores, in presenting itself as the story of Borges's start as a fiction writer, that he had written fiction before "Pierre Menard." But "Menard" does represent the start of that special type of writing we think of as "Borgesian," as well as the beginning of that stage in Borges's career when his principal output would be fiction. Monegal goes on to describe Borges's accident as a symbolic "death (by suicide) and a rebirth" (*JLB*, 326), implicitly associating Borges's unintentionally self-inflicted wound with the type of death that concludes a duel between doubles.

Like Borges, Dahlmann had also run up a flight of stairs (he had been hurrying home to examine "an imperfect copy of Weil's edition of *The Thousand and One Nights*" [*F*, 167]), had felt something graze his head ("the edge of a recently painted door" [*F*, 168]), had gotten blood poisoning from the wound and been carried on the point of death to a sanitarium where after several weeks of fever and delirium he eventually recovered. But where Borges on his recovery wrote a short story (a story in which Menard's doubling the *Quixote* is a figure for Borges's doubling the Dupin stories), Dahlmann on his recovery makes a trip to the south. This parallel equates the journey to the south with the act of writing, in particular, with the attempt at some new type of writing, some imaginative exploration. And here again we see the influence of Poe, for in several of his best-known stories Poe figuratively represents the act of writing as an exploratory journey into *terra incognita,* into some new realm of the human imagination. And in two of these—"MS. Found in a Bottle" and *The Narrative of A. Gordon Pym*—where virtually every aspect of the act of writing is metaphorized, the exploratory journey is specifically a journey to the south, an attempt to reach the South Pole. In both stories, the central character tries to reach the limits of the imagination, tries to gain, as the narrator of "MS. Found in a Bottle" says, "some exciting knowledge—some never-to-be-imparted secret, whose attainment is destruction" (2:145). And both the narrator of "MS. Found in a Bottle" and Arthur Gordon Pym die in the quest, but with this difference. Where the narrator of "MS. Found in a Bottle" dies during the course of the journey when his ship enters the polar abyss, Arthur Gordon Pym dies some ten years after the journey during the writing of his narrative, dies at precisely that point in the narrative at which he should have died in the journey (i.e., when his canoe enters the polar abyss), but which he had survived in some unexplained manner. The displacement of the main character's death from the voyage of exploration to the act of writing makes clear the journey's metaphoric status.

Like the journeys of Arthur Gordon Pym and the narrator of "MS. Found in a Bottle," Juan Dahlmann's trip to the south turns out to be fatal. Riding the train to his ranch, Dahlmann occupies himself by reading the first volume of *The Thousand and One Nights* that he had acquired on the day of his accident, feeling somehow that he is "traveling into the past and not merely south" (*F*, 171). Disembarking at a station near his ranch, Dahlmann becomes involved in a senseless quarrel in a café with three drunken toughs, and one of them challenges him to a knife fight. Dahlmann knows that he should refuse, that he does not have a chance, but he has chosen the life of the south and part of that life is this death. Dahlmann is without a weapon, but suddenly an old gaucho—"in whom Dahlmann saw a summary and cipher of the South (his South)—threw him a naked dagger, which landed at his feet. It was as if the South had resolved that Dahlmann should accept the duel. . . . He felt that if he had been able to choose, then, or to dream his death, this would have been the death he would have chosen or dreamt" (*F*, 174). Ironically, the drunken toughs pick a fight with Dahlmann precisely because they see him as a stranger from the city, a northerner, but Dahlmann accepts the challenge because he thinks of himself as a southerner. With his acceptance of the challenge (and of his almost certain death), Dahlmann decides the outcome of that duel within himself between a northern and southern heritage, decides in favor of "his ancestor of the romantic death." But in a final (though not unexpected) twist, this duel between north and south also turns out to be one between the intersecting polarity of east and west; for Dahlmann's opponent, the southern country dweller, is also an easterner, a tough "whose features hinted at Chinese blood" (*F*, 172–73), and in this context Dahlmann, the northern city dweller of German ancestry, is very much a representative of the West. (The Spanish word translated as "Chinese" [*rasgos achinados*, Chinese features] is commonly used in Argentina to refer to Indians of the pampas, or people of Indian ancestry, whose Asiatic features suggest an ancient origin in the East.)

That Dahlmann has been reading the eastern story *The Thousand and One Nights* on his southern journey reminds us that it was a favorite work of Borges's, although it is probably being invoked here as an allusion to Poe's *Pym*. In his 1975 collection *The Book of Sand*, Borges names as one of his models in writing the stories in this volume "Poe, who, around 1838, gave up a very rich style in order to bequeath us the admirable final chapters of his *Narrative of Arthur Gordon Pym*" (*BS*, 7–8). Of course, "the admirable final chapters" of *Pym* recount Pym's voyage to the south, a voyage that ends with Pym's canoe being swept, "under the influence of a powerful current" (*P*, 3:240), toward the South Pole and toward that gigantic white figure in the mist that, as the text hints, is Pym's own unrecognized shadow. One of the two tales from *The Thousand and One Nights* that Borges says Dahlmann read on his southern journey is the story of "the magnetized mountain" (*F*, 170), the opening of the Third Kalandar's Tale recounting King Ajib's marvelous voyage to the west. Blown off course during a storm, Ajib's ship is caught by a strong current that carries it toward the Magnet Mountain, a gigantic lodestone that wrecks ships by drawing the nails from their planks and that bears on its top the figure of a bronze horseman which Ajib must topple.[2] According to Burton, Arabic legend located the Magnet Mountain, with its bronze horseman, in the Fortunate Isles or Eternal Isles (i.e., the Canaries), depicting it as a kind of western limit of the world (Burton, 1:141 n. 1). The broad similarities between Pym's voyage to the south and Ajib's to the west—the fact that the direction of each voyage is the polar opposite of the direction associated with the voyager's culture; the powerful current that captures each boat; the attractive force of the polar abyss and the Magnet Mountain; the gigantic white figure and the bronze horseman—all suggest that the reference to the story of "the magnetized mountain" in "The South" may well be an oblique evocation of Poe's *Pym* as an influence on Dahlmann's southern journey. And this possibility seems even more likely when we recall that Poe, an admirer like Borges of *The Thousand and One Nights*, published in 1845 a parody entitled "The Thousand-and-Second Tale of Scheherazade" which recounts the aged Sinbad's last voyage, his voyage to the modern West as a prisoner on board an English steamship. The point of the tale is that the scientific and technological marvels of the West far surpass the Eastern marvels that fill the Arabian Nights. As the list of these amazing Western phenomena mounts, Scheherazade's husband the king becomes more incredulous and angry until he finally orders that his wife be strangled with a bowstring—the true ending of Scheherazade's own story, says Poe. If Borges's reference to the tale of the magnetized mountain is indeed an allusion to Poe's parody of the voyage to a polar opposite and those other Poe voyage tales that lie behind Dahlmann's southern journey, then it is an allusion that seems to say, "As the western storyteller Poe has served the eastern storyteller Scheherazade, so the southern storyteller Borges will serve the northern storyteller Poe." Need I add that the other tale from the Arabian Nights which Borges says Dahlmann read on his journey to the south was that of "the genie who swore to kill his benefactor" (*F*, 170), for of course what Borges learned from Poe—how to achieve his own originality by making the most of his southernness—would be put to its ultimate test in establishing his difference from a major North American writer, Poe.

19 *The Red Thread; The Locked-Room Problem; The Hidden-Object Problem; The Continuity of Inner and Outer; The Turning of a Glove; Locked Room, Letter, and Labyrinth*

IN "THE SOUTH" BORGES NOT only thematizes his development as a fiction writer in terms of a north/south polarity, he also alludes at several points to the "invisible" project that enacts his struggle for a regional identity within the writing of the Americas, the doubling of the Dupin stories. One of his subtler allusions occurs when Dahlmann, glancing from the train window during his journey, notes that the "limitless country" contained "only a solitary bull" (*F*, 171). Given Borges's practice in the detective stories of figuring the protagonists' meeting place as a labyrinth, this detail, in the context of Dahlmann's trip to an unexpected fatal duel in the south (like Lönnrot's in "Death and the Compass"), evokes the opponent characteristically associated with the labyrinth—the Minotaur. Although Borges uses the labyrinth image in all three detective stories, he explicitly mentions the Minotaur only in the third tale, "Ibn Hakkan al-Bokhari." However, in his 1970 note to the English translation of "Death and the Compass," he does make an oblique but highly significant allusion to the myth of Theseus and the Minotaur, an allusion meant to remind us of an original link between this myth and the detective genre.

Recall that in the note Borges directs our attention to "a thread of red" that "runs through the story's pages"—a thread that, as we saw, continues into the pages of his other two detective stories as well. We interpreted this recurrence of the color—particularly in such details as the relationship of the *Dream of the Red Chamber* to the figure of Stephen Albert; Erik Lönnrot's name; and the image of a "red-haired king," a "scarlet maze," and a lion "the color of the sun"—as an effect of the recurring symbolic action underlying these stories: the checkmating of the Red King (borrowed from Carroll's *Through the Looking-Glass* to evoke the self-defeating nature of the attempt at absolute mental reflexivity).

Yet this "thread of red," which the author so obligingly isolates from the fabric of his story, as if to suggest that it is a clue whose unraveling will lead to the tale's solution, is also meant to recall the origin of the word that, perhaps more than any other, is associated with the analytic detective story. Under the spelling "clew," *Webster's New World Dictionary* gives "1. a ball of thread or yarn: in Greek legend, a thread was used by Theseus as a guide out of the labyrinth; hence, 2. something that leads out of a maze, perplexity, etc., or helps to solve a problem: in this sense generally spelled *clue*" (*W*, 273). A clue is literally, then, a ball of thread, and its common metaphoric meaning (as a hint to solve a mystery) is a function of the myth of Theseus and the Minotaur. Given that the thread running through the labyrinth of Borges's detective stories is specifically a red one, it is worth noting that in the ancient world one of the more common color schemes used in visually representing the labyrinth pattern, particularly as a decorative border design (the meander), was a red line on a yellow or pale background (*ML*, 31), a fact which suggests that for Borges the red line delineating the shape of the labyrinth (e.g., the red ink line forming the triangle on the map in "Death and the Compass") and the red thread leading us out of the story's labyrinth may be continuous.

In giving us this clue to the origin of *clue*, this hieroglyph of the object from which the word's usual meaning derives, Borges is engaged at once in the work of antithetically doubling the Dupin stories and of interpreting them. And what Borges's reading focuses on in this instance is Poe's repeated use of the word *clue* in the three tales with what seems to be a clear sense both of its original meaning (a ball of thread) and of the association of its figurative meaning with the myth of Theseus and the Minotaur; though, curiously, Poe makes no explicit reference to the myth—an omission that, as we shall see, assumes greater significance in light of the fact that another Greek myth eventually becomes associated with the analytic detective story (and particularly with the Dupin tales) as a kind of classical archetype of the genre's structure, that of Oedipus.

The word *clue*, or *clew*, occurs seven times in the Dupin stories, and at least two of the occurrences are of special significance. In "The Purloined Letter," for example, the word is used only once, but in a position of great formal importance (the story's final paragraph). Oddly enough, however, it does not occur in a context where one would have expected it, which is to say that Poe uses the word to refer not to the hints that led Dupin to solve the mystery of where and how the Minister D—— had hidden the letter but rather to the trace Dupin himself leaves in the substituted letter to reveal his identity to his double. Explaining his decision not to leave the interior of the substituted letter blank, Dupin says,

That would have been insulting. D——, at Vienna once, did me an evil turn, which I told him, quite good-humoredly, that I should remember. So, as I knew he would feel some curiosity in regard to the identity of the person who had outwitted him, I thought it a pity not to give him a clue. He is well acquainted with my MS., and I just copied into the middle of the blank sheet the words—

—Un dessein si funeste,
S'il n'est digne d'Atrée, est digne de Thyeste.

They are to be found in Crébillon's "Atrée." (3:993)

This reference to Dupin's manuscript, that is, to his immediately recognizable handwriting, as a clue to his identity suggests an imagistic association of that meandering line of ink on paper (which reveals the opponent concealed in the letter) with that equally meandering line of thread which leads to and from the opponent concealed in the labyrinth, an association clearly present in the detective story that Borges balances against "The Purloined Letter." In "Death and the Compass" the clue Scharlach gives Lönnrot to their meeting place in the maze—a line of red ink on a map— is also a veiled signature, its redness suggesting the doubly red name (Red Scarlet) of the man who is Lönnrot's double.

That Poe associates a line of ink inscribed on a sheet of paper with a line of thread running through a labyrinth seems even more likely when we consider the elaborate hieroglyphic action he constructs in "The Murders in the Rue Morgue" around the word *clue*. What with the tale's startling device of a simian culprit, we often forget that Poe's first detective story initially presents itself as a locked-room mystery: Dupin's first problem is the murderer's "means of egress" (2:551) from the L'Espanayes' apartment. When the police arrive, they find that the "large back chamber in the fourth story," from which the women's screams had issued, is "locked, with the key inside" (2:537), and upon forcing the door, they find that the front and rear windows are "down and firmly fastened from within" (2:542). Examining the chamber's two rooms, Dupin satisfies himself that the murderer could not have exited through either of the doors to the hall, since each was locked with the key inside, nor through the chimneys, which are too narrow at the top to admit "the body of a large cat" (2:551), nor through the windows in the front room from which "no one could have escaped without notice from the crowd in the street" (2:551). All of which leads him to concentrate his investigation on the two windows in the back room. Each has a "gimlet-hole" drilled in its frame with "a very stout nail . . . fitted therein, nearly to the head" (2:552). The police had tried to raise the sashes but, failing, had concluded that the murderer had exited in some other way. Dupin, however, carries out a closer examination. With some difficulty, he removes the nail from one of the frames and then tries to raise the sash, only to find that it still cannot be budged. He theorizes that the sash must be fastened by a hidden spring which snaps into place when the sash is lowered. He quickly discovers the spring, but this still leaves him with the problem of the nail inserted in the frame. Even if the sash had fastened automatically when lowered, how had the murderer reinserted the nail in the gimlet hole on the inside of the closed window?

With this in mind, Dupin turns his attention to the other window, seemingly identical to the first, with a nail inserted in the frame and a hidden spring that fastens automatically. Dupin reasons that since all the other possible means of escape have been logically eliminated, this window must have been the murderer's way out; and although it seems identical to the other one, it must, he concludes, be different in some respect, and the difference must involve the nail in the frame. As he explains to the narrator,

> You will say that I was puzzled; but, if you think so, you must have misunderstood the nature of the inductions. To use a sporting phrase, I had not been once "at fault." The scent had never for an instant been lost. There was no flaw in any link of the chain. I had traced the secret to its ultimate result,—and that result was *the nail*. It had, I say, in every respect, the appearance of its fellow in the other window; but this fact was an absolute nullity (conclusive as it might seem to be) when compared with the consideration that here, at this point, terminated the clew. "There *must* be something wrong," I said, "about the nail." I touched it; and the head, with about a quarter of an inch of the shank, came off in my fingers. The rest of the shank was in the gimlet-hole, where it had been broken off. (2:553)

The murderer had indeed, then, exited through this window, with the hidden spring automatically fastening the lowered sash, and the police mistaking "the retention of this spring" (2:554) for that of the apparently undamaged nail. Dupin's description of the unbroken, step-by-step process that led him to the nail is significant for several reasons. First, the "clew" that terminates at the nail clearly suggests, in the context of the imagery of following a marked path (i.e., tracking a scent), that Poe is using the word here to evoke both its literal, original meaning and also that mythic account of following a thread out of a labyrinth from which the word derives its standard figurative meaning, and that he is doing so precisely because of (and perhaps to call attention to) the structural similarity between a locked-room mystery and a labyrinth. In both, the problem is one of understanding how an apparently exitless enclosure may be exited, in one instance by following a figurative clue that leads to the discovery of the criminal's "means of egress," in the other by following a literal clew that leads out of the maze. (One might note here in passing that Poe's image of a clew terminating at a nail in the exit's frame implicitly raises the question of how Theseus kept the thread in place at the labyrinth's entrance as he unwound the clew along his path. Although the question is not addressed in any of the major classical versions of the myth, the Scholiast on Apollodorus explains that Theseus fastened "one end of the thread to the lintel of the door on entering into the labyrinth" [Apollodorus, 2:135 n. 3], and one might easily imagine the thread's being tied to a nail driven into the lintel.)

What seems clear is that Borges's antithetical reading/rewriting of the Dupin stories registers not only the resemblance between the mystery of a locked room and the puzzle of a labyrinth, but also the resemblance between these two structures and the purloined letter. The basic similarity of the three turns upon each one's problematic representation of the relationship between inner and outer. In a locked-room mystery, for example, the notion that a solid body requires a physical opening to pass from inside a room to outside it seems to have been violated. Inside the room there is physical evidence, usually a dead body, of the earlier presence of another body in the room, that of the killer. But when the room, with all its entrances locked from within, is broken into by the police, that other physical body is absent—a situation that seems to question assumptions as basic as the physical continuity of inner and outer and the noninterpenetrability of solid bodies. A locked-room mystery confronts us with an enclosure that appears, from both inside and outside, to be unopened, indeed unopenable without there being left some physical trace of the operation, such as a broken lock from the police's forced entry or an unfastened window from the murderer's escape. The solution generally involves showing that the room's appearance of being unopened is only an appearance, an illusory outer show that does not represent an inner reality.

In contrast to the locked room, a labyrinth is always open from the outside but appears to be unopenable from within. It permits a physical body access to its interior but denies it exit by subtly disrupting the link between relative and absolute bearing, by confusing the self's control of itself through the disorientation of the body. A labyrinth is in a sense a self-locking enclosure that uses the body's directionality as the bolt in the lock.

The relationship of inner and outer is even more problematic in the case of the purloined letter, for there it is a matter not only of the letter's being turned inside out as part of its concealment in the open, but also of whether the letter is hidden inside or outside a given physical space, the minister's house. During the prefect's account of his minute but unsuccessful search of the minister's dwelling, the question arises as to whether the minister might in fact carry the letter about with him or whether he might have "concealed it elsewhere than upon his own premises" (3:978).

The prefect maintains that the letter cannot possibly be in the minister's possession, since he has twice had the minister "waylaid, as if by footpads, and his person rigorously searched" (3:979). As to the letter's being hidden somewhere other than the minister's house, Dupin reasons that since "the instant availability of the document—its susceptibility of being produced at a moment's notice" is "a point of nearly equal importance with its possession" (3:978), the letter must be hidden in the minister's residence.

The mystery depends, of course, on this rigorous circumscription of the letter's possible hiding places. If the minister had the whole world in which to conceal the letter, what would be mysterious about the prefect's inability to find it? Only because it is logically certain that the letter is hidden in a specific finite enclosure whose space has been painstakingly searched does its continued nonappearance become mysterious. All of which is to say that as opposed to a locked-room mystery in which the criminal's patent absence from an internally sealed space constitutes the problem, the mystery of the purloined letter turns upon an object's unperceived presence within what we might call an externally sealed space, a space that is closed off not physically but logically, since all the possible external hiding places for the object must be analytically eliminated if there is to be something odd about the object's nonappearance. A locked-room mystery asks how a solid body got out of (or into) an internally sealed space without violating the space's appearance of closure, while a hidden-object mystery asks how a solid object remains present within a finite physical space without, as it were, making an appearance. In one case we are certain that what we seek is not inside a given space, in the other that what we seek cannot possibly be outside it.

Part of the peculiar force of hidden-object and locked-room detective stories is that they seem to present us with a physical embodiment, a concrete spatialization, of that very mechanism of logical inclusion/ exclusion on which rational analysis is based, indeed, present this as an apparent confounding of rational analysis. In the case of the purloined letter the problematic relationship of inner and outer takes on an added twist. For while the object must be present *inside* the minister's house without its making an appearance, the relationship of appearance to reality as outer to inner is itself further put in play by the fact that the object is hidden *out in the open* within this enclosed space. The letter is concealed in plain sight on the surface, *on the outside of this inside* (the house), a concealment accomplished by, and symbolized in, the turning of the letter itself inside out. Thus everted, its outside—the part of the letter whose appearance is known to the prefect and Dupin from the queen's description, the part that usually serves to conceal, to envelop, the letter's contents—now becomes the content to be concealed from the eyes of the police; while the inside—the reality that gives this letter its special significance, the part of it that is not known to the prefect and Dupin—becomes a new outside that gives the letter a different appearance.

Analyzing the structure of hidden-object and locked-room mysteries in terms of an inner/outer problematic not only allows us to see that the first and last Dupin stories are variations on the same mystery of consciousness, it also reveals a further link between these stories and the labyrinth, a link involving the intersection of the inner/outer and right/left oppositions. Recall that Poe compares the turning of the letter inside out to the turning of a glove, and that the reversal of a glove's inner and outer surfaces is also a reversal of its handedness. But the reversal of inner and outer depends upon the fact that these two poles are not separate entities but opposing aspects of the same entity. And this sense of inner and outer as opposing appearances presented by a single continuous surface recalls one of the traditional methods for finding the center of and, more important, the exit from a labyrinth, a method that works by aligning the continuity of the inner and outer surfaces with the handedness of the individual exploring the labyrinth. In *Mazes and Labyrinths*, W. H. Matthews describes the method's application to the navigation of a hedge maze:

> When it is impracticable to place marks, or even to use, like Theseus, a clue of thread, it is still possible in the majority of cases to make certain of finding the goal by the simple expedient of placing one hand on the hedge on entering the maze, and consistently following the hedge around, keeping contact all the time with the same hand. Blind turnings present no difficulty, as they will only be traversed first in one direction and then in the other. The traveller being guided by his contact with the hedge alone is relieved of all necessity for making a choice of paths when arriving at the nodes.
>
> The only case in which this method breaks down is that in which the goal is situated anywhere within a loop. Where this occurs the explorer adopting the method described will discover the fact by finding himself eventually back at the starting-point without having visited the goal. (*ML*, 191)

This method postulates that if the interior and exterior surfaces of a labyrinth are continuous, so that the inner surface inevitably leads back to the outer, then the inner surface can guide one back to the exit, if one can find a way of maintaining the body's orientation in relation to this surface. And that constant orientation of the body is established, of course, by the uninterrupted use of the same hand to trace the continuity. Suppose, for example, that on entering a labyrinth we decide to use the wall on our right as the guiding thread into and out of the maze and, as we begin walking, guide our progress by keeping our right hand in contact with the wall. We will, as Matthews notes, eventually trace the interior surface of the entire labyrinth and return to the entry point. But the wall that was on our right as we entered, and with which we maintained continuous contact, will as we return be on our left, and the wall which on exiting we touch with the right hand will be the one that was on our left as we entered. All of which is a way of saying that on returning to the entry point we will be facing the other way, outward from the labyrinth rather than into it.

This rather involved description is necessary to make clear the connection between the structure of a labyrinth and the structure that Poe proposes for the purloined letter by comparing its everting to that of a glove. In everting a glove, the inner and outer surfaces exchange places. This movement reverses not only the glove's handedness, but also the direction in which its fingers point. Imagine a right-hand glove lying palm downward on a flat surface with its fingers pointing away from us; if we turn it inside out while maintaining its palm-downward orientation, we will have a left-hand glove with its fingers pointing toward us. In following the interior surface of a labyrinth to its exit, we are exploiting the same topological phenomenon that makes possible the turning of a glove. The difference, of course, is that in turning a glove the surface continuity is traced by *the movement of the surface itself*, while in navigating a labyrinth the continuity is traced by *the movement of a hand along the surface*. Nevertheless, the various reversals effected by these movements correspond: as the glove's inner surface becomes its outer, the direction in which its fingers point and its handedness are reversed; and as the labyrinth's inner surface leads us back to the entrance, the direction in which we are facing is reversed, as well as what we might call the handedness of the wall (the wall that was on our right on entering is now on our left).

What all this suggests is that the labyrinth derives its special appeal for Borges in part from the fact that it combines the features of both Poe's locked room and his purloined letter in a single structure, a fact Borges seems to acknowledge at the start of "Ibn Hakkan al-Bokhari" (the only one of his detective stories to contain a real rather than symbolic labyrinth) when he invokes the purloined letter and locked room as examples of the simplicity he considers essential to true mystery. To Dunraven's listing of the oddities surrounding the case, Unwin replies, "Don't go on multiplying the mysteries. . . . They should be kept simple. Bear in mind Poe's purloined letter, bear in mind Zangwill's locked room." Having returned once more to this passage in exploring Borges's detective story labyrinth, we can now appreciate that the simplicity Borges commends in citing the purloined letter and locked room is that single-fold sameness which, by turning in or bending back upon itself, produces a difference with/in itself, creates a mutually constitutive opposition between aspects of the same entity (like that between the inner and outer surfaces of a labyrinth or a letter). And this notion of dual, opposing aspects of a single entity, aspects that are reversible because of the continuity of their ground, evokes not only the physical structure of the labyrinth in "Ibn Hakkan al-Bokhari," but also the solution to the murder committed within it: the fact that a single person plays a dual role in order to commit the crime and escape without his presence being detected—the murderer Zaid masquerading as the victim in order to lure the real Ibn Hakkan into the labyrinth and leave him dead in his place.

What is particularly significant in the passage quoted above from "Ibn Hakkan al-Bokhari" is that Borges refers to "Poe's purloined letter" but not to "Poe's locked room," an odd omission given that "The Murders in the Rue Morgue" is generally acknowledged as not only the first detective story but also the first locked-room mystery. Instead, Borges specifically refers to "Zangwill's locked room," a much later example of the locked-room problem from the English author Israel Zangwill's novella *The Big Bow Mystery* (1892). But the omission as regards Poe is only apparent, for anyone familiar with the novella knows that the reference to Zangwill's story is a veiled allusion not only to "The Murders in the Rue Morgue" but also to the very notion of an analytic detective story tradition, a tradition constituted precisely by the self-conscious relatedness of later detective stories to the Dupin tales as origin. Consequently, before we can fully appreciate the reading of Poe's locked-room problem that Borges gives in his detective stories, we must digress for a moment to consider the reading Zangwill gives in his.

20 The Big Bow Mystery; *Poe's Locked Room and the Sense of a Tradition; The Collapsing of Roles into One; An Original Solution; The Locked Room's Solution as Hidden Object; The Locked Room and Handedness*

ZANGWILL'S *The Big Bow Mystery* begins with the discovery of Arthur Constant's body by his landlady and her neighbor, retired police detective George Grodman. When Constant does not appear at breakfast one morning or respond to a knock on his locked bedroom door, the landlady Mrs. Drabdump summons Grodman who breaks open the door and discovers the young man in bed with his throat cut. Examining the room, Grodman finds that the windows are bolted from the inside and that the only door has not only been locked with a key from within but fastened a second time on the inside by a slide bolt. Grodman also discovers that though Constant's throat has apparently been cut with a razor, there is no instrument in the room capable of inflicting the wound. As a result, at the inquest there is a balance between evidence appearing to rule out the possibility of murder (i.e., the locked room) and evidence appearing to rule out the possibility of suicide (i.e., the absence of a weapon). The jury cannot agree on a decision, although one juror "insists on a verdict of 'Death from visitation by the act of God.'"[1]

While the authorities are unable to solve the mystery, the letter writers to the popular press are far from stumped. One of these correspondents, "a professional paradox-monger," pointed

> triumphantly to the somewhat similar situation in "the murder in the Rue Morgue," and said that Nature had been plagiarising again—like the monkey she was—and he recommended Poe's publishers to apply for an injunction. More seriously, Poe's solution was re-suggested by "Constant Reader" as an original idea. He thought that a small organ-grinder's monkey might have got down the chimney with its master's razor, and, after attempting to shave the occupant of the bed, have returned the way it came. This idea created considerable sensation, but a correspondent . . . pointed out that a monkey small enough to get down so narrow a flue would not be strong enough to inflict so deep a wound. This was disputed by a third writer. . . . The bubble was pricked by the pen of "Common Sense," who laconically remarked that no traces of soot or blood had been discovered on the floor, or on the nightshirt, or the counterpane. (*BBM*, 176–77)

In calling attention to the resemblance between his novella and Poe's first detective story, Zangwill not only locates his work in the tradition of locked-room mysteries begun by "The Murders in the Rue Morgue," but also alerts the reader to a series of more or less subtle allusions to Poe throughout the story. Thus, for example, one of the characters in the novella is a down-at-heels poet named Denzil Cantercot given to using the word *nevermore* (*BBM*, 197) at dramatic moments. Cantercot supports himself by doing prose piecework, one of his projects having been the ghostwriting of George Grodman's memoirs, *Criminals I Have Caught*. The combination of Grodman's experience and Cantercot's artistry is characterized by Cantercot as a blending of the former's "cold, lucid, scientific" qualities with the latter's poetry (*BBM*, 199), a blend probably meant to recall Poe's notion of the analytic power as a combination of the creative and resolvent personified as poet and mathematician. We should, however, be a bit skeptical of Zangwill's openness in pointing out the resemblance between his story and Poe's, for it may simply be sleight of hand— his open acknowledgment of a device borrowed from the first Dupin story in effect concealing a stratagem borrowed from the third, that of hiding something most effectively by hiding it in the open.

After the passage of several weeks, Edward Wimp, Grodman's successor at Scotland Yard, causes a sensation by arresting the young political agitator Tom Mortlake for Constant's murder. In the course of his investigation, Wimp has discovered that Mortlake, an acquaintance of Constant's, had apparently been his rival both professionally and for the affections of a young woman and that, in addition, Mortlake had once lodged in the room where Constant was murdered and thus had a key to the locked room. He theorizes that Mortlake, using this key to enter Constant's bedroom, killed his sleeping rival, and then, leaving Constant's own key set loosely in the lock on the inside so as not to impede the locking mechanism, he locked the door from the outside with his own key. But since this solution leaves unanswered the problem of the second fastening on the door (the slide bolt that can only be locked from the inside), Wimp further theorizes that before leaving the room Mortlake pried "the staple containing the bolt from the woodwork" (*BBM*, 268), so that when Grodman broke open the locked door (a door fastened only by the keyed lock) and saw the staple "torn away from the lintel" (*BBM*, 269), he assumed he had broken the staple of the fastened slide bolt in forcing his way in.

Although the evidence against Mortlake is circumstantial, he is tried, found guilty, and condemned to death. However, in thinking over Wimp's solution to the locked-room mystery, the reader begins to suspect Zangwill's candor in pointing out the resemblance between the situation in his novella and Poe's first Dupin story, particularly since the immediate effect of this gesture is to dismiss the significance of the resemblance, it being clearly nonsense to think that the murder was committed, as "Constant Reader" suggests, by "a small organ-grinder's monkey" that had gotten "down the chimney with its master's razor." But of course Zangwill, in the guise of "Constant Reader," has misrepresented Poe's story. First, and most obviously, Poe's ape does not come down the chimney; indeed, Poe specifically notes that the chimney in the L'Espanaye apartment would not at its narrowest point admit the body of a large cat. Second, and more importantly, in Poe's story the bizarre identity of the killer is not, strictly speaking, the solution to the locked-room mystery. The solution to this problem is the two different locks on the window, one that can be locked from the outside (the concealed spring) and is actually fastened, another that can be locked only from the inside (the nail in the frame) and is only apparently fastened (the broken nail). And it is, of course, this solution that Edward Wimp reproduces almost exactly. There are two locks on Constant's door, one that can be locked from the outside (the keyed lock) and is actually fastened, another that can be locked only from the inside (the slide bolt) but is only apparently fastened (the broken staple). When one realizes that Zangwill has made Wimp reinvent Poe's solution as his own, one appreciates the wittiness of Zangwill's clue, in commenting on the theory of the razor-wielding monkey, that "Poe's solution" had been "re-suggested by 'Constant Reader' as an original idea," a comment not at all appropriate to Constant Reader's solution (which is not Poe's) but only too appropriate to Wimp's.

But Zangwill has even more tricks up his sleeve. As the date of Tom Mortlake's execution approaches, George Grodman reinvolves himself in the case to try to prove Mortlake's innocence. At the last possible moment, Grodman arrives at the residence of the Home Secretary to announce that he has solved the crime and that Mortlake is not the killer. As the Home Secretary listens in mounting disbelief, Grodman explains that it was he (Grodman) who killed Arthur Constant, not out of enmity but out of the pure "desire to commit a crime that should baffle detection" (BBM, 303), in particular, baffle detection by Edward Wimp, Grodman's successor at Scotland Yard whose reputation had begun to eclipse Grodman's own. The victim, Arthur Constant, had simply been a target of opportunity, though Grodman does wryly admit that it was Constant's humanitarian-ism that recommended him: "He was a lovable young fellow, an excellent subject for experiment. . . . From the moment I first set eyes on him, there was a peculiar sympathy between us. . . . I felt instinctively he would be the man. I loved to hear him speak enthusiastically of the Brotherhood of Man—I, who knew the brotherhood of man was to the ape, the serpent, and the tiger" (BBM, 304). Although Zangwill's killer is not a razor-wielding ape, he is, to judge by these remarks, someone who understands only too well the meaning embodied in the first Dupin story's manlike killer animal: that the duel between protagonists in an analytic detective story externalizes the struggle between the animal and human elements in the self, the struggle to prevent a master/slave reversal that would put human reason in the service of instinctual ferocity.

Having decided on Constant as the most likely (and most worthy) victim, Grodman devises a plan of startling simplicity and waits for his chance. On the evening before the murder, Constant pays a social call on Grodman, and in the course of their conversation he mentions that he has been suffering from a toothache and in consequence has gotten very little sleep. Seeing the elements for enacting his plan come together, Grodman uses an image Borges must have appreciated, "Of old I should have connected these . . . facts and sought the thread; now, as he spoke, all my thoughts were dyed red" (*BBM,* 305). Grodman makes Constant "promise to secure a night's rest . . . by taking a sleeping draught" and gives him "a quantity of sulfonal in a phial," a "new drug, which produces protracted sleep" (*BBM,* 305). He also makes him promise "to bolt and bar and lock himself in so as to stop up every chink or aperture by which the cold air of the winter's night might creep into the room" (*BBM,* 305). Constant leaves, and Grodman waits for morning to see if the second stage of his plan can be put into effect. The key to this second stage, as Grodman explains to the Home Secretary, is "feminine psychology" (*BBM,* 306), that is, Grodman's knowledge of his neighbor Mrs. Drabdump's personality and her probable conduct in the situation he has contrived. For what Grodman expects is that when Constant does not appear for breakfast or respond to the knock at his locked door, Mrs. Drabdump will imagine the worst, rush hysterically from the house in search of help, and come straight to her neighbor the retired police detective, who will be waiting in his house across the street, with his razor in his pocket. (The date, by the way, is December 4, the same date [using the Hebrew system of reckoning the start of a new day at sundown] as that of the first murder in "Death and the Compass." And of course Grodman's plan to kill Constant had been put in motion on the previous evening, December 3.)

The plan works perfectly, with the result that Grodman is the first person to enter the locked room:

> As I broke open the door of the bedroom in which Arthur Constant lay sleeping, his head resting on his hands, I cried, "My God!" as if I saw some awful vision. A mist as of blood swam before Mrs. Drabdump's eyes. She cowered back, for an instant (I divined rather than saw the action) she shut off the dreaded sight with her hands. In that instant I had made my cut—

precisely, scientifically. . . . I covered up the face quickly with a handkerchief to hide any convulsive distortion. But as the medical evidence (in this detail accurate) testified, death was instantaneous. I pocketed the razor and the empty sulfonal phial. With a woman like Mrs. Drabdump to watch me, I could do anything I pleased. (*BBM*, 307–8)

Grodman admits that his decision to reveal himself as the murderer was prompted not by concern for Mortlake—he cares no more for Mortlake's life than he did for Constant's—but by his desire to prevent Wimp from gaining credit for having solved a mystery contrived precisely "to shake his reputation," indeed, solved it "by dint of a colossal mistake" (*BBM*, 311). The final revelation, however, belongs to the Home Secretary: he had just reprieved Mortlake on the basis of new evidence only moments before Grodman arrived, so that "Wimp's card-castle would have tumbled to pieces" (*BBM*, 313) without Grodman's assistance. As the Home Secretary watches, Grodman draws a pistol and shoots himself through the heart.

In the classic pattern of analytic detection, Zangwill's tale involves a battle of wits between detective and criminal, but in this case the splitting/doubling that links the roles of detective, criminal, and victim is so circumscribed, so doubled back upon itself—the three roles seeming at first to be filled by three persons, then two, then one—that the resulting intellectual duel turns out to be a highly oblique one. Wimp, for example, never realizes during the contest that his opponent is Grodman. The role of the detective is, of course, split and doubled at the start with both Grodman and Wimp involved in the case. And this division/duplication is further compounded by one of the detectives also being the criminal and the other, in effect, the intended victim. For clearly the real aim of Grodman's plan is not the death of the ostensible victim Constant (anyone could have served as the corpse, says Grodman) but the victimizing of Grodman's analytic rival Wimp, who is to be presented with a sensational, insoluble mystery that will remain a permanent blot on his reputation. And indeed the retired detective seems to have achieved his goal when the coroner's jury cannot decide on a verdict. But, as Grodman admits to the Home Secretary, his "own ingenuity" (*BBM*, 310) would not let him rest with this success. In language suggesting his divided, dual status, Grodman remarks,

I tried to stand outside myself, and to look at the crime with the eyes of another, or of my old self. I found the work of art so perfect as to leave only one sublimely simple solution. The very terms of the problem were so inconceivable that, had I not been the murderer, I should have suspected myself, in conjunction, of course, with Mrs. Drabdump. The first persons to enter the room would have seemed to me guilty. I wrote at once (in a disguised hand and over the signature of "One who looks through his own spectacles") to the *Pell Mell Press* to suggest this. By associating myself thus with Mrs. Drabdump I made it difficult for people to dissociate the two who entered the room together. To dash a half-truth in the world's eyes is the surest way of blinding it altogether. This pseudonymous letter of mine I contradicted (in my own name) the next day, and in the course of the long letter which I was tempted to write, I adduced fresh evidence against the theory of suicide. (*BBM*, 310)

But with this last flourish Grodman overreaches himself, for the evidence he presents against the theory of suicide is so convincing and his comments on Scotland Yard's ineptitude in handling the case so stinging that Wimp applies himself with renewed energy to the mystery and ultimately "by dint of persistent blundering" stumbles "into a track which— by a devilish tissue of coincidences . . . —seemed to the world the true" (*BBM*, 311). Since Grodman's aim had been to produce a sensational mystery his successor couldn't solve, the public's acceptance of Wimp's solution threatens to give the victory to his opponent and thus compels Grodman to take up the role of detective again (in effect, to revert to his "old self") and produce the correct solution, apprehending himself in the process. Yet since it is Wimp's blundering (that is, his ingenuity in finding a plausible solution to the locked-room problem) that ultimately causes the criminal's discovery, the question of who won the battle of wits remains open—a not-unexpected outcome in the analytic detective genre, where winning a mental duel with an antithetical double means defeating a specular image of one's own mind.

The self-enclosed character of this intellectual battle is emphasized by the progressive centering of the three roles of criminal, detective, and victim in one person. Early in the tale, these roles appear to be filled respectively by Mortlake, Wimp, and Constant. But with Grodman's revelation of the mental duel that forms the story's real action, they seem to be filled by only two people—the detective/criminal Grodman and the detective/intended victim Wimp. Yet by the story's end, all the roles in the analytic contest have been played by Grodman—the detective/criminal whose overreaching ingenuity forces him to solve his own crime and thus, in the last analysis, to victimize himself, as symbolized by his death at his own hand. One is reminded of Borges's remark, in the note to "Death and the Compass," that since "the killer and the slain, whose minds work in the same way, may be the same man," Lönnrot, in "walking into his own death trap," is "in a symbolic way, a man committing suicide."

The mental duel between detective and criminal is not, however, the only battle of wits in Zangwill's novella. In drawing attention to the resemblance between his locked-room mystery and Poe's original, Zangwill suggests a contest of ingenuity between himself and Poe as writers of detective fiction. The locked-room problem Poe created in his first detective story exists for his successors in the tradition as *the problem of Poe's solution to the locked room,* that is, the problem of whether there is only one solution to such a mystery (the two-lock ploy invented by Poe) or whether other original solutions are possible. Indeed, it would seem that Zangwill's ultimate purpose in first citing "The Murders in the Rue Morgue" and then having Wimp unwittingly reproduce Poe's ploy was to set up a direct contest between Poe's solution and his own, a contest Zangwill wins not so much because Poe's solution turns out in this case to be incorrect but because Zangwill actually succeeds in producing an original alternative—the killer is the first person to break into the room.

However, the battle of wits between Zangwill and Poe does not end here. It goes on to encompass another intellectual duel characteristic of the genre as originated by Poe (the battle of wits between writer and reader) and another mystery from Poe's third detective story (the hidden-object problem). By presenting early in the novella the correct solution to the locked-room mystery through the device of Grodman's writing a pseudonymous letter to the press pointing out the only possible answer (a letter printed in the text of the story, along with the reply Grodman writes in his own name), Zangwill makes, I would argue, an essentially correct interpretation of the hidden-object problem's significance within the structure of the genre, an interpretation that sees this device as having been generated precisely by the battle of wits between writer and reader.

As we noted, that battle in an analytic detective story is typically a contest to see if the reader can solve the mystery before the detective does. Obviously, the contest depends upon the writer's playing fair by giving the reader access to the same clues the detective has, so as to make it a contest of attention and reasoning. And it is in light of this contest that we can understand the significance of Poe's hidden-object problem, for although this problem seems at first glance to be simply one type of story within the genre, there is a sense in which every analytic detective story, as a contest between writer and reader for priority of solution, is a hidden-object problem—the object in question being the mystery's solution, that is, the clue or clues that must, if the writer plays fairly, be hidden in plain view on the surface of the same text that presents the mystery. This is why the hidden object in Poe's story is specifically a text whose distinctive feature is its susceptibility to being concealed in the open, a text whose specific manner of concealment at the minister's residence (its being everted and exposed to view) is itself hidden out in the open in Poe's text when the prefect tells Dupin at the start how the queen tried to hide the letter in plain sight on a table. As we noted earlier, the larger mystery evoked by the purloined letter concerns the way the metaphysicality of meaning is contained or concealed on the physical surface of writing, but the immediate form this larger mystery takes in the story is the concealment of that special meaning whose pursuit animates the genre—the mystery's solution. The brilliance of Zangwill's interpretation of Poe's hidden-object problem (and thus of his reading of its relationship to the locked-room problem) is that Zangwill hides the solution to his own locked-room mystery in plain sight within the text by means of a letter (Grodman's pseudonymous missive to the press) that, like Poe's purloined letter, is in effect turned inside out and exposed to public view, a letter whose contents are published in a newspaper. In revealing the correct solution to the mystery, Grodman's letter also evokes the split and doubled self of its author, the split being suggested by the "half-truth" which associates the guilty Grodman with the innocent other (Mrs. Drabdump) and the doubling by the reply in Grodman's own name contradicting the letter. Indeed, the detail of Grodman's writing the pseudonymous letter "in a disguised hand" may even be an antithetical allusion to the letter Dupin leaves in place of the purloined letter to reveal his identity to the minister—an unsigned letter disclosing its author's name through his recognizable hand.

From our description of Zangwill's novella, the extent of its influence on and thus its importance as an allusive background to Borges's own contest with Poe should be clear. Borges's reference to "Zangwill's locked room" seems meant at once to acknowledge the influence and invoke the background. Among the many things Borges would have found useful in *The Big Bow Mystery*, perhaps the most significant for our purposes is Zangwill's explicit linking of the locked-room problem to the question of handedness, that is, to the same question that Poe associates with the purloined letter both when he compares the turning of the letter to the everting of a glove and when he has Dupin reveal himself through his familiar hand in the substituted letter. One of the mysteries presented by Constant's death concerns the direction of the wound on his throat. To pose the problem in the coroner's words:

> The medical evidence says deceased was lying with his hands clasped behind his head. Now the wound was made from right to left, and terminated by a cut on the left thumb. If the deceased had made it he would have had to do it with his right hand, while his left hand remained under his head—a most peculiar and unnatural position to assume. Moreover, in making a cut with the right hand, one would naturally move the hand from left to right. It is unlikely that the deceased would move his right hand so awkwardly and unnaturally, unless,

of course, his object was to baffle suspicion. Another point is that on this hypothesis, the deceased would have had to replace his right hand beneath his head. But Dr. Robinson believes that death was instantaneous. If so, deceased could have had no time to pose so neatly. It is just possible the cut was made with the left hand, but then the deceased was right-handed. (*BBM*, 168–69)

And even if we suppose that Constant *had* used his left hand, there would still have been no time for him to place this hand behind his head if death were instantaneous. Nor would his using his left hand explain the cut on his left thumb that terminated the right-to-left direction of the throat wound. Given that Poe evokes the mysterious nature of handedness through the figure of turning a glove, should we add, in good detective fashion, that Zangwill specifically locates his locked room in a house on "Glover Street" (*BBM*, 136)?

Certainly, we can recognize, in Zangwill's raising the issue of handedness within the context of a locked-room mystery, a mingling of elements from "The Murders in the Rue Morgue" and "Maelzel's Chess-Player." It is as if in his imagination part of the "Rue Morgue"'s action (the animal slave's imitating its human master shaving himself in a mirror, as a prelude to its casting off that mastery by cutting another's throat in the repetition of the imitated act) had been combined with a key notion from the essay (the idea of dominant handedness as a sign of the difference between a master mind and a slave mechanism) in order to produce the coding of handedness in *The Big Bow Mystery*.

Given that the usual method of cutting one's throat with a razor involves drawing the blade across the throat, Constant's right-handedness should have produced, if the wound was self-inflicted, a cut running from left to right rather than the right-to-left one found. The right-to-left wound would indicate the act was done by someone who stood on the left side of the bed and drew the razor across the victim's throat. What is significant here for our purposes is that Zangwill clearly connects the problem of the locked room—the question of whether the death is suicide or murder and thus whether the perpetrator we are seeking is the victim's self or another—with the victim's handedness and with the direction (given in terms of handedness, i.e., right/left) of a trace made by the V-shaped edge of a blade. Put in more general terms, we could say that in Zangwill's locked room the test that differentiates self and other is the relationship of the self's privileged hand to the right/left directionality of a division or split (the cut). Zangwill's association of these images with the locked room is significant precisely because a similar grouping of images is to be found around the Carian word *labrys* (a double axe), the generally accepted root of the word *labyrinth,* a grouping of images that we shall eventually examine in detail as we continue to follow the Borgesian thread linking the labyrinth and the myth of Theseus to the analytic detective story.

21 *The Battle of Wits between Writer and Reader;*
A Clue to a Clew; The Coding of Head and Body;
Dupin's Doubleness

TO PICK UP THAT THREAD again, we must return to the passage in "The Murders in the Rue Morgue" where Dupin explains how a process of logical elimination led him to the broken nail at which "terminated the clew." As I suggested earlier, the passage is significant for reasons that go beyond its association of locked room and labyrinth through the image of a threadlike clew leading to an entrance/exit. It marks as well, for example, a crucial moment in the development of the battle of wits between writer and reader in the analytic detective genre. At this point in Poe's first detective story, Dupin is about to reveal the solution to the tale's initial mystery (the locked-room problem) as a prelude to revealing the tale's principal mystery (the identity of the killer). Dupin's method of revelation in both instances is not a sudden announcement of his conclusions but rather a gradual presentation of his train of thought, a retelling of the crime or re-presentation of the scene that indicates and organizes salient points in a way that might, but does not, enable the listener—Dupin's unnamed companion—to anticipate the detective's conclusions. Moreover, Dupin conceives of this method of revelation as a game played with his friend the narrator, for in addition to showing him the clues that influenced his own deductions, Dupin gives the narrator added hints—often in the imagery he uses to characterize a situation—that point to the ultimate solution. For example, in describing the reasoning process that led him to the nail, he says, "To use a sporting phrase, I had not been once 'at fault.' The scent had never for an instant been lost. . . . I had traced the secret to its ultimate result,—and that result was *the nail.* . . . Here, at this point, terminated the clew" (2:553). Although Dupin is describing how he solved the locked-room problem, the imagery—"a sporting phrase," the "scent" that "had never . . . been lost"—hints at the solution to the larger mystery of the killer's identity by evoking the sport of hunting and thus suggesting that the object of Dupin's pursuit is in fact an animal. And since human hunters do not have the olfactory ability to track game by scent, there is perhaps a hint here as well of an animal quality to Dupin (the traditional image of the sleuth as bloodhound) of which we will have more to say later. Dupin's suggestion that the culprit is nonhuman is reinforced, of course, by the image of the threadlike clew, for while the thread followed one way in the Theseus myth leads back to the entrance, the thread running the other way marks the track Theseus took in hunting down the Minotaur.

The game Dupin plays with the narrator is at once a part and a figure of the game the author plays with the reader, as Poe suggests by making the terminus of the clew (the problem's solution) a nail, thereby testing the reader's linguistic skill and attention. Dupin is, of course, French; and although the narrator's nationality is not specified, he does reside in Paris, so we can take it that he is fluent in the language. Consequently, we can assume that Dupin's conversations in English with the narrator represent the tale's "translations," as it were, of ones originally conducted in Dupin's native tongue. As we recall, Dupin's account of his solution to the locked-room problem minutely describes the two windows at the rear of the victims' apartment, mentioning again and again the nail inserted in each window frame. And, of course, the French word for *nail,* the word Dupin would have used repeatedly, is *clou.* Which is simply Poe's way of giving the reader a linguistic clue (hint) that the clew (thread) will ultimately terminate at a *clou* (nail)—although even the most attentive reader will probably experience this pun as a clue only retrospectively, so that Poe remains one up. But there is more at work here than just a pun, for the structure of this linguistic clue—two words with similar sounds but different meanings (a hidden, i.e., metaphysical, difference)—mirrors the structure of the solution to which the threadlike clew leads—two windows apparently "identical in character" (2:553) but with a hidden difference, a concealed break in the *clou* embedded in one of them. (In this connection we should note that in the bilingual pair clew/*clou* with their phonetic similarity and their orthographic and lexical differences, the English half is split and doubled again—clew/clue—by an orthographic difference and a phonetic and lexical sameness.) The hidden difference between the windows is hinted at in Dupin's first description of them: "There are two windows in the chamber. One of them is unobstructed by furniture, and is wholly visible. The lower portion of the other is hidden from view by the head of the unwieldy bedstead which is thrust close up against it" (2:551). The window whose "lower portion . . . is hidden from view by the head" of the bed is, of course, the same window in which the broken, lower portion of the nail is hidden from view by the nail's undamaged head. The language of the subsequent passage in which Dupin recounts his discovery of the break in the nail clearly echoes his earlier description of the windows:

> I touched it; and the head, with about a quarter of an inch of the shank, came off in my fingers. The rest of the shank was in the gimlet-hole, where it had

been broken off. The fracture was an old one (for its edges were incrusted with rust), and had apparently been accomplished by the blow of a hammer, which had partially *imbedded*, in the top of the bottom sash, *the head portion* of the nail. I now carefully replaced this head portion in the indentation whence I had taken it, and the resemblance to a perfect nail was complete—the fissure was invisible. Pressing the spring, I gently raised the sash for a few inches; the head went up with it, remaining firm in *its bed*. I closed the window, and the semblance of the whole nail was again perfect.

The riddle, so far, was now unriddled. (2:553, italics mine)

Clearly, Poe is playing a game of verbal clues with the reader in having the head of the bed conceal the lower portion of the same window in which the head of the nail, "firm in its bed," conceals the broken shank. Moreover, in the very act of unriddling one riddle, he leads us to another, for he gives us a clue not just to the solution of the locked-room problem (the broken *clou*) but also to a larger pattern of imagery that runs through the entire story and hints at both the identity of the killer and the meaning of the tale—I refer to the tale's recurring allusions to decapitation, the separating of a higher portion from a lower. The most striking instance is literal, the corpse of Mme. L'Espanaye. In the words of the newspaper account of the body's discovery:

After a thorough investigation of every portion of the house, without farther discovery, the party made its way into a small paved yard in the rear of the building, where lay the corpse of the old lady, with her throat so entirely cut that, upon an attempt to raise her, the head fell off. The body, as well as the head, was fearfully mutilated—the former so much so as scarcely to retain any semblance of humanity.

To this horrible mystery there is not as yet, we believe, the slightest clew. (2:538)

Poe indicates the significance of this head/body separation when he notes that the torso was so badly mutilated "as scarcely to retain any semblance of humanity": that is, in the differential relationship he sets up between head and body, Poe codes the body as nonhuman (lacking "any semblance of humanity") and thus the head as human in opposition—the standard equation of head, mind, rationality, humanity on the one hand, and of body, instinct, irrationality, animality on the other. The concluding image of "the clew" links the puzzle of Mme. L'Espanaye's corpse being found *outside* the locked room to the nail that is the solution to the locked-room mystery. And this linking of the corpse, whose head has been severed from its body, to the nail, whose head is broken from its shank, reinforces our interpretation of the clew-leading-to-the-nail as an allusion to the myth of Theseus and the labyrinth. For while one end of Theseus's clew marks the labyrinth's entrance and exit, the other, as we noted, marks the location of the corpse of the labyrinth's inhabitant, a creature itself characterized by a head/body separation. The Minotaur, with its animal head and human torso, symbolizes the destructive reversal of the proper relationship between mind and body in man, the kind of reversal that occurs, for example, when instinctual ferocity masters reason in the taking of a human life. (As we recall, the Minotaur is killed because it is a mankiller, the slaughterer of the Athenian youths sent to Crete every nine years as tribute.) And this same master/slave reversal is symbolized by the manlike killer-animal of "The Murders in the Rue Morgue," whose cries are mistaken for human speech, whose name literally means "man of the forest," and whose murderous rampage is triggered by its attempt to mimic a self-reflective action, its master's shaving himself in a mirror.

Dupin does not, of course, engage in a battle of wits with the unthinking killer of "The Murders in the Rue Morgue." Rather, in the absence of a rational culprit in the first analytic detective story, the mental duel between detective and criminal that will become the genre's mainstay is replaced by Dupin's outwitting of both the ape's master and the prefect of police. Dupin does not himself capture the ape, indeed, he never even sees it. It is only by outwitting the animal's master through a false newspaper advertisement luring him to Dupin's lodgings that Dupin is able to verify his theory of the killer's identity. We should also note that when Dupin later reveals the solution to the police, the prefect reacts to the amateur detective's analytic success as if it were very much a defeat for himself. Unable to "conceal his chagrin at the turn which affairs had taken," he remarks on "the propriety of every person minding his own business" (2:568).

Interestingly enough, Poe's imagery in describing the battle of wits between Dupin and the prefect tends to associate the prefect with Theseus's opponent in the labyrinth, even to the point of using a head/body separation to characterize the policeman's methods. Dupin says of the prefect,

> I am satisfied with having defeated him in his own castle. Nevertheless, that he failed in the solution of this mystery, is by no means that matter for wonder which he supposes it; for, in truth, our friend the Prefect is somewhat too cunning to be profound. In his wisdom is no *stamen*. It is all head and no body, like the pictures of the Goddess Laverna,—or, at best, all head and shoulders, like a codfish. But he is a good creature after all. (2:568)

As Theseus overcame the Minotaur in its dwelling, so Dupin defeats the prefect "in his own castle." And as Theseus's opponent was a creature with an animal head and a human body, so Dupin's opponent the prefect, "a good creature after all," is compared to a mythical being traditionally represented as a head without a body (Laverna, "the Roman goddess of thefts" [2:574 n. 40]) and an animal that is "all head and shoulders," the codfish. The point of this comparison, which figures the prefect's reasoning as "cunning" rather than "profound" (L. *profundus*, "deep, low"), as higher rather than lower ("all head and no body"), seems to be the same point Dupin makes in "The Purloined Letter"—that the prefect cannot imagine the workings of a mind substantially different from his own, a rule always true when the level of the other's intellect is above his own "and very usually when it is below" (3:985). These two extremes are illustrated by the prefect's failure to comprehend the operations of a mind (the minister's) almost superhuman in comparison to his and of a "mind" literally subhuman, the ape's.

That Dupin *does* recognize in the savagery of the L'Espanaye murders the signature of an animal mind is in some degree a function of Dupin's own doubleness—not that doubleness of the creative and resolvent elements in the self Dupin discusses in "The Purloined Letter," but rather a doubleness that makes the detective and the criminal reciprocals of one another, precisely because the impulses that have mastered the criminal are those that have been mastered in the detective. Dupin recognizes the marks of "*brutal* ferocity" (2:557) in the deed because it is an animal ferocity, an irrationality, that he knows exists within himself, an irrationality that grounds rationality as the physical body grounds the human mind. Summing up the distinctive marks of the criminal—"an agility astounding, a strength superhuman, a ferocity brutal, a butchery without motive, a *grotesquerie* in horror absolutely alien from humanity, and a voice foreign in tone to the ears of men of many nations, and devoid of all distinct or intelligible syllabification"—Dupin asks the narrator what this combination of features suggests, and the narrator replies, "A madman . . . has done this deed—some raving maniac, escaped from a neighboring *Maison de Santé*" (2:558). The response is significant because earlier, in describing his and Dupin's shared style of living as a reflection of "the rather fantastic gloom" of their "common temper," the narrator says, "Had the routine of our life . . . been known to the world, we should have been regarded as madmen—although, perhaps, as madmen of a harmless nature" (2:532). The fact that the ape's rampage and Dupin's fantastic temperament both suggest madness to the narrator underlines the instinctual, not to say irrational, element shared by the culprit and the detective. Indeed, one might interpret that intellectual power which both Poe and Dupin consider to be the culmination of rational analysis—the power of intuition—as being in large part the rational mind's reliance upon, its translation into consciousness of, the animal instincts of the body in which it is lodged, the kind of physical intuition whose lack prevents the prefect, with his all-head-and-no-body reasoning, from recognizing and interpreting the signs of *"brutal* ferocity" in the crime.

Theseus in the Locked Room; Oedipus and the Detective Story; "Thou Art the Man"; The Bible or Sophocles; Solving a Riddle and Enacting a Mystery

OUR ANALYSIS OF DUPIN'S INGENIOUSLY phrased solution to the locked-room problem suggests the care with which Poe constructed this passage in "The Murders in the Rue Morgue," indeed, suggests a poet's attention to word and image. And given this degree of attention (a degree characteristic of Poe's best stories), one naturally wonders why in his first detective story he subtly evokes the myth of the labyrinth through the images of a clew leading to an exit, a manlike animal adversary, and a head/body separation, yet does not explicitly invoke Theseus's encounter with the Minotaur as an analogue of Dupin's with the killer ape. Moreover, one wonders how Borges, who would use both the labyrinth image and the myth of the Minotaur in *his* detective stories, interpreted Poe's hints on the one hand and his reticence on the other, a reticence noteworthy not merely because it is uncharacteristic of Poe to miss the chance at a classical allusion (particularly one that draws a parallel between an ancient and a modern action), but because in the absence of such an explicit reference to Theseus and the Minotaur, another myth, as we noted, becomes associated with the analytic detective genre.

This is not to suggest that the association with Oedipus represents in any way a distortion of the genre. Indeed, if one had to choose a classical model for that innovation in the Gothic double story that Poe created in moving from "The Fall of the House of Usher" (1839) and "William Wilson" (1839) to the first Dupin story (1841), one would immediately think of Oedipus, with his double role as culprit and detective and his clear-sighted blindness in following clues that lead to a moment of blinding self-recognition. It is just that to judge from the structure of the first Dupin story, it seems not to have been the Greek myth that immediately occurred to Poe. But this may be only an appearance. We should not, at any rate, assume that the initial association of Oedipus with the analytic detective story occurred at a much later date, that it was, for example, a function of twentieth-century psychoanalytic readings of the Dupin stories such as Marie Bonaparte's analysis of "The Murders in the Rue Morgue" or Lacan's of "The Purloined Letter." Rather, this association seems to have been present early on, as we can see from another of Poe's tales of ratiocination, "Thou Art the Man" (1844), published a month after the last Dupin story.

It is interesting that Poe not only originated the analytic detective genre but also produced the first parody of it in "Thou Art the Man," a tale, in Mabbott's words, "generally recognized as the first comic detective story" (3:1042). (That the inventor of the analytic detective story was also the first to parody the form both reminds us of and perhaps accounts for the fact that during the same period when Borges was writing his first two serious detective stories he was also collaborating with his friend Bioy-Casares on a collection of parody detective tales entitled *Six Problems for Don Isidro Parodi*, which they published under their joint pen name H. Bustos Domecq. And this reminds us in turn of Borges's comment about his third serious detective story, that it became during the writing "a cross between a permissible detective story and a caricature of one. The more I worked on it, the more hopeless the plot seemed and the stronger my need to parody" [*A*, 274].)

"Thou Art the Man" concerns the apparent murder of Barnabas Shuttleworthy and the efforts of his friend Charley Goodfellow to discover the killer. Shuttleworthy sets out on horseback one morning from Rattleborough on a trip to a nearby city. Two hours after his departure, his horse comes home "without his master, and without his master's saddlebags, and all bloody from a pistol-shot, that had gone clean through and through the poor animal's chest without quite killing him" (3:1046). The townspeople begin a search for Shuttleworthy under Charley Goodfellow's direction, and though they are unable to find his body, they turn up further evidence suggesting that he has been the victim of foul play, evidence that clearly points to Shuttleworthy's nephew Mr. Pennifeather as the killer. Pennifeather is arrested, found guilty on a "chain of circumstantial evidence" (3:1054), and condemned to death.

By this point, however, the narrator, as we learn at the story's end, has begun to suspect Charley Goodfellow. He knows that Goodfellow hates Pennifeather and has sworn revenge for an affront. He also notes that all the evidence against Pennifeather has been uncovered by Goodfellow, including the single most damaging piece, a rifle ball Goodfellow claims to have found in the wound in Shuttleworthy's horse, "a bullet of very extraordinary size" that fits the bore of Pennifeather's rifle but is "far too large for that of any other person in the borough" (3:1054). Yet it is just this piece of evidence—which convinces the townspeople of Pennifeather's guilt—that convinces the narrator of his innocence, for when Shuttleworthy's wounded horse returned without its master, the narrator had noticed that the bullet "had gone clean through and through the poor animal's chest," which is to say that if "there was a hole where the ball had entered the horse, and another where it *went out*," then for the ball to be found in the animal "after having made its exit, . . . it must have been deposited by the person who found it" (3:1058). The narrator concludes that since Goodfellow has fabricated evidence to frame Pennifeather, Goodfellow is probably the murderer.

In secret the narrator carries out his own search for Shuttleworthy's body, using as his guiding principle the determination to search "in quarters as divergent as possible from those to which Mr. Goodfellow conducted his party" (3:1058–59). Following this procedure, the narrator discovers Shuttleworthy's body hidden in a dry well and immediately sets in motion a plan to trap Goodfellow into an admission of guilt. Recalling that several weeks earlier Shuttleworthy had promised to have his agents send Goodfellow "a double box" (3:1055) of his favorite wine, the narrator forges a letter from the agent informing Goodfellow that the box of wine will be delivered the next day, a letter that leads Goodfellow to invite a group of townspeople to sample the wine. The narrator places Shuttleworthy's corpse in a wooden box, thrusts "a stiff piece of whalebone" down the corpse's throat, and then manages to "double the body up" (3:1059) before nailing down the lid. He arranges for the box to be delivered to Goodfellow's house during the party, and then, with the eyes of the assembled company on the host and his box of wine, the narrator loosens the lid:

> The top of the box flew suddenly and violently off, and, at the same instant, there sprang up into a sitting position, directly facing the host, the bruised, bloody and nearly putrid corpse of the murdered Mr. Shuttleworthy himself. It gazed for a few moments, fixedly and sorrowfully, with its decaying and lacklustre eyes, full into the countenance of Mr. Goodfellow; uttered slowly, but clearly and impressively, the words—"Thou art the man!" and then, falling over the side of the chest as if thoroughly satisfied, stretched out its limbs quiveringly upon the table. (3:1057)

Stunned by the terrifying scene and the corpse's words (an effect produced by the narrator's ventriloquism), Goodfellow confesses the murder and expires.

Obviously, Poe is having fun with the genre he invented in making the conclusion of the tale hinge on the device of a corpse rigged up as a combination jack-in-the-box and ventriloquist's dummy. Yet for all the absurdity of its ending, "Thou Art the Man" is an important step in the development of the analytic detective story. Goodfellow's stratagem with the rifle ball is one of the earliest uses in fiction, and certainly the first use in the analytic detective genre, of ballistic evidence. In addition, critics have, as Mabbott notes, pointed to the tale as " 'a trail blazing tour de force' in its first use of the least-likely-person theme, of the 'scattering of false clues by the real criminal,' and of 'the psychological third degree'" (3:1042). However, the most interesting feature of the story for our purposes is its clear linking of the analytic detective genre to the Oedipus myth, a link that can be seen in the story's title and climactic exclamation.

Most annotators of the tale identify the phrase "Thou art the man" as a quotation from 2 Samuel 12:7 in the King James Version of the Bible— the words of the prophet Nathan to King David denouncing him for the sins of adultery and murder. In the Biblical account David commits adultery with Bathsheba, the wife of Uriah the Hittite, and then arranges for Uriah to be killed in battle. Angered by David's sins, the Lord sends Nathan to reveal the king's guilt and announce his punishment. Nathan appears before David and tells him the story of two men living in the same city, one rich, the other poor. The rich man has "many flocks and herds," the poor man "nothing, save one little ewe lamb," yet when a traveler visits the rich man, he does not "take of his own flock" to feed the visitor but takes "the poor man's lamb" (2 Sam. 12:2–4). Incensed by the tale, David declares, "The man that hath done this thing shall surely die," and Nathan replies, "Thou art the man" (2 Sam. 12:5, 7). In pointing out the Biblical source of the words, however, Poe's annotators overlook the fact that these same words are occasionally used in English translations of Sophocles' *Oedipus the King* to render Tiresias's denunciation of Oedipus, a translator's choice clearly based on the similarity of the situations in the Biblical story and the Greek play.

In the play, Oedipus, seeking to punish the murderer of his predecessor Laius and thereby free the city from a plague, consults the seer Tiresias to learn the killer's identity. Tiresias admits that he knows the man but refuses to reveal his name. Angered by the seer's continued refusal, Oedipus finally accuses Tiresias of being a conspirator in Laius's murder. To which Tiresias replies (Storr's translation in the Loeb series is typical):

> Is it so? Then I charge thee to abide
> By thine own proclamation; from this day
> Speak not to these or me. Thou art the man,
> Thou the accursed polluter of this land.[1]

In both the Bible and Sophocles, a prophet denounces the crimes of a ruler, crimes of sexual misconduct and violence—in one case adultery and murder, in the other patricide and incest. And in each instance the prophet's denunciation involves revealing the ruler's identity to himself, since each king has already condemned the criminal without realizing that he himself is the man. Moreover, in each instance the ruler's recognition of himself in the other is initiated by a thou-art-that formula, a recognition easily achieved in the case of David but one that is resisted by Oedipus (who accuses Tiresias of conspiring with Creon to depose him) and that requires the course of the play to effect. In the latter case there is also the sense that as Oedipus comes to recognize himself in the other, so the audience comes to recognize the other in the self, comes to see a constitutive blindness or unconsciousness of the self to itself.

That Poe had in mind the subsequent use of the words "Thou art the man" to translate Tiresias's denunciation of Oedipus rather than their original use in the Bible can be judged from the tale's opening image. The narrator begins, "I will now play the Oedipus to the Rattleborough enigma" (3:1044), meaning that he will explain the natural causes behind the sudden appearance and apparent reanimation of Shuttleworthy's corpse in the heart of Rattleborough society, an event that had not only provoked the confession and expiration of Goodfellow but had also "put a definite end to infidelity among the Rattleburghers" (3:1044). Playing Oedipus to an enigma refers, of course, to the event that had made Oedipus the ruler of Thebes—his ridding the city of the Sphinx by answering the monster's riddle. And in the Sophoclean context suggested by the tale's title, the image recalls the angry exchange that immediately follows Tiresias's denunciation of Oedipus, an exchange in which king and seer compare their reputations as interpreters of dark sayings. Seeking to dismiss Tiresias's revelation, Oedipus asks,

> hast thou ever proved thyself
> A prophet? When the riddling Sphinx was here
> Why hadst thou no deliverance for this folk?
> And yet the riddle was not to be solved
> By guess-work but required the prophet's art;
> Wherein thou wast found lacking; neither birds
> Nor sign from heaven helped thee, but *I* came,
> The simple Oedipus; *I* stopped her mouth
> By mother wit, untaught of auguries. (Sophocles, 1:39)

In reply Tiresias repeats his charge and then asks, "Dost know thy lineage?" (Sophocles, 1:41). When Oedipus taunts the seer with loving "to speak in riddles and dark words," the sparring continues:

> TIRESIAS: In reading riddles who so skilled as thou?
> OEDIPUS: Twit me with that wherein my greatness lies.
> TIRESIAS: And yet this very greatness proved thy bane.
>
> (Sophocles, 1:43)

Clearly, the point of this argument over Tiresias's failure to solve the Sphinx's riddle and Oedipus's failure to unriddle the oracle's mystery is that answering a riddle and solving a mystery are two very different things. Part of the play's ironic effect, of course, is that Oedipus's "very greatness" as a riddle answerer, in leading to his being made ruler of Thebes, has put him in a position where he must discover the mysterious identity of Laius's killer. It is as if, for Oedipus, *answering* a riddle inevitably led to *enacting* a mystery, as if his success with the Sphinx's enigma caused him to mistake mere human cleverness for superhuman insight at the same time that it set in motion events that would punish that illusion by forcing him to play out the mystery of a split and doubled identity, a mystery whose only solution is the enactor's disillusion/dissolution. It is precisely this dramatic trajectory—from the *hybris* born of riddle-answering to the tragedy involved in mystery-solving—that Tiresias evokes when he poses the mystery of Oedipus's self-alienation as if it were a riddle ("Dost know thy lineage?") and challenges him to answer. Indeed, a further indication that Poe intends the phrase "Thou art the man" as an Oedipal allusion is that the two activities linked to the figure of Oedipus (answering a riddle and enacting a mystery) are both included in his parody detective story, although assigned to separate figures. While the narrator plays "Oedipus to the Rattleborough enigma" by revealing that Shuttleworthy's reanimation is a conjurer's trick, Goodfellow enacts the mystery of a dual identity (killer and false detective), a duality that for Goodfellow is, if not less mysterious, certainly less unself-conscious than for Oedipus, since Goodfellow not only knows that he is the murderer but also knows in advance that he must play the role of detective to accomplish his real purpose of taking revenge on Pennifeather.

If, as our analysis of Poe's parody of the genre suggests, the figure of Oedipus is associated in his mind with the analytic detective story virtually from the start, then his subtle evocation of, but omission of an explicit reference to, the myth of Theseus and the labyrinth in the first Dupin story takes on, if not a greater, at least a different significance. It becomes not a matter of a carelessly omitted reference to Theseus that accidentally opens the way for another mythic figure to become linked with the genre later in the tradition, but rather of a reference suppressed by the genre's originator who clearly associates Oedipus with the detective story and yet, oddly enough, does not carry out this suppression of Theseus's name in order to mention Oedipus in his place. Poe's reference to Oedipus only occurs in his parody of the genre. And this in turn suggests that these two omissions may be of the same order, that what is important for Poe about Theseus and Oedipus is not their difference but their similarity and that what caused the suppression of the reference to one was precisely his resemblance to the other. It is that resemblance we must now examine more closely.

23 *Oedipus and Theseus; Recognition and Acknowledgment; Exiles and Parricides; Oedipus's Spiritual Heir; Incest; Theseus and Hippolytus; Incest and Differentiating the Human; The Sphinx's Riddle; Numbers; The Three/Four Oscillation*

CERTAINLY, THE ANCIENT GREEKS THOUGHT of Oedipus and Theseus not as opposed but as closely related figures, their similarity invoked explicitly in Sophocles' *Oedipus at Colonus.* Banished from Thebes, the blind Oedipus, led by his daughter Antigone, comes at the end of his wanderings to Colonus, a deme of Athens. Mindful of the city's reputation for hospitality, Oedipus seeks protection from Athens and burial in Attic soil. In granting these requests, the city's ruler Theseus says that his welcome of Oedipus is prompted in part by a resemblance in their early lives:

> I too was reared,
> Like thee, in exile, and in foreign lands
> Wrestled with many perils, no man more.
> Wherefore no alien in adversity
> Shall seek in vain my succour, nor shalt thou;
> I know myself a mortal, and my share
> In what the morrow brings no more than thine. (Sophocles, 1:203)

The similarity Theseus cites recalls (as it was probably meant to) a series of unmentioned similarities between the two stemming from the fact that neither was raised by his natural father, a series of structural resemblances that sheds light not only on the link between the two figures but also on their association with (and thus on the structure of) the analytic detective story. In examining these resemblances, our focus will be on each man's relationship to three other figures—father, mother, and a third being, a part-human, part-animal adversary whose death the hero causes.

Oedipus and Theseus belong to a class of mythic characters often referred to as "heroes of consciousness," a designation that generally indicates two things about their stories. First, their myths tend to emphasize the hero's mental rather than physical abilities. This is not to suggest that they lack physical prowess but rather that their distinctive character as heroes is more a function of intelligence or cleverness than brute strength. Second, their myths tend in part to be parabolic expressions of the development and stabilization of individual self-consciousness. That is, a prominent theme in these stories is the relationship between self-recognition or self-knowledge on the one hand and self-mastery on the other, a relationship that has in these cases not only personal but communal significance. Since these mythic figures are usually rulers, their knowledge and mastery of themselves determine their understanding and control of their subjects.

Often in this type of myth the hero's self-knowledge is directly linked to the recognition and acknowledgment of him by his father. In Oedipus's case (a negative example) the man who, as ruler of Thebes, sets out to find Laius's murderer is literally a man who does not know who he is because he does not know who his real father was. Laius had ordered his infant son to be killed because of a Delphic prophecy that his son would someday kill him. But the shepherd charged with the task gave the child instead to a messenger who took him to Corinth where King Polybus and Queen Meropè raised him as their own. As a young man, Oedipus himself consults the Delphic oracle and is told that he will kill his father and marry his mother. Believing Polybus and Meropè are his parents, he decides not to return to Corinth, thereby avoiding his fate. But in his flight he encounters Laius and his retinue at a point where three roads meet on the way from Delphi. Not recognizing one another, father and son argue over which one will give way, and in the ensuing battle Oedipus kills Laius, subsequently assuming his father's position as ruler.

Paternal recognition is similarly an issue in Theseus's myth. In Plutarch's *Lives*, Theseus's father Aegeus, king of Athens, "desiring to have children," receives from the Pythian priestess at Delphi "the celebrated oracle" in which she bids him "to have intercourse with no woman" until he comes to Athens.[1] On the way back from Delphi, Aegeus stops at the little town of Troezen whose ruler Pittheus persuades or beguiles him "to have intercourse with his daughter Aethra" (*PL*, 1:9). Suspecting that Aethra is with child by him, Aegeus leaves "a sword and a pair of sandals hidden under a great rock." He tells "the princess [Aethra] alone about this," and bids her, "if a son should be born . . . , to send that son to him with the tokens, in all secrecy," for Aegeus fears that the sons of his brother Pallas, who despise him "on account of his childlessness" (*PL*, 1:9) and plot against him, might harm the child. At the very start, then, Theseus's story focuses on the question of a father's recognition and acknowledgment of his son, even to the extent, as Plutarch notes, of finding this theme at the root of Theseus's name. Aethra calls her son Theseus, "as some say, because the tokens for his recognition had been *placed* in hiding; but others say that it was afterwards at Athens, when Aegeus *acknowledged* him as his son" (*PL*, 1:9), a play on the similarity of the Greek noun θέσις (a setting or placing) and the aorist participle θεμένος (acknowledged) to the name Θησεύς (Theseus). The similarity springs from the fact that all three words derive from the same stem as the Greek verb τίθημι, meaning both "to set, put, or place" and "to reckon, regard as, or acknowledge" (a mental placing or establishment). Thus the name Theseus literally means "The Settler."

When Theseus comes of age, his mother reveals his father's identity, and the young man, having recovered the sword and sandals from beneath the rock, sets out for Athens. The sorceress Medea is living with Aegeus, having promised to relieve his childlessness through her magic. Medea learns of Theseus's arrival in Athens and convinces Aegeus, who does not recognize the stranger, that the young hero's presence is a threat to Aegeus's rule. She persuades Aegeus to invite the stranger to a banquet and poison him. But at the banquet Theseus manages to call attention to his sword, and the king, recognizing the weapon and realizing its bearer's identity, dashes "down the proffered cup of poison" (*PL*, 1:25) at the last instant. Embracing Theseus, Aegeus formally acknowledges him as his son and banishes Medea.

As Aegeus's heir, Theseus immediately sets out to ingratiate himself with the citizens of Athens. He volunteers to be one of the group of youths sent to Crete every nine years to be sacrificed to the Minotaur as punishment for the death of King Minos's son Androgeos in Athens years before. Since the Athenian youths are traveling to their death, their ship is rigged with a black sail. However, when Theseus tells his father that he intends to kill the Minotaur, Aegeus gives the pilot a second, white sail, ordering him to hoist it if he returns with Theseus safe but the black one if Theseus has been killed. Theseus sails to Crete and, with Ariadne's help in solving the maze, kills the Minotaur. But for some reason on the return voyage he fails to hoist the white sail. As the ship approaches Athens, Aegeus, who has been keeping watch for his son's return, sees the black sail betokening Theseus's death and throws himself off the acropolis in despair. With Aegeus's death, Theseus becomes ruler of Athens.

Significantly, in Plutarch's opinion (which seems to reflect the general opinion of the ancients), Theseus was directly responsible for his father's death:

> Theseus . . . for his forgetfulness and neglect of the command about the sail, can hardly, I think, escape the charge of parricide, be the plea of his advocate ever so long and his judges ever so lenient. Indeed, a certain Attic writer, conscious that would-be defenders of Theseus have a difficult task, feigns that Aegeus, on the approach of the ship, ran up to the acropolis in his eagerness to catch sight of her, and stumbled and fell down the cliff; as though he were

without a retinue, or was hurrying down to the sea without any servants. (*PL*,
1:197)

As this summary suggests, when Theseus in welcoming Oedipus to
Athens cites the resemblance of their childhood exiles as a reason for his
hospitality, he leaves a lot unsaid. For in addition to the similarity of an
expatriate upbringing, they each had a father who attempted, wittingly or
not, to kill his son; they were each responsible, wittingly or not, for that
father's death; and they each, as a result of that death, succeeded to the
father's position as ruler of a city. But now one of them has been over-
whelmed by tragedy. Blind, banished, and hounded by his successor Creon, Oedipus, seeking sanctuary, presents himself before Theseus, and
Theseus's greeting, with its acknowledgment of the likeness in their early
lives, amounts to a moment of self-recognition—that as their beginnings
were similar, so may their endings be. Exiled from Thebes as an infant,
Oedipus will die in exile as an old man, and faced with this example of a
banished ruler, Sophocles' Theseus—no arrogant overreacher—makes,
if not a thou-art-that, then certainly a thou-might-become-that acknowledgment of their common humanity, with its several uncertainties and its
ultimate certainty: "I know myself a mortal, and my share / In what the
morrow brings no more than thine."

The irony of this, as an Athenian audience would have noted, is that at
the end of his life Theseus is himself driven into exile by his enemies and
treacherously murdered on the island of Scyros by its ruler Lycomedes,
from whom Theseus had sought protection. As Plutarch describes it:
"Lycomedes, either because he feared a man of such fame, or as a favour
to Menestheus, led him [Theseus] up to the high places of the land, on
pretence of showing him from thence his lands, threw him down the cliffs,
and killed him. Some, however, say that he slipped and fell down of
himself while walking there after supper, as was his custom" (*PL*, 1:83).
On the one hand, Theseus's end seems to be an ironic reversal of
Oedipus's: where the banished ruler of Thebes had the noble Theseus to
shelter him, the banished ruler of Athens has no one of like nobility to
shelter *him*. But on the other hand, the manner of Theseus's death (a fall
from a cliff) and its alternative explanations (murder or accident) recall
the end of Theseus's father Aegeus, who also fell from a cliff and whose
death, as Plutarch records, also had alternative explanations (suicide or
accident). The resemblance suggests that the son's death is a repetition of,
and thus perhaps a punishment for, the father's, and this in turn points to
the problem lying at the heart of the father/son relationship in the myths
of Oedipus and Theseus. For while the son's self-knowledge (his knowing
who he is) is a function of knowing who his father is (i.e., a function of the

father's recognition and acknowledgment of the son and thus a form of the son's dependence on the father's will), the son's self-mastery, his creation of a stable, independent personality, is in some sense a function of his freeing himself from his father's will.

The contrary impulses that arise from the son's sense of self-worth involving a simultaneous dependence upon and independence from the father show themselves most clearly in regard to paternal authority—the marker of (in)dependence. The son wants what the father has—the authority of a father. And there are two ways he can gain it—with or against the father's will. He can receive it as a transmission from the father (a patrimony), or he can seize it from the father by force. But each method has its drawbacks. If the son receives the father's authority as a gift or inheritance, then that authority, whose possession should be the mark of independence, still represents in some measure a dependence on the father's will—not to mention that the price exacted for such a gift is often a long, debilitating subservience to the father. But if, on the other hand, the son seizes the father's power by overthrowing or killing him, then the very manner in which he takes possession of that authority seems to destroy the thing possessed. For if the son's identity depends in part on being recognized and acknowledged by the father, the father's authority also depends in part on being recognized and acknowledged by the son. If the son refuses that recognition, how can he then expect others to recognize *his* paternal authority, a sway whose unchallengeable character is based not on physical force but on an irreversible generative precedence? The seizure of paternal authority renders it useless as a principle to be employed in the future to bolster the usurper's rights. And the inevitable punishment for such a seizure is that the precedent of not recognizing the father's rule is transmitted to the next generation, so that the son who has overthrown his own father must now kill or banish his own son before the child becomes old enough to turn on him.

In regard to paternal authority, the son's desires are at cross purposes. On the one hand, wanting the father's power before the father is willing to give it up, the son ends up wanting the father out of the way. Clearly a murderous desire, but not quite, as it turns out, a desire for murder. For on the other hand, the son wants that paternal authority intact; he does not want it discredited by the father's overthrow or violent death. The problem facing the son, then, is how to bring about the father's absence from the paternal role while maintaining the unchallenged character of that role, how to make his parent a dead father whose honored memory grounds an orderly patriarchal succession rather than a murdered one whose bloody remembrance justifies filial rebellion. This conflict in the son's desires accounts for the oblique manner of the father's death in the stories of Oedipus and Theseus, a death brought about in each case either by fate or by accident but not by the son's deliberate intention to kill his father. The two myths dramatize, in effect, the fantasy of an impersonal or indirect accomplishment of the son's desire that simultaneously satisfies the conflicting demands of desire and repression.

The similarity of the two heroes' relationships to their fathers is the basis for Sophocles' resolution of the father/son conflict in *Oedipus at Colonus*, a resolution in which Oedipus and Theseus act out in their treatment of one another the proper relationship between father and son. On the one hand, Theseus like a good son shelters the homeless Oedipus, promises to protect his daughters Ismene and Antigone, and provides him with a fitting burial on Attic soil. On the other, Oedipus like a loving father confers on Theseus what can only be described as a patrimony and a blessing—a paternal transmission denied his own sons Polyneices and Eteocles, who had consented to his banishment. Indeed, Oedipus curses his sons for their treachery, a curse fulfilled when they kill each other in an internecine struggle for the rule of Thebes. But to Theseus who has performed the office of a son, Oedipus grants a favor withheld even from his beloved daughters:

> O son of Aegeus, for this state will I
> Unfold a treasure age cannot corrupt.
> Myself anon without a guiding hand
> Will take thee to the spot where I must end.
> This secret ne'er reveal to mortal man,
> Neither the spot nor whereabouts it lies,
> So shall it ever serve thee for defence
> Better than native shields and near allies.
> . . . Not to any of thy subjects, nor
> To my own children, though I love them dearly,
> Can I reveal what thou must guard alone,
> And whisper to thy chosen heir alone,
> So to be handed down from heir to heir.
> Thus shalt thou hold this land inviolate.
> . . . Blessing on thee, dearest friend,
> On thee and on thy land and followers!
> Live prosperous and in your happy state
> Still for your welfare think on me, the dead.   (Sophocles, 1:285–87)

Obviously, the similarity between Oedipus and Theseus as regards their fathers is substantial, yet when we consider their relationships with their mothers the resemblance seems to vanish. In contrast to Oedipus who unwittingly marries his mother Jocasta and sires four children/siblings, Theseus seems to have had, by all accounts, an unremarkable relationship with his mother Aethra. Certainly there is no hint in Theseus's story of any incestuous attachment. Yet this difference regarding the element of incest in the two myths may be only apparent, simply a function of the transformation process linking the two stories that, in shaping Theseus's story as a variation or further development of Oedipus's, includes the latter myth's basic structure of agonistic self-knowledge and self-mastery but arranges individual elements in a more complex pattern that alters or reverses their form and thus conceals their identity. What makes the question of incest particularly significant here is its structural connection to the analysis of self-consciousness, that is, to that structure of splitting and doubling (constituting self-reflection) that is doubled back again on itself in the analysis of mind. I have discussed at length in another work the relationship between doubling and incest and for present purposes need only summarize salient points from that study.[2]

The quest for absolute self-knowledge has characteristic dangers associated with it, some of which arise from the fact that the pursuit of such knowledge is often simply a form of narcissistic self-absorption—the self's attempt to know absolutely what it loves absolutely, with all the perils of suffocating self-enclosure that that implies. We have already noted in the analytic detective story, for example, how the battle of wits with an antithetical double typically results in self-defeat, if not self-destruction. One thinks of Borges's comment on the suicidal character of Lönnrot's death or the actual suicide of Grodman in Zangwill's novella. In a similar vein, this tendency of the narcissistic self to find its own reflection wherever it looks is frequently evoked in incest scenarios where the self's inability to break out of the circle of self-love is dramatized as a character's inability to break out of the family circle (that ring of faces resembling his own) in choosing a love-object. The extremes of incest and suicide represent in effect the poles of love and hate in the self's relationship to itself and, as is the nature of polar opposites, they tend to reverse into one another. The self's incestuous entrapment within the family becomes a form of self-destruction, and the self-destructive duel with a double becomes an incestuous *Liebestod*.

In two tales Poe published in the autumn of 1839 that represent crucial steps in the development of the analytic detective story ("The Fall of the House of Usher" and "William Wilson"), this tendency of scenarios of incest and suicidal doubling to reverse into one another is particularly clear. In the first, Roderick Usher, who shares his ancestral home with his twin sister Madeline, projects his own morbid self-absorption onto the figure of his dying sibling, in effect turning his twin into an external

mirror image of his deteriorating mental state. But this reflection of
Usher's narcissistic self-regard back upon itself only serves to accelerate
the disintegration of his personality, for his twin sister's wasting illness
confronts him with an image of what the narcissistic self fears most—the
inevitability of its own dissolution. This image so frightens Usher that it
threatens to cause, through a rapid increase of his own debilitating terror,
the very death he fears. To free himself from this destructive cycle in
which "the consciousness of the rapid increase" of his "superstition . . .
served mainly to accelerate the increase itself" (2:399), Roderick tries to
remove the terrifying image of his psychic deterioration by prematurely
burying Madeline, who suffers from cataleptic seizures, in the family
crypt. But like any destructive act aimed at an image of the self, this one
rebounds on the self. In a real or fantasized return from the grave, Madeline presents herself at her brother's bedroom door:

> There was blood upon her white robes, and the evidence of some bitter strug-
> gle upon every portion of her emaciated frame. For a moment she remained
> trembling and reeling to and fro upon the threshold—then, with a low moan-
> ing cry, fell heavily inward upon the person of her brother, and in her violent
> and now final death-agonies, bore him to the floor a corpse, and a victim to the
> terrors he had anticipated. (2:416–17)

Witnessing this last, deadly embrace of the twins, the terrified narrator
flees the family mansion, a dwelling figuratively evoked as a gigantic
human body, bearing on its front "a barely perceptible fissure" (2:400)
running from roof to foundation. As the narrator rushes from the house,
this fissure, an external split that corresponds to the doubling of the twins
within, suddenly widens, and the family home containing the bodies of its
last members collapses Narcissus-like into the mirroring tarn at its base.

The other tale published in the autumn of 1839, "William Wilson,"
ends with a similar moment of destructive mirroring as Wilson literally
duels with his own reflection, a specular double representing his con-
science. Wilson kills his moral self, but the mirror image's last words
pronounce Wilson's doom: "*You have conquered, and I yield. Yet, henceforward
art thou also dead—dead to the World, to Heaven and to Hope! In me didst thou
exist—and, in my death, see by this image, which is thine own, how utterly thou hast
murdered thyself*" (2:448). That Poe intended this suicidal duel as an incestuous *Liebestod* consummating Wilson's morbid self-love is made clear by
the incident's context. Throughout the story the double thwarts or ex-
poses Wilson's evil deeds, but it is only with the interruption of his final
villainy—the attempted seduction of an Italian nobleman's young wife—
that Wilson challenges his moral self to a duel to the death, with the result
that the duel substitutes for (and is thus equated with) the lovers' tryst to

which Wilson had been hastening. This reading is supported by an earlier Poe story "The Assignation" (1834) in which a similar situation—the thwarted passion of a romantic Englishman and the young wife of an Italian nobleman—ends with that passion being consummated in a double suicide. The woman's reply in that tale to her lover's proposal that they be joined in death—"Thou hast conquered, . . . thou hast conquered" (2:155)—is echoed five years later by the dying words of Wilson's double—"*You have conquered, and I yield.*"

The same structural connection between doubling and incest lies at the heart of the Oedipus myth. The figure of Oedipus is, of course, split by the difference between who he really is (the son of Laius and Jocasta) and who he believes he is (the son of Polybus and Meropè), and this splitting grounds his double role as criminal and detective—the man who kills his father and marries his mother, and the avenger who hunts that man down. As Sophocles makes clear, Oedipus's doubleness is transmitted by and embodied in his incestuous union and its offspring, for what this marriage of mother and son produces is the splitting and doubling of familial relationships. Oedipus is Jocasta's son and husband; he is the father and half-brother of their children; and Jocasta is their mother and grandmother. As Tiresias had said in amplifying his taunt to Oedipus ("Dost know thy lineage?"):

> Nay, thou know'st it not,
> And all unwitting art a double foe
> To thine own kin, the living and the dead;
> Aye and the dogging curse of mother and sire
> One day shall drive thee, like a two-edged sword,
> Beyond our borders.   (Sophocles, 1:41)

The division and duplication of relationships produced by this marriage threatens a return to chaos, for in "mingling the blood of fathers, brothers, children, / Brides, wives and mothers" (Sophocles, 1:129), an incestuous union dissolves the very notion of kinship, the sense of a clear network of relationships within which the self is located. And with this dissolution, the self in turn begins to disintegrate, gradually ceasing to know who it is. In the Oedipus myth, incest's disintegrative effect on the notion of kinship (considered as a differential ground of the self) is symbolized by the proliferating self-destruction, like a chain reaction in a house of mirrors, that occurs within Oedipus's family in the wake of the incest's revelation. Jocasta hangs herself, Oedipus blinds himself, and the messenger who recounts these events comments, "Such evils, issuing from the double source, / Have whelmed them both, confounding man and wife" (Sophocles, 1:119). Their sons Polyneices and Eteocles kill each other in battle. Their daughter Antigone, condemned to a slow death by her maternal uncle Creon (who is also her father's uncle and brother-in-law), hangs herself and is joined by (and conjoined with) her betrothed Haemon (Creon's son and her cousin) in a double suicide clearly understood as a *Liebestod:*

> Then the boy,
> Wroth with himself, poor wretch, incontinent
> Fell on his sword and drove it through his side
> Home, but yet breathing clasped in his lax arms
> The maid. . . . So there they lay
> Two corpses, one in death. His marriage rites
> Are consummated in the halls of Death.   (Sophocles, 1:409)

On learning of her son's suicide, Haemon's mother Eurydice stabs herself, and the slaughter of relatives is completed.

As the myth of a hero of consciousness, Oedipus's story illustrates the link between the structure of the self's cognitive relatedness to itself (the splitting and doubling that constitutes self-reflection) and the two major scenarios dramatizing the extremes of love and hate in the self's emotional relatedness to itself (incest and the suicidal duel with a double). Given the structural connection between doubling and incest and between the stories of Oedipus and Theseus as myths of the development and stabilization of the self, the presence of incest in the former myth leads us to look for this element in the latter (albeit transformed or displaced). As it happens we do not have far to look, for in Theseus's story the incest motif appears in his relationship not to his father and mother but to his wife and son, Phaedra and Hippolytus.

In Euripides' *Hippolytus,* Theseus's son by the Amazon Hippolyta is a young man renowned for his virtue (particularly chastity), a hunter devoted to the service of the virgin goddess Artemis. To punish Hippolytus for his rejection of physical love and her worship, the goddess Aphrodite makes Theseus's wife Phaedra, the sister of Ariadne, fall in love with her stepson. Resisting the illicit passion, Phaedra chooses to die of lovesickness rather than dishonor her name. Phaedra's nurse, learning the cause of her mistress's illness, takes it upon herself to approach Hippolytus, hoping that the young man will satisfy Phaedra's passion and thus save her life. Outraged at the nurse's proposal, the chaste Hippolytus expresses his contempt for her and her mistress, though he is prevented from informing his father by a vow of secrecy he had sworn as a condition of the nurse's speaking. Hearing of her nurse's rash action and Hippolytus's response, Phaedra, overcome with shame, decides to kill herself to protect her reputation and preserve her children from any taint of disgrace. But first, in order to punish Hippolytus for his callousness and forestall any suspicion of her guilty passion, she leaves a letter saying she has taken her life because Hippolytus had violated her by force. When Theseus finds her body and the letter, he invokes in his anger one of the three curses promised him by Poseidon, charging the sea god to destroy his son that very day. He then banishes Hippolytus, refusing to believe his protestations of innocence. Going into exile, Hippolytus drives his chariot along the coast, and Poseidon, fulfilling Theseus's curse, sends a gigantic bull from the sea that frightens Hippolytus's horses, causing them to smash the chariot against the rocks and mortally wound their master. Appearing to Theseus, Artemis reveals his wife's ruse and his son's innocence. The dying Hippolytus is carried into their presence, and with Artemis's assurance that these events were fated and that neither Theseus nor Hippolytus is to blame, father and son are reconciled, Hippolytus dies, and Euripides' version of the episode ends. (We should note that the "similarities in diction between parts of the *Oedipus* and the *Hippolytus*" are "so striking" that, as the classicist Frederick Ahl points out, some critics have "suggested Euripides must have derived his lines" from Sophocles' play and thus have proposed dating "*Oedipus* to 429 B.C. and *Hippolytus* to 428" since both plays "seem to respond to the great plague in Athens [430–28 B.C.]."[3])

Although Phaedra and Hippolytus are not related by blood, they are related by marriage, and clearly in the play both Theseus's outrage at the alleged violation of his wife and Phaedra's revulsion at her illicit passion are not simply violent reactions to the crimes of rape or adultery but instinctual aversions to the incestuous character of this involvement of stepmother and stepson. And just as in a case of actual mother/son incest (the primal affront to the father's authority), the father in this instance wills the son's death. The incest motif thus links the myths of Oedipus and Theseus as each hero enacts one of the two opposing male roles in the Oedipal triangle.

That Euripides associates Hippolytus's situation with Oedipus's, associates the alleged technical incest of the one with the actual genetic incest of the other, is implied by an exchange between Hippolytus and Theseus about the latter's decision merely to banish Hippolytus for his alleged crime:

HIPPOLYTUS: Nay, but I marvel, father, at this in thee;—
For, if my son thou wert, and I thy sire,
I had slain thee: exile should not be thy mulct,
If on my wife thou hadst dared to lay a hand.
THESEUS: Good sooth, well said: yet not so shalt thou die—

Not by the doom thou speakest for thyself!
Ay, easiest for the wretched is swift death.
But from the home-land exiled, wandering
To strange soil, shalt thou drain life's bitter dregs;
For this is meet wage for the impious man.[4]

As Oedipus's sons agreed to their father's banishment from Thebes, so Theseus banishes his son from Athens. The irony in the reciprocity of Oedipus's role as the son in one incestuous triangle and Theseus's as the father in another springs, of course, from the symbolic father/son relationship between the two. In Sophocles' *Oedipus at Colonus* Theseus's conduct shows that he has learned from Oedipus's example the dangers inherent in the son's role in the family triangle, in effect learned how to behave as a dutiful son by sheltering his spiritual father Oedipus. But to judge from Euripides' *Hippolytus*, Theseus has not learned the dangers inherent in the father's role. Perhaps Theseus assumes from Oedipus's example that committing incest with the father's wife is the desire of every son, an assumption on the father's part that is as much a factor in the father/son conflict as the desire would be on the son's.

What is most significant for our purposes about this passage from Theseus's life is that both Phaedra's ancestry and the manner of Hippolytus's death link this episode to the most famous incident in Theseus's myth, his slaying of the Minotaur. Phaedra is, as we noted earlier, the sister of Ariadne, and thus, as a daughter of Minos and Pasiphae, a half-sister of the Minotaur. Pasiphae's unnatural passion was a punishment for an offense of Minos against the sea god Poseidon. According to Apollodorus, Minos, finding his claim to rule Crete opposed,

> alleged that he had received the kingdom from the gods, and in proof of it he said that whatever he prayed for would be done. And in sacrificing to Poseidon he prayed that a bull might appear from the depths, promising to sacrifice it when it appeared. Poseidon did send him up a fine bull, and Minos obtained the kingdom, but he sent the bull to the herds and sacrificed another. . . . Angry at him for not sacrificing the bull, Poseidon made the animal savage, and contrived that Pasiphae should conceive a passion for it. (Apollodorus, 1:303–5)

Aided by an artifice of Daedalus, Pasiphae coupled with the bull and

> gave birth to Asterius, who was called the Minotaur. He had the face of a bull, but the rest of him was human; and Minos, in compliance with certain oracles, shut him up and guarded him in the Labyrinth. (Apollodorus, 1:305)

The resemblance between this incident and the passion of Phaedra for Hippolytus seems clear enough: In each case a deity punishes an offending male by afflicting a female relative with an unnatural passion. Thus Poseidon punishes Minos by making his wife copulate with a bull and conceive a monstrous child, and Aphrodite punishes Hippolytus by striking his stepmother Phaedra with an incestuous passion for her husband's son. The two episodes are linked by a bull from the sea sent by Poseidon—the sacrificial bull whose appearance begins the earlier episode and leads to the fathering of the Minotaur, and the bull that ends the later episode by causing Hippolytus's death. In each instance the animal appears in response to a human request: Minos's prayer for a god-given sign to confirm his kingly authority against those who would oppose it, and Theseus's curse invoking the death of a son who has apparently defied his authority. And of course the two episodes are also linked by the figure of Theseus who slays the Minotaur and whose own son is in turn slain by a bull from the sea.

Euripides explicitly connects Phaedra with the Minotaur when he has her compare her plight to those of her mother and sister:

PHAEDRA: O hapless mother!—what strange love was thine!
NURSE: Love for the bull, my child?—or what wouldst name?
PHAEDRA: And thou, sad sister, Dionysus' bride.
NURSE: What ails thee, child?—dost thou revile thy kin?
PHAEDRA: And I the third—how am I misery-wrecked!

(Euripides, 4:189–91)

In fleeing from Crete with Theseus, Ariadne (depending on which version of the story one chooses) was either intentionally abandoned or accidentally left on the island of Naxos or else forcibly abducted by Dionysus. But in most versions she ends up as Dionysus's bride. Phaedra thus likens her passion for her stepson not only to her mother's lust for the bull but to her sister Ariadne's union with the god who, in the Apollo/Dionysus opposition, represents the instinctual, animal side of human nature. Euripides again alludes to the link between the slaying of the Minotaur and Phaedra's incestuous love for Theseus's son in a passage immediately following Hippolytus's departure for exile. The chorus laments, "When doubt whispereth 'Ah but to *know*!' / No clue through the tangle I find of fate and of life for my tracing" (Euripides, 4:249)—an image that, in recalling the clew of thread leading Theseus away from the slain Minotaur and out of the labyrinth, underscores the reversal that occurs when Theseus's son, fleeing a fatal tangle of family relationships, is killed by a bull.

Euripides' linking of the plight of Phaedra and Hippolytus to the Minotaur is important for our purposes because the implied reason for this association—the similarity of a divinely inspired, unnatural passion in Phaedra's incestuous desire for her stepson and in Pasiphae's mating with the bull—sheds light on the meaning of that third figure (Sphinx and Minotaur) who appears as a common structural element in the myths of Oedipus and Theseus. As we suggested earlier, the myths of heroes of consciousness are, in one degree or another, symbolic accounts of the development and stabilization of the self, with one form of this drama of self-mastery being a scenario of self-recognition based on parental acknowledgment. But in addition to this personal recognition, there is a more general form that the hero enacts—that broader self-knowledge involved in discovering not so much who he is as a person but what it means to be a person at all, to be a man rather than a god or an animal. And it is in the context of this generic self-recognition that we can understand not only the principal function of the incest motif in these myths but also the significance of the part-animal, part-human figure connected with each.

What the incest taboo clearly represents in the Oedipus myth is a cultural means of signifying the difference between human and nonhuman, the difference between beings who, as individuals, know who they are precisely because they recognize their kin, and creatures who do not know themselves because they do not recognize their kin (as evidenced by the fact that they mate with them). In this connection it is significant that a recurring motif in Sophocles' Oedipus trilogy is the image of incest as a deformer of the generative process, a producer of malformed children. Oedipus's children are not, of course, physically deformed (although we recall that Oedipus's name [literally "swollen foot"] clearly associates him with physical deformity, and specifically with a deformity inflicted on an infant by its father). Rather, Oedipus's offspring are psychically deformed, fated by their regressive origin to destroy themselves. But it is quite clear that underlying and coloring the image of destinies deformed by an incestuous origin is the notion of inbreeding as a cause of physically deformed children, offspring who lack a human shape. And this presumed link between incestuous generation and physical deformity undoubtedly underlies Euripides' comparison of Phaedra's incestuous passion for Hippolytus to Pasiphae's mating with a bull.

The chain of associations seems clear enough: If the incest taboo differentiates human from animal, humans who commit incest are behaving like animals and run the risk of producing by their inbreeding inhuman (deformed) offspring. Euripides suggests the animal character of incest and the risk of inhuman progeny through the image of Phaedra's mother, who literally mated with an animal and bore a monstrous child. Similarly, in *Oedipus the King* Sophocles invokes the connection between incest and unnatural births in describing the unlucky offspring of Oedipus and

Jocasta: "the mother left to breed / With her own seed" produced "a monstrous progeny," a "double brood" (Sophocles, 1:117). The sense is that the doubling, and consequent blurring, of familial relationships has deprived these children of the basic means of establishing their personal identities and thus their common humanity. It is as if the duality of the children's relationship to their parents has literally made them monstrous, made them biform creatures who are at once the children and grandchildren of their mother and the children and siblings of their father. (The fact that the disastrous [L. *aster,* "star"] fates of Oedipus's incestuous brood, their ill-starred, unnatural births, are compared to a physical defect recalls a similar link between the stars and a monstrous birth in the Theseus myth—the name Asterion.)

In this context the significance of the Sphinx and the Minotaur becomes clear. If the incest taboo serves as a principle of differentiation between human and animal and if the failure to observe that taboo results in monstrous offspring, then the biform creatures in the myths of Oedipus and Theseus are dramatic means of posing, in a sense personifications of, the problem confronting the hero of consciousness—the question of differentiating the human. On the one hand, the Sphinx and Minotaur symbolize the monstrous condition resulting from the failure to solve that problem, the condition of humans who behave like animals, with instinct overruling reason, body directing mind; while on the other, these creatures function within their respective myths as posers of specific problems requiring an analytic solution by the hero. The Sphinx presents Oedipus with a riddle; the Minotaur confronts Theseus with a three-dimensional puzzle. If the hero fails to solve the riddle or unravel the labyrinth, then he dies. But if he succeeds, then the monster dies. And since the hero's triumph in each case is the result not of brute force but of human reason, the analytic solution to the specific problem associated with each creature enacts, at the same time, the solution to that larger problem of human differentiation they embody. Which is to say that the hero's very exercise of reason in solving the monster's riddle or puzzle constitutes the difference between human and animal.

But of course in these myths the problem of differentiation is not simply one of distinguishing human from subhuman but of distinguishing human from superhuman. One lesson these myths teach is that although humans have animal-like bodies, they are not animals, and although they have godlike minds, they are not gods. In defeating the Sphinx, Oedipus learns one of these points but not the other. Using reason to solve the riddle, he enacts the difference between human and animal, but he mistakes this power for something higher, comparing his analytic ability to Tiresias's prophetic gift. His punishment for thinking himself more than human is to be made less than human by mating with his own mother like an animal, a punishment that suggests how in these myths the subhuman and superhuman realms cooperate in establishing man's proper place in the hierarchy of things. This mythic joint venture by gods and animals to define the human accounts for the divine aura of the two biform creatures. The Minotaur is the offspring of a bull sent by Poseidon, while the Sphinx is sent to Thebes by Apollo.

This link between gods and animals also explains why incest functions in mythology as a marker not only of the subhuman but of the superhuman as well. Which is to say that if incest theoretically characterizes creatures who, lacking personal self-recognition, do not recognize close relations as *their own* (as belonging to the self) and thus mate with them, it also characterizes beings who, knowing their own uniqueness, recognize *only* their close relations as possible breeding partners, a coding of incest as a privilege of the gods reflected in the marriage practices of Egyptian pharaohs whose divinity required that they mate with their equals (their own family), the divine archetype of this being the incestuous union of Isis and Osiris. Significantly, the figure of the Sphinx originated in Egypt, and in its earliest form it seems to have been a type of the king.[5]

That the Sphinx and Minotaur personify the problem of human differentiation confronting the hero is clearly suggested by the Sphinx's riddle—a verbal problem that uses the number of feet on which a creature walks as the differential criterion for establishing its identity, a riddle whose answer, predictably enough, is "man." There are, of course, several variants of the Sphinx's enigma. The earliest complete form is in Athenaeus's *The Deipnosophists* (ca. A.D. 200), which cites as its source Asclepiades' *Tragdoumena* ("Subjects of Tragedy"), a work of the mid-fourth century B.C.:

> There walks on land a creature of two feet and four feet, which has a single
>   voice,
> And it also has three feet; alone of the animals on earth it changes its
>   nature,
> Of animals on the earth, in the sky, and in the sea.
> When it walks propped on most feet,
> Then is the speed of its limbs the least.[6]

In the more common form of the riddle and its explanation, the varieties of pedal locomotion are explicitly linked to different stages in the creature's development:

> "What creature," the Sphinx asked him, "goes on four feet in the morning, on two at noonday, on three in the evening?" "Man," answered Oedipus. "In

childhood he creeps on hands and feet; in manhood he walks erect; in old age he helps himself with a staff."[7]

What makes the Sphinx's question a riddle, of course, is the way that it simultaneously proposes and then calls into question the notion of "foot-edness" as a means of differentiating creatures, calls it into question not simply through the contradictory image of a being who walks on two, three, and four feet, but through the apparent noncorrespondence of each of these types of pedal locomotion to an identifiable creature. This latter problem is particularly clear in the earliest complete version, where the description of the unnamed creature begins by invoking two naturally occurring categories of footedness and then proceeds to add a third for which there seems to be no natural example. That is, the riddle, by ini-tially describing the creature as two-footed and four-footed, categorizes it immediately in terms of pedal modes that, although usually opposed to one another as markers of animal types, are nevertheless linked by a natural reciprocity. Some two-footed creatures, such as humans, can go on all fours and some four-footed creatures, such as dogs, can walk on their hind legs; while some creatures, such as apes, alternate easily be-tween the two modes. At this point in the riddle we may be puzzled about the creature's identity, but we are not puzzled about the categories of identification. But with the next category (three-footedness), we find our-selves not only unable to name the specific three-footed creature the riddle describes, but unable to name any three-footed creature, a diffi-culty that renders transparent the question of differential categories. The solution to the problem of three-footedness (an old man using a staff) points to the real differential criteria underlying the riddle's apparent criterion of footedness—criteria based on oppositions between art and nature and between the figurative and the literal. Which is to say that man, as distinguished from other animals, is evoked in this riddle as a creature of artifacts and figurative representations, one who makes and uses tools (such as a staff for walking) and then figuratively represents this literal object as a third foot.

Perhaps the most significant aspect of the Sphinx's enigma from our point of view is its character as a counting riddle, a riddle whose cryptic description of man involves both counting from one to four (a creature with a *single* voice who walks on *two, three,* and *four* feet) and distinguishing between two types of numbers within that series. For quite clearly the earliest form of the riddle divides its numerical evocation of man into two parts, describing him first as "a creature of two feet and four feet" and then as a creature who "also has three feet." The distinction the riddle thus makes between numbers that refer to natural modes of pedal locomotion (two and four) and a number that refers to an artificial mode *as if* it were a natural one (three) not only presents the oppositions between natural and artificial and between literal and figurative as differential criteria of the human, but also aligns these oppositions with that between even and odd, an association that reminds us both of Poe's use of the game of even and odd as a figure for the analysis of mind within the larger work of differentiating the human and of Borges's similar use of the three/four oscillation in imaging the doubly specular character of the analysis of self-consciousness. Indeed, given the structural connection between Oedipus and the analytic detective story and given the importance in his myth of a riddle depicting the hidden identity of a creature in terms of the number of feet on which it walks, we should perhaps treat as an Oedipal allusion Inspector Treviranus's remark at the scene of the first murder in "Death and the Compass": "We needn't lose any time here looking for three-legged cats" (*A*, 66). Just as Treviranus's image of a four-legged animal with only three legs encodes the solution to the serial character of the crimes (the fact that there are four events but only three murders, the third of which will occur only if the prospective victim correctly deciphers the number of events in the series and presents himself at the fourth point of the compass for his own unexpected execution), so the Sphinx's image of a creature with a single voice who walks on two, three, and four feet encodes not only the solution to the generic identity of the creature in the riddle (man) but also, I would suggest, the solution to that mystery of a specific human identity in Oedipus's story.

One of the curious aspects of Sophocles' *Oedipus the King* is that although much is made of Oedipus's riddle-solving ability and although the Sphinx's riddle is mentioned several times, the riddle itself is never given in the play. If we assume that Sophocles' audience was so familiar with the riddle's terms that there was no need to include it, and if we are correct in characterizing the Sphinx's enigma as primarily a numerical riddle that involves counting from one to four and distinguishing between even and odd, then one can argue that although Sophocles omits the riddle's words, he does use its numerical imagery (whose source he would expect the audience to recognize) to reveal the mystery of Laius's killer to Oedipus. Reading the play with an eye to the link between numerical imagery and the Sphinx's riddle, we find only one place where great significance is attached to an exact determination of numbers. In trying to persuade Oedipus that Tiresias's identification of him as the killer is mistaken, Jocasta tells him what she knows of the circumstances of Laius's murder— that Laius was killed "by highwaymen . . . at a spot where three roads meet," "roads from Delphi and from Daulis" (Sophocles, 1:67, 69). But this information only increases Oedipus's misgivings, for he knows that, years before, near these same "triple-branching roads" (Sophocles, 1:75) he was involved in an altercation with a group of men and in the ensuing struggle killed several of them. Accordingly, Oedipus asks Jocasta about the size of Laius's party:

OEDIPUS: Had he but few attendants or a train
Of armed retainers with him, like a prince?
JOCASTA: They were but five in all, and one of them
A herald; Laius in a mule-car rode.
OEDIPUS: Alas! 'tis clear as noonday now. But say,
Lady, who carried this report to Thebes?
JOCASTA: A serf, the sole survivor who returned.   (Sophocles, 1:71)

There are two possible ways of interpreting Jocasta's statement about the number of men in Laius's party, and this ambiguity is clearly present in the Greek text, as commentaries on the play have noted.[8] Either we can take her remark "They were but five in all" as a statement that refers only to Laius's retainers, in which case the entire party would consist of five retainers plus Laius, for a total of six. Or we can interpret it as a statement that refers to the entire party including Laius, for a total of five. I would suggest that the latter is the correct interpretation and that since one member of Laius's party escaped the slaughter and returned to tell the tale, Oedipus killed four men out of a five-man party at the crossroads. Which is to say that the man who solved the Sphinx's numerical riddle about the identity of a creature that speaks with a *single* voice and walks on *two, three,* and *four* feet also solves the numerical mystery of the identity of Laius's killer—the mystery of a *single* man named Oedipus who discovers that he has a *dual* identity (killer and detective) by recognizing himself in Jocasta's account as the same person who, at a spot where *three* roads meet, slew *four* men. Indeed, the ambiguity of Jocasta's remark about the size of Laius's party may be meant to suggest the ambiguity of a riddle and thus recall the link between numbers (especially these numbers) and the Sphinx's enigma. Throughout the play, of course, verbal doubleness, like that associated with the Sphinx's riddle and the Delphic oracle, serves as the linguistic embodiment of the play's central theme—the essential doubleness of human nature personified in the doubleness of one particular man.

That Sophocles means for the audience to notice the use of numbers in the play is emphasized by a subsequent exchange between Oedipus and Jocasta. Oedipus, puzzled by Jocasta's remarks about Laius's assailants, says,

In thy report of what the herdsman said
Laius was slain by robbers; now if he
Still speaks of robbers, not a robber, I
Slew him not; "one" with "many" cannot square.
But if he says one lonely wayfarer,
The last link wanting to my guilt is forged.   (Sophocles, 1:79)

(The herdsman had, of course, lied about Laius's being killed by robbers because he was afraid to identify the new ruler of Thebes as the killer.) Oedipus's emphatic "'one' with 'many' cannot square" calls attention not only to the drama's numerical determination of identity (and to the logical certainty associated with mathematics) but also to the way this determination becomes problematic in the case of one man with a dual identity, which is to say, calls attention to self-consciousness's fundamental condition of being at odds, of not squaring, with itself.

If, as I have suggested, Oedipus ultimately realizes his *dual* identity by recognizing himself as the same *one* who at a place where *three* roads meet killed *four* men, then the mathematical/geometrical imagery in Borges's "Death and the Compass" may well be an allusion to the numerical determination both of *personal* identity in Oedipus's quest for the truth and of collective *human* identity in the Sphinx's riddle—though an allusion with a typically Borgesian twist. For while in the Oedipus myth there are four bodies at a geographical spot where three roads meet, in "Death and the Compass" there are three bodies (Yarmolinsky, Azevedo, Lönnrot) distributed within a pattern of four geographical locations. The allusive link between Borges's modern configuration and Sophocles' classical one seems even more likely when we recall that on the one hand Borges describes the diamond shape formed by the crimes' locations as a labyrinth and that on the other "a spot where three roads meet" is the basic structural unit of a multicursal labyrinth (one in which the path branches at nodal points, as distinguished from a unicursal labyrinth made up of a single winding path). Regarding the latter point, W. H. Matthews notes,

> Using the word *node* to signify a point of branching, and the terms *odd* and *even* to describe respectively those nodes at which odd or even numbers of paths are to be found, we see that there must be at least three paths meeting at a point to form a node, for two paths meeting at a point constitute only a change of direction of the path without formation of branches, whilst the arrival of one path only at a point also precludes the idea of "branching" at that point, and can only occur at the end of a blind alley, at the entrance of the maze, or at the goal. We find it convenient, however, to regard the latter arrangement as an odd node of the lowest order, the lowest possible order of even nodes being, of course, that at the meeting of four paths. (*ML,* 190)

The numbers three and four, as the minimum number of paths needed to form an odd and an even node, have, then, a special connection with the type of labyrinth composed of forking paths; and there is reason to believe that Sophocles intended the image of four bodies at a triple-branching crossroads as an allusion not only to the numerical imagery of the Sphinx's riddle but also to that other puzzle associated with the Sphinx's counterpart in the Theseus myth, that labyrinthine structure of forking paths containing the bodies of the Minotaur's victims and ultimately the corpse of the Minotaur itself. At the beginning of *Oedipus the King* the chorus, citing Oedipus's success in solving the Sphinx's riddle, asks him to solve the mystery of the plague afflicting Thebes. Oedipus replies that in his musings (literally, "in his wanderings") he has "gone over many roads of thought and care" and found only one solution: He has sent Creon to the Delphic oracle to ask "how I might save the State by act or word" (Sophocles, 1:11). The image of Oedipus wandering "over many roads of thought and care" suggests, of course, someone trapped in a maze, a suggestion emphasized by Oedipus's decision to send Creon to the Delphic oracle. For in so doing, he sends him along the road leading to that same mazelike, triple-branching crossroads at which Oedipus killed Laius, sends him to the scene of the event that brought the plague and prompted Creon's mission. The labyrinth image implicit in Oedipus's description of himself wandering "over many roads of thought and care" is made explicit in several English translations of the passage, Storr's version being typical:

> Many, my children, are the tears I've wept,
> And threaded many a maze of weary thought.
> Thus pondering one clue of hope I caught,
> And tracked it up.   (Sophocles, 1:11)

This association of Oedipus with a maze and a clue not only foreshadows his final blind wanderings over many roads to find shelter with the man who conquered the Cretan labyrinth, but also underlines the analogous status of the Sphinx's riddle and the Minotaur's maze in both stories. And this in turn suggests for us that, as a recurring element in the scenario of differentiating the human through the analysis of self-consciousness, the Sphinx and its riddle, the Minotaur and labyrinth, the manlike killer ape and locked room in Poe's "Murders in the Rue Morgue," and the trio of faceless corpses and the crimson labyrinth in Borges's "Ibn Hakkan al-Bokhari" all have essentially the same function. On the one hand, these figures (two biform creatures composed of human and animal parts, an ape mistaken for a man, a group of human and animal bodies reduced to a faceless equivalence) evoke a blurring of the difference between human and nonhuman that represents a threatened reversal of the master/slave relationship between mind and body. And on the other, they are each associated with either a riddle or a spatial puzzle whose problematic form encrypts the mystery of human identity and whose solution enacts, through the hero's exercise of reason, the difference between the rational and the irrational.

We will examine presently, in the same detail as we did the Sphinx and its riddle, the relationship of the Minotaur and labyrinth when we discuss this recurring image in Borges's fiction. But first we must return to the question that originally prompted the present digression, the question of why Poe omits in "The Murders in the Rue Morgue" any mention of Theseus's name in connection with the labyrinthlike locked room, the clew/*clou* that leads Dupin to the exit/solution, and the manlike killer animal.

24 *The Repressed Name; The Mother-Substitute; Psychological Incest; The Dying Woman Stories; Womb/Tomb; Violence against the (M)other; Dying Woman and Female Victim*

GIVEN THAT THE RESEMBLANCE BETWEEN Oedipus and Theseus as figures of analytic detection derives in part from their each having solved a problem associated with a potentially murderous, semihuman creature, they are both obvious classical models for Dupin's solving the problems of the locked room and the killer's identity in Poe's original detective story. Although the scenario of "The Murders in the Rue Morgue" is more closely related to Theseus's encounter with the Minotaur than Oedipus's with the Sphinx, still one can infer Oedipus's presence in the text from the narrator's early remark that "the analyst" is a type of person "fond of *enigmas,* of conundrums, of hieroglyphics" (2:528, my italics); and we know from the opening sentence of "Thou Art the Man" the figure Poe associates with solving enigmas in a detective story context: "I will now play the Oedipus to the Rattleborough enigma" (3:1044).

Clearly, the mythological link between Oedipus and Theseus is so close that, for anyone familiar with classical literature, to name the latter is immediately to recall the former, an inevitability of association that more than likely lies behind the omission of Theseus's name in the first Dupin story. For it is precisely the figure of Oedipus that Poe cannot tolerate in this context, and it is ultimately the repression of his name that causes by association the repression of Theseus's. Poe's apparent uneasiness with the figure of Oedipus in his first detective story springs, I would suggest, from a combination of two factors—the nature of the crime (an irrational, murderous assault on a mother and daughter, an assault almost sexual in nature) and the association of Oedipus (the classical archetype of the doubling of detective and criminal) with incest. Recall that the man who invented the analytic detective story in 1841 at the age of thirty-two had, some five years earlier, married his thirteen-year-old first cousin Virginia Clemm. Poe was to live for the next eleven years in a family unit consisting of himself, Virginia, and her mother Maria Clemm (Poe's aunt and proba-bly the most important of the various surrogate mothers in his life). It was an arrangement that involved not just a doubling, but in some sense a tripling, of relationships, for Poe called his beloved cousin/wife "Sis" and his no-less-beloved aunt/mother-in-law "Muddy." Given the nature of this household, one might read the manlike animal's assault on Mme. and Mlle. L'Espanaye as an oblique expression of Poe's feeling that his union with his cousin was in some sense an "incestuous" violation of mother and daughter. According to such an interpretation, the bizarre crime (committed by the temporarily escaped irrational double and witnessed by the helpless human master outside the window) would represent the return of a repressed content, of Poe's sense that as his aunt Maria had been a substitute for his real mother (Eliza), so Maria's daughter Virginia was to some extent a substitute for her mother and that consequently his marriage was a means of possessing through the daughter the mother-substitute Maria, and through Maria, the absent mother who died when Poe was two.

To judge from Poe's correspondence, one of his motives in proposing to Virginia was a desire to keep together the family unit he had lived with since returning to Baltimore from West Point in 1831 (an arrangement whose continuation had been threatened, in the wake of his grandmother's death and the loss of her pension, by the offer of Neilson Poe, another cousin, "to provide for Virginia's education and support" [Quinn, 219]), in effect, Poe's desire to maintain the household in which "Eddie" was mothered by "Muddy." This is not to suggest that Poe did not love his cousin/wife but simply to note that love is an emotion compounded of various desires. The complexity of Poe's relationship with mother and daughter can be seen in his tribute to Maria Clemm, the 1849 sonnet "To My Mother":

> Because I feel that, in the Heavens above,
>   The angels, whispering to one another,
> Can find, among their burning terms of love,
>   None so devotional as that of "Mother,"
> Therefore by that dear name I long have called you—
>   You who are more than mother unto me,
> And fill my heart of hearts, where Death installed you
>   In setting my Virginia's spirit free.
> My mother—my own mother, who died early,
>   Was but the mother of myself; but you
> Are mother to the one I loved so dearly,
>   And thus are dearer than the mother I knew
> By that infinity with which my wife
>   Was dearer to my soul than its soul-life.   (1:466–67)

Even allowing for a degree of hyperbole, the poem suggests the intensity of Poe's feelings about the ideal embodied in a mother-substitute.

Now while it is certainly possible to interpret the assault on a mother and daughter in the first Dupin story as an expression of Poe's repressed feelings about his psychically incestuous union with a related pair of mother-substitutes, such a reading does not do full justice to the complexity of the message encrypted in the odd crime that begins the detective genre. Which is simply to say that although the image of such a forbidden union seems to be an important component of that message, there is another component of equal if not greater importance, one that emerges when we consider the crime not simply as an evocation of psychosexual transgression but as literal mayhem, a brutal murder of mother and daughter committed within an internally sealed space from which the killer is inexplicably absent.

From what we know of Poe's life, he was a man whose relationships with women characteristically involved the need to be mothered. But to judge from his fiction, he was highly ambivalent about this need, at once wanting maternal care and affection from women and yet resenting it as an entrapment in childish dependency. Apparently, for Poe the reverse side of the need to be mothered was the fear of being smothered, of being buried alive in the womb of the family, and in his fiction wherever we find the imagery of a claustrophobic enclosure or of premature burial, we usually find not far away this fear of being (s)mothered to death.

Nowhere is this clearer than in the series of "dying woman" stories he published between 1835 and 1841, a series that includes "Berenicë" (1835), "Morella" (1835), "Ligeia" (1838), "The Fall of the House of Usher" (1839), and "Eleonora" (1841). From these tales we can abstract a general structure that leads into, and sheds light on, the Dupin stories with their series of female victims. The various structural elements of the "dying woman" scenario do not, of course, all appear in any one of the tales, nor does any element of the structure (with the exception of the mortally ill female figure and her male companion) necessarily appear in all the tales. In its most general form, the dying woman story concerns a sensitive, often "artistic" young man (usually the story's narrator) whose precarious psychic stability is undermined by the illness and death of a woman to whom he is closely related. The nature of their relationship varies. Often the woman is the wife or betrothed of the young man as in "Morella" and "Ligeia," or a close relative (a twin) as in "The Fall of the House of Usher," or both as in "Berenicë" and "Eleonora" where she is the man's cousin and his betrothed. Sometimes the man and woman have been raised together in the same dwelling from childhood ("Berenicë," "The Fall of the House of Usher," "Eleonora"), and almost as frequently the man's unstable temperament is presented as an hereditary disposition embodied in and to some degree transmitted by the claustrophobic home. In "Berenicë," for example, the "gloomy, gray, hereditary halls" of "the

family mansion" embody the visionary character of the narrator's fore-
bears, a character expressed in the building's architectural style, "in the
gallery of antique paintings—in the fashion of the library chamber—and,
lastly, in the very peculiar nature of the library's contents":

> The recollections of my earliest years are connected with that chamber, and
> with its volumes. . . . Here died my mother. Herein was I born. But it is mere
> idleness to say that I had not lived before—that the soul has no previous
> existence. . . . There is . . . a remembrance of aerial forms—of spiritual and
> meaning eyes—of sounds, musical yet sad; a remembrance which will not be
> excluded; a memory like a shadow—vague, variable, indefinite, unsteady; and
> like a shadow, too, in the impossibility of my getting rid of it while the sunlight
> of my reason shall exist.
>
> In that chamber was I born. . . . I loitered away my boyhood in books, and
> dissipated my youth in revery; but it *is* singular, that as years rolled away, and
> the noon of manhood found me still in the mansion of my fathers—it *is*
> wonderful what stagnation there fell upon the springs of my life. . . .
>   **************
> Berenicë and I were cousins, and we grew up together in my paternal halls.
> (2:209–10)

In his most explicit diagnosis of the psychic malady afflicting the heroes of these tales, Poe figures the library as a womb/tomb in which the
narrator was born and his mother died (presumably in giving birth), and
he evokes the narrator's sense of preexistence as a kind of amniotic
dreamworld, an ideal of all-encompassing maternal care whose remembrance falls like a shadow across the narrator's life, causing the psychic stagnation that reduces his present existence to a series of meditative
reveries within the womblike chamber. Indeed, one might argue that this
idealized prenatal condition had become associated in Poe's own life with
the image of a dead mother, an association that linked the sleep of the
womb with that of the grave and the goal of reunion with the means of
reunion (the mother with Death). It is this deathly shadow that seems to
fall across the women in Poe's life, a dark image of the dead mother as
Mother Death superimposed on the living faces of the women he cared
for. One might argue as well that his cousin Virginia ultimately surpassed
his aunt Maria as a mother-substitute precisely by dying, by coming to
resemble Poe's real mother in that most important of aspects.

Whatever the truth of Poe's own inner life, the men in these tales find
themselves emotionally bound (often inexplicably so) to women who are
mortally ill and who, because of the life-threatening effect of their illness
on the precarious mental state of their consorts, come to embody Death
for these men. But while the women in these tales are weak in body, they

are prodigiously strong in spirit, gifted with a power of will that enables them either to return from the grave in their own person (as in the case of Madeline Usher) or to return in spirit and take over another's body (as with Morella and Ligeia). The case of Morella seems particularly relevant to Poe's own situation in that there the spirit of a dead mother comes back from the crypt to inhabit the body of her daughter. Moreover, in several of these stories the woman's strength of spirit manifests itself as an over-mastering intelligence that reduces the man to childlike dependence, as if he were at his mother's knee. The narrator of "Morella" remarks that because his wife's "powers of mind were gigantic" he "became her pupil" (2:229); while the narrator of "Ligeia" says, "I was sufficiently aware of her infinite supremacy to resign myself, with a child-like confidence, to her guidance through the chaotic world of metaphysical investigation" (2:316).

The dying woman tends, then, to be coded as a mother-surrogate, and to the extent this makes her an object of the man's desire, it also makes her, in a double sense, a threat to his life. On the one hand, since she serves as a kind of Psyche figure, the beloved woman's physical deterioration in the grip of a wasting illness mirrors (and thereby exacerbates) the man's psychic deterioration. On the other hand, as a mother figure the woman serves to keep the man in a state of childlike dependence, and since Poe's standard rite-of-passage scenario for depicting a character's progress from adolescence to maturity involves a symbolic death and rebirth, this arresting of the man in emotional immaturity by the mother figure is frequently depicted as a symbolic death without a subsequent rebirth, a living entombment in the womb of the family evoked either as a psychically incestuous union with a close relative or an inability to leave the ancestral home, or both. Indeed, precisely because overcoming the fear of death is at once the principal task and goal in the passage from childhood to adulthood, this arresting of the man in a psychic state where that fear remains unmastered makes the woman's gradual decline all the more terrifying, as in "The Fall of the House of Usher" where Roderick predicts that his own inordinate terror of death, in being aggravated by the sight of his dying twin, will inevitably cause, through his mental collapse, the very thing he fears.

It is to protect himself from being destroyed by the woman he desires that the man tries in several of these tales to rid himself of her terrifying presence by literally inflicting on her the living entombment she personifies for him. But with the woman's premature burial, a characteristic reversal occurs. As long as the dying woman is still alive, she represents death-in-life; but once she has been prematurely interred, she represents life-in-death, embodying the man's narcissistic obsession with survival enacted as the woman's real or hallucinated return from the grave to bring not life but madness or death. We should note that in "Berenicë" the narrator's disinterment of the woman's body, a body "enshrouded, yet still breathing" (2:218), involves as well an act of grotesque physical violence. The narrator, using "instruments of dental surgery" (2:219), pulls out Berenicë's teeth. Apart from the act's symbolic significance—a figurative attempt to defang the *vagina dentata* of the grave, the flesh-eating maw/womb of (Mother) Earth/Death—that violence against the woman (as an expression of the man's hatred of the debilitating familial entrapment his cousin/betrothed personifies) clearly exhibits the link between the dying woman stories (where the man tries to save himself from a living death in the womb of the family by prematurely consigning the woman to the family tomb) and the first detective story (with its brutal murder of a mother and daughter in a locked room from which the killer has inexplicably escaped). Which is to say that the locked room of "The Murders in the Rue Morgue" is simply a structural transformation of the womblike family crypt or narrow room of the grave from the dying woman stories, and the resemblance between the two enclosed spaces is emphasized by the supererogatory entombment of Mlle. L'Espanaye, whose body is forced "head downward . . . up the narrow aperture" of the chimney "for a considerable distance" (2:538).

Although mother and daughter are both murdered within the room, only the daughter's body is found there when the police break in. As we noted, Mme. L'Espanaye's corpse, with its head almost severed, is discovered in "a small paved yard in the rear of the building" (2:538). This difference in the disposition of the two bodies (one inside, one outside the locked room), along with the daughter's enclosure in the womblike space of the chimney and the mother's decapitation, is indicative of the repressed Oedipal character of the scene. As we recall, the revelation of Oedipus's incest causes his mother to commit suicide, an act of self-violence immediately doubled by Oedipus's own self-mutilation as he gouges out his eyeballs with the brooches from Jocasta's robe. Based on the above/below equation of eyeballs and testicles, the usual psychoanalytic interpretation of Oedipus's blinding explains it as a symbolic self-castration, an interpretation that suggests as well the appropriateness of the instruments of mutilation. For just as the brooches fastening Jocasta's robe had been unpinned during her marriage to unveil to Oedipus's gaze what, as a son, he should not have seen and to permit his entrance where he should not have gone, so they are unpinned one last time by Oedipus in order to punish the offending organs of sight and, by extension, the offending sexual organ.

The fact that Oedipus's incest with his mother results in mirroring acts of self-violence sheds light on the detail of Mme. L'Espanaye's near-decapitation by the razor-wielding ape. As the agency of violence in "The Murders in the Rue Morgue" is divided (the human master outside the room watching through the window as the animal slave inside slaughters the two women), so the object of that violence is also divided (the mother in the paved yard outside and the daughter entombed in the chimney within). This inside/outside division suggests the splitting and doubling of agent and object found in the dying woman stories, where the man's action against his female double, the outer embodiment of his inner life, amounts to self-destruction. And this in turn suggests that the difference in the disposition of the victims' bodies (the objects of violence) in the first detective story can be read as a reflection of the division within the agency of the violence, a division of desire against itself that is ultimately self-canceling. Thus, if the daughter's entombment in the chimney and the culprit's absence from the locked room express the male's desire to escape from the suffocating womb of the family by inflicting on the female the literal entombment that she symbolically represents for him, then the decapitated body found outside the room evokes in turn the ultimate effect on the male of this violent escape, his psychic castration, projected here onto the female double (whose gender betokens as well the feminization of the male that results from self-mutilation). There are, of course, Oedipal resonances to these roles and actions in both groups of Poe stories, resonances that evoke not only Jocasta's suicide and Oedipus's self-mutilation at the discovery of their incest but also their daughter Antigone's living entombment by her uncle Creon, an entombment that results in the double suicide of Antigone and her cousin/betrothed Haemon. We will pursue these later, but for the moment we must consider which character in the Dupin tales corresponds most closely in terms of his psychic situation to the male protagonist of the dying woman stories and what this correspondence means in terms of the triadic structure of the detective story.

25 _Sexual Victims; "Eleonora"; Borges and His Mother; The Test of the Hero; The Birth Trauma and the Sphinx_

GIVEN THE DOUBLING OF DETECTIVE and criminal characteristic of the genre, it seems clear that in the Dupin tales the structural equivalent of the recurring male figure from the dying woman stories is Dupin himself, though an equivalence somewhat disguised due to Poe's rather obvious identification with the archreasoner. Several details in the stories suggest this notion. For example, in his initial description of Dupin, the narrator presents him as someone out of contact with, or perhaps estranged from, his "illustrious family" (2:531). He notes that "a variety of untoward events" had reduced Dupin "to such poverty that the energy of his character succumbed beneath it" (2:531), with no apparent aid forthcoming from his relatives. Consequently, when the narrator and Dupin take up residence together, it is the narrator who rents and furnishes the house, serving in effect as a kind of surrogate family. Further, in establishing this residence, they isolate themselves so completely from the world that it seems like a withdrawal into a kind of womblike security. The narrator notes, "Our seclusion was perfect. We admitted no visitors. . . . We existed within ourselves alone" (2:532). Add to the mansion's isolation the fact that Dupin keeps the shutters closed during the day, creating an artificial night in which he and the narrator busy their "souls in dreams— reading, writing, or conversing" (2:533), and one is reminded of the narrator's amniotic reveries in the library in "Berenicë" and Roderick's meditations in his gloomy chamber in "The Fall of the House of Usher." Indeed, it seems only fitting that a master analyst who lives in a kind of womblike retirement should be presented with, as his first case of detection, the problem of the "locked room" murder of a mother and daughter and further fitting that he confirms his solution to the murders by luring the killer's human master to his secluded mansion and locking him in his chamber (2:563).

We can appreciate by this point how pervasive the Oedipal resonances are in Poe's first detective story and thus how powerful is the force of repression directed against mentioning Oedipus's name, powerful enough even to submerge the name of a mythic figure (Theseus) associated with him. For to mention or suggest by resemblance the name of the man whose incest led to his mother's suicide and his own self-mutilation would be to recall, in the context of a brutal murder of a mother and daughter, Poe's own psychically incestuous relationship and thus to suggest that the irrational violence directed against the L'Espanayes is an unconscious expression or artistic sublimation of a real, repressed resentment Poe felt toward that other mother/daughter pair evoked by these characters.

Again, this is not to imply that Poe did not love Virginia and Maria but simply to suggest that by marrying his cousin in order to keep intact the family he had shared for several years, Poe had secured for himself an emotionally supportive domestic circle at the cost of assuming both a heavy financial and a psychologically complex familial responsibility. One can well imagine that at moments Poe thought the price he had paid for a measure of domestic stability was too high and resented those associated with the stifling of his independence, a resentment of which he would undoubtedly have been ashamed and would have repressed precisely because he knew that without this family unit he would not have been emotionally or financially independent but, as his later life was to demonstrate, hopelessly adrift.

Whether or not such resentment is an underlying factor in the dying woman stories and thus in the brutal assault on the mother and daughter in the first detective story, there can be little doubt about the structural link between the two groups of tales, a link that serves to explain why the victims in the Dupin stories are all women and why their victimization has in each case a sexual dimension. We noted already the sexual resonances of the ape's assault on the mother and daughter in "The Murders in the Rue Morgue." This undercurrent of sexual violence becomes explicit in "The Mystery of Marie Rogêt" where "the general impression" of the crime given by the newspapers was that Marie had been raped and murdered by "*a gang* of desperadoes" (3:734). Although Dupin refutes the gang-rape theory, there is no reason to believe, given the cause of death in the actual case on which the tale is based, that had Poe chosen to maintain the parallel between the fictive case and the real one, the cause of Marie Rogêt's death would have been any less sexually motivated, since the victim in the real case, Mary Cecilia Rogers, died as the result of an abortion. (In a January 1848 letter to George Eveleth, Poe, discussing "The Mystery of Marie Rogêt," refers to Rogers's "accidental death arising from an attempt at abortion" and adds cryptically that "the whole matter is now well understood—but, for the sake of relatives, this is a topic on which I must not speak further" [3:788 n. 120].) In the final Dupin story, of course, the queen is the victim not of physical but of psychological violence (blackmail); and once again the violence has a sexual dimension, for the letter the minister holds over her head apparently implicates her in an adulterous affair.

The notion that the Oedipal implications of the detective stories for Poe's personal life ultimately account for the repression of Oedipus's name in the text is further confirmed by two related Poe tales in which the name does appear—"Thou Art the Man" and the most idyllic of the dying woman tales, "Eleonora." Poe can mention Oedipus's name in the first sentence of the former precisely because the victim in the tale is not a woman but a man and the apparent motive for the crime greed rather than sexual revenge. The tale thus allows most of the elements associated with Oedipus as an archetype of analytic detection to function, while excluding the one element (the difference in gender between murderer and victim) that evokes the disturbing sexual component of Oedipus's story.

Poe's reference to Oedipus in "Eleonora," published some three years before "Thou Art the Man," is equally revealing, for just as "Thou Art the Man" deletes the element of female victimization found in the detective stories, so "Eleonora" dispels the sense of mutual victimization (the man's feeling of being psychologically buried alive by the mother figure and his literal retaliation) found in the dying woman stories. Indeed, the tale's mood of mutual release and conciliation between man and woman probably permits as well the remarkably close resemblance of the narrator's domestic situation to Poe's own. Presenting himself as a divided consciousness, the narrator introduces the description of his family with a reference to Oedipus's riddle solving:

> There are two distinct conditions of my mental existence—the condition of a lucid reason, not to be disputed, and belonging to the memory of events forming the first epoch of my life—and a condition of shadow and doubt, appertaining to the present, and to the recollection of what constitutes the second great era of my being. Therefore, what I shall tell of the earlier period, believe; and to what I may relate of the later time, give only such credit as may seem due; or doubt it altogether; or, if doubt it ye cannot, then play unto its riddle the Oedipus.
>
> She whom I loved in youth, and of whom I now pen calmly and distinctly these remembrances, was the sole daughter of the only sister of my mother long departed. Eleonora was the name of my cousin. We had always dwelled together, beneath a tropical sun, in the Valley of the Many-Colored Grass. No unguided footstep ever came upon that vale. . . . Thus it was that we lived all alone, knowing nothing of the world without the valley,—I, and my cousin, and her mother. (2:638–39)

Maria Clemm was not, of course, the sister of Poe's mother, Eliza Arnold, but of his father David Poe, Jr., so that in altering his own personal history to produce the narrator's, Poe emphasizes the direct line of descent, the unbranching chain of substitutes, that runs from the betrothed cousin back to the dead mother: "the *sole* daughter of the *only* sister of my mother long departed" (my italics).

When the narrator is twenty and Eleonora fifteen, they fall in love, and with this change in their relationship the character of the enclosed valley changes: "And now, too, a voluminous cloud . . . sank, day by day, lower and lower, until its edges rested upon the tops of the mountains, . . . shutting us up, as if forever, within a magic prison-house of grandeur and glory" (2:641). That the awakening of sexual love between the cousins transforms the idyllic enclosure of their childhood into a "prison-house" (albeit of "grandeur and glory") is no more surprising in the psychic economy of these tales than that Eleonora should be struck almost immediately with a wasting illness. In Poe, death is the handmaiden of sex. As Eleonora grows weaker, she is affected less by "the terrors of the grave" than by the thought that the narrator, "having entombed her in the Valley of the Many-Colored Grass," will "quit forever its happy recesses, transferring the love which now was so passionately her own to some maiden of the outer . . . world" (2:642). To quiet her fears, the narrator vows never to marry and invokes a curse upon himself should he break his promise. Comforted by his vow, Eleonora promises that after her death she will remain with him in spirit, giving him "frequent indications of her presence" (2:642). With Eleonora's passing, "the second era" of the narrator's existence begins in which, as he says, "a shadow gathers over" him. He leaves the valley for "a strange city" where "the pomps and pageantries of a stately court" efface the memories of his earlier life, and "the indications of the presence of Eleonora" which "were still given" to him "in the silent hours of the night" suddenly cease. There the narrator weds "the ethereal Ermengarde" (2:644), but the curse he had invoked to seal his vow to Eleonora is not "visited upon" him (2:645). One last time in the silence of the night, he hears the voice of Eleonora: "Sleep in peace!—for the Spirit of Love reigneth and ruleth, and, in taking to thy passionate heart her who is Ermengarde, thou art absolved, for reasons which shall be made known to thee in Heaven, of thy vows unto Eleonora" (2:645).

If this had been one of the earlier dying woman stories, it would have ended with the revelation that Ermengarde was the reincarnation of Eleonora, that Eleonora's spirit had either forcibly taken over Ermengarde's body (as in "Ligeia") or been reborn in a new body (as in "Morella"). But that expected ending is precisely what does not occur. Eleonora's absolution of the narrator from his vow and her parting benediction sound a note of release at odds with the terror of the earlier stories. One wonders, however, whether this change reflects the fact that "Eleonora" was published almost six months after the appearance of the first Dupin story and thus whether the current of sexual resentment running through the earlier dying woman stories had been diverted into the new genre whose subject matter offered greater scope for the violent expression of these impulses.

We should note in passing that just as there is in the genealogy of Southern gothic writing a structural line of descent linking the decapitation of Mme. L'Espanaye by the razor-wielding ape in the first Dupin story to the decapitation of Joanna Burden by the razor-wielding black, Joe Christmas, in Faulkner's *Light in August*, so there is also, I would suggest, a related line of descent (within the gothic structures of doubling and incest) linking Poe's psychically incestuous household with its cousin/wife "Sis" and aunt/mother-in-law "Muddy" to Quentin Compson's incestuous obsession with his sister Candace in *The Sound and the Fury*—an obsession with a mother-substitute that is also an obsession with death, the combination of the two being encoded for Quentin in the recurring image of Candace's "muddy drawers" first seen by her brother when Candace as a child climbs a tree outside their parlor window to look in at the funeral of their grandmother "Damuddy."[1]

This dual line of descent linking Poe and Faulkner as Southern gothic detective writers is significant for our purposes because, as I suggested earlier, the principal contemporary mediator of Poe's influence for Borges in his detective story project seems to have been Faulkner. Borges's acquaintance with Faulkner's work dates from at least the mid-1930s. In a review of *Absalom, Absalom!* published in the periodical *El Hogar*, Borges describes the novel as "comparable to *The Sound and the Fury*," adding "I know of no higher praise" (*BR*, 93); in another he proposes Faulkner as "the leading novelist of our time" (*BR*, 94). In addition to these early reviews, the most visible example of Borges's admiration for Faulkner's work was his translation of *The Wild Palms* published by Sudamericana in 1941, the same year as "The Garden of Forking Paths." Monegal notes that "the importance of this translation for the new Latin American novel was considerable," a translation thought by many to be "as good as or even better than the original. . . . The hardness and intensity of the novel's best passages (praised by Borges in his review as 'notoriously exceeding the possibilities of any other author') indicate how much he put into the translation—in spite of his claims that it was Mother who really did it" (*JLB*, 373).

Monegal's closing comment refers to Borges's remark in "An Autobiographical Essay" that many of the translations bearing his name were actually the work of his mother, Leonor Acevedo de Borges. The passage in the essay is particularly interesting for the picture it gives of the lifelong companionship of mother and son:

> My mother has always had a hospitable mind. From the time she learned English, through my father, she has done most of her reading in that language. After my father's death, finding that she was unable to keep her mind on the printed page, she tried her hand at translating William Saroyan's *The Human Comedy* in order to compel herself to concentrate. . . . Later on, . . . she also produced some of the translations of Melville, Virginia Woolf, and Faulkner that are considered mine. She has always been a companion to me— especially in later years, when I went blind—and an understanding and forgiving friend. For years, until recently, she handled all my secretarial work, answering letters, reading to me, taking down my dictation, and also traveling with me on many occasions both at home and abroad. It was she, though I never gave a thought to it at the time, who quietly and effectively fostered my literary career. (*A*, 207–8)

As we noted earlier, in "An Autobiographical Essay" Borges associates the start of his career as a fiction writer with a symbolic death and rebirth in which his mother plays a crucial role in bringing his new persona into existence. In the same year his father died (1938), Borges himself almost died of blood poisoning, hovering "all unknowingly, between life and death" for a month (*A*, 243). As he began to recover, he feared that the prolonged fever had destroyed his "mental integrity" (*A*, 243). Borges's mother had tried to read to him during his convalescence, but he kept putting her off. At last she prevailed, and after a page or two Borges began to cry, so he tells us, grateful to find that he could still understand. Soon after, as a test of whether he could still write as well, he began his first story in a new style, "Pierre Menard, Author of *Don Quixote*."

It would, I think, be difficult to overestimate the importance of Borges's mother to his work. That she in fact "quietly and effectively fostered" his "literary career" seems certain, as emblemized by this scene in which a mother reads to her son as a means of ultimately enabling his writing. And given this importance, one wonders about the significance of Borges's decision, in doubling the Dupin stories, to suppress the element of female victimization (with its implied sexual motivation) in favor of a series of male victims and motives of politics, revenge, or greed, that is, in favor of a configuration resembling "Thou Art the Man."

Now if it is accurate to say that Poe's mother (who died when he was two, abandoning him to the care of strangers) remained figuratively present to him for the rest of his life as an absence of, as an unfulfilled and perhaps unfulfillable need for, maternal affection that he tried to satisfy through a series of mother-substitutes, then it may also be accurate to say that Borges's mother (who lived into her nineties, serving as a "companion . . . especially in later years" when he "went blind" and as "an understanding and forgiving friend") remained present to her son for most of his life as the very embodiment of maternal care. This is not to say that for a grown man a lifelong companionship with his mother would not have its difficulties and consequent resentments but simply to suggest that where the figure of the mother signifies for Poe an abiding absence, this figure exists for Borges as a lifelong, literal presence. And this difference, reflected perhaps in Borges's decision to reverse the gender of the victims in doubling Poe's detective stories, corresponds to a significant difference in the two classical myths underlying both groups of stories. When Poe in "Thou Art the Man" abandons the structure of a female victim and sexual motive in favor of a male victim and the motive of greed, the name that suddenly appears in the text is Oedipus's, but when Borges in his three detective stories adopts this configuration of male victim and apparently nonsexual motive, the classical myth evoked in all three stories (and explicitly named in the third) is Theseus's slaying of the Minotaur.

In reading the myths of Oedipus and Theseus as symbolic accounts of the development and stabilization of self-consciousness, one tends to treat Theseus as a later, more developed stage in this process. A clear instance of what this difference in development amounts to can be seen in the cognate episodes of the Sphinx and Minotaur. One of the traditional tasks of the hero is, of course, to slay a monster threatening the community, a monster representing the fear of death, which must be overcome if the human community is to survive, if its members are to function in a world of risk. That the communal mastering of the personal fear of death is what the hero's act at once accomplishes and portrays can be seen in the standard association of the monstrous figure with either a descent into the underworld or with the image of a terrifying primordial mother. In *The Trauma of Birth* (1929), Otto Rank argues that when the hero masters the fear of death he is in essence overcoming the repressed primal trauma of birth, mastering the fear of that terrifying threshold whose crossing in one direction is the movement from the womb's security to the mortal world by means of a violent expulsion through the smothering, narrow gate (a trauma whose memory must be repressed if the fragile life is to survive) and whose crossing in the other direction is the return to the womb of earth, the flesh-eating maw of the grave. According to Rank, the tests of the hero (by which he passes from the human to the heroic plane) are evoked as symbolic deaths and rebirths not so much because this is the standard rite-of-passage structure for figuring the end of one stage of human development and the beginning of another, as because the symbolic mastering of the primal trauma of birth is itself, as far as self-consciousness is concerned, the archetypal heroic act, the act whose structure is superimposed on any significant transition from one stage of life to another. Thus in a rite-of-passage scenario, for example, one reason for symbolizing the passage from childhood to adulthood as a death to the former and rebirth to the latter is precisely to equate the movement from one stage of life to another with the passage from life to death, *thereby coding the state after death as simply another stage of life.* In such a ritual the community incorporates death into the world of meaning by figuring it as the stage preceding (re)birth.

In this connection Rank contends that the monster who confronts Oedipus with the riddle of human differentiation represents "the primary birth anxiety" in the form of "a mother symbol" and that "her character as 'strangler' makes the reference to the birth anxiety unambiguous."[2] The Greek word *sphinx* ("strangler") derives from the verb *sphingein*, "to draw or bind tight," a verb that is also the root of our word *sphincter*, "a ring-shaped muscle that surrounds a natural opening in the body and can open or close it by expanding or contracting" (*W*, 1403). The Sphinx is generally depicted with a human head and neck, the breast, feet and tail of a lion, and the wings of a bird. In the Egyptian version the human portion is male, but in the Greek version (the monster who confronts Oedipus) the human portion is female. In Hesiod's *Theogony* the Sphinx is identified as the offspring of the goddess Echidna and her son "Orthus the hound of Geryones,"[3] and is thus, as a product of mother-son incest, an appropriate figure to pose the riddle whose successful solution ultimately leads to Oedipus's being made king of Thebes and marrying his own mother.

Noting that the Oedipus saga is "a duplicate of the Sphinx episode," Rank suggests that the story represents "the repetition of the primal trauma at the sexual stage (Oedipus complex), whereas the Sphinx represents the primal trauma itself" (Rank, 144). And certainly the Sphinx comes by her "man-swallowing character" (Rank, 144), her association with the womb of the grave, through legitimate succession, as Hesiod makes clear in his description of the Sphinx's mother Echidna, a monster "who is half a nymph with glancing eyes and fair cheeks, and half again a huge snake, great and awful, with speckled skin, eating raw flesh beneath the secret parts of the holy earth" where "she has a cave deep down under a hollow rock far from the deathless gods and mortal men" (Hesiod, 101). Rank argues that the Sphinx, conforming to its character as strangler, represents not only in its latent content the wish to return into the mother, as the danger of being swallowed, but it also represents in its manifest form parturition itself and the struggle against it, in that the human upper body grows out of the animal-like (maternal) lower body without finally being able to free itself from it. (Rank, 145)

Rank further suggests that the biform creatures who confront the heroes of Greek mythology with some life-threatening test of their heroic mission not only evoke in a symbolic form the individual birth trauma (as the partial emergence of a human from an animal body) but also figure the more general trauma of the birth of the "human" from the "natural" world, of self-consciousness (the awareness of an individual life and death) from the animal world's amniotic sleep.

In the case of Theseus and the Minotaur the symbolic evocation of the birth trauma seems clear. The winding subterranean passages of the labyrinth are, says Freud, "the twisting paths" of "the bowels" in a mythic "representation of anal birth"[4] (i.e., the type of birth associated with "the animal kingdom" in childhood theories of birth [*SE*, 7:196]), "and Ariadne's thread is the umbilical cord" (*SE*, 22:25). The Minotaur, who resides at the center of the labyrinth, is, of course, a biform creature and thus by Rank's standard an image of the primal birth trauma. However, unlike the Sphinx whose upper part is human and lower part animal (a configuration that accords with Rank's idea of the higher [human] form emerging from the lower [animal] one), the Minotaur is usually depicted as having a human body and an animal head, a fact that apparently leads Rank to theorize that the Minotaur, considered as a "mis-shapen form" (Rank, 154), may represent the human embryo as an animal-like, partially formed being trapped in the "prison" of the womb, "unable to find the exit" (Rank, 154). For our purposes, however, the major difference between the biform creatures confronting Oedipus and Theseus is that the human portion of the Sphinx is female, while that of the Minotaur is male. Which is to say that the female monster who poses the riddle of man in the Oedipus story (threatening to devour the hero if he fails to answer correctly) is replaced by a male monster in the Theseus story, with the female element being transposed into a loving companion and helper (Ariadne) who aids Theseus in entering the womb of the labyrinth, defeating the monster of the grave, and returning to the upper world by means of the umbilical thread.

For the hero to defeat the killer animal is in effect for him to defeat the animal in himself, that irrational part which in its instinctual terror of death threatens to overwhelm the rational and bring about the destruction it fears. The hero's mastery of the fear of death is figured in the

Theseus myth, then, not simply in the defeat of the subterranean monster but in the transformation of the mother figure, a change in the female image apparent in the gender difference of the victims in the two episodes—from a terrifying female to be defeated to a terrifying male who can only be defeated with the help of a woman. And this difference is played out again in a subsequent episode of each myth. Thus Oedipus, who causes the female Sphinx to leap off a cliff by answering her riddle, later causes his mother Jocasta to hang herself by solving the mystery of his identity, causes her in effect to strangle in midair, thus associating her with the Strangler who leaps to her death and who embodies the son's fear of the desired return to the matrix. In contrast, Ariadne, who aids Theseus in being reborn from a lower to a higher realm by means of the umbilical thread (a symbol of the unrealized threat of strangulation), accompanies Theseus when he leaves Crete and, in most versions of the myth, is herself translated to a higher realm when she becomes the consort of Dionysus and, upon her death, has the crown Dionysus had given her transformed into a constellation, the Corona Borealis.

Since the gender difference of the monsters slain by Oedipus and Theseus corresponds to the difference in the victims' genders in Poe's and Borges's detective stories, one might see this assimilation of Poe's tales to Oedipus's myth and Borges's to Theseus's as suggesting that the transformational process governing the two myths (the translation of the terrifying mother of the underworld into the idealized female helpmate of the heavens) governs the two groups of stories as well, a possibility to keep in mind as we look more closely at the myth of the Minotaur and labyrinth in Borges's work.

26 *The* Labrys; *The House of the Double Axe;*
Evans and Frazer; The Ritual Marriage of Sun
and Moon; The House of Asterion

SO IMPORTANT IS THE MYTHIC configuration of Minotaur and labyrinth not only to Borges's detective stories but to his work as a whole that it is virtually impossible to understand the overall shape of his fiction without knowing something of the ancient practices associated with this myth. Recall that in *The Book of Imaginary Beings* (1967) Borges cites the generally accepted derivation of the word *labyrinth* in his essay on the Minotaur: "The worship of the bull and of the two-headed ax (whose name was *labrys* and may have been at the root of the word *labyrinth*) was typical of pre-Hellenic religions, which held sacred bullfights" (*BIB*, 159). The entry for *labyrinth* in the eleventh edition of the *Britannica* clarifies this etymology, noting that *labrys* is "a Lydian or Carian word meaning a 'double-edged axe' (*Journal of Hellenic Studies*, xxi. 109, 268), according to which the Cretan labyrinth or palace of Minos was the house of the double axe, the symbol of Zeus" (*EB*, 16:32). In "The House of Asterion," Borges explicitly invokes this origin when he says that from the entrance to the labyrinth the Minotaur could see "the temple of the Axes" (*L*, 139).

The modern scholarly source for this derivation is the 1901 article by Arthur J. Evans in *The Journal of Hellenic Studies* cited in the *Britannica*. As we noted earlier, Borges acquired the eleventh edition of the *Britannica* in 1929, and he seems to have used it consistently as a starting point for his research. Moreover, since Borges worked as a librarian for a large part of his adult life, it would have been second nature for him to look up a reference to a subject that interested him as much as the labyrinth did. What he would have found is an essay entitled "Mycenaean Tree and Pillar Cult and Its Mediterranean Relations" in which Evans, the excavator of the Palace of Knossos at Crete, argues that among the ancient inhabitants of the island the double-edged axe "stood as the visible impersonation" of the Cretan Zeus, not a symbol but "the actual material shape of the divinity, the object into which his spiritual essence might enter as it did into his sacred pillar or tree."[1] Evans notes that there is ample evidence in the ancient Mediterranean world of the association of the double axe with the cult of the bull, an association based on the fact that the bull, like the double axe, was a sacred object representing "the material form or

246

Figure 26.1

indwelling-place of the divinity" (Evans, 107) and that the double axe was an instrument used in the periodic ritual sacrifices of the animal to the god. Evans cites as an example a painted Mycenaean vase showing "the repeated delineation of a double axe apparently set in the ground between pairs of bulls, which also have double axes between their horns" (Evans, 106–7) (see fig. 26.1). He points out that at the foot of the axe handle placed between the bulls' heads appears a "distinctive piece of Mycenaean ritual furniture elsewhere described as 'the horns of consecration.' It occupies the same position in relation to the double axe as in other cases it does to the pillar or tree forms of the divinity" (Evans, 107).

Since the Cretan Zeus was, according to Evans, essentially a solar deity, the association of the bull's horns with other phallic objects evoking the engendering power of the sun (such as pillar and tree) is understandable. However, the linking of the double axe with the bull and the stone pillar (considered as embodiments of the solar deity) depends upon a further association which Evans finds present throughout the Palace at Knossos, culminating at the "centre of the building" in "two small contiguous chambers" (see fig. 26.2):

> In the middle of each . . . rises a square column . . . on every side . . . of which in one case and on three sides of the other is engraved a double axe. There can . . . be little doubt that these chambers are shrines, probably belonging to the oldest part of the building, and the pillars thus marked with the sign of the God are in fact his aniconic images. The double axe is thus combined with the sacred pillar. (Evans, 110–11)

For Evans the evidence linking the double axe to the pillar and bull cults is of such weight that it leads him to recognize "in the great prehistoric Palace . . . at Knossos . . . the true original of the traditional Labyrinth" (Evans, 110). Citing the Palace's "long corridors and succession of magazines with their blind endings, its tortuous passages, and maze of

Figure 26.2

lesser chambers, . . . its huge fresco-paintings and reliefs of bulls, grap-
pled perhaps by men, as on a gem impression from the same site, the
Mycenaean prototype of Theseus and the Minotaur," Evans pronounces
the "at present partially excavated" structure both a palace and "a
sanctuary"—"the 'House of the Double Axe'" (Evans, 110). And he invokes as further proof of the building's status as a sanctuary of the god the
fact that its "chief corner stones and doorjambs . . . are incised with the
double axe sign, implying consecration to the Cretan Zeus" (Evans, 110).

   Now whether the Palace at Knossos is, as Evans argued in 1901, "the
true original of the traditional Labyrinth" is obviously not the issue here.
Nor is the issue whether the word *labyrinth* actually derived from the
Carian word *labrys*. Indeed, in the same volume of *The Journal of Hellenic
Studies* in which Evans's article appears, there is a note by W. H. D. Rouse
casting doubt both on the derivation of *labyrinth* from *labrys* and on the
identification of the Palace at Knossos with the Cretan labyrinth. For our
purposes the point is that the lack of any certain etymology for *labyrinth,*
combined with Evans's prestige as excavator of one of the great archae-
ological sites of the Mediterranean world, led to the derivation of *labyrinth*
from *labrys* (with its appealing background of bull cult and double axe)
becoming the etymology usually cited by dictionaries, even when they

Figure 26.3

designate it as questionable (a questionableness reflected in Borges's remark that *labrys* "may have been at the root of the word *labyrinth*"). All of which is to say that although Borges was aware of the uncertainty of this derivation, he nevertheless (judging from "The House of Asterion" and the Minotaur essay) seems to have used Evans's work linking the labyrinth, double axe, and bull cult in much the same way that he used the writings of Jung or "Pliny or Frazer's *Golden Bough*"—"as a kind of mythology, or as a kind of museum or encyclopedia of curious lores" (Burgin, 109).

One of the most significant passages in Evans's 1901 article concerns the double axe's "janiform" character, its status as the material form of a dual or conjoined deity. Interpreting the scene represented on a "large gold signet from the Akropolis treasure at Mycenae" (see fig. 26.3), Evans explains,

> Here, above the group of the Goddess and her handmaidens, and beneath the conjoined figures of the sun and moon, is seen a double axe, which is surely something more than a mere symbol. It stands in a natural relation to the small figure of the warrior God to the left, and probably represents one of the cult forms under which he was worshipped. . . . The curious reduplication of the axe blades suggests indeed that it stands as an image of the conjunction of the divine pair—a solar and a lunar divinity. This primitive aspect of the cult, in which the double axe was actually regarded as a pair of divinities, receives in fact a curious illustration from the human imagery of later Greek cult. On the reverse of the coins of Tenedos, as on so many Carian types, the old double axe form of the divinity is still preserved, while on the obverse side appears its anthropomorphic equivalent in the shape of a janiform head, which has been identified with Dionysos and Ariadnê. (Evans, 107–8)

In effect, Evans interprets the doubleness of the axe symbol—its two edges facing in opposite directions—as a representation of "a pair of divinities" (or perhaps of a single divinity with a dual aspect) whose faces point in opposite directions like those of Janus, the Etruscan sky god who became the Roman god of doorways and of endings and beginnings. That the two-faced "janiform head" is, in later Greek cult, the "anthropomorphic equivalent" of "the old double axe form of the divinity" is illustrated, says Evans, by their appearance on the opposite faces of coins from Tenedos. Noting that the pair of divinities have in this case been "identified with Dionysos and Ariadnê" and that in Tenedos Dionysos is a solar deity, Evans will argue later in the essay that the name Ariadne is simply an epithet of the lunar deity who served either as "the female consort of the warrior Light-God" or as "his female form" (Evans, 172, 173). In Greek myth Dionysus is, of course, a god of dual aspect—the instinctual, subterranean half of a pair whose intellectual, solar aspect is Apollo. In a similar manner the moon goddess, whose heavenly body is composed of light and dark portions, is characteristically represented as a deity of divided aspect. All of which supports Evans's reading of the symbol of the double axe on the signet as "an image of the conjunction of the divine pair" whose union is represented in celestial terms at the top of the signet by "the conjoined figures of the sun and moon." One might also speculate that "the curious reduplication of the axe blades," which Evans takes as a sign of deities' union, is more specifically a sign of the union of two deities each of whom is already understood to have a double aspect.

What Evans's essay suggests is that the story of Theseus and the Minotaur is linked to an ancient ritual representing the conjunction of a solar and a lunar divinity, deities of various designations two of whose possible names are respectively Dionysus and Ariadne. The link between myth and ritual is indicated in Theseus's story by the episode in which Ariadne, fleeing with Theseus from Crete, becomes the consort of Dionysus and is ultimately translated into the heavens. To understand what is involved in this linking of the Theseus myth to a ritual marriage of sun and moon, we must turn for a moment to another of those works Borges used "as a kind of mythology, . . . or encyclopedia of curious lores"—Sir James Frazer's *The Golden Bough.*

In *The Dying God* (1911), the third part of *The Golden Bough*, Frazer discusses the theory that "the reign of many ancient Greek kings was limited to eight years, or at least that at the end of every period of eight years a new consecration" was needed "to enable them to discharge their civil and religious duties."[2] Frazer notes that this was the case with "Minos, king of Cnossus in Crete, whose great palace has been unearthed in recent years":

The tradition plainly implies that at the end of every eight years the king's sacred powers needed to be renewed by intercourse with the godhead, and that without such a renewal he would have forfeited his right to the throne. We may surmise that among the solemn ceremonies which marked the beginning or the end of the eight years' cycle the sacred marriage of the king with the queen played an important part, and that in this marriage we have the true explanation of the strange legend of Pasiphae and the bull. (Frazer, 4:70–71)

The legend, in which Pasiphae, the wife of King Minos, mates with "a wondrous white bull" that

rose from the sea, . . . appears to reflect a mythical marriage of the sun and moon, which was acted as a solemn rite by the king and queen of Cnossus, wearing the masks of a bull and cow respectively. To a pastoral people a bull is the most natural type of vigorous reproductive energy, and as such is a fitting emblem of the sun. . . . Indeed, we are expressly told that the Cretans called the sun a bull . . . [and] the identification of Pasiphae, "she who shines on all," with the moon was made long ago by Pausanias. . . . The horns of the waxing or waning moon naturally suggest the resemblance of the luminary to a white cow. (Frazer, 4:71–72)

To explain why the term of eight years was "selected as the measure of a king's reign," Frazer, invoking this identification of king and queen with solar and lunar deities, notes that

the difficulty of reconciling lunar with solar time is one of the standing puzzles which has taxed the ingenuity of men who are emerging from barbarism. Now an octennial cycle is the shortest period at the end of which sun and moon really mark time together after overlapping, so to say, throughout the whole of the interval. Thus, for example, it is only once in every eight years that the full moon coincides with the longest or shortest day; and as this coincidence can be observed with the aid of a simple dial, the observation is naturally one of the first to furnish a base for a calendar which shall bring lunar and solar times into tolerable, though not exact, harmony. (Frazer, 4:68–69)

Thus Frazer suggests, "When the great luminaries had run their course on high, and were about to renew the heavenly race, it might well be thought that the king should renew his divine energies, or prove them unabated, under pain of making room for a more vigorous successor" through his "deposition or death" (Frazer, 4:69). Frazer points out that although "the sun and moon are in conjunction once every month," their conjunction "takes place at a different point in the sky, until eight revolving years have brought them together again in the same heavenly bridal chamber where first they met" (Frazer, 4:74). Thus on the "principles of sympathetic magic," the union of the king and queen would have been "consummated with unusual solemnity every eight years" at the time "when the moon was thought to rest in the arms of the sun" (Frazer, 4:73, 74).

Frazer further theorizes that "the tribute of seven youths and seven maidens" sent to Minos "every eight years had some connexion with the renewal of the king's power for another octennial cycle" (Frazer, 4:74). Among the ancients "the common view" of the young people's fate was

> that they were shut up in the labyrinth, there to be devoured by the Min-otaur. . . . Perhaps they were sacrificed by being roasted alive in a bronze image of a bull, or of a bull-headed man, in order to renew the strength of the king and of the sun, whom he personated. This at all events is suggested by the legend of Talos, a bronze man who clutched people to his breast and leaped with them into the fire. . . . According to one account he was a bull, according to another he was the sun. Probably he was identical with the Minotaur, and stripped of his mythical features was nothing but a bronze image of the sun represented as a man with a bull's head. (Frazer, 4:74–75)

Frazer goes on to note that

> the same cunning artist Daedalus who planned the labyrinth . . . was said to have made a dance for Ariadne, daughter of Minos. . . . When Theseus landed with Ariadne in Delos on his return from Crete, he and the young companions whom he had rescued from the Minotaur are said to have danced a mazy dance in imitation of the intricate windings of the labyrinth; on account of its sinuous turns the dance was called "the Crane." (Frazer, 4:75)

Now since there is reason to believe "that Cnossus was the seat of a great worship of the sun, and that the Minotaur was a representative or embodi-ment of the sun-god," Frazer wonders whether Ariadne's dance may not

> have been an imitation of the sun's course in the sky . . . [,] its intention . . . , by means of sympathetic magic, to aid the great luminary to run his race on high. . . . If there is any truth in this conjecture, it would seem to follow that the sinuous lines of the labyrinth which the dancers followed in their evolu-tions may have represented the ecliptic, the sun's apparent annual path in the sky. It is some confirmation of this view that on coins of Cnossus the sun or a star appears in the middle of the labyrinth, the place which on other coins is occupied by the Minotaur. (Frazer, 4:77)

Summing up, Frazer says,

> On the whole the foregoing evidence, slight and fragmentary as it is, points to the conclusion that at Cnossus the king represented the sun-god, and that

every eight years his divine powers were renewed at a great festival, which comprised, first, the sacrifice of human victims by fire to a bull-headed image of the sun, and, second, the marriage of the king disguised as a bull to the queen disguised as a cow, the two personating respectively the sun and the moon. (Frazer, 4:77–78)

The speculations of Evans and Frazer on the ritual significance of the labyrinth and Minotaur (many of which are summarized in Matthews's popular *Mazes and Labyrinths*) present us with a network of associations underlying Borges's treatment of the subject. In "The House of Asterion," for example, Borges clearly associates the Minotaur with the sun. Asterion remarks that although everything in the world "is repeated many times, . . . two things in the world seem to be only once: above, the intricate sun; below, Asterion" (*L*, 139–40), as if Asterion in the subterranean labyrinth were the embodiment of the sun during its nightly sojourn through the underworld. Borges's description of the sun as "intricate" ("el intrincado sol") more than likely refers to the complexity of the sun's apparent path through the sky during the year, the same intricate path (the ecliptic) represented, suggests Frazer, in "the sinuous lines of the labyrinth" and mimed in the "sinuous turns" of the "Crane" dance as the dancers "aid the great luminary to run his race on high." Indeed, if the labyrinth's winding path is the ecliptic, then the word *house* in the story's title ("La Casa de Asterión") may well have an astrological resonance. In astrology the ecliptic is divided into twelve sections called "houses" (*casas* in Spanish), each bearing the name of a different constellation, the twelve together constituting the signs of the zodiac (literally, "the circle of animals"). As the Minotaur runs through the winding path of his house, so the sun runs through the circular path of the zodiacal houses, a path that was called in ancient Babylonia "the Furrow of Heaven, ploughed by the heavenly Directing Bull, our Taurus, which from about 3880 to about 1730 B.C. was the first" of the zodiac's twelve signs (Allen, 1).

The connections of the Minotaur and labyrinth with the zodiac are numerous. The Minotaur, for example, is associated with at least two zodiacal signs—Taurus and Sagittarius. As we noted earlier, in one "myth of early spring" Taurus was identified with the bull who fathered the Minotaur on Pasiphae (Allen, 379); while the figure of Sagittarius, now generally represented as a centaur with a bow and arrow, was in many early versions depicted with the hind quarters of a bull (Allen, 352), producing that alternate form of the Minotaur "with a man's head and a bull's body" that Borges associates with Dante's representation of the creature (*BIB*, 159). Moreover, the Minotaur's house is often linked with the zodiac as a whole. In *Mazes and Labyrinths*, Matthews notes that a medieval representation of the labyrinth in the church of San Savino at Piacenza has "the signs of the Zodiac . . . placed in juxtaposition" to the maze (*ML*, 57), and earlier, in our discussion of Jung's psychoanalytic reading of alchemy, we cited an illustration from Van Vreeswyck's *De Groene Leeuw* (see fig. 6.7) showing the *lapis* sanctuary as a labyrinth whose circular paths are planetary orbits and whose center (the site of the sacred marriage of the king and queen of heaven) is marked by the conjunction of sun and moon. Since in astrology "the positions of the planets at the birth of an individual constitute a symbolic language"[3] governing the individual's character and destiny, a language whose basic elements are each planet's position with respect to the zodiac (sign), the Earth's rotation on its axis (house), and the other planets (aspects), one might well read the illustration from *De Groene Leeuw* as a figure of the planets' journey through the zodiac's circular labyrinth, a journey whose conjunctions and oppositions would have directly affected the alchemist's achievement of the great work. As Jung notes, alchemists thought of the zodiac as a pathway to be followed in their art, a kind of clocklike "mandala . . . with a dark centre, and a leftward *circumambulatio* with 'houses' and planetary phases" (*PA*, 206). The notion that the movement through the zodiac involves a leftward circumambulation recalls, of course, Borges's dictum about "turning always to the left" to reach "the central courtyard of certain labyrinths" (*F*, 93).

The most interesting aspect of the illustration from Van Vreeswyck's *De Groene Leeuw* for our purposes is that the event depicted at the center of the labyrinth—the sacred marriage of king and queen symbolized as the conjunction of sun and moon—is essentially the same event Frazer theorizes took place every eight years at the center of the Cretan labyrinth. In both cases the sacred marriage represents a conjunction of opposites as a return to an original condition of undifferentiated unity. Given Frazer's suggestion that the marriage was enacted "as a solemn rite by the king and queen of Cnossus, wearing the masks of a bull and cow respectively," we should note in the illustration from *De Groene Leeuw* what appear to be a young bull and cow shown in the lower right-hand corner, an iconographic gloss perhaps on the sun and moon signs conjoined above the *lapis* sanctuary.

If one connotation of the Spanish *casa* in "La Casa de Asterión" is an astrological house, another connotation evokes the labyrinth's connection with the game of chess, a connection with its own astrological resonance. In Spanish, *casa* is used for the individual squares on a chessboard, and certainly Borges would have remembered that in *The Garden of Cyrus* Browne links the labyrinth, chess, and astrology through the shared figure of the quincuncial network. On the one hand, Browne maintains that "the Labyrinth of *Crete,*" the "lodging of the *Minotaur*" (*SW,* 175), was shaped like a quincunx; while on the other he points out the quincuncial pattern "in Chesse-boards" and says that if "we had their true and ancient description, farre different from ours," we might well discover that the game was "an invention as High as *Hermes* the Secretary of *Osyris,* figuring the whole world, the motion of the Planets, with Eclipses of Sunne and Moon" (*SW,* 172–73). By virtue of their sharing a common pattern, then, the labyrinth becomes for Browne a kind of chessboard and the chessboard a kind of labyrinth, and both in turn astrological representations of the world. Note that the illustration from the seventeenth-century *De Groene Leeuw* cited above is a representation not only of "the motion of the Planets" but probably of a solar eclipse as well, for such an eclipse can occur only during a "conjunction of the Sun and the Moon, in which the Moon passes directly between the Earth and the Sun" (*Larousse,* 100). Evans notes in this regard that in a Roman version of the sacred marriage, Mars "in the aspect of a Sun God" is united with Rhea Silvia in a cave, their conjunction "being accompanied by an eclipse" (Evans, 129).

The linking of labyrinth and chessboard as quincuncial networks may well have suggested to Borges a further association of the actions played out within these structures (the slaying of the Minotaur, the checkmating of the king)—an association reinforced by Evans's and Frazer's inter- pretation of the bull connected with the Cretan labyrinth as an animal embodiment of the solar deity and thus a surrogate of the king (the deity's human embodiment). Indeed, the symbolic linking of King Minos and the Minotaur would have been further heightened by the Cretan king's wear- ing a bull mask in the ritual marriage of sun and moon, reproducing in effect the Minotaur's combination of a bull's head and a man's body. But if the Minotaur is a symbol of the king, then Theseus's slaying of Asterion becomes, as we shall see in the following sections, a much more complex and problematic allusive background for Borges's detective stories.

27 *Labyrinth and Chessboard; The Red King and Fire; Light and Mirroring; The Double Axe as Lightning Bolt; Plato's Myth of Origin; Zeus as Splitter and Doubler; Geometric Figure of the* Labrys; *A Square and Its Diagonals*

IF BROWNE'S QUINCUNCIAL ASSOCIATION OF chessboard and labyrinth suggested to Borges an assimilation of the scenarios enacted in these spaces, an assimilation reinforced by the symbolic equation of king and bull as embodiments of the solar deity (the principle of light), then one can see how the mythic and ritual structures surrounding the Cretan labyrinth, precisely because they resemble in many respects the scenario underlying Borges's detective stories (the checkmating of the Red King from Carroll's *Through the Looking-Glass*), could have been easily annexed as an allusive background for his three tales. For example, Carroll clearly associates the Red King with firelight as a figure of mind. In the scene where Tweedledum and Tweedledee tell Alice that she exists only in the Red King's dream, the king's consciousness and Alice's being are both imaged as a candle flame: "If that there King was to wake . . . you'd go out—bang!—just like a candle!" (*AA*, 238). This equation of mind and light is foreshadowed at the very start of the book when Alice, drowsing in the drawing room, anticipates the great bonfire the next day (Guy Fawkes Day) and wonders whether there is a fire in the fireplace in the room she sees reflected in the mirror: "I can see all of it when I get upon a chair," Alice says, "—all but the bit just behind the fireplace. . . . I want so much to know whether they've a fire in the winter: you never *can* tell, you know, unless our fire smokes, and then smoke comes up in that room too—but that may be only pretence, just to make it look as if they had a fire" (*AA*, 181).

Since light and mirroring are probably the two most common figures of mind (figures often combined as in Hawthorne's famous description of the imagination in *The Scarlet Letter*), it is not surprising that, in the mirror asymmetry governing the relationship of Alice's waking and dreaming worlds, she should fall asleep wondering whether there is a fire in the fireplace of Looking-glass House and then, as if in response to this, be shown (by the mirror-image twins) a figure whose consciousness, imaged as a candle flame, reflects Alice as if in a mirror. Moreover, because mirroring is a function of the reflection of light, it is also not surprising that the two are frequently conjoined as a figure of the mind's dual status as

256

source of illumination and reflector of images. Inasmuch as one of the issues in Alice's encounter with the Red King is which is the dreamer (the mental light source) and which the dreamed (the reflection), Alice's question about whether there is a fire in the fireplace of Looking-glass House is in effect one about whether that world is an independent source of mental light or only a reflection. Given the impossibility of making the reflected image of mind completely reproduce the reflecting power, it is only appropriate that part of Alice's drawing room (the world of waking consciousness that figures the act of thinking) should not be contained in the reflected image of that room (the world of dreams that figures the content of thought), and further appropriate that that unseen part should be the place where light is generated.

Just as there is in the chessboard-labyrinth-garden of Looking-glass House a conjunction of firelight and mirroring in Alice's encounter with the Red King, so in the Cretan labyrinth, as interpreted by Evans and Frazer, there is a conjunction of a light source and a reflector in the marriage of sun and moon. Indeed, the figure of the moon as a mirror is fairly common in antiquity and one Borges himself employs in his poem "Mirrors" (1959):

> Now, after so many troubling years
> of wandering underneath the wavering moon,
> I ask myself what accident of fortune
> handed to me this terror of all mirrors.   (BR, 277)

We should note that although in the sacred marriage of the Cretan king and queen, as in Alice's encounter with the Red King, the light source is associated with the male figure and the mirroring object with the female, this master/slave polarity is subsequently reversed in both the ancient and modern scenarios when Ariadne, who like her mother Pasiphae is a mask of the moon goddess, brings about the death of the Minotaur (the surrogate of sun and king) and when Alice, after having been promoted from pawn to queen, checkmates the Red King.

In his story "The Circular Ruins," Borges invokes Carroll's association of the Red King with firelight when he uses a line from Alice's encounter with the sleeping monarch ("And if he left off dreaming about you . . .") as the epigraph to his tale of a magician who dreams another man into existence with the aid of the god of fire. As the figure within Alice's dream is the Red King, so the figure within the magician's first dream is compared to the Gnostics' "red Adam" (A, 59), a man molded from the "red earth" that is the origin of his name. But it is only when the color of the figure changes from the redness of earth to that of fire that the magician's work succeeds:

> Having exhausted his prayers to the gods of the earth and river, he threw himself down at the feet of the stone image that may have been a tiger or a stallion, and asked for its blind aid. That same evening he dreamed of the image. He dreamed it alive, quivering; it was no unnatural cross between tiger and stallion but at one and the same time both these violent creatures and also a bull, a rose, a thunderstorm. This manifold god revealed to him that its earthly name was Fire, that there in the circular temple . . . sacrifices had once been made to it, . . . that through its magic the phantom of the man's dreams would be wakened to life in such a way that—except for Fire itself and the dreamer—every being in the world would accept him as a man of flesh and blood. . . . In the dreamer's dream, the dreamed one awoke. (*A*, 59)

The magician spends two years "initiating his disciple into the riddles of the universe and the worship of Fire" and then sends him off to the ruined temple downstream, having first taken care to erase his disciple's memory of his "long years of apprenticeship," so that "the boy would never know he was a phantom" (*A*, 60). For, as the magician says, "not to be a man but to be the projection of another man's dreams" is "an unparalleled humiliation" (*A*, 61). But it is this humiliation that the magician himself must suffer when, in a kind of Heraclitean, cyclic return to the condition of fire, "the ruins of the fire god's shrine" are once again "destroyed by fire" (*A*, 61): "The magician saw the circling sheets of flame closing in on him. . . . They did not bite into his flesh, but caressed him and flooded him without heat or burning. In relief, in humiliation, in terror, he understood that he, too, was an appearance, that someone else was dreaming him" (*A*, 61–62).

The stone image of the fire god in Borges's tale is a multiform figure that, like the biform Minotaur embodying the fiery solar deity, combines in some mysterious way the shapes of several entities (including a bull). One of these shapes is, appropriately enough, a thunderstorm, for of course before humans had learned how to generate fire, its most common source (and still one of its most dramatic) was lightning striking a tree during a storm. In his essay on the Mycenaean tree and pillar cult, Evans suggests not only a connection between this cult and the *labrys* but also a connection between these two and the lightning or fire from heaven, a link that suggests in turn the reason for the imagistic association of the double axe with Zeus.

As we recall, Evans treats the *labrys* as an aniconic image of the divinity, an "object into which his spiritual essence might enter as it did into his sacred pillar or tree" (Evans, 107), and he offers as evidence for this equation of double axe and stone pillar as embodiments of the god the square stone columns engraved with the sign of the double axe that he found in the two small chambers at the center of the Palace of Knossos.

While the sanctity of the stone pillar or *baetylos* was due to "a variety of causes," Evans notes that

> there is . . . a good deal of evidence to show that certain natural blocks derived their baetylic qualities from the fact that they were of meteoric origin. According to Sanchoniathon "Baetylos" is "the son of Ouranos," in other words sky-fallen. The phenomena associated with aerolites seem indeed to a certain extent to have attached themselves to the whole class of sacred stones. The early cults of the Greek world supply a good illustration of this class of ideas in the "rude stone," or ἀργὸς λίθος, that stood near Gythion in Laconia, and was known as Zeus Kappôtas—in other words the Zeus "fallen down" from heaven. Allied to this are the *keraunia* or thunderstones, which, as the "bolts of heaven," were naturally recognized in the stone axes of an earlier age. (Evans, 118)

Regarding this last point, Evans refers us to Pliny's discussion of thunderstones in his *Natural History*. Pliny notes that

> among the bright colourless stones there is also the one called "ceraunia" ("thunder-stone") which catches the glitter of the stars. . . . Zenothemis . . . describes it as "containing a twinkling star." . . . Sotacus distinguishes also two other varieties of the stone, a black and a red, resembling axe-heads. According to him, those among them that are black and round are supernatural objects; . . . their name being "baetuli," while the elongated stones are "cerauniae." These writers distinguish yet another kind of "ceraunia" which is quite rare . . . because it is found only in a place that has been struck by a thunderbolt.[1]

Evans adds that Pliny's word *baetuli* is the Latin form of the Greek βαίτυλοι, "sacred stones." Pliny's comments on the ceraunia or thunderstone grow out of his discussion of three astriated gems: the "asteria" or "star stone" which when "held up to the sun . . . reflects bright beams radiating as if from a star"; the "astrion" or "little star" which "has inside it at the centre a star shining brightly like the full moon"; and the "astriotes," or "star stone" again, "used in the practice of magic" (Pliny, 10:271–73). As we recall, in *The Garden of Cyrus* Browne mentions two of these stones in noting the correspondence between the quincuncial shape of certain heavenly bodies ("the single Quincunx of the *Hyades* upon the head of *Taurus*") and that of certain "bodies in the Earth" ("subterraneous concretions . . . in the *Asteria* and *Astroites*" [*SW*, 177])—the latter names not only evoking the link between astral and subterranean light bearers/reflectors but also recalling the name of that other light-related figure housed in the subterranean, quincuncially shaped labyrinth of Crete.

Quite clearly for the ancients, meteorites and lightning were related phenomena, two forms of the fire from heaven, and as such both were associated with the sky god Zeus, the *keraunia* or thunderstones being, as Evans suggests, "bolts of heaven" analogous to the lightning bolts hurled by Zeus—a link between the two confirmed by Pliny's comment that one type of *keraunia* was thought to be "found only in a place that has been struck by a thunderbolt." But what is the basis of that further connection among lightning, meteorites, and those "stone axes of an earlier age" that the ancients took to be a form of *keraunia* (as indicated by Sotacus's description of certain varieties of thunderstones "resembling axe-heads")? The answer would seem to be that an ancient image of the lightning bolt, derived no doubt from the splitting of trees by lightning during thunderstorms, was that of a fiery celestial axe, Zeus's axe. If, as Evans maintains, one source of the "baetylic qualities" (the sacredness) of certain pillars was their construction from stone blocks of meteoric origin, then clearly one source of the sacredness of trees was the special relationship between certain types of trees and lightning (that other form of fire from heaven), a relationship manifested in their power either to ward off or to attract lightning in a storm. Evans cites, for example, "the traditional sanctity of the fig-tree . . . in the later cult of Greece," a sacredness explained in part by "the prophylactic powers of these trees against lightning": "A fig-tree is said to have sprung where Gaia sought to ward off the bolts of Zeus from her son Sykeas" (Evans, 104). In contrast, Frazer suggests in *The Golden Bough* that the "reverence which the ancient peoples of Europe paid to the oak, and the connexion which they traced between the tree and their sky-god, were derived from the much greater frequency with which the oak appears to be struck by lightning than any other tree of our European forests" (Frazer, 11:298). Citing contemporary statistics to support this observation, Frazer theorizes that the ancients would have noticed this peculiarity of the tree and have accounted for it "by supposing that the great sky-god . . . loved the oak above all the trees of the wood and often descended into it from the murky cloud in a flash of lightning" (Frazer, 11:299).

Evans points out that stone axes or celts were "regarded as thunderbolts" by a variety of cultures throughout the world, and he cites the extensive documentation of this provided by his father, the archaeologist Sir John Evans, in *The Ancient Stone Implements, Weapons, and Ornaments, of Great Britain* (1872). The elder Evans records examples of this folklore from virtually every country in Europe, that of Sweden being typical, where prehistoric stone axe heads "are preserved as a protection against lightning" because they are "regarded as the stone-bolts that have fallen during thunder-storms."[2] He argues that the origin of the common name for these stone axe heads, "celts," is the Latin *caelum* ("sky, heavens") and notes that "in Greece the stone celts are known as *Astropelekia* [star axes], and have long been held in veneration" (J. Evans, 50, 53). He adds,

> The hatchet appears in ancient times to have had some sacred importance among the Greeks. It was from a hatchet that, according to Plutarch, Jupiter Labrandeus received that title; and M. de Longpérier has pointed out a passage, from which it appears that Bacchus was in one instance, at all events, worshipped under the form of a hatchet, or πέλεκυς. He has also published a Chaldean cylinder on which a priest is represented as making an offering to a hatchet placed upright on a throne, and has called attention to the fact that the Egyptian hieroglyph for *Nouter,* God, is simply the figure of an axe. (J. Evans, 54)

Significantly, the passage from Plutarch concerning Zeus Labrandeus which the elder Evans cites here is the same one his son invokes in 1901 as the principal philological evidence for interpreting the sign of the double axe inscribed in the winding passages of the Palace at Knossos as that *labrys* symbol of the solar deity from which the name "labyrinth" derives. In *The Greek Questions* Plutarch records "that the statue of the Labrandean Zeus in Caria is fashioned holding an axe, but not a sceptre or a thunderbolt," and he notes that the god was called Labrandeus because "the Lydians call the axe *labrys*."[3] The point of Plutarch's remark seems clear. Where one would have expected to find, in this plastic representation of the god, the traditional thunderbolt, one finds instead the double axe; and although Plutarch cites an episode from Carian history which explains the axe in the statue's hand as a dedicatory token presented to Zeus from the spoils captured in the Lydian war, the specific reason for choosing the axe as an offering appropriate to the god was undoubtedly the link between thunderbolt and axe head that Sir John Evans documents, a symbolic equivalence allowing one to be substituted for the other. Indeed, the imagistic association between lightning's splitting a tree in a storm and the falling of the sky god's double axe has a further resonance for the figure of Zeus, for in the *Symposium* Plato includes a story of human origins as a divinely dispensed splitting and doubling. Plato assigns the story to Aristophanes who says that "in the beginning" human beings

> were nothing like we are now. For one thing, the race was divided into three; that is to say, besides the two sexes, male and female, which we have at present, there was a third which partook of the nature of both, and for which we still have a name, . . . "hermaphrodite."[4]

Moreover,

each of these beings was globular in shape, with rounded back and sides, four arms and four legs, and two faces, both the same, on a cylindrical neck, and one head, with one face one side and one the other, and four ears, and two lots of privates, and all the other parts to match. . . . The three sexes . . . arose as follows. The males were descended from the Sun, the females from the Earth, and the hermaphrodites from the Moon, which partakes of either sex, and they were round and they *went* round, because they took after their parents. (Plato, 542–43)

So great was "their arrogance, that they actually tried . . . to scale the heights of heaven and set upon the gods" (Plato, 543). Zeus "didn't want to blast them out of existence with thunderbolts," so he decided "to cut them all in half," making each one "only half as strong" and leaving "twice as many of them": "And if, said Zeus, I have any more trouble with them, I shall split them up again, and they'll have to hop about" on one leg (Plato, 543).

When the work of bisection "was complete it left each half with a desperate yearning for the other, and they ran together and flung their arms around each other's necks, and asked for nothing better than to be rolled into one" (Plato, 543). In pity for them Zeus "moved their members round to the front and made them propagate among themselves," so that, says Aristophanes, we can see how

our innate love for one another . . . is always trying to redintegrate our former nature, to make two into one, and to bridge the gulf between one human being and another. . . . We are all like pieces of the coins that children break in half for keepsakes—making two out of one, like the flatfish—and each of us is forever seeking the half that will tally with himself. (Plato, 544)

While Plato does not say what method was used to split these spherical beings, he does mention the thunderbolt as Zeus's traditional means of dealing with unruly subjects (though here it is associated with the ultimate sanction of blasting them out of existence rather than reshaping their persons). Perhaps the most significant detail in this story for our purposes is Zeus's threat to "split them up again, and they'll have to hop about." For this remark indicates that the threatened split will be along the vertical axis of the body separating right and left sides and thus suggests that for Plato the human form's bilateral asymmetry may well have looked, at least figuratively, like the result of a splitting and unfolding of a more compact being into a kind of V-shaped, hingelike structure.

What seems clear from Plato's description is that the original bisection Zeus inflicted on the spherical beings and the subsequent one he threatened to inflict would have been at right angles to each other (see fig. 27.1).

Figure 27.1

And this quadrantlike schema again suggests the extent to which Plato's story of human origins as the splitting of a four-armed, four-legged being into two complementary halves derives from (because it is meant to accord with) the body's present directional symmetry—that intersection of a front/back polarity by a right/left polarity in terms of which a human being orients himself, an intersection of two mirror folds producing the fourfold figure of self-consciousness as self-location.

As regards the body's directional symmetry, Plato tends to associate the number four (as embodied in a square) with the figure of the just man, which is to say, he images the ideal of human rectitude as geometric rectification. In the *Protagoras,* for example, he quotes a poem of Simonides that employs this imagery:

> Hard it is on the one hand to become
> A good man truly, hands and feet and mind
> Foursquare, wrought without blame.   (Plato, 333)

We are perhaps most familiar with the practice of arraying the body within, and thus equating its proportions with, a square in the Neoplatonic tradition that runs through alchemy and the cabala, as illustrated by a diagram from Heinrich Cornelius Agrippa's *Three Books of Occult Philosophy* (see fig. 27.2).[5] S. K. Heninger notes that this figure "presents man in his most natural position, inscribed within a square and therefore approximated to the tetrad" (i.e., the four elements, directions, seasons, humors, etc.) (Heninger, 145–46). Agrippa says that "the four square measure is the most proportionated body; for, if a man be placed upright with his feet together, and his arms stretched forth, he will make a quadrature equilateral, whose center is in the bottom of his belly" (Heninger, 146). In another illustration even more significant for our purposes, Agrippa shows how "if the Heels being unmoved, the feet be stretched forth on both sides to the right and left, and the hands lifted up to the line of the head, then the ends of the fingers and Toes do make a square of equall sides, whose center is on the navile, in the girdling of the body"

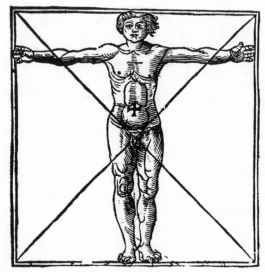

Figure 27.2

(Heninger, 147) (see fig. 27.3). Noting that "the signs of the zodiac are arranged counterclockwise around the sides of the square, with Aries at the head," Heninger explains that "in this diagram, man is directly correlated with the annual unit of time, repeating the perfection of the macrocosm in its temporal aspect" (Heninger, 147).

What one notices about both these figures is that the diagonals intersecting at each square's center superimpose upon the body the image of the fourfold, which is to say that the two mirror folds represented by the diagonals each divide the square into two triangles or V shapes hinged at a common base. It is as if the square were a sheet of paper that could be doubled back upon itself by being folded along either diagonal. In its folded state it figures self-conscious reflection's attempt to make the self coincide absolutely with itself (an *attempted* coincidence evoked in the figure by the fact that although two of the triangle's sides coincide, the third, strictly speaking, is not a side but a hinge). And in its unfolded state it figures the fourfold directional presence of self-consciousness (the double mirror fold) in the physical world.

In the second of the two figures from Agrippa, the X shape of the intersecting diagonals is aligned with the bodily decussation formed by the extended arms and legs, and the addition of a second square within, and rotated 45 degrees from, the first produces a series of decussations, a quincuncial network like that which Browne associates with the Cretan labyrinth. Finally, distributed counterclockwise around the square, three to a side, are the signs of the zodiac, forming a pathway that begins with

Figure 27.3

Aries at the head and proceeds in a leftward circumambulation, recalling that continual turning to the left by which one reaches the center of certain labyrinths. (Note as well that the disposition of the geometrical shapes within the zodiac in Agrippa's diagram suggests the notion of astrological "aspects," those angular relationships "between two planets or important points on the zodiac" that govern a person's birth and that are considered in astrology to be "the building blocks of character"— aspects with names such as *conjunction, opposition, square, trine,* and *quincunx* [*Larousse,* 15].)

By this point we have accumulated enough data to trace a fairly clear chain of associations linking the *labrys* or double axe with its namesake. But bear in mind that the issue here is not how clear these associations were for the ancients (there is, after all, a millennium between the high Mycenaean civilization of Crete and Plato's Greece), but rather how clear they were for a reader in the 1920s and '30s like Borges, whose interest in classical myth and history (particularly in the labyrinth) would have led him to the works of contemporary authorities such as Evans and Frazer as encyclopedias of curious lore. Indeed, even though many of the theories of Evans and Frazer (such as the belief in the existence of sacral kingship in ancient Greece) are now largely discounted by classical scholars, this does not affect Borges's use of the two as modern mythographers, as writers who, based on the best available information of the day, produced powerfully coherent and poetically appealing readings of ancient myth and ritual that allowed the first generation of modernists a renewed (be-

cause ostensibly scientific) access to the classical world. With that in mind
let us now turn our attention to the way this chain of associations surrounding the myth and ritual of the labyrinth imaginatively meshed with the
structure of the detective stories.

Axe and Axis; Fold as Incision; Matching Edges and Coinciding Parts; Labrys *and Quincunx; The Square's Double Axes;* Labrys *and Chess; The Number Eight; A Riddle Whose Answer Is Father*

PLATO'S STORY OF HUMAN ORIGINS as a primordial splitting and doubling seems clearly related to a tradition of Zeus as wielder of the lightning bolt's fiery axe. Moreover, this myth of an original division that transformed spherical beings into four-sided ones gives added resonance to the geometrical representation of the *labrys* Evans found at Knossos. While the most common image of the *labrys* shows both the axe head and haft ⋈ , some show the axe head alone ⋈ .

This figure, composed of two triangles joined at their apices, brings together in a single shape several of the motifs associated with the labyrinth. As an image of the sky god, the *labrys* suggests the form of his originating presence to the human race, for the axe's splitting edge is itself doubled. Moreover, as an axe with two faces pointing in opposite directions on a single haft, its form resembles that of the beings whom Zeus divided, beings with "two faces, both the same, on a cylindrical neck, and one head, with one face one side and one the other" (Plato, 542). In bisecting these creatures, Zeus transformed them into beings whose directionality is a function of two intersecting axes (front/back, right/left), and the geometric representation of the *labrys* Evans found at Knossos is quite clearly a figure formed by two intersecting axes ⋮✕⋮ . Indeed, it is a short imaginative step to assimilate this aniconic image of the god as Platonic splitter/doubler to that geometric schema superimposed on the human body in the Neoplatonic illustrations from Agrippa—the square crossed by intersecting diagonals, *its* double axes ⊠ , a figure that clearly contains within it the geometric image of the *labrys* ⊠ . And, certainly, if the double axe evokes Zeus in his role as originator of the human race, then it is only appropriate that the square (as an image of the rectified proportions of the human body) should bear within it the mark of Zeus as *labrys,* the mark of the differentiating power who gave the body its four-sided directionality through an original act of bisection.

In assimilating the geometric representation of the double axe to that of a square and its diagonals, we have treated the intersecting lines at the center of both figures as polar axes, an association of axe and axis that may reflect the words' possible derivation from the same root. Eric Partridge suggests that *axe* and *axis* (as well as all the words related to *axis—axle, axilla, aisle, aileron,* etc.) have their common source in the Indo-European *aks-* (Partridge, 34). In his discursive dictionary of Indo-European roots, Joseph Shipley describes *aks* as "a strengthened form of *ag:* to move, drive. Gk, *axon.* L, *axis. axil:* point where branch extends to twig; *axilla:* point where shoulder extends to arm: *armpit. axillary.* By extension (L *agsla?, ala:* wing), *alar, alate; aliped; aileron. aisle. axial, coaxial.* Gc, *axle.*"[1] Shipley derives *axe,* however, from the Indo-European word *agu(e)si* rather than from the root *aks-,* although it is possible that *agu(e)si,* like *aks-,* comes from the still more basic *ag* and thus that *axe* and *axis* share a common root one step further back.

But whether or not the English words *axe* and *axis* derive from the same linguistic root is finally less the point than whether there exists a semantic association between them, whether the concepts or things signified by these two words (or, for example, by the words *pelekus* [axe] and *polos* [axis] or *axinē* [axe] and *axōn* [axle] in Greek) have become mentally linked because of some basic resemblance they share. What underlying image, then, do the words *axe* and *axis* have in common that would make such a semantic association possible? Of the several meanings of *axis,* two are of particular significance here. First, an axis is "the straight line about which the parts of a body or system are symmetrically arranged"; and second, in geometry it is "any line in a regular figure which divides it into two symmetrical parts, e.g., which joins opposite angles or the centres of opposite sides."[2] What is common to both these definitions is the image of an axis as a real or imaginary dividing line (a differential edge) between two symmetrical parts of an entity, and if we conceive of differentiation as a separation or cutting and imagine the edge of difference as an incision made by a cutting tool, then the model for this differentiating cut could easily be the V-shaped trace left by an axe blade driven into a surface. Obviously, not every incision with a blade divides an entity into symmetrical parts, but it does leave two matching surfaces, the sides of the cut (A and B), that face each other $\overline{A\backslash B}$. And if we imagine that this V-shaped incision could be unfolded $\ulcorner \overline{A | B} \urcorner$ and then refolded again so that the matching sides of the incision were rejoined $\overline{A | B}$, then we would have a structure resembling the fold along a square's diagonal that produces two mirror-image figures hinged at their base so that their surfaces meet and their edges match.

Note in this regard that the culminating image in Plato's story of human origins as a primordial division-as-duplication is precisely that of matching edges or surfaces. Aristophanes says that "we are all like pieces of the coins that children break in half for keepsakes—making two out of one, like the flatfish—and each of us is forever seeking the half that will tally with himself." Although the image here is one of breaking rather than cutting, it is clearly being applied to Zeus's division of the original beings, so that Plato's final image associates in effect the *matching* of two severed edges with the *symmetry* of the two separated parts they bound.

Since in Plato's story splitting and doubling are associated with the body's vertical axis, and since this division was caused by a deity often represented as a double axe, there would seem to be an obvious imagistic association of axis and axe that allows us to see the body's vertical axis (whether between the two faces of the original globular being or between the right and left sides of the human body) as the place where the matching faces of an axe blade are replicated in the mirror-image asymmetry of the parts severed, the place where splitting is necessarily doubling (unfolding) as the V shape of the blade's edge is translated into the V shape of the mirror fold. In this structural network, axe and axis are inextricably linked as mutually constitutive (and thus reversible) cause and effect. On the one hand, the axis is the trace of, the striking point for, the axe's edge. The axe's stroke creates an axis. But on the other, it is the place where the V shape of intelligibility, of differentiation as the power to separate (materialized in the blade's edge) translates itself into the double mirror fold of reflective self-consciousness, so that the axis is the ideal form physically embodied both in the axe's edge and in the twin faces of the *labrys* on either side of the haft. The axis creates an axe.

That the imaginary line between the right and left sides of the body was for the ancients the most obvious example of an "axis," of a dividing line "about which the parts of a body . . . are symmetrically arranged," can be inferred from the word's etymological link with such words as *axilla* ("armpit") and *alar* ("winglike," from Latin *ala,* "wing") that refer to appendages symmetrically disposed on, or branching from, the sides of a body. Note as well that *axis* is linked etymologically to the word *axil,* "the upper angle between a leaf, twig, etc. and the stem from which it grows" (*W,* 104). And recall in this connection that in "The Garden of Forking Paths" the Spanish word translated as "forking" (*bifurcan*) connotes the branching of limbs from a tree, a connotation particularly appropriate for Borges's labyrinthine detective story given that Evans's derivation of labyrinth from *labrys* occurs in an essay on the Mycenaean tree and pillar cult and given further that the quincuncial pattern Browne associates with the shape of the Cretan labyrinth was originally a pattern for planting trees in a garden, a pattern resembling a series of straight lines with V-shaped branches (see fig. 28.1).

Let me emphasize again that what we are attempting to reproduce

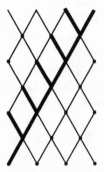

Figure 28.1

here is a network of associations surrounding the labyrinth based on Borges's known or probable reading. With that in mind, it is a short imaginative step from the derivation of the word *labyrinth* and the geometric representation of the *labrys* in Evans to the Cretan labyrinth's quincuncial shape in Browne, for the figure of the double axe formed by two triangles joined at their apices is clearly contained within the quincuncial network as the decussation or X shape that provides the basic pattern for grouping five trees (see fig. 28.2). Obviously, the difference between the double axe figure and the decussation is that the opposite ends of the latter are left open, producing two V shapes joined at their apices; while the opposite ends of the former are closed, producing two triangles. But the essential element is the same in each: the intersecting axes that create two identical shapes oriented 180 degrees apart. Indeed, both the double-axe figure and the decussation could be seen as deriving from a square and its diagonals ⊠, a figure whose sides have been partially removed in the case of the *labrys* ⋈ and entirely removed in the case of the decussation ✕ .

The presence of the *labrys* figure within the quincuncial pattern Browne associates with its namesake is particularly significant for Borges's detective stories. In "Death and the Compass" Borges creates a geometric labyrinth (whose four angles, as the four points of the compass, are the opposite ends of intersecting polar axes) by reversing the orientation of a triangle to produce a figure that is the reciprocal of the double-axe shape: a diamond arrived at by projecting downward from the triangle on the map a second one pointing in the opposite direction. Now if we accept Evans's description of the *labrys* as "janiform" (like the opposite faces of the god Janus), then the story of a deity figured as the *labrys*, who bisects a creature with two faces pointing in opposite directions to produce a new race of beings able to face one another in acts of opposition and conjunction, gives an added resonance to Borges's geometric labyrinth where the

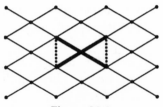

Figure 28.2

doubles meet face to face. For if the bases of the two triangles forming the *labrys* figure ▷◁ represent the faces of the double axe, then in Borges's diamond-shaped labyrinth, these figurative janiform faces come face to face as well ⬦. Scharlach, of course, conceived this labyrinth during that period of delirious self-alienation at Triste-le-Roy when he "swore by the god who looks with two faces and by all the gods of fever and of mirrors" to "weave a maze around the man" who sent his brother to prison.

This image of a face-to-face encounter between doubles within a diamond-shaped labyrinth should remind us of another geometric figure (also associated with face-to-face meetings) that has the same shape as the *labrys*. I refer, of course, to the schema used earlier to illustrate the difference between the facing encounter of two human bodies and that of a body with its mirror image. That these figures resemble the geometric representation of the *labrys* is no accident. The diagrams represent the simplest form of a straight-line figure showing the possible relationships of a human being's hands to those of a facing human or those of its mirror image. When two humans square off, their hands are disposed as if at the corners of a square. In this configuration any given hand can be related to those of the person opposite in only two possible ways—directly or diagonally. In these diagrams, then, two intersecting, differential oppositions (right/ left, direct/diagonal) have been subsumed under the broader category of differentiation itself (sameness/difference) to show that in a facing encounter of persons, the hands with the same name are diagonally opposed, while those with different names are directly opposed, and that in a facing encounter of a person with his mirror image the reverse is the case.

This account of the diagrams' generation suggests two things: First, it evokes the *necessary* character of this *labrys*-like figure ▷◁ as *the simplest straight-line diagram* of the only two possible relationships between the hands of humans facing one another. And second, it suggests that this figure is part of, in effect derives from, the Platonic figure of a square and its diagonals superimposed on the image of a body to show its foursquare proportions. As we noted earlier, one of the meanings of the word *axis* pertaining to geometry is "any line in a regular figure which divides it into two symmetrical parts, e.g., which joins opposite angles or the centres of opposite sides." Since a square is a regular figure with four sides and four angles, it has two axes joining its opposite angles ⊠ and two joining the centers of its opposite sides ⊞ . Which is to say that a square by its very nature is a figure with a double set of double axes. Note that in the second of the two illustrations from Agrippa showing the superimposition of a square on the body's proportions (see fig. 27.3), the two lines that intersect at the navel are the axes joining both the opposite angles of the outer square and the centers of the opposite sides of the inner square.

These two configurations are, of course, the basis for the diagrams used earlier to describe the physical structure of chess. The figure with the axes joining the centers of the opposite sides illustrated the positioning of the players on opposite sides of the chessboard, the diagram's horizontal axis dividing the white side of the board from the black (a plane midway between the opponents) and its vertical axis dividing the king side from the queen side (a plane coinciding with the one dividing the right and left sides of the opponents' bodies) (see fig. 12.6). And the figure with the axes joining the opposite angles illustrated the difference between the face-to-face encounter of the two players on the one hand and the mirror-image asymmetry in the alignment of the chess pieces on the other (see figs. 12.1, 12.3, and 12.4).

In returning us to the image of the chessboard as labyrinth and to chess as an encounter with an antithetical mirror image of one's own mind that evokes the mental duel between doubles in the detective story, these diagrams (based on a square's double set of double axes) bring us back to a geometric configuration (the chessboard) whose basic numerical component is the number eight (the number of its intersecting ranks and files). And the association of chess with that particular number brings us back in turn to Borges's choice of exactly eight stories for his first volume of pure fictions *The Garden of Forking Paths,* a volume whose tales are dominated by images of chess and the labyrinth. As we saw, Frazer's interpretation in *The Golden Bough* of the ritual lying behind the myth of the Minotaur is part of a discussion centering on the number eight, specifically, on the "octennial tenure of the kingship" in ancient Greece. Frazer explains that the need for the king to be replaced or reconsecrated every eight years was a reflection of "those astronomical considerations which determined the early Greek calendar" (Frazer, 4:68), in particular the attempt to reconcile solar and lunar time through such simple observations as the octennial coincidence of the full moon with the longest or shortest day. This association of the number eight with the harmonizing of solar and lunar time sheds light in turn on Browne's speculation that originally "Chesse-boards" were symbolic representations "figuring the whole world, the motion of the

Planets, with Eclipses of Sunne and Moon" (*SW*, 173). For since solar
eclipses can occur only during a new moon (a conjunction of sun and
moon) and lunar eclipses only during a full moon (an opposition of sun
and moon), Browne's notion that the chessboard's ancient form in some
way figured the periodicity of eclipses means that its symbolism in effect
reconciled solar and lunar cycles. And since Frazer associates this same
project with the ritual conjunction of king and queen as sun and moon
enacted in the labyrinth every eight years, one wonders whether the
chessboard's structure of ranks and files, that labyrinthine network of
squares on which kings and queens enact geometric patterns of conjunction and opposition, preserves in its structure of intersecting eights the
ancient effort to harmonize solar and lunar time. (Indeed, might this be a
riddle whose answer is chess, whose answer in turn is time?)

In his prologue to *The Garden of Forking Paths*, Borges calls attention to
the number of stories in the volume in a way that subtly suggests a link
between the number eight and chess:

> The eight pieces of this book do not require extraneous elucidation. The
> eighth piece, "The Garden of Forking Paths," is a detective story; its readers
> will assist at the execution, and all the preliminaries, of a crime, a crime whose
> purpose will not be unknown to them, but which they will not understand—it
> seems to me—until the last paragraph. (*F*, 15)

In using the phrase "eight pieces" (*ocho piezas* in the Spanish text), Borges
seems to be playing on two senses of the word *piece*. The Spanish *pieza*,
like the English *piece*, can refer not only to a piece of fiction but also
to the carved figures on a chessboard (chess pieces), and specifically to the
eight chessmen aligned on the first rank at the start of the game (king,
queen, two rooks, two knights, two bishops) as distinguished from the
pawns aligned on the second rank. Borges's use of the phrase to refer to
the stories in his volume may be his way of suggesting that as a chess player
begins a game with eight pieces on the first rank, so he has begun his
career as a serious fiction writer with a collection of eight pieces (presumably, of the first rank) through which he means to engage the reader in a
chesslike battle of wits, a mental duel explicitly hinted at in the volume's
"eighth piece" through Stephen Albert's wittily problematic dictum that
in a riddle whose answer is chess, the only prohibited word is *chess*.

In this connection, recall for a moment two other references to the
game in *The Garden of Forking Paths*. In the volume's sixth story, "An
Examination of the Work of Herbert Quain," the narrator, summarizing
Quain's literary career, outlines the plot of his detective novel *The God of
the Labyrinth:*

An indecipherable assassination takes place in the initial pages; a leisurely discussion takes place toward the middle; a solution appears in the end. Once the enigma is cleared up, there is a long and retrospective paragraph which contains the following phrase:

"Everyone thought that the encounter of the two chess players was accidental." This phrase allows one to understand that the solution is erroneous. The unquiet reader rereads the pertinent chapters and discovers *another* solution, the true one. The reader of this singular book is thus forcibly more discerning than the detective. (*F*, 74)

The other reference is from the volume's opening story, "Tlön, Uqbar, Orbis Tertius." Near the end of the tale, Borges describes the imaginary world of Tlön as a "labyrinth plotted by men, . . . destined to be deciphered by men," a structure created by "the discipline of chess players" (*F*, 34)—a remark meant to remind us that Herbert Ashe, one of the men involved in the creation of these imaginary counterworlds, was a chess player and that Ashe and Borges's father "would beat one another at chess, without saying a word" for hours on end (*F*, 20). To this seemingly irrelevant reminiscence, Borges adds the fact that Ashe's "limp squared beard had once been red" (*F*, 20), a detail that resonates in the epigraph to the volume's fourth story ("The Circular Ruins"), taken from Alice's encounter with the sleeping Red King in *Through the Looking-Glass:* "And if he left off dreaming about you. . . . "

Now if we consider these references to the game in the volume's eighth, sixth, and first tales as forming a trajectory that runs across the collection and back toward the origin of Borges's interest in chess, then we might summarize them in this way: In the eighth tale, chess is evoked as the answer to a riddle, the solution to a mystery; in the sixth, it is linked to the structure of a detective story and to the notion of a rereading that reveals a true solution; and in the first, it is associated with Borges's father and the invention of a world of "extreme idealism" (*F*, 24) created by "the discipline of chess players." Earlier in this study we suggested that the various references to chess in *The Garden of Forking Paths* are meant to evoke the game as a figure of the analysis of mind within the tradition of the analytic detective story. We went on to argue that in his detective stories Borges in effect presents us with a riddle whose answer is chess by constructing the three tales around a scenario based on the game (the checkmating of the Red King from *Through the Looking-Glass*) and that the references to the game in Borges's first volume of pure fictions are clues to the existence of this riddle. We also suggested that for Borges the Red King, as a figure of the dreaming self contained in the dream of the Other, evokes the self-destructive potential inherent in the analysis of mind, a potential realized in the Red King's ultimate checkmate. However, given the network of associations surrounding the myth and ritual of the labyrinth in the works of Evans and Frazer and given Borges's association of the labyrinth with chess (and thus the implicit linking of the actions played out within each of these spaces), one wonders whether this scenario of checkmating the Red King represents in fact the deepest meaning of that riddle whose answer is chess, or whether there is a still deeper level on which the game of chess possesses within Borges's work an uncanny power as a figure of combative, life-threatening self-knowledge.

I would suggest that such a level does exist and that Borges gives us a clue to its significance in his very first mention of the game in *The Garden of Forking Paths*. I refer to his description in "Tlön, Uqbar, Orbis Tertius" of the chess games between Herbert Ashe and Borges's father, a description that associates the elder Borges not only with the game but, more particularly, with the attempt to checkmate a man whose "limp squared beard had once been red," a man whose secret work involves dreaming up imaginary counterworlds characterized by their "extreme idealism." Indeed, I would further suggest that the chess games between Herbert Ashe and Borges's father are the real referent of that laconic sentence from Herbert Quain's (whose given name echoes that of Herbert Ashe) detective novel *The God of the Labyrinth*, "Everyone thought that the encounter of the two chess players was accidental," a remark that leads "the unquiet reader," says Borges, to reread "the pertinent chapters" and discover another solution. In his association of chess with his father and with the image of a world of "extreme idealism," Borges gives us a clue not only to the deepest meaning of the riddle but also a clue, as we shall see, to reconciling the two opposing scenarios associated respectively with the myth and the ritual of the labyrinth: a scenario of opposition in the myth of Theseus and the Minotaur and of conjunction in the ritual marriage of king and queen as solar bull and lunar cow.

29 Zeno's Paradoxes; Chess as Sublimated Violence; The Dream in Athens; The King of the North; The False Artaxerxes; The Sleeping King in the Garden; The Game of Kings and Queens; Tropes of Impotence

IN ASSOCIATING HIS FATHER WITH the game of chess in "Tlön, Uqbar, Orbis Tertius," Borges seems simply to have transposed into art a link already present in life. Borges's father was a chess player; he taught his son the game; and, as Borges tells us in his "Autobiographical Essay," he used the chessboard to begin his son's philosophical education: "When I was still quite young, he showed me, with the aid of a chessboard, the paradoxes of Zeno—Achilles and the tortoise, the unmoving flight of the arrow, the impossibility of motion. Later, without mentioning Berkeley's name, he did his best to teach me the rudiments of idealism" (A, 207).

During Borges's visit to Baltimore in 1983, I asked how his father had demonstrated Zeno's paradoxes at the chessboard. He said the elder Borges had used the eight pieces aligned on the first rank, showing him that before he could travel the distance between the king's rook and the queen's rook he had first to go half that distance (i.e., from the king's rook to the king), but that before he could go from the king's rook to the king he had first to go half *that* distance (i.e., from the king's rook to the king's knight), and so on. (That Borges's father used the eight pieces on the first rank for this demonstration gives an added resonance to the "eight pieces" of Borges's first volume of pure fictions and their recurring chess imagery.) To the extent that Zeno's paradoxes reveal "the impossibility of motion," they are in effect tropes of helplessness, of impotence. And if motion is impossible, then our physical world in which motion seems constantly to occur must be an illusion. This world does not have a real, independent (i.e., material) existence; its existence is wholly a function of mental states. From the paradoxes of Zeno, it is a short step, then, as the passage from the "Autobiographical Essay" implies, to the "rudiments of idealism" and the philosophy of George Berkeley. But if the paradoxes of Zeno are, as we suggest, tropes of impotence, then a father's decision to teach these paradoxes to his young son might seem at best ill-considered and at worst faintly hostile. Indeed, if there is an element of veiled hostility in this act—a sense on the father's part that he has accomplished little of what he set out to do, not because he failed, but because nothing could really be achieved in a world where motion is an illusion; and a warning to the son not to show his father up, not to defeat him, by trying to accomplish something on his own—then certainly the chessboard is the right place for the father to convey that message, for virtually every psychoanalytic reading of the game's structure and symbolism sees it as a ritual sublimation of father murder.

The game's goal is, of course, the checkmate of the king. One seeks to place the king under a direct attack from which he is powerless to escape, so that on the next move he can be captured and removed from the board. But this capture and removal (the killing of the king) never actually takes place in the game, for the game always ends a move before this with the king's immobilization in check. Which is simply to say that in the game's sublimation of aggression, even the killing of the father in a symbolic form is repressed. According to the psychoanalyst and chess master Reuben Fine, since "genetically, chess is more often than not taught to the boy by his father, or by a father substitute," it naturally "becomes a means of working out the father-son rivalry."[1] In this ritual mime of the conflicts surrounding the family romance, the mother plays a major role. In his essay on the American chess champion Paul Morphy, the psychoanalyst Ernest Jones points out that "in attacking the father the most potent assistance is afforded by the mother (=Queen)" (Cockburn, 23), the strongest piece on the board. As one chess critic has noted,

> Chess is a matter of both father murder and attempts to prevent it. This mirror function of chess is of extreme importance; obviously the player appears both in a monstrous and in a virtuous capacity—planning parricide, at the same time warding it off; recreating Oedipal fantasy, yet trying to disrupt it. Yet the stronger urge is the monstrous one; the player wants to win, to kill the father rather than defend him, although one could clearly speculate on the problems of players who habitually lose at the last. (Cockburn, 100–101)

Fine argues that the king not only represents the father but, as a hand-manipulated, carved figure, "stands for the boy's penis in the phallic stage, and hence rearouses the castration anxiety characteristic of that period. . . . It is the father pulled down to the boy's size. Unconsciously it gives the boy a chance to say to the father: 'To the outside world you are big and strong, but when we get right down to it, you're just as weak as I am'" (Cockburn, 42).

That Borges understood the Oedipal component of chess is clear from a passage in the last book he published before his death, *Atlas* (1984), a collection of short essays devoted for the most part to geographic locales associated with the psychic terrain of his past. The meditation on Athens begins:

> On the first morning, my first day in Athens, I was proffered the following dream. In front of me stood a row of books filling a long shelf. They formed a set of the *Encyclopaedia Britannica,* one of my lost paradises. I took down a volume at random. I looked up Coleridge: the article had an end but no beginning. I looked up Crete: it concluded but did not begin. I looked up the entry on Chess. At that point the dream shifted. On an elevated stage in an amphitheater filled to capacity with an attentive audience, I was playing chess with my father, who was also the False Artaxerxes. (His ears having been cut off, Artaxerxes was found sleeping by one of his many wives; she ran her hand over his skull very gently so as not to awaken him; presently he was killed.) I moved a piece; my antagonist did not move anything but, by an act of magic, he erased one of my pieces. This procedure was repeated various times.
>
> I awoke and told myself: *I am in Greece, where everything began, assuming that things, as opposed to articles in the dream's encyclopedia, have a beginning.*[2]

It seems only fitting that this dream, with its images of castration and father murder, should have been "proffered" to Borges in Athens, the city where the blind parricide Oedipus ultimately finds shelter with Theseus who, according to Plutarch, cannot himself "escape the charge of parricide" because of his forgetfulness about the sail.

Borges's dream in Athens begins as a search for origins, an attempt to return to a "lost paradise" represented in the dream by a set of the *Encyclopaedia Britannica*. In terms of an individual's biological origin, that lost paradise is the maternal womb, and the fact that Borges's attempt to penetrate the "lost paradise" of the encyclopedia (by delving into one of its volumes) leads almost immediately to an image of conflict with the father and the threat of castration suggests that the *Britannica* functions here as a figure of the mother's body. Moreover, since the *Britannica* is one of Borges's favorite examples of a textual Aleph (a book that contains within it a verbal image of everything in the universe at the same time that it is itself contained within that universe), the encyclopedia as a figure of the matrix gives an added resonance to the image of total self-inclusion evoked by Borges's Aleph-like objects. Which is to say that the microcosmic Aleph is like the child contained within its mother's womb who in turn contains within itself its parents' image. Seen in this light, the desire for total self-inclusion present in the analysis of mind (the desire to include within the mind an absolute image of itself) appears as an intellectualization of the fantasy of a total return to the womb, a sublimation figuring the self as a mental rather than a bodily entity.

In the Athens dream Borges takes a volume of the *Britannica* from the shelf (the volume for the womblike letter *C*, to judge from its entries) and finds that in the first two articles he reads (on Coleridge and Crete) the attempt to return to the origin is frustrated. Each article has an end "but no beginning." The reference to Crete seems to be a fairly straightforward allusion to the Cretan labyrinth, whose winding passageways Freud takes to be an image of the matrix from which Theseus is reborn, with the help of the umbilical thread, after having slain the male monster who embodies the fear of castration or death.

In contrast, the dream reference to Coleridge seems less clear at first glance, but a passage from Borges's essay on nightmares in his 1980 volume *Seven Nights* gives us a clue. According to Borges, Coleridge says that

> it doesn't matter what we dream, that the dream searches for explanations. He gives an example: a lion suddenly appears in this room, and we are all afraid; the fear has been caused by the image of the lion. But in dreams the reverse can occur. We feel oppressed, and then search for an explanation. I, absurdly but vividly, dream that a sphinx has lain down next to me. The sphinx is not the cause of my fear, it is an explanation of my feeling of oppression. Coleridge adds that people who have been frightened by imaginary ghosts have gone mad. On the other hand, a person who dreams a ghost can wake up and, within a few seconds, regain his composure.
>
> I have had—and I still have—many nightmares. The most terrible, the one that struck me as the most terrible, I used in a sonnet. It went like this: I was in my room; it was dawn (possibly that was the time of the dream). At the foot of my bed was a king, a very ancient king, and I knew in the dream that he was the King of the North, of Norway. He did not look at me; his blind stare was fixed on the ceiling. I felt the terror of his presence. I saw the king, I saw his sword, I saw his dog. Then I woke. But I continued to see the king for a while, because he had made such a strong impression on me. Retold, my dream is nothing; dreamt, it was terrible.[3]

The progression of images in this passage forms an instructive gloss on the association of images in Borges's dream at Athens. Starting with the name of Coleridge and the dictum that "the dream searches for explanations" by creating images that correspond to, and thus account for, emotions we feel, the passage introduces the example of a lion as a symbolic expression of fear. To which Borges adds the example of his own dream that a sphinx has lain down beside him, the image of the sphinx serving as "an explanation of my feeling of oppression." The associative link between the images of lion and sphinx seems plain enough: the multiform sphinx is traditionally depicted with a lion's body. But the Sphinx is, of course, the monster associated with Oedipus.

The passage's imagery now shifts from the figure of a sphinx to that of a ghost, with the dictum that people frightened by an imaginary ghost in waking life have gone mad but that those who dream a ghost can wake up and regain their composure. The link between sphinx and ghost seems unclear at first, until we recall that in "Ibn Hakkan al-Bokhari" the three faceless corpses found in the labyrinth are those of a king, a slave, and a lion and that the explanation of the crime contrived by the killer is that the three have been murdered by the ghost of the king's vizier. Given the associative link between sphinx and lion in Borges's discussion of nightmares and that among king, ghost, and lion in "Ibn Hakkan al-Bokhari," the progression of images in the nightmare passage becomes easier to follow. The lion (the king of the beasts) serves as a middle term connecting the sphinx (with its lion's body) to the king. But this linking of sphinx and king also implicitly connects the images of sphinx and ghost, for the king in Borges's nightmare is clearly coded as a spectral apparition. Thus the associative chain underlying the passage from the nightmare essay runs: lion (king of the beasts) → sphinx (creature with a lion's body who tests King Oedipus) → king → ghost (of a king). But in the passage Borges reverses the order of the last two links in the chain by moving directly from the dream image of the sphinx to a discussion of ghosts in waking life versus ghosts in dreams, and only then goes on to describe his "most terrible" nightmare about "a very ancient king." Since it is dawn and the king is at the foot of Borges's bed, one assumes that within the dreamed scene Borges is just awakening from a night's sleep and that the uncertainty as to whether he is awake or dreaming, whether the king is an imaginary ghost or a dreamed one, forms part of the image's terror, a frightening sense of ambiguity that is confirmed when Borges actually awakens and yet continues "to see the king for a while" because the image has "made such a strong impression."

That the figure of the "ancient king" is coded as a ghost is clear from the way Borges's account of the nightmare grows out of his comment about the difference between thinking we see and dreaming we see a ghost. Moreover, this "King of the North" is a very specific ghost indeed. Borges identifies him as the king of Norway, but that is probably a displacement within the dream. He is the king of Denmark, the ghost of Hamlet's father returned to confront his son with the Oedipal task of avenging the father's murder and with the epistemological dilemma of whether this demanding appearance is a real ghost, a dream, or an hallucination. (At the start of Shakespeare's play we are told that Hamlet had killed Fortinbras, the king of Norway, in combat, thus causing young Fortinbras to seek revenge for his father's death.) In the dream the king's "blind stare" is "fixed on the ceiling," at once a reminder of the punishment Oedipus inflicted on himself for incest and parricide (for usurping the true king's place) and an evocation of Borges's own father who went blind from an hereditary eye ailment, an ailment he passed on to his son who also went blind. Indeed, the imagery of the dream suggests the extent to which Borges may have experienced his blindness on some unconscious level as an Oedipal transmission. The blind king's sword would seem to be both a phallic symbol of the father's authority and a metonym for the punishment meted out to those who would usurp that authority; while his dog probably bears the same relationship to the dreamer that the Sphinx does to Oedipus and the Minotaur does to Theseus—a symbol of the animal (sexual) realm who confronts the aspirant (son) with a life-threatening test by which the real king (or his lawful successor) is distinguished from usurpers or impostors.

If we are correct in thinking that the image of the encyclopedia entry on Coleridge in the dream at Athens represents the dreamwork's condensation of the chain of associations grouped around Coleridge's name in the essay on nightmares, then it seems clear that the progression of images in the Athens dream is essentially the same as that in the nightmare essay, but with this difference: In the nightmare essay Borges can directly allude to Oedipus through the mention of a sphinx precisely because the king is *not* explicitly identified as Borges's father. But in the Athens dream the figure whom Borges confronts across a chessboard in a ritual sublimation of father murder *is* so identified; and consequently, the direct allusion to Oedipus is repressed in favor of a veiled reference to an Oedipal screen-figure (Theseus) evoked by the encyclopedia entry on Crete (i.e., the Cretan labyrinth → the Minotaur → the Minotaur's slayer). In any case the two passages culminate in an uncanny reciprocity: the terrifying image of a blind king with a sword balanced against the image of Borges's father (who went blind) as a false king mutilated by a sword.

Perhaps the most striking detail in the Athens dream is the description of Borges's father as "the False Artaxerxes" whose ears have been cropped. It seems only fitting that since the dream begins with an image of the *Encyclopaedia Britannica*, we should turn to it for an explanation of this figure. The eleventh edition identifies the false Artaxerxes as one Bessus, a "satrap of Bactria and Sogdiana under Darius III": "When Alexander pursued the Persian king [Darius III] on his flight to the East (summer 330), Bessus with some of the other conspirators deposed Darius and shortly afterwards killed him. He then tried to organize a national resistance against the Macedonian conqueror in the eastern provinces, proclaimed himself king and adopted the name Artaxerxes." Taken prisoner by treachery, Bessus was sent by Alexander to Ecbatana where he was condemned to death: "Before his execution his nose and ears were cut off, according to the Persian custom; we learn from the Behistun inscription that Darius I punished the usurpers in the same way" (*EB,* 3:824). Bessus, the false Artaxerxes, was, then, a usurper, able to kill a king but unable to take his place, like the vizier Zaid in "Ibn Hakkan al-Bokhari." In Borges's dream the cutting off of the usurper's ears is an obvious image of castration, reminiscent of the destruction of Oedipus's eyeballs with the pin of Jocasta's brooch; and the suggestion of maternal complicity in the attack on the father is present as well: "Artaxerxes was found sleeping by one of his many wives; she ran her hand over his skull very gently so as not to awaken him; presently he was killed."

This image of a woman discovering a sleeping false king cannot help but remind us of another scene associated with the recurring scenario underlying Borges's detective stories—Alice's discovery of the sleeping Red King (whom she will ultimately checkmate) in the chessboard-labyrinth of Looking-glass House. We should note, regarding Borges's nightmare image of a ghostly king of Norway, that in the poem "Mirrors" Borges implicitly associates Claudius's murder of the king of Denmark as he lies sleeping in his orchard with Alice's coming upon a dreaming king within her dream:

> Claudius, king for an evening, king in a dream,
> did not know he was a dream until that day
> on which an actor mimed his felony
> with silent artifice, in a tableau.   (*BR,* 278)

As we saw earlier, Borges, in his essay "Partial Enchantments of the *Quixote,*" singles out this scene (in which Shakespeare "includes on the stage of *Hamlet* another stage, where a tragedy almost like that of *Hamlet* is being presented" [*OI,* 45]) as one of those Aleph-like textual moments that are structural analogues of Alice's encounter with the Red King.

Regarding Alice's promotion in the chess game from pawn to queen, Rodríguez Monegal points out that when Borges and his younger sister Norah were children they used to play in the garden of their Buenos Aires home a game of Kings and Queens in which Borges enacted the role of the prince and Norah the role of the queen mother. "It is significant," remarks Monegal,

> that, in playing Kings and Queens, Norah (who was two years younger) became the Queen Mother and not the Princess, as might have been expected at that healthy incestuous stage of their lives. . . . In changing his sister (his equal) into his "mother" (a superior; thus an unreachable being), Georgie was exorcising a potential incestuous relationship that would have been normal at

their age. The garden . . . was to be Eden; no serpent was allowed to weave its way into that secluded space. (*JLB,* 36)

Given Monegal's association of the childhood garden where Borges and Norah played their game of Kings and Queens with the Garden of Eden, we should recall, first, that the Athens dream with its imagery of an unreachable origin begins with a description of the *Britannica* as one of Borges's "lost paradises" (Greek *paradeisos,* "garden") and, second, that Alice's chess game takes place in the garden of Looking-glass House. All of which raises the question of whether the promotion of Norah from the role of princess to queen in the game of Kings and Queens constituted, as Monegal contends, a "powerful repression of the Oedipal conflict" (*JLB,* 36) that coded the sister, at that "healthy incestuous stage of their lives," as "an unreachable being," or whether it constituted instead an oblique expression of a more basic incestuous attachment for which the brother-sister relationship is a substitute formation—that between son and mother. In this case the promotion of the princess (sister) to the role of the queen (mother), instead of coding the sister as an unreachable being, would code the mother as a playfellow and helpmate. The writer José Bianco, who was a friend of Borges and his family from 1935 on, recalls that Borges made much of his mother's youthful appearance in introducing her to his friends, so that "she didn't seem to be her son's eldest sister but his sister merely" (*JLB,* 285).

With this in mind, consider again Borges's dream in Athens. While the image of paternal mutilation and death would seem to be simply an expression of the son's desire to inflict on the father the same violence with which he feels threatened, the nature of the paternal threat to the son's power, as figured in the moves of the chess game, is more complex than that reading suggests. For the image of the father in Borges's dream is not that of a true king with absolute power to inflict whatever injury he chooses on the son but that of a false king who is castrated and put to death. Which is to say that the father in Borges's dream threatens the son's potency by presenting himself as a castrated son trapped within a generational line and doomed to death, threatens him by showing that the father is not an absolute source but merely the son's immediate predecessor who has been rendered helpless, made unoriginal, by his own predecessor. Describing the moves of the chess game, Borges says, "I moved a piece; my antagonist did not move anything but, by an act of magic, he erased one of my pieces. This procedure was repeated various times." When we recall that Borges's father had used the chessboard to teach his son the paradoxes of Zeno, tropes of impotence figuring "the impossibility of motion," then the logic of the scene becomes clear: To play a game of chess, one must move pieces from one square to another until finally one places the king in a check from which he cannot escape. But if checkmating the king is a symbolic murder of the father, then the father who teaches this game to his son might well try to protect himself from the combat for paternal power by convincing his son that no such power exists. Thus in the dreamed chess game, Borges moves a piece, but his father does not move anything (motion is impossible). Instead "by an act of magic" (the paradoxes of Zeno which reveal the magical, i.e., illusory, nature of action), he erases one of his son's pieces, he makes it vanish like the dream it is. In so doing, the father castrates his son, not physically by exercising superior strength, but psychologically by convincing him that in this illusory world nothing can be done, that everyone is helpless, father and son alike. (It is worth noting in this regard that Borges's poem "Chess" [1960] concludes by questioning that traditional scholastic explanation of the origin of motion which traces movement, through a series of intermediate causes, back to an unmoved first mover, the All-Father: "God moves the player, he, in turn, the piece. / But what god beyond God begins the round / of dust and time and dream and agonies?" [*BR*, 281].)

No wonder, then, that when Borges awakens from this dream in Athens of unreachable origins and illusory grounds, this dream in which (like Alice in the labyrinthine chessboard-garden) he discovers, during the course of a chess game, the person who conceived him depicted as a sleeping king (when he discovers himself [the dreamer of the Athens dream] as a figure in the dream of the Other), no wonder that the force of the dream persists into waking consciousness as a doubt about whether origins and original power exist in real life, a persistence of the dream state that seems to blur the distinction between material reality and illusion (as when Borges awakened from his nightmare of the blind King of the North yet "continued to see the king for a while"): "I awoke and told myself: *I am in Greece, where everything began, assuming that things, as opposed to articles in the dream's encyclopedia, have a beginning.*"

Mirrors and Fatherhood; Encyclopedias as Matrix Symbols; Labyrinths, Mirrors, and Masks; The Secret of Copulation; The Encounter in Geneva; The Monster in the Labyrinth; The Dreaming Minotaur; The Amphisbaena and William Wilson; The Sublimation of the Body

WHEN ONE UNDERSTANDS THE PSYCHOLOGICAL background of Borges's association of his father with chess, then "the encounter of the two chess players" (the elder Borges and Herbert Ashe) in "Tlön, Uqbar, Orbis Tertius" seems far from accidental indeed. And this encounter takes on still greater significance when we consider that "the faded English engineer Herbert Ashe" is, according to Borges's friend José Bianco, simply "a portrait" of Borges's father (*JLB,* 285). That Borges should imagine a chess game in which his father competes against a portrait of himself is not surprising, given his use of the game's mirror-image structure to evoke the detective genre's mental duel between doubles. But this image of a specular chess game played by the father becomes even more interesting when we recall that at the beginning of "Tlön" fatherhood and mirroring are invoked as analogous forms of duplicating human beings. Borges says there that he owed the discovery of the idealist worlds of the story's title to "the conjunction of a mirror and an encyclopedia." He and his friend Bioy-Casares had dined one evening and talked well into the night. During their conversation, Borges noticed that

> from the far end of the corridor, the mirror was watching us; and we discovered, with the inevitability of discoveries made late at night, that mirrors have something grotesque about them. Then Bioy Casares recalled that one of the heresiarchs of Uqbar had stated that mirrors and copulation are abominable, since they both multiply the numbers of man. (*F,* 17)

Asking for the source of this "memorable sentence," Borges is told by Bioy that it comes from the article on Uqbar in the *Anglo-American Cyclopaedia.* As it happens, the villa where they are staying has a copy of the work, but try as they might, they cannot find the article on Uqbar. The next day Bioy telephones to say that he has found in another copy the article in question and that the passage he had paraphrased the night before reads: "For one of those gnostics, the visible universe was an illusion or, more precisely, a sophism. Mirrors and fatherhood are abominable because they multiply it and extend it" (*F,* 18). Borges and Bioy compare the two versions of the encyclopedia and find that the sole difference is the additional four pages of the article on Uqbar, a discovery that ultimately reveals the existence of a secret project to introduce the idealist world of Tlön into this one and thereby alter the shape of reality. (We should note that in his essay "Poetry" in *Seven Nights* Borges associates his fear of mirrors and their terrifying duplication of reality with Poe: "It is truly awful that there are mirrors. . . . I think that Poe felt it too. There is an essay of his . . . on the decoration of rooms. One of the conditions he insists on is that the mirrors be placed in such a way that a seated person is not reflected. This tells us his fear of seeing himself in the mirror. We see it in his story 'William Wilson' about the double, and also in *The Narrative of Arthur Gordon Pym*, where there is an Antarctic tribe, and a man from that tribe sees a mirror for the first time and collapses, horrified. We are accustomed to mirrors, but there is something terrifying in that visual duplication of reality" [*SN*, 88].)

The opening image of "Tlön" ("the conjunction of a mirror and an encyclopedia") is almost certainly an allusion to the medieval practice of referring in Latin to a work of encyclopedic knowledge as a *speculum* (e.g., the thirteenth-century *Speculum majus* of Vincent of Beauvais), a name that figures the encyclopedia as a written "mirror" of the universe. Given the sexual connotation of *conjunction* (*conjunción* in the Spanish text), the opening image also sets the stage for the subsequent association of a mirror, first with copulation, and then with fatherhood. And if, in this conjunction of mirror and encyclopedia, the mirror is equated with the male principle, then it would seem only natural to equate the encyclopedia with the female (the matrix)—the same association found in Borges's dream at Athens where the *Britannica* is described as a "lost paradise" and then immediately linked to the image of the womblike labyrinth through the reference to Crete. (Significantly enough, *The Anglo-American Cyclopaedia* in "Tlön" is described as "a literal if inadequate reprint of the 1902 *Encyclopaedia Britannica*" [*F*, 17].)

If for Borges mirror and encyclopedia are gender-coded as male and female respectively, then the description he gives in *Seven Nights* of two of his recurring nightmares, two dreams that frequently blend into one, seems like a gloss on the conjunction of mirror and encyclopedia that begins "Tlön":

> I have two nightmares which often become confused with one another. I have the nightmare of the labyrinth, which comes, in part, from a steel engraving I saw in a French book when I was a child. In this engraving were the Seven Wonders of the World, among them the labyrinth of Crete. The labyrinth was a great amphitheater, a very high amphitheater. . . . In this closed structure—ominously closed—there were cracks. I believed when I was a child (or I now

believe I believed) that if one had a magnifying glass powerful enough, one could look through the cracks and see the Minotaur in the terrible center of the labyrinth.

My other nightmare is that of the mirror. The two are not distinct, as it only takes two facing mirrors to construct a labyrinth. . . .

I always dream of labyrinths or of mirrors. In the dream of the mirror another vision appears, another terror of my nights, and that is the idea of the mask. Masks have always scared me. No doubt I felt in my childhood that someone who was wearing a mask was hiding something horrible. These are my most terrible nightmares: I see myself reflected in a mirror, but the reflection is wearing a mask. I am afraid to pull the mask off, afraid to see my real face, which I imagine to be hideous. There may be leprosy or evil or something more terrible than anything I am capable of imagining. (*SN*, 32–33)

As the dream at Athens begins with the image of a book (the *Britannica*) and immediately moves (via the reference to Crete) to the image of the labyrinth, so this passage from the nightmare essay begins with the image of the labyrinth and moves immediately to the image of a book—a French book in which Borges saw a steel engraving of the labyrinth when he was a child. Although Borges does not say what kind of book it was, the mention of a "steel engraving" recalls a remark from the "Autobiographical Essay" about the books he enjoyed most as a child in his father's library: "I have forgotten most of the faces of that time . . . and yet I vividly remember so many of the steel engravings in *Chambers's Encyclopaedia* and in the *Britannica*" (*A*, 209).

In the engraving from the French book, the labyrinth is shown as a "very high amphitheater," a description that gives added meaning to the setting of the chess game in the Athens dream: "On an elevated stage in an amphitheater filled to capacity with an attentive audience, I was playing chess with my father, who was also the False Artaxerxes." That Borges imagines the labyrinth as an enclosed amphitheater suggests yet again that the site of the chess game with his father, a game of kings and queens played out on a labyrinthine network of squares, represents the maternal space of origin for whose possession they are competing. And the fact that the labyrinth is closely associated in these passages with another womb symbol (the image of a book as a "lost paradise") suggests that the real-life arena into which the Oedipal struggle between Borges and his father has been displaced is not the game of chess but the realm of literature in which the virgin space of the page, inseminated by ink from the phallic pen, can produce an offspring longer-lived than any child, an offspring almost immortal if the author only be original enough.

If the images that dominate Borges's two recurring nightmares (mir-

ror and labyrinth) are associated respectively with fatherhood and motherhood, then Borges's assertion that "the two are not distinct" suggests a
union of male and female principles reminiscent of "the conjunction of a
mirror and an encyclopedia" at the beginning of "Tlön." This blending of
mirror and labyrinth in Borges's dreams, like the conjunction of mirror
and encyclopedia in the tale, seems to be a symbolic figuration of the
primal scene, an evocation of the dreamer's parents in the act of engendering the dreamer. And to judge from the imagery that follows from this
blending of mirror and labyrinth in Borges's account, the product of that
union is experienced as something monstrous—a masked figure whose
mask conceals "something more terrible than anything" the dreamer is
"capable of imagining."

According to the passage's associative logic, two of Borges's nightmare
images, in becoming "confused with one another," are in effect equated—
labyrinth and mirror. As the labyrinth contains a monstrous figure (the
Minotaur with a man's body and a bull's head), so the mirror contains an
equally monstrous figure (a masked man with a human body and a concealed face). In one case the bull's head, in the other the masked face,
makes the figure terrifying. But what is that frightening content at once
concealed and evoked by the mask and the animal head? In his entry on
the Minotaur in *The Book of Imaginary Beings*, Borges says that the Cretan
labyrinth was built "to confine and keep hidden" Queen Pasiphae's "monstrous son" (*BIB*, 158), the product of an unnatural union of animal and
human. And if the bull's head is the visible trace of a monstrous copulation, then are we to assume, given the equation of the labyrinth's bull-
headed monster and the mirror's masked figure, that the masked face also
evokes the image of a monstrous copulation, or more precisely, evokes the
image of copulation as something monstrous?

Noting the "revulsion for the act of fatherhood . . . or copulation"
found in "Tlön," Monegal wonders how much this feeling "has to do with
the discovery of the primal scene through the complicity of a mirror"
when Borges was a child. He points out as evidence for this possibility a
passage from Borges's poem "The Mirror":

> Infinite I see them, elementary
> executors of an old pact,
> to multiply the world as the generative
> act, sleepless and fatal.   (*JLB*, 33)

Monegal also notes that in the tale "The Sect of the Phoenix" (1952)
Borges imagines a pagan cult bound together by a shared secret that
assures them immortality, a secret hinted at in the tale but never named.
Borges says that although the secret "is transmitted from generation to

generation . . . usage does not favor mothers teaching it to their sons" (*F*, 165). He continues,

> Initiation into the mystery is the task of individuals of the lowest order. . . . In itself the act is trivial, momentary, and does not requires description. . . . The Secret is sacred, but it is also somewhat ridiculous. The practice of the mystery is furtive and even clandestine, and its adepts do not speak about it. There are no respectable words to describe it, but it is understood that all words refer it, or, better, that they inevitably allude to it. . . . A kind of sacred horror prevents some of the faithful from practicing the extremely simple ritual; the others despise them for it, but they despise themselves even more. (*F*, 165)

To many members of the sect, the secret seemed "paltry, distressing, vulgar and (what is even stranger) incredible. They could not reconcile themselves to the fact that their ancestors had lowered themselves to such conduct" (*F*, 166). When asked by the critic Ronald Christ about the secret shared by the sect of the Phoenix, Borges replied, "The act is what Whitman says 'the divine husband knows, from the work of fatherhood.'— When I first heard about this act, when I was a boy, I was shocked, shocked to think that my mother, my father had performed it. It is an amazing discovery, no? But then too it is . . . a rite of immortality, isn't it?"[1]

Borges had earlier used this image of a child shocked by the thought of parental intercourse in his tale "Emma Zunz" (1948). In order to avenge her father who had killed himself after being framed for embezzlement, Emma Zunz plans to kill the real embezzler, her father's former employer Aaron Loewenthal. She will claim that Loewenthal lured her to his office, raped her, and that she killed him with the gun he kept in his desk. To make the plan work, Emma, who is apparently a virgin, must have intercourse on the afternoon of the murder. She goes to the waterfront, picks up a sailor in a bar, and while they are together in a dingy room, the narrative voice speculates,

> Did Emma Zunz think *once* about the dead man who motivated the sacrifice? It is my belief that she did think once, and in that moment she endangered her desperate undertaking. She thought (she was unable not to think) that her father had done to her mother the hideous thing that was being done to her now. She thought of it with weak amazement and took refuge, quickly, in vertigo. (*L*, 135)

So great is her feeling of violation from this sexual encounter that when she confronts Loewenthal she feels, "more than the urgency of avenging her father, . . . the need of inflicting punishment for the outrage she had suffered. She was unable not to kill him after that thorough dishonor" (*L*, 136). It is as if the man who caused her father's suicide had become a substitute for her father, a substitute for the man who, by doing that same "hideous thing" to her mother, had engendered Emma, dooming her to a material body and thus making her subject to having the "hideous thing" done to her in a waterfront dive. It is as if the effort to avenge the father had subtly metamorphosed into vengeance against the father for the act of fatherhood.

If, as we suggested, the masked figure in the mirror evokes for Borges the bull-headed monster of the labyrinth ("it only takes two facing mirrors to construct a labyrinth") considered specifically as the product of an unnatural copulation, and if that bull-headed figure symbolically represents in turn the act of copulation as something monstrous, as a male animal's assault on the mother (Freud notes that in the fantasy of the primal scene the child frequently misinterprets parental intercourse as an act of violence by the father against the mother), then the terror Borges feels at the nightmare image of seeing his masked reflection would seem to be compounded of two related emotions. First, there is probably, in Monegal's words, a "revulsion for the act of . . . copulation," a sense (left over from childhood or adolescence) of the reproductive act as terrifying or humiliating, unworthy of those godlike beings one's parents and, as an origin, unworthy of oneself, that spiritual entity imprisoned (as a result of this engendering) in the earthy cave of the body (with its physical constraints and sexual drives) as surely as the Minotaur (a symbol of the sun during its daily descent into the underworld) is imprisoned in the subterranean labyrinth. Second, there is the son's feeling of helplessness, of being trapped in the cycle of generation, doomed to repeat and transmit this cycle by doing the thing his father did. Indeed, for Borges, part of the peculiar terror of the dream's masked figure seems to be the sense that the face hidden beneath the mask of his mirror image is not his own but his father's, that in this reversal of the master/slave relationship between self and mirror image the son is simply a reflection of the father helplessly repeating his gestures.

Commenting on a passage from Borges's tale "The Other" in *The Book of Sand* (1975), Monegal speculates on the biographical sources of this fear and revulsion at the body's instinctual demands. The tale recounts how Borges as an old man meets his youthful double, the adolescent Borges who spent the years of the First World War in Geneva. One morning, sitting on a bench facing the Charles River in Cambridge, Massachusetts, Borges has the uncanny feeling of "having lived that moment once before" (*BS*, 11). The Charles reminds him of the Rhone in Geneva and the days of his youth. Suddenly Borges notices that a young man has taken a seat at the other end of the bench and that it is, to his astonishment, himself as a teenager. When Borges introduces himself, the young man is incredulous. To convince his younger self that he is who he says, Borges tells him things that only he could know, including the fact that hidden behind the other volumes in his wardrobe is "a book in paper covers about sexual customs in the Balkans" (*BS*, 13). He concludes by reminding the young man of an event whose nature, though unspecified, is apparently related to the subject of the concealed book:

> "Nor have I forgotten one evening on a certain second floor of the Place Dubourg."
> "Dufour," he corrected.
> "Very well—Dufour. Is this enough now?"
> "No," he said. "These proofs prove nothing. If I am dreaming you, it's natural that you know what I know." (*BS*, 13)

Monegal suggests that this memory of an evening spent "on a certain second floor" of the Place Dufour refers to an actual event in Borges's adolescence, an event that had a profound effect on Borges's personal life and on the shape of his imagination:

> Only gossip is available to elucidate the reference, but it is gossip that has been around long enough to acquire a certain respectability. According to Borges' confidences to several friends, he was once taken by Father to one of those complaisant Geneva girls who catered to foreigners, loners, and young men in distress. He performed his task so quickly that he was overcome by the power of orgasm. The "little death," as the French call it, was too close to real death for him. From then on Georgie viewed sex with fear. There is another side to the story which may have more complex implications. In being initiated into sex through the offices of his father, Georgie may have assumed that the girl had performed the same services for Father; having to share the same woman with Father disturbed deep-seated taboos. (*JLB*, 113)[2]

Indeed, one wonders if the second floor room on the Place Dufour contained, as such rooms often do, a large mirror for its occupants to observe themselves in the act. If so, the association of mirrors and copulation in "Tlön" (and the combined fear, revulsion, and fascination linked with this association) takes on a deeper biographical resonance.

The most significant aspect of Borges's recollection of the encounter in the Place Dufour is his self-conscious parapraxis in recalling the location as the Place Dubourg, for the name Dubourg may well be meant to link a frightening scene of sexual initiation to the brutal murders in Poe's first detective story. When the sailor who owns the escaped orangutan in "The Murders in the Rue Morgue" asks Dupin if the ape (whose capture Dupin had advertised in the newspaper) is on the premises, Dupin replies, "He is at a livery stable in the Rue Dubourg, just by" (2:563)—a name that immediately recalls the murders of the mother and daughter. For the first witness deposed in the newspaper account of the crime had been a Parisian laundress, Pauline Dubourg, who did the L'Espanayes' washing. (Interestingly enough, the first school Poe attended as a child during his foster parents' stay in England was kept by two sisters named Dubourg,[3] and one cannot help but wonder how much his memories of the Dubourgs as teachers [as mother substitutes] was mixed up with the image of the murdered mother and daughter in the tale.) The echoing of Poe's Rue Dubourg (the fictitious location of the killer ape) by Borges's Place Dubourg (the misremembered location of Borges's first sexual encounter) suggests that in Borges's mind two scenarios evoked by the name had become blended: on the one hand, the murderous (almost sexual) assault of a male animal on a mother and daughter, and on the other, a bookish adolescent's sexual contretemps with a Geneva prostitute, a physical encounter in which the little death of sex seemed "too close to real death" for the young man, and perhaps too close to home as well, if, as Monegal suggests, Borges suspected that he was sharing this young woman with his father, thus making him aware of a repressed desire to share another woman with the father. While the former scenario invests violent death with a sexual aura, the latter invests a sexual encounter with the aura of death. And in both cases sexuality is coded as something animal, violent, and life-threatening.

In this connection we should note that in Borges's last book, *Atlas,* the piece on Athens (recounting the dream of a chess game played against his father) is immediately followed by a piece on Geneva recalling the various revelations Borges experienced there as an adolescent: "the revelation of love, of friendship, of humiliation and of the temptation to suicide. In memory, everything is gratifying, even mischance. These reasons are personal" (*Atlas,* 38). Indeed, one wonders whether several of these revelations refer to the same event, that rumored encounter with the prostitute which may have revealed physical love as humiliation to the shy adolescent and have led him to contemplate suicide. One recalls the rueful comment in "The Sect of the Phoenix" about the fear of copulation: "A kind of sacred horror prevents some of the faithful from practicing the extremely simple ritual; the others despise them for it, but they despise themselves even more." Borges ends the Geneva essay, "I know that I will always return to Geneva, perhaps after the death of my body" (*Atlas,* 38). He died there in June 1986.

That Borges's use of the name Dubourg in "The Other" is meant to recall Poe's first detective story seems likely, given that in both the preface and afterword to the volume containing the tale, Borges goes out of his way to point out Poe's influence on his writing. In the "Author's Note" at the start of *The Book of Sand,* he acknowledges the debt these late stories owe to Wells, Swift, and "Poe, who, around 1838, gave up a very rich style in order to bequeath us the admirable final chapters of his *Narrative of Arthur Gordon Pym*" (*BS,* 7–8); while in the "Afterword," he describes Poe's indirect influence on his tale "There Are More Things": "Life, which everyone knows is inscrutable, left me no peace until I perpetrated a posthumous story by H. P. Lovecraft, a writer whom I have always considered an unconscious parodist of Poe" (*BS,* 124). Clearly, if Borges considers Lovecraft an unconscious parodist of Poe, then his attempt to write a posthumous Lovecraft story implies that Borges must himself act as a conscious parodist in imitating the Poesque elements he finds in Lovecraft's work, a move that seems less a commentary on Lovecraft's unconscious borrowing than an oblique acknowledgment of Borges's own highly self-conscious use of Poe in his own work.

In "There Are More Things," Borges reworks the monster-in-the-labyrinth theme as a modern horror story that brings together for one final going over most of the autobiographical elements he associates with the labyrinth. The tale's narrator, a philosophy student at the University of Texas, learns that his uncle Edwin Arnett has died at his home, Casa Colorada, on the outskirts of Buenos Aires. It was this uncle who "had first revealed" to him "philosophy's beautiful perplexities": "One of the after-dinner oranges was his aid in initiating me into Berkeley's idealism; a chessboard was enough to illustrate the paradoxes of the Eleatics" (*BS,* 51). The image of an older man "initiating" a younger man into a mystery, along with the references to Berkeley's idealism and Zeno's paradoxes explained at a chessboard, code the figure of the uncle as Borges's father, an association supported by the detail that the uncle had been "an engineer . . . with the railroad" (*BS,* 52) like Herbert Ashe in "Tlön," another portrait of Borges's father. (This substitution of uncle for father is, of course, evoked by the story's title. "There Are More Things" is taken from act I, scene V of *Hamlet,* the scene in which the ghost of Hamlet's father tells him of his murder by his brother Claudius and the usurpation of his crown, as well as that further usurpation by Hamlet's uncle in his semi-incestuous marriage to Gertrude.) Just as Herbert Ashe and Borges's father "would beat one another at chess" for hours on end, so the narrator's uncle (a freethinker) and his friend (a Calvinist architect named Alexander Muir) carried on for years a theological argument which the narrator describes as "a long game of chess, demanding of each player the collaboration of his opponent" (*BS,* 54).

When the narrator returns to Buenos Aires, he finds that his uncle's home, Casa Colorada, has been sold to a mysterious stranger named Max Preetorius. On taking possession of the house, Preetorius had visited the architect Muir, who originally designed the building, "and proposed certain alterations that the architect indignantly rejected" (*BS*, 53) on the grounds that they would turn the building into "a monstrous thing" (*BS*, 54). Preetorius finds someone else to make the alterations, and soon after he moves in, strange events start happening in the neighborhood, beginning with the discovery one morning of the uncle's sheepdog "dead on the walk, headless and mutilated" (*BS*, 53). Since Preetorius has turned the Casa Colorada into the dwelling place of a monster, the association of the headless sheepdog with the labyrinthine dwelling (the linking of decapitation as symbolic castration [the punishment for incest, for copulating as animals do] with a matrix symbol) recalls the mutilated king, slave, and lion in the labyrinth from "Ibn Hakkan al-Bokhari" and the blind king of Norway with his sword and dog from the essay "Nightmares." Moreover, given Borges's association of the labyrinth with the color red— the Chinese *Dream of the Red Chamber* in "The Garden of Forking Paths," the triangular maze inscribed in red ink on the map in "Death and the Compass," the circular crimson labyrinth in "Ibn Hakkan al-Bokhari," and the hidden Red King at the center of them all—it seems only appropriate that the labyrinthine house in "There Are More Things" should be called the Casa Colorada, the red house.

Obsessed with discovering the secret of the Casa Colorada, the narrator explains his compulsive behavior in images reminiscent of one of Poe's mentally unstable narrators justifying his self-destructive persistence in a perilous adventure:

> I know that my most obvious trait is curiosity—that same curiosity that brought me together with a woman completely different from me only in order to find out who she was and what she was like, to take up (without appreciable results) the use of laudanum, to explore transfinite numbers, and to undertake the hideous adventure that I am about to tell. (*BS*, 53)

In implicitly comparing the narrator's "hideous adventure" in penetrating the labyrinthine house to a sexual adventure (his involvement with the woman), Borges once again codes the labyrinth as matrix symbol and sexuality as something threatening. And just as clearly the reference to laudanum is an allusion to Poe's reputed use of the drug, supposedly to produce altered states of consciousness; while the image of exploring transfinite numbers (Georg Cantor's Aleph) recalls the list of "horrible fancies" in Borges's essay "The Total Library," a list of intellectual monstrosities that includes "the Platonic ideas, the chimera, the sphinx, the abnormal transfinite numbers (where the parts are no less abundant than the whole), masks, mirrors, operas, the monstrous Trinity: the Father, the Son, and the unresolvable Ghost, all articulated into one single organism"

(*BR*, 96). So obsessed does the narrator become with the sinister Casa Colorada that he begins to dream about labyrinths in imagery already familiar from Borges's account of his childhood:

> I dreamed about an engraving . . . ; it was in the style of Piranesi, and it had a labyrinth in it. It was a stone amphitheater ringed by cypresses, above whose tops it reached. There were neither doors nor windows; rather, it displayed an endless row of narrow vertical slits. With a magnifying glass, I tried to see the Minotaur inside. At last, I made it out. It was a monster of a monster, more bison than bull, and, its human body stretched out on the ground, it seemed to be asleep and dreaming. Dreaming of what or of whom? (*BS*, 55)

The image of a dreaming Minotaur and the question of whom it is dreaming make explicit Borges's symbolic equation of the labyrinth's monstrous inhabitant with the dreaming Red King discovered by Alice in the labyrinthine chessboard-garden. And this equation clarifies in turn the linking of the scenarios associated with each figure (the slaying of the Minotaur and the checkmating of the Red King) as attempts to free the self from the mastery of the Other (whether that mastery takes the form of the animal body's instinctual urges or the mental gaze of the master mind [i.e., the introjected figure of the father as superego, that being whose thought created the self and holds it in existence]), attempts that turn out to be self-defeating, if not self-destructive, precisely because the specular relationship with the Other is constitutive of the self.

In "There Are More Things" the narrator's curiosity finally overcomes his fear. He enters the Casa Colorada one stormy evening just before midnight on the nineteenth of January, Poe's birthday. Once inside the labyrinthine building the narrator immediately loses his sense of direction: "Right or left, I'm not sure which, I tripped on a stone ramp" (*BS*, 57). He finds the strange house full of "meaningless shapes" that don't correspond "to the human figure" (*BS*, 58) and on the upper floor

> a sort of long operating table, very high and in the shape of a U, with round hollows at each end. I thought that maybe it was the bed of the house's inhabitant, whose monstrous anatomy revealed itself in this way, implicitly, like an animal's or a god's by its shadow. From some page or other of Lucan there came to my lips the word "amphisbaena." . . . I also remember a V of mirrors that became lost in the upper darkness. (*BS*, 58–59)

As the narrator is descending the ladder from the second floor, he senses that "something, slow and oppressive and twofold" is "coming up the ramp" behind him: "Curiosity overcame my fear, and I did not shut my eyes" (*BS*, 59). The amphisbaena, as Borges tells us in *The Book of Imaginary Beings,* was a mythical serpent with two heads, "one in its proper place and the other in its tail," capable, as Lucan reports in the *Pharsalia,* of moving "on at both of its heads" (*BIB,* 24). Borges adds that "in the Antilles and in certain parts of America, the name is given to a reptile commonly known as the *doble andadora* (both ways goer)" (*BIB,* 24–25).

The monstrous inhabitant of the labyrinthine house is, then, a double goer (*Doppelgänger*) with a head at either end of its body—an appropriate figure of the labyrinth's double animal (man/bull) as an animal double of man. Significantly, Borges goes out of his way to evoke this doubling in imagery reminiscent of Poe's most famous double story "William Wilson" by making the amphisbaena's bed U-shaped and its looking glass V-shaped—details that, besides suggesting the V-shaped fold of mirror doubling, recall the way Poe emblemizes William Wilson's doubleness not only by doubling his initials but by choosing for those initials a letter already doubled (double U, which is to say, double you). Of course, the letter called "double U" in English (and "double V" in French) is usually written as a double V—a V shape doubled, not as in the diamond-shaped labyrinth of "Death and the Compass" by the projection of a second V downward from an inverted V ◇ , but by the flipping of the V to one side or the other V V. That Borges consciously associated this animal "double goer" and its V-shaped appurtenances with Poe's Wilson and his double double-U initials is further suggested by the fact that in making the narrator enter the Casa Colorada on Poe's birthday, Borges repeats Poe's own use of January 19th in "William Wilson" as the birthday of the tale's hero and his double (2:432).

If the autobiographical details Borges gives to the narrator's uncle code him as Borges's father and if in the wake of this father figure's death the narrator enters the domestic space (the matrix) that had belonged to the older man, then the terrifying (phallic) serpent inhabiting the house symbolizes (in the detail of a second head at its tail) the renunciation that the young man must make to enter that forbidden space. The opposition between mind and body figured in the human physique as the high/low one between head and genitals is represented in the monster's physique as that between head and tail, the placement of another head at the tail in effect signifying a substitution of the intellectual for the sexual. But if this substitution is the price the good son pays to enter the father's realm, it is a high one, for it represents nothing less than the decision to psychically withdraw from the game rather than face the risk of conflict and possible defeat, the decision to do something debilitating to oneself rather than having it done by another.

31 *Mental Fatherhood; Writing as Paternal Inheritance; A Father's Disappointment; (Re)writing a Patriarchal Text; Cervantes and Autobiographical Resonances; Arms versus Letters; Renewal of the King; Animal Sacrifice and Sacred Marriage; Light in the Cave; Dionysus and Ariadne*

THE SUBSTITUTION OF MIND FOR body, of the intellectual for the sexual, lies at the core of many of Borges's best-known stories, a substitution whose autobiographical dimension is almost always present in the text. In "Tlön, Uqbar, Orbis Tertius," for example, this sublimation of the bodily reaches its limit in a world (Tlön) where reality is understood as simply "a series of mental processes" (*F*, 24). Since "the nations of that planet are congenitally idealist" (*F*, 23), there is "only one discipline, that of psychology" (*F*, 24). Consequently, "among the doctrines of Tlön, none has occasioned greater scandal than the doctrine of materialism. . . . To clarify the general understanding of this unlikely thesis, one eleventh century heresiarch offered the parable of nine copper coins, which enjoyed in Tlön the same noisy reputation as did the Eleatic paradoxes of Zeno in their day" (*F*, 26).

The irony, of course, is that in an idealist world a parable of materialism seems as paradoxical as Zeno's antimaterialist parables do in ours. But this mention of Zeno also suggests the autobiographical link between the world of Tlön and the detail of Herbert Ashe's chess games with Borges's father. For if the fictive games between the elder Borges and Ashe (an image of the father) are based on those real ones during which the elder Borges taught his son Zeno's paradoxes, and if it was a natural transition from these lessons to his father's instructing him in "the rudiments of idealism" without ever "mentioning Berkeley's name" (*A*, 207), then that trajectory in Borges's personal life—from paradoxes at the chessboard demonstrating "the impossibility of motion" to a philosophical system that treats the material world as an illusion—is evoked in the story by having the same person who plays chess with Borges's father be one of the secret inventors of an imaginary idealist world, a world created through the writing of its fictive encyclopedia—through fiction writing.

Tlön is a world of perfect sublimation, and its significance for Borges is clearly a function of the way his knowledge of Berkeley's idealism grew out of a scene of sublimated conflict with his father at the chessboard, a scene that suggested idealist philosophy as an effective means of extending to life as a whole chess's sublimation of (sexual) conflict, its transformation of physical confrontation into a mental duel where opponents match wits but remain ultimately untouchable because physical motion is an impossibility. No wonder, then, that the world of Tlön is described as exhibiting "the discipline of chess players" or that one of the members of that "benevolent secret society" which "came together" in the seventeenth century "to invent a country" (the society that counted Herbert Ashe among its latter-day members) was "George Berkeley" (*F*, 31).

What the imaginary world of Tlön represents for Borges, then, is the substitution of a mental life for a physical one, of inventing stories for living them. Recalling his boyhood in "An Autobiographical Essay," Borges says that he "felt ashamed, quite early, to be a bookish kind of person and not a man of action" (*A*, 208). And in one of the essays from *Other Inquisitions*, he speaks of his as "a lifetime dedicated less to living than to reading" and recalls that "Plotinus was said to be ashamed to dwell in a body" (*OI*, 60) so devoted was he to the life of the mind, a remark Borges applied to himself and his own lifetime devoted to the imagination in a conversation we had during his visit to Baltimore in 1983.

Given that Borges's predilection for idealist philosophy is to some degree a function of its valorization of mind at the expense of body, and given further that his acquaintance with it began as a child in the context of a combative game favoring mental acuity rather than physical strength, a game of sublimated father-murder taught him by his own father, it is not surprising that in Borges's stories concerned with idealist philosophy there is usually some form of veiled father/son competition, a competition in which the son not infrequently tries to occupy the father's place by effecting a wholly mental procreation. In "The Circular Ruins," for example, the magician sets out "to dream a man" (*A*, 56) into existence, but the relationship of dreamer and dreamed soon becomes that of father and son: "On closing his eyes he would think, 'Now I will be with my son.' Or, less frequently, 'The son I have begotten awaits me and he will not exist if I do not go to him'" (*A*, 60). The magician takes steps to insure that his son will never know he is only a mental apparition, for "not to be a man but to be the projection of another man's dreams" is "an unparalleled humiliation" (*A*, 61). But at the end of the tale the magician learns that another dream-father had taken the same precaution with him.

Similarly, in "The Other" Borges comes to feel that his younger self, a character he has (re)created in the text, is like his son:

> I, who have never been a father, felt for that poor boy—more intimate to me even than a son of my flesh—a surge of love. Seeing that he clutched a book in his hands, I asked what it was.

"The Possessed, or, as I believe, *The Devils,* by Fëdor Dostoevski," he answered, not without vanity.

 . . . I asked what other volumes of the master he had read. He mentioned two or three, among them *The Double. (BS,* 15).

The young man with the book represents not just Borges's youth or that early decision of a "rather frail" nearsighted youngster to be "a bookish kind of person" but also that other of the self constituted in and by Borges's writings, that *Borges* whose italicized name stands not for a physical body but for a body of work. In his essay "Borges and I," he says of his relationship with this literary other:

> It would be an exaggeration to say that ours is a hostile relationship; I live, let
> myself go on living, so that Borges may contrive his literature, and this litera-
> ture justifies me. . . . I am destined to perish, definitively, and only some
> instant of myself can survive in him. . . . I shall remain in Borges, not in myself
> (if it is true that I am someone). *(L,* 246)

During Borges's visit to Johns Hopkins in 1983, one of the students in my Poe-Borges seminar asked him if he thought he had created any characters who had "their own identity," who had taken "on a life of their own outside of the author like Cervantes' Don Quixote." Borges replied, "I have no characters. Every character is myself very thinly disguised. . . . I'm not Dickens, I'm not Balzac. . . . I imagine myself in different circumstances, in different times, in different lands. And that's that. But I haven't created any characters, as far as I know." When the student pressed him about his most memorable characters, Borges replied with a level of emphasis that in someone of his courtly manners could only be described as vehement, "But I have no characters. I am barren, I haven't begotten any characters as far as I know."[1]

Borges's response, like the passage quoted from "Borges and I," evokes the writer as the mental father of his creations—a father who knows that "some instant" of himself will survive in that other Borges, and yet who also feels that he is "barren," that he hasn't "begotten any characters." What Borges acknowledges in these apparently conflicting comments is that the mental fatherhood of his fiction writing does not produce an independent identity but only a "very thinly disguised" image of himself. One senses that part of the terror in Borges's nightmare of seeing his masked face in a mirror is the feeling that father and son must share the same substance, that if one of them is a dreamed image, a mental reflection, so is the other—the revelation that ends "The Circular Ruins." Which is to say, if the fictional characters Borges has fathered are thinly disguised images of their creator, then perhaps the masked mirror image of himself in the nightmare reveals that even as a writer he is only a disguised reflection of his own father.

Borges supports this reading of the nightmare's masked figure when in the "Autobiographical Essay" he depicts his decision to become a fiction writer as a paternal inheritance. Noting that "a tradition of literature ran through" his "father's family," Borges recalls,

> My father wrote a novel, which he published in Majorca in 1921, . . . called *The Caudillo*. He also wrote (and destroyed) a book of essays, and published a translation of FitzGerald's Omar Khayyám in the same meter as the original. He destroyed a book of Oriental stories—in the manner of the Arabian Nights—and a drama, *Hacia la nada* (Toward Nothingness), about a man's disappointment in his son. . . . From the time I was a boy, when blindness came to him, it was tacitly understood that I had to fulfill the literary destiny that circumstances had denied my father. . . . I was expected to be a writer.
>
> I first started writing when I was six or seven. . . . I had set down in quite bad English a kind of handbook on Greek mythology, no doubt cribbed from Lemprière. This may have been my first literary venture. My first story was a rather nonsensical piece after the manner of Cervantes, an old-fashioned romance called "La visèra fatal"—(The Fatal Helmet). . . . When I was nine or so, I translated Oscar Wilde's "The Happy Prince" into Spanish, and it was published in one of the Buenos Aires dailies, *El País*. Since it was signed merely "Jorge Borges," people naturally assumed the translation was my father's. (*A*, 210–11)

In describing the origin of his writing career, Borges evokes a dual inheritance from his father's side of the family—literature and blindness. When the latter interferes with the practice of the former in the father's case, the faithful son must "fulfill the literary destiny that circumstances had denied" his parent. And the title of Borges's first story, "La visèra fatal," suggests the blending of the two in the son's fate, for what Borges translates as "The Fatal Helmet" is literally "The Fatal Visor"—the part of a helmet that pertains to the eyes and that, when lowered to protect them, wholly or partially masks the face. If the helmet's visor is fatal in the sense of an inherited destiny, then Borges's remark about the story being "after the manner of Cervantes" may well be meant to evoke both the *Quixote* (particularly the prologue, in which Cervantes plays with the image of authorship as fatherhood) and an English work (performed two years before the appearance of the *Quixote* [1605]) that begins with the image of a father, clad in armor and a visored helmet, imposing a fatal task on his son Hamlet.

In the prologue to the *Quixote*, Cervantes writes,

Idle reader, you can believe without any oath of mine that I would wish this book, as the child of my brain, to be the most beautiful, the liveliest and the cleverest imaginable. But I have been unable to transgress the order of nature, by which like gives birth to like. And so, what could my sterile and ill-cultivated genius beget but the story of a lean, shrivelled, whimsical child, full of varied fancies that no one else has ever imagined? . . . It may happen that a father has an ugly and ill-favored child, and that his love for it so blinds his eyes that he cannot see its faults. . . . But I, though in appearance Don Quixote's father, am really his step-father, and so will not drift with the current of custom, nor implore you, almost with tears in my eyes, as others do, dearest reader, to pardon or ignore the faults you see in this child of mine.[2]

The passage's imagery—a father's disappointment in his child, a kind of paternal blindness regarding that offspring, and the renunciation or undercutting of authorial fatherhood in favor of being simply a stepfather—forms a resonant background to Borges's account of inheriting his literary career from his father, an account that includes paternal blindness, a father's "disappointment in his son," and a paternal corpus largely composed of imitative works written and then destroyed as if in renunciation of authorial fatherhood. (Recall in this connection that Borges's remark during the Poe-Borges seminar in 1983—"I am barren, I haven't begotten any characters"—was in response to a question about whether he had created any figures who had taken on a life of their own "like Cervantes' Don Quixote.")

As we indicated, the allusive resonance of "La visèra fatal" also extends to *Hamlet* (which Borges explicitly links with Cervantes' novel as examples of self-reflexive literature in "Partial Enchantments of the *Quixote*"), for the fatal visor of Borges's first childhood story recalls in this context Horatio's recognition of the armor-clad ghost of Hamlet's father precisely because the visor of his helmet is raised (act I, scene II). If the fatal visor is in part an allusion to the opening of *The Tragicall Historie of Hamlet, Prince of Denmarke*, then the next work Borges mentions—his Spanish translation of Oscar Wilde's "The Happy Prince"—continues the association of ideas, particularly since the expectation implicit in the word *prince* (the son's eventual succession to the father's position) seems to have already been enacted in the public's reception of the son's translation as the father's.

"The Happy Prince" is a children's tale dominated by imagery of mutilation. In the tale a swallow, flying south to join its companions in Egypt, alights on a column bearing a statue of the prince. The statue, covered with gold leaf and precious stones, is crying. When the swallow asks why, the prince says that he is weeping for the poverty and suffering of his people, and he asks the swallow to help him lessen that suffering by taking the jewels and gold leaf from his statue and distributing them to the poor. The swallow agrees and begins to progressively mutilate the prince's statue, even to the point of removing the sapphires that are its eyes. Winter is approaching, and the swallow knows it must fly south or die; but it has grown to love the prince and decides to stay with him now that he is blind. He perches on his shoulder telling him stories of the many things he has seen in strange lands, including "the Sphinx, who is as old as the world itself, and lives in the desert, and knows everything."[3] The prince says he is happy the swallow is going to Egypt, but the swallow replies, "It is not to Egypt that I am going. . . . I am going to the House of Death" (Wilde, 21). The swallow kisses the prince on the lips and falls dead at his feet. For the aging Borges recalling his initial literary ventures, the prince's progressive mutilation by the phallic bird (even to the Oedipal blinding) may well have seemed, in retrospect, Wilde's oblique evocation of sexuality as something psychically destructive (indeed, self-destructive since the bird also dies), and his linking of the translation to "La visèra fatal" and adding the detail of the translation's being mistaken for his father's gives a deeper sense of what was at stake by the time Borges came to recollect (or reconstruct) his origin as a writer.

Given that the translation of "The Happy Prince" was from English to Spanish and that Borges's "first literary venture" as a child was a translation of a "handbook on Greek mythology" into "quite bad English," we should note that the whole question of translating a text into or out of English was coded for Borges as a paternal inheritance. The bilingual character of the Borges household had its origin in the marriage of Borges's paternal grandparents, the Argentinean Colonel Francisco Borges and the Englishwoman Fanny Haslam. In consequence, Shakespeare and Cervantes, as the patriarchal figures of English and Spanish literature, evoke for Borges, through the characters of Hamlet and Don Quixote, not only the trope of authorship as fatherhood (or stepfatherhood) but also the problematic father-son relationship between a young writer and the patriarchal figures of his literary tradition, a relationship made even more problematic if one's own father was a writer.

Certainly it cannot have been an emotionally neutral detail for Borges to record in "An Autobiographical Essay" that his father had written a play about "a man's disappointment in his son." Although observing that the play *Hacia la nada* was undoubtedly about the disappointment of Borges's grandfather in *his* son rather than about that of Borges's father in Borges, Rodríguez Monegal notes that this theme of paternal disappointment runs through the work of both Borges and his father:

> There is in both writers a preoccupation, almost an obsession, with a certain kind of confrontation: between powerful, primitive men and weak, educated men. Father was (like his son) an intellectual who learned to make his living through the practice of law and the teaching of psychology. But his own father had been a colonel, a man of action. In Father's situation one can already recognize the conflict between arms and letters that Georgie would have to face later. (*JLB*, 83)

In his novel *The Caudillo*, Borges's father explored, according to Monegal, "the feeling of inadequacy he felt in contrasting his fate with that of his own father," while in *Hacia la nada* he expressed his "recognition of his shortcomings as a man, when measured against the heroic proportions of his father, Colonel Borges. The feeling was inherited by Georgie" (*JLB*, 83–84).

As a young man Borges must have felt that his inherited writing career put him in a double bind. On the one hand, writing, as a kind of imaginative fatherhood, gave him access to the father's role while allowing him to avoid the sexual conflicts (and possible physical humiliations) associated with actual fatherhood. (Indeed, in becoming a writer, Borges was not rebelling against but fulfilling his father's will.) But, on the other hand, since Borges's father was himself a published author, the son's choice of authorial rather than actual fatherhood simply transferred the father-son competition into the realm of the imagination. Although Borges's career was meant "to fulfill the literary destiny that circumstances had denied" his father, it must have seemed that the only way to accomplish this was to become the successful writer his father had never been, to best him in an implicit literary competition, thus becoming a better man than his father—a course almost as fraught with guilt as any physical confrontation with a parent would have been.

It may well have been Borges's conflicting feelings about his writing career that kept him from pure fiction (his father's domain) until after the elder Borges's death. And, as we noted earlier, it is significant that his first fictional work in the new style was a tale about a man who sets out to (re)write the patriarchal figure of Spanish literature, "Pierre Menard, Author of *Don Quixote*." Interestingly enough, the parts of the *Quixote* Menard intends to recreate out of his own experience—"the ninth and thirty-eighth chapters of Part One . . . and a fragment of the twenty-second chapter"—all have autobiographical resonances for Borges, related in one way or another to his story of a writing career inherited from his father and the notion of authorship as a sublimation of fatherhood. In chapter 9, for example, Cervantes explains that his book is simply a trans-

lation of an Arabic work whose manuscript he had bought in the mar-
ketplace at Toledo, an admission that immediately recalls his remark in
the prologue that he, "though in appearance Don Quixote's father," is
"really his step-father." That Cervantes presents a book he has written as a
translation into Spanish of another man's work and thus characterizes
himself as the book's stepfather rather than father resonates in Borges's
linking of "La visèra fatal" (written "after the manner of Cervantes") and
his Spanish translation of "The Happy Prince" (mistaken by the public for
the work of his father). Again, in chapter 38 ("Don Quixote's curious
Discourse on Arms and Letters"), the knight presents a series of arguments demonstrating the superiority of the life of a soldier to that of a
scholar—a motif evoking the sense of inferiority Borges and his father
both felt in relation to Colonel Borges, their shame at being "a bookish
kind of person and not a man of action."

Menard's third excerpt from the *Quixote*, "a fragment of the twenty-
second chapter," is clearly the episode of the rogue Gines de Pasamonte,
one of a group of galley slaves Don Quixote sets free after defeating their
guards in a fight. When Quixote asks Gines for his life story, the rogue says
he has already written it in a book that surpasses even the picaresque
Lazarillo de Tormès, being "such well-written, entertaining truth that there
is no fiction that can compare with it" (Cervantes, 176). And he adds that
he was not unhappy to be going back to the galleys because, since he had
not finished living his life, he would have had time to continue his book.
Gines's comment recalls the tradition that Cervantes conceived the *Quixote*, and even began writing it, while imprisoned in Seville in the late
1590s, a tradition supported by Cervantes' remark in the Prologue that
his poor book, the offspring of his brain, was like a child "engendered in
prison" (Cervantes, 25). If this reflexive moment (in which the composition of a fictive picaresque book in prison mirrors that of the real picaresque novel that contains it) evokes a self-conscious autobiographical
component in Cervantes' fiction writing, then Menard's citing chapter 22
as a part of the *Quixote* he means to rewrite is simply Borges's way of
pointing out his own autobiographical presence in the fictive Menard,
and specifically, in Menard's choice of excerpts with a special resonance
for Borges's life. For of course Menard (re)writing the patriarchal work of
Spanish literature is a figure of Borges at the start of his career as a writer
of pure fiction, a form of writing he had always considered his father's
province.

That Borges and his father both thought of his career as involving to
some degree the son's literal (re)writing of a paternal text can be judged
from a comment in his "Autobiographical Essay." Noting that he had
thought about the plot of his story "The Congress" for almost twenty

years before writing it, Borges adds, "I have another project that has been pending for an even longer period of time—that of revising and perhaps rewriting my father's novel *The Caudillo,* as he asked me to years ago. We had gone as far as discussing many of the problems; I like to think of the undertaking as a continued dialogue and a very real collaboration" (*A,* 259). Borges never did rewrite, or even revise, his father's novel (about a local military strongman named Tavares who ends up killing his young neighbor and rival Carlos DuBois because he believes that DuBois has abducted and seduced Tavares's daughter), though, as Monegal suggests, some of the novel's themes resurface in Borges's gaucho stories. Nor did he rewrite a work of Cervantes (though one might argue that the tension between arms and letters in both his life and writing repeats the polarities of Cervantes' life as soldier and writer). Instead, he chose to double Poe's Dupin stories, to make an interpretive rewriting of the detective genre's origin and to begin this project with the title story of the volume in which "Pierre Menard" appears.

Borges seems to hark back to the autobiographical resonance of Menard's excerpts from the *Quixote* (specifically to the parallel between Menard's project with Cervantes and his own with Poe) by echoing a moment from the episode of Gines de Pasamonte in his second detective story. When Quixote tells the sergeant of the guard to release the galley slaves in his charge, the sergeant replies, "Get along with you, sir, and good luck to you! Put that basin straight on your head, and don't go about looking for a cat with three legs [*y no ande buscando tres pies al gato*]" (Cervantes, 178)—a proverbial phrase reprised in Treviranus's first words to Lönnrot at the scene of Yarmolinsky's murder, "We needn't lose any time here looking for three-legged cats [*No hay que buscarle tres pies al gato*]" (*A,* 66). In each case the proverb, whose sense is not to go looking for trouble, for something out of the ordinary, is put in the mouth of a police official and addressed to the story's main character, an indication (along with the fact that the more common form of the proverb is "Don't go looking for five-legged cats") that the phrase's appearance in Borges's story is no mere coincidence but a repetition meant to link Menard's fictive doubling of Cervantes with Borges's real doubling of Poe. Nor is it coincidental, given the centrality of the labyrinth image to Borges's detective stories, that in another of the chapters Menard selects (chapter 38) Don Quixote compares the debate between arms and letters to "a very difficult labyrinth to find a way out of [*laberinto de muy dificultosa salida*]" (Cervantes, 343). For if the debate between arms and letters represents for Borges the opposition between action and intellection, then the analytic detective story, as we argued earlier, enacts this body/mind opposition as that between crime and solution, between the physicality of the former and the intellectuality of the latter. And unlike Quixote's discourse on arms and letters, the analytic genre decides the dispute in favor of mind.

Indeed, it was probably the conflict between arms and letters in Poe's own life that partly attracted Borges to the project of doubling Poe and to the analytic detective genre as an analogue of this conflict. For, as we saw, Poe, like Borges, had a paternal grandfather who was a military hero, and he had even tried to follow a career in the military before becoming a full-time man of letters and creating a genre that made the sedentary life of intellectual analysis seem the better part of valor. Certainly Borges credited Poe, as part of his invention of the genre, with originating the convention of the sedentary detective, and he seems to have understood that the dexterity and brute strength of the killer in Poe's first detective story was meant to contrast with (and thus emphasize) the detective's physical inactivity as a pure reasoner. Moreover, Borges realized that the development of the figure of the sedentary detective over the genre's history was in effect the challenge presented to later writers of finding new ways of enforcing or accounting for the detective's restricted physical activity. Thus in *Six Problems for Don Isidro Parodi,* the collection of parody detective stories Borges and Bioy-Casares published in 1942, this convention is given a new twist by making the detective a convict. In their satiric preface to the book, Borges and Bioy briefly sketch the convention's history:

> In the stirring annals of criminal investigation, the honor of being the first detective to be a jailbird goes to don Isidro. Any critic with a sound nose can, however, point to several possible derivatives. Without leaving his nightly den in the Faubourg St. Germain, the gentleman Auguste Dupin captures the troublesome ape who caused the tragedies in the Rue Morgue; . . . [while] Max Carrados carries with him everywhere the portable jail cell of his blindness. Such sedentary sleuths, such strange *voyageurs autour de la chambre,* are, if only in part, forerunners of our Parodi. . . . Parodi's lack of mobility is the symbol and epitome of intellectuality.[4]

Note that the trajectory of analytic sedentariness here begins with Poe but culminates with Ernest Bramah's blind detective Max Carrados, for while the analytic detective story evokes the superiority of an intellectual life to an active one, this choice of letters over arms was nevertheless determined in large part for Borges both by his own poor eyesight and by his father's blindness. And certainly if Borges's choice of a writing career seems overdetermined, his decision to double Poe's Dupin stories seems equally so.

For Poe, of course, the necessity of choosing a career in arms or in letters was in part the result of a conflict with his foster father John Allan and the consequent need to support himself after Allan disowned him.

Indeed, any association in Borges's mind of his own career choice with Poe's probably carried with it this resonant detail of a father-son conflict that, along with the Oedipal component of the detective stories, made Borges's doubling of the Dupin tales an even more appropriate means of enacting and thematizing the element of paternal inheritance-fulfillment-competition he felt in his writing career. For what seems clear is that Borges experienced his career in some sense as a contest of wills in which he had bowed to his father's wishes in becoming a writer, in choosing a life of intellectual sedentariness over one of physical action (unlike his father who had not followed in Colonel Borges's footsteps), only to find that the fulfilling of his father's literary destiny involved an implicit competition between them that reinscribed in the intellectual realm the very conflict he had sought to avoid. And this reversal is reenacted in effect in his doubling of the Dupin stories; for while on the one hand he (re)writes a patriarchal work (the origin of a genre) in a kind of symbolic fulfillment of his father's interrupted writing career, on the other he personalizes the detective genre's Oedipal content by filtering it through the Carrollian scenario of checkmating the dreaming Red King (which is to say, the scenario of immobilizing that paternal figure at the chessboard who taught his son that physical action is an illusion and existence a dream).

In *The Garden of Forking Paths* this motif of paternal inheritance-fulfillment-competition is a thematic trajectory that runs across the stories: from "Tlön" with its association of fatherhood and mirrors and its description of Borges's father playing chess with a man who is not only the father's disguised mirror image but one of the writers of an imaginary idealist world's fictive encyclopedia; to "Pierre Menard" with its implicit imagery of fiction writing as mental fatherhood and of a writing career as a paternal inheritance that involves the doubling of a patriarchal text; to "The Circular Ruins" in which one man dreams another into existence in an act of mental fatherhood only to find at the moment of his death that father and son share the same dream-substance; and on to "The Garden of Forking Paths" in which the doubling of a patriarchal work involves the refiguring of its Oedipal content (through the combination of the myth of the labyrinth and the scenario of checkmating the Red King) in order to enact a self-defeating release from an introjected image of the Other (father) as origin. It is precisely in this context that we can understand at last not only the deeper relationship between the myth of the labyrinth (Theseus's slaying of the Minotaur) and the ancient ritual Frazer associates with it (the sacred marriage of king and queen) but also how this relationship between the myth and ritual meshes with Borges's use of idealist philosophy as a figure of bodily repression/sublimation in his doubling of the Dupin stories.

Recall again that in *The Golden Bough* Frazer discusses the labyrinth as part of his interpretation of the octennial cycle of Greek kingship and the notion of a periodic renewal of the king's powers. Sometimes this renewal involved, according to Frazer, the deposition, castration, or execution of the old king and his replacement by a vigorous young ruler. But often the killing of the aging king was replaced both by the sacrifice of an animal substitute and the ceremonial enactment of the king's restored vigor in a ritual marriage. Discussing "the ritual renewal of the Cretan kingship, which had to follow after every 'great year' of eight years' duration," Erich Neumann notes,

> Just as the renewal of kingship is to be interpreted as a late substitute for the original sacrifice of the annual king, so, too, in Crete we can follow the road leading from his castration and yearly death to the substitution of a human and eventually an animal victim, and, last of all, to the festival of renewal, when the kingly power was ritually restored. The human sacrifices to the Minotaur, the bull-king of Crete, which according to the Greek legend originally consisted in a tribute of seven youths and maidens, can probably be explained in this manner, likewise the passion evinced by Queen Pasiphaë, mother of the Minotaur, for the bull.[5]

(The rationale for invoking the Jungian Neumann as a commentator on this myth, like that for citing the Jungian Carl Kerényi later, is Borges's comment that he used Jung's work "in the same way" he did Frazer's *Golden Bough*, "as a kind of mythology, . . . or encyclopedia of curious lores" [Burgin, 109]. Neither Neumann nor Kerényi is invoked as having any special authority as a classicist.)

As we recall, Frazer explains the eight-year cycle of the festival of renewal on astronomical grounds. Noting that among "the barbarous Dorians of old" the deposition of the king occurred "whenever at a certain season a meteor flamed in the sky," Frazer argues that this practice suggests the people's basic sense of the relationship of the celestial and the earthly realms, their sense either that an extraordinary sign, such as a meteor, "signified the dissatisfaction of the higher powers with the state of the commonwealth" as embodied in the person of the king or that "every man had his star in the sky, and that he must die when it fell" (Frazer, 4:68), the king being no exception to the rule. Pursuing this link between the kingship's renewal and an extraordinary astronomical occurrence, Frazer argues that the recurring celestial event by which the Greeks measured the cycle of kingship was the coincidence of the full moon with the longest or shortest day of the year, an event that occurs only once in every eight years and that was one of the first astronomical observations that furnished a base for a calendar reconciling "lunar and solar times" (Frazer, 4:69). Consequently, in the as-above-so-below structure of homeo-pathic magic, the king and queen at the festival of renewal demonstrated the king's restored potency by reenacting the celestial marriage in the labyrinth with the king as solar bull and the queen as lunar cow.

Because his interpretation depends upon the symbolic equivalence of king, sun, and bull as embodiments of the god's generative power, Frazer cites numerous examples in the ancient world of the king's vitality being imaged as that of both sun and bull, imagery that ultimately suggests, as regards the link between ritual and myth, the identification of the king who wears a bull mask in the *ritual* with the figure who has a bull's head and a human body in the *myth* (the Minotaur), suggests that in the multi-level economy of the myth, the killing of the Minotaur is a symbolic killing of the masked king. Taking a hint from Neumann, one could read the story of Theseus's slaying of the Minotaur, then, as an evocation of the different stages leading from "the original sacrifice of the annual king . . . to the substitution of a human and eventually an animal victim, and, last of all, to the festival of renewal, when the kingly power was ritually re-stored." Thus the story begins at a point where human sacrifice (in the form of Athenian youths sent periodically to Crete) has already been substituted for the original sacrifice of the king, and Theseus's saving of the youths by slaying the Minotaur represents the replacement of human victims by an animal (whose role as a substitute for human sacrifice is embodied in its part-human, part-animal shape).

But clearly there is more at work in the story of Theseus and the Minotaur than such a reading of its ritual significance would suggest. The very fact that the hero who effects the substitution is the same figure who shelters the aged Oedipus at Athens (and becomes his spiritual son) sug-gests that the young man's slaying of an animal representing the king amounts to a veiled Oedipal drama. And this reading of the Minotaur's death would have been reinforced for Borges by Frazer's association of the bull-headed monster with the bull-masked king who mates in the labyrinth, the two together evoking the Borgesian nightmare figure of the father-as-animal copulating with the mother to engender the son. If the Oedipal component of the Theseus myth is veiled by a generational displacement in which the queen's son (the Minotaur) represents the king (father), then this displacement extends as well to the figure who aids The-seus in overcoming the Minotaur. Which is to say that the queen's daugh-ter (Ariadne) would seem to represent the mother, so that Theseus's flight with Ariadne symbolically enacts his union with the mother.

Ariadne's role as mother figure in this scenario is further confirmed by the precise form of aid she gives Theseus in his task (the umbilical thread), Ariadne in effect giving birth to the hero. Her symbolic role would also explain the ill-fated character of her liaison with Theseus. All the versions of the story agree that Theseus and Ariadne are separated on Naxos, and most accounts record Ariadne's death (indeed, one version has her dying in childbirth). If the parricidal nature of Theseus's slaying of the Minotaur is a latent content subsequently made explicit in Theseus's "accidental" slaying of his father, then Ariadne's and Theseus's liaison as a symbolic mother-son union is in turn a latent content made explicit later in the myth when Theseus marries Ariadne's sister Phaedra and she accuses Theseus's son Hippolytus of having raped her. (The affront Theseus performed as son he must now suffer as father.) Ariadne's symbolic role as the mother is also suggested by the fact that in the ancient world she was associated with the moon (her mother's name meant "she who shines for all" and her own epithet in Crete, Aridela, meant "the utterly clear"[6]) and that in the sacred marriage consummated in the labyrinth the queen (mother) is a lunar deity.

Indeed, it is precisely the light symbolism in the myth of the labyrinth—the association of the king and Minotaur with the sun and the queen and Ariadne with the moon—that in part underlies Borges's linking of idealist philosophy (as a figure of bodily repression/sublimation) with the labyrinth scenario. Frazer identifies the dance that Daedalus, the builder of the labyrinth, made for Ariadne with the dance Theseus and his companions performed on the island of Delos during the return voyage from Crete, "a mazy dance in imitation of the intricate windings of the labyrinth" (Frazer, 4:75). Arguing that "the Minotaur was a representative or embodiment of the sun-god," Frazer goes on to suggest that Ariadne's dance may "have been an imitation of the sun's course in the sky," with "the sinuous lines of the labyrinth which the dancers followed in their evolutions" representing "the ecliptic" (Frazer, 4:77).

If the Minotaur tracing the winding subterranean paths of the labyrinth is indeed a figure of the sun following its "apparent annual path in the sky," then this image emphasizes the fact that half the sun's annual journey is through the darkness of the underworld (between its setting and rising). And this in turn evokes the solar journey as a contest between light and dark, a contest that the sun seems to be winning in its progress toward summer as days grow longer and losing as winter comes on and they grow shorter. Hence, the need, as Frazer says, "to aid the great luminary to run his race on high" (Frazer, 4:77) by an act of sympathetic magic such as Ariadne's dance, an act that was probably felt to be most necessary at the winter solstice. Theseus's entrance into and reemergence from the labyrinth, as a descent into darkness and a reascent to the light, parallels the sun's daily struggle with darkness—as is only appropriate, given that the labyrinth's inhabitant and his conqueror, as figures evocative respectively of physical light (the sun) and intellectual light (the mind), are antithetical doubles. The defeat of the Minotaur by Theseus evokes the ascendancy of the mental over the physical within the self and of spirit over matter in the world. And there is in this scenario a further appropriateness in Ariadne's association with the moon, for just as Ariadne gives Theseus the thread to lead him through the darkness of the labyrinth back to the light, so the moon serves as a guide through the darkness of night back to dawn.

The connection of light imagery and of symbolic death and rebirth with the labyrinth scenario suggests that what we are dealing with here is a form of the light-in-the-cave or light-under-ground structure usually associated in the ancient world with the myth of a vegetative god such as Dionysus. And Dionysus does, of course, enter into most versions of the labyrinth story: He finds, or carries off, Ariadne on Naxos, makes her his consort, and upon her death translates the crown he had given her into the constellation Corona Borealis. This pairing of Dionysus and Ariadne in the myth suggests that Theseus, in his own interaction with Ariadne, is a hero imitating a divine model, a mortal symbolically enacting the vegetative god's cycle of death and resurrection as a descent into the darkness of the labyrinth (womb/tomb) and a reascent to the daylight world. In his essay on the Mycenaean tree and pillar cult, Evans notes the solar aspect of Dionysus ("under his earlier Thracian form of Sabazios," Dionysus "was himself a Sun-God") and thus his similarity to the Cretan Zeus, and he remarks, "This solar aspect of Dionysos gives a special value to the fact that at Argos the 'tomb of Ariadnê' was shown in the sanctuary of the Cretan Dionysos" (Evans, 120). For if Dionysus is associated with the sun and Ariadne with the moon, then their conjunction in the sanctuary/tomb (particularly when linked to the motif of an ultimate stellar translation for Ariadne's crown) would be the divine counterpart of that ritual marriage of sun and moon performed by the king and queen in the Cretan labyrinth.

32 *Dionysus and Christ; The Daystar versus the Thinking Fire; Epiphanies of Light; Plato's Allegory of the Cave; Womb Fantasies; Sublimation of the Matrix*

THE CENTRAL MYSTERY EMBODIED IN a vegetative god such as Dionysus is the cyclical generation of life out of death—the mystery of the natural world's death in winter and its rebirth in spring, of the seed's burial in the dark earth and its reemergence into the light. And paralleling this generation of life out of death in the seasonal cycle is the gradual waning of daylight in the passage from summer to winter and its gradual waxing from winter back to summer (a battle repeated daily in the setting and rising of the sun). The parallel between the vegetative cycle and the light cycle underlies the broad symbolic equivalence (common to ancient mystery religions) between life, light, and ascent on the one hand and death, darkness, and descent on the other. And in many of these religions a common figuration of the mysterious persistence of life in death was the image of a light enclosed in darkness (in a cave or tomb), a light in the subterranean world of death. In his book on Dionysus, Carl Kerényi suggests that in Crete "the festival of the light in the cave was a mystery rite" in which the fermentation of mead from honey and of wine from grapes (the creation of life-giving, illuminating drink from the corruption and decay of vegetable matter) was celebrated in connection with the early rising of the star Sirius: "The star appeared in the sky; the light emerged from a cave" (where the ritual fermentation occurred) (Kerényi, 118). He adds,

> At Knossos the way to the "mistress of the labyrinth" and back again was danced publicly on a certain dance ground. The mistress was at the center of the true labyrinth, the underworld; she bore a mysterious son and conferred the hope of a return to the light. In antiquity the Cretan origin of the mysteries of Eleusis, Samothrace, and Thrace, that is, the Orphic mysteries, was deduced from the fact that in the Greek period everything that was kept secret in those mysteries was still open to the public at Knossos. (Kerényi, 118)

Indeed, Kerényi suggests that the Minoan word for "labyrinth" (*da-pu-ri-to-jo*) signified for them "a way to the light" (Kerényi, 95).

The light-in-the-cave structure is most familiar nowadays from the Dionysian and Orphic elements in Christianity. Like Dionysus, Christ is a god who dies and is resurrected, whose birth and death/rebirth are associated respectively with the winter solstice and the vernal equinox, and whose symbols (bread, wine, fish) are characteristic of the mystery cults of vegetative gods. But where the worship of Dionysus celebrated the fact that physical life mysteriously persists in the vegetative and animal worlds in spite of, and in some sense by means of, the death of individual living things, the worship of Christ celebrates the persistence of individual human life in spite of (and often by means of) the physical death of the body. Christianity personalizes the generic Dionysian immortality (an immortality of physical nature as a whole achieved at the expense of individual beings) precisely by translating the notion of life from a material to a spiritual plane, from body to mind. As in the cult of Dionysus, Christianity images this indestructible life as light. But where part of what was signified by the symbol of light in Dionysian or Orphic cults was the actual light of the sun with its life-giving power, in Christianity light represents not material illumination but thought, the divine *logos* John describes at the beginning of his gospel: "In the beginning was the Word, and the Word was with God, and the Word was God. . . . In him was life; and the life was the light of men. And the light shineth in darkness; and the darkness comprehended it not. . . . That was the true Light, which lighteth every man that cometh into the world" (John 1:1, 4–5, 9).[1] In invoking the Platonic equation of *logos*, life, and light, John makes clear that the god he serves is not a solar deity, a mythic personification of the daystar, but the divine *nous*, the thinking fire. Yet while Christianity excises the element of sun worship in translating the image of light from a material to a spiritual plane, it retains the light-in-the-cave structure both for the incarnation of the Word (the descent of the Light into the dark cave of a physical body) and for Christ's resurrection from the grave (the reascent of the Light).

    In the case of the nativity—depicted as an epiphany of light in the dark, dead time of year—the Magi (the knowers) are led by a celestial light (a star) to the ultimate knowledge, the divine light enclosed in a human body and lodged in a manger. And the manger at Bethlehem is, of course, traditionally understood to have been located in a grotto or a hollowed-out space in a hillside, which is simply to say that the light which "shineth in darkness" was born in a cave. Similarly, in the case of the resurrection, Christ's body is laid in a "new tomb . . . hewn out in the rock" (Matt. 27:60), and although the gospels do not describe Christ's actual exit from the tomb, they do describe the first discovery of his absence when the two Marys come to anoint his body at sunrise, the time of day clearly linking the Light's rising from the cave/grave with the sun's ascent from the darkness of the underworld. (According to Christian lore, during the time Christ was in the tomb, he descended into the underworld to harrow hell and complete the defeat of death, the heroic slaying of the flesh-eating monster of the grave.) When the two Marys arrive at the tomb, they find an "angel of the Lord" sitting on the stone rolled back from the door: "His countenance was like lightning, and his raiment white as snow" (Matt. 28:2, 3), a description obviously meant to recall Christ's transfiguration, when he showed Peter, James, and John his divine nature by allowing the light of the spirit to shine through his physical body. In the words of the gospel, he "was transfigured before them: and his face did shine as the sun, and his raiment was white as the light" (Matt. 17:2). Christ himself links this epiphany of the Light to his resurrection by warning his disciples, "Tell the vision to no man, until the Son of man be risen again from the dead" (Matt. 17:9).

In figuring the struggle of life against death as the battle of light against encompassing darkness, the light-in-the-cave scenario often takes the form of a god's or hero's battle with a subterranean monster who threatens to swallow him, a structure Christ explicitly associates with his own resurrection when he compares his descent into the grave to Jonas's being swallowed by a whale: "For as Jonas was three days and three nights in the whale's belly; so shall the Son of man be three days and three nights in the heart of the earth" (Matt. 12:40). In this same vein, the hero Theseus descends into the subterranean labyrinth to defeat the man-killing monster with the bull's head who represents the solar bull trapped in the darkness of the underworld. In slaying the Minotaur, Theseus frees the principle of light from the dominance of the material world (a dominance of body over mind symbolized by the Minotaur's animal head and human body), and by establishing the ascendancy of the human in his own nature he releases himself from the monster's subterranean realm and reascends to the light.

In the myth of Theseus and the Minotaur, a human being takes on godlike qualities in his heroic overcoming of the fear of death, while in the Christian gospel a god becomes man, slays death, and gives humanity the divine gift of immortality. And in each case the light-in-the-cave structure evokes the human condition as the entrapment of a godlike principle of light in the physical cave of the body and human destiny as the ultimate return of this light/life to its origin, either in an undifferentiated form (as in Dionysianism) or a differentiated one (as in Christianity). But where the Greek myth, as we said, retains elements of sun worship and of a solar deity in its association of life with light, the Christian gospel excises these in its Platonic identification of light with mental existence. And certainly Plato's is the right name to invoke here. For in order to complete the structural trajectory linking Greek myth to Christian gospel, we must interpose as a mediating moment between the two another light-in-the-cave episode, perhaps the best-known moment in ancient Greek philosophy. In Plato's allegory of the cave, light is explicitly equated with mental existence as part of a scenario depicting human destiny as an ultimate escape from a subterranean cavern into a higher realm of spirit.

This powerful figuration in Book VII of *The Republic*—with its firelit cave and fettered men looking at shadows cast on a wall; its prisoner, released to the upper world, gradually accustoming himself to the sight of objects until he can look directly at the sun; and its interpretation of this higher realm as the domain of the idea of the good (which gives birth to light in the visible world and to truth and reason in the intelligible)—is, of course, one of the constitutive moments of idealist philosophy, a moment in which much of the major imagery of Platonism is linked together in a single structure. And the central mechanism around which this imagery is organized is the light-produced relationship between a physical object and its shadow. Not only does the master/slave relationship between object and shadow serve as a figure of that between the higher, intelligible world and the lower world of physical things (as the sunlit world of objects is to the dim world of shadows, so the bright world of transparent intelligible forms is to the opaque world of physical objects—an analogy that ends up making sunlight itself a shadow), this relationship also points to the visible image on which Plato based both his conception of ideal forms and his notion of truth as a correspondence between an idea and its material embodiment. Which is simply to say that in reversing the master/slave relationship between a physical object and its shadow, Plato seems to have imagined the ideal form or archetype as a kind of bright shadow-image, a geometric schema or two-dimensional outline whose pure intelligibility was expressed by its transparency, by its lacking an opaque third dimension to mask parts of itself from the intellectual gaze. That Plato conceived his ideal forms on the analogy of geometric projection is further suggested by Socrates' comment later in Book VII that the two most important areas of education as regards the higher realm of intelligible forms are mathematics and geometry. These two fields compel "the soul to contemplate essence," and since "geometry is the knowledge of the eternally existent," its study "would tend to draw the soul to truth, and would be productive of a philosophical attitude of mind, directing upward the faculties that now wrongly are turned earthward" (Plato, 759).

Given that Plato's allegory represents a basic structuring of the imagery of idealism and that it is, like the myth of Theseus and the labyrinth, a light-in-the-cave scenario, we can appreciate both the appropriateness and the ease with which Borges combines idealist philosophy (along with its autobiographical resonances evoked by the figure of the Carrollian Red King) with the labyrinth imagery of his detective stories; for the

Platonic allegory and the Greek myth share the same basic structure. And
this linking of Platonic idealism and the myth of the labyrinth seems even
more appropriate when we consider that the allegory of the cave bears all
the marks of a sublimated womb fantasy. As with Theseus's exit from the
subterranean labyrinth, the prisoner's exit from Plato's cave into the world
above is associated with a birth into a higher state of existence, an association that codes the cave as a symbolic womb and that is supported by
Socrates' claim in the *Theaetetus* that in aiding others to reach the world of
intelligible forms by means of dialectic, he is practicing his mother's art of
midwifery. Expressing surprise that Theaetetus does not know that Socrates' mother Phaenarete was a midwife, Socrates outlines the duties of
midwives and then adds,

> My art of midwifery is in general like theirs; the only difference is that my
> patients are men, not women, and my concern is not with the body but with the
> soul that is in travail of birth. And the highest point of my art is the power to
> prove by every test whether the offspring of a young man's thought is a false
> phantom or instinct with life and truth. I am so far like the midwife that I
> cannot myself give birth to wisdom, and the common reproach is true, that,
> though I question others, I can myself bring nothing to light because there is
> no wisdom in me. . . .
>
> In yet another way those who seek my company have the same experience as
> a woman with child; they suffer the pains of labor and, by night and day, are
> full of distress far greater than a woman's, and my art has power to bring on
> these pangs or to allay them. . . .
>
> Accept, then, the ministration of a midwife's son who himself practices his
> mother's art, and do the best you can to answer the questions I ask. (Plato, 855–
> 56)

The associative connection between the allegory of the cave and the image
of the philosopher as midwife seems clear enough: Just as the person
released from the cave into the realm of intelligible forms must return to
help his fellow prisoners out of the womblike cavern into the light, so the
philosopher as spiritual midwife must aid his pupils to be born into a
higher condition of existence by helping them give birth to thoughts that
are not false phantoms but forms "instinct with life and truth."

Perhaps the most significant question that arises from our point of
view in reading the allegory of the cave as a sublimated womb fantasy
turns upon its apparent reversal of the directionality usually associated
with such fantasies: the fact that the allegory seems to evoke not a return
to the matrix but a flight from it. In the usual form of the fantasy the
individual seeks to escape from the world, from the realm of frustration,
trauma, and the sense of the self's alienation from its environment, back

into the condition of interuterine existence with its fantasized sense of encompassing physical security and perfect integration of self and environment. But in the allegory, the individual apparently flees from the cave into the world. I say "apparently" because, of course, in Socrates' explanation it is the cave that represents the physical world. In escaping from this enclosure, the prisoner is in fact acting out the fantasy's flight from the outer world, but instead of retreating to the inner space of the womb he leaves the material realm altogether for that of pure thought. In effect, Plato sublimates the womb fantasy by subliming away (in the sense of turning a solid directly into a vapor) the physical. The bright world of intelligible forms becomes the sublime womb, the ultimate escape from the trials of bodiliness. And in this translation of the matrix from body to mind, mental values are substituted for physical goods: intellectual certainty takes the place of physical security, and the interpenetrability of mental (bodiless) forms (of objects as diaphanous as light that lack the material solidity to enforce the self's separateness from its environment) substitutes for the encompassing of one physical body by another as a means of merging the self with its environment.

33 *The Fantasy of a Total Return; Dematerializing the Body; Making the Invisible Visible; Abstraction and Dematerialization; Mathematics as Symbol; The Calculus of Probabilities; The Mere Mathematician and the True Mathematician*

IF THE ALLEGORY OF THE CAVE, considered as a constitutive moment in the imagery of idealist philosophy, represents a sublimation of a womb fantasy, then not only is there a structural fit between Borges's use of idealist philosophy (with its evocation of his father [his personal origin]) and the labyrinth scenario (evocative of the matrix) in the detective stories, but a further fit of these two with the Poe stories Borges sets out to double. Earlier, we noted that in "The Murders in the Rue Morgue" the irrational assault on a mother and daughter by a male animal within a locked room was a continuation of that violence against the female double by a male figure trapped within the symbolic womb of the family/home in the dying woman stories, a continuation that in effect codes the locked room as a matrix. In the basic scenario underlying the dying woman stories, the male figure tries to release himself from an incestuous relationship with a Psyche-figure (whose physical deterioration mirrors and exacerbates his mental deterioration), and thereby release himself from the womb of the family/home, by prematurely consigning the female double to the womb of the grave. Although the attempt to escape ultimately fails, this structure of one body entering the womb of the grave as the condition for one body exiting the womb of the family/home sheds light on the physical disposition of the bodies of mother and daughter in the first detective story. For what the bodies' disposition—the daughter's inside the room, shoved feet first up the chimney; the mother's, almost decapitated, outside in the paved courtyard—evokes is the fantasized alternative responses to the physical barrier preventing the child's actual return to its mother's womb, a barrier that necessarily makes such a return a fantasy (i.e., a function of thought's translation of the physical body into the mental image of a body). Obviously when a child has grown, its size in relation to the mother effectively precludes a total return to the womb without violence being done either to one body or the other—either by the child's being violently reduced in size or the mother's torn open. Thus in the story the daughter's body inside the locked room has been shoved up the chimney until the narrowness of the passage prevents its further progress, even with the application of brute force; while the mother's

318

body outside the room has been savagely mutilated. At first glance, of course, the form of mutilation in Mme. L'Espanaye's case (decapitation) evokes castration rather than the ripping open of the womb. Yet given the equation of head and genitals in Oedipus's castratory blinding, the beheading of Mme. L'Espanaye could be interpreted as a wounding of the mother's genitals in an "as-above-so-below" structure. Moreover, since Poe is ultimately the source of the womb fantasies in these stories, the element of symbolic castration in the mother's beheading could be seen as reflecting Freud's observation that for the son the fantasized return often involves his identification with the mother, an identification that, because it is achieved by the son's castration, figures the mother's womb as the site of a sexual wounding—the removal of the penis.

In tracing the figuration of the womb fantasy across the three Dupin stories, one can detect a clear trajectory running from a physical sense of return to origin to a mental one. The trajectory begins at the literal, bodily end of the spectrum with "The Murders in the Rue Morgue," where the impossibility of a total physical return (brutally attempted by a childlike instinctual being) is evoked through the condition and location of the mother's and daughter's bodies in relation to the locked room's symbolic matrix. The trajectory then leads to "The Mystery of Marie Rogêt" where what looks at first like a crime resulting from a violent entry into the womb (the initial explanation of the "murder" in the newspapers theorizes a gang rape) turns out to be, in the real life case on which the story is based, a death resulting from a violent exit from the womb, from an abortion (an event whose effect on the story, as we shall see, is abortive as well). And the trajectory concludes in "The Purloined Letter" where physical violence has been translated into mental violence (blackmail) and the notion of physical containment rendered problematic in the figure of the self as letter. Not only does the letter, as an entity composed of physical and mental "parts" (writing and meaning), evoke the conjunction/opposition of body and mind in the self (as well as the implicit question of how the physical body "contains" the nonphysical mind), it also raises in regard to the womb fantasy the problem of imaging the return to origin as a *physical* containment when the very condition for this return (as it applies to the self after death) is the leaving of physicality behind. As we noted earlier, the turning of the purloined letter inside out suggests that the written text "contains" its meaning in an essentially different way from that in which the letter folded in on itself "contains" the written text. By putting in play the container/contained structure for imaging the relationship of text to meaning and body to mind, the turning of the purloined letter is analogous to the movement from the subterranean cavern to the upper world of light in Plato's allegory of the cave. While the movement in Plato's story seems at first glance to be from inner to outer (from the physical enclosure of the cavern to the outside world), it is, as a return to origin, a figure of the movement from outer to inner (from the external, physical world to a nonphysical world which, though it is associated with the interuterine world before birth, is clearly represented in Plato as an apotheosis of the "inner world" of mind).

In the allegory of the cave, the movement from the real world of objects to the ideal world of forms in effect turns the matrix (the space of origin) inside out, thus signifying through the reversibility of the poles of this opposition that the physical world has been transcended. As the matrix and the returning self are dematerialized, intellectual certainty, as we said, replaces physical security as the goal of the return, and the interpenetrability of mental forms replaces the physical containment of one body by another as the means of uniting the self with its environment, of rendering the self godlike. This dematerialization or disembodiment of the self and of the space of origin is figured in Poe's story by the turning of the purloined letter inside out like a glove, a reversal of one opposition that, as we noted earlier, implies the reversal of another, the difference between the right and left hands. And this reversal of right and left is in turn associated, from Möbius's work to Wells's "The Plattner Story," with the notion of a fourth dimension, an invisible, mental realm whose transcendence of the three-dimensional world is simply an imaginative extension of the three-dimensional world's "transcendence" of two-dimensionality. It is indicative of the symbolic dematerialization of the purloined letter (in its circular journey from the queen's initial possession until its eventual return to her) that the blindness either to the letter's presence (on the part of the king in the first instance and the police in the second) or to the fact of its unconcealment (on the part of the queen in the first instance and the minister in the second) amounts to a form of invisibility for the letter, its invisibility either to a certain order of intellect (king and police) or to an intellect geometrically fixed, so to speak, in a point of view determined by the letter's possession.

Poe's problem, of course, in using the letter as a figure of the self was to find a way to make a visible object embody the condition of invisibility (i.e., mental existence), a way for such an object to evoke the process of mentally abstracting a form from a physical thing, or a meaning from a written word, or a sound from an alphabetic character. In "The Gold-Bug," for example, Poe uses the cryptographic writing of Captain Kidd's note (a physical writing that is literally invisible until heat is applied to the scrap of parchment) to evoke the invisibility of a text's meaning compared to the visibility of its writing: As the coded writing of the note contains in a hidden manner the plain text, so the plain text contains in an unexplained manner the invisible meaning.

In contrast to this, Poe evokes in the Dupin stories another type of "coded" formulaic writing subtly meant to direct the reader's attention to the relationship between visible sign and invisible meaning, and thus to the process of abstracting the mental from the physical. I refer to the abstract use of letters in algebra and calculus. As the intelligible objects of Plato's ideal world are associated with geometric shapes and numerical relationships (i.e., with abstract, dematerialized forms), so the logical certainty that characterizes this world is associated with mathematics and geometry (the certainty of abstract generalization). Significantly, the trajectory of increasing abstraction, of increasing sublimation of the physical, in the figuration of the self and of the space of origin that runs across the Dupin stories is paralleled by a progressive increase in the importance of mathematical and geometrical imagery as one moves from the first to the last of the three tales. In the lengthy discussion of the analytical power that begins "The Murders in the Rue Morgue," the narrator mentions mathematics only in passing, while concentrating his attention on specific examples of analysis in chess, draughts, and whist. He says merely, "The faculty of re-solution is possibly much invigorated by mathematical study, and especially by that highest branch of it which, unjustly, and merely on account of its retrograde operations, has been called, as if *par excellence,* analysis. Yet to calculate is not in itself to analyse" (2:528).

In contrast, at the start of the second Dupin story, the narrator presents the tale as being in effect an illustration of the calculus of probabilities. The tale begins with an epigraph from Novalis that uses the Platonic opposition of real and ideal to pose the question of coincidence and divergence in two series of events, a quotation that subtly evokes the three tales' Platonic trajectory running from the figure of the self as animal body to that of the self as textual, symbolic entity:

> There are ideal series of events which run parallel with the real ones. They rarely coincide. Men and circumstances generally modify the ideal train of events, so that it seems imperfect, and its consequences are equally imperfect. Thus with the Reformation; instead of Protestantism came Lutheranism.
> —Novalis, *Moralische Ansichten*

There are few persons, even among the calmest thinkers, who have not occasiónally been startled into a vague yet thrilling half-credence in the supernatural, by *coincidences* of so seemingly marvellous a character that, as *mere* coincidences, the intellect has been unable to receive them. Such sentiments— for the half-credences of which I speak have never the full force of *thought*—

are seldom thoroughly stifled unless by reference to the doctrine of chance, or, as it is technically termed, the Calculus of Probabilities. Now this Calculus is, in its essence, purely mathematical; and thus we have the anomaly of the most rigidly exact in science applied to the shadow and spirituality of the most intangible in speculation.

The extraordinary details which I am now called upon to make public, will be found to form, as regards sequence of time, the primary branch of a series of scarcely intelligible *coincidences*, whose secondary or concluding branch will be recognized by all readers in the late murder of MARY CECILIA ROGERS, at New York. (3:723–24)

(Reading this opening passage in the context of Borges's doubling of Poe, one has the uncanny feeling that the story, with its references to ideal and real series of events, to primary and secondary branches in the series of "scarcely intelligible *coincidences*," might easily have been written by Borges to illustrate the theory of parallel, bifurcating narratives proposed in "The Garden of Forking Paths.")

In the tale, Poe gives the epigraph in both the original German (omitted here) and in an English translation, as if the two versions were a textual embodiment of the serial parallelism that the epigraph invokes, a parallelism Poe means to reproduce in the writing by making the ideal (i.e., imaginary) series of events in the text of the fictive case of Rogêt correspond to the real series in the newspaper "text" of the case of Rogers, a newspaper text incorporated at various points into the story. And what the narrator seems to be raising in his use of mathematical imagery is not just the specific issue of the calculus of probabilities but the larger question of the application of calculus, of mathematical reasoning per se, "the most rigidly exact in science," to what appears to be a supramathematical order, "the shadow and spirituality of the most intangible in speculation." The phrase "Calculus of Probabilities" is, as critics have noted, a reference to the writings on probability of the French mathematician Pierre Laplace whose *Théorie analytique des probabilities* was published in 1812. And what the narrator seems to envision with this reference is a method of estimating the odds that, if two series of events (such as the cases of Rogêt and Rogers) coincide in a certain number of significant particulars, they will coincide in others, that is, that the solution to one series will turn out to be the solution to the other.

Poe has, of course, effected a sort of Platonic reversal in the relationship of the real and imaginary cases, for although the imaginary case of Rogêt is derived from the real one of Rogers, the imaginary case is said to form "as regards sequence of time, the primary branch of a series of scarcely intelligible *coincidences*" and the real one the "secondary or concluding branch." In raising the issue of applying numerical calculation to "the shadow and spirituality" of intangible speculations, Poe seems to be qualifying the use of mathematical reasoning in the second Dupin tale in much the same way as he did in the first by arguing that although "the faculty of re-solution is possibly . . . invigorated by mathematical study," yet "to calculate is not in itself to analyse."

Although Poe refers to the theory of probability several times in "The Mystery of Marie Rogêt" and cites at various moments the odds for or against a given event, the lengthy discussion of probability that concludes the story seems to contradict his original intention in basing the case of Rogêt on that of Rogers and as a result calls into question yet again the efficacy of purely mathematical reasoning. Obviously, the difficulty Poe faced in finishing the story was that during its serial publication in Snowden's *Ladies' Companion* the real case of Mary Rogers was solved by the deathbed confession of the woman on whose premises the abortion had been performed. The confession, which occurred in November 1842 after two of the story's three installments had been printed, meant that the solution toward which the tale had been moving (the murder of Marie by a secret lover) was no longer feasible. Since no murder had been committed, Poe was deprived of the tale's expected dramatic conclusion—the analytic solution and the criminal's apprehension. In place of Dupin's solving the case, Poe had to content himself with the general correctness of portions of Dupin's reasoning, most notably, his demonstration of the improbability of the two most widely held theories of the murder—that Marie had been raped and murdered by a gang of ruffians, or that she had been killed by her former employer. And in place of a dramatic finish, he had to come up with a conclusion that retained as much as possible of the reasoning leading up to his original solution while diverting the reader's attention from the fact that there would be no solution to a murder.

The compromise Poe worked out shows the economy of genius, for what he saw was that whether Mary Rogers was murdered by a secret lover or died as the result of an abortion, the ultimate cause of death in both scenarios was her having a secret lover and that the identification of this figure would eventually lead to an explanation of her death, whatever the immediate cause. For either this individual murdered Mary Rogers, or else, as Poe assumes, he helped procure the abortion, conveyed Mary to the place where it was to be performed, then helped dispose of her body by dumping it in the river. With only minor changes in the text, then, Poe's tale could accommodate both the actual cause of death and most of the reasoning associated with his original theory of the crime—as can be seen from the slight modifications Poe made in the opening passage of Dupin's summary of the evidence, modifications made between the story's first serial publication and its appearance in the *Tales* (1845). In the 1845 version he adds, for example, a key phrase (indicated by my italics) that makes it seem as if the possibility of Marie's accidental death had been envisioned from the start. Dupin says, "Let us sum up now the meagre yet certain fruits of our long analysis. We have attained the idea *either of a fatal accident under the roof of Madame Deluc, or* of a murder perpetrated, in the thicket at the Barrière du Roule, by a lover, or at least by an intimate and secret associate of the deceased" (3:768). Poe proceeds to identify several characteristics of this individual (dark complexion, a sailor, etc.), suggests a general line of investigation for his discovery, and then suddenly breaks off the narrative of the case with a fictive editorial comment claiming that, for unspecified but obvious reasons, the portion of the manuscript detailing "the *following up* of the apparently slight clew obtained by Dupin" has been omitted, but that "the result desired was brought to pass; and . . . the Prefect fulfilled punctually, although with reluctance, the terms of his compact with the Chevalier" (3:772). Poe then concludes the story with a discussion of the ultimate noncoincidence of the cases of Rogers and Rogêt and a final word on the calculus of probabilities.

By breaking off the narrative of the case with the perfunctory editorial note, Poe tries to make it seem as if solving the murder of Mary Rogers had never really been the point of the tale and that consequently the reader's expectations have not been violated. Indeed, by ending with a discussion of mathematics, Poe implies that the real goal all along had been the more or less abstract demonstration of the link between chance and necessity, probability and predictability in human events as exhibited by the two parallel cases. Obviously, this is a trick to divert our attention from the story's missing solution, as Poe himself acknowledged in his letter to George Eveleth in January 1848. Noting that Mary Rogers had died an "accidental death arising from an attempt at abortion" and that this was a topic on which he "must not speak further," he admits that the editorial note with its reference to omitted material is nothing but pure "mystification" (3:788 n. 120). What is significant for our purposes, however, is the specific form of mystification that Poe substitutes for the missing solution. In place of the suppressed explanation of the cause of death, there is a discussion of coincidence and of mathematical probability, a substitution that, in the context of our present inquiry, becomes more understandable. For if, as we suggested, the symbolic trajectory of the Dupin stories involves a Platonic sublimation of a womb fantasy that (as in the allegory of the cave) translates the return to origin from a physical to a mental plane, a sublimation that (as in Christianity's use of Platonism) suppresses the self's bodily component in order to figure death as a rebirth of the self in its essentially mental character, then it is not surprising that Poe, given this Platonic-Christian tendency to represent death as birth, substitutes for the image of birth as death (an aborted birth that kills mother and child) that imagery of bodiless abstraction (mathematics) associated with the Platonic realm of pure light into which the self is reborn after leaving the cave of the material world. (We should note in passing that Poe's first two detective stories both involve the death of a mother and child—in the first instance as the ostensible subject of the tale, in the second as a repressed content—a recurrence that could be read as part of that structure discussed earlier in which the association of death and motherhood produces the figure of Mother Death who, in symbolizing the child's reunion with the lost mother through its own death, merges the images of tomb and womb.)

Given the association of mathematical imagery with Plato's realm of intelligible forms and given that this realm provides the philosophical basis for the notion of the "otherworldly" in Christianity, it is also not surprising that Poe begins the concluding passage on probability with a reference to the supernatural or, more precisely, with a denial of preternatural intervention as regards the remarkable series of coincidences in the two cases. Remarking that he has "no faith in praeter-nature" and that no thinking man can deny "that Nature and its God are two," the narrator nevertheless admits that only "the insanity of logic" would claim that "the Deity *cannot* modify his laws" (3:772). However, he argues that it is not a question of divine power but of divine will, that in effect we insult the deity "in imagining a possible necessity for modification. In their origin these laws were fashioned to embrace *all* contingencies which *could* lie in the Future" (3:772). Having said this, the narrator reaffirms that he is speaking only of coincidence in the parallelism of the two cases and not divine intervention, yet his interpretation of the meaning of this parallelism seems to be exactly the reverse of that with which he began the tale. Albeit that the epigraph from Novalis invokes the principle that while ideal and real series of events may often run parallel they "rarely coincide," the whole point of Poe's tale, as the narrator introduces it, is precisely that with Rogêt and Rogers such a rare coincidence between two series of events has indeed occurred. And, of course, why should it not have, since one of the series is Poe's own creation and could be made to duplicate the real events as faithfully as he chose? Indeed, Poe acknowledges this in a footnote at the very start of the story in the 1845 *Tales:* "The author has followed, in minute detail, the essential, while merely paralleling the inessential facts of the real murder of Mary Rogers. Thus all argument founded upon the fiction is applicable to the truth: and the investigation of the truth was the object" (3:723n).

Poe's remark about the applicability to a real case of an argument

founded on a fictive one implies that the remarkable coincidence between
these two series of events in so many points along the way *raises* the probability of their coinciding to the end, so that the solution to the fictive case
will turn out to be the solution to the real one. Yet when he takes up the
issue of coincidence at the end of the tale this implied principle is explicitly
contradicted. The narrator says,

> But let it not for a moment be supposed that, in proceeding with the sad
> narrative of Marie from the epoch just mentioned, and in tracing to its *dénoue-*
> *ment* the mystery which enshrouded her, it is my covert design to hint at an
> extension of the parallel, or even to suggest that the measures adopted in Paris
> for the discovery of the assassin of a grisette . . . would produce any similar
> result.
>
> For, in respect to the latter branch of the supposition, it should be consid-
> ered that the most trifling variation in the facts of the two cases might give rise
> to the most important miscalculations, by diverting thoroughly the two courses
> of events; very much as, in arithmetic, an error which, in its own individuality,
> may be inappreciable, produces, at length, by dint of multiplication at all
> points of the process, a result enormously at variance with truth. And, in
> regard to the former branch, we must not fail to hold in view that the very
> Calculus of Probabilities to which I have referred, forbids all idea of the exten-
> sion of the parallel:—forbids it with a positiveness strong and decided just in
> proportion as this parallel has already been long-drawn and exact. (3:772–73)

The narrator claims that a "trifling variation in the facts" might have
caused miscalculations "by diverting thoroughly the two courses of
events," and yet to judge from the footnote at the start of the story in
which Poe says that he "followed, in minute detail, the essential, while
merely paralleling the inessential facts of the real murder," it would seem
that it was just such a possibility he had guarded against. What this suggests is that in writing most of the tale after the real death and the preliminary investigation but before the solution, Poe could not be certain which
were the essential and which the inessential facts. To illustrate how a
seemingly inessential fact could divert the two courses of events, Poe gives
an example from mathematics in which an inappreciable error at an early
stage of an operation produces by repeated multiplication an enormous
error at the end. While this is not a particularly apt example for the case at
hand (indeed, it is much more suited to the tale Poe published four
months later, "The Gold-Bug," where he uses a similar example to account
for the characters' initially digging for the treasure in the wrong spot), it
does allow Poe to reintroduce the image of mathematics at the very end of
the tale, thereby substituting this figure (evocative of the transcendent
world of Platonic forms) for the image of birth as death that he would have

been led to had he pursued the parallel between the cases.

It is in the context, then, of mathematical imagery as a substitute for the repressed solution of a mystery (the mystery of the self's possible dissolution evoked by the reversal of the traditional figure of death as rebirth) that Poe reinvokes the calculus of probabilities in order to reverse the principle implied at the start of the tale, for now the long-term coincidence of events in two parallel series, instead of raising the probability of their continued coincidence to the end, "forbids all idea of the extension of the parallel . . . just in proportion as this parallel has already been long-drawn and exact"—a principle the narrator backs up with assertions of dubious mathematical theory. This reversal in Poe's argument can be accounted for only in part by the fact that the real case did not turn out to be a murder as expected and the real solution could not, for a variety of reasons, be reproduced in fiction. It probably resulted as well from Poe's realizing that the unexpected divergence between the actual solution of Rogers's death and the one he had originally envisioned, although it disrupted his plans for "Marie Rogêt," could nevertheless be made to serve a larger theme of the Dupin stories as a whole. Which is to say that if Poe's detective stories are about the way that the analytic effort to include the process of thinking wholly within the content of thought ultimately reveals the essential noncoincidence of the self with itself, then Poe's unsuccessful attempt to double the real case of Mary Rogers with the imaginary one of Marie Rogêt becomes, through the reader's experience of this ultimate noncoincidence of parallel lives, a textual embodiment of this theme. Thus when the narrator gives a mathematical illustration of the principle of prolonged coincidence *decreasing* the probability of continued coincidence, the example he chooses seems to have more relevance for the imagery of the self's structure in the Dupin stories than for the principle it is invoked to demonstrate. The narrator says that this principle is

one of those anomalous propositions which, seemingly appealing to thought altogether apart from the mathematical, is yet one which only the mathematician can fully entertain. Nothing, for example, is more difficult than to convince the merely general reader that the fact of sixes having been thrown twice in succession by a player at dice, is sufficient cause for betting the largest odds that sixes will not be thrown in the third attempt. A suggestion to this effect is usually rejected by the intellect at once. . . . The chance for throwing sixes seems to be precisely as it was at any ordinary time—that is to say, subject only to the influence of the various other throws which may be made by the dice. And this is a reflection which appears so exceedingly obvious that attempts to controvert it are received more frequently with a derisive smile than with

The Mystery to a Solution

anything like respectful attention. The error here involved—a gross error redolent of mischief—I cannot pretend to expose within the limits assigned me at present; and with the philosophical it needs no exposure. It may be sufficient here to say that it forms one of an infinite series of mistakes which arise in the path of Reason through her propensity for seeking truth *in detail*. (3:773–74)

One senses that the intentional "mystification" Poe introduced into the tale several paragraphs earlier to disguise its lack of a proper solution is still at work. Yet to describe this passage as "mystification" is by no means to suggest that it is meaningless, that one cannot read Poe's intention from the specific form this mystification takes. We should not, of course, interpret the narrator's remarks as indicating mathematical ignorance. To judge from Poe's school records, mathematics was one of his three best subjects (along with French and Latin), and it is clear from the narrator's comments that Poe knew the correct probability of "throwing sixes" on the third roll after sixes had already been thrown twice in succession was "precisely as it was at any ordinary time"—the odds being 1 in 36 if there are two dice. That Poe knew this and yet still had the narrator deny it in favor of the principle that the two previous throws of the dice raised the odds against throwing sixes on the third roll can almost certainly be accounted for by the distinction the narrator makes in this passage between two orders of intellect—a lower order which he characterizes as that of the "merely general reader" and a higher order which he characterizes as being at once mathematical ("only the mathematician can fully entertain" this principle) and philosophical ("with the philosophical it needs no exposure").

This distinction is, of course, one we are already familiar with from the first and third Dupin stories. In "The Murders in the Rue Morgue," it is the difference between, on the one hand, "most men," who in respect to Dupin, wear "windows in their bosoms," and, on the other, the mastermind himself whose dual intellectual power suggests to the narrator "the fancy of a double Dupin—the creative and the resolvent." In "The Purloined Letter," it is the distinction between the prefect and his men on one side and Dupin and the Minister D—— on the other, with the dual intellectual power shared by Dupin and his adversary being characterized as that of both poet and mathematician. The pattern seems clear: The half of this dual power described as "resolvent" in the first Dupin story is characterized as mathematical in the second and third, while the half described as "creative" in the first story is characterized as philosophical in the second and poetic in the third. Thus when the narrator states the correct mathematical principle regarding the odds of throwing sixes on

328

the third roll only to dismiss it in favor of an unstated higher principle, Poe is in effect repeating that qualification of purely mathematical ability voiced in the first Dupin story when the narrator noted that "to calculate is not in itself to analyse." For Poe the purely or merely mathematical is not the truly mathematical. For this latter ability, there must be joined to the resolvent power a creative one. Only when the two operate together does rational analysis become fully empowered by acknowledging the existence and claims of something that lies beyond rational analysis—a "beyond" symbolized in the final paragraph of "Marie Rogêt" by that unspecified higher principle the narrator invokes, a "beyond" that is simultaneously at the edge and the center of rational analysis, existing in a mutually constitutive relationship with it. As Dupin says of the Minister D——, "As poet *and* mathematician, he would reason well; as mere mathematician, he could not have reasoned at all" (3:986). Which brings us back to "The Purloined Letter" and to the lengthy discussion of mathematics that follows Dupin's remark about the minister's being both poet and mathematician, a discussion constituting in some sense the latent intellectual core of the three detective stories.

34 Poet and Mathematician; Analysis and Algebra; The Rise of Algebra; Two Senses of Abstraction; The British Resistance to Analytics; The Cambridge Curriculum

DUPIN'S DISCUSSION OF MATHEMATICS IN "The Purloined Letter" grows out of his comment on a logical flaw in the prefect's reasoning process, a point worth noting precisely because much of the ensuing discussion turns upon the logical claims of mathematical analysis. In explaining how he recovered the letter by identifying his "intellect with that of his opponent" (3:984), Dupin suggests that the prefect failed in this identification through his supposing

> "that the Minister is a fool, because he has acquired renown as a poet. All fools are poets; this the Prefect *feels;* and he is merely guilty of a *non distributio medii* in thence inferring that all poets are fools."
>
> "But is this really the poet?" I asked. "There are two brothers, I know; and both have attained reputation in letters. The Minister I believe has written learnedly on the Differential Calculus. He is a mathematician, and no poet."
>
> "You are mistaken; I know him well; he is both. As poet *and* mathematician, he would reason well; as mere mathematician, he could not have reasoned at all, and thus would have been at the mercy of the Prefect."
>
> "You surprise me," I said, "by these opinions, which have been contradicted by the voice of the world. You do not mean to set at naught the well-digested idea of centuries. The mathematical reason has long been regarded as *the* reason *par excellence*." (3:986)

But, of course, it is precisely this idea of equating mathematical analysis with the highest form of reason that Poe means "to set at naught" (to make equal to zero, in the narrator's mathematical imagery), just as in the first Dupin story he disputed the name "analysis" for the "highest branch" of "mathematical study" (as if it represented analysis "*par excellence*") and in the second story invoked an unspecified higher intellectual power to correct the merely mathematical reading of probability. In his ensuing argument against the primacy of "mathematical reason," Dupin in effect repeats the method he used to dispose of the prefect's faulty syllogism. He shows that two words usually treated as synonyms are not such, because the classes of things they name do not coincide. Thus, according to Dupin, the prefect concludes that the minister is a fool through a syllogism that runs

All fools are poets.
The Minister is a poet.
The Minister is a fool.

But, as Dupin points out, the prefect commits the logical error of using an undistributed middle term, for while the major premise affirms that all fools are poets, it is not necessarily the case that all poets are fools. Which is to say that the premise "All fools are poets" is not a reversible equation (i.e., not a *mathematical* equation). It is part of the irony implicit in Poe's method that Dupin moves from the prefect's faulty syllogism, which associates the terms *poet* and *fool* in the person of the minister, to a discussion that links the terms *poet* and *mathematician* in the same individual, as if, in this associative logic, the common term *poet* had remained a constant, while the term *mathematician* had been substituted for *fool* in such a way as to identify the two, an identification supported by Dupin's remark that "as mere mathematician" the minister "could not have reasoned at all."

And just as Dupin argued that the class of fools is predicated in the prefect's syllogism as forming part, but not the whole, of the class of poets, so in the discussion of mathematics that follows he argues that the class "mathematical reason" forms part, but not the whole (and not even the better part), of the class "reason itself." Replying to the narrator's comment that mathematical reason "has long been regarded as *the* reason *par excellence*," Dupin suggests that mathematicians themselves "have done their best to promulgate the popular error to which you allude":

> "With an art worthy a better cause, for example, they have insinuated the term 'analysis' into application to algebra. The French are the originators of this particular deception; but if a term is of any importance—if words derive any value from applicability—then 'analysis' conveys 'algebra' about as much as, in Latin, '*ambitus*' implies 'ambition,' '*religio*' 'religion,' or '*homines honesti*,' a set of *honorable* men."
>
> "You have a quarrel on hand, I see," said I, "with some of the algebraists of Paris; but proceed." (3:987)

The distinction Dupin draws between "algebra" and "analysis" not only serves to particularize the difference between "mathematical reason" and "reason itself" but also allows him to *enact* at that very moment this algebra/analysis (mathematics/reason) distinction by carrying out a form of "analysis" that has nothing to do with mathematics—a linguistic analysis in which English words are reduced to their etymological roots. Dupin

argues that the words *analysis* and *algebra* are as different in meaning as
the English words he cites are from their Latin originals, and the implication is that the reader can verify this difference by conducting his own
etymological analysis. In a group of stories that begins with the author's
oblique announcement of his intention to analyze the analytical power
(oblique because what he announces is how "little susceptible of analysis"
that power is), it is an appropriately Poesque touch that this endlessly
reflexive examination of self-reflection should be symbolically enacted in
the final story by the reader's own linguistic analysis of *analysis*.

The word *analysis* comes, of course, from the Greek roots *ana-* ("up,"
"throughout") and *lysis* ("a loosing," from the verb *lyein*), and a standard
dictionary definition makes clear the original image behind the word: "a
separating or breaking up of any whole into its parts so as to find out their
nature, proportion, function, relationship, etc." (*W*, 53). In contrast, the
word *algebra* derives from the Arabic *al-jebr* (the "reunion of broken
parts," from the roots *al*, "the," and *jabara*, "to reunite"), and one of its
Arabic meanings is "the surgical treatment of fractures, bone-setting"
(*OED*, 55). The word's application to mathematics comes from its use in
the title of a mathematical treatise, *Al-jabr w'al muqâbala*, written in A.D.
830 by Mohammed ibn Musa al-Khowârizmi. As the mathematician Morris Kline notes, "The word *al-jabr* meant . . . , in this context, restoring the
balance in an equation by placing on one side of an equation a term that
has been removed from the other; thus if -7 is removed from $x^2 - 7 = 3$,
the balance is restored by writing $x^2 = 7 + 3$."[1] To judge from their
origins, then, the words *analysis* and *algebra* are exact opposites. One
means "the breaking of a whole into parts," the other "the reuniting of
broken parts." Thus, on linguistic grounds Dupin rightly objects to any
attempt to turn antonyms into synonyms. But Poe did not, of course,
choose these two words at random for his performative demonstration of
the difference between mathematical and nonmathematical analysis. He
chose them precisely because they evoked a contemporary controversy in
the mathematical world over whether analysis was to be done solely by
algebraic methods to the exclusion of geometrical ones—a controversy
that the narrator alludes to in his remark about Dupin having "a quarrel
. . . with some of the algebraists of Paris." Poe's point is that it makes no
sense to apply a solely mathematical significance to the word *analysis* if
mathematicians themselves cannot agree on the meaning or applicability
of the term within their own field.

To understand what was at issue in the controversy over algebra as the
sole method of mathematical analysis and thus understand Poe's reason
for invoking it in "The Purloined Letter," we must consider for a moment
the historical relationship of analysis, geometry, and algebra. For the

Greeks, mathematical analysis was done by means of geometry, and algebra was simply an aid to working out geometrical proofs. As Morris Kline points out, algebra remained "tied to geometry" from ancient times until the beginning of the sixteenth century, indeed, so much so that "equations of higher degree than the third were considered unreal" (Kline, 278). The German mathematician Stifel, for example, argued that "going beyond the cube just as if there were more than three dimensions . . . is against nature" (Kline, 279). But with the work of François Vieta in the sixteenth century and of René Descartes in the seventeenth, this situation began to change. Descartes expanded the reach of algebra, seeing in it "a powerful method wherewith to carry on reasoning, particularly about abstract and unknown quantities" and judging it to be more fundamental than, that is, "logically prior to," geometry (Kline, 280). As Kline says,

> Descartes's view of algebra as an extension of logic in treating quantity suggested to him that a broader science of algebra might be created, which would embrace other concepts than quantity and be used to approach all problems. Even the logical principles and methods might be expressed symbolically, and the whole system employed to mechanize all reasoning. Descartes called this idea a "universal mathematics." (Kline, 281)

This broader notion of algebra, though never followed up by Descartes, was pursued by Leibniz in his *De Arte Combinatoria* (1666), and ultimately led, through the work of nineteenth-century mathematicians such as Augustus De Morgan and George Boole, to the creation of symbolic logic.

Apart from his broad conception of the science of algebra, Descartes's specific contribution to its use in mathematics was the invention of coordinate geometry. "By arguing that a curve is any locus that has an algebraic equation," Descartes dramatically extended the scope of mathematics and made it, according to Kline, "a double-edged tool. Geometric concepts could be formulated algebraically and geometric goals attained through the algebra. Conversely, by interpreting algebraic statements geometrically one could gain an intuitive grasp of their meanings as well as suggestions for the deduction of new conclusions" (Kline, 322). The establishment of algebra as an independent branch of mathematics resulted in large part from the practical success of coordinate geometry in providing seventeenth-century science with the mathematical tool it needed to quantify its investigations. Indeed, so successful was this quantification of knowledge that, as Kline notes, "algebra, which Descartes had thought was just a tool, an extension of logic rather than part of mathematics proper, became more vital than geometry. . . . Whereas from Greek times until about 1600 geometry dominated mathematics and algebra was subordinate, after 1600 algebra became the basic mathematical subject" (Kline, 323). The decisive factor in establishing the ascendancy of algebra over geometry was the invention of the calculus by Newton and Leibniz. Both men thought of the calculus as simply "an extension of algebra; it was the algebra of the infinite, or the algebra that dealt with an infinite number of terms, as in the case of infinite series" (Kline, 324).

The process by which algebra went from being ancillary to geometry, to being independent of and equal to geometry as a branch of mathematics, to being at last the dominant area in mathematical study is known as "the arithmetization of mathematics." At the time Poe wrote the Dupin stories in the 1840s, the arithmetization of mathematics had been in progress for more than two hundred years and was entering its final decisive phase with the work of the French mathematician Augustin-Louis Cauchy. But another process, one that we might call the arithmetization of reasoning, was just beginning with the work of the Scottish philosopher Sir William Hamilton and that of the mathematicians Augustus De Morgan and George Boole, an effort to reform Aristotelian logic by quantifying the reasoning process, which would lead to the algebraic formulations of symbolic logic. Interestingly enough, Poe seems to be evoking both these processes in Dupin's acerbic comments about mathematics and analysis, for while Dupin quarrels, on the one hand, with the "algebraists of Paris," objecting to any attempt on their part to make algebra the sole means of doing mathematical analysis (i.e., to their identifying analysis with algebra), he quarrels, on the other, with those mathematicians or educators who would try to make mathematical reasoning synonymous with reason itself (i.e., to their identifying all logical analysis with mathematical analysis).

As one might expect, the gradual arithmetization of mathematics over several centuries led to a certain wandering in the meaning and application of the word *analysis*. Commenting on the "confusion in mathematical terminology" that resulted, Kline observes,

> The word "analysis" had been used since Plato's time to mean the process of analyzing by working backward from what is to be proved until one arrives at something known. In this sense it was opposed to "synthesis," which describes the deductive presentation. About 1590 Vieta rejected the word "algebra" as having no meaning in the European language and proposed the term "analysis" . . . ; the suggestion was not adopted. However, for him and for Descartes, the word "analysis" was still somewhat appropriate to describe the application of algebra to geometry because the algebra served to analyze the geometric construction problem. . . . Thus Jacques Ozanam (1640–1717) said in his *Dictionary* (1690) that moderns did their analysis by algebra. In the famous eighteenth-century *Encyclopédie*, d'Alembert used "algebra" and "analysis" as

synonyms. Gradually, "analysis" came to mean the algebraic method, though the new coordinate geometry, up to about the end of the eighteenth century, was most often formally described as the application of algebra to geometry. By the end of the century the term "analytic geometry" became standard and was frequently used in titles of books.

. . . In the eighteenth century the view that algebra as applied to geometry was more than a tool—that algebra itself was a basic method of introducing and studying curves and surfaces . . . —won out, as a result of the work of Euler, Lagrange, and Monge. . . .

In the meantime the calculus and extensions such as infinite series entered mathematics. . . . Since algebra and analysis had been synonyms, the calculus was referred to as analysis. In a famous calculus text of 1748 Euler used the term "infinitesimal analysis" to describe the calculus. This term was used until the late nineteenth century, when the word "analysis" was adopted to describe the calculus and those branches of mathematics built on it. (Kline, 323–24)

This wandering of the meaning and application of the word *analysis* was further complicated by the fact that, as the principal means of doing mathematical analysis, geometry was not to be supplanted by algebra without a struggle, a struggle that often left mathematicians divided into opposing camps of geometers and algebraists, each with a different stake in the meaning of the term *analysis*.

The objections that mathematicians raised most frequently to the algebraic method of analysis tended to fall into two main categories—one having to do with logical rigor, the other with mental abstraction. The first class of objections, the more serious of the two, turned upon the fact that algebra had never been established on a logical basis of axioms and proofs as geometry had. The rules of algebra had come into existence piecemeal over many centuries, and the practical success of algebra and the calculus in providing mathematical tools for the rapidly developing physical sciences from the seventeenth century onward tended to obscure their uncertain logical status. Consequently, as the number system grew more complicated with the addition of new types such as negative, irrational, and complex numbers, and as it became increasingly difficult to reason about these numbers by analogy with the positive integers or illustrate their properties by geometric figures, mathematicians found themselves uncertain about the logical correctness of their work and about the reality of the numbers they were manipulating. Thus the sixteenth-century mathematician Stifel in his *Arithmetica Integra* argued that while irrational numbers seem to be true numbers judging "by the results which follow from their use—results which we perceive to be real, certain, and constant," yet "when we seek to subject them to numeration [decimal representation] . . . we find that they flee away perpetually." And since a true number is one that can "be apprehended precisely in itself," an irrational number "is not a true number, but lies hidden in a kind of cloud of infinity" (Kline, 251). Similarly, Stifel thought of negative numbers as "absurd"; Cardan "considered them . . . mere symbols"; and Vieta discarded them entirely (Kline, 252). As for complex numbers (e.g., $\sqrt{-1}$), Descartes "coined the term 'imaginary'" to describe them (Kline, 253); while Newton considered them of little significance probably because at that period "they lacked physical meaning" (Kline, 254). Paradoxically, then, many of those whose work contributed most to the triumph of algebra over geometry in doing mathematical analysis were the very people whose emotional attachment to geometry, on the grounds of tradition and the authority of the ancients, was the greatest and thus whose skepticism about the algebraic method was correspondingly great. As Kline observes, Newton "not only constantly expressed great admiration for the geometers of Greece but censured himself for not following them more closely than he did" (Kline, 392). Indeed, he even went so far as to remark in a letter that "algebra is the analysis of the bunglers in mathematics," but at the same time in his own work *Arithmetica Universalis* he "set up arithmetic and algebra as the basic science, allowing geometry only where it made demonstrations easier" (Kline, 392).

The second major class of objections raised by mathematicians to the algebraic method concerned its abstract, symbolic character—a character that seemed ultimately to distance it from the real world. As Kline summarizes the problem,

> Up to 1550 the concepts of mathematics were immediate idealizations of or abstractions from experience. By that time negative and irrational numbers had made their appearance and were gradually gaining acceptance. When, in addition, complex numbers, an extensive algebra employing literal coefficients, and the notions of derivative and integral entered mathematics, the subject became dominated by concepts derived from the recesses of human minds.
>
> . . . Mathematicians were contributing concepts, rather than abstracting ideas from the real world. (Kline, 392–93)

Certainly, the geometric figure of a square has a seemingly much clearer, more self-evident relationship to the physical world than does, for example, the algebraic expression $\sqrt{-1}$. Consequently, no matter how successful algebra and the calculus were in allowing early scientists to manipulate the material world (thereby proving that these methods of analysis did have "some ties to physical reality" [Kline, 393]), there was nevertheless a sense on the part of many mathematicians (particularly during those centuries when science and religion were still close to one another) that the relationship of geometry to the physical world was a simple, necessary one (a more or less straightforward abstracting from nature of the divine shapes in which God had written the world), while the relationship of algebra and calculus to the physical world was, by contrast, an increasingly complex and arbitrary one (a study not of the necessary, God-given shapes of nature but of the contingent operations of the human mind). As Kline reminds us, Descartes did "not regard algebra as a science in the sense of giving knowledge of the physical world"; such knowledge came, he thought, from "geometry and mechanics" (Kline, 280). And, indeed, even into the late nineteenth century, mathematicians continued to object to the distancing from reality that arbitrary algebraic symbols seemed to create as compared to the visible presence of the real world in the almost pictographic shapes of geometry. In his *Théorie générale des fonctions* (1887) the French mathematician Du Bois-Reymond voiced his concern that "the arithmetization of analysis" in separating analysis "from geometry and consequently from intuition and physical thinking" reduced it "to a simple game of symbols where the written signs take on the arbitrary significance of the pieces in a chess or card game" (Kline, 973). Yet whatever the objections were to the arithmetization of analysis and however long they persisted, it is clear that by the beginning of the eighteenth century the trajectory of mathematics was increasingly away from the world of physical reality toward the world of mental constructs.

By 1844, then, when Poe described Dupin's quarrel with "the algebraists of Paris" over whether analysis and algebra were synonymous, the question of how mathematical analysis was to be done had been a central issue for mathematicians for almost two centuries, and the distinction in Paris (the center of the mathematical world at the time) between those whose primary analytic interest centered on the algebraic method and the calculus (the algebraists) and those whose primary interest centered on geometry (the geometers) was fairly clear. Within this latter group it is worth making a further distinction between the vast majority of geometers, who used algebra and the calculus as a tool in their analytic work, and a small group of geometers (mainly British) who tried to restore a purely geometrical analysis. In the introduction to his *Treatise on Algebraic Geometry* (1831), Dionysius Lardner, professor of natural philosophy at the University of London, points out that while

> the analytical methods have been almost universally adopted by the moderns in all questions which pass the mere elements of geometry . . . , it is fair to state, that in Great Britain the ancient geometry is not altogether without some remaining partisans, who, in spite of the many proofs of its inefficiency, and in

opposition to the judgment of the great mass of scientific talent of Europe, wish to found upon its principles the whole theory of curve lines.[2]

Lardner cites the 1813 volume *Geometry of Curve Lines* by the Scottish mathematician and physicist Sir John Leslie as an example of this fore-doomed effort "to produce a counter revolution in geometrical science in Great Britain, and to restore it to the state it had been in before the introduction of the modern analysis" (Lardner, xli). Leslie's hopeless at-tempt "to restore . . . the state" prior to "the introduction of the modern analysis" can be seen as the last gasp of British resistance (extending over the entire eighteenth and first decade of the nineteenth centuries) to continental (read "French") analytic methods. As Kline notes, "Excessive reverence for Newton's geometrical work in the *Principia,* reinforced by the enmity against the Continental mathematicians engendered by the dispute between Newton and Leibniz" over priority in the invention of the calculus, "caused the English mathematicians to persist in the geometrical development of the calculus. But their contributions were trivial com-pared to what the Continentals were able to achieve using the analytical approach" (Kline, 392).

Lardner (whom Poe cites, by the way, in the *Marginalia*) describes the debilitating effect this reverence for Newton had on British mathematical education and the revolutionary curricular measures needed to remedy the stagnation it caused:

> In the hands of Newton the powers of the ancient geometry were extended to their extreme limit. . . . Deeply impressed with the wonders they thus beheld effected and guided by his avowed judgment, the English schools of science, until a few years since, have uniformly pursued the ancient geometrical meth-ods. The consequence has been, that the progress of mathematical science has been much slower in Great Britain than elsewhere. . . .
>
> The immense advantage thus gained upon us by the philosophers of Europe in mathematical and physical science became at length too apparent to be longer overlooked. The university of Cambridge was the first to begin the reformation. (Lardner, xxxiv–xxxvi)

Lardner attributes the dramatic change in the British mathematical cur-riculum to the efforts of Dr. Bartholomew Lloyd who, "about the year 1811, . . . was elected to the professorship of mathematics" at Cambridge. Through Lloyd's exertions, "the works of Euler, and the French mathe-maticians Laplace, Lagrange, Lacroix, and numerous others, were intro-duced and studied with activity. The notation of fluxions and fluents was superseded by the more elegant and powerful algorithm of the Differen-tial and Integral Calculus." In short, Lloyd "singly and unassisted, con-

ceived and executed the most important and rapid revolution ever effected in the details of a great public institution" (Lardner, xxxvi–xxxviii).
Given that Lardner describes these changes as a "revolution," it is not
surprising that he also describes Sir John Leslie's effort "to restore . . . the
state" of geometrical science in Great Britain to what it had been "before
the introduction of the modern analysis" as a "counter revolution." Indeed, Lardner's imagery was undoubtedly meant to remind his readers
that during the very years when Britain was leading the counterrevolu-
tionary forces of Europe against the French Revolution, culminating in
the defeat of Napoleon at Waterloo and the restoration of the French
monarchy, a revolution in mathematical education was going on in Britain in which the work of "the French mathematicians Laplace, Lagrange,
Lacroix, and numerous others" was gaining the day in spite of the native
influence of Newton and an attempted counterrevolution in favor of "the
ancient geometry."

35 *Mathematics and Politics in Nineteenth-Century France;*
The Dupin Brothers; Poe's Mathematical Education;
West Point and the École Polytechnique; A Chain
of Associations in "The Murders in the Rue Morgue";
A Subliminal Drama of High and Low

THE LINKING OF MATHEMATICS AND politics implicit in Lardner's imagery would probably not have struck his readers as either arbitrary or far-fetched, for a great many of the most distinguished French mathematicians in the late eighteenth and early nineteenth centuries were eminent political figures as well. For example, Gaspard Monge, perhaps the foremost French geometer of his day, was a staunch republican and Bonapartist. The inventor of descriptive geometry, Monge had already had a long and distinguished career as a teacher of mathematics when he was appointed to important administrative and political positions during the Revolution and the Empire.[1] In 1792–93 he served briefly as minister of the navy. Working to provide the technological expertise needed for the republic's defense, he took an active part in establishing the École Polytechnique where he taught descriptive geometry. In 1796 he made the acquaintance of Napoleon and later accompanied him on his expedition to Egypt. Returning to France in 1798, he was named the first president of the Institute of Egypt and resumed teaching at the Polytechnique. A loyal supporter of Bonaparte, Monge was subsequently appointed a member of the Senate and given the title of count of Pelusium. Upon Napoleon's fall, he was stripped of his offices and titles by Louis XVIII and died soon after (*EB,* 18:710).

When Monge was expelled in 1816 from the Académie des Sciences, his place was filled by the appointment (not the election) of Augustin-Louis Cauchy, a devout Catholic and royalist and perhaps the foremost French algebraist of the day. A professor first at the École Polytechnique and later at the Faculté des Sciences and the Collège de France, Cauchy published in 1821 his famous *Cours d'Analyse,* which revolutionized mathematical analysis by basing it on limits, functions, and calculus. But just as Monge had seen the political part of his career overwhelm the scientific part with the fall of Napoleon in 1815, so Cauchy experienced the same fate in 1830 when the July Revolution replaced the Bourbon Charles X with the Orléans Louis Philippe. Refusing to take the oath of allegiance to the new king, Cauchy lost his academic positions and went into self-imposed exile. In 1833 Cauchy "was called to Prague, where Charles X had settled, to assist in the education of the crown prince" and was eventually made a baron by the ex-king as a mark of his esteem. With the Revolution of 1848 and the establishment of the Second Republic, the oath of allegiance was repealed, and "Cauchy resumed his chair at the Sorbonne. . . . He retained this chair even when Napoleon III reestablished the oath in 1852, for Napoleon generously exempted the republican Arago and the royalist Cauchy."[2]

The fact that leading figures from two distinct mathematical camps in nineteenth-century France—the geometer Monge and the algebraist Cauchy—were deeply involved, from opposite ends of the political spectrum, in the governmental turmoil of the period explains in part the appropriateness of Poe's including a reference to mathematical partisanship (Dupin's quarrel with "some of the algebraists of Paris") in a tale of French political intrigue such as "The Purloined Letter." For in both the political and the mathematical spheres it must have seemed that revolution and counterrevolution, exile and return, were the order of the day. Indeed, this association of politics and mathematics in the affairs of the time sheds light on Poe's choice of a name for his detective. The traditional explanation of the detective's surname holds that Poe took it from one André-Marie-Jean-Jacques Dupin (1783–1865), a well-known "French advocate" and "president of the chamber of deputies" (*EB*, 8:686). And the evidence most frequently cited for this identification is the fact that in the same issue of *Graham's Magazine* (April 1841) in which he published the first Dupin story, Poe reviewed a book translated by R. M. Walsh entitled *Sketches of Conspicuous Living Characters of France* that contains a chapter devoted to the political career of André Dupin. Moreover, the book's author, Louis Léonard de Loménie, describes André Dupin in terms that bear a striking resemblance to Poe's detective. He says, for example, that Dupin is "a perfect living encyclopaedia. From Homer to Rousseau, from the Bible to the civil code, from the laws of the twelve tables to the Koran, he has read every thing, retained every thing."[3] He also notes that Dupin's character seems to be compounded of nothing but antithetical qualities, a description recalling the narrator's sense of his friend as "a double Dupin" whose dual powers of intellect remind him of "the old philosophy of the Bi-Part Soul":

> He is the personage for whom the painters of political portraits, make the most enormous consumption of antithesis. In the same picture, he will be drawn as both great and little, courageous and timid, . . . white and black; there is no understanding it. . . . If, like every one else, and even more than every one else, the honourable deputy of Nièvre has his contrasts of light and shade, is it therefore to be supposed, that so many heterogeneous elements are combined

in him in such equal proportions, as to render his character a jumble so strange
as to be absolutely monstrous? (Loménie, 210–11)

Perhaps the most interesting piece of information Loménie provides
about André Dupin for our purposes is that he has a brother, the Baron
Charles Dupin (1784–1873), who is a famous mathematician. Now while
it seems fairly clear that Poe had the lawyer and politician André Dupin in
mind when he chose a name for his detective in the first Dupin story, it
seems equally clear that Poe had Charles Dupin in mind as well when he
provided his detective with an antithetical double, the Minister D——, in
the third story. In giving the minister the same initial as Dupin (and as the
word *double*), Poe suggests a structural kinship between the two opponents, a kind of antithetical "family resemblance." And Poe guided himself in creating this resemblance by taking biographical details from both
Dupin brothers and giving them to the characters of the detective and his
rival, the Minister D——.

We can see this process more clearly if we examine for a moment the
career of the mathematician Charles Dupin. He graduated "in 1803 from
the École Polytechnique . . . as a naval engineer," having been a student
there of the geometer Monge.[4] When Dupin published his *Développements
de géométrie* in 1813, he acknowledged his discipleship by dedicating the
work to his "illustre maître" Monge. Occupying himself mainly with naval
engineering projects during the first two decades of the nineteenth century, Charles Dupin eventually became "professor of mechanics at the Paris
Conservatoire des Arts et Métiers, a position he held until 1854." In 1824
he was made a baron by Louis XVIII; in 1828, elected deputy for Tarn; in
November 1834, served briefly as minister of marine affairs; in 1838, was
made a peer; and finally in 1852, became a member of the Senate (Struik,
4:257).

In "The Purloined Letter" Poe indicates that he has both the Dupin
brothers in mind by having the narrator remark of the Minister D——:
"There are two brothers, I know; and both have attained reputation in
letters. The Minister I believe has written learnedly on the Differential
Calculus" (3:986). Undoubtedly one reason Poe associates both the Du-
pins with this story is that the tale is set against the complex political
backdrop of the French court, a court with which both brothers were
involved to varying degrees. From internal evidence we can make a fairly
accurate estimate of the political period in which the action of "The
Purloined Letter" takes place. In all of the Dupin stories, Poe refers to the
prefect of the Paris police as G——, and Poe scholars have generally taken
this to be the initial, as Mabbott notes, of "Henri-Joseph Gisquet . . .
prefect of police in Paris, 1831–1836. . . . Baudelaire in 1865 identified

G—— as Gisquet" in a footnote to his translation of "The Mystery of Marie Rogêt" (2:573 n. 31). Given that Gisquet was prefect from 1831 to 1836, the French king and queen in the tale would then be Louis Philippe and his queen Maria Amelia.

Louis Philippe, the duke of Orléans, had, of course, gained the throne as a result of the Revolution of 1830, in which Charles X attempted to abdicate in favor of his grandson the comte de Chambord (with Louis Philippe as regent) but was deposed instead by the Chamber of Deputies who "proclaimed Louis Philippe 'King of the French, by the grace of God and the will of the people'" (*EB*, 17:51). André Dupin, as one of the leading members of the Chamber of Deputies, played a major role in the events of July 1830.

In the political spectrum of the period, André Dupin seems to have maintained a fairly consistent stance of liberal opposition to absolute rule. In 1815, as a member of the Chamber of Deputies, he "strenuously opposed the election of the son of Napoleon as emperor after his father's abdication" (*EB*, 8:686). After the restoration Dupin was not reelected to the Chamber of Deputies, and the new monarchy "made an effort to win the distinguished advocate" with the offer of a position as secretary general in the Department of Justice (Loménie, 218). Dupin refused, choosing instead to defend "with great intrepidity the principal political victims of the reaction," most notably Marshal Ney (*EB*, 8:686). Like many liberals of the period, André Dupin found Louis Philippe, who had been a republican hero at the battle of Jemappes and had courted the favor of the liberal bourgeoisie throughout his adult life, an attractive political alternative to the other members of the royal family, and he became Louis Philippe's personal friend and political ally, serving from 1817 as one of his "legal counselors . . . and as his business agent."[5] In 1820 Louis Philippe appointed André Dupin "a member of his private council" (Loménie, 218). In 1827 Dupin was again elected to the Chamber of Deputies, taking "his seat in the left centre" (Loménie, 218), and, after the accession of Louis Philippe in 1830, Dupin became president of the Chamber of Deputies in 1832, an office "he held successively for eight years" (*EB*, 8:686).

At the period, then, in which "The Purloined Letter" is set— somewhere in the five-year space between 1831 and 1836 when Gisquet was prefect of the Paris police, and probably after late 1832 when Dupin became president of the Chamber of Deputies—André Dupin's relationship with Louis Philippe (first as his business agent and a member of his private council, then as a deputy who worked for his accession to the throne, and finally as president of the Chamber of Deputies) was certainly as intimate as the Minister D——'s was with the king in the tale, which is to say, a relationship close enough that it permitted the Minister D—— to enter the royal boudoir for an audience with the king and, after conducting "business transactions," to converse "for some fifteen minutes, upon the public affairs" (3:977), as if his visit were an everyday occurrence. The difficulty here is that Poe gives D—— the title "Minister," a title that allows for some confusion; for while André Dupin had served briefly as minister without portfolio in the first cabinet formed after the Revolution of 1830, his brother Charles, as we have noted, had also served briefly as minister of marine affairs in 1834. One might wonder, then, whether Poe had taken the name of his detective from one brother (the politician André) and the character of the Minister D—— from the other brother (the mathematician Charles, who, in his application of differential calculus to geometry in the *Développements* could certainly have been said to have "written learnedly on the Differential Calculus," as the narrator says of the Minister D——). Yet to judge from Loménie's description of the way the press portrayed André Dupin at the time of the July Revolution (a portrayal Loménie feels is unjust and attempts to correct), the character of the Minister D—— (whom Poe describes as a man of "daring, dashing, and discriminating ingenuity" [3:990] given to political intrigue and the use of influence to satisfy his personal ambition for power) seems to be derived from the popular image of the politician André rather than from his brother Charles. It would seem, then, that Poe took the surname and some of the mental traits of his detective as well as the broad outline of the Minister D——'s political character from one brother (André), while in "The Purloined Letter" he added to the characters of both the detective and the minister features taken from the other brother (Charles). In so doing, Poe was able to superimpose upon the figures of the detective and the minister an image of structural kinship (the antithetical twinship of doubles) and thus personify the creative/resolvent power of mind they shared as that of poet and mathematician, a move that took advantage of the fact that one of the Dupin brothers was actually a famous mathematician. (Whatever the Dupin brothers' poetic talents might have been—and certainly writing verse was a standard accomplishment for men of their class and era, as evidenced by the reams of bad poetry produced by the mathematician Cauchy—history seems to have ignored them as poets.)

In mingling details from the careers of the two Dupin brothers in "The Purloined Letter," Poe may well have been reflecting the combined influence that nineteenth-century French politics and mathematics had had on his own mathematical education. Recall that after his withdrawal from the University of Virginia and his two years of service as an enlisted man in the Army, Poe sought an appointment to West Point. He entered the U.S. Military Academy as a cadet in July 1830—the same month in which

André Dupin was, according to Loménie, continually mentioned in the French press for his active role in the events of the July Revolution that brought Louis Philippe to the throne. And the school that Poe entered at West Point that summer was one whose curriculum had been modeled since 1817, when Major Sylvanus Thayer became superintendent, on that of the École Polytechnique in Paris, the school created by Gaspard Monge in 1794 to train engineers and scientists for republican France.

In 1815 Thayer and another American officer had been sent abroad by the War Department "to look into the military systems of Europe, particularly of France."[6] Thayer, who had graduated from West Point in 1808 and taught mathematics there from 1810 to 1812, was a Francophile, and most of the two and a half years he stayed in Europe were spent in Paris examining the organization of various technical schools.[7] In 1816 Thayer was informed by the War Department that, upon his return to the United States, he would become superintendent of the U.S. Military Academy, and it was with the reform of West Point's curriculum in mind that Thayer focused his attention on the École Polytechnique. Thayer was able to "spend time with faculty members at *Polytechnique*" through the help of Lafayette and General Simon Bernard, "who was about to sail for the United States as Chief of the Board of Fortifications" (Molloy, 388).

Bernard, an early graduate of the Polytechnique, had entered the French army's corps of engineers and eventually risen to become Napoleon's aide-de-camp in 1813 and a field marshal the following year.[8] With the fall of Napoleon, he emigrated to the United States, having accepted an appointment in the "Corps of Engineers, with the title of Brigadier General" (Molloy, 368). In the United States Bernard "executed a number of extensive military works for the government, notably at Fortress Monroe, Virginia, and around New York, and did a large amount of the civil engineering connected with the Chesapeake and Ohio Canal" (*EB*, 3:799). (As an enlisted man in the U.S. Army, Poe was stationed at Fort Monroe, Virginia, from December 1828 to April 1829 [*Log*, 87–90].) In 1830, after the July Revolution, Bernard returned to France and was appointed a lieutenant general by Louis Philippe. He became aide-de-camp to the king in 1832, served briefly as minister of war in November 1834, and was again appointed minister of war in 1836 (*EB*, 3:799). Bernard would thus have been minister of war in 1834 at the same time that Charles Dupin was minister of marine affairs and André Dupin was president of the Chamber of Deputies. It was this Simon Bernard, then, who helped Thayer find his "way in Parisian scientific circles" in 1815–16, arranging for him "to receive instruction in descriptive geometry, advanced stonecutting, and techniques of wooden construction" at the École Polytechnique (Molloy, 374), and it was Bernard again who, as a

brigadier general in the Corps of Engineers and chief of the Board of
Fortifications, acted as Thayer's staunch supporter in modeling the curriculum of the Military Academy on that of the French technical school.

   To understand what that modeling involved, we must consider for a
moment the original purpose of the Polytechnique as it was conceived by
Gaspard Monge in 1794, compared to its purpose in 1816 when Thayer
saw it. When Monge drew up the original curriculum for the Polytechnique, he planned to create a pure engineering school, a single institution
to train France's civil, military, and naval engineers, and for the first five
years of its existence this was the role the Polytechnique filled. But in 1800
the curriculum began to change. As a result of constant political pressure
from the Écoles d'Application (specialized schools of advanced training in
science and engineering), the Polytechnique gradually became a prepara-
tory school for the advanced schools, with its length reduced from three
years to two and its curriculum devoted to pure and applied mathematics
rather than to engineering (Molloy, 70, 78). In 1804 Napoleon militarized
the Polytechnique, requiring the students to wear uniforms, perform
infantry drill, and live in barracks at the school (Molloy, 80), for the emper-
or's main interest in the institution was as a source of engineers and
artillery officers for the army. But his decision to place the students under
military discipline was prompted as well by the fact that the Polytechnique
was a bastion of republican sentiment, manifested in early 1804 in a series
of anti-Bonapartist acts by the student body. Indeed, this strong republican bias remained an ongoing aspect of the school, as demonstrated some
twenty-five years later when the students "went in a body to the barricades
to fight for the Liberals in the Revolution of 1830" (Molloy, 85).

   The Polytechnique Thayer saw in 1815–17, then, was a military school
with long-standing republican traditions and a curriculum devoted to
pure and applied mathematics. But

> Thayer had no intention of modeling West Point's curriculum after the ad-
> vanced and highly abstract curriculum of the *École Polytechnique* of 1815; in-
> stead he looked back to the curriculum of the years 1795–1804, when *Poly-
> technique* had been a genuine engineering school. Perhaps Thayer was
> influenced in this respect by General Bernard, an early graduate of *Polytech-
> nique*. (Molloy, 388–89)

Although mathematics was at the core of the curriculum Thayer established, the emphasis was on its practical applications, with a specific bias
against the theoretical: "The Cadets were not encouraged to express
themselves in abstract terms" (Molloy, 432–33). Indeed, one wonders
whether Dupin's quarrel with "some of the algebraists of Paris" reflects a

bias against theoretical mathematics left over from Poe's education at West Point.

Thayer copied not only West Point's curriculum and its system of examinations from the Polytechnique, but even specific regulations, such as that forbidding cadets to have any books in their rooms "beyond prescribed texts and reference works" (Molloy, 390). In addition, he employed a graduate of the Polytechnique, Claude Crozet, to teach engineering. Crozet, who had been an artillery officer in Napoleon's army, had accompanied Bernard to the United States in 1816, serving first as an engineer in the U.S. Army and then on the engineering faculty at West Point from 1816 to 1823. Like Charles Dupin, Crozet had been a student of Monge's at the Polytechnique, and he introduced into the United States the study of descriptive geometry, the field Monge had invented. In 1821 Crozet published *A Treatise of Descriptive Geometry for the Use of Cadets of the U.S.M.A.*, a text that was "the standard work for third and fourth classmen until 1832" (Molloy, 444) and would thus have been available to Poe.

When Poe entered the Military Academy in 1830, Thayer's Polytechnique-derived curriculum had already been in place for thirteen years, so we can be fairly certain what Poe's course of studies involved. For the first two years at West Point, a cadet concentrated on two subjects—mathematics and French. In the examination system "subjects were weighted according to their importance. Thus for freshmen, who studied only mathematics and French, the former subject received a weight of 2, the latter a weight of one." Included in the study of mathematics was "a little drawing, and a fair amount of descriptive geometry." In his first year a cadet, "even in the slowest section, mastered algebra, plane geometry, plane analytic geometry, plane trigonometry, and basic techniques of surveying; the advanced section covered advanced plane and spherical geometry in addition to the previous subjects" (Molloy, 438, 441–42). Poe was in the advanced section in mathematics, as he bragged to his foster father John Allan in a letter dated 6 November 1830: "I have a very excellent standing in my class—in the first section in every thing and have great hopes of doing well." But he adds that "the study requisite is incessant, and the discipline exceedingly rigid." He goes on to note, "I am very much pleased with Colonel Thayer, and indeed with every thing at the institution."[9]

As one of Poe's contemporaries at West Point, A. B. Magruder, recalled, Poe "was an accomplished French scholar, and had a wonderful aptitude for mathematics" (*Log*, 107). Indeed, Poe's standing in his studies, as he told Allan, was excellent: after the January examinations in 1831 he was third in French and seventeenth in mathematics in a class of eighty-seven (*Log*, 112). And since "the performance of each Cadet was charted on a daily basis," with the grades being turned over to the superintendent weekly (Molloy, 428), Poe's ranking in these areas for his five months of classes at West Point is a significant gauge of his ability, particularly of his mathematical aptitude, for at the time Poe attended West Point, and for several decades after, the Military Academy was "unquestionably the most influential mathematical school in the United States" (Cajori, 121).

Poe's sense of his high academic standing in his class can be seen in a subsequent letter to the superintendent. After getting himself court-martialed in February 1831 and dismissed from West Point, Poe wrote Thayer on 10 March requesting a letter of recommendation:

> I intend by the first opportunity to proceed to Paris with the view of obtaining, thro' the interest of the Marquis de La Fayette, an appointment (if possible) in the Polish Army. In the event of the interference of France in behalf of Poland this may easily be effected. . . . A certificate of "standing" in my class is all that I have any right to expect. Any thing farther—a letter to a friend in Paris—or to the Marquis—would be a kindness which I should never forget. (*Letters*, 1:44–45)

One wonders whether Poe's plan to go to Paris to continue his military career had been influenced by the recent return to France of General Bernard. Indeed, one wonders whether Bernard was Thayer's "friend in Paris" mentioned by Poe. French army records show that Bernard had "returned to active service in the Corps of Engineers" as of 12 February 1831 (Carter, 307), a month before Poe's letter.

To judge, then, from the curriculum at West Point in Poe's day, it seems fairly certain that his course of studies there would have indelibly linked in his mind the subject of mathematics with contemporary French politics. It would have done so not just because Poe was required to spend five of the nine hours a day that cadets devoted to their studies on learning mathematics and the other four on French, but because the very reason for this odd, two-subject curriculum for new cadets was rooted in the events of recent French history—the founding of the École Polytechnique in revolutionary France to provide civil and military engineers for the fortification and defense of the republic; the militarization of the school in 1804 by Napoleon; the departure from France, upon the fall of Napoleon and the restoration of the monarchy, of some of the Polytechnique's most distinguished graduates (such as Bernard and Crozet) to follow careers in the U.S. Army; the modeling of West Point's curriculum on that of the Polytechnique and the resultant need for the cadets to know French well enough to keep up with the latest mathematical developments at the school (Thayer had purchased over a thousand technical books in France for the West Point library during his 1815–17 sojourn); and the return of

Simon Bernard to France, upon the accession of Louis Philippe, to rejoin the French army and ultimately become minister of war, serving alongside his fellow Polytechnician Charles Dupin who was minister of marine affairs.

We can see the influence Poe's Polytechnique-based West Point education had on the French setting of the detective stories in that initial example the narrator gives of Dupin's extraordinary mental powers in "The Murders in the Rue Morgue," his uncanny ability to intuit and follow the narrator's unspoken train of thought. The two men had been walking one evening through the streets of Paris in the vicinity of the Palais Royal. "Being both, apparently, occupied with thought," neither of them "had spoken a syllable for fifteen minutes," when suddenly Dupin breaks in on the narrator's meditations with the comment, "He is a very little fellow, that's true, and would do better for the *Théâtre des Variétés*" (2:533–34). The narrator says that he had just been thinking of an actor named Chantilly, "a *quondam* cobbler of the Rue St. Denis, who, becoming stage-mad, had attempted the *rôle* of Xerxes, in Crébillon's tragedy so called, and been notoriously Pasquinaded for his pains" (2:534), and he expresses his astonishment at Dupin's ability to read his thoughts. In response Dupin explains the deductive method that allowed him to eavesdrop on his friend's meditation. He points out that some fifteen minutes earlier the narrator had been jostled in the street by a "fruiterer, with a large basket upon his head." The man, "brushing quickly past," had thrust the narrator upon "a pile of paving-stones collected at a spot where the causeway is undergoing repair." The incident, says Dupin, had clearly launched the narrator on a train of thought, and by close observation of his facial movements and gestures and by a series of deductions based on his knowledge of the narrator's thought processes, Dupin had reproduced the associative logic governing his companion's meditation, until the moment he decided to test the accuracy of his method by agreeing with the narrator's last mental comment. As Dupin explains, the "larger links" in the narrator's chain of thought "run thus—Chantilly, Orion, Dr. Nichol, Epicurus, Stereotomy, the street stones, the fruiterer" (2:535).

Dupin's subsequent explanation of this chain is, as we shall see, a remarkable exercise in the association of ideas. But what is most interesting about the passage, in which Dupin theorizes the associations that produced the linking of ideas in the narrator's mind, are the actual associations in Poe's mind that led him to create this particular sequence of thoughts as an example of associative logic, associations linking the realms of mathematics and politics in revolutionary and postrevolutionary France and centering on the word *Stereotomy*.

Noticing that the narrator, in the wake of being thrust against the paving stones, keeps looking at the rough pavement as he walks, Dupin concludes that he is "still thinking of the stones," and when they reach "the little alley called Lamartine, which has been paved, by way of experiment, with the overlapping and riveted blocks," he notes that the narrator's lips move, and he assumes that he is murmuring "the word 'stereotomy,' a term very affectedly applied to this species of pavement" (2:535–36). Literally, the word *stereotomy* refers to "the science or art of cutting, or making sections of, solids; . . . the art of cutting stone or other solid bodies into measured forms, as in masonry" (*OED*, 2:3044). Thus the application of the word to a particular form of road paving does seem, as Dupin says, somewhat affected. But what interests us here is not so much the fictive chain of associations in the narrator's mind as the real chain of associations in Poe's. By calling attention to the affected use of the word *stereotomy*, Poe encourages the reader to inquire into its more normal use. And as one of the historical citations in the *OED* makes clear, *stereotomy* was, at the time and place in which the story is set, a word with very specific technical connotations: "Stereotomy, . . . in the scientific language of the Polytechnic School, signifies that part of stone-cutting, on which Frezier and De la Rue have written so much" (*OED*, 2:3044). In the curriculum for the Polytechnique that Monge drew up in 1794, half of the time allotted for mathematical study "would be given over to 'stereotomy,' or civil and military engineering," an area of study that "included descriptive geometry, mechanical drawing, theories of shadows and perspective and their applications to stone and wood cutting techniques" (Molloy, 104) for use in road building, bridge and canal construction, harbor improvements and fortifications. Poe's use of the word, then, almost certainly reflects his Polytechnique-based schooling at West Point and possibly reflects as well his sense of the influence that the Polytechnique's scientific innovations had had on daily life in France by the 1830s.

The chain of associations that led Poe to use this odd technical term connected with the Polytechnique in his tale would seem to begin with his choice of a name for "the little alley" whose paving reminded the narrator of the word *stereotomy*. He calls the alley "Lamartine." Mabbott is undoubtedly correct in thinking the name is an allusion to "the voluminous poet" Alphonse de Lamartine. According to Mabbott, Poe considered Lamartine "a bore, and slyly gave his name to a little alley" (2:571 n. 18). But there is clearly more involved in his use of the name than just a passing slap at a boring poet. Like André Dupin, Lamartine was one of the figures discussed at length in Loménie's *Sketches of Conspicuous Living Characters of France*, the book Poe reviewed in the same issue of *Graham's Magazine* in which he published "The Murders in the Rue Morgue." In the chapter devoted to him, Lamartine is depicted as a man who has succeeded in a dual career—being both a brilliant poet and an adept politician. Having held various diplomatic posts under the restored monarchy, Lamartine eventually became a member of the Chamber of Deputies in 1834, serving in that body at the same period when André Dupin was its president and when Charles Dupin, another member, was appointed minister of marine affairs.

At the beginning of his political career, Lamartine endeavored, says Loménie, "to respond both to the inspirations of the poet and the functions of the deputy," but as time passed, he tended to regard poetry as the "humble vassal of politics" and to resent those who "would confine him to his poetic inaction" at the expense of his "social labour." The sight of one of France's greatest poets preferring political involvement to artistic achievement gave rise, says Loménie, "in the literary world to grave discussions upon the mission of the poet in modern societies," as well as to a feeling on the part of many in France that while the country had "no want of politicians" it had "only one poet" like Lamartine (Loménie, 121–23). The image of Lamartine that emerges, then, from the book is that of a poet-politician; and since Charles Dupin (who is mentioned in the chapter on his brother André) was an eminent mathematician-politician, one wonders whether, in designating the Minister D—— as both "poet *and* mathematician," Poe recalled from Loménie's work that a famous poet and a renowned mathematician had both been important political figures in the Chamber of Deputies over which André Dupin presided.

If for Poe the name of the poet-politician Lamartine was associated with the name of his opposite, the mathematician-politician Charles Dupin, then it would have been a short step from the latter individual, a star pupil of Monge's at the Polytechnique, to a word closely associated with the Polytechnique's curriculum—*stereotomy*. That Poe's use of the word was prompted by its association with the Polytechnique is further confirmed by the fact that in the narrator's train of thought, as explicated by Dupin, "stereotomy" leads him to think immediately of atomies, the theories of Epicurus, and finally of the way in which "the vague guesses of that noble Greek had met with confirmation in the late nebular cosmogony" (2:536); and we know from *Eureka* the name of the French mathematician Poe always associated with that "most magnificent of theories"—"the Nebular Cosmogony of Laplace" (*P,* 16:245). Pierre Simon Laplace, whose calculus of probabilities provides, as we saw earlier, a kind of mathematical-philosophical background for the second Dupin story, was, like Monge, associated with the École Polytechnique in both a mathematical and political capacity, though often this relationship was more adversarial than otherwise. When Napoleon seized power in 1799, Monge became the director of the Polytechnique, and Laplace became for a brief period minister of the interior, head of the governmental department that administered the school. Laplace favored the legislative bill changing the curriculum of the Polytechnique from an engineering school to a school of pure and applied mathematics, and the bill became law in December 1799 (Molloy, 78). Several years later Laplace again altered the structure of the Polytechnique when, after the fall of Napoleon, he headed a commission to reorganize the school in 1816 (Molloy, 88). It would seem, then, that in addition to being linked in Poe's mind with the calculus of probabilities, the author of the nebular cosmogony may also have been associated with that peculiarly French blend of mathematics and politics that characterized the Polytechnique.

If the mention of the nebular cosmogony (with its implicit link to Laplace and thence to the Polytechnique) does, indeed, represent another echo of the connection between mathematics and politics in France at this period, then we can perhaps detect the image pattern that triggered Poe's own mental associations as he created the narrator's fictive train of thought. The incident begins with the narrator's being bumped by a laborer in the street and his falling against a pile of paving stones. Since the narrator seems to be of the same upper-class social stratum as the Chevalier C. Auguste Dupin, his being jostled, inadvertently or not, by a common laborer tends to give added significance to the detail of his falling against the paving stones. For since the French Revolution the most readily available weapons for the Parisian mob in the periodic uprisings that convulsed the country were the paving stones in the streets, torn up and hurled at the enemy. And the narrator is in fact slightly injured by being thrust against the pile of stones.

I would suggest that what governs the imagery in the narrator's train of thought is precisely this opposition between low and high, between common laborer and aristocrat, between the lowly paving stones (at which the narrator continues to gaze for several minutes as he walks) and the constellation Orion (to which he directs his attention when the chain of associations leads him to think of the nebular cosmogony). At the period in which the tale is set, the most recent example of a popular uprising in Paris would have been the Revolution of 1830, the uprising in whose wake the poet Lamartine, a descendant of an upper-class family, became a member of the popularly elected Chamber of Deputies. If we are correct in thinking that Poe antithetically associated Lamartine with the Baron Charles Dupin—one a poet, one a mathematician; both involved in politics as members of the legislature; one bearing the same name as the detective who traces the associations in the narrator's thoughts—then there is probably both a high road and a low road leading to the next link in the chain (the word *stereotomy*). The high road leads from Lamartine to Charles Dupin, and then to Dupin's association with the Polytechnique and the use of the word *stereotomy* in its curriculum to refer to the type of civil engineering that included techniques of stonecutting for road building. The low road leads from the laborer who jostles the narrator against the pile of paving stones, to the little street called Lamartine, to the sufferings of Lamartine's aristocratic family at the hands of the mob during the French Revolution as recounted by Loménie, to Lamartine's survival to become a popular figure and a member of the Chamber of Deputies (a body that both represents the populace and tries to prevent its rising up and restoring the chaos of the revolution), and finally to the particular form of paving in the little alley named Lamartine, a paving that employs "overlapping and riveted blocks" (2:536) that are clearly difficult to dislodge, stones that cannot rise up out of their place and hurt the people who walk on them. (We should note that after its militarization in 1804 the Polytechnique changed from being a school open to any bright young student of whatever social class to a school "for the sons of the middle and upper classes" [Molloy, 86], so that this road-building technique meant to keep the paving stones in their place [and associated with the Polytechnique through the word *stereotomy*] suggests the way in which the technical and scientific advances that grew out of the revolutionary spirit which created the Polytechnique eventually became middle-class tools for discouraging continued revolution by the lower class.)

Clearly, the symbolic equation at work in the narrator's train of thought identifies the members of the lower class (the laborers in the road) with the paving stones beneath the narrator's feet—each (person and stone) being a basic, atomlike element in a larger structure (state and street). Given this implied comparison, it is not surprising that Dupin continues his explication of the narrator's thought processes by remarking, "I knew that you could not say to yourself 'stereotomy' without being brought to think of atomies, and thus of the theories of Epicurus; and since, when we discussed this subject not very long ago, I mentioned to you how singularly, yet with how little notice, the vague guesses of that noble Greek had met with confirmation in the late nebular cosmogony, I felt that you could not avoid casting your eyes upward to the great *nebula* in Orion" (2:536). From the implicit imagery of common laborers and paving stones as atoms in a larger body, the chain of associations runs to the theory of the ancient Greek philosopher Epicurus that all things are composed of atoms, and then on to a modern derivation from that theory, Laplace's nebular cosmogony. In *Eureka* Poe discusses the link between the work of Epicurus and Laplace, noting that Laplace's original idea seems to have been a compound of the true Epicurean atoms with the false nebulae of his contemporaries; and thus his theory presents us with the singular anomaly of absolute truth deduced, as a mathematical result, from a hybrid datum of ancient imagination intertangled with modern inacumen. Laplace's real strength lay, in fact, in an almost miraculous mathematical instinct: . . . in the case of the Nebular Cosmogony, it led him, blindfolded, through a labyrinth of Error, into one of the most luminous and stupendous temples of Truth. (*P*, 16:266)

When Dupin originally listed the "larger links" in the narrator's chain of thought, the list ran: "Chantilly, Orion, Dr. Nichol, Epicurus, Stereotomy, the street stones, the fruiterer." But in his subsequent explanation of this sequence, Dupin never tells us who Dr. Nichol is or how he fits into the chain of associations. Mabbott notes that "Dr. John Pringle Nichol (1804–1859), Regius Professor of astronomy at Glasgow University, published in 1837 . . . [a] popular presentation of the findings and theories of current astronomy," in which he quoted at length from the work of Sir William Herschel on the Orion nebula and described "the nebular hypothesis" (2:570 n. 16). Nichol's book thus forms the connecting link between Laplace's nebular cosmogony (the modern scientific restatement of Epicurean atomism) and the constellation Orion. (Poe's failure to include Nichol in Dupin's explication of the narrator's associative logic may be either a simple oversight or the skipping of a step he considered obvious for his contemporaries.)

As the narrator's gaze rises from the individual paving stones to the great nebula in Orion, the sociopolitical aspect of this movement from low to high is made clear by the final link in the associative chain. Having seen the narrator look up at the constellation Orion, Dupin says,

> But in that bitter *tirade* upon Chantilly, which appeared in yesterday's "*Musée*," the satirist, making some disgraceful allusions to the cobbler's change of name upon assuming the buskin, quoted a Latin line about which we have often conversed. I mean the line
>
> Perdidit antiquum litera prima sonum
>
> I had told you that this was in reference to Orion, formerly written Urion. . . . It was clear, therefore, that you would not fail to combine the two ideas of Orion and Chantilly. (2:536)

Earlier the narrator had told us that when Dupin suddenly broke in on his unspoken chain of thought the subject of his meditation had been this same Chantilly, "a *quondam* cobbler of the Rue St. Denis, who, becoming stage-mad, had attempted the *rôle* of Xerxes, in Crébillon's tragedy so called, and been notoriously Pasquinaded for his pains." The Latin line

Dupin cites is, as Mabbott notes, from a passage in Ovid's *Fasti* (5.536) "concerning the birth of the 'Boeotian Orion'" and the derivation of his original name Urion (2:571 n. 22). According to Ovid, Jupiter, Neptune, and Mercury had been journeying one day and accepted at nightfall the hospitality of a farmer named Hyrieus. In return for his kindness, they granted him a favor. Hyrieus was old and widowed and had never had a son but wanted one. The three gods granted his request: they took a bullock's hide, urinated on it, then covered it with earth, and in ten months a son was born. Hyrieus called the boy Urion because of the manner of his begetting, the name deriving from the Greek word for urine; although as Ovid remarks in the line Dupin quotes, "The first letter has lost its original sound." Dupin's learned allusion, evoking the notion of a name change that masks a laughable, not to say faintly obscene, origin, is undoubtedly meant as a further slap at Chantilly, suggesting that the cobbler's change of name may hide an equally comic origin.

According to Dupin, then, the link between the ideas of Orion and Chantilly is simply that each has undergone a change of name, but for Poe the connection between the two is more complex than that. Clearly, within the high/low opposition that governs the passage's imagery, Chantilly is a member of the lower class who has attempted to rise above his station by playing the role of a king, and his new name, the same as the French town famous for fine lace, makes his upper-class aspirations obvious. Given Poe's association of the lower class with paving stones, it is only appropriate that Chantilly should be a former cobbler, someone whose trade depended upon the contact between shoe leather and paving stones (*cobbler* and *cobblestone* share a common root). (Poe emphasizes the persistence of Chantilly's former employment in his new calling when he has the satirist from the *Musée* refer to the cobbler's choice of an acting career as his "assuming the buskin," evoking Chantilly's career change as a move from repairing boots to wearing the boots associated with Greek and Roman tragedy.) The associative link between the constellation of stars called Orion and the actor Chantilly is, then, not just that both had had other names at one time but that Chantilly has attempted to rise in society from his former cobblestone-oriented trade by becoming a star in the theater in the tragic role of a king. The use of "star" to refer to the principal actor in a theatrical production had become commonplace by the 1820s.

From a would-be theatrical star to the image of stars in the heavens is an easy mental step, but a stellar translation, whether in the theater or in ancient mythology, is more difficult for a groundling to effect, particularly when the groundling in question is built too close to the ground to reach that high. Dupin says that when the narrator thought of "the poor cobbler's immolation" by the press, he changed his posture: "So far, you had been stooping in your gait; but now I saw you draw yourself up to your full height. I was then sure that you reflected upon the diminutive figure of Chantilly. At this point I interrupted your meditations to remark that as, in fact, he *was* a very little fellow—that Chantilly—he would do better at the *Théâtre des Variétés*" (2:536–37). That the narrator interprets the public slapping down of this lowly upstart as having a larger social significance, a significance that bears on his being jostled in the street by a common laborer, seems clear from the fact that after gazing down at the pavement and stooping in his gait following the incident with the laborer, he appears to recover himself, to remember who and what he is by drawing himself up to his full height. This almost subliminal drama of the tensions between high and low in postrevolutionary France is, of course, wholly appropriate to a tale in which a humanlike animal slave first mimics, or if you will, apes its master (the shaving episode) and then breaks loose from its master's control to spread terror through the streets of Paris. That the fallen aristocrat Dupin intervenes in this case of master/slave reversal to help restore order bespeaks a political orientation that becomes explicit in "The Purloined Letter" when he intervenes again, this time on the side of royalty, to thwart another master/slave reversal—an orientation that no doubt reflected the aristocratic sentiments of the fallen Virginia gentleman who invented Dupin.

36 *Mathematics and Logic; Wallace's* Stanley;
William Hamilton and the Cambridge Curriculum;
The Analytical Society; D-*ism versus* Dot-*age;*
Liberalism and Analytics; Cambridge Mathematics
at Virginia

CLEARLY, FOR A LAYMAN POE possessed not only a fairly sophisticated knowledge of mathematics but also a fairly accurate sense of the relationship between mathematics and politics in postrevolutionary France, a sense, as one historian of science has remarked, that "mathematics represented . . . republicanism, rationality."[1] And what we must keep in mind is that Poe deploys this knowledge in "The Purloined Letter" to maintain that distinction between a mere mathematician and a true mathematician discussed earlier. In this vein, Dupin, replying to the narrator's remark that he has a quarrel with the algebraists of Paris, sets out to combat a particular form of the popular notion that "mathematical reason" is "*the* reason *par excellence*": the claim that mathematical study provides the best training in reasoning. He says,

> I dispute the availability, and thus the value, of that reason which is cultivated in any especial form other than the abstractly logical. I dispute, in particular, the reason educed by mathematical study. The mathematics are the science of form and quantity; mathematical reasoning is merely logic applied to observation upon form and quantity. The great error lies in supposing that even the truths of what is called *pure* algebra, are abstract or general truths. And this error is so egregious that I am confounded at the universality with which it has been received. (3:987)

Dupin's argument turns upon two different senses of the word *abstract* as applied to reasoning. On the one hand, he claims that the truths of mathematics are not abstract enough, in the sense that they are not "general truths." But on the other, he implies that this lack of universality is due to the fact that mathematical truths are too abstract, too much a product of abstruse, individual minds. Such truths, says Dupin, lack "availability" as compared to the "abstractly logical," that is, to truths directly abstracted from the common-sense ground of the physical world.

To illustrate that "mathematical axioms are *not* axioms of general truth," Dupin gives examples of fields in which mathematical reasoning does not apply:

What is true of *relation*—of form and quantity—is often grossly false in regard to morals, for example. In this latter science it is very usually *un*true that the aggregated parts are equal to the whole. In chemistry also the axiom fails. In the consideration of motive it fails; for two motives, each of a given value, have not, necessarily, a value when united, equal to the sum of their values apart. There are numerous other mathematical truths which are only truths within the limits of *relation*. But the mathematician argues, from his *finite truths*, through habit, as if they were of an absolutely general applicability—as the world indeed imagines them to be. Bryant, in his very learned "Mythology," mentions an analogous source of error, when he says that "although the Pagan fables are not believed, yet we forget ourselves continually, and make inferences from them as existing realities." With the algebraists, however, who are Pagans themselves, the "Pagan fables" *are* believed, and the inferences are made, not so much through lapse of memory, as through an unaccountable addling of the brains. (3:987–88)

As scholars have noted, Poe borrowed several of the examples and even some of the language in this passage from Horace Binney Wallace's 1838 novel *Stanley; or The Recollections of a Man of the World.* In one of the many learned discussions that fill the book, the main character and a Mr. Tyler turn from a lengthy conversation on religion to the subject of mathematics, maintaining that "the predominance which in this country is given to mathematical studies in the education of youth, is unfavourable to their best advancement in future life."[2] Mr. Tyler rehearses the various fields in which mathematics is no help to good judgment, along with the reasons for this (the passage on which Poe drew for Dupin's discussion of the topic), and he concludes, interestingly enough for our purposes, with an example of the unsuccessful incursion of mathematics into French politics: "We constantly see results anticipated by the prophetic eye of political wisdom, which strict reason could not educe. . . . The comprehensive generalisation of Napoleon could rarely satisfy with a reason the bigoted scrutiny of that great analyst who 'carried into the cabinet the doctrine of infinitesimals'" (Wallace, 1:209). Wallace does not name the "great analyst" because he undoubtedly assumed that Napoleon's remark was so well known no identification was needed. When Napoleon seized power in 1799, he appointed Laplace minister of the interior. But the new minister was such a stickler for details and, as a result, so complete a failure as an administrator that Napoleon was obliged to replace him after six weeks with his brother Lucien Bonaparte and subsequently explained his firing of the most distinguished mathematician-scientist in France with the remark quoted by Wallace (*EB*, 16:201).

That Wallace had Laplace in mind as an instance of mathematical training undermining good judgment suggests the specific form of mathematics against whose incursion into other fields Wallace inveighs—the calculus of probabilities. In his *Philosophical Essay on Probabilities* Laplace argues for the application of probability theory not only to the physical sciences and games of chance but to "the moral sciences"[3] as well, and he gives examples of the way the calculus of probabilities can be applied to such areas as testimony in court, the selection and decisions of assemblies, and the judgments of tribunals. Indeed, one wonders whether Dupin's argument in "The Purloined Letter" against the applicability of mathematical analysis to questions of morals and motives refers specifically to the calculus of probabilities, given its rather striking lack of success in "The Mystery of Marie Rogêt." One also wonders whether Dupin's position reflects the fact that during the period in which the stories are set the mathematician Charles Dupin was involved in a public debate in France over the application of the calculus of probabilities to the moral sciences. As Florian Cajori notes,

> In 1835 and 1836 the Paris Academy was led by S. D. Poisson's researches to discuss the topic, whether questions of morality could be treated by the theory of probability. M. H. Navier argued on the affirmative, while L. Poinsot and Ch. Dupin denied the applicability as "une sorte d'aberration de l'esprit;" they declared the theory applicable only to cases where a separation and counting of the cases or events was possible.[4]

We should note that the political sentiments expressed in Wallace's *Stanley* reflect the same upper-class concern with the rise of the masses seen earlier in that subliminal drama of high and low from "The Murders in the Rue Morgue." While the remarkable strides made in mathematics in the wake of the French Revolution had the effect of associating the field with the triumph of rationalism and republicanism, this association had changed by the 1830s, as reflected in the evolution of the Polytechnique from a school open to students of any social class to one for the sons of the well-to-do. The main character in *Stanley* contends, "One of the advantages which mathematics has in the present time . . . is its tendency to check and chill the airy dreams of modern philosophy; dreams . . . which are of fatal influence in political action. I should regard as a general blessing any thing which would dispel the heated visions of speculative reform, and arrest the progress of revolution in Europe." To which Mr. Tyler replies, "I look upon the spirit of change as already crushed in the old world, . . . and the destiny of Europe as settled for the next century in favour of conservatism." Tyler argues that "principles so unnational as those of radicalism" could never have succeeded in England, where "patriotism is toryism," and that in America "our experience has shown that a democracy is merely one of the forms of despotism" (Wallace, 1:209). Claiming that there exists in America "a fair prospect of the speedy establishment of a formal monarchy," Tyler rhapsodizes about "what a splendid nation America would become . . . if some great man were to place himself at the head of the government, who should have spirit and the power to strike from the body politic the dull cancer of democracy" (Wallace, 1:209, 211).

Just as Dupin disputes "the value . . . of that reason which is cultivated in any especial form other than the abstractly logical," and in particular that "educed by mathematical study," so Tyler maintains that mathematics, as a means of "cultivating the intellect," is "a study of little value as compared with moral logic" and "is often injurious to the practice of the world" (Wallace, 1:206). The issue for each is whether the best training in logical reasoning is the study of mathematics or the study of logic itself, and at the time Poe and Wallace wrote, this question, much discussed in learned journals of the day, tended to center on the curriculum of Cambridge University. In the January 1836 issue of the *Edinburgh Review*, for example, the Scottish philosopher William Hamilton published a lengthy essay-review of a volume entitled *Thoughts on the Study of Mathematics as a part of a Liberal Education* by the scientist-philosopher William Whewell, a fellow and tutor at Trinity College, Cambridge, or as Hamilton characterizes him, "the principal public tutor of the principal college of his university."[5] As we noted earlier, although Hamilton's work in reforming Aristotelian logic (particularly in the so-called quantification of the predicate) ultimately led, along with the efforts of the mathematicians De Morgan and Boole, to the arithmetization of logic, Hamilton himself was no partisan of mathematics, and in his review of Whewell he addresses himself to the question of "whether . . . the study of mathematics conduces to the developement of the higher faculties." Hamilton censures that "revolutionary tendency . . . regarding the objects and the end of education" that seeks to substitute "the extended study of mathematics" for those "ancient branches of discipline which our innovators would retrench." And he finds the center of this movement to be the university at which Whewell teaches: "In opposition to the general opinion of the learned world . . . , the University of Cambridge stands alone in making mathematical science the principal object of the whole liberal education it affords" (Hamilton, 409).

As the historian Philip Enros notes, the prominence of mathematics in Cambridge's curriculum was one of the two features distinguishing this university from others in Britain. The second was its "final examination, the Senate House examination, which later evolved into the Mathematical Tripos."[6] Young men at Cambridge in the early part of the nineteenth century enrolled in "one of its seventeen colleges" which "controlled to a large extent the instruction of students. Besides classics, college lectures concentrated on mathematics. . . . A fairly good basic training in mathematics was available to, and expected of, almost all Cambridge students enrolled for a Bachelor of Arts degree" (Enros, 138). And the "main motivation" for this knowledge was "the Senate House examination, most of which was devoted to mathematics. The examination was held at the end of . . . about 3¹/₃ years, and was by far the most important and most rigorous test in qualifying for that degree." Enros notes that "although a very little knowledge might suffice for passing in the early nineteenth century, there was no maximum for the competition to be a wrangler, that is, to be in the first class of the honours list. . . . Besides fame and glory the reward for the Cambridge wrangler almost certainly included a valuable college fellowship" (Enros, 139). Thus, William Whewell, for example, who had been "second wrangler in 1816" (*EB*, 28:587), went on to become a fellow and tutor of his college and eventually master in 1841.

In his review of Whewell's book, Hamilton, aiming to refute the notion that "mathematical study" should serve "as the principal mean in the cultivation of the reasoning faculty" (Hamilton, 411), invokes the controversy between algebraists and geometers as part of his argument—a forensic strategy significant for our purposes because of its resemblance to the progress of Dupin's own argument in "The Purloined Letter" as he moves from denying that mathematical reason is "*the* reason *par excellence*," to challenging the identification of analysis with algebra, to disputing "the availability, and thus the value," of the "reason educed by mathematical study." Hamilton notes that while "some intelligent mathematicians" admit that mathematical study is no aid to the higher faculties and may even do harm, other mathematicians

> endeavour to vindicate the study in general, by attributing its evil influence to some peculiar modification of the science; and thus hope to avoid the loss of the whole, by the vicarious sacrifice of a part. But here unfortunately they are not at one. Some are willing to surrender the modern analysis as a gymnastic of the mind . . . [,] its formulae mechanically transporting the student with closed eyes to the conclusion, whereas the geometrical construction leads him to the end, more circuitously indeed, but . . . with a clear consciousness of every step in the procedure. Others, on the contrary, . . . recommend the algebraic process as that most favourable to the powers of generalization and reasoning; for, concentrating into the narrowest compass the greatest complement of meaning, it . . . enables the intellect to operate for a longer continuance, more energetically, securely, and effectually. The arguments in favour of the study, thus neutralize each other. (Hamilton, 411–12)

Hamilton points out that while Whewell is a staunch advocate of mathematical study, he "willingly allows the worst that has been urged against it to be true of certain opinions and practices, to which he is opposed" (Hamilton, 412). But his opposition to these opinions and practices does not seem to reflect, says Hamilton, a bias on Whewell's part in favor of either the geometric or the analytic method. Whether or not this lack of a methodological bias on Whewell's part existed in 1836, there was certainly a bias both earlier and later in his career. For Whewell began as a strong partisan of the analytic method in his student days at Cambridge, only to reverse his position later as he came to question the value of studying analytics in a liberal education.

As we noted earlier, England had lagged behind the Continent in mathematical research during the eighteenth century because English mathematicians had persisted for various reasons "in the geometrical development of the calculus" (Kline, 392). But this situation began to change around 1810 with the introduction of Continental methods and textbooks into the Cambridge curriculum. As we saw, Dionysius Lardner attributed the beginning of this change to the appointment of Bartholomew Lloyd as professor of mathematics at Cambridge in 1811, but an even more important event in creating a new openness to the work of Continental mathematicians was the founding in 1812 of the Analytical Society by three Cambridge undergraduates—George Peacock, J. F. W. Herschel, and Charles Babbage. J. F. W. Herschel, whose father was the eminent eighteenth-century astronomer Sir William Herschel, was senior wrangler in 1813, and Peacock was second wrangler in the same year; while Babbage, who was later to achieve fame for his invention of the calculating engine, was one of the most imaginative young mathematicians enrolled in the university. Much impressed by the teaching of Robert Woodhouse and by his *Principles of Analytical Calculation* published at Cambridge in 1803, the three students agreed to form a society "with the object of advocating the general use in the university of analytical methods and of the differential notation."[7] The Analytical Society published a collection of essays in 1813 and a translation of Lacroix's *Elementary Differential Calculus* in 1816 (Ball, 120, 125), and its members, particularly George Peacock who held the office of moderator in 1818–19 and was by virtue of this an examiner, worked to introduce analytics and the differential notation into the university examination.

As Philip Enros points out, analytics denoted for these young men at Cambridge "a particular style of mathematics" involving "the formal manipulation of equations, or expressions; analytics implied an algebraic . . . operational approach to a topic. The alternative style was synthetics. This was all that was not algebraic. . . . Hence the Newtonian style of the calculus, the theory of fluxions, was synthetic because it involved the idea of motion, a concept which was held as not algebraic" (Enros, 136–37). The most visible sign of the triumph of analytics in the Cambridge curriculum was the eventual supplanting of the Newtonian fluxional notation by the differential. Babbage, "who gave the name to the Analytical Society," had stated that one of the society's goals was "to advocate 'the principles of pure d-ism as opposed to the dot-age of the university'" (Ball, 125), "d-ism" and "dot-age" referring respectively to the characteristic symbols of the differential and the Newtonian notations. In the differential script the letter d is used to signify the operation represented in the Newtonian by the use of a dot above a letter. Thus, for example, the derivative written as $\frac{dz}{dx}$ in the former method would be written as $\dot{z}:\dot{x}$ in the latter.[8] Newton began the use of dots or "pricked letters" in 1665, and this form of notation continued in use in Britain well into the nineteenth century.

Babbage's famous remark about d-ism versus dot-age is significant for our purposes both because the pun on "dotage" evokes the Newtonian fluxional notation as symbolic of an outmoded social and cultural system that is to be reformed out of existence by the young men of the Analytical Society and because the pun on "deism" associates analytics with a world view in which science and logic dictate the shape of religious and political belief, one whose concomitants are rationalism, reform, and republicanism. As the historian of science David Bloor points out, "In the Cambridge context the advocates of symbolical algebra were reformers and radicals. . . . They stood . . . for an end to traditional authority in mathematics teaching. . . . They jokingly looked upon themselves as bringers of light into darkness, as reformers with 'extensive schemes for enlightening and improving the human race,'" as Babbage wrote to Herschel in 1814.[9] Bloor goes on to note that "themes of reform, change and autonomy" characterize "the broader spectrum of attitudes that were adopted by the formalists of the Cambridge group. Babbage is perhaps an extreme case, but he certainly threw himself vigorously into the world of liberal politics and electioneering. . . . Even his theology implies that science is an activity independent of any higher spiritual authority" (Bloor, 224). Indeed, Babbage claimed that it was a religious controversy which originally gave rise to the founding of the Analytical Society. The stimulus was "the founding of the Cambridge branch of the British and Foreign Bible Society" and the subsequent "controversy . . . over whether the Bible should be distributed with or without an accompanying commentary" (Bloor, 223). The Evangelical students opposed a commentary, the High Church group favored one, the point being "whether people could be trusted to reach acceptable conclusions from the Bible when left to their own devices. From the High Church point of view the Evangelicals were dissenters, and little better than the sectarian fanatics of old" (Bloor, 223), the fanatics who overthrew the monarchy and executed the king in the seventeenth century:

> Babbage reports that on hearing about this issue his mind leapt to the idea of a society for distributing copies of Lacroix—one of the French textbooks of analysis. It would be a shining example of the truth which everyone could see for themselves by the light of the reason. The new society, Babbage decided, would maintain "that the work of Lacroix was so perfect that any comment was unnecessary." (Bloor, 223–24)

In wanting to distribute copies of Lacroix without a commentary, Babbage was in effect replicating the position of the Evangelicals in the Bible society controversy, for both the Cambridge formalists and the Evangelicals saw themselves as representing a liberal, or even radical, challenge to established authority. It is perhaps further revealing of Babbage's taste for puns that he chose Lacroix's as the text to occupy within his movement the place held by the Bible in the other, since the name Lacroix in English means "the cross." No wonder, then, that Bloor describes "Babbage's oft-quoted witticism about the Cambridge group advocating 'Pure D-ism'" as "perhaps more than a pun about their mathematical notation" (Bloor, 225). What is most interesting for our purposes in Babbage's using the term *D-ism* to evoke the differential notation and analytics (as well as the association of mathematical reforms at Cambridge with political and religious reforms) is the added resonance this gives to Poe's decision to designate Dupin's antithetical double (who has "written learnedly on the Differential Calculus" and tries to manipulate the royal authority) by the letter *D*.

As a Cambridge undergraduate, William Whewell had been closely associated with the Analytical Society and had helped his friend George Peacock insure the prevalence of differential symbolism in the university examination (symbolism that Peacock had introduced in 1817) by continuing its use during the period when he (Whewell) was an examiner. But while the society succeeded in introducing analytics into the Cambridge mathematical curriculum, the ultimate fate of analytics within that curriculum tended to parallel the political/mathematical shift that occurred in Whewell's own position during his subsequent career at Cambridge, first as tutor of Trinity College and then as master. The undergraduates associated with the Analytical Society were political liberals, but while Whewell "in early life was not altogether averse from the Whig party, which included some of his firmest friends" such as Peacock, "he became in the end a Conservative" (Bloor, 227), gradually moving away from "the symbolical approach in his mathematical writings" (Bloor, 229–30) as well. As Philip Enros points out,

> increasing criticism of Cambridge, particularly in the 1830s and 1840s, gave rise to a defensive reaction within the University. This response manifested itself in mathematical studies by an emphasis in the curriculum on geometry and elementary mathematics and by an assertion of the subservience of mathematics to the goals of intellectual discipline. (Enros, 145–46)

Indeed, the reaction was sufficiently vigorous that "by 1850 Whewell was able to rejoice in the successful checking of the 'mischievous tendency' of analytics" (Enros, 146). What all this makes clear is the shift that occurred in the image of mathematical study in England from the first three decades of the nineteenth century (when mathematics was associated with liberal, not to say radical, political sentiments) to the 1830s and '40s (when it became increasingly associated with conservative social sentiments), a shift reflected by Wallace's remark in *Stanley* (1838) about "one of the advantages" of mathematics "in the present time" being "its tendency to check . . . the airy dreams of modern philosophy" that are "of fatal influence in political action."

Hamilton's review of Whewell is significant for our purposes for several reasons: first, because it shows that the contemporary debate about the place of mathematics in a liberal education was largely a function of mathematics having become synonymous with the study of analytics; second, because Dupin's discussion of mathematics in "The Purloined Letter" parallels Hamilton's in revealing ways and may even echo it at some points (either directly or through Wallace's *Stanley*); and finally, because in associating specifically with Cambridge University this dual question of the place of analytics in a mathematical curriculum and the place of mathematical study in a liberal education, the review recalls another way in which the principal mathematical controversy of the day may have impinged on Poe's schooling.

Poe's formal education in mathematics at the college level seems to have been confined to the period he spent at West Point. In his year at the University of Virginia, Poe took no courses in mathematics, although he does seem to have evinced an interest in the subject and may have studied it informally. Upon entering Virginia in 1826, he enrolled in the Schools of Ancient and Modern Languages, taking courses in Latin and French from two professors. At some point during that year, his foster father John Allan sent him "a packet of books" that included "the Cambridge Mathematics in 2 vols," although Allan did not see fit to provide him with the financial "means of attending the mathematical lectures" (*Letters,*

1:40). In a January 1831 letter upbraiding Allan for this penurious treatment, Poe recalls that though he only had enough money at Virginia "for
attendance upon 2 professors . . . you even then did not miss the opportunity of abusing me because I did not attend 3" (*Letters*, 1:40). And one
assumes, given the books Allan sent him, that this third course of study
expected of Poe was in mathematics. It is worth noting that in a November
1830 letter to Allan from West Point, in which Poe bragged about his class
standing, he asked his foster father to send him "a Box of Mathematical
Instruments" and this same "copy of the Cambridge Mathematics" (*Letters*, 1:38).

The Cambridge Mathematics or, more accurately, the Cambridge
Course in Mathematics took its name not from Cambridge University in
England but from Cambridge, Massachusetts, and referred to a series of
English translations of mathematical works (mostly French) done by John
Farrar, professor of mathematics and natural philosophy at Harvard Col-
lege. Farrar, "the first American . . . to place translations of Continental
works on mathematics in the hands of students in the New World," pub-
lished in 1818 translations of S. F. Lacroix's *Elements of Algebra* and *An
Elementary Treatise on Arithmetic*, in 1819 a translation of Legendre's *Geometry*, and in 1820 a translation of Lacroix's *Trigonometry* (Cajori, 128–29).
Cajori remarks that "Farrar's translations and selections from French
authors" were used as textbooks "at the U. S. Military Academy and at the
University of Virginia" (Cajori, 130).

Since Poe had a copy of the Cambridge Mathematics as an undergraduate at Virginia and since, to judge from his January 1831 letter to
Allan, it was his foster father's wish (and perhaps his own as well) that he
study mathematics in addition to languages, it would not have been extraordinary for Poe to ask one of his fellow students at Virginia who was
enrolled in the mathematical lectures either to help him make his way
through the texts in the Cambridge Mathematics or to lend him his lecture notes. If this had been the case, or even if Poe's mathematical interests had led to nothing more formal than conversations with fellow students equally interested in the subject, he would have found that
mathematical instruction at Virginia was dominated by the curriculum of
Cambridge University. Thomas Hewett Key, the professor of mathematics at the time Poe attended Virginia, was a graduate of Trinity College,
Cambridge; and the professor of natural philosophy, Charles Bonnycastle, although educated at the Royal Military Academy at Woolwich, belonged "to that coterie of English mathematicians of which Herschel,
Peacock, Whewell, and others were members, and which introduced the
Leibnitzian notation . . . into Cambridge" (Cajori, 192). The textbooks
Bonnycastle used in his courses when he succeeded Key as professor of

mathematics in 1827 clearly indicate his affinity with the goals of the Cambridge Analytical Society: "The text-books . . . in pure mathematics . . . were the Arithmetic, Algebra, and Differential Calculus of Lacroix, the first two in Farrar's translation" (Cajori, 193). The *Arithmetic* and *Algebra* of Lacroix were, of course, both included in the two-volume Cambridge Mathematics that Poe had with him at the university. One can see, then, that whatever exposure Poe might have had at Virginia to mathematical discussions with, or informal instruction from, his fellow students, these would almost certainly have been influenced (because of the presence of Key and Bonnycastle) by the kinds of questions that had been raised by the Analytical Society's efforts to reform the mathematics curriculum at Cambridge, questions about the relative merits of algebra versus geometry (analytics versus synthetics), about whether the study of mathematics was the best training for logical reasoning (better than the study of logic itself), and about the place of mathematical study in a liberal education if that study had become solely a matter of analytics.

37 *Bryant's* Mythology; *Mathematical and Linguistic Roots;*
Quadratic Equations; The Diagonal of a Square; Euclid,
the Pythagoreans, and Incommensurability; Even and Odd;
Reductio ad Absurdum *and* Reductio ad Infinitum

WHAT SHOULD BE CLEAR BY this point is not just the variety and extent of Poe's mathematical education and thus his exposure to the various issues implicit in Dupin's digression on mathematics in "The Purloined Letter," but also the extent to which these mathematical issues (with their political and religious resonances) were discussed and written about in Poe's day—so much so that when Poe began the Dupin stories by pointing out the difficulty inherent in analyzing the analytical power, he must have been aware that for most of his educated readers the contemporary associations of the word *analysis* would have been largely mathematical. Clearly, Poe felt the need to reclaim the word for an older, wider range of meaning. And his solution was, on the one hand, to argue the case for the word's primary philosophical sense, while, on the other, to enact literally its philological sense through the suggested application of etymological analysis to mathematical terms such as *algebra*. By introducing a quotation from Jacob Bryant's *Mythology* into his discussion of mathematics, Poe emphasizes this latter method of questioning the solely mathematical sense of the word *analysis* in the tale. For anyone familiar with Bryant's work knows that its correct title is not simply *Mythology* but rather *A New System, or, An Analysis of Ancient Mythology* (1774) and that Bryant's method of examining ancient myths is to carry out a minute, albeit at times fanciful, etymological analysis of "ancient names."[1] He notes that these "names seem to be composed of the same, or similar, elements; and bear a manifest relation to the religion in use among the Amonians, and to the Deity, whom they adored. This Deity was the Sun" (Bryant, 1:xv).

Bryant begins his work with a section entitled "Radicals"—a "list of some Amonian terms, which occur in the mythology of Greece; and in the histories of other nations." To each of these radicals Bryant subjoins "a short interpretation" and "examples of names, and titles, which are thus compounded," and he adds, "From hence the Reader will see plainly my method of analysis; and the basis of my etymological enquiries" (Bryant, 1:xv). He follows this with a brief essay entitled "Of Etymology, As it has been too generally handled," and then goes on to apply his own methods of linguistic analysis to mythology to show that its proper names can all be reduced to one of forty-odd roots and that these can all be reduced in turn to a narrow group of meanings such as heat, light, a place of solar worship, and so on, all referring ultimately to the pagan concept of a single solar deity. Indeed, one might remark, considering the structure underlying Borges's three detective stories, that part of the burden of Bryant's work is to uncover the hidden red king who lies at the root of all pagan mythology. Bryant's book, which went through three editions between 1774 and 1807, was highly influential during the late eighteenth and early nineteenth centuries, particularly in literary circles. As Burton Feldman notes, echoes of Bryant's work can be found throughout Blake's poetry, while "Bryant's discussions of mythic zodiacal astronomy show in Shelley's 'Alastor,'" and "Bryant's discussion of sunworship" in Coleridge's "The Wanderings of Cain" and "Kubla Khan" (Bryant, 1:vi).

Certainly, Bryant's book and its method of etymological analysis were well enough known in Poe's day that he would have expected his readers to get the point of Dupin's invoking the work in a discussion of mathematical analysis, expected them to understand that to say "Bryant's 'Mythology'" in such a context was to say "linguistic analysis and etymological roots," as opposed to "mathematical analysis and the roots of an equation." Thus by applying specifically to mathematicians Bryant's remark about people who make inferences from pagan fables, Poe in effect suggests that just as Bryant used etymological analysis on the proper names of ancient mythology, so he (Poe) applies the same type of analysis to the language and symbols of modern mathematical mythology, a point he immediately underlines with a turn on the dual mathematical and philological senses of the word *root*. Dupin says,

> "With the algebraists . . . who are Pagans themselves, the 'Pagan fables' *are* believed, and the inferences are made, not so much through lapse of memory, as through an unaccountable addling of the brains. In short, I never yet encountered the mere mathematician who could be trusted out of equal roots, or one who did not clandestinely hold it as a point of his faith that $x^2 + px$ was absolutely and unconditionally equal to q. Say to one of these gentlemen, by way of experiment, if you please, that you believe occasions may occur where $x^2 + px$ is *not* altogether equal to q, and, having made him understand what you mean, get out of his reach as speedily as convenient, for, beyond doubt, he will endeavor to knock you down.
>
> "I mean to say," continued Dupin, while I merely laughed at his last observations, "that if the Minister had been no more than a mathematician, the Prefect would have been under no necessity of giving me this check. I knew him, however, as both mathematician and poet, and my measures were adapted to his capacity." (3:988)

Dupin's remark about "equal roots" assumes the reader's knowledge of the two senses in which *root* is used in mathematics. First of all, it refers to "a number, quantity, or dimension, which, when multiplied by itself a requisite number of times, produces a given expression" as, for example, a square root, a cube root, and so on; and second, it refers to "the value or values of an unknown quantity which will satisfy a given equation" (*OED*, 2:2574) as, for example, in the expression "to solve for the roots of an equation." That Poe had both of these meanings in mind is clear from the fact that Dupin immediately introduces into his argument an algebraic equation—$x^2 + px = q$—whose solution or root involves solving for a square root. But it is equally clear that in using the word *root* in this passage, Poe expects the reader to register its philological sense as well: "one of those ultimate elements of a language, that cannot be further analyzed, and form the base of its vocabulary; a primary word or form from which others are derived" (*OED*, 2:2574). For Dupin's lengthy digression on mathematics begins, of course, with his suggesting (through the citation of three English words, each differing significantly in meaning from its Latin root) that the linguistic equation the algebraists have made between the words *analysis* and *algebra* is an equation that, if subjected to etymological analysis, is found to be based on unequal roots— the original meaning of one word being "to take apart," that of the other "to put together." Dupin's remark about mere mathematicians who cannot be "trusted out of equal roots" seems, then, to be a subtle comment on this false linguistic equation.

The point of the remark depends as well on the reader's understanding the difference between equations with equal roots and those with unequal ones. The equation $x^2 - 2x + 1 = 0$, for example, has equal roots in that it can be factored into $(x - 1) \cdot (x - 1) = 0$, and the single value $x = 1$ makes both factors vanish. In factoring this equation, we have, so to speak, found its square root, which is to say, found the expression which, when multiplied by itself one time, produces $x^2 - 2x + 1$; and the roots are "equal" precisely because a single value of x satisfies the equation. In contrast, an equation such as $x^2 - x = 0$ can be factored into $(x - 0) \cdot (x - 1) = 0$, where the expressions $(x - 0)$ and $(x - 1)$ are obviously not equal, and the equation has in consequence two solutions or roots, two values of x ($x = 0$, $x = 1$) that satisfy the condition $x^2 - x = 0$.

The wit of Dupin's remark also depends on the reader's knowing that equations with equal roots are, generally speaking, less complicated and therefore easier to solve than those with unequal roots but also that the former are less common than the latter and thus less important mathematically. Claiming in effect, then, that a mere mathematician can be trusted only in simple tasks with limited applicability, Dupin goes on to cite an example of a mere mathematician's simple trust in basic formulas—the belief that $x^2 + px$ is "absolutely and unconditionally equal" to q. Given that Poe wrote his stories with a poet's attention to detail, the specificity of this equation suggests that he intended his readers to recognize its significance. Yet even if the reader fails to recognize the equation, he still understands the rhetorical point of Dupin's remark about not denying its unconditional status in the presence of a mere mathematician unless one is prepared to be knocked down. Which is to say that whatever this particular equation means, it is obviously cited by Dupin as "a paradigm of elementary correctness," to use the classicist Walter Burkert's phrase, cited as an algebraic expression so basic and self-evident that, like the arithmetical expression $2 + 2 = 4$, the attempt to deny it is virtually a sign of madness in oneself and capable of inciting madness in others. We can also see that Poe's point in questioning the equation's unconditional status is (as with his denying of a basic principle of probability theory for the calculation of odds at the end of "Marie Rogêt") an attempt to distinguish the mere mathematician's slavish adherence to accepted principles from the true mathematician's intuitive ability to question such givens, no matter how irrational that might seem, in search of a higher understanding. All of which is clear from the passage, whether one recognizes the equation or not. But the question still remains: what is the expression $x^2 + px = q$ that Poe should invoke it as a paradigm of elementary correctness, and what, if any, is its specific significance for his story of the purloined letter?

To answer the first part of this question, we must turn to that compendium of mathematical texts Poe owned as a student at the University of Virginia and later asked his foster father to send him when he was a cadet at West Point—John Farrar's "Cambridge Course in Mathematics," and specifically Farrar's translation of S. F. Lacroix's *Elements of Algebra*. That Poe was well acquainted with this work seems certain, since it was the required text in elementary algebra for first-year students at the U.S. Military Academy when he was enrolled there. Discussing equations of the second degree with one unknown, Lacroix writes, "Any equation whatever of the second degree may be resolved, by referring it to the general formula $x^2 + px = q$."[2] Since the mathematical expression Dupin cites in his argument is not some random collection of letters and numbers but a well-established formula for solving quadratic equations, Poe probably intends it to evoke the general notion "quadratic equation" in much the same way that his earlier reference to "Bryant's 'Mythology'" was meant to evoke the concepts "linguistic analysis and etymological roots" in the midst of his discussion of mathematical analysis and the roots of equations. But why would Poe want to call our attention to the notion of a quadratic equation, particularly when he has Dupin immediately question this formula's unconditional status, has him theorize within a paradigm of elementary correctness and logical rigor a possible irruption of the alogical (i.e., that it may not always be true that $x^2 + px = q$)? Which is to ask, in effect, what the notion of a quadratic equation has to do with the story of the purloined letter.

In addressing this question, it seems only appropriate, given the context in which Poe introduces the formula, that we start with a linguistic analysis of the word *quadratic* to discover why equations of the second degree (equations containing a mathematical expression of the form x^2) are so named. The word derives from the past participle of the Latin verb *quadrare* ("to make square"), from the noun *quadrus* ("a square"), and ultimately from the Latin *quattuor* ("four") (*W*, 1188). There lies behind the term, then, both a geometric figure and a number, and clearly the use of the term to designate equations of the second degree derives from the fact that one finds the area of a rectangle by multiplying the lengths of two of its adjacent sides by each other, an operation that in the case of a square involves multiplying a number by itself, "squaring" it.

Now if the algebraic formula Poe introduces into the text is meant to evoke the general notion "quadratic equation" along with its implicit relationship to the figure of a square, then we must ask ourselves whether, considering the undercurrent of imaginative associations Poe creates in his lengthy digression on mathematics, there exists some other aspect of a square that corresponds to, and is thus meant to be evoked by, Poe's denial of the formula's unconditional status, by his associating with this elementary paradigm of logical rigor and mathematical certainty the possibility of an irrational incursion, of a destabilizing uncertainty or indeterminacy at the geometrical figure's core. Put that way, the answer seems obvious. For if we consider the relationship between a square's side and its diagonal, the figure of a square contains within itself, indeed is bisected by, an irrational element—a diagonal line whose length is arithmetically incommensurable with the length of the square's side.

As we recall from the Pythagorean theorem, in a right triangle the square on the hypotenuse is equal to the sum of the squares on the two sides. Since the diagonal of a square bisects it into two isosceles right triangles, the diagonal is the hypotenuse of each; and its length can be determined accordingly. For example, in a square the length of whose side is 1, the diagonal is the $\sqrt{2}$. But the $\sqrt{2}$ is an irrational number. It cannot be expressed as a whole number or as the ratio of two whole numbers. In decimal form, it can be carried out to an infinite number of places (1.4142135 . . .) without coming out even. Thus, a square—the classical perfect figure, a traditional image of rectitude and stability proverbially evoked in such phrases as "on the square" or "a square deal"—contains at its heart a quantity that, as regards commensuration, opens up an infinite abyss into which certainty leaks away. Since irrationality inhabits, not to say bisects, the figure of a square, Dupin's questioning of the unconditional status of the formula $x^2 + px = q$ may reflect Poe's sense that the indeterminacy associated with the geometrical figure extends as well to the form of algebraic expression that both derives its name from the figure and involves solving for square roots.

The specific case of incommensurability cited above is not, of course, an instance chosen at random but a well-known classical example associated with the supposed discovery of irrationals by the Pythagoreans. In his edition of Euclid's *Elements*, Sir Thomas Heath notes that whatever the opinions of ancient writers may have been concerning the discovery of the so-called Pythagorean theorem, there seems to have been general agreement among them "that the *Pythagoreans* discovered the irrational" and that "everything goes to show that this discovery of the irrational was made with reference to $\sqrt{2}$, the ratio of the diagonal of a square to its side."[3] In his introductory note to Book X, Heath continues,

> The first scholium on Book X of the *Elements* states that the Pythagoreans were the first to address themselves to the investigation of commensurability. . . . The scholium quotes further the legend according to which "the first of the Pythagoreans who made public the investigation of these matters perished in a shipwreck," conjecturing that the authors of this story "perhaps spoke allegorically, hinting that everything irrational and formless is properly concealed, and, if any soul should rashly invade this region of life and lay it open, it would be carried away into the sea of becoming and be overwhelmed by its unresting currents." There would be a reason also for keeping the discovery of irrationals secret for the time in the fact that it rendered unstable so much of the groundwork of geometry as the Pythagoreans had based upon the imperfect theory of proportions which applied only to numbers. (Heath, 3:1)

Clearly, the subject of Pythagoreanism is relevant to our discussion of Poe's mathematical knowledge on several counts. First, if one had to characterize the blend of mathematical and poetic skill Poe associates with the true mathematician, one could hardly do better than the word *Pythagorean*. Indeed, one can easily imagine the author of *Eureka* being particularly attracted to the blend of mathematics and mysticism Pythagorean philosophy represents, and in fact Poe refers to Pythagoras or the Pythagoreans at various points in his writing with what seems to be a general awareness of their doctrines. In the *Marginalia*, for example, Poe cites "Pythagoras' definition of beauty" as "the reduction of many into one";[4] and in "Morella" he says that one of the ongoing topics of conversation between the narrator and his wife was "the modified Παλιγγενεσια of the

Pythagoreans" (2:230), which is to say, palingenesis or reincarnation.

This latter example is significant for our purposes because it suggests one of the ways in which the subject of Pythagoreanism may have become linked in Poe's mind with the detective story. Clearly, Poe was influenced in the creation of the detective story's triangular structure (in which doubling connects the three principal roles of criminal, victim, and detective) by the two related but distinct types of double stories he had been writing in the late 1830s: on the one hand, the dying woman stories with their male/female doubling in which the male is psychologically victimized by the female and the female physically victimized by the male, and on the other, a story such as "William Wilson" with its male/male doubling in which the good self hunts down the bad. Poe seems to have created the detective story structure by combining these two types of doubling to produce the male/female pairing of criminal and victim and the male/male pairing of detective and criminal. "Morella" is, of course, one of the principal dying woman stories, and the subject of these stories (the form of the self's possible survival after death) is closely related to the subject of the detective stories (the analysis of the self's structure), there being a natural connection between the notion of the self's destiny as an endless return (reincarnation) and the concept of the self's structure as essentially reflexive. Consequently, since Poe associated the Pythagorean notion of reincarnation with the former subject (as the narrator's comment in "Morella" about palingenesis indicates), it is not surprising that a Pythagorean element should be present in the detective tales which developed from these earlier exercises in doubling. Indeed, the presence of such an element is especially likely if, as I have suggested, a Platonic trajectory runs across the Dupin stories, a trajectory that figures the self's structure (within the arc of its movement from the real to the ideal world in the allegory of the cave) as that of a bodily entity whose shape has been idea-lized (i.e., dematerialized and schematized, in effect, rendered two-dimensional) to produce the mathematical-geometrical "givens" of consciousness. For, of course, in Plato the markers of this ideal world are precisely those elements in his work that have traditionally been identified as Pythagorean—the blend of mathematics, geometry, and mysticism that one finds, for example, in the *Timaeus*.

There are, as we said, several reasons for introducing the subject of Pythagoreanism into our discussion of Poe's mathematical knowledge. The most immediately relevant of these is the association of the Pythagoreans with the notion of the irrational and thus the possible connection between their discovery of irrationality through the incommensurability of a square's diagonal and Dupin's remark questioning the unconditional status of a quadratic equation. In his edition of Euclid's *Elements*, Sir Thomas Heath notes that

> the actual method by which the Pythagoreans proved the incommensurability of $\sqrt{2}$ with unity [in a square whose side was 1 and diagonal the $\sqrt{2}$] was no doubt that referred to by Aristotle (*Anal. prior.* I.23, 41a 26–7), a *reductio ad absurdum* by which it is proved that, if the diagonal is commensurable with the side, it will follow that the same number is both odd and even. The proof formerly appeared in the texts of Euclid as X. 117. (Heath, 3:2)

In Aristotle's mind the *reductio ad absurdum* (or proof *per impossibile*) and the incommensurability of the diagonal seem to have been closely related notions. In the passage from the *Prior Analytics* Heath cites, Aristotle says,

> All who reach a conclusion *per impossibile* infer by syllogism what is false, proving by a hypothetical argument the original proposition, when something impossible results from assuming its contradictory; e.g. they prove that the diagonal of a square is incommensurable with its side by showing that, if it is assumed to be commensurable, odd numbers will be equal to even.[5]

Later in the *Prior Analytics* (I. 44. 50a 35–38), he again links the two notions in virtually the same terms, while in the *Posterior Analytics* (I. 33. 89a 29) he says that "the idea that you can have a true opinion that the diagonal is commensurable is absurd" (*Math.*, 23).

Certainly, Aristotle's linking of the *reductio ad absurdum* with the incommensurability of the diagonal was due in part to the fact that the proof of the latter in Book X of Euclid's *Elements* was undoubtedly the best-known example of the argument by *reductio* in the ancient world (as it is in the modern). But there was probably another reason for Aristotle's frequently associating the two, for they both have to do, in different but related ways, with the concept of the irrational or alogical. Indeed, we might say that in one case we have a reduction to the absurd in terms of logical reasoning, while in the other we have a reduction to a surd in terms of mathematical quantities. In mathematics the word *surd*, meaning an "irrational number or quantity, especially a root," derives from the Latin *surdus* ("deaf," "silent," "indistinct"). As the *OED* points out, "The mathematical sense 'irrational' arises from L. *surdus* being used to render Gk. ἄλογος (Euclid bk x. Def.)" (*OED*, 2:3171). And of course the word *absurd*, in the sense of something illogical or unreasonable, derives from this same Latin root. There would seem, then, to be a natural symmetry between the fact of the incommensurability of a square's diagonal and the form of its proof in Euclid: In one case, the reasoning process is pushed to the point where reason contradicts itself, where rationality begins to dissolve; in the other, the mathematical process is pushed to the point where numeration, in pursuing the exact determination of a quantity such as $\sqrt{2}$, sees itself start to vanish in the endlessly receding vista of infinite decimal places.

That the *reductio ad absurdum* and the *reductio ad infinitum* are related logical figures is something Aristotle himself implies in the *Prior Analytics* (II. 17. 65b 16–21) when he links the proof of incommensurability to Zeno's infinite regress. He remarks,

> To assign the not-cause as cause is just this: suppose, for example, that a person wishing to prove that the diagonal is incommensurable should attempt to apply the argument of Zeno that motion is impossible, and should reduce the impossibility (that the diagonal should be commensurable) to *this*; for the false conclusion (of Zeno) is not connected in any way whatever with the original assumption. (*Math.*, 30)

Heath notes that the meaning of the passage is not entirely clear and that "the Greek commentators do not throw much light" on it (*Math.*, 30). However, Heath thinks that

> Aristotle's remark may point to some genuine attempt to prove the incommensurability of the diagonal by means of a real "infinite regression" of Zeno's type. Euclid, in fact, succeeded in proving (in Book X) the property of the incommensurable by an "infinite regression," but found the correct result whereas Zeno deduced an incorrect one. Euclid proves in his Prop. 2 of Book X that, if we apply to two incommensurable magnitudes the process of finding the greatest common measure, the process will never come to an end. His proof by *reductio ad absurdum* shows that, if the process *did* come to an end, the magnitudes would be commensurable and not incommensurable. It seems, therefore, as if the argument referred to by Aristotle, beginning with the assumption that the diagonal is commensurable with the side of a square, revealed some "infinite regress," and it was then inferred that Zeno's argument, as, for example, in the *Achilles*, to prove that motion is impossible (which is, of course, absurd), would apply in this case. (*Math.*, 31)

Aristotle's linking of the incommensurability of the diagonal (and its associated geometric figuration ▱) with Zeno's notion of an infinite regress along a straight line (the Achilles paradox) would seem to shed light on Borges's strategy at the end of "Death and the Compass." There, Lönnrot proposes that Scharlach, in their next "incarnation" (a Pythagorean metempsychosis, no doubt), trap him by using not a four-sided labyrinth (made up of two equilateral triangles sharing the same base ◇) but a straight-line labyrinth (which Borges says in the concluding note "comes out of Zeno the Eleatic" [*A*, 269]). Earlier we had pointed out that just as the movement from three sides to four in Borges's diamond-shaped maze adumbrates an infinite progression toward totality, so the movement involved in halving the straight line's length, then halving the half, and so on adumbrates an infinite regression to indivisibility, the two alternatives representing for Lönnrot different pathways to an ultimate unity. What strikes one, of course, is the resemblance between Borges's diamond-shaped maze and the geometrical shape associated with the Pythagorean proof of incommensurability. Each is a four-sided figure containing a straight line that bisects a pair of opposing angles and divides the figure into two identical triangles, the only differences being that the square has four equal angles and is differently oriented on the page. Indeed, were it rotated 90 degrees, it could just as easily be described as diamond-shaped. Given, then, the resemblance between the two figures and given Borges's encyclopedic reading, one wonders whether some memory of Aristotle's having linked the diagonal's incommensurability to Zeno's infinite regress suggested the shift at the end of "Death and the Compass" from the figure of a four-sided labyrinth to that of a single straight-line maze. We will, of course, have more to say about these geometric figures and their manipulation presently, but for the moment we must turn our attention to discovering the link between the notion of incommensurability (evoked by the Pythagorean proof of the diagonal's irrationality) and Dupin's questioning of the unconditional status of a quadratic equation that culminates his digression on mathematics in "The Purloined Letter."

38 *Even and/or Odd; A Figure of God's Relation to the Universe; A Geometric Image of the Self; The Alogical Ground of the Self; Coincidence at Infinity; Other Geometries; Logic and Reality-Correspondence*

IF DUPIN'S QUESTIONING OF THE quadratic equation's absolute status in "The Purloined Letter" is meant to evoke that element of incommensurability or alogicality lying at the core of the geometric figure from which the equation's name derives, then what point does Poe mean to make by this? To answer this question, we must remember that the immediate context of Dupin's mathematical digression is his explanation of the way one doubles the thought processes of an opponent in order to be one up on him, as specifically illustrated by the children's game of even and odd. We noted earlier the importance of this game within the tale. It serves not only as an illustration of Dupin's analytic method but also as a linguistic clue to his motive for involving himself in the affair: his desire to get even with a person with whom he has been at odds. We also noted the game's place in the numerical-geometrical structure of the tale: the fact that the prefect first pronounces the affair of the letter a "*very* simple" matter only to reverse himself immediately and describe it as "excessively *odd*"; Dupin's emphasizing the contradictoriness of the prefect's remarks by repeating the words "simple and odd" and thus preparing the reader to hear the phrase's resemblance to the "game of 'even and odd,'" a resemblance underlined by Dupin's remarking that "this game is simple"; the fact that together the two pairs of words (simple/odd, even/odd) reproduce the three/four structure in which three things are made to fill four spaces by doubling one of them; and finally the fact that at the root of each word lies a number (simple: one; even: two; odd: three). However, what we have not noted so far is that the *name* of the "game of 'even and odd'" is itself odd. Surely it should be called the game of even or odd, for in playing it one is never given the opportunity to choose both even and odd but only one or the other, as Dupin makes clear when he tells the narrator that the boy holding the marbles always asks, "Are they even or odd?" (3:984).

In naming the game, then, did Poe like Homer simply nod, or is there some deeper point here? Obviously the form "even and odd" more closely resembles the phrase "simple and odd," increasing the probability of the reader's noticing the link between the two; and this was surely part of Poe's

378

intention. But there is also probably a subtler reason for his choice of the name, for although the phrase does not describe the actual either/or alternative faced by the players, it does describe the oddly contradictory but highly successful analytic method of that schoolboy whose skill allows him to win all the marbles, his ability simultaneously to identify his intellect with those of his opponents (making his mind in effect even with theirs) and yet to end up always one jump ahead of them (adding, as it were, one to that evenness to make it odd). As we noted earlier, what Dupin has to say about the process of doubling an opponent's thoughts, especially as illustrated by this game, applies less to the confrontation of two opposing minds than to the essentially oppositional character of individual self-consciousness.

Given this larger frame of reference for the game of even and odd and given that the game forms part of the context for Dupin's digression on mathematics, Dupin's questioning the unconditional status of a quadratic equation (considered as an allusion to the incommensurability inhabiting the geometric figure from which its name derives) becomes easier to understand. For, as we noted, the Pythagorean proof of incommensurability from Book X of Euclid is a *reductio ad absurdum* demonstrating that if the diagonal and side of a square *are* commensurable, then the same number (the side's length) must be both even and odd. And it would have been no great associative leap for Poe to go from Dupin's game of even and odd (in which self-consciousness's interplay of sameness and difference is figured by the schoolboy's contradictory analytic position) to the notion of incommensurability as represented by a classic mathematical proof (in which logic itself is reduced to absurdity if a square's side and diagonal are commensurable and thus the same number both even and odd). And this imaginative leap from Dupin's game to Euclid's proof seems even more likely when we recall that the geometric figure associated with the proof of incommensurability is also a traditional figure of the self. Whether it is Plato in the *Protagoras* quoting Simonides on the "foursquare" character of the just man and thus imaging human rectitude as geometric rectification, or the writers of the Neoplatonic tradition arraying the human body within a square and thus approximating its proportions to the tetrad of the elements, directions, or seasons, this figurative association is a well-established element in idealist philosophy.

Earlier we noted that in those cabalistic diagrams that superimpose a square and its diagonals on the image of a body, the X shape formed by the diagonals corresponded to the body's outstretched limbs and seemed to suggest a further correspondence between the mirror-fold structure of the body's right and left sides and the two identical triangles formed by each diagonal. And in fact the figure of a quadrangle produced by the "unfolding" of two overlapping triangles sharing a single base line is a fairly common image in cabalistic literature for the mirror relationship between the triune God and His creation. Recall that in "Death and the Compass" Lönnrot discovers the location of the fourth event in the series by projecting a second triangle downward from the "equilateral and mystical" one inscribed on the map, that fourth point where, as Lönnrot still believes at this juncture in the story, he will learn God's secret name and perhaps have an unmediated encounter with the deity. Borges gives us a clue to the type of cabalistic design on which Scharlach's labyrinth is based when he tells us that among the books written by Rabbi Yarmolinsky and found in his room at the time of his death was "a *Study of the Philosophy of Robert Fludd*" (A, 67), the seventeenth-century English physician and Christian cabalist whose work on geomancy ("a method of divination by means of marking the earth with a pointed stick" [Poe, 2:420 n. 20]) Poe had included a century earlier in his catalogue of Roderick Usher's favorite reading (2:409). In Fludd's major work, *Utriusque cosmi majoris scilicet et minoris metaphysica, physica atque technica historia* (1617–19), we find a geometric diagram illustrating the relationship between God and the universe (see fig. 38.1).[1]

At the center of the upper triangle (whose angles represent the three persons of the Trinity) is the Tetragrammaton, and along one side a Latin legend reading "That most divine and beautiful counterpart visible below in the flowing image [mirror] of the universe" (Heninger, 83). In the lower triangle are "the three regions of the universe—empyreal, ethereal, and elemental" which correspond to "the triangular form of the trinitarian deity," and along one side of this is the Latin legend: "A shadow, likeness, or reflection of the insubstantial [incomprehensible] triangle visible in the image [mirror] of the universe," the lower triangle being "a projection of an idea" in the divine mind and thus a mirror image of the deity (Heninger, 83–84). Surrounding both triangles is a flamelike effulgence suggesting at once the radiant nature of this Platonic projection or emanation, the symbolic character of the deity as fire or pure light (mind), and the traditional imagistic association (going back at least to the Egyptians) of the triangle with the tip of a flame (pyramid and obelisk being stone flames above a grave) and thus with eternal life.

One finds this same diamond-shaped figure composed of an upper and lower triangle in the medieval painting that adorns the inside of the wooden canopy above the tomb of the Black Prince in Canterbury Cathedral (see fig. 38.2). Although the ornate scalloping surrounding the figure of God the Father partially obscures the diamond shape, it increases the sense of the fold across the middle of the figure's body, a fold that, in being unfolded, has created the above/below symmetry in which the circular

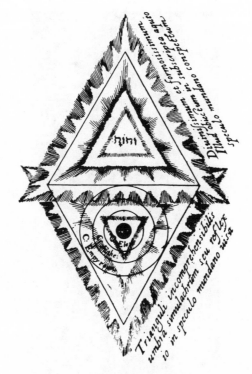

Figure 38.1

globe of the universe at His feet corresponds to the circular nimbus around His head (appropriately so, since the universe is simply a projection of an idea in His mind). And this symmetry is further heightened by the correspondence, first, between the figure's upraised hands and its outstretched feet and, second, between the two pairs of animals at the top and bottom of the painting (each symbolic of one of the four Evangelists).

Since an "unfolded" quadrangle is a common figuration in the Neo-platonic tradition for God's mirroring of Himself in the universe, it would have required no great imaginative leap for Poe to associate this figure (depicting the relationship of Absolute Mind and contingent matter) with that of a square bisected by its diagonals and superimposed upon the image of a body in the same occult geometrical tradition. No great imaginative leap, that is, for him to think of the square's diagonal as a fold between two identical triangles and thus to associate this fold both with the body's bilateral asymmetry and the reflexive structure of self-consciousness. And clearly Poe's further point in associating *this* geometric figure with the same figure from the Pythagorean proof of incommensurability is that there exists an analogy between the odd character of the square's diagonal in each case. In the former, the diagonal fold creates a reflexive

Figure 38.2

structure that, in its oscillation between unfolded and folded states, is both even and odd, four-sided and three-sided; while in the latter, the diagonal is mathematically incommensurable (and thus logically noncontradictory) only if the same numerical quantity (the side's length) *cannot be* both even and odd. What this analogy between the two diagonals does, then, is to associate the reflexive principle that grounds the structure of self-consciousness with the notion of alogicality, suggesting that this principle, while serving as the basis for the system of logic created within self-consciousness, itself transcends (in its interplay of sameness and difference, evenness and oddness, of one and more than one) the law of noncontradiction.

Or, to put it another way, the reflexive principle represents a transcendent logic in much the same way that (recalling Aristotle's association of the Pythagorean proof of incommensurability with Zeno's paradoxes of infinite regression) a square's diagonal is commensurable with its side at infinity. Which is to say, the length of the diagonal will be commensurable at the point where its numerical value has been carried out to an infinite number of decimal places. One also assumes, given the *reductio-ad-absurdum* form of the proof of incommensurability in Euclid, that if diagonal and side are commensurable at infinity, then the same number (the side's length) will be both even and odd at infinity as well. This way of phrasing the matter is, of course, formed by analogy with a more familiar type of mathematical statement: parallel lines meet at infinity. What the use of the term *infinity* unconsciously (and sometimes not so unconsciously) figures in such contexts is the dominance of mind over matter; the concept of infinity serving in effect as a marker of the mind's transcendence of the three-dimensional world in much the same way that, in relation to the folding and refolding of the purloined letter, the oscillation of inner and outer and the reversal of handedness do.

We should note that during the 1830s and '40s when Poe was writing his tales, three mathematicians—the German Carl Friedrich Gauss, the Russian Nikolai Lobatchevsky, and the Hungarian Wolfgang Bolyai—working separately on the problem of Euclid's parallel axiom, "grasped the idea," as Morris Kline remarks, "that there could be a logical geometry in which Euclid's parallel postulate did not hold" (Kline, 871). They saw that it was possible to construct logically consistent geometries other than the Euclidean. Moreover, Gauss was the first to realize that non-Euclidean geometries could "be used to describe the properties of physical space as accurately as Euclidean geometry does," understanding that the latter was "not the necessary geometry of physical space" and that its physical truth could not be "guaranteed on any a priori grounds" (Kline, 869–70). As Kline notes, Euclidean geometry had been considered "the correct idealization of physical space . . . from 300 B.C. to about 1800" (Kline, 863), and the realization that alternative geometries were possible which violated neither logic nor reality-correspondence caused subtle but important changes to both these concepts. As Euclid's geometry had for two millennia been considered "the correct idealization of space," so it had also been considered synonymous with logic, being in effect the commonly available paradigm of logical proof. The understanding that in the field of geometry the domain of Euclid's *Elements* and the domain of logic did not absolutely coincide, that the domain of logic was larger than had been thought, able to accommodate other geometric representations of the world, led to a sense that the domain of logic was itself being extended as these non-Euclidean geometries were developed. (As we saw, it was in this same period of the nineteenth century that formal logic, through the work of Hamilton, Boole, and De Morgan, was undergoing its most sweeping revision since Aristotle.)

And just as the logical consistency of non-Euclidean geometries seemed to put in play the old stable relationship between geometry and logic, so the validity of these geometries as descriptions of physical space also put in play the relationship between logic and reality-correspondence. For if there are any number of logically consistent geometries that are as accurate descriptions of reality as the Euclidean (and some even more accurate when it comes to astronomical calculations), then no one of these systems is a necessary rendering of reality, an insight that suggests that the domain of reality-correspondence exceeds the domain of logic.

Such insights have long been associated with mystical philosophy and religion. But in the first half of the nineteenth century the changes that occurred in mathematics and formal logic were such that a relatively knowledgeable layman like Poe could quite understandably have felt that even in these decidedly nonmystical fields no principle or rule or equation, of however long standing, was absolutely certain or unconditionally true. After all, part of the impetus for doing analysis by algebra had been to develop for arithmetic as sound a logical foundation as that which existed for Euclidean geometry, but the development of non-Euclidean geometries showed that a logical foundation did not guarantee that a particular geometry was a *necessary* description of reality. It would have been, then, very much in the spirit of the times for Poe to feel the conditionality of many of the traditional certainties in mathematics and logic. Consequently, Dupin's questioning the unconditional status of a quadratic equation would seem to be much of a piece with Poe's use of the Neoplatonic figure of a square folded along its diagonal as an image of reflective self-consciousness, for it is clearly a figure that, in its association of the reflexive principle with a line that is numerically incommensurable, evokes that principle as something beyond logic.

39 *The Three/Four Oscillation; Playing Poe's Game; Self-Mirroring; Dupin's Numerically Ambiguous Location; The Minister's Initial; An Arabesque in D*

SINCE DOUBLING IS A CENTRAL element in the Dupin stories and since a continuing motif in "The Purloined Letter" is the oscillation between three and four, the simplest structure that will accommodate both these elements is a square folded along its diagonal. The numerical doubling of three produces six, while that of four produces eight. But the only kind of "doubling" that turns four into three (or, when reversed, three back into four) is that reflexive doubling-back that occurs along a square's diagonal.

One might raise, however, a question at this point about the presence of the three/four oscillation as a motif in Poe's text. For while it is clear that doubling is a central element in his detective stories, is it in fact equally clear that the three/four oscillation is a recurring element in "The Purloined Letter" itself? Or is it simply a recurring element in various interpretations of the story, such as Borges's rewriting of Poe's tale in "Death and the Compass" or Lacan's and Derrida's readings of the story's structure? What this question implicitly raises, of course, is the issue of Poe's own degree of self-consciousness in constructing these stories about self-consciousness. What tends to be overlooked in readings of "The Purloined Letter" that treat it as a pretext for examining the analytic act in a specific discipline such as psychoanalysis, or that make it the more or less naive starting point for an agon of ever-increasing methodological self-awareness, is just how self-conscious Poe was about the interpretive effect produced by a literary text ("The Purloined Letter") that includes within itself a symbolic text (the purloined letter) whose attributes are clearly those of the literary text itself.

Such readings tend to ignore how painstakingly Poe thematized *within* the story the reader's interpretive interaction *with* the story and how he then proceeded to make the discovery of that thematization a further form of interaction with the reader, a subtler game of hide-and-seek, of clues and solutions. For example, the solution to the mystery of the purloined letter (the mystery of its concealment in the minister's house so that the prefect cannot find it) is that the minister has turned the letter inside out and hidden it in plain sight. But this trick of reversing the object and leaving it in view is also the solution to *Poe's* concealment of *this* solution within the text. On his first visit to Dupin the prefect presents us with the mystery: the letter's theft and the fact of its continued nonappearance despite his repeated searches. But this standard scene in the analytic detective story (the presentation of the mystery) is in effect turned inside out by Poe, for in describing how the minister took the letter, Poe simultaneously shows us the secret of its subsequent concealment by giving us the detail of the queen's turning the letter over and leaving it in the open on a table to conceal it from the king. What Poe confronts us with, of course, is the central mystery of the analytic detective story itself: the fact that in a genre where the reader is encouraged to engage in a battle of wits with the detective to see who solves the mystery first, the same text that presents the reader with the mystery must also present him with the clues to solve it, clues that have been hidden in plain sight on the text's surface.

Similarly, in Dupin's presentation of the game of even and odd as a figure of the attempt to be one up on a specular double, Poe again hides in plain sight that other, subtler game of simple/odd, even/odd—the game figuring the reader's battle of wits with the author as a specular encounter in which the reader plays or tries to avoid playing the game of even and odd with Poe through the author's opposing masks of detective and criminal. Poe hides *this* game in the open by having Dupin pointedly note that the game of even and odd "is simple," a verbal gesture that directs us back to his earlier emphatic repetition of the prefect's claim that the affair of the letter was "simple and odd." If one were to represent in a geometric figure the opposing players in the game of simple/odd, even/odd, the basic form of the figure would look familiar (see fig. 39.1).

It is only through the battle of wits between Dupin and the Minister D——, through their fictive encounter in the story, that the reader can engage in a real battle of wits with Poe, can try to outwit the author for the interpretive possession of "The Purloined Letter," much as Dupin outwits the minister for the letter's physical possession. Because the reader cannot directly confront his adversary Poe, he has to engage him indirectly through his opposing masks in a triangular structure of reader, Dupin, minister. And similarly Poe can only confront the reader indirectly through these same masks in a triangular structure of author, Dupin, minister. Poe and the reader square off, then, as specular doubles, each meaning to outwit a self-projected image of the other, within a quadrangular figure composed of two triangles whose vertices point in opposite directions (Poe and the reader) but whose bases are a single line linking the opposing positions of Dupin and the minister.

In this structure the reader is obviously at a disadvantage, since in having to match wits with Poe through the game of even and odd played

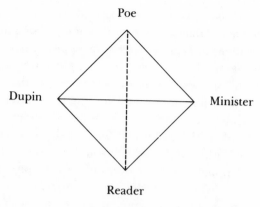

Figure 39.1

by the author's adversarial masks he is clearly playing Poe's game: If, within that quadrangular figure representing the indirect confrontation of author and reader through the direct one of criminal and detective, we were to try, for example, to bring together the positions of Poe and the reader for a direct confrontation (like that between the specular doubles Lönnrot and Scharlach at the fourth point of the compass), try to make the upper and lower vertices representing author and reader coincide, then we would be enacting that mirror fold along a square's diagonal that for Poe figures the antithetical structure of individual self-consciousness.

Thus the answer to our earlier question about whether the three/four oscillation is actually a recurring motif in "The Purloined Letter" or simply a recurring element in subsequent interpretations of the story turns out to be a dual one: To the extent that the game of simple/odd, even/odd can be said to be "present in the text," then the three/four oscillation that forms its core is also present. But clearly the game of simple/odd, even/odd is not present in "The Purloined Letter" in the same way that, for example, Dupin's game of even and odd is. For while the latter is explicitly presented by Dupin and then explained as a figure of the mental duel between detective and criminal, the game of simple/odd, even/odd is wholly an effect of the reader's interpretation of the story. It is an effect of the reader's seeing that the game of even and odd, as a figure of the mental duel between specular doubles, has been unfolded from within the tale to cover the reader's oblique battle of wits with the author; and then an effect of the reader's realizing that this oblique confrontation with the author through his masks of detective and criminal enacts the four-sided structure that is Poe's geometric model of self-consciousness.

Like a child playing at hide-and-seek, Poe wants to be found out, but only by those whose wit and perseverance (in this process of self-selection as self-mirroring) match his own. Yet as one pursues Poe through the

winding mazes of the Dupin stories, one realizes that he has constructed
the tales in such a way that the closer the reader follows the author's trail
the more the reader's interpretive stance takes on a numerical or geometrical structure planned in advance by Poe. Moreover, since being one
jump ahead of the opponent is the object not only of the game the detective plays with the criminal but also the one the reader plays with the
author, Poe is always ready to raise the level of subtlety a notch. Thus,
having thematized in the game of simple/odd, even/odd the indirect
confrontation of author and reader through the direct one of criminal
and detective, Poe makes the discovery of this thematization a further
form of interaction with the reader by planting clues to that three/four
oscillation that evokes the quadrangular figure's mirror fold. In the very
first sentence of "The Purloined Letter," for example, the narrator gives
us the complete street address of Dupin's residence in Paris, a level of
specificity that in the economy of a Poe story is almost always significant,
particularly where numbers are concerned. The address is *"au troisième,
No. 33, Rue Dunôt, Faubourg St. Germain"* (3:974). We already know from
the first Dupin story that the house is located in the Faubourg St. Germain, an authentic section of Paris. The street name, however, is Poe's own
invention and is perhaps an appellation that, in echoing the sound of an
elided "don't know," is meant to suggest, like Samuel Butler's Erewhon,
the nonexistent character of the place it names. More significantly (for
reasons that will be apparent in a moment), the name of the street begins
with the letter *D*. The crucial information, however, which Poe provides in
this address is that Dupin lives *"au troisième"* at *"No. 33."* No annotated
edition of the tale ever fails to point out that the French *"au troisième"* (*le
troisième étage*), the third floor, is what Americans call the fourth floor.
Dupin resides, then, in a numerically ambiguous spot—on a floor that in
France is called the third but in America the fourth. And it is only appropriate that this third/fourth floor should be located in a building whose
street number is 33 (double 3), for in the folding of Poe's quadrangular
figure, the twin shapes that result are three-sided, a doubling of threes
paralleled in the game of simple/odd, even/odd by the repetition of a
word whose root (the Old Norse *oddi*) means "triangle."

That Borges understood the clue contained in Dupin's residing *"au
troisième"* at *"No. 33"* can be seen from a detail in "Death and the Compass." The murder of Rabbi Yarmolinsky, the first in the series, takes place
at the Hôtel du Nord in the rabbi's "room on floor R, across from the suite
occupied . . . by the Tetrarch of Galilee" (*A*, 66). Since the name of the
hotel is French, one assumes that the designation of its floors follows the
French custom and that the *R* of "floor R" is the first letter of *rez-de-chausée*
(much as in this country the letter *M* in a building directory stands for

mezzanine or *B* for basement). The first murder occurs, then, on a floor that the French call the ground floor and Americans call the first, a difference in the naming/numbering of the first term in a series that gives rise (and in this case is certainly meant to allude) to the numerical ambiguity of Dupin's residence "*au troisième.*" It is only appropriate, of course, that Yarmolinsky's murder on the *first* floor should initiate a series of events that ultimately brings Lönnrot, who thinks of himself as "a kind of Auguste Dupin," to that *fourth* point of the compass where the *third* murder will occur as the *two* doubles, who "may be the same man," confront one another. And appropriate as well that the first murder in this series was the chance result of the jewel thief Azevedo's mistaking Yarmolinsky's room for "the suite occupied . . . by the Tetrarch of Galilee," whose title, as we saw, originally derived from the historical division of a realm into four parts in order to distribute it among three persons.

Yet another instance of Poe's planting a clue in the text to the three/four oscillation is the naming of Dupin's rival, the Minister D——. In a tale entitled "The Purloined Letter" any manipulation of a letter, such as the substitution of an initial for a name, should attract our attention. Examining the letter's roots (as we did those of the words *simple, even,* and *odd*) reveals that the shape of our capital *D* derives from that of the capital *delta* (Δ) in Greek. In the Greek alphabet, *delta* is the fourth letter, as *D* is in ours; and it also serves as a sign for both the cardinal and ordinal forms of the number four.[1] The minister's initial derives, then, from a triangular-shaped Greek letter that stands for the number four, the same initial as that of his double who lives on the third/fourth floor at No. *33* Rue *D*unot. We should also note in this connection that *delta* is the root of the Greek word *deltos,* "*a writing-tablet,* from the letter Δ (the old shape of tablets)" (*Lexicon,* 178), the letter *D* thus being a doubly appropriate designation for the purloiner and the recoverer of the letter (themselves characters composed of letters) in this drama of inscribed surfaces.

Indeed, at one point in the tale, Poe's delight in weaving clues around the letter produces an alliterative arabesque in the key of D: Dupin says that the more he "reflected upon the daring, dashing, and discriminating ingenuity of D——," the more certain he became that the minister must have kept the letter "*at hand*" by resorting to the "sagacious expedient of not attempting to conceal it at all" (3:990). While the amount of alliteration in this passage would not be extraordinary for Poe's poetry, it is remarkable in his prose, as if Poe wanted us to notice not the minister's but his own "ingenuity" in manipulating a letter. And when we further consider that the three adjectives beginning with *D* are used to describe the mental features of a character with the same initial and that the pattern of this alliteration falls into a three/four grouping (three words plus a fourth initial), then it seems fairly clear that Poe means for us, first, to associate the minister's consciousness with the figure of a reflexive fold producing a three/four division (Dupin says he "*reflected* upon the daring, dashing, and discriminating ingenuity of D——" [my italics]), then, second, to connect this figurative fold with that refolding that allows D—— to conceal the letter by "not attempting to conceal it at all," and perhaps, finally, to link this manipulation of the letter (which permitted D—— to keep it "*at hand*") with the V-shaped fold of the hand (the letter's refolding is, after all, compared to the turning of a glove).

That Borges spotted the clue concealed in the minister's initial can be judged from Lönnrot's parting flourish in "Death and the Compass." Trapped in Scharlach's quadrangular labyrinth, Lönnrot makes one last attempt to best his enemy intellectually by proposing a simpler, more economical labyrinth composed of "a single straight line" (*A*, 78). But Lönnrot's ploy is a trick, his labyrinth's vaunted economy more apparent than real. For what is at issue here is not the number of lines in a geometric figure but the number of steps in a mental operation. And just as there are four steps in Scharlach's labyrinth designated by the four points of the compass, so there are four steps in Lönnrot's designated by the first four letters of the alphabet: "Scharlach, when in another incarnation you hunt me down, stage (or commit) a murder at A, then a second murder at B, eight miles from A, then a third murder at C, four miles from A and B, halfway between the two. Lay in wait for me then at D, two miles from A and C, again halfway between them. Kill me at D, the way you are going to kill me here at Triste-le-Roy." Lönnrot's suggestion that their specular duel will be replayed again in a future existence is simply Borges's implicit acknowledgment that this meeting of the doubles at the letter *D* (Δ, four) has already been played in a previous incarnation.

40 *The Overdetermined D; Radicals and Roots; Signs of the Calculus; Infinity; Cantor, Russell, and Reflexiveness; Royce's Map; The Fold between Even and Odd; Rouge et Noir*

POE'S FREIGHTING OF THE LETTER D with significance is by no means confined to evoking the three/four oscillation associated with his geometric model of self-consciousness. Just as Poe has overdetermined the meaning of the purloined letter, so he has made this other purloined letter, this initial D displaced from the rest of the letters in a name, equally overdetermined, standing within the story for any number of words with this initial. As we shall see, Poe uses the letter D as a nodal point to link the subject of algebraic analysis (and the notion of a "mere mathematician" which he associates with it) to that of Platonic/Pythagorean mathematics (and the notion of a true mathematician) and then uses the initial once more to link these subjects to the physical manipulation of the stolen letter.

Earlier, in discussing the Analytical Society, we cited Charles Babbage's widely quoted remark that the society, in pressing for the introduction of continental methods of analysis at Cambridge, had advocated "the principles of pure d-ism as opposed to the *dot*-age of the university," d-ism referring, as we said, to the Leibnizian notation of the calculus and *dot*-age to the Newtonian. And we noted that, given the influence of Cambridge University on mathematical instruction at the University of Virginia in Poe's era, this remark of Babbage's may well have played some part in determining Poe's use of the letter D in the tale. Thus, in Dupin's description of the refolded letter's physical appearance, Poe literally affixes the initial D to the letter, and the imagery of the passage plays on the earlier discussion of algebra and analysis: Dupin says that in scanning the minister's apartment on his first visit his eye fell upon a pasteboard "card-rack" hanging by a ribbon from the mantelpiece, a card-rack that contained several visiting cards "and a solitary letter" (3:991):

> This last was much soiled and crumpled. It was torn nearly in two, across the middle—as if a design, in the first instance, to tear it entirely up as worthless, had been altered, or stayed, in the second. It had a large black seal, bearing the D—— cipher *very* conspicuously, and was addressed, in a diminutive female hand, to D——, the minister, himself.

Dupin says that no sooner "had I glanced at this letter, than I concluded it to be that of which I was in search," even though "it was, to all appearance, radically different from the one of which the Prefect had read us so minute a description" (3:991).

That Dupin's attention should be immediately attracted to the letter is not surprising; for not only does it exhibit all the signs (which Dupin has just described to the narrator) of having been conspicuously hidden in plain view, it exhibits as well the odd characteristic of being addressed to the minister but marked with the minister's own seal. Since a letter usually bears the seal of the person who sends it rather than the one who receives it, this anomaly alone would have been enough to catch Dupin's eye. (The letter could, of course, have been from a female member of D——'s family, but if this were the case, then how account for the careless, even contemptuous, fashion in which the letter has been treated and then exhibited for any visitor to see?) And just as Dupin's attention would have been caught by the presence of D——'s seal on a letter addressed to D——, so the reader's attention should be caught by Dupin's remarking on this letter's *difference* in appearance from the one he is seeking. For clearly the problem posed by the purloined letter is one of identity, the problem of finding the *same* letter beneath a *different* appearance—the letter's identity-in-difference being a figure for that larger problem of personal identity, the "sameness of a rational being," as Poe says in "Morella," quoting Locke. Consequently, when Dupin characterizes the letter as being "*radically* different" (my italics) in appearance from the missing one, the reader should recall the terms of Dupin's lengthy discussion of mathematics a few pages earlier. That inquiry had begun with Dupin's invoking *linguistic radicals* (L. *radix,* "root") to suggest the nonidentity of the words *analysis* and *algebra,* and it had ended with the imagery of *radicals in mathematics* and with Dupin's contention that a "mere mathematician" could not "be trusted out of equal roots" (as if this had been the cause of their equating the two words). In elaborating his description of the letter he saw at the minister's, Dupin goes out of his way to emphasize its difference from the one he is seeking:

> Here the seal was large and black, with the D—— cipher; there it was small and red, with the ducal arms of the S—— family. Here, the address, to the Minister, was diminutive and feminine; there the superscription, to a certain royal personage, was markedly bold and decided; the size alone formed a point of correspondence. But, then, the *radicalness* of these differences, which was excessive; the dirt; the soiled and torn condition of the paper, so inconsistent with the *true* methodical habits of D——, and so suggestive of a design to delude the beholder into an idea of the worthlessness of the document; these

things, together with the hyperobtrusive situation of this document, full in the view of every visiter, and thus exactly in accordance with the conclusions to which I had previously arrived; these things, I say, were strongly corroborative of suspicion, in one who came with the intention to suspect. (3:991)

It is precisely the "*radicalness*" of the difference in appearance of the minister's letter not only from the queen's but from the minister's own character (the letter's soiled and torn condition being "inconsistent with the *true* methodical habits of D——") that convinces Dupin that this is the same letter taken from the queen. The passage not only evokes the notion of identity as a sameness constituted by difference, it also links a series of differential oppositions (e.g., red/black, small/large, masculine/feminine) to the image of the letter in its folded and refolded states. And this in turn suggests that one of the possible words represented by the overdetermined letter *D* is *difference,* and that one of the words represented by its reciprocal, the initial imprinted on the seal of the original letter before it was everted and resealed (the letter *S*), is *sameness.*

But Poe knows something more about the letters *D* and *S* that he means for us to register as we watch this game in which the same letter (missive) is inscribed with two different letters (alphabetic characters signifying "sameness" and "difference") to indicate its self-identity. For *D* and *S* are also signs in mathematical analysis. In the differential calculus the lower-case *d* stands for the differential of a variable, which is to say, for an infinitesimal difference, as in the expression dx; while the Greek capital *delta* Δ stands for a finite difference, as in the expression Δx. Similarly, in the integral calculus the $\int$ sign, "a slender, elongated form of the letter" *S* (*Notations,* 2:243), stands for the integral, that is, for an infinite sum of infinitesimal differences, as in the expression $\int \sin [x] \, dx$. The $\int$ sign was first introduced by Leibniz in 1675 and signified the Latin word *summa* or the French *somme,* "sum" or "total." Leibniz used "the symbol $\int l$ for *omn. l,* that is, for the sum of the *l*'s" (*Notations,* 2:242). (One senses that the narrator's earlier remark about the Minister D——'s having "written learnedly on the Differential Calculus" is partly meant as a clue to this marking of the purloined letter with symbols from the calculus.)

As the differential represents an infinitesimal difference, so the integral represents an infinite sum of such differences, and the reciprocity of integration and differentiation rests upon the fact that the procedure for finding the area under a curve is the inverse of the procedure for determining the slope (or direction) of a curve. Now since the relationship Poe establishes between the letter in its original (folded) and its subsequent (refolded) state is one of reciprocity (the reversible mutuality of inner and outer), it is only appropriate that the alphabetic characters marking these states should evoke—whether they stand for the words *sameness* and *differ-ence* or for the mathematical signs for the integral and the differential in calculus—relationships that are similarly reciprocal. Indeed, in associat-ing the calculus's reciprocity of integration and differentiation with the reversible mutuality of inner and outer in the refolding of the letter, Poe sets up a further equation of images: For just as the refolding of the purloined letter (considered as a figure of reflexive self-consciousness) is assimilated to the Platonic/Pythagorean image of folding a square along its diagonal, so the reciprocity of integration and differentiation (associ-ated with the former image through the marking of the letter's folded and refolded states with the initials *S* and *D*) is assimilated to the incommen-surability of the diagonal and the infinite regression/progression (evoked by the three/four oscillation) that form part of the latter image. And this assimilation is appropriate because both the calculus and the notion of incommensurability address the same mathematical problem—the con-cept of infinity.

As Morris Kline notes, Newton and Leibniz, the inventors of the calcu-lus, thought of it as simply "the algebra of the infinite, or the algebra that dealt with an infinite number of terms, as in the case of infinite series." Thus the differential and the integral calculus (dealing respectively with the infinitesimal and the infinite sum of infinitesimals) represent the at-tempt to determine the infinite in opposite directions—the infinitely small (whose limit is represented by the concept of absolute indivisibility or zero) and the infinitely many (whose limit is represented by the concept of absolute totality). And in the case of the incommensurability of the diago-nal, we find ourselves confronting the same problem; for in attempting to determine the length of a square's diagonal in terms of a system of numera-tion that forms a common measure for the square's side, we are faced with a number that resists closure. And as with the reciprocity of integration and differentiation, we are left with the sense of the infinite proceeding simul-taneously in opposite directions—the number of decimal places infinitely increasing (e.g., $\sqrt{2}$ or 1.4142135 . . .), while the degree of difference in the numerical determination of the length is endlessly decreasing.

In effect, what Poe has done in associating the turning of the pur-loined letter with the calculus is to link the notion of a reflexive fold to the concept of infinity—the same association we find in the figure of a square folded along its diagonal, where the site of the fold can only be numer-ically represented by an irrational number. As Morris Kline points out, "An irrational number is not just a single symbol or a pair of symbols, such as a ratio of two integers, but an infinite collection. . . . The irrational number, logically defined, is an intellectual monster" (Kline, 987).

In linking reflexiveness with infinity, Poe exhibits what seems to be a remarkable intuition about the nature of the infinite, the kind of insight that the mathematician Georg Cantor was to pursue some thirty years after Poe's death in creating the theory of sets. Cantor, who invented the concept of transfinite numbers and used the Hebrew *aleph* (א) as their mathematical symbol, was, of course, an important influence on Borges's thinking. Borges refers to Cantor's work in such essays as "The Doctrine of Cycles" (1936), "The Total Library" (1939), and "Avatars of the Tortoise" (1939), and he told Selden Rodman in an interview that he took the title for his story "The Aleph" from "the symbol for transfinite numbers"[1] which he had come upon in Bertrand Russell's *Introduction to Mathematical Philosophy*. Invoking the Aleph symbol in his discussion of Cantor's work, Russell points out that "Cantor used reflexiveness as the *definition* of the infinite" (*IM*, 88). Which is to say that Cantor defined a set as infinite if it could be put into a "one-to-one correspondence with part of itself" (Kline, 995). "When this can be done," says Russell, "the correlator by which it is done may be said to 'reflect' the whole class into a part of itself; for this reason, such classes" are "called 'reflexive'" (*IM*, 79–80).

The most obvious example of mathematical reflexiveness is to be found in the set of natural or inductive numbers $(1, 2, 3, 4 \ldots)$. This set of numbers is infinite, proceeding by the relation of n to $n + 1$ without limit, and it is, of course, commonly divided into two parts—even and odd. And, odd as it may seem, these subsets, these "halves" of the whole, are also infinite. The set of natural numbers can, for example, be used to count (can be put in a one-to-one correspondence with, be "reflected" into) the set of even numbers, as in the parallel series

| 2 | 4 | 6 | 8 | 10 | 12 | 14 | 16 | 18 | *ad infinitum* |
| 1 | 2 | 3 | 4 | 5 | 6 | 7 | 8 | 9 | *ad infinitum.* |

It is worth noting that the first example Russell gives of the principle of "reflexion" is "Royce's illustration of the map" of England constructed "upon a part of the surface of England" (*IM*, 80)—the same example, as we saw earlier, that Borges used in his essay "Partial Enchantments of the *Quixote*" to explain literary reflexiveness. Of Royce's illustration Russell remarks,

> Whenever we can "reflect" a class into a part of itself, the same relation will necessarily reflect that part into a smaller part, and so on *ad infinitum*. For example, we can reflect . . . all the inductive numbers into the even numbers; we can, by the same relation (that of n to $2n$) reflect the even numbers into the multiples of 4, these into the multiples of 8, and so on. This is an abstract analogue to Royce's problem of the map. The even numbers are a "map" of all the inductive numbers; the multiples of 4 are a map of the map; the multiples of 8 are a map of the map of the map; and so on. (*IM*, 81)

Regarding this image of the set of natural numbers reflected back into a part of itself, we should note that in the figure of a square folded along its diagonal the association of reflexiveness and infinity (the fact that the site of the fold, in being mathematically irrational, represents an infinite collection) is implicitly linked to the reciprocity of even and odd numbers. Which is to say that the reflexive fold, in changing the figure from a shape with an even number of sides into one with an odd number of sides, figuratively assimilates this "halving" of the geometric shape to the "halving" of the infinite set of natural numbers (its division into the two infinite subsets of even and odd). And it seems only appropriate that this fold along the diagonal (the hinge, as it were, about which the infinite subsets of even and odd endlessly oscillate) should itself be a quantity whose numerical expression involves an infinitely increasing number of decimal places used to specify an infinitely decreasing level of difference. Further, in associating, as figures of reflective self-consciousness, the image of a square folded along its diagonal with that of the purloined letter folded and refolded so as to reverse its inner and outer surfaces, Poe assimilates the limitless alternation of even and odd within the set of natural numbers to the equally limitless oscillation of inner and outer as two opposing aspects of a single continuous surface.

In his description of the letter Dupin sees at the minister's residence, Poe subtly links the inner/outer reversal characterizing the letter to the three/four oscillation of a diagonally folded square. Remarking that the letter was displayed in a pasteboard card-rack hanging from the mantelpiece, Dupin notes that the rack "had three or four compartments" into one of which the letter was "thrust carelessly" (3:991). That the exact location of the refolded letter involves an uncertainty about the numbers three and four (as does the location of Dupin's residence, the letter being after all an image of the self) is no coincidence. And this three/four indeterminacy regarding the letter's location is emphasized by a further detail Dupin volunteers about the color of its seals. He tells us that in its original state the letter carried a red seal marked with *S*, while in its refolded state it bore a black seal marked with *D*. As Poe has freighted the alphabetic characters with meaning, so he has made the color of the seals meaningful as well. The words "red and black" in Dupin's native tongue are, of course, *rouge et noir*, and Poe, ever the gamesman, would have known that *Rouge et Noir* was the name of a French gambling game, "one of the two . . . played in the gambling rooms at Monte Carlo, roulette being the other" (*EB*, 27:251). Poe would also have been aware that *Rouge et Noir* (which was played with cards at a special table marked with triangular and diamond shapes) was better known by another name—*Trente et*

Quarante ("Thirty and Forty")—a name that evokes the three/four oscillation multiplied by ten (a linking of the numbers three, four, and ten to keep in mind later when we consider the relationship of Poe's figure of reflexivity to the Pythagorean "tetractys").

41 *A Platonic Dialogue;* Eureka *as Detective Story; Marked with a Letter; The Tetractys and the Line of Beauty; Letter as Nodal Point; A Shared Structure; Thematizing the Act of Reading*

THAT REFLEXIVENESS IS ASSOCIATED WITH infinity in Poe's figurations of self-consciousness should not surprise anyone familiar with his writings, for Poe was intrigued by the subject of infinity and dealt with it in several works, including his late mystical-mathematical treatise on cosmology, *Eureka.* Of his various discussions of the topic, the one most significant for our present purposes is the imaginary dialogue entitled "The Power of Words" (1845) published less than a year after the appearance of "The Purloined Letter." The fact that "The Power of Words" is a Platonic dialogue between two spirits named Oinos and Agathos (the One and the Good) is especially relevant to Poe's detective stories, given the Platonic trajectory that we suggested runs across the three tales. (Regarding the name Agathos, recall that the goal of the journey from the cave to the realm of pure light is the idea of the good.)

The dialogue between Oinos and Agathos takes place in the future, after the destruction of the world. Oinos, a recent inhabitant of the earth, is "a spirit new-fledged with immortality" seeking instruction about the afterlife from the angel Agathos, who informs him that this questioning is only proper since "not in knowledge is happiness, but in the acquisition of knowledge." But Oinos wonders whether, if a spirit's happiness consists in acquiring knowledge, there must eventually be a limit to such happiness, for "must not *at last* all things be known," the mind and the objects of its knowledge absolutely coincide? In reply Agathos invites Oinos to look around himself at the "infinity of matter"—an infinity whose "*sole* purpose," Agathos speculates, "is to afford infinite springs, at which the soul may allay the thirst *to know* which is for ever unquenchable within it— since to quench it, would be to extinguish the soul's self" (3:1211–12).

The shape of this argument is not essentially different from the one underlying the detective stories (the contention that the analytic power is itself "but little susceptible of analysis"). In one case, Agathos claims that the object of knowledge (the universe) is infinite and thus the process of knowing this object unending; in the other, Poe implies that the process of knowing the self absolutely, resists closure and that consequently this object of knowledge (the self) is for all practical purposes infinite. Were

398

such an absolute coincidence ever to be effected it would, like the possibility of Oinos's exhausting the objects of knowledge in the universe, "extinguish the soul's self" by doing away with the difference that constitutes identity.

What makes "The Power of Words" particularly interesting for our purposes is the explicit connection Poe subsequently makes between infinity and algebraic analysis, between the infinite objects of knowledge and the indefinite advancement of mathematics as a means of comprehending that infinity. Noting that "as no thought can perish, so no act is without infinite result," Agathos continues,

> The mathematicians who saw that the results of any given impulse were absolutely endless—and who saw that a portion of these results were accurately traceable through the agency of algebraic analysis— . . . saw, at the same time, that this species of analysis itself, had within itself a capacity for indefinite progress—that there were no bounds conceivable to its advancement and applicability, except within the intellect of him who advanced or applied it. (3:1213–14)

And he adds, "It was deducible from what they knew, that to a being of infinite understanding—one to whom the *perfection* of the algebraic analysis lay unfolded—there could be no difficulty in tracing every impulse given the air—and the ether through the air—to the remotest consequences at any even infinitely remote epoch of time." Agathos says that "this faculty of referring at *all* epochs, *all* effects to *all* causes" is "in its absolute fulness and perfection" the "prerogative of the Deity alone," although in every degree "short of the absolute perfection" the "power itself" is "exercised by the whole host of the Angelic Intelligences" (3:1214–15).

Yet only four years later, in *Eureka,* Poe imagines an ultimate goal in which this "absolute fulness and perfection" of the analytic power will no longer be solely a prerogative of the deity, since at that period all individual intelligences will have merged with the divine intelligence. According to Poe, God "passes his Eternity in perpetual variation of Concentrated Self and almost Infinite Self-Diffusion," the current state of the universe being simply his "present expansive existence," in which all his creatures are but "infinite individualizations of Himself." These creatures are more or less conscious intelligences, "conscious, first, of a proper identity; conscious, secondly and by faint indeterminate glimpses, . . . of an identity with God." Poe predicts that of these two classes of consciousness the former will grow weaker "during the long succession of ages," and the latter will grow stronger, until "the sense of individual identity will be gradually merged in the general consciousness" and man, "ceasing imperceptibly to feel himself Man, will at length attain that awfully triumphant epoch when he shall recognize his existence as that of Jehovah" (*P*, 16:314–15).

Eureka is, of course, relevant to a discussion of the Dupin stories because of the numerous similarities between the cosmological treatise and the detective tales. The first and most obvious of these is that *Eureka* is structured like a detective story: The question of the essence, origin, and end of the universe is presented as a cosmic mystery to be solved by a combination of rational analysis and imaginative intuition. Indeed, at one point in *Eureka* Poe explicitly likens his analytic speculations in cosmology to Dupin's detective work: Noting the resemblance (in terms of their shared peculiarity) between the problem of the unequal distribution of matter in the universe and the "*outré* character" (2:547) of the crime in "The Murders in the Rue Morgue," Poe argues that it is precisely by "such peculiarities—such protuberances above the plane of the ordinary—that Reason feels her way . . . in her search for the True" (*P*, 16:228). *Eureka* is, of course, written in a voice that one immediately recognizes as Dupin's. And, predictably enough, the solution this voice seeks to the mystery of the universe must be both mathematically correct and aesthetically satisfying, both true and beautiful, a solution that will always remain beyond the power of those who are "mathematicians *solely*" (*P*, 16:223) and reveal itself only to those with the instinct for mathematics and poetry (indeed, Poe represents the mathematical/metaphysical speculations of *Eureka* as being "an Art-Product alone: . . . a Poem" [*P*, 16:183]).

According to Poe, such a solution must also explain the universe in terms of the interplay of simplicity and complexity. It must account for the complexity of matter through the simplicity of mathematical and geometrical principles, which is to say, account for the complexity of the universe's present state in terms of the absolute simplicity of its origin. And it is in this connection that we confront the most striking resemblance between *Eureka* and the Dupin stories; for just as Poe makes the ongoing mystery at the heart of his three detective tales the mystery of the self's structure, the puzzle of self-consciousness, so in *Eureka* by presenting the universe as an apotheosized self, he makes this same mysterious structure the central puzzle of the universe. For the universe in its present state is nothing but God's self in a condition of "almost Infinite Self-Diffusion," nothing but "his present expansive existence." And just as God's self passes through eternity in a "perpetual variation" between "Concentrated Self" and "Infinite Self-Diffusion," between ultimate self-contraction and ultimate self-expansion, original simplicity and final complexity, so in that model of the human self evoked in "The Purloined Letter" (the figure of a square folded and unfolded along its diagonal) we find adumbrated this same interplay between simplicity and complexity, the figure's unfolding

foreshadowing its infinite progression or expansion and its folding foreshadowing its infinite regression or contraction. Moreover, as we identified this reflexive fold with the notion of infinity (as Russell says, "Whenever we can 'reflect' a class into a part of itself, the same relation will
necessarily reflect that part into a smaller part, and so on *ad infinitum*"), so
Poe in *Eureka* links the concept of infinity to the reflexive structure of self-
consciousness by claiming that "the word, 'Infinity'" as applied to the
physical universe represents simply "the *thought of a thought*" (*P*, 16:200).

Given that the central mystery in both the Dupin stories and *Eureka* is
the structure of the self (whether human or divine), we should note one
further resemblance between "The Purloined Letter" and Poe's cosmological treatise, a resemblance that brings us back to our discussion of
the alphabetic characters impressed on the purloined letter's seals. For
just as Poe inscribes this symbol of reflexiveness, in its folded and refolded
states, with the characters *S* and *D*, so he notes in *Eureka* that our galaxy, a
symbol of the gigantic self that is the universe (God's self), also seems to be
inscribed with an alphabetic character. Remarking that "in nearly all our
astronomical treatises" the "*shape* of the Galaxy . . . is said to resemble that
of a capital Y" (*P*, 16: 271), Poe explains that the galaxy's Y shape is simply
an appearance based on our earthly perspective, that is, a function of
human self-consciousness. Yet despite this qualification, he still goes on to
use the alphabetic figure as the most effective means of describing our
solar system's astronomical location.

Just as the meanings of the letters *S* and *D* inscribed on Poe's symbol of
the human self are overdetermined, so the meaning of the letter *Y* inscribed on his symbol of the divine self is equally overdetermined. For
though it might seem at first glance that *Y* is simply the initial of the deity
whose self the universe is (Yahweh), an appearance reinforced by Poe's
closing remark about man's ultimately recognizing his existence as that of
Jehovah, there is at least one other relevant meaning that critics have
found in the letter—the capital *Y* being interpreted as the so-called *littera
Pythagorae*. Thus Joan Dayan in her reading of *Eureka* identifies "Poe's Y"
as "the Samian letter used by Pythagoras as an emblem of the two roads of
Virtue and Vice."[1] Called the Samian letter from the place usually associated with Pythagoras (the island of Samos), the *Y* was said to have been
regarded by him as "a symbol of human life (Servius, on Vergil, *Aeneid* vi.
136)" (*EB*, 28:890). Poe would undoubtedly have known of the Pythagorean significance of the letter from references to it in English and Latin
poetry. Dayan, for example, points to the lines from Pope's *Dunciad* (4,
151–52): "When Reason doubtful, like the Samian letter, / Points him two
ways, the narrower is the better" (Dayan, 238 n. 44). Given Poe's proficien-
cy in Latin, he would probably have known as well the original on which

Pope's lines are based, a passage from the third satire of Persius:

> Et tibi quae Samios diduxit littera ramos
> surgentem dextro monstravit limite callem.   (*EB*, 28:890)

>   . . . the Samian's parable, Y
> Displaying its two forks, revealed to you
> The stony climb which rises to the Right.[2]

(There was, of course, a readily available translation of Persius's third satire by Dryden that Poe could also have known.) It is interesting to note, in light of our earlier discussion of the cultural coding of directionality, that in the Latin poem the righteous path is literally the path to the right, and that, given the way the letter *Y* is usually printed by hand with a single straight line slanted toward the right and a second line that deviates from it to the left, the righteous path was also the straight one.

A Pythagorean significance for Poe's Y seems more than likely considering the tone of Poe's mathematical-mystical speculations in *Eureka*. And the likelihood of the letter's being an allusion to the notion of human existence as a decision at a crossroads is increased by Poe's description of our solar system's astronomical position in the Y-shaped galaxy: "Our Sun" is "actually situated at that point of the Y where its three component lines unite" (*P*, 16:272). The sun is, of course, a traditional symbol of self-consciousness, and Poe's description of its location as being the point where the Y's "three component lines unite" creates an image that resonates backward and forward in time across several texts concerned with human self-awareness that we have discussed: backward first to the figure of Oedipus and that epiphany of self-consciousness that turns upon his understanding what happened at a place where three roads meet; backward as well to the figure of Theseus and the innumerable crossroads composing the labyrinth, a place where self-definition (the differentiation of the human) is figured as a problem of self-location; and backward also to Sir Thomas Browne and the quincuncial network as an image of man's place in the world; and then forward to Borges and "The Garden of Forking Paths," in which the human condition is evoked in terms of a labyrinth whose paths branch endlessly in time.

Given the structural resemblance between Poe's marking of the purloined letter with alphabetic characters and his noting that our galaxy is shaped like a letter, we should not be surprised that as one of the significances of the galactic *Y* seems to be Pythagorean, so too does one of the significances of the purloined letter's *D*. As we noted earlier, our capital *D* derives from the Greek capital *delta* (Δ), a three-sided letter that, as the fourth character in the Greek alphabet, is used as a sign for the number

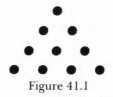

Figure 41.1

four. And this same combination of a deltalike triangular shape and the number four recalls the most sacred symbol of the Pythagoreans— the tetractys or "four-group," the "kernel of Pythagorean wisdom,"[3] the brotherhood's "shibboleth or *symbolon*," as the classicist Walter Burkert describes it (Burkert, 187).

The symbol was composed of "the numbers, 1, 2, 3, 4 . . . represented in a pebble figure, in the form of the 'perfect triangle'" (Burkert, 72), which is to say, an equilateral triangle each of whose sides contains four points, a triangle of fours (see fig. 41.1). The highest oath that a Pythagorean could take was to swear by the tetractys, since it emblemized for Pythagoras's followers their belief that "number is the essence of all things," as Aristotle says in the *Metaphysics* (Aristotle, 17:41). And indeed the tetractys served as a compendium of number symbolism: The four numbers 1, 2, 3, 4 add up to 10, the root of the decimal system and the Pythagorean perfect number (as evidenced, for example, in the original decad of oppositions that make up the Pythagorean table of opposites). Further, these four numbers contain not only the basic musical intervals of fourth (4:3), fifth (3:2), and octave (2:1), "but also, according to the Platonic pattern, point, line, plane, and solid" (Burkert, 72). That is, the figure exhibits the way in which the material world, considered in terms of dimensionality, is built up out of numbers: Beginning at the triangle's apex with the geometric point, we move downward to the next level, the two points that are the minimum number needed to determine a line; then to the next level, the three points that are the minimum needed to determine a plane; and then to the last level, the four points that are the minimum needed to determine a solid.

In making the tetractys a symbol of the material world's origin from the realm of numbers, the Pythagoreans simply substituted for the four basic elements of earth, air, fire, and water (considered as the building blocks of all things) the first four numbers, and they arranged them so as to show the origin of all things in unity as well as the way that unity flows out or falls down into multiplicity. (One is reminded of the opening of Borges's story "The Book of Sand," which combines the symbolism of dimensionality [contained in the tetractys] with the concept of infinity to create an image of beginning a tale with the most basic elements: "The line is made up of an infinite number of points; the plane of an infinite number of lines; the volume of an infinite number of planes; the hypervolume of an infinite number of volumes. . . . No, unquestionably this is not— *more geometrico*—the best way of beginning my story" [*BS*, 117].) Since, as Burkert points out, "The harmonic ratios, the 'perfection' of 10, and the role of the pebble figures are all part of what Aristotle attributes to the Pythagoreans" (Burkert, 72), Poe's knowledge of the tetractys's significance would not have required much more than an acquaintance with Book I of Aristotle's *Metaphysics*.

There is one further significance of the tetractys that seems to have a tantalizing connection with the Dupin stories. Burkert notes that the Neoplatonic philosopher Iamblichus, whose work is a principal source of our knowledge of Pythagorean lore, links the Pythagoreans' sacred number symbol to the oracle of Delphi: In his *De Vita Pythagorica* Iamblichus responds to the question "What is the oracle of Delphi?" with the answer "The tetractys; that is, the harmony in which the Sirens sing" (Burkert, 187). As Burkert explains, since the tetractys contains within itself "the harmonic ratios of fourth, fifth, and octave" and since

> the Sirens produce the music of the spheres, the whole universe is harmony and number. . . . The tetractys has within it the secret of the world; and in this manner we can also understand the connection with Delphi, the seat of the highest and most secret wisdom. Perhaps Pythagorean speculation touched upon that focal point, or embodiment, of Delphic wisdom, the bronze tripod of Apollo. Later sources speak of its mysterious ringing, which must have been "daemonic" for Pythagoreans. (Burkert, 187)

This bit of Pythagorean lore about the tetractys and the Sirens' song reminds us of the epigraph to "The Murders in the Rue Morgue," taken from the fifth chapter of Browne's *Urn Burial:* "What song the Syrens sang, or what name Achilles assumed when he hid himself among women, although puzzling questions, are not beyond *all* conjecture" (2:527). Since Poe uses this quotation as an introduction to the first of three related stories, stories whose whole point is that puzzling questions can indeed be solved through rational conjecture, it seems only appropriate for him to allude in the last of these stories to just such a conjectural answer to the famous question of the Sirens' song, which is to say, to allude, through the letter *D* and the three/four oscillation associated with it, to the ancient dictum identifying the Sirens' song with the harmonic ratios contained in the tetractys (the triangle of fours), one of these ratios being, of course, that of 4:3 (a fourth). Moreover, since the Pythagorean lore in question not only links the tetractys to the Sirens' song but also both of these to the oracle of Delphi, there is a further appropriateness in Poe's epigraphically invoking the Sirens' song in his first detective story. For, as we saw, the figure from Greek mythology whose story represents the archetypal pattern for the detective genre is Oedipus, and the Delphic oracle is central to his story. It is on the way from Delphi that Oedipus meets Laius and his retinue at the crossroads. And when Oedipus, as king of Thebes, sets out to solve the mystery of Laius's murder, the problem presents itself as a puzzle built upon the four numbers contained in the tetractys.

Of course, the general appropriateness of Poe's having in mind a Pythagorean significance for one of the meanings of the letter D stems from what we have described as the Pythagorean tone of his discussion of analysis and algebra, his sense of the true mathematician as someone who combines the resolvent and the creative powers, at once mathematician and poet. But if we are correct in seeing a reference to the Pythagorean tetractys among the possible meanings Poe associates with the letter D, then this raises a further question. For with the two earlier significations suggested for the letter (the initial of "Difference" and the sign for the differential in calculus), there was a reciprocal signification in each case for the letter S (the initial of "Sameness" and the sign for the integral in calculus), so that one naturally wonders whether, in a similar fashion, there exists for the letter S a meaning that is the reciprocal of the Pythagorean significance proposed for D.

Since the letter D evokes in a Pythagorean context a symbolic figure (the triangle of fours) rather than the initial of a word, we should probably seek the significance of the letter S in terms of its graphic symbolism as well. And indeed there does exist a symbolic association of the letter that immediately comes to mind, an association originating with a graphic artist whose work Poe admired—William Hogarth. In his art treatise *The Analysis of Beauty* (1753) Hogarth, discussing the serpentine line or elongated S curve, notes that in the frontispiece to the 1745 edition of his engraved works he had drawn "a serpentine line lying on a painter's pallet, with these words under it, THE LINE OF BEAUTY," a designation that caused widespread curiosity in the art world, with painters and sculptors applying to him "to know the meaning of it."[4] In his preface Hogarth cites various authorities to support his view that the serpentine line is the most beautiful in painting and design because it is the most fit to express motion, "the greatest grace and life that a picture can have," and he quotes a passage from the sixteenth-century painter Giovanni Lomazzo citing Michelangelo's advice to a young artist to "*alwaies make a figure Pyramidall, Serpentlike, and multiplied by one two and three*" (Hogarth, v–vi). As we noted earlier, the pyramidal shape had been associated with the tip of a flame since at least the time of the ancient Egyptians, and this same association is made by Lomazzo, who notes that "the forme of the flame . . . is most apt for motion: for it hath a *Conus* or sharpe pointe . . . that so it may ascende to his proper sphere," and by the seventeenth-century French painter Dufresnoy, whom Hogarth quotes to the effect that "a fine figure and its parts ought always to have a serpent-like and flaming form" because these sorts of lines have a "life and seeming motion in them, which very much resembles the activity of the flame and of the serpent" (Hogarth, vi–vii).

This linking of the images of pyramid, serpent, and flame has a Pythagorean/Platonic ring to it, and Hogarth goes on to note that for the painters and sculptors of ancient Greece "Pythagoras, Socrates, and Aristotle, seem to have pointed out the right road in nature" for their study (Hogarth, xii). Indeed, on the specific subject of Pythagoras, Hogarth cites the translator's preface to Ten Kate's *Beau Ideal* and its discussion of "the Analogy of the ancient Greeks." The translator says that this "Analogy" is "the true key for finding all harmonious proportions in painting, sculpture, architecture, musick, etc." and that it was "brought home to Greece by Pythagoras . . . after this great philosopher had travell'd into Phoenicia, Egypt and Chaldea, where he convers'd with the learned" (Hogarth, xiii). Of what this Analogy consists, the translator does not say, but clearly it seems to be based on the sense that harmony or proportion in the arts is a function of mathematical ratios—a notion the ancient world associated with Pythagoras. Not only were the harmonic ratios in music (such as those contained in the tetractys) thought to be Pythagorean discoveries, but also certain proportions in painting and architecture, the most famous of these being the "golden section." Burkert notes that "Euclid gives the construction of the golden section . . . in book 4, which is ascribed 'as a whole' to the Pythagoreans" (Burkert, 452).

The golden section or golden mean is the Euclidean problem of dividing a straight line in extreme and mean ratios, and it enters into ancient painting and architecture as the notion of a perfect proportion achieved by dividing "a straight line or rectangle . . . into two unequal parts" such that "the ratio of the smaller to the greater part is the same as that of the greater to the whole."[5] Like "the mathematical value pi," the ratio of the golden section "cannot be expressed as a finite number, but an approximation is 8:13 or 0.618:1" (*ODA*, 210). Indeed, some historians of mathematics such as G. J. Allman have suggested that "it was rather in connexion with the line cut in extreme and mean ratio than with reference to the diagonal and side of a square that the Pythagoreans discovered the incommensurable" (Heath, 3:19). Suffice it to say that like the incommensurability of the diagonal, the incommensurability of the golden section has been associated since antiquity with the Pythagoreans in their legendary capacity as discoverers of the irrational. And undoubtedly part of the aura of the golden section's mysterious perfection for the ancients was its irrationality, the fact that its exact numerical determination vanished in infinity. Besides its importance in Euclid, Plato, and Vitruvius (who used it in his work *De architectura* "to establish architectural standards for the proportions of columns, rooms, and whole buildings"[6]), the golden section was a topic of intense study in the Renaissance and the subject of a book entitled *Divina Proportione* (1509) by Luca Pacioli, the best-known mathematician of the period and a friend of Leonardo and Piero della Francesca. Maintaining that this "divine proportion" possesses mystical properties, Pacioli explains that the ratio "cannot be expressed by a number and, being beyond definition, is in this respect like God, 'occult and secret'; further, this three-in-one proportion is symbolic of the Holy Trinity" (*ODA*, 210), the "three-in-one proportion" referring to the three lengths compared in the figure—the smaller segment, the larger, and the whole line.

It is precisely in the spirit, then, of an inquiry into hidden ancient wisdom, into Pythagorean lore, that Hogarth invokes the translator's preface to Ten Kate's *Beau Ideal,* with its reference to the "Analogy of the ancient Greeks" as a *"great key of knowledge,"* and in this vein he continues, "As every one has a right to conjecture what this discovery of the ancients might be, it shall be my business to shew it was a key to the thorough knowledge of variety both in form, and movement" (Hogarth, xv–xvi). Quoting Shakespeare, Hogarth sums up "all the charms of beauty in two words, INFINITE VARIETY," the sense being that beauty inheres in *"an infinite variety of parts"* (Hogarth, xvi–xvii) brought together in a single, harmonious whole, the effect of an interplay of complexity and simplicity, difference and sameness. (One is immediately reminded of Poe's reference in the *Marginalia* to "Pythagoras' definition of beauty" as "the reduction of many into one.") In a distinctly Pythagorean tone, Hogarth continues, "The ancients made their doctrines mysterious to the vulgar, and kept them secret from those who were not of their particular sects . . . by means of symbols, and hieroglyphics" (Hogarth, xvii), and indeed Hogarth may have had in mind those two recognition symbols used by members of the Pythagorean brotherhood—the tetractys and the pentagram or star-pentagon, which the Pythagoreans called Health. (Interestingly enough, the relationship between the pentagram ☆ and the pentagon ⬠ seems to have involved for the Pythagoreans a problem in geometric construction that depended for its solution on another problem, that of the golden section [Heath, 2:99].)

Hogarth invokes the notion of ancient wisdom concealed in symbols and hieroglyphical emblems here because he is about to give an oblique gloss on the emblem that appears on the title page of *The Analysis of Beauty,* an emblem constructed from the shapes of a pyramid and serpentine line

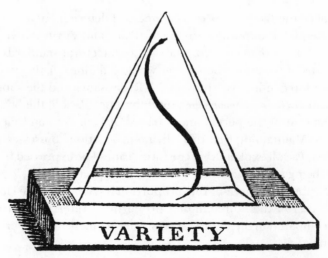

Figure 41.2

and from the word *variety* (see fig. 41.2). Hogarth begins his explanation
of the figure with a quotation from Lomazzo: "The Grecians in imitation
of antiquity searched out the truly renowned proportion, wherein the
exact perfection of most exquisite beauty and sweetness appeareth; dedicating the same in a triangular glass unto Venus the goddess of divine
beauty" (Hogarth, xvii). And he adds, giving the quotation specific reference to the figures he has discussed, "The symbol in the triangular glass,
might be similar to the line Michael Angelo recommended; especially, if it
can be proved, that the triangular form of the glass, and the serpentine
line itself, are the two most expressive figures that can be thought of to
signify not only beauty and grace, but the whole *order of form*" (Hogarth,
xvii).

We know that at the University of Virginia Poe had something of a local
reputation for his talent in drawing, one of his classmates remarking that
so great was his artistic skill his fellow students were "in doubt whether Poe
in future life would be Painter or Poet" (*Log*, 69). And we also know that at
the university in May 1826 Poe came upon "a rare edition of Hogarth's
prints" in a second-hand shop and tried to buy it (*Log*, 71). Although the
edition ultimately went to someone else, Poe had apparently examined it
with great care. In later years, Poe was fond of quoting approvingly
Hogarth's remark that genius is "but *diligence* after all" (3:1145, 1149 n.
47), suggesting that his early regard for the artist's work stayed with him
all his life. And certainly if Poe knew Hogarth's work, he would have
known of his association with the serpentine line. For as Hogarth himself
points out in the preface to *The Analysis of Beauty*, the self-portrait pub-

lished as a frontispiece to his engraved works showed "a serpentine line, lying on a painter's pallet" and beneath it the words "THE LINE OF BEAU-TY." Finally, it seems hard to believe that anyone as interested as Poe was in questions of analysis and in the subject of the sublime and beautiful would not have made it a point to read a work entitled *The Analysis of Beauty,* particularly if it had been written by an artist whose work he admired.

The question is, then, if Poe did know *The Analysis of Beauty,* as seems more than likely, what would he have made of the emblem Hogarth had created for the title page, an emblem combining a "triangular form" and a "serpentine line" as the "two most expressive figures" to signify "not only beauty and grace, but the whole *order of form.*" I would suggest that, given Poe's taste for deciphering cryptograms, he would have almost certainly seen the two combined shapes as letters, the "triangular form" evoking the Greek capital *D* (the legend on which the emblem is based is, after all, Greek in origin, according to Lomazzo) and the "serpentine line" evoking the letter *S*. Moreover, given the Pythagorean resonances in Hogarth's preface, Poe might well have assimilated these letters to the two powers he associated with the true mathematician—the resolvent and the creative, the analytic and the poetic—the *D* evoking the triangular tetractys as a figure of the mathematical component of reality and the *S* evoking the line of beauty as a figure of the aesthetic, the two together (one inscribed within the other) presenting an emblem of the conjunction of these two orders in the creation of the universe. Indeed, the sexual resonances of these conjoined symbols (the phallic serpent within the pubic triangle) suggest the image of a sacred marriage, a *hieros gamos* of beauty and mathematics. (Hogarth had, of course, quoted Lomazzo to the effect that the Greeks placed the perfect aesthetic shape "in a triangular glass" and dedicated it "unto Venus," the goddess of love.) And certainly a sexual resonance is present as well in the conjunction of these two alphabetic characters on the seals of the purloined letter. Not only are the two states of the letter gender-coded (the address on the original letter written in a bold, masculine hand; that on the refolded letter in a diminutive, feminine one), but the letter itself is undoubtedly an amorous communication between the duke of S—— (or some male member of his family) and the queen, a form of written intercourse meant to evoke another form of intercourse—hence the letter's susceptibility to being used for blackmail by the minister and hence the appropriateness, in Lacan's reading of the tale, of associating the letter with the phallic signifier, with the linking third term that both unites and differentiates masculine and feminine.

So far we have suggested three sets of possible significations for the *S* and *D* impressed on the purloined letter's seals, and there is at least one more we should note, a set that bears directly on the nature of the fold, specifically, on the turning of the letter inside out like a glove. For, as we noted, the everting of a glove reverses its handedness, and certainly Poe with his knowledge of Latin would have noticed that *S* and *D* are the initials of the words for left and right in that language—*sinistra* and *dextra*—a signification that reinforces the sense of mirror-image reciprocity between the terms in the other differential pairs and that points once again to the V-shaped fold of the hand as the bodily given that grounds a linguistic system of differential oppositions.

What becomes clear, then, is that in making the purloined letter a figure of the reflexive nature of the self, Poe has made it a nodal point at which a series of differential oppositions intersect—oppositions that are presented either through the manipulation of the letter (inner/outer, depth/surface), through the handwriting of the address (masculine/feminine), or through the possible significances of the initials on the seals (such as sameness/difference). But to grasp the full point of Poe's evoking the letter as the intersection of these oppositions, we must understand its position within the overall structure of the tale, a structure that "The Purloined Letter" shares with the myths of Oedipus and Theseus and with the first Dupin story.

Taking the myth of Oedipus as the general form of this scenario, we can identify its recurring elements as follows: There is a protagonist (Oedipus) whose fated task is to enact the mysterious relationship of sameness and difference that constitutes self-identity, enact it by confronting an antagonist (the Sphinx) who poses the internal problem of self-identity or self-difference (a problem figured within the self as the mind/body difference) as the external problem of differentiating human from animal. The antagonist, a physical embodiment of the external problem, is literally a monster, a combination of animal and human parts in which the feral predominates. But the antagonist poses the problem in a form that, although it bears an animal sanction for failure (death by being devoured), demands a human (i.e., mental) solution. When Oedipus answers the riddle correctly, the Sphinx kills herself. But Oedipus, having successfully confronted the general question of human identity, must now face the individual problem of personal identity, enacting the dark half of the riddle's truth by discovering not the difference that separates human from animal but the sameness that unites them, a discovery ultimately made through a scenario structured around the same set of numbers that governs the Sphinx's riddle of human differentiation. Since the incest taboo is a traditional cultural marker of the difference between animal and human, incest functions in the Oedipus myth as a structural means of linking the general problem of human differentiation within the natural world to the specific problem of personal identity within a human community (i.e., the recognition of kinship and its rules). This same broad structure is repeated in the Theseus myth with slight modifications. The protagonist is Theseus, his half-animal, half-human antagonist the Minotaur, and the mental problem associated with the antagonist the labyrinth. Unlike the Sphinx's riddle (a puzzle of words and numbers), the labyrinth poses the problem of human differentiation in terms of oppositions such as right/left and inner/outer that figure self-consciousness as self-location.

In the first Dupin story Poe adapts these mythic structures to his own ends. The protagonist is Dupin, and the antagonist the manlike killer ape, or more precisely, a combination of the ape's human master (the sailor) and his animal slave (the orangutan). The mental problem linked with the antagonist (the locked-room puzzle) is, as we noted earlier, a variant of the labyrinth, employing in its figuration of the self's structure many of the same oppositions associated with the Minotaur's dwelling and presenting at the same time (as in Poe's manipulation of the word *clew*, for example) a self-conscious commentary on its mythic antecedents. For of course what characterizes the Dupin stories is precisely the degree of self-consciousness they exhibit about their *own* literary origin, tradition, and structure as they pursue the task of reflecting on the structure of self-consciousness. The major change Poe makes in adapting the Oedipus/Theseus scenario for the first Dupin story concerns the transition from the general problem of differentiating the human to the individual one of self-identity within the family unit, a transition effected, as we said, in terms of the incest taboo as a cultural marker of the difference *animal/human*. For in "The Murders in the Rue Morgue" the incest motif and the element of familial violence are not associated with the protagonist Dupin but with the protagonist's creator, the killing of a mother and daughter within a claustrophobic family setting suggesting the more or less conscious translation of Poe's ambivalent feelings about his own semi-incestuous family circle evident in the dying woman stories.

We should note, in moving from the first to the last Dupin story, that the absence from "Marie Rogêt" of the structure we have been discussing is probably due to Poe's abandoning his original design for the tale in order to parallel the real case of Mary Cecilia Rogers. But with the third Dupin story, the scenario appears once more. The protagonist is again Dupin and the antagonist the Minister D——, whose character Poe presents as a combination of animal and human traits. The prefect describes the minister as one "who dares all things, those unbecoming as well as those becoming a man" (3:976); while Dupin refers to him as "that *monstrum horrendum*, an unprincipled man of genius" (3:993). As a figure of superior human intelligence in the service of base instincts, the minister culminates the structure's genealogy of "horrifying monsters." Similarly, the incest taboo and the element of familial violence characteristic of the structure are evoked by the substitutive Oedipal triangle (king, queen, and minister) in the original scene in the royal boudoir. The coding of the minister's role within the triangle is accomplished, first, by his taking possession of the phallic communication from the queen's lover and using it against her (the mental violence of blackmail), and second, by Dupin's inscribing a quotation from Crebillon's *Atrée* in the letter he leaves at the minister's house. The quotation in effect compares the minister's scheme to the ancient tale of Atreus and Thyestes: As Thyestes seduced the wife of his brother King Atreus, so the minister has tried to blackmail the king's wife with evidence of an adulterous affair. Atreus punishes his brother by having Thyestes' two children boiled and served to their unwitting father. And when Thyestes discovers the truth, he curses the house of Atreus, a curse that ends up consuming his brother's offspring for generations to come.

There is, of course, a natural appropriateness to the punishment Atreus inflicts on his brother, for in most cultures the taboos against incest and cannibalism, considered as markers of the animal/human difference, are structurally linked. Which is to say that just as human beings are forbidden to mate with their own kin, so they are forbidden to eat their own kind. Indeed, we can even see a faint trace of this connection between the two taboos running through the Oedipus myth, starting with the animal threat of the Sphinx to devour Oedipus if he fails to answer her riddle and ending with the self-devouring fates of Oedipus's incestuous offspring.

As the minister fills the role in the third Dupin story of the part-human, part-animal antagonist, so the mental puzzle associated with this role is the hidden-object problem. And just as the first Dupin story's locked-room problem is a conscious reworking of the labyrinthine puzzle associated with the Minotaur (as well as a commentary on the meaning of such puzzles), so the hidden-object problem is Poe's summation of this commentary. In effect, Poe makes the purloined letter a compendium of the oppositions and motifs connected with these mental tests—to which he adds his own interpretive embellishments, as, for example, when the inner/outer opposition associated with the labyrinth is translated into the endless reversibility of inner and outer as a figure of mind; or when the numbers governing the Sphinx's riddle become associated with the figure of a square folded along its diagonal as an image of self-consciousness; or when the right/left opposition from the labyrinth is linked, through the image of the quincuncial network, to the body's mirror asymmetry and the V-shaped fold of the hand. For Poe, the purloined letter figures the point of intersection in the self's structure where reflexiveness, infinity, and incommensurability are joined. And like the V shape in Browne's *Garden of Cyrus*, the purloined letter with its myriad associations is meant to evoke the interface between mind and body as the point where alphabetic characters, numbers, and geometric shapes can be converted into one another on the basis of a common physical form—a bilateral or bipolar, mirror-image relationship figured as a fold.

The self is, then, for Poe essentially a structure of number and geometry (number spatially extended as relation) within language. It is an identity in difference, a unity that is halved and doubled, an always-about-to-be-accomplished evenness constituted by its being originally and essentially at odds with itself, a shifting marker of positions within geometrical as well as grammatical relationships—indeed, one could go on indefinitely multiplying its numerical expressions within speech. Small wonder, then, that as Poe attempts to analyze the analytic power in the Dupin stories the amount of mathematical reference and imagery increases almost exponentially from tale to tale. And small wonder, too, that in pursuing a Pythagorean/Platonic trajectory in the stories Poe is ultimately led to the task of distinguishing the true mathematician (in the Pythagorean sense of the term) from the mere mathematician, of distinguishing analysis from algebra. For what Poe has done is to take the task of differentiating the human that he found in the myths of Oedipus and Theseus and reflect its mind/body opposition into one of the two differential terms (mind). Which is simply to say that just as there is a difference between mind and body, so there is a difference between the aspects of mind related to each, between a mental power reflecting the mind's abstract structure and one reflecting the body's physical instincts. Poe makes this distinction at the very start of the Dupin stories with the narrator's remark about "the Bi-Part Soul" and his notion of "a double Dupin—the creative and the resolvent." These powers, personified later in the figures of poet and mathematician, represent respectively the intuitive and the ratiocinative aspects of mind: the former concerned with the sensual, the emotional, the aesthetic—translating into consciousness the realm of animal instinct and bodily knowledge; the latter concerned with the ideal, the abstract, the logical—reflecting into consciousness the mind's own numerical/geometrical form: the two together as necessary to the definition of a true poet as to that of a true mathematician. For just as Poe believes that the true mathematician must possess powers of imagination and aesthetic insight, so he also believes—as "The Philosophy of Composition," "The Rationale of Verse," and "The Poetic Principle" make clear—that the true poet must be literally a man of numbers, in that ancient sense of verse as a kind of counting.

In "The Purloined Letter" Poe is able to take this structure of self-consciousness (in which the whole is reflected into a part of itself) one step further by naming the story after the central symbolic object the story presents and by making that symbolic object a text—an identity-in-difference that allows Poe to embody the theme of analyzing the analytic power in the tale's oblique analysis of its own ontological/epistemological status. Indeed, the notion of the text's describing its own status suggests one of the practical concerns that may have led Poe to the invention of the detective story. Poe supported himself for most of his adult life as a writer for and editor of literary magazines during a period when the reading public in America was growing and its character changing. As both writer and editor, Poe undoubtedly tried to learn as much as he could about the composition of his audience, about its interests and its taste in reading, in order to give his work as broad an appeal as possible. We know that Poe prided himself on the fact that as an editor he dramatically increased the circulation of all the magazines with which he was associated. And in this regard one can well imagine Poe asking himself whether there existed a single interest or activity shared by all readers, one that a writer or editor could take advantage of. To which one can equally well imagine Poe replying, in one of those mental shortcuts that constitute genius, that, obviously, there does exist one activity that all readers share and that, one assumes, they are all interested in—the act of reading itself. Consequently, if one were to invent a type of story that thematized the act of reading, that presented reading as the analytic interpretation, the decipherment, of a text contained within the framing text of the tale, then one would have created a form of both universal interest and unparalleled immediacy for readers, a form in which the emotional energy generated by the reader's effort to interpret the text would flow directly into the main character's activity of solving the mystery, a genre in which the reader would be asked to interpret the author's intentions by participating in the detective's attempt to interpret the criminal's.

Poe makes this thematization of the act of reading explicit in the first two Dupin stories by having Dupin and the narrator analyze lengthy newspaper accounts of the cases. In "The Murders in the Rue Morgue" the entire presentation of the crime is accomplished by two excerpts (running to eight pages in the Mabbott edition) from the "Gazette des Tribunaux," excerpts from which Dupin extracts a crucial clue by noting that each witness identifies the killer as speaking a different foreign language, but always one that that particular witness does not himself speak. And as the entire exposition phase in the first story is accomplished through Dupin's reading newspaper reports before visiting the scene of the crime, so in "The Mystery of Marie Rogêt" the entire investigation is carried out without Dupin ever viewing the crime scene. In effect, the story consists of nothing but Dupin's analysis of written reports of the case. The narrator tells us that he "procured, at the Prefecture, a full report of all the evidence elicited, and, at the various newspaper offices, a copy of every paper in which, from first to last, had been published any decisive information in regard to this sad affair" (3:728–29). With Poe once again introducing lengthy journalistic excerpts into the text, Dupin and the narrator sift through the various accounts of the crime, comparing versions, eliminating various theories of the murder advanced by different reporters, rejecting seemingly important clues as red herrings, and singling out details that may lead somewhere. Pausing midway in this exercise in textual analysis (an analysis that demonstrates who didn't commit the crime), Dupin sends the narrator out to verify certain details and adds, "I will examine the newspapers more generally than you have as yet done. So far, we have only reconnoitred the field of investigation; but it will be strange indeed if a comprehensive survey . . . of the public prints, will not afford us . . . a *direction* for inquiry" (3:752).

With this flourish, Poe emphasizes that Dupin's vaunted powers of detection amount in the first two stories to little more than a highly developed form of close reading; and in thus heightening the reader's awareness of the text-within-a-text motif in the first two tales, Poe prepares the reader to notice the change he makes in the motif in the final tale. For while in the first two, the actual words of the self-included text (the newspaper accounts of the crime) appear within the framing tale, in the third story it is simply a description of the self-included text that appears, the text-within-a-text being made to signify not in its own words (we are never shown the contents of the letter) but in ways more elliptical and problematic (i.e., the oppositions associated with its manipulation, the gender of the hand in which it is addressed, the initials on the seals, and so on). Indeed, in some sense it is the verbal "blankness" of the self-included text (the purloined letter with its letters purloined), its empty, mirrorlike quality, that makes it possible for Poe to superimpose on it the framing tale that bears its name, to fold that framing tale back into itself so that it becomes its own content. And this move, which sets up a ceaseless oscillation of outer and inner figuring the reflexive structure of the self, seems to lead immediately to the use of mathematical and geometrical images as the most natural and accurate means of representing the necessary intersection of reflexiveness, infinity, and incommensurability—a not unpredictable transition from the imagery of letters to that of numbers and geometrical shapes reflecting the way the V-shaped fold, as a figure of reflexiveness, forms a graphic conversion point for these three registers of signification or inscription.

In understanding that the structure of self-consciousness involves a necessary relationship among reflexiveness, infinity, and incommensurability, Poe in effect reproduced an insight of the ancient Greeks, and in choosing to make the analysis of the analytic power the central mystery in the Dupin stories, he committed himself to a notion of mystery best characterized as "Pythagorean." Poe's aesthetic task, like that of the creators of the myths of Oedipus and Theseus, was to find mysteries that would serve as dramatic correlatives for the central mystery of the human condition, and the fact that the mysteries he created were ones associated with the commission of crimes simply evokes the ancient sense that the structure of self-consciousness, as something constituted by an original and essential oddness, is basically transgressive.

IT IS IN REGARD TO the Pythagorean/Platonic character of the central mystery in the Dupin tales (and its accompanying imagery) that we must look one last time at Borges's project of doubling Poe. For not only does Borges employ the imagery of mathematics and geometry in a way that clearly invokes Poe's tales (the cabalistic aura of Borges's mathematics recalling the Pythagorean character of Poe's), he also uses mathematics to determine the order in which his three stories will double Poe's, a sequence Borges encodes in the order of the stories' historical settings. Perhaps the best way to gain a sense of Borges's engagement with Poe's mathematics is to recall that in his third detective story, "Ibn Hakkan al-Bokhari," he makes his two young detectives, Dunraven and Unwin, a poet and a mathematician respectively, alluding to Poe's personification of the dual creative/resolvent power in these two callings in "The Purloined Letter." He says that Dunraven "thought of himself as the author of a substantial epic, which his contemporaries would barely be able to scan and whose subject had not yet been revealed to him" and that Unwin "had published a paper on the theory supposed to have been written by Fermat in the margin of a page of Diophantus" (*A*, 115).

This latter detail is the most interesting of Borges's several allusions to Poe in the story, both because it suggests his sense of the Pythagorean character of Poe's mathematical imagery and because it illustrates his practice of doubling Poe by giving a Borgesian twist to a salient feature from the Dupin tales. Fermat's "Last Theorem," as it is called, is one of the most famous mysteries in the history of mathematics. In Kasner and Newman's *Mathematics and the Imagination* (reviewed by Borges in *Sur* in 1940), the problem is described in a section devoted to theorems "believed to be true, but never proved": "In the margin of his copy of Diophantus, Fermat wrote: 'If n is a number greater than two, there are no whole numbers, a, b, c such that $a^n + b^n = c^n$. I have found a truly wonderful proof which this margin is too small to contain'" (*MI*, 187–88). Noting that "almost every great mathematician since Fermat" has tried to duplicate this proof but that "none has ever succeeded," the authors continue:

Many pairs of integers are known, the sum of whose squares is also a square, thus:

$$3^2 + 4^2 = 5^2; \text{ or, } 6^2 + 8^2 = 10^2.$$

But no three integers have ever been found where the sum of the cubes of two of them is equal to the cube of the third. It was Fermat's contention that this would be true for all integers when the power to which they were raised was greater than 2. By extended calculations, it has been shown that Fermat's theorem is true for values of *n* up to 617. But Fermat meant it for *every n* greater than 2. Of all his great contributions to mathematics, Fermat's most celebrated legacy is a puzzle which three centuries of mathematical investigation have not solved and which skeptics believe Fermat, himself, never solved. (*MI,* 188)[1]

As Morris Kline explains, the seventeenth-century French mathematician Pierre de Fermat had written his famous marginal comment in a copy of Diophantus's *Arithmetica* "alongside Diophantus' problem: To divide a given square number into (a sum of) two squares" (Kline, 276). A Greek mathematician of the third century A.D., Diophantus of Alexandria produced during his eighty-four-year lifespan mathematical treatises that represent in Kline's words "the highest point of Alexandrian Greek algebra" (Kline, 138). One of his major innovations was the introduction of algebraic symbolism. Kline notes that although the precise symbols Diophantus employed are uncertain, "it is believed that the symbol he used for the unknown was ς," and that this terminal form of the Greek *sigma* or *s* "may have been chosen because it was not a number in the Greek system of using letters for numbers" (Kline, 139).

In telling us that his young mathematician/detective Unwin had published a paper on Fermat's Last Theorem, Borges is making several mathematical allusions at once. First, there is an obvious appropriateness in invoking Fermat's theorem in a story about an old unsolved mystery, for that theorem is itself an old unsolved mystery of mathematics, evoking in effect a complex tradition of unsuccessful detection. Second, the story of the theorem's origin—its inscription by Fermat in the margins of the work of an earlier writer—obliquely calls attention to Borges's own project of inscribing *his* three detective stories within the margins of Poe's. Further, the fact that Fermat wrote his marginal comment alongside this specific problem of Diophantus's seems to have been clearly understood by Borges as a reference to Pythagorean mathematics and thus intended in turn in his own detective story as an allusion to the Pythagorean element in the Dupin tales.

Diophantus's problem of dividing a square number into the sum of two squares refers, of course, to the Pythagorean theorem for finding the length of the hypotenuse in a right triangle. Diophantus's problem seeks, in effect, a means of generating whole numbers for the hypotenuse and sides of these triangles, thereby avoiding the problem of the hypotenuse's length being an irrational number, as in the diagonal of a square. As we recall, the equation for the Pythagorean theorem is $a^2 + b^2 = c^2$, an equation whose most famous whole number solution ($a = 3, b = 4, c = 5$) is specifically associated with Pythagoras. And indeed the very fact that there *are* whole-number solutions to this equation is precisely what evoked Fermat's supposed proof that there are *no* whole number solutions for equations of this form of the third power and above (e.g., $a^3 + b^3 = c^3$). So one could accurately say that Pythagorean mathematics was the ultimate origin of Fermat's theorem.

But Borges intends by this reference an even more specific allusion to Poe's mathematics. As we saw, in the third Dupin story Poe introduces an algebraic equation into Dupin's digression on analysis and algebra, a standard formula ($x^2 + px = q$) for solving quadratic equations with one unknown given in Farrar's translation of Lacroix's *Elements of Algebra*. And just as Poe includes a second-degree equation in *his* story (an equation meant to evoke the notion of solving for square roots and, by implication, the Pythagorean theorem), so Borges goes Poe one better and invokes in his tale a mathematical proof involving equations of the third degree and above, a proof that is at once a famous unsolved mystery of mathematics and a direct reference to the Pythagorean theorem.

This strategy of antithetically doubling specific details from the Dupin stories is one we have seen before—in Borges's reversal of the genre's right over left (righteous over sinister) privileging, for example, or in opposing the gender homogeneity of the genre's triad of detective/criminal/victim in his tales to its gender heterogeneity in Poe's. But in Borges's invocation of Fermat's Last Theorem, this strategy is probably given an added twist, for since the types of equations covered by Fermat's theorem can only have irrational solutions, Borges's balancing of this image of the irrational against the apparent rationality of the Dupin stories may also be a case of his making explicit in his tales what is implicit in Poe's—that sense of rationality's ultimate discovery, in analyzing itself, of the alogicality of its own ground.

Borges does not limit himself, however, to antithetically doubling specific elements from the Dupin stories; he repeats larger structures as well, repeats them in such a way that each of his detective stories ends up being keyed to one of Poe's. It is as if the reversal of details provided the element of difference while the repetition of larger structures provided the element of sameness in his project of doubling Poe one hundred years later.

And what we should note regarding these larger structures is that though Borges apparently set out to publish his three tales in the centennial years of the Dupin stories (a schedule he maintained for his first two stories of 1941 and 1942), he did not duplicate these structures in the sequence in which they appear in Poe's tales.

Although Borges's first detective story, "The Garden of Forking Paths," was published in the centennial of the genre's origin, it takes its central structure not from the "The Murders in the Rue Morgue," but from Poe's second story, "The Mystery of Marie Rogêt." The strategy seems clear: Borges wanted to commemorate the genre's anniversary, recover the form's original impulse, and perhaps in the process match his own skill against the genre's originator. But for his initial effort he decided to test his talent not against the genre's original story but against the weakest of the Dupin tales, a tale flawed by Poe's having to alter his original plan midway in its composition. Indeed, what Borges seems to have aimed for in repeating a structure from "Marie Rogêt" was to recover Poe's design and bring it to a successful, if slightly altered, conclusion.

In "The Mystery of Marie Rogêt" Poe had set out, through the mask of his detective Dupin, to reanalyze the facts in the Rogers murder case and indicate the identity of the killer. In effect, he would send this information, encrypted in the form of a fictive account, through the public medium of a magazine (Snowden's *Ladies' Companion* for November and December of 1842 and February 1843) to the New York authorities, who would decrypt the message by realizing the similarity of the Rogêt story to the Rogers case and follow Dupin's line of reasoning to the real culprit. That, of course, didn't happen.

What happened instead was that an Argentine fiction writer took Poe's original plan for "Marie Rogêt" and in 1941 published a tale in which Dr. Yu Tsun, a German agent in England during the First World War, sends a piece of secret information, encrypted in a newspaper account of a murder, to his chief who sits in his Berlin office, leafing "infinitely through newspapers, looking . . . for news" from his agents in England (*F*, 91). The spy trusts his chief will understand that his "problem was to shout . . . above the tumult of war, the name of the city called Albert" (*F*, 101) by murdering the Sinologist Stephen Albert.

The brilliance of Borges's adaptation turns in part upon the way that Borges, à la the purloined letter and the Aleph, transforms container into contained by making what had been an external principle of form in Poe's story (the author's original intention in writing the tale) a matter of content in his own (the main character's intention in concocting his plan). In each case the central idea is to send an important piece of information in an oblique form (a detective story; a newspaper account of a murder) through a public medium (Snowden's *Ladies' Companion;* the British tabloids) to a specific reader (the New York police; the spymaster in Berlin). And what probably suggested the notion of encrypting the French place name Albert in the English surname Albert (two names with the same spelling but different pronunciations) was a combination of Poe's encrypting the English name Mary Rogers in the French Marie Rogêt and his pun, in "The Murders in the Rue Morgue," on the English and French words clue/*clou*.

As Borges's first detective story repeats a structure from Poe's second, so Borges's second story, "Death and the Compass," repeats a structure from Poe's third, "The Purloined Letter." We have seen already how the three/four oscillation that lies at the heart of Poe's geometric model of reflexiveness was adapted by Borges to create the uncertainty of the triangular/quadrangular pattern of murders in "Death and the Compass," the pattern within which the antithetical doubles confront one another. Borges was also able to make use of the structural dynamics associated with this pattern in Poe, dynamics in which, as Lacan points out, a character's place within a triangular structure of glances is shifted from a position of insight to blindness as soon as he takes possession of the letter.

In "Death and the Compass" Borges adapts this ploy of position-shifting to the triad of victim, criminal, and detective by coding the three positions in terms of the differential opposition *hunter/hunted*. Which is to say that as the relationship of killer to victim is that of hunter to hunted, so is that of detective to killer. Consequently, in "Death and the Compass" the reader identifies Lönnrot as the detective for most of the story because he is the person in pursuit of the killer, but at the end of the tale the reader suddenly finds that Lönnrot has shifted from detective to victim, indeed, realizes that he has occupied that position almost from the beginning, when Scharlach used the circumstances of an accidental murder to concoct a plan to kill a double-crosser and take revenge on an old enemy. The criminal has counted on Lönnrot's own perception of himself as the hunter to blind him to his true status and has used the detective's own powers of analysis to lure him into a trap. But Scharlach is ultimately able to switch Lönnrot from detective to victim only because Scharlach has himself shifted at one point into that same role by playing the apparent third victim Gryphius-Ginzberg. Using a kind of hunter's magic, Scharlach enacts the role of victim in jest to get Lönnrot to play it in earnest. And the psychological mechanism Scharlach uses to distract his opponent is clearly one that Borges has adapted from the triangular structure of glances in "The Purloined Letter." For just as the second glance within Poe's structure, in observing the blindness of the first, mistakes its own view for an ultimate understanding in comparison and misses the superi-

or insight of the third glance, so Lönnrot, in observing Treviranus's blindness to the correct number of events in the series, interprets his own
numerical reading as a final insight and misses the possibility of Scharlach's superior grasp of Lönnrot's mental processes.

The vulnerability to a blind spot that the letter's possession brings
extends beyond the triangular structure of glances within "The Purloined
Letter" to the observer of that structure as well. As Derrida points out,
Lacan's interpretation of the two "narrated" scenes ignores the narrator's
presence, misses the fact that it is from the narrator's point of view (the
fourth glance) that the triangular structure of these scenes is constituted.
And what this implies is that in ignoring the narrator's involvement, Lacan
in effect overlooks the reader's involvement, that is, his own involvement
as the story's interpreter, in this same structure. For it is precisely from a
fourth point presumed to be outside the triangular structure of glances
that Lacan sees that structure *as* triangular. By contrast, when Derrida
observes Lacan looking at this structure, *he* sees a quadrangular configuration in which Lacan's privileged fourth position is equally subject to that
mechanism of position-shifting from insight to blindness at work in the
story.

In "Death and the Compass" Borges creates his own version of this
dilemma of hermeneutic reflexiveness in the problem of whether Lönnrot or Treviranus achieves the correct numerical solution to the murders.
Lönnrot is right about the number of events in the series but wrong about
the number of murders; Treviranus wrong about the number of events
but right about the number of murders. The blindness and insight of each
complements that of the other: It is only because Lönnrot's insight about
the number of events leads him to present himself at the time and place
planned for the last murder, blind to what is really going on, that Treviranus's blindness about the true number of events turns into an insight
about the actual number of murders. But while Treviranus and Lönnrot
(who embody the first and second glances) are both seeking the solution to
the mysterious series of murders, Scharlach (who embodies the third) is
seeking the solver of that mystery, seeking possession of the "text" that is
Lönnrot's self, a text he had already shrewdly read in concocting his plan.
But once Scharlach has captured Lönnrot, then something very much like
that shift from insight to blindness caused by the sought-after object's
possession takes place. Not that Scharlach is in danger of losing possession
of Lönnrot to someone else, of seeing him suddenly rescued by Treviranus, for example; but rather that Scharlach himself intends to lose this
object by killing Lönnrot. And the insight that allowed him to gain the
object now turns into blindness, or more precisely, becomes an insight that
is blinding; for in carrying his plan through to its conclusion he has come

to realize how much of his own existence is bound up with that of his antithetical double, that to do away with Lönnrot is to do away with his own reason for living. Indeed, Borges says that Lönnrot hears all this in Scharlach's voice, hears "the weariness of final triumph, a hatred the size of the universe, a sadness as great as that hatred" (A, 75). This is a game that Scharlach both wants and does not want to win, an object he both wants and does not want to capture; for winning is losing, possession is loss.

Scharlach's emotions simply reflect within the frame of the tale the reader's own mixed feelings in finishing an analytic detective story—on the one hand, the satisfaction in a solution (a satisfaction heightened if the reader has been able to defeat the author in their battle of wits by beating the detective to the answer) and, on the other hand, the reader's feeling of disappointment if the solution exhausts the sense of mystery and thus forecloses the pleasure of unlimited rereadings.

The originator of the analytic detective genre understood this as the main challenge the form presents the writer, and in consequence he made the central mystery in his three detective stories the problem of human self-consciousness, appreciating that for a work to reflect on the nature of reflexiveness would create the kind of double-mirror structure that infinitely deferred a final solution. Each reading of these stories presents the reader with an evolving solution that continually reorients his sense of where the central mystery in the tales lies, thus empowering another reading, in much the same way that the analysis of the analytic power always requires one more step to effect closure. Borges expresses his own sense of the genre's challenge when he says of Dunraven that, being "steeped in detective stories," he "thought that the solution of a mystery is always less impressive than the mystery itself" (A, 123). And he reflects into the plot of "Death and the Compass" the reader's own desires regarding the genre when he has Lönnrot, defeated in the battle of wits with Scharlach and about to be killed, suggest the infinite deferral of any final solution, suggest that because Scharlach's plan was not perfect, they must meet again in another incarnation to replay their duel. In any detective story whose central mystery is the self-conscious description of its own workings, there will always be one more step needed, precisely because self-consciousness by its very nature can never really think its own ending, its own absence.

43 *Linking First to Last; Doubling the Origin; The Man Who Knew Too Much; Originating a Hybrid Genre; Poe's Borgesian Quality*

THAT BORGES'S FIRST TWO DETECTIVE stories are keyed to the second and third Dupin tales is due in part, as we suggested, to Borges's desire to begin his project by doubling Poe's weakest story. But it is probably also due to his wanting to save the most difficult part of the project for last, the writing of the story that would confront the genre's origin, "The Murders in the Rue Morgue." Certainly his final tale, "Ibn Hakkan al-Bokhari, Dead in His Labyrinth," is his most explicit attempt both to create something resembling a locked-room problem and to link it to the question of differentiating human from animal. Borges's first two detective stories involve, of course, labyrinths that are only metaphoric (a Chinese novel whose narrative branches fork in time; a geometric design on a map leading to a house of "meaningless symmetries"). And in neither case is an animal associated with the structure, beyond the metaphoric animality involved in one human being killing another. But in Borges's third tale, there is a real labyrinth and a problem of personal identity posed by a trio of faceless corpses (both animal and human) at the labyrinth's center.

Among the difficulties Borges faced in trying to double the tale that originated the analytic detective genre, perhaps the main one was that he simply knew too much about what he was doing, had read too many detective stories to be able to reproduce the uncontaminated state of mind out of which the first detective story came, that unembarrassed innocence of later developments which necessarily attends a genre's origin. Without a doubt, Borges had problems in writing "Ibn Hakkan al-Bokhari," and he registers his sense of these in the note to the English translation of the tale. He observes that after the "first two exercises of 1941 and 1942" his third effort in the detective genre, which was to be his "swan song,"

> became a cross between a permissible detective story and a caricature of one. The more I worked on it, the more hopeless the plot seemed and the stronger my need to parody. What I ended up with I hope will be read for its humor. I certainly can't expect anyone to take seriously or to look for symbols in such pictorial whims as a black slave, a lion in Cornwall, a red-haired king, and a

scarlet maze so large that on first sight its outer ramparts appear to be a straight blank wall. (*A*, 274)

This final demurrer is, of course, Borges's way of calling attention to the very opposite: that these details are included precisely for their symbolic significance. The image of the king, slave, and lion in the labyrinth, in evoking the question of animal/human differentiation, recalls that in Poe's original story this question was associated with the role of the killer (the manlike ape and his human master), while in Borges's attempt to double that story it is associated with the role of the victim. And it is precisely this switching of roles, combined with a distinctive color-coding, that suggests how much Borges's effort to duplicate the origin of the genre had become contaminated by his knowledge of subsequent detective stories, particularly "The Purloined Letter." The red-haired king, the black slave, and the lion "the color of the sun" (presumably a reddish gold) evoke the red/black opposition associated not with the first Dupin story but with the last (the red and black wax seals affixed to the folded and refolded states of the letter), a color differentiation that Poe in effect links to the letter's container/contained oscillation and thus to the notion of reflexiveness as the defining principle of the self.

Indeed, the presence of details from the third Dupin story in Borges's doubling of the first suggests the way he ultimately tried to handle the impossible task of duplicating the genre's origin, and it suggests as well the deeper significance of that passage from "Ibn Hakkan al-Bokhari" cited earlier—the exchange between the amateur detectives regarding simplicity and complexity: Unwin's caution, "Don't go on multiplying the mysteries. . . . They should be kept simple. Bear in mind Poe's purloined letter, bear in mind Zangwill's locked room," and Dunraven's response, "Or made complex. . . . Bear in mind the universe." Since the notion of an origin is usually associated with simplicity, it is not surprising that the locked-room problem with which Poe began the genre should be invoked here. What is surprising, though, is that Borges refers to it not as Poe's locked room but Zangwill's and that he does not mention the locked room first, as befits its status as the genre's original mystery, but mentions it after the reference to Poe's last story, "The Purloined Letter."

It would seem that in referring to "Zangwill's locked room" rather than Poe's, Borges meant to allude to that tradition of detective stories that attempt new solutions to the locked-room puzzle and thus to evoke that ongoing project of doubling the genre's original problem as a figure of his own project. For just as Poe's last Dupin story is structurally linked to his first through the reciprocity of the locked-room and hidden-object problems, and just as that last story reflects the detective form back into itself by naming the tale after the concealed text that is its subject, so Borges, in referring to "Zangwill's locked room" in the last of his three stories, means to reflect back into *his* tale the whole tradition of the detective genre synecdochically evoked through one specialized strand in that tradition, a strand constituted precisely by the notion of continuous relatedness to an origin (Poe's womblike locked room).

Since the doubling of Poe's first detective story by Borges's last clearly fits into a larger Borgesian pattern of linking ends to beginnings as a figure of temporal reflexiveness, and since Borges saw this technique as replicating a pattern already present in the Dupin tales, it is no wonder that Borges's final detective story, while taking the structure of its mystery from "The Murders in the Rue Morgue," takes the structure of its solution from "The Purloined Letter." Which is to say that "Ibn Hakkan al-Bokhari" presents us with what at first glance appears to be a locked-room problem (and its associated question of animal/human differentiation) but then gives us, as the solution to the mystery of how the murderer made his escape without a trace, not some ploy concerning the way in which the exits were sealed (as in "The Murders in the Rue Morgue") but a structure of position-shifting and final substitution (as in "The Purloined Letter"). For what the two young detectives Dunraven and Unwin finally conclude is that the murderer (Zaid) first shifted positions within the triad by masquerading as the would-be victim (Ibn Hakkan) and then made a final substitution (not unlike Dupin's in switching letters at the minister's residence) by leaving the real Ibn Hakkan dead in the labyrinth and having the fake Ibn, whom no one knew existed, vanish into thin air— though Borges, always the contrarian, reverses the pattern from the ending of "The Purloined Letter," where the fake letter is left behind and the real one carried off.

As we saw, Borges had used the device of position-shifting within a triad in "Death and the Compass" (the tale specifically intended to double the structure of "The Purloined Letter"), but he had also employed it in another story that appeared between the publication of "Death and the Compass" (1942) and "Ibn Hakkan al-Bokhari" (1951). In late 1942 Borges and Bioy-Casares published a collection of parody detective stories called *Six Problems for Don Isidro Parodi*. The name of their detective suggests the intent of the work, although the volume is meant as a parody more of the French-dominated, highbrow literary tastes of Buenos Aires society than of a genre that Borges and Bioy-Casares both admired. The pompously learned foreword to the book, signed by the fictional "Gervasio Montenegro, Member, Argentine Academy of Letters" (*DIP*, 13), comments both on the history of the genre and on the individual tales in the volume and, as we recall, notes of the last story "Tai An's Long Search" that it is "a new and original treatment of the classic problem of the hidden object" which "Poe began . . . with 'The Purloined Letter'" (*DIP*, 10).

In the story the Chinese cultural attaché in Buenos Aires comes to Parodi's jail cell on visiting day to seek his help in solving a mystery. Almost twenty years earlier in China, a thief had stolen a jewel from a shrine and fled the country. The priests of the shrine had sent someone in pursuit, and this emissary, Tai An, arriving in Buenos Aires, had spent several years looking for the stolen jewel. Recently, Tai An's dwelling had been destroyed by fire, and Tai An subsequently murdered. As the cultural attaché tells his story, the reader expects that the hidden object in this tale will be the stolen jewel, much as the stolen letter was in Poe's. But the reader discovers at the end that the real hidden object is the identity of the thief, or more precisely, the identities of hunter and hunted. For Parodi demonstrates that Tai An, the apparent hunter sent from China to recover the jewel, is in fact the thief and that the man Tai An had been shadowing (even to the point of having him share his dwelling), a certain Fang She, is the real emissary sent in pursuit. Tai An had told the cultural attaché that he was the emissary, and this had seemed plausible at the time because the apparent suspect Fang She had arrived in Buenos Aires almost a year before Tai An, the assumption being that since the thief had fled China before the emissary had started in pursuit this same temporal lag (which coded one as hunted and the other as hunter) applied to their arrivals in Buenos Aires. But apparently Fang She had anticipated Tai An's ultimate destination and arrived before him.

What Borges does in "Death and the Compass," the parody "Tai An's Long Search," and "Ibn Hakkan al-Bokhari" is to systematically make his way through a series of possible position-shifts within the triad of victim/criminal/detective, shifts that refigure the hidden-object problem as that of identifying the characters who fill the three roles in each story. In "Death and the Compass" the apparent detective is the real victim; in "Tai An's Long Search" the apparent detective is the real criminal; and in "Ibn Hakkan al-Bokhari" the apparent victim (the false Ibn Hakkan) is the real criminal (the impostor Zaid). At one point in "Tai An's Long Search," Borges explicitly alludes to the numerical/geometrical strategies of "Death and the Compass" by having the cultural attaché note that after Tai An's dwelling had been burned the four principal characters in the drama—Tai An, his mistress Madame Hsin, his business partner Nemirovsky, and Fang She—had dispersed to various locations that formed "on the map of Buenos Aires an interesting shape not unlike that of a triangle" (*DIP*, 149). Inasmuch as this pattern (in which four people are dispersed among three points arranged in a triangle on a city map) evokes the three/four oscillation governing the locations of the murders in "Death and the Compass," there exists the distinct possibility that in "Tai An's Long Search" Borges and Bioy-Casares are parodying not so much Poe's original hidden-object problem as Borges's attempt to double the structure of "The Purloined Letter" in "Death and the Compass," parodying the notion that it is possible to produce an "original treatment" of this classic problem. For, of course, Borges's stratagem of position-shifting within the genre's triad of roles had already been anticipated to some extent by the shifting that occurs within the triad of glances in the third Dupin story.

Given the possibility that with the *Parodi* stories Borges had begun to parody his own project of doubling the Dupin tales, begun to thematize the impossibility of recovering an origin, we can understand his difficulty, once he turned his attention back to that project, in bringing "Ibn Hakkan al-Bokhari" to a conclusion, understand why, as he says, "the more I worked on it, the more hopeless the plot seemed and the stronger my need to parody," until "it became a cross between a permissible detective story and a caricature of one." And in this regard we can also see more clearly both what is at stake in Borges's strategy of linking beginning to end and what "Tai An's Long Search" may have contributed to that strategy.

In a circular, a temporally reflexive, system where the end leads back into the beginning, the end often comes to seem prior to the beginning, as original or more original than the origin. A kind of temporal reversal occurs in which beginning and end seem to change places. In linking his last detective story to Poe's first, Borges meant to create, among other things, a structure of temporal reflexiveness appropriate to a genre whose central theme was the reflexive nature of self-consciousness. The difficulty Borges experienced in doubling the genre's original story sprang, as we suggested, from the fact that that origin no longer existed for him in an uncontaminated form. But at some point, probably after finishing *Six Problems for Don Isidro Parodi* and while working on his last detective story, Borges seems to have understood that this difficulty was in fact the real point of his project. He understood that by creating a structure in which Poe's three detective stories and his own three were treated, respectively, as the beginning and end points of the genre, the linking of his last story to Poe's first—to the extent that this figure of temporal reflexiveness produced a reversal in which the endpoint seemed prior to, and more original than, the beginning—mirrored the effect produced by tradition, by the accumulated works within a genre as they act retrospectively to alter our reading of the genre's origin. In effect, Borges understood that the only way to double (and thus recover) the origin of the analytic detective genre was to originate a new, hybrid genre springing from the detective story's thematizing of analytic reading. Perhaps as a result of writing *Six Problems for Don Isidro Parodi*, he saw that just as the parody analytic detective story is a different genre from analytic detective fiction, so the type of story he was writing to double Poe's Dupin tales was also a different genre from the one Poe had invented. For while Borges's stories, like Poe's, analyze the analytic power and reflect on the nature of reflexivity, they also constitute highly self-conscious exercises in literary history and criticism, sophisticated critical readings of the genre's origin (and, implicitly, of the tradition arising from that origin) that make Poe's Dupin stories seem almost Borgesian, as if they had been written by Borges or by someone who had read him.

That Borges ultimately intended his detective stories to create this effect can be judged from his essay "Kafka and His Precursors," published in the same year "Ibn Hakkan al-Bokhari" appeared. In the essay Borges sets out to make a brief "survey of Kafka's precursors," noting that although he had at first thought Kafka was "as singular as the fabulous Phoenix," when he came to know his work better he "recognized his voice, or his habits, in the texts of various literatures and various ages" (*OI*, 106). Included in these precursors are texts by Zeno, Han Yu, Kierkegaard, Browning, Leon Bloy, and Lord Dunsany. Borges concludes,

> If I am not mistaken, the heterogeneous selections I have mentioned resemble Kafka's work: if I am not mistaken, not all of them resemble each other, and this fact is the significant one. Kafka's idiosyncrasy, in greater or lesser degree, is present in each of these writings, but if Kafka had not written we would not perceive it; that is to say, it would not exist. The poem "Fears and Scruples" by Robert Browning is like a prophecy of Kafka's stories, but our reading of Kafka refines and changes our reading of the poem perceptibly. Browning did not read it as we read it now. The word "precursor" is indispensable in the vocabulary of criticism, but one should try to purify it from every connotation of polemic or rivalry. The fact is that each writer *creates* his precursors. His work modifies our conception of the past, as it will modify the future. (*OI*, 108)

One is perhaps most familiar nowadays with "the word 'precursor' . . . in the vocabulary of criticism" from Harold Bloom's studies of poetic influence, its anxieties and defense mechanisms, but Bloom has always acknowledged that one of his own major precursors in the theory of influence was Borges in the Kafka essay. And certainly the germ of the idea in this essay was present as early as that first short story in a new manner, "Pierre Menard, Author of *Don Quixote*." For in terms of the text of the novel, what does Menard's project of recreating chapters of the *Quixote* word for word out of his own experience amount to except the reader's recognizing Menard's "voice, or his habits" in Cervantes' work? And in fact the ending of the story speculates about the way the interpretation of virtually every passage in the novel changes once one assumes the text was written by a twentieth-century Frenchman rather than a seventeenth-century Spaniard.

Menard's project of doubling the *Quixote* is, as we argued earlier, an oblique version, or perhaps preliminary sketch, of Borges's own project regarding the Dupin stories. But we should also note the ways this project differs both from Menard's with the *Quixote* and from Kafka's with those precursor texts mentioned in Borges's essay. There is never a sense in Borges's essay that Kafka set out to double any of the earlier texts in question. Rather, Borges, the omnivorous reader, having become well acquainted with Kafka's writings, notices in the works of other, earlier writers turns of phrase or habits of thought that, because of Kafka's highly distinctive body of work, he can now retrospectively recognize (and name) as Kafkaesque. Kafka may have read some of the authors and texts in question and may even have been influenced by them, but that is not really Borges's concern in the essay. His focus is on the way that a major writer can take elements of thought or style that may have been present, though in a virtually unrecognizable form, in earlier writers and make so much of those elements (and thus make them so much his own) that they are ultimately perceived as literary historical entities. Although these elements of thought or style may have operated in one temporal direction in the writing of a fictional work (through the influence of an earlier writer on a later), Borges's essay argues that for readers they come into self-conscious existence in the opposite direction (from later to earlier) through an interpreter's perception of resemblances. In the essay Borges never suggests that Kafka consciously intended his fiction as a commentary on, or critique of, the tradition of literary elements that form his distinctive style. The self-conscious awareness of such a tradition of precursors required a different type of writing—Borges's critical essay.

In contrast, for both Borges and Menard in their fiction-writing projects, the task of doubling a specific work by an earlier writer is from the very start an intentional, highly self-conscious act. Obviously, in Borges's case the writer he chose was a major influence on his own work. But the difference between Borges's and Menard's projects is that the latter, as Borges says, is invisible; it produces no new text that differs linguistically from Cervantes'. The distinction between Cervantes' work and Menard's is wholly interpretive, the hermeneutic effect of attributing the authorship of a seventeenth-century Spanish novel to a twentieth-century Frenchman. But Borges's project of doubling Poe produces three new detective stories, texts that are linguistically different from the Dupin tales though clearly meant to have this "difference" understood in light of their sameness with those stories. As Borges manipulates elements and structures from the Dupin tales, he creates his own readings of them, interpretations that reveal what he takes to be the essential components and dynamics of the genre Poe invented. As a result, Borges's detective stories can only be fully understood when the Dupin stories are placed over them like templates and variations from the originals measured.

If Borges meant his detective story project to be a recovery of the original impulses and intentions of the genre, it was clearly because he believed the detective tradition that sprang from the Dupin tales had developed only the most superficial aspects of the form, missing the original stories' central meaning. Thus, for example, the real significance of the locked-room problem's animal killer and threadlike clew had been almost completely lost by the time of Conan Doyle's Sherlock Holmes story "The Adventure of the Speckled Band," in which the ape has been replaced by a swamp adder and the threadlike clew by a bell-rope leading from a ventilator to the victim's bed. I say almost completely lost because in the Holmes mystery the intended victims are twin stepdaughters, while the killer is their stepfather who penetrates (with a phallic serpent) the sealed space of the victim's bedroom through a ventilator pipe—the point being that there is just enough Oedipal resonance to the tale to suggest Doyle had some inkling of what was at issue in "The Murders in the Rue Morgue." But certainly by the time of Zangwill's *The Big Bow Mystery,* the deeper significance of the locked-room problem had been erased in the effort to create an alternate solution to Poe's. Just as the deeper significance of virtually everything else in the Dupin stories, so Borges seems to have felt, was eventually lost in the English country-house school of detective fiction and lost again in the American hard-boiled school (although in Dashiell Hammett's *The Dain Curse* and Raymond Chandler's *The Big Sleep* there are Oedipal resonances suggesting some understanding of Poe's original story). This is not to say that Borges did not admire the work of Doyle and Zangwill or Hammett and Chandler but rather that he thought the kinds of detective stories they wrote bore only a minimal relationship to the central structures and literary/epistemological seriousness of the genre Poe founded. Indeed, one senses that Borges thought of himself as the only writer in the tradition who fully understood what Poe had created, and to the extent that one accepts the interpretation Borges gives of the Dupin tales in his own three stories, he was probably right.

What seems clear is that between the publication of *Six Problems for Don Isidro Parodi* and his third detective story "Ibn Hakkan al-Bokhari," Borges became more self-conscious about the way that doubling the origin of the detective genre meant originating a new genre. And we can see the effect of this increased self-consciousness in a major difference in narrative technique between "Ibn Hakkan al-Bokhari" and the two earlier stories. In both the earlier tales the narrative viewpoint is associated with participants in the events (the criminal Yu Tsun in "The Garden of Forking Paths" and the detective Erik Lönnrot in "Death and the Compass"), and the narration is more or less contemporary with the incidents narrated. (There is a slight sense of historical displacement created by the first story's introductory paragraph, which places the events of 1916 within the context of Liddell Hart's book *A History of the World War* published in 1934, but that sense of events long past is quickly effaced by the immediacy of Yu Tsun's first-person narrative written on the eve of his execution.)

By contrast, in "Ibn Hakkan al-Bokhari" the narrative viewpoint is lodged with Dunraven and Unwin who have no personal involvement in the affair, and the narration takes place "about a quarter of a century" (*A*, 115) after the crime. On a visit to his hometown in Cornwall, Dunraven tells his friend the story of Ibn Hakkan's murder. Since most of his narrative has been learned second-hand from Mr. Allaby, the rector of the village, Dunraven, struck by the logical difficulties in what he recounts, asks Unwin, "Can this story be explained?" (*A*, 121). Together they reexamine his account, because, as Unwin tells his friend, although the facts in the case "could be thought of as true, . . . told the way you told them they were obviously lies." Unwin theorizes that if the intended victim was indeed Ibn Hakkan, then the impostor who built the labyrinth (and killed the king) must have been his vizier Zaid. Reinterpreting the story in this light, they find that all its "difficulties" now make sense, leading Dunraven to remark at last, "I admit . . . that my Ibn Hakkan could have been Zaid. Such metamorphoses are classic rules of the game, are accepted *conventions* demanded by the reader" (*A*, 125).

In referring to "classic rules of the game" and "*conventions* demanded by the reader," Dunraven indicates just how much he has separated himself from his own account of these events, how much he has come to think of it as detective fiction and himself as a critic able to identify its rules and conventions. Moreover, the correctness of the two young men's solution is never actually established by their turning detective in earnest and tracking down Zaid. Their solution remains within the field of speculation to the end, its correctness based on how well their reading reorganizes the salient features of Dunraven's narrative to achieve maximum coherence and plausibility in terms of character, motive, plot, and so on, which is to say, a correctness based on wholly formal, literary critical principles. Not only, then, has Borges in his third tale made the emotional/intellectual identification of the reader with the detective (implicit in the Dupin stories) explicit by presenting his two young sleuths as close readers of a detective story, he has also self-consciously confronted the fact that his project of doubling the genre's origin, a genre whose central subject is the analysis of reflexivity, has led him to create a new origin precisely by reflecting an old one back on itself, combining in a single form detective fiction with a critical commentary on the origin and traditions of detective fiction.

44   *The Dupin Tales' Sequence of Publication; The Order*
of Borges's Doubling; A Cyclic Permutation; Parody
or Trial Run; Parody versus Serious Detective Story

TO INSURE THAT HIS READERS understood the Poe-related project governing his three detective stories, Borges had to give textual clues not only to these stories' relationship to the Dupin tales (as he does through explicit references to Auguste Dupin in "Death and the Compass" and to the purloined letter in "Ibn Hakkan al-Bokhari") but also to the significance of the sequence in which his three stories double the earlier trilogy. And here again Borges seems to have taken his lead from Poe. For one of the odd things about the Dupin stories that a close reader like Borges would certainly have noticed is that the sequence of their publication is incorporated into the text of the tales. Near the beginning of "The Mystery of Marie Rogêt," the narrator refers to his "article entitled 'The Murders in the Rue Morgue'" which had appeared "about a year ago" (3:724), and at the start of "The Purloined Letter" he says that he and Dupin had been discussing earlier that evening "the affair of the Rue Morgue, and the mystery attending the murder of Marie Rogêt" (3:974). Since the second and third Dupin stories, in naming the tales that precede them, establish the series' order of appearance, Borges is simply replicating another element in Poe's trilogy by subtly making the texts of his three tales indicate a sequence of their own, a sequence that takes for granted the reader's knowledge of the order of Borges's three tales' publication and demands instead that the reader attend to the chronology of their historical settings.

As we saw, Borges's first story ("The Garden of Forking Paths") is keyed to the central structure in the second Dupin tale ("The Mystery of Marie Rogêt"), his second story ("Death and the Compass") to the third Dupin tale ("The Purloined Letter"), and his third ("Ibn Hakkan al-Bokhari, Dead in His Labyrinth") to the first Dupin tale ("The Murders in the Rue Morgue"), so that the sequence in which Borges's three detective stories double Poe's is 2–3–1. The historical setting of Borges's first story is July 1916; that of the second sometime after 1917 (Rabbi Yarmolinsky had survived "three years of war in the Carpathians" [*A*, 66]); and of the third the summer of 1914. The first tale is thus the second latest in the chronology of settings, the second tale the third latest, and the third tale the earliest, giving us an order of 2–3–1 that replicates within the texts the sequence in which these tales double the individual Dupin stories.

That the sequence 2–3–1 had a special significance for Borges can be judged from a remark made by his principal English translator Norman Thomas di Giovanni at a seminar on translation he and Borges attended at Columbia University in 1971. Commenting on two possible ways of translating a sentence from one of Borges's stories, di Giovanni argues that the structure of one is demonstrably superior to the other because "a good sentence in English has a structure that begins with the second most important element, moves to the least important element, and ends with the strongest element. The pattern is 2–3–1" (*BOW*, 135). Since this comment was made with Borges present and since he and di Giovanni collaborated on the English translations of his stories, one can assume at the very least that Borges agreed with this principle and at most that di Giovanni was stating a rule learned from working with Borges. And quite clearly since one of Borges's objects in taking on the Dupin stories in the order he did was to save the most important (and most difficult) task for last (doubling the story that originated the genre), his practice and di Giovanni's dictum coincide. We should note that the sentence whose alternative translations had evoked di Giovanni's comment was from the opening paragraph of "The Garden of Forking Paths."

But what Borges does, in matching the sequence of his stories' publication (1–2–3) against the sequence of their chronological settings (2–3–1) as a means of textually encoding the order in which they double the Dupin tales, is something more complicated than the procedure indicated by di Giovanni's remark. In mathematical terminology this shifting of the sequence 1–2–3 into 2–3–1 is known as a cyclic permutation. To visualize it as a mathematician would, imagine two concentric circles with the numbers 1, 2, 3 distributed around each and aligned with their equivalent numbers (see fig. 44.1). If we let the numbers distributed around the inner circle represent the order of the appearance of Poe's detective stories and those distributed around the outer the order of the appearance of Borges's, then rotating the outer circle counterclockwise by one numerical position while maintaining the inner circle in place gives the order in which Borges's stories double Poe's (see fig. 44.2). (Of course, this same cyclic permutation could be achieved from the original figure by rotating the inner circle clockwise one numerical position while maintaining the outer circle in place.)

But why distribute the numbers within the original figure in this particular fashion? After all, we could just as easily put the 2 on the right and the 3 on the left and achieve the same results by rotating either the inner or the outer circle by a single numerical position while maintaining the

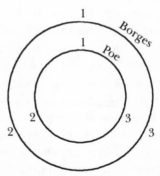

Figure 44.1

other circle in place. However, when contrasted with this alternative form, the significance of the original configuration becomes clear, for it is one that Borges himself authorizes in "Death and the Compass" when he has Scharlach send Treviranus the map showing the locations of the three crimes. The first murder occurred in the north, the second in the west, and the apparent third murder in the east, forming on the map an equilateral triangle that Scharlach has drawn in red ink. Given the standard spatial symbology of maps, this distribution of the events in sequence would place the number 1 at the top (north), the number 2 below and to the left (west), and the number 3 below and to the right (east), all within the circle of the compass. Since in the analytic detective story's battle of wits between author and reader the author plays the role of the criminal and the reader the detective, Scharlach's sending Treviranus the map highlighting this configuration is in effect Borges's presenting the reader with the sequence 1–2–3 in precisely this spatial arrangement to see whether he will make anything of it or whether, like Lönnrot, he will go on to the number 4 and be trapped.

But what might the reader make of it? Suppose he were to take this configuration of numbers within a circle and double it with the same configuration in a surrounding concentric circle, as we did in the first diagram. Would the reader be able to make the connection between this figure and the numerical sequence given by the order of historical settings in Borges's detective stories (2–3–1) and then make the further connection between these and Borges's dictum that the way to find the center of certain labyrinths is by always turning to the left? For, of course, in starting from our initial diagram, the operation of turning the outer circle of numbers counterclockwise by one numerical position is simply a turn to the left that produces the sequence 2–3–1. And Borges gives us an added clue to this operation by putting the instruction about turning to the left in his *first* and *third* detective stories, in effect showing us through this

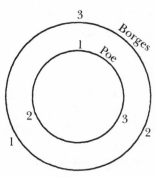

Figure 44.2

textual coincidence that the goal of the leftward turn is an alignment of the numbers 1 and 3, of beginning and end (the alignment achieved in our second diagram).

Complicated as this manipulation of sequences might seem, it would have been child's play compared to the kind of numerology Rabbi Yarmolinsky dealt with in writing his *Vindication of the Kabbalah* or the kind of number symbolism Borges was exposed to in reading Sir Thomas Browne, Gershom Scholem, or any number of alchemical or cabalistic texts. Indeed, Borges's interest in this kind of cyclic permutation can be judged from the opening story of *Six Problems for Don Isidro Parodi*—"The Twelve Figures of the World." Recall that the volume's final story, "Tai An's Long Search," is described in Gervasio Montenegro's foreword as "a new and original treatment" of the hidden-object problem which "Poe began . . . with 'The Purloined Letter'" and that in the story Borges makes a clear allusion to the plot of "Death and the Compass" (the tale meant to double "The Purloined Letter") when he disperses the four principal characters to three locations forming a triangle "on the map of Buenos Aires." Given Borges's habit of linking the first and last stories in a collection (as he did in *The Garden of Forking Paths*), we should not be surprised to find that this ploy of dispersing the number four among three positions is balanced by a similar mathematical ploy in *Parodi*'s first story, one that bears, like that in the volume's final tale, an obvious relationship to the central plot device of "Death and the Compass."

In "The Twelve Figures of the World" Achilles Molinari, a suspect in the murder of Dr. Ibn Khaldun, seeks Parodi's help in clearing himself. On his first visit to Parodi's jail cell he explains that Khaldun, an acquaintance who belonged to a sect of Druses, had invited Molinari to join the sect. Molinari had agreed, and on the evening that he arrives at Khaldun's home for the initiation rite (after having spent the day memorizing the twelve signs of the zodiac in their correct order), he finds the Akils (the initiates of the sect, some 150 in number) wearing identical robes and masks, assembled in a room around the large metallic statue of a bull. Khaldun takes Molinari upstairs to his office and explains the initiation ceremony:

> You shall seek out the four masters who make up the veiled tetragon of the Godhead. Right now, entrusted with a pious mission, they are gathered around the metal bull, praying with their brothers, the Akils, who are also veiled. No mark distinguishes them, but your heart will recognize them. I command you to bring Yusuf. You will descend to the auditorium, remembering in their exact order the twelve figures of the heavens. When you reach the last figure, the sign of Pisces, you shall return to the first, which is Aries, and so on in rotation. Thrice you will weave a circle round the Akils and your steps will lead you to Yusuf—so long as you have not changed the order of the figures. You will tell him, "Ibn Khaldun summons," and you will bring him here. Then I shall command you to bring the second master, then the third, then the fourth. (*DIP*, 24–25)

Following Khaldun's instructions, Molinari returns with the first veiled master, and Khaldun, after taking the master into a small room adjoining his office, returns and tells Molinari the name of the second master. The same process is then repeated with the second and third veiled figures, but when it comes time for Molinari to seek the fourth, Khaldun offers to find this veiled master himself because, he says, it is clear Molinari is exhausted from his task. Khaldun returns to the office with the final veiled figure, and the four are then unmasked to reveal the men Khaldun had named. Later in the evening during the course of a further initiation ceremony Molinari comes upon the body of Ibn Khaldun, stabbed to death. Molinari flees the house in panic and looks back to see the building in flames.

The problem of who killed Ibn Khaldun and why (it was another member of the sect—Khaldun's bookkeeper—who had been embezzling from him and feared exposure) assumes secondary importance in the economy of the story to the mystery of how Molinari was able to find the four veiled men Khaldun had designated. And it is this latter problem that Parodi sets out to solve, revealing the identity of the murderer and his motive only as an afterthought. Parodi assumes that the initiation rite had been simply an elaborate practical joke the Druses pulled on a gullible outsider and that the test of finding the four veiled masters was a device adapted from an old card trick. As Parodi explains, Khaldun had named the first man to be found, and Molinari had returned to Khaldun's office with a veiled figure. Khaldun had taken the man into a small room adjoining the office, lifted his veil to find out who he was, and then returned to the office to tell Molinari to find the man he had just brought. This same procedure was repeated until the third veiled figure had been found, and then Khaldun offered to find the fourth figure himself. He fetched the fourth, who was in fact the first man that he had named (indeed, named precisely because he knew him so well that he was sure he would recognize him even veiled), returned with him to the office, and had the four men unmask themselves. As Parodi phrases it, "He ordered you to seek out Druse number one, and you brought him number two. He asked for number two, and you brought him three. He asked for three and you brought him four. He told you he'd find number four himself, and he brought number one" (*DIP*, 34–35). Which is simply to say that this trick is based on a cyclic permutation: the four men are named in a sequence that runs 1–2–3–4 but found in a sequence that runs 2–3–4–1.

What strikes one first about this story is how many of its details resemble elements in "Death and the Compass." Each tale involves, for example, a progressive movement through the sequence 1–2–3–4 (the locations of the serial crimes in one and the finding of the veiled masters in the other). Moreover, the four points of the compass are associated with the four letters of the Tetragrammaton in Lönnrot's quest for the secret name of God, while the four masters whom Molinari must seek out are described as constituting "the veiled tetragon of the Godhead." And just as the crime scenes in "Death and the Compass" form a geometric figure described as a labyrinth, through which Lönnrot must make his way; so Molinari's initiation rite contains elements associated with the passage through the Cretan labyrinth. According to Frazer, the Minotaur running through the labyrinth is a figure of the sun's annual movement through the ring of the zodiac, and, as we saw, Molinari must repeat the twelve signs of the zodiac as he circles the metallic figure of a bull. Further, as the labyrinth composed of compass points involves an oscillation or uncertainty between the numbers three and four, so Molinari's initiation rite (a rite of passage) turns upon an interplay between these same numbers. In order to find each of the veiled masters, Molinari must circle the figure of the bull three times while repeating the twelve signs of the zodiac before he makes each choice—three circuits of the bull for each of four choices makes twelve circuits, the same number as the signs of the zodiac, which are themselves arranged in a circle and subdivided into four groups of three signs each for the three months that compose each of the four seasons.

Given the similarities between "The Twelve Figures of the World" and "Death and the Compass," the presence of a cyclic permutation in the former lends further weight to the argument for Borges's having adumbrated a cyclic permutation governing the tales' arrangement in the latter, a permutation evoked by the notion of rotating the triangular arrangement of the crime scenes displayed on Scharlach's map one numerical position to the left (within the kind of schema shown in fig. 44.1) to reveal the combination that aligns, like tumblers in a lock, the order of the three stories' historical settings with the order in which they double the three tales that are the genre's historical origin.

Indeed, there is a distinct possibility that, unlike the reference to the triangular arrangement of four people distributed among three locations in the last tale of *Don Isidro Parodi,* the cyclic permutation contained in the volume's first tale may not be a retrospective evocation of elements in "Death and the Compass" but a trial run for the second of Borges's serious detective stories. "Death and the Compass" first appeared in *Sur* in May 1942, and while *Six Problems for Don Isidro Parodi* was published almost six months later (the foreword by Gervasio Montenegro is dated November 20, 1942), the volume's first story, "The Twelve Figures of the World," is dated December 27, 1941, and was published in *Sur* in January 1942. If "The Twelve Figures of the World" *was* written before "Death and the Compass" and served as a testing ground for elements in the latter story, then this suggests two points about the relationship between Borges's serious detective stories and the six parodies he wrote with Bioy-Casares.

First, it indicates that the play of influence between the two groups of stories ran in both directions—the parody stories being used to burlesque elements in the analytic genre but also serving as a means of testing devices Borges would use in the serious tales. This evidence of a mutual influence would reinforce the argument that Borges's collaboration on the six parody stories of 1942 contributed to the difficulty he had in completing the last of his serious tales but that this experience ultimately deepened his understanding of the Poe project and allowed him to bring it to a conclusion—deepened his understanding precisely because the level of self-consciousness about a genre's origin, tradition, and structures that is the essence of parody is, when transposed into a different analytic register, the stuff of literary history and criticism as well.

The second point raised by the possibility of Borges's having used "The Twelve Figures of the World" as a testing ground for "Death and the Compass" is the difference in his practice between writing a parody and a serious detective story. When Borges makes a cyclic permutation part of the arrangement of his three serious stories, this mathematical ploy, though highly complex and buried deeply within (and across) the tales, is a significant element of their meaning, consciously intended as a key to the sequence used in doubling the Dupin stories. It is not a trick meant to hoodwink the reader.

In contrast, the cyclic permutation in "The Twelve Figures of the World" represents a quite different use of the device. The explanation that Parodi gives of Molinari's finding among the 150 veiled figures the four men selected by Ibn Khaldun is that while Khaldun named them in the sequence 1–2–3–4, they were actually retrieved in the sequence 2–3–4–1. Parodi's solution is correct insofar as it explains how such a feat could have been accomplished, but the catch is that it doesn't explain the feat as Molinari narrated it. Molinari says that Ibn Khaldun told him to fetch Yusuf, Ibrahim, Izz-al-Din, and Kahlil in that order. Now the ploy only works if the first man named is the last one retrieved and if the person (Ibn Khaldun) who retrieves the last man has arranged a way to recognize him beneath his veil. Yet a few pages later in the tale, when Parodi offers his solution to the problem, he says that the man whom Khaldun would have had no trouble recognizing in a crowd of veiled figures was "his closest friend" (*DIP*, 35) and business partner Ibrahim, and that consequently when he named the four veiled figures, "Number one was Ibrahim" (*DIP*, 35). But Molinari had said repeatedly that the first man named was Yusuf and the second was Ibrahim.

When one notices this discrepancy between the order of names in Molinari's account and in Parodi's solution, then the satiric point of the device becomes clear. From the very beginning of the tale the reader has been encouraged to laugh at Molinari for being tricked into a phony initiation rite, and to laugh particularly at his pedantic obsessiveness in memorizing the twelve signs of the zodiac in their correct order and then being unable to put that order out of his mind for a long time after. But if the reader laughs at someone obsessed with remembering a sequence of twelve names, he will probably miss the fact that someone else is laughing at him. For Borges assumes that this same reader won't be able to remember, over the space of a few pages separating Molinari's account and Parodi's solution, the correct sequence of four names. If Borges is right, then the reader swallows the hook that is Parodi's "solution," a solution that explains theoretically how Ibn Khaldun's practical joke could have worked but that does not correspond to Molinari's account of the events. The trick that Borges plays on the inattentive reader is a mirror image of the one the Druses play on the pedantic Molinari. And the difference between Borges's serious detective stories and his parodies is, then, that while in the former he always plays by the rules governing the battle of wits between writer and reader, in the latter he doesn't feel he has to.

45 Borges's Reading of Poe; Borges and Lacan; Buried in a Footnote; Originality Anxiety or the Privileging of Psychoanalytic Discourse; Borges and Derrida

IF BORGES'S DOUBLING OF THE Dupin stories was not just a project in fiction writing but to some extent a project in literary history and criticism as well, then the measure of his success becomes not solely a question of whether his detective stories, judged purely as fiction, are better than Poe's, but a question of whether Borges's interpretation of the Dupin tales, his imaginative reading/rewriting of them in his own detective stories, is so strong that it has become normative for *our* reading of Poe.

To address this question, we must adopt the Borgesian strategy, already familiar from the detective stories, of turning back to the opening of this study to link end to beginning. We started with a discussion of Lacan's "Seminar on 'The Purloined Letter'" and its subsequent critiques by Derrida and Johnson. There are, of course, any number of other essays we could have mentioned that take Lacan's "Seminar" either as their starting point or their principal intellectual underpinning.[1] Indeed, it is fair to say that in the last twenty-five years, the current of critical discussion initiated by Lacan's essay has been the most powerful interpretive tradition for Poe's detective stories in this country and has significantly raised the level of critical discourse about Poe's work as a whole, with the result that Poe's corpus has become a (if not the) principal site for psychoanalytic, structuralist, and poststructuralist readings in American literature. What is important about this for our purposes is that there exists the distinct possibility that Borges's "Death and the Compass" originally directed Lacan's attention to the numerical/geometrical dimension of "The Purloined Letter" and thus suggested Poe's tale as an ideal text for an analytic reading that would project the structure of the Oedipal triangle onto the reciprocity of blindness and insight in the psychoanalytic encounter. And if Borges's story *was* instrumental in evoking Lacan's seminal reading of "The Purloined Letter," then this would be a clear measure of the success of Borges's project regarding Poe, a measure of how much his rewriting-as-interpretation formed the ultimate basis for the strongest current readings of the Dupin tales.

The evidence for Borges's influence on Lacan, though ample, is circumstantial, but surely no psychoanalyst would object to that. One of the first promoters of Borges's work in France was Roger Caillois, the noted critic and sociologist whose writings influenced Lacan. Rodríguez Monegal notes that Borges's friend Victoria Ocampo had invited Caillois to lecture in Argentina on the eve of the Second World War and that Caillois remained there for the duration. With Ocampo's help, he started a magazine in Buenos Aires called *Lettres Françaises,* and in its October 1944 issue he published French translations of two Borges stories, "The Babylon Lottery" and "The Library of Babel." The relationship between Caillois and Borges, not an entirely friendly one, turned in part on their mutual interest in the detective genre. Monegal notes that Borges wrote

> a rather catty article in *Sur* (April 1942) reviewing one of Caillois' pamphlets, on the detective novel. Against Caillois' statement that the detective story was born when Joseph Fouché created a well-trained police force in Paris, Borges observes that a literary genre invariably begins with a literary text and points out that the text in question is one of Edgar Allan Poe's stories. An exchange of notes ensued, and the relationship between Borges and Caillois cooled considerably. That did not affect Caillois' admiration for Borges' writings. He continued to promote Borges unflinchingly. (*JLB,* 382)

In 1951 Caillois published in Paris a translation (by P. Verdevoye and Nestor Ibarra) of Borges's *Ficciones,* the collection that contains both "The Garden of Forking Paths" and "Death and the Compass" (*JLB,* 420). There was, then, a translation of "Death and the Compass" widely available in France under the aegis of Caillois some five years before the publication of Lacan's "Seminar on 'The Purloined Letter.'" And given Caillois's interest in the detective story and his ongoing promotion of one of the genre's most sophisticated modern practitioners, and given further the influence of Caillois's writings on Lacan and the psychoanalyst's professional interest in analytic detection, it seems hard to believe that Lacan had not read "Death and the Compass" sometime in the early 1950s. Such an acquaintance with the story would at least explain in part the extremely odd reference to Borges in the "Seminar on 'The Purloined Letter.'"

In presenting the purloined letter as a model of the Lacanian signifier, Lacan points out the letter's property (as the signifier of an absence) of simultaneously being and not being present in a particular place, adding that "between *letter* and *place* exist relations for which no French word has quite the extension of the English adjective: *odd.*" He asks, "Must a letter then, of all objects, be endowed with the property of *nullibiety:* to use a term which the thesaurus known as *Roget* picks up from the semiotic utopia of Bishop Wilkins?" (53). To which question he appends the curious note: "The very one to which Jorge Luis Borges, in works which

harmonize so well with the phylum of our subject [*dans son oeuvre si har-
monique au phylum de notre propos*], has accorded an importance which
others have reduced to its proper proportions. Cf. *Les Temps modernes*,
June–July 1955, pp. 2135–36 and Oct. 1955, pp. 574–75" (Lacan, 53
n. 20).

The citation of the June–July issue of *Les Temps modernes* refers to the
opening pages of a translation of Borges's "The Analytical Language of
John Wilkins" (one of six essays by Borges in that issue), while the item
cited in the October issue is a letter to the editor from M. Pobers commenting on the Wilkins essay. In "The Analytical Language of John Wilkins,"
Borges describes the universal language proposed by the seventeenth-
century Englishman Wilkins, bishop of Chester and first secretary of the
Royal Society, in his book *An Essay towards a Real Character and a Philosophical Language* (1668). Borges notes that in this language "each word defines
itself":

> Wilkins divided the universe into forty categories or classes, which were then
> subdivisible into differences, subdivisible in turn into species. To each class he
> assigned a monosyllable of two letters; to each difference, a consonant; to each
> species, a vowel. For example, *de* means element; *deb*, the first of the elements,
> fire; *deba*, a portion of the element of fire, a flame. (*OI*, 102)

In his letter to the editor, Pobers points out that this philosophical language, which replaces arbitrary words and expressions with a system of
letters and syllables each having a particular sense, was not original with
Wilkins. It had been invented by another Oxford scholar, George Dalgarno, and Wilkins's work simply completed and perfected the project presented in Dalgarno's 1661 treatise *Ars Signorum vulgo character universalis et
Lingua Philosophica*.

Now while it is always good to learn new things for their own sake, one
cannot help but wonder what exactly Lacan's footnote to Borges is meant
to note. There is, according to Lacan, this special property possessed by a
signifier (the present sign of an absence) of simultaneously being and not
being present in a particular place, an odd relationship between letter and
place; and to evoke this property he has found the perfect word, *nullibiety*
(the condition of being nowhere existent), a word that Roget's *Thesaurus*
tells him was first used in a work by John Wilkins. And oh, by the way, says
Lacan, this is the same John Wilkins whose universal analytic language
Borges has discussed in an essay that harmonizes "so well with the phylum
of our subject." (One should note that in mentioning the name Roget in a
footnote on Borges, Lacan evokes, unconsciously or not, his sense of the
link between Borges and the author of "Marie Rogêt.")

Is the point of Lacan's footnote, then, simply to remark on a mere coincidence, this note that Lacan appends to an essay he considered important enough to place at the start of his *Écrits*? Or is it meant to acknowledge (although it does not say so) some debt of influence to, or sense of priority of, Borges as regards a knowledge of Wilkins's work? Perhaps, for example, Lacan, in discovering from Roget's *Thesaurus* that the word *nullibiety* had originated with Wilkins, recognized Wilkins's name because he had read Borges's essay. Such a debt would have been minor, easy to acknowledge, and yet in the last analysis no less trivial a matter than the noting of a coincidence. So why did Lacan go to the trouble of including this footnote?

Although the property that the word *nullibiety* designates is important for Lacan's notion of the signifier, the word itself is not that important; he has described this property of the signifier often and with other words as good. Still less important and less obvious is the word's connection with Wilkins, and least important and least obvious of all is Wilkins's connection with Borges—both of which Lacan goes to the trouble of pointing out to the reader. Clearly, there is something odd about this footnote, an uncanny feeling that is usually the aura of an unconscious mechanism, of a repression and a return. For while it is not at all clear that Borges's essay on Wilkins "harmonizes so well" with the subject of Lacan's "Seminar" that it was worth calling attention to that essay in a footnote, it is quite clear that another work of Borges's harmonizes only too well with the subject of Lacan's "Seminar," and it is that work, the detective story "Death and the Compass," of which, I would suggest, the essay on Wilkins reminds Lacan at crucial moments.

We can see just such a moment in the passage quoted above in which Borges illustrates Wilkins's analytic language by constructing the word for flame, *deba*. He starts with a two-letter root *de*, an element; then in the second step adds the consonant *b* to specify the element fire; and in the third adds the vowel *a* to specify a portion of that element, a flame—a three-step process to produce a four-letter word that cannot help but remind us of the way that the successive murders in "Death and the Compass" each add, as part of a supposed cabalistic rite, another letter to the spelling of a four-letter name composed of three different letters, the Tetragrammaton. The resemblance between essay and story seems even more striking when Borges remarks that in "the words of John Wilkins's analytical language . . . every letter is meaningful, as the letters of the Holy Scriptures were meaningful for the cabalists," the analytical language being "a universal key and a secret encyclopedia" (*OI*, 103). One recalls the cabalistic texts Lönnrot read in trying to solve the mystery of the murders: a work on "the magic and the terror of the Tetragrammaton, which is God's unspeakable name," another on

the doctrine that God has a secret name in which (as in the crystal sphere that
the Persians attribute to Alexander of Macedonia) His ninth attribute, Eternity, may be found—that is to say, the immediate knowledge of everything under
the sun that will be, that is, and that was. Tradition lists ninety-nine names of
God; Hebrew scholars explain that imperfect cipher by a mystic fear of even
numbers; the Hasidim argue that the missing term stands for a hundredth
name—the Absolute Name. (*A*, 68)

This Absolute Name, which is "the immediate knowledge" of everything
that is, was, or will be, is in effect "a universal key and a secret encyclopedia." It is the apotheosis of that linguistic totality of representation Wilkins sought in his analytical language, and as such it confronts us with the
paradox of self-inclusion on the cosmic level. Like "the crystal sphere that
the Persians attribute to Alexander" or that other crystal sphere that
Borges named the Aleph, the Absolute Name evokes the ultimate vanishing of signification in the infinite as one pursues an absolute coincidence
between the cosmos and its self-included image, and this terrifying possibility probably accounts for the cabalists' "mystic fear of even numbers,"
the fear that the secret, hundredth name of God, representing a symbolic
apotheosis of evenness, invokes the condition of zero difference where
ubiquity and nullibiety are indistinguishable.

Given the several resemblances between "Death and the Compass" and
"The Analytical Language of John Wilkins" (the two were published within fifteen months of each other), one can see that Lacan's reference to the
Wilkins essay may indeed represent the return of a repressed content, the
resurfacing of Lacan's sense of how much his own reading of "The Purloined Letter" either owed directly to, or was anticipated by, Borges's
reading/rewriting of Poe's story. And certainly if Lacan had any misgivings, any anxiety about the originality of his reading, these misgivings
could only have been increased and given focus by Pobers's "letter" to the
editor pointing out that the analytical language Borges attributed to Wilkins did not originate with him but was the invention of another man.
Might another Pobers write a letter pointing out that Lacan's reading of
"The Purloined Letter" did not originate with *him*, a letter arguing that
Lacan's reading had either been influenced, or at least anticipated, by
Borges's reading/rewriting, so that Lacan's reading, like the purloined
letter itself, was out of place, not the first but the second instance of this
particular interpretation of the tale?

If this originality anxiety existed for Lacan, then his footnote to Borges
would be the trace of an inner division, the visible mark of his inability, on
the one hand, to acknowledge explicitly a debt of influence to, or the
simple priority of, Borges in a matter so central to his interpretation of

Poe's tale, and of his equal inability, on the other, not to acknowledge in some oblique manner his sense of this debt or priority. Or perhaps it is less a matter of Lacan's unwillingness to acknowledge Borges as a precursor than of his reluctance as a psychoanalyst, which is to say, as a scientist, a writer of nonfiction prose, to acknowledge an interpretive influence or priority originating in a work of fiction, since such an acknowledgment would seem to undermine the privileged "scientific" status of Lacan's reading of Poe by suggesting the imaginative (not to say, fictive) component in psychoanalytic interpretation. If this were the case, then the footnote could be a compromise that lets Lacan acknowledge Borges not by citing one of his stories but by referencing one of his analytic essays, a nonfiction work whose veiled resemblance to "Death and the Compass" allows it to serve as a screen figure for the tale. In either case—originality anxiety or, more likely, the privileging of psychoanalytic discourse—the result would be the same: the oddly gratuitous footnote pointing out a trivial coincidence, the trace of a burial within the self that recalls the idiom of burying something in a footnote or at the foot of a page.

That the structures of specular self-consciousness elaborated in Borges's "Death and the Compass" and in Lacan's "Seminar on 'The Purloined Letter'" involve essentially the same geometric configuration—a figure formed by the doubling of a triangle—can be seen quite clearly in a diagram Lacan included as part of a commentary on the "Seminar" in the *Écrits*. Discussing "the dialectic of intersubjectivity"[2] presented in the "Seminar," Lacan identifies its central mechanism as that reciprocal imaginary objectification of self and Other found in the Lacanian mirror stage. According to Lacan, the mirror stage in human development occurs between the sixth and the eighteenth months when the child, lacking motor control of his body, "anticipates on the imaginary level the future acquisition and mastery of his bodily integrity." This "imaginary integration . . . brought about through identification with the image of a similar being . . . as a total form . . . is illustrated and realized by the concrete experience in which the child perceives his own image in a mirror."[3] To illustrate the specular nature of "the dialectic of intersubjectivity," Lacan uses a diagram, the so-called *Schéma L* (*Écrits*, 1:66) (see fig. 45.1). This figure representing the doubling of two triangles is the reciprocal of the geometric shape Borges uses in "Death and the Compass" to figure the encounter of two men "whose minds work in the same way" and who "may be the same man" (*A*, 269). The difference is that Borges represents the doubling as the projection downward of a second triangle from the base of the first, while Lacan represents this same doubling as the projection upward of a second triangle from the vertex of the first. Both of these shapes are indebted, of course, to the type of Neoplatonic figure (representing the

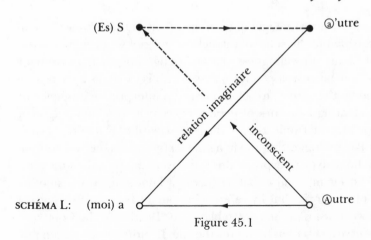

SCHÉMA L: (moi) a

Figure 45.1

mirror-image relationship between the divine mind and the material universe) cited earlier, and both can be assimilated to the figure of a square folded along either of its diagonals that emblemizes, in the Neoplatonic tradition, the split and doubled nature of self-consciousness, assimilated simply by adding a diagonal to Borges's figure and two sides to Lacan's.

That Lacan chose to present his reading of the psychoanalytic encounter in the context of the analytic detective story's triad of criminal/victim/detective and to schematize its dynamic (the dialectic of intersubjectivity) in a figure of doubled triangles would seem to reflect his sense that the face-to-face encounter between analyst and analysand casts each in a dual role, the analysand as the self-conscious victim of his own victimizing unconscious, the analyst as the self-conscious detective who helps track down the source of the victimization by ventriloquizing the speech of the analysand's unconscious (in effect, enacting its role) to help the analysand understand its language. In the encounter between the two, the analysand, whose situation is one of relative helplessness in the face of the unconscious, is led, through the transference, to double the analyst's role, exchanging his own passive role as victim for the analyst's active one as detective, the mark of the successful exchange being the completion of the counter-transference in which the analyst is rendered passive, is decathected by the analysand.

The probability of Lacan's having been influenced by Borges should come as no surprise to anyone familiar with the enormous appeal Borges's work had for French intellectuals in the 1950s, '60s, and '70s. Lacan, Derrida, and Foucault, to name a few, all cite Borges's writings with evident admiration. Foucault, for example, says that the idea for *Les mots et les choses* (1966) "first arose out of a passage in Borges,"[4] a passage, interestingly enough, from "The Analytical Language of John Wilkins" that he quotes in the book's preface. Indeed, one might speculate further that if Borges's rewriting of "The Purloined Letter" in "Death and the Compass" influenced Lacan's numerical/geometrical reading of the Poe tale, then the triangular/quadrangular structure at the heart of Borges's story may also have influenced Derrida's critique of Lacan, his playing the number four to Lacan's three. In the discussion following Derrida's paper at the Johns Hopkins structuralism conference in 1966, Richard Macksey, pursuing the notion of "free play" developed in the essay, asked about those "players" who could join Derrida's "team in the critique of metaphysics represented by" his "tentative game-theory," and Macksey suggested as a possible player "that writer who has made the shifting center of his fictional poetics the narrative game in 'the *unanimous* night,' that architect and prisoner of labyrinths, the creator of Pierre Menard."[5] To which Derrida replied, "You are thinking, no doubt, of Jorge Luis Borges" (Macksey, 269).

46 *Circling Back to the Beginning; Progression/Regression; Saying a Final Word*

WHAT STILL REMAINS TO BE said about the success of Borges's project with the Dupin stories? Clearly, Borges set out to double Poe's three tales with three of his own and ended up replicating that series with a greater fidelity than he perhaps intended. For just as Poe had produced two masterpieces of detective fiction and one flawed example of the genre ("The Mystery of Marie Rogêt"), so Borges in his three stories produced two masterpieces and one flawed tale ("Ibn Hakkan al-Bokhari"). If Borges implicitly acknowledged in the writing of his third story that the only way he could rival Poe in the detective form was by originating a new genre in which fiction enacts to some degree a literary historical and critical agenda, then we must in turn acknowledge that it is precisely the critical distance of his two young detectives from the tale's events that flaws "Ibn Hakkan al-Bokhari," both a historical distance that prevents them from apprehending the supposed killer and an emotional distance that makes the question of whether theirs is the correct solution largely academic. Appropriately enough, in unintentionally doubling Poe's flawed tale with a flawed one of his own, Borges in effect reproduces a major weakness of "Marie Rogêt," for in that tale Dupin and the narrator, by functioning solely as critical readers of newspaper accounts of the crime, end up intellectually distanced from and emotionally uninvolved in the events, as emblemized by the tale's anticlimactic ending.

That Borges needed to create a mixed genre in order to double Poe seems in retrospect almost predictable given the type of story Poe had invented and the shape of his literary career. For the man who originated the analytic detective genre was not only one of the first great American fiction writers, he was also the first major American literary critic. Indeed, given that the form Poe invented enacts its theme of reflexiveness through his tales' self-conscious mirroring of their own status as writing, it seems inevitable that an author such as Borges, who wrote both short fiction and critical essays and was as devoted to the analytic detective story as its originator, would take the form to its next logical stage by reflecting not just an individual story back upon itself as in "The Purloined Letter" but the entire genre back upon its origin in an act of critical and historical self-consciousness.

Can it seem, then, any less inevitable that a work whose subject is the relationship between Poe's and Borges's detective stories would itself turn back at its ending to reflect on the way its method mirrors the structure of these tales? We began this study by examining a series of three cumulative readings of "The Purloined Letter" and by noting that the self-including structure of the tale draws into its progressive/regressive vortex any interpretation of it. Just as Lacan and Derrida in reading the tale replay in a critical register the game of even and odd, so I have, in reading the Dupin stories, borrowed a dynamic from Borges by replaying Lönnrot's geometrical response to Scharlach's quadrangular maze. Which is to say that in beginning this study by observing the quadrangular hermeneutic figure formed by a literary text ("The Purloined Letter") and a cumulative series of three interpretations, I have in effect added one more side to that hermeneutic figure, a fifth side adumbrating an infinite progression of interpretations. But at the same time I have, like Lönnrot with his regressive straight-line labyrinth, introduced between points A and B in the hermeneutic figure (between Poe's tale and Lacan's reading) another story/interpretation (Borges's "Death and the Compass") that adumbrates an infinite regression of influence/priority in the interpretive tradition of the analytic detective story, a movement pursued to some extent in this study by introducing between "Death and the Compass" and "The Purloined Letter" Israel Zangwill's *The Big Bow Mystery* (1892); and between Borges and Zangwill, H. G. Wells's "The Plattner Story" (1897); and between Zangwill and Poe, Lewis Carroll's *Through the Looking-Glass* (1872), and so on, through any number of digressions.

One comes, then, to the end, balancing potential infinities of interpretation, progressive and regressive, and facing the necessity of saying a final word, even though one knows that the finality of that word is always provisional, that there is always another interpreter ready to add one more point or to subdivide the field of inquiry one more time. Since the last word is always in another voice, or more precisely within this double-mirror structure, always in the voice of the Other, the best one can do, given the way that the end of anything foreshadows the end of everything, is to speak that word in a voice whose otherness we must all share at last. Since one must choose a voice for this, I choose the one that sounds at the beginning of the detective story prior to Poe's own, the voice of the author of the epigraph to "The Murders in the Rue Morgue"—Sir Thomas Browne. An echo taken not, as in Poe's epigraph, from the last chapter of *Urn Burial*, affirming that "puzzling questions . . . are not beyond *all* conjecture," but from the last chapter of its companion work *The Garden of Cyrus*, expressing at once the necessity and the impossibility of a last word:

> A large field is yet left unto sharper discerners to enlarge upon this order, to search out the *quaternio's* and figured draughts . . . to erect generalities, disclose unobserved proprieties . . . affording delightful Truths, confirmable by sense and ocular Observation, which seems to me the surest path, to trace the Labyrinth of Truth. . . .
>
> But the Quincunx of Heaven runs low, and 'tis time to close the five ports of knowledge; We are unwilling to spin out our awaking thoughts into the phantasmes of sleep, which too often continueth praecogitations; making Cables of Cobwebbes and Wildernesses of handsome Groves. (*SW*, 209–10)

Notes

Preface

1. Just as my first two critical books (*Doubling and Incest / Repetition and Revenge* and *American Hieroglyphics*) formed a larger work of triangulation with the poet John Bricuth's volume *The Heisenberg Variations*, so the three books of literary criticism now being completed form a larger work of quadrangulation with Bricuth's long poem in progress *Just Let Me Say This About That*, the three critical works and the poem representing a three/four oscillation between the analytic and the creative. In addition, the present book forms a bridge between the first two critical volumes, many of whose motifs and structures it completes, and the two critical volumes to follow, whose motifs and structures it initiates.

2. The game was played June 20, 1965, in the Oahu Championship, Honolulu, Hawaii. White: John T. Irwin. Black: Fred Borges. 1. e4, c5; 2. Nf3, d6; 3. d4, cd; 4. c3, dc; 5. Nc3, Nc6; 6. Bc4, e6; 7. O-O, Be7; 8. Bf4, Nf6; 9. Qe2, O-O; 10. Rfd1, Ne8; 11. Rac1, a6; 12. a4, Bd7; 13. Rc2, Qc7; 14. Rcd2, Rd8; 15. e5, d5; 16. Bd5, ed5; 17. Nd5, Qa5; 18. Ne7+, Ne7; 19. Rd7, Rd7; 20. Rd7, Ng6; 21. Bd2, Qa4; 22. e6, Kh8; 23. Rf7, Qa1+; 24. Be1, Rg8; 25. Ng5, h6; 26. Rb7, Nf6; 27. Nf7+, Kh7; 28. g3, Rc8; 29. Kg2, Rc1; 30. Bc3, Nd5; 31. Ng5+, Kg8; 32. Rg7+, Kf8; 33. e7+, Nge7; 34. Qf3+, Ke8; 35. Qf7+, Kd7; 36. Qe6+, Kc7; 37. Re7+, Ne7; 38. Qe7+, Kc6; 39. Qe6+, Kb5; 40. Qd5+, Kb6; 41. Bd4+, Kc7; 42. Ne6+, Kc8; 43. Qd8+, Kb7; 44. Qd7+, Ka8; 45. Qa7 mate. Black kept playing after move 34 when his position was clearly lost because White might have forfeited the game on time before being able to enforce checkmate.

1

1. Raymond Chandler, "The Simple Art of Murder," in *Detective Fiction: Crime and Compromise*, ed. Dick Allen and David Chacko (New York: Harcourt Brace Jovanovich, 1974), 398.

2. Edgar Allan Poe, *Collected Works of Edgar Allan Poe*, 3 vols., ed. Thomas Ollive Mabbott (Cambridge: Harvard University Press, 1969–78), 2:521n. All subsequent quotations from Poe's fiction and poetry are taken from this edition unless otherwise noted.

3. Jorge Luis Borges, "Ibn Hakkan al-Bokhari, Dead in His Labyrinth," in *The Aleph and Other Stories, 1933–1969,* trans. and ed. Norman Thomas di Giovanni (New York: Dutton, 1978), 123. Subsequent citations of this volume in text as *A*.

4. Jorge Luis Borges, "Chesterton and the Labyrinths of the Detective Story," in *Borges: A Reader*, ed. Emir Rodríguez Monegal and Alastair Reid (New York: Dutton, 1981), 72–73. Subsequent citations of this volume in text as *BR*.

5. Jacques Lacan, "Seminar on 'The Purloined Letter,'" trans. Jeffrey Mehlman, *Yale French Studies* 48 (1972): 41. Unless otherwise noted, all subsequent quotations from the "Seminar on 'The Purloined Letter'" are taken from this edition.

6. Barbara Johnson, "The Frame of Reference: Poe, Lacan, Derrida," in *The Critical Difference* (Baltimore: Johns Hopkins University Press, 1980), 118. All

subsequent quotations from Johnson are taken from this edition.

7. Jacques Derrida, "The Purveyor of Truth," trans. W. Domingo, J. Hulbert, M. Ron, and M.-R. Logan, *Yale French Studies* 52 (1975): 100. All subsequent quotations from "The Purveyor of Truth" are taken from this edition.

2

1. Jorge Luis Borges, "Time and J. W. Dunne," in *Other Inquisitions, 1937–1952*, trans. Ruth L. C. Simms (New York: Simon and Schuster, 1964), 18–19. Subsequent citations of this volume in text as *OI*.

2. Jorge Luis Borges, "Tlön, Uqbar, Orbis Tertius," trans. Alastair Reid, in *Ficciones*, ed. Anthony Kerrigan (New York: Grove Press, 1962), 23. Subsequent citations of this volume in text as *F*.

3. Jorge Luis Borges, "The Zahir," trans. Dudley Fitts, in *Labyrinths*, ed. Donald A. Yates and James E. Irby (New York: New Directions, 1964), 163. Subsequent citations of this volume in text as *L*.

4. Lewis Carroll, *The Complete Works of Lewis Carroll* (New York: Vintage, 1976), 617. Subsequent citations of this volume in text as *LC*.

5. James Joyce, *Finnegans Wake* (New York: Viking Press, 1972), 628. All subsequent quotations from *Finnegans Wake* are taken from this edition.

3

1. *Webster's New World Dictionary of the American Language*, College Ed. (Cleveland: World Publishing Co., 1964), 1359, "simple." The etymologies of "even" and "odd" are also taken from this edition. Subsequent citations of this volume in text as *W*.

2. D. P. Simpson, *Cassell's Latin Dictionary* (New York: Macmillan, 1978), 556, "simplex." Subsequent citations of this volume in text as *Cassell's*.

4

1. *McKay's Modern English-Swedish and Swedish-English Dictionary* (New York: David McKay, 1959), 110, "lönn." Although the actual meaning of the word *lönnrot* in Swedish is "maple tree," Borges's identification of the last syllable in the word as the German *rot* ("red") authorizes an inquiry into the meaning of the first syllable. And certainly in the context of Borges's remark that the similarity in the minds of Lönnrot and Red Scharlach "is hinted at by the similarity of their names" (*A*, 269), the meaning of "lönn" as the prefix "hidden" accords with the notion of a concealed similarity that must be "hinted at." Given Borges's interest in Old Norse and Icelandic sagas, he probably took the proper name Lönnrot from Elias Lönnrot (1802–84), the compiler of the Finnish national epic *The Kalevala*.

2. *Encyclopaedia Britannica*, 11th ed., 29 vols. (New York: Encyclopaedia Britannica Co., 1911), 27:254. Subsequent citations of this work in text as *EB*.

3. Edgar Allan Poe, *The Complete Works of Edgar Allan Poe*, 17 vols., ed. James A. Harrison (New York: Thomas Y. Crowell, 1902), 16:314–15. Subsequent citations of this edition in text as *P*.

4. Ralph Waldo Emerson, *The Complete Works of Ralph Waldo Emerson*, 12 vols., ed. E. W. Emerson (Boston: Houghton Mifflin, 1903–4), 9:195. See also Borges, *OI*, 69.

5

1. Howard Haycraft, *Murder for Pleasure: The Life and Times of the Detective Story* (New York: Carroll and Graf, 1984), xxi.

2. Jorge Luis Borges, "The Garden of Forking Paths," trans. Anthony Boucher, *Ellery Queen's Mystery Magazine* 12, no. 57 (August 1948): 101–10.

3. G. W. F. Hegel, *The Phenomenology of Mind*, trans. J. B. Baillie (New York: Harper and Row, 1967), 239. All subsequent quotations from Hegel are taken from this edition.

6

1. Richard Burgin, *Conversations with Jorge Luis Borges* (New York: Holt, Rinehart and Winston, 1969), 109. Subsequent citations of this volume in text as Burgin.

2. C. G. Jung, *Psychology and Alchemy*, 2d ed., trans. R. F. C. Hull (Princeton: Princeton University Press, 1980), 25–26. Subsequent citations of this volume in text as *PA*.

3. C. G. Jung, *Psychology and Religion*, 2d ed., trans. R. F. C. Hull (Princeton: Princeton University Press, 1969), 72. Subsequent citations of this volume in text as *PR*.

4. C. G. Jung, *Mysterium Coniunctionis*, 2d ed., trans. R. F. C. Hull (Princeton: Princeton University Press, 1977), 90. Subsequent citations of this volume in text as *MC*.

5. Jorge Luis Borges, "The Mirror and the Mask," in *The Book of Sand*, trans. Norman Thomas di Giovanni (New York: Dutton, 1977), 78. Subsequent citations of this volume in text as *BS*.

6. Benedict de Spinoza, *Works of Spinoza*, 2 vols., trans. R. H. M. Elwes (New York: Dover, 1951–55), 1:xxii. All subsequent quotations from Spinoza are taken from this edition.

7

1. W. H. Matthews, *Mazes and Labyrinths: Their History and Development* (New York: Dover, 1970), 161. Subsequent citations of this volume in text as *ML*.

2. Janet Bord, *Mazes and Labyrinths of the World* (London: Latimer New Dimensions Ltd., 1976), 36, fig. 48, and 16, fig. 2.

3. Heinrich Schliemann, *Ilios: The City and Country of the Trojans* (New York: Arno Press, 1976), 347, fig. 243. All subsequent quotations from Schliemann are taken from this edition.

4. *American Hieroglyphics* (New Haven: Yale University Press, 1980).

9

1. Lewis Carroll, *The Annotated Alice: Alice's Adventures in Wonderland and Through the Looking-Glass*, with introduction and notes by Martin Gardner (Cleveland: World Publishing Co., 1963), 199. Subsequent citations of this volume in text as *AA*.

2. Bertrand Russell, *Introduction to Mathematical Philosophy* (New York: Simon and Schuster, n.d.), 88. Subsequent citations of this volume in text as *IM*.

3. Emir Rodríguez Monegal, *Jorge Luis Borges: A Literary Biography* (New York: Dutton, 1978), 40–41. Subsequent citations of this volume in text as *JLB*.

4. Jorge Luis Borges, *Discussion,* trans. Claire Staub (Paris: Gallimard, 1966), 151.

5. Edward Kasner and James Newman, *Mathematics and the Imagination* (New York: Simon and Schuster, 1940), 32. Subsequent citations of this volume in text as *MI.*

10

1. Barbara W. Tuchman, *The Guns of August* (New York: Bantam, 1980), 135. All subsequent quotations from Tuchman are from this edition.

2. *The New York Times,* Mid-Week Pictorial, vol. 3, no. 24 (August 17, 1916), front cover.

3. William L. Shirer, *The Rise and Fall of the Third Reich* (New York: Ballantine, 1983), 962.

4. Tsao Hsueh-Chin and Kao Ngoh, *Dream of the Red Chamber,* trans. Chi-Chen Wang (London: Routledge, n.d.), reverse of title page. Subsequent citations of this volume in text as *DR.*

5. Adolfo Bioy Casares, "On Fantastic Literature," in *Prose for Borges,* ed. Charles Newman and Mary Kinzie (Evanston: Northwestern University Press, 1974), 171.

11

1. Jorge Luis Borges, *Borges on Writing,* ed. Norman Thomas di Giovanni, Daniel Halpern, and Frank MacShane (New York: Dutton, 1973), 54. Subsequent citations of this volume in text as *BOW.*

2. Jorge Luis Borges, *Doctor Brodie's Report,* trans. Norman Thomas di Giovanni (New York: Dutton, 1978), 9.

3. H. G. Wells, *The Plattner Story and Others* (London: Methuen, 1897), 12. Subsequent citations of this volume in text as *PS.*

4. Michael J. Crowe, "August Ferdinand Möbius," in *Dictionary of Scientific Biography,* 16 vols., ed. Charles C. Gillispie (New York: Scribner's, 1970), 9:430.

12

1. Curtis Hardyck and Lewis F. Petrinovich, "Left-Handedness," *Psychological Bulletin,* 84, no. 3 (May 1977): 385, 392; Jerre Levy and Ruben C. Gur, "Individual Differences in Psychoneurological Organization," in *Neuropsychology of Left-Handedness,* ed. Jeannine Herron (New York: Academic Press, 1980), 206.

2. Edward Lasker, *The Adventure of Chess,* 2d ed. (New York: Dover, 1959), 204.

13

1. Aristotle, *Metaphysics,* trans. Hugh Tredennick, in *Aristotle,* 23 vols., Loeb Classical Library (Cambridge: Harvard University Press, 1980), 17:35, 37. Subsequent citations from this edition in text as Aristotle.

2. Plutarch, *Isis and Osiris,* trans. Frank Cole Babbitt, in *Moralia,* 16 vols., Loeb Classical Library (Cambridge: Harvard University Press, 1969), 5:119.

3. Jorge Luis Borges, *Selected Poems 1923–1967,* ed. Norman Thomas di Giovanni (New York: Dell, 1972), 111. Subsequent citations of this volume in text as *SP.*

4. G. W. Leibniz, *Leibniz: Selections,* ed. Philip P. Wiener (New York: Scribner's, 1951), 536. Subsequent citations of this volume in text as *LS.*

5. See also G. W. Leibniz, *New Essays on Human Understanding*, trans. and ed. Peter Remnant and Jonathan Bennett (Cambridge: Cambridge University Press, 1981), 144–45.

14

1. Taped interview with Borges conducted on April 18, 1983.

2. Robert Louis Stevenson, *Memories and Portraits* (New York: Scribner's, 1896), 59–60.

3. Suetonius, *Suetonius*, 2 vols., trans. J. C. Rolfe, Loeb Classical Library (Cambridge: Harvard University Press, 1979), 1:393. Subsequent citations of this volume in text as Suetonius.

4. Sir Thomas Browne, *Selected Writings*, ed. Sir Geoffrey Keynes (Chicago: University of Chicago Press, 1970), 124–25. Subsequent citations of this volume in text as *SW*.

15

1. Frank Livingstone Huntley, *Sir Thomas Browne: A Biographical and Critical Study* (Ann Arbor: University of Michigan Press, 1968), 209–10. Subsequent citations of this volume in text as Huntley.

2. H. J. R. Murray, *A History of Chess* (Oxford: Oxford University Press, 1913), 757, facing illustration.

3. Sir Thomas Browne, *Hydriotaphia (Urn Burial) and The Garden of Cyrus*, ed. F. L. Huntley (New York: Appleton-Century-Crofts, 1966), x. Subsequent citations of this volume in text as *GC*.

17

1. Richard Hinckley Allen, *Star Names: Their Lore and Meaning* (New York: Dover, 1963), 379. Subsequent citations of this volume in text as Allen.

2. Apollodorus, *The Library*, 2 vols., trans. J. G. Frazer, Loeb Classical Library (Cambridge: Harvard University Press, 1976), 1:299. Subsequent citations of this edition in text as Apollodorus.

3. Jorge Luis Borges with Margarita Guerrero, *The Book of Imaginary Beings*, trans. Norman Thomas di Giovanni (New York: Avon Books, 1970), 159. Subsequent citations of this volume in text as *BIB*.

4. Eric Partridge, *Origins: A Short Etymological Dictionary of Modern English* (New York: Greenwich House, 1983), 439. Subsequent citations of this volume in text as Partridge.

5. J. Chelhod, "A Contribution to the Problem of the Pre-eminence of the Right, Based upon Arabic Evidence," trans. James J. Fox, in *Right and Left: Essays on Dual Symbolic Classification*, ed. Rodney Needham (Chicago: University of Chicago Press, 1973), 247.

18

1. Arthur Hobson Quinn, *Edgar Allan Poe: A Critical Biography* (New York: Appleton-Century, 1942), 15. Subsequent citations of this edition in text as Quinn.

2. *The Book of the Thousand Nights and a Night*, 17 vols., trans. Richard F. Burton (printed by the Burton Club in a limited edition for private subscribers, n.d.), 1:139–41. Subsequent citations of this edition in text as Burton.

20

1. I. Zangwill, *The Big Bow Mystery* in *The Grey Wig: Stories and Novelettes* (New York: Macmillan, 1923), 175. Subsequent citations of this volume in text as *BBM*.

22

1. Sophocles, *Sophocles,* 2 vols., trans. F. Storr, Loeb Classical Library (Cambridge: Harvard University Press, 1968), 1:35. Subsequent citations of this edition in text as Sophocles. If one compares a late eighteenth-century translation of *Oedipus* (such as Potter's from 1788) with an early twentieth-century version (like Way's from 1909), the association of Tiresias's words denouncing Oedipus with Nathan's denouncing David amounts to little more than the interpolation of an appositional phrase. Thus Potter translates Tiresias's words as "For thou / Art the accursed polluter of this land" (*The Tragedies of Sophocles Translated* [London: G. G. J. and J. Robinson, 1788], lines 377–78), while Way translates the same passage as "Thou art the man!— / The god-accurst polluter of this land!" (*Sophocles in English Verse* [London: Macmillan, 1909], 20). The similarity of the "thou-art" form in Potter's translation and in the King James version of the Bible, plus the striking resemblance in the dramatic situations, made the assimilation of the two speeches both obvious and inevitable.

23

1. Plutarch, *Plutarch's Lives,* 11 vols., trans. Bernadotte Perrin, Loeb Classical Library (Cambridge: Harvard University Press, 1982), 1:7. Subsequent citations of this edition in text as *PL*.

2. See John T. Irwin, *Doubling and Incest / Repetition and Revenge: A Speculative Reading of Faulkner* (Baltimore: Johns Hopkins University Press, 1975).

3. Frederick Ahl, *Sophocles' Oedipus: Evidence and Self-Conviction* (Ithaca: Cornell University Press, 1991), 114.

4. Euripides, *Euripides,* 4 vols., trans. A. S. Way, Loeb Classical Library (Cambridge: Harvard University Press, 1980), 4:243–45. Subsequent citations of this edition in text as Euripides.

5. *The Oxford Classical Dictionary,* 2d ed., ed. N. G. L. Hammond and H. H. Scullard (London: Oxford University Press, 1977), 1009, "Sphinx."

6. Athenaeus, *The Deipnosophists,* 10.456B, English translation of the riddle by Lowell Edmunds. See also Athenaeus, *The Deipnosophists,* 7 vols., trans. Charles Burton Gulick, Loeb Classical Library (Cambridge: Harvard University Press, 1930), 4:569.

7. Edith Hamilton, *Mythology* (New York: New American Library, 1960), 257.

8. See, for example, J. C. Kamerbeek, *The Plays of Sophocles: Commentaries,* 7 vols. (Leiden: E. J. Brill, 1953–84), vol. 4 (*The Oedipus Tyrannus*), 156, note to line 752.

25

1. See Irwin, *Doubling and Incest,* 44–45.

2. Otto Rank, *The Trauma of Birth* (New York: Harper and Row, 1973), 144. Subsequent citations of this volume in text as Rank.

3. Hesiod, *The Homeric Hymns and Homerica,* trans. Hugh G. Evelyn-White, Loeb Classical Library (Cambridge: Harvard University Press, 1977), 101. Subsequent citations of this volume in text as Hesiod.

4. Sigmund Freud, *The Standard Edition of the Complete Psychological Works of Sigmund Freud,* 24 vols., ed. James Strachey (London: Hogarth Press, 1978), 22:25. Subsequent citations of this edition in text as *SE.*

26

1. Arthur J. Evans, "Mycenaean Tree and Pillar Cult and Its Mediterranean Relations," *Journal of Hellenic Studies* 21 (1901): 106–7. Subsequent citations of this article in text as Evans.

2. James G. Frazer, *The Golden Bough,* 3d ed., 12 vols. (London: Macmillan, 1911–15), vol. 4 (*The Dying God*), 58. Subsequent citations of this edition in text as Frazer.

3. Jean-Louis Brau, Helen Weaver, and Allan Edmands, *Larousse Encyclopedia of Astrology* (New York: McGraw-Hill, 1980), 218. Subsequent citations of this volume in text as *Larousse.*

27

1. Pliny, *Natural History,* 10 vols., trans. D. E. Eichholz, Loeb Classical Library (Cambridge: Harvard University Press, 1971), 10:273–75. Subsequent citations of this edition in text as Pliny.

2. John Evans, *The Ancient Stone Implements, Weapons, and Ornaments, of Great Britain* (New York: Appleton, 1872), 51–52. Subsequent citations of this volume in text as J. Evans.

3. Plutarch, *Moralia,* 16 vols., trans. Frank Cole Babbitt, Loeb Classical Library (Cambridge: Harvard University Press, 1972), 4:233–35.

4. Plato, *The Collected Dialogues of Plato,* ed. Edith Hamilton and Huntington Cairns (Princeton: Princeton University Press, 1973), 542. Subsequent citations of this volume in text as Plato.

5. S. K. Heninger, Jr., *The Cosmographical Glass: Renaissance Diagrams of the Universe* (San Marino, Calif.: Huntington Library, 1977), 145, fig. 85a. Subsequent citations of this volume in text as Heninger.

28

1. Joseph T. Shipley, *The Origins of English Words: A Discursive Dictionary of Indo-European Roots* (Baltimore: Johns Hopkins University Press, 1984), 4.

2. *The Compact Edition of the Oxford English Dictionary,* 2 vols. (New York: Oxford University Press, 1977), 1:150, "axis," nos. 6, 7. Subsequent citations of this edition in text as *OED.*

29

1. Alexander Cockburn, *Idle Passion: Chess and the Dance of Death* (New York: Simon and Schuster, 1974), 42. Subsequent citations of this volume in text as Cockburn.

2. Jorge Luis Borges with María Kodama, *Atlas,* trans. Anthony Kerrigan (New York: Dutton, 1985), 37. Subsequent citations of this volume in text as *Atlas.*

3. Jorge Luis Borges, *Seven Nights,* trans. Eliot Weinberger (New York: New Directions, 1984), 36. Subsequent citations of this volume in text as *SN.*

30

1. Ronald J. Christ, *The Narrow Act: Borges' Art of Allusion* (New York: New York University Press, 1969), 190 n. 19.

2. Where Monegal, writing in 1978, describes the source of this account of Borges and the Geneva prostitute as gossip that had "been around long enough to acquire a certain respectability," Estela Canto in her 1989 book *Borges a Contraluz* (Madrid: Espasa-Calpe) gives a somewhat different version of the Geneva incident and names as her source Borges's psychologist, Dr. Cohen-Miller, who told her the story during a meeting she had with him at Borges's request. Canto says that in 1945 Borges asked her to marry him, and she replied that, being "a disciple of Bernard Shaw," she couldn't marry him if they hadn't gone to bed together first (p. 98). Borges said that she was right, that it was necessary for them to have a physical relationship before getting married, but "he added that he was a prisoner 'of his ghosts'" (p. 111). Subsequently, Borges asked Canto to visit the psychologist he had been seeing for some months, Dr. Cohen-Miller. Canto says that the doctor had requested the meeting because "at this point of the analysis" her presence "was thought necessary" (p. 112). According to Canto, Cohen-Miller told her the following:

> Borges was far from being impotent. On the physical plane he was a victim of an extreme sensitivity, of a fear of sex and of a feeling of guilt. His sensitivity would be tempered by time and by gradually adapting to reality; the fear would disappear with marriage, which would also diminish considerably the feeling of guilt. . . .
>
> He then recounted a painful experience Borges had at age eighteen or nineteen, when he and his family were living in Geneva. Borges was a sensitive teenager, with eyesight and speech difficulties. Concerned by the shyness of his son, Jorge Borges asked Georgie one day if he already had had physical contact with a woman. . . . Georgie answered that he had never been with a woman. As would many other contemporary Argentine gentlemen, Señor Borges thought that this situation had to be remedied immediately. . . .
>
> A few days later Señor Borges announced to his son that he had found a solution for his case. He provided an address and told him he should be there at a certain hour. A woman would be waiting for him.
>
> Georgie set out on foot, as was his habit, in order to consider the situation and to arrive at the assigned address as naturally as possible, with no extra pressures. He was overwhelmed by his father's admonitions. Maybe his flesh was rebelling obscurely against the act that was being imposed on him; maybe the certainty of failure was in him before failure itself. Maybe this failure was his way of rejecting what was so deeply distasteful to his body and to his soul. In any case, an idea crossed his mind: his father had ordered him to go to bed with a woman he, Georgie, did not know. If this woman was willing to go to bed with him, it was because she already had done so with his father. This kind of intimate, personal favor cannot be asked from anybody—not even a prostitute—unless there is already an intimate connection between the persons involved. This way of reasoning was logical and precise, and even if untrue, it was what Borges believed. He had no doubts about it.

He arrived at the specified house, saw the woman, and nothing happened, of course.

Beyond the brutality of the mere facts—enough to induce impotence in an adolescent of delicate feelings—the images conjured by Borges's mind were also there. The woman that was offered him was a woman that he was going to *share* with his father. The reaction of his body and of his soul was natural. This was the "South American fate" of failure and death that he would later write about in the "Conjectural Poem," where so many things and meanings lurk between the lines. . . .

What came to light then, explosively, was the most humiliating of words: impotence. . . .

Borges was doubly humiliated: He had not been able to execute his father's command; he was incapable, he was impotent.

But impotence, as I have said, was not the explanation that Dr. Cohen-Miller subscribed to. . . .

He told me that I should try to inspire confidence in him, that I should be tender with him. He believed that with patience all the obsessions that troubled Georgie would disappear. . . .

In this long conversation Dr. Cohen-Miller never made reference to the strong bond between Georgie and Doña Leonor, his mother. Perhaps he intuited our mutual antagonism and tried not to exacerbate it. He might also have thought that, were Borges to normalize his life, the overwhelming influence of his mother would wane and that he would stop acting like a child whose growth had been arrested.

I believe that Cohen-Miller's diagnosis was correct. Several years later Borges told me that he had had sexual intercourse with one or two women. I have no reason to doubt his words. . . .

There is something that must be made clear: It was not Doña Leonor who castrated her son. It was his father. But she took advantage of Georgie's weakness and made him an unhappy person. Without the toughness, the cruelty, the devotion, the total attention, the unquenchable thirst for power of Doña Leonor, the Borges that the world knows would have never existed. (114–21; trans. by Edgar Krebs)

Whether, as in Monegal's version, the adolescent Borges "performed his task so quickly that he was overcome by the power of orgasm" or, as in Canto's, he "arrived at the specified house, saw the woman, and nothing happened," the ultimate source of this story of Borges's one-on-one encounter with the prostitute can only have been Borges himself, and what remains common to each account is Borges's reaction to the incident, the way in which this encounter epitomized his fear of sex and remained an image, even in his seventies, of intercourse as something humiliating and life-threatening, the fear of either being castrated by the father or engulfed by the mother.

3. Dwight Thomas and David K. Jackson, *The Poe Log: A Documentary Life of Edgar Allan Poe 1809–1849* (Boston: G. K. Hall, 1987), 29–30. Subsequent citations of this volume in text as *Log*.

31

1. Jorges Luis Borges, videotape of Poe-Borges Seminar at Johns Hopkins University, April 18, 1983.

2. Miguel de Cervantes Saavedra, *The Adventures of Don Quixote,* trans. J. M. Cohen (Baltimore: Penguin Books, 1963), 25. Subsequent citations of this volume in text as Cervantes.

3. Oscar Wilde, *Complete Works of Oscar Wilde,* 10 vols., ed. Robert Ross (Boston: David D. Nickerson, 1909), 3:19. Subsequent citations of this volume in text as Wilde.

4. Jorge Luis Borges and Adolfo Bioy-Casares, *Six Problems for Don Isidro Parodi,* trans. Norman Thomas di Giovanni (New York: Dutton, 1981), 12. Subsequent citations of this volume in text as *DIP.*

5. Erich Neumann, *The Origins and History of Consciousness,* trans. R. F. C. Hull (Princeton: Princeton University Press, 1971), 78–79. Subsequent citations of this volume in text as Neumann.

6. C. Kerényi, *Dionysos: Archetypal Image of Indestructible Life,* trans. Ralph Manheim (Princeton: Princeton University Press, 1976), 104, 116. Subsequent citations of this volume in text as Kerényi.

32

1. All quotations from the Bible are taken from the King James Version.

34

1. Morris Kline, *Mathematical Thought from Ancient to Modern Times* (New York: Oxford University Press, 1972), 192. Subsequent citations of this volume in text as Kline.

2. Dionysius Lardner, *A Treatise on Algebraic Geometry* (London: Whittaker, Treacher, and Arnot, 1831), xl. Subsequent citations of this volume in text as Lardner.

35

1. René Taton, "Gaspard Monge," in *Dictionary of Scientific Biography,* 9:470. Subsequent citations of this article in text as Taton.

2. Hans Freudenthal, "Augustin-Louis Cauchy," in *Dictionary of Scientific Biography,* 3:132. Subsequent citations of this article in text as Freudenthal.

3. Louis Léonard de Loménie, *Sketches of Conspicuous Living Characters of France,* trans. R. M. Walsh (Philadelphia: Lea and Blanchard, 1841), 224. Subsequent citations of this volume in text as Loménie.

4. Dirk J. Struik, "Pierre-Charles-François Dupin," in *Dictionary of Scientific Biography,* 4:257. Subsequent citations of this article in text as Struik.

5. Robert Brown, "Andre-Marie-Jean-Jacques Dupin," in *Historical Dictionary of France from the 1815 Restoration to the Second Empire,* 2 vols., ed. Edgar Leon Newman (Westport, Conn.: Greenwood Press, 1987), vol. A–L, p. 354.

6. Florian Cajori, *The Teaching and History of Mathematics in the United States* (Washington: U.S. Government Printing Office, 1890), 114. Subsequent citations of this volume in text as Cajori.

7. Peter M. Molloy, *Technical Education and the Young Republic: West Point as America's École Polytechnique, 1802–1833,* diss., Brown University, 1975 (Ann Arbor: UMI, 1976), 386–87. Subsequent citations of this volume in text as Molloy.

8. William H. Carter, "Brevet Major-General Simon Bernard," *Professional Memoirs* (Corps of Engineers, U.S. Army) 5 (May–June 1913): 307. Subsequent citations of this article in text as Carter.

9. Edgar Allan Poe, *The Letters of Edgar Allan Poe,* 2 vols., ed. John Ward Ostrom (New York: Gordian Press, 1966), 1:38. Subsequent citations of this edition in text as *Letters.*

36

1. Luke Hodgkin, "Mathematics and Revolution from Lacroix to Cauchy," in *Social History of Nineteenth Century Mathematics,* ed. Herbert Mehrtens et al. (Boston: Birkhäuser, 1981), 62.

2. Horace Binney Wallace, *Stanley; or The Recollections of a Man of the World,* 2 vols. (Philadelphia: Lea and Blanchard, 1838), 1:206. Subsequent citations of this edition in text as Wallace.

3. Pierre Simon Laplace, *A Philosophical Essay on Probabilities,* trans. Frederick W. Truscott and Frederick L. Emory (New York: John Wiley and Sons, 1902), 108.

4. Florian Cajori, *A History of Mathematics,* 3d ed. (New York: Chelsea Publishing, 1980), 379.

5. William Hamilton, Review of William Whewell's *Thoughts on the Study of Mathematics as a part of a Liberal Education,* in the *Edinburgh Review* 62 (January 1836): 410. Subsequent citations of this article in text as Hamilton.

6. Philip C. Enros, "Cambridge University and the Adoption of Analytics in Early Nineteenth-Century England," in *Social History of Nineteenth Century Mathematics,* 138. Subsequent citations of this essay in text as Enros.

7. W. W. Rouse Ball, *A History of the Study of Mathematics at Cambridge* (Cambridge: Cambridge University Press, 1889), 120. Subsequent citations of this volume in text as Ball.

8. Florian Cajori, *A History of Mathematical Notations,* 2 vols. (Chicago: Open Court Publishing, 1928–29), 2:198. Subsequent citations of this volume in text as *Notations.*

9. David Bloor, "Hamilton and Peacock on the Essence of Algebra," in *Social History of Nineteenth Century Mathematics,* 222–23. Subsequent citations of this essay in text as Bloor.

37

1. Jacob Bryant, *A New System, or, An Analysis of Ancient Mythology,* 2d ed., 3 vols., intro. Burton Feldman (New York: Garland Publishing, 1979), 1:xv. Subsequent citations of this edition in text as Bryant.

2. S. F. Lacroix, *Elements of Algebra,* trans. John Farrar (Cambridge, Mass.: Hilliard and Metcalf, 1818), 117.

3. Euclid, *The Thirteen Books of Euclid's Elements,* 2d ed., 3 vols., trans. Sir Thomas Heath (New York: Dover, 1956), 1:351. Subsequent citations of this edition in text as Heath.

4. Edgar Allan Poe, *The Brevities: Pinakidia, Marginalia, Fifty Suggestions, and Other Works,* ed. Burton R. Pollin (New York: Gordian Press, 1985), 229.

5. Sir Thomas Heath, *Mathematics in Aristotle* (Oxford: Oxford University Press, 1949), 22. Subsequent citations of this volume in text as *Math.*

38

1. From Heninger, *The Cosmographical Glass,* 83, fig. 52b.

39

1. *An Intermediate Greek-English Lexicon* (Oxford: Oxford University Press, 1980), 171. Subsequent citations of this volume in text as *Lexicon*.

40

1. Selden Rodman, *Tongues of Fallen Angels* (New York: New Directions, 1974), 19.

41

1. Joan Dayan, *Fables of Mind: An Inquiry into Poe's Fiction* (New York: Oxford University Press, 1987), 238 n. 44. Subsequent citations of this volume in text as Dayan.

2. *Latin Poetry in Verse Translation,* ed. L. R. Lind (Boston: Houghton Mifflin, 1957), 251.

3. Walter Burkert, *Lore and Science in Ancient Pythagoreanism,* trans. Edwin L. Minar, Jr. (Cambridge: Harvard University Press, 1972), 72. Subsequent citations of this volume in text as Burkert.

4. William Hogarth, *The Analysis of Beauty* (London: Scolar Press, 1974), x–xi. Subsequent citations of this volume in text as Hogarth.

5. *The Oxford Dictionary of Art,* ed. Ian Childers and Harry Osborne (Oxford: Oxford University Press, 1988), 210. Subsequent citations of this volume in text as *ODA*.

6. Ralph Mayer, *A Dictionary of Art Terms and Techniques* (New York: Crowell, 1969), 169–70.

42

1. While this book was in production in June-July 1993, an English mathematician, Andrew Wiles, who teaches at Princeton, announced in a series of three lectures at Cambridge University that he had solved the problem of Fermat's Last Theorem. Wiles's method, which makes use of many recent developments in twentieth-century mathematics, seems to be correct, though of course its ultimate correctness will only be established after extensive peer review. Whatever the ultimate mathematical verdict is on Wiles's method, clearly his proof cannot have been the one that Fermat had in mind when he wrote his famous marginal comment in Diophantus, for Wiles's method employs mathematical techniques Fermat could not have conceived of.

45

1. See, for example, *The Purloined Poe: Lacan, Derrida and Psychoanalytic Reading,* ed. John P. Muller and William J. Richardson (Baltimore: Johns Hopkins University Press, 1988).

2. Jacques Lacan, *Écrits,* 2 vols. (Paris: Éditions du Seuil), 1:66. Subsequent citations of this volume in text as *Écrits*.

3. Jean Laplanche and J.-B. Pontalis, "Mirror Stage (*Stade du miroir*)," trans. Peter Kussell and Jeffrey Mehlman, *Yale French Studies* 48 (1972): 192.

4. Michel Foucault, *The Order of Things* (New York: Random House, 1973), xv.

5. *The Structuralist Controversy,* ed. Richard Macksey and Eugenio Donato (Baltimore: Johns Hopkins University Press, 1972), 268–69. Subsequent citations of this volume in text as Macksey.

Index

John T. Irwin is Decker Professor of the Humanities and chairman of the Writing Seminars at the Johns Hopkins University. A former editor of the *Georgia Review*, he now edits the series Johns Hopkins: Poetry and Fiction for the Johns Hopkins University Press. His books include *Doubling and Incest / Repetition and Revenge, American Hieroglyphics*, and *The Heisenberg Variations*, all available from Johns Hopkins.